new mexico

new mexico

a new guide to the colorful state

LANCE CHILTON
KATHERINE CHILTON
POLLY E. ARANGO
JAMES DUDLEY
NANCY NEARY
PATRICIA STELZNER

UNIVERSITY OF NEW MEXICO PRESS
Albuquerque

Drawings © 1984 by Katherine Chilton
Design by Emmy Ezzell and Katherine Chilton
Maps by Carol Cooperrider

Manufactured in the United States of America.
International Standard Book Number (clothbound) 0-8263-0732-9
International Standard Book Number (paperbound) 0-8263-0733-7
Library of Congress Catalog Card Number 83-27351

Third paperbound printing 1985

Library of Congress Cataloging in Publication Data
Main entry under title:

New Mexico, a new guide to the colorful state.

  Bibliography: p.
  Includes index.
  1. New Mexico—Description and travel—1981–
—Guide-books.   1. Chilton, Lance, 1944–
F794.3.N49   1984   917.89   83-27351
ISBN 0-8263-0732-9
ISBN 0-8263-0733-7 (pbk.)

TO OUR FAMILIES
Annelise and Noël
John, Carlos, Francesca, Pilar, and Nicolas
Mary, Claire, and Rosemary
Stephen and Sarah
Luis, Sarah, and Alex

contents

introduction

Forty-four years after publication of the first edition of *New Mexico: A Guide to the Colorful State*, a new group of writers presents the first major revision of the guide. The initial volume was produced as one of a series of guides to each of the then forty-eight states, and to Alaska, Puerto Rico, and the District of Columbia. The writers were members of the Writers' Program of the Work Projects Administration; they followed a set of uniform guidelines developed in Washington, D.C.

Previous revisions of the guide, occurring in 1953 and 1962, were minor and consisted largely of updating census figures. When some of the current group of writers first came to New Mexico in the late 1960s, the *Guide* provided for us an excellent introduction and travel companion, but it was clearly a dated and nostalgic source.

Because of the vast changes in New Mexico since 1940, we have chosen to rewrite the book while maintaining much of its original structure. We have traveled virtually every mile of the highways described. We have spoken with specialists in many fields and with residents of every part of the state who have generously given of their knowledge to help us write the tours and essays. Above all, we have read.

What, then, has changed about New Mexico in this time span? Progress has come; its good and bad effects are evident in every corner of the state. The first paved road in southeastern New Mexico did not arrive until 1936; in 1984, four-lane divided highways, lined with shopping centers, crisscross the newly prosperous region. Albuquerque has a proud new civic plaza, a fine, modern library, and beautiful new museums. However, in the name of progress, most of the highlights of the 1940 tour of Albuquerque, such as the Huning Castle and the Alvarado Hotel, have fallen to the wrecker's ball. Rural poverty has decreased, but continued migration to the cities has robbed many small settlements of their young.

The population of New Mexico increased 145 percent between 1940 and 1980. New Mexicans have continued to deplete their state's natural resources; oil, gas, and uranium reserves may not last long into the twenty-first century, and water supplies are stretched to their limits in many parts of the state. Several species of animals, beginning with the once-countless bison and including bear, antelope, and even Carlsbad Caverns' bats, have moved closer to extinction within the state's borders. For better or for worse, the more than 1,3 million New Mexicans now have better access to the wonders of their state, as do millions of other Americans and many foreign visitors.

Roads finished since 1940 have dictated the creation of new tours in this book. A new cross-state highway has been completed. The magnificent and varied country accessible by U.S. 64 makes a new Tour 2 essential. A combination of roads, almost all paved, makes Tour 17 a handsome additional route from north to south near the Arizona border. Tour 11 departs from the format of straight-line routes; the circle from Santa Fe to Taos and back by "high road" and "low road" is a popular pattern of travel for many natives and visitors. We have elected to keep the circle intact. An entirely new aspect of the book is the many pen-and-ink drawings by Kathy Chilton, which illustrate either particular scenes or common sights in New Mexico. Earlier editions of the *Guide* included photographs by excellent young photographers, including Ernest Knee and Laura Gilpin. Although this edition does not include their work, we have solicited and published pictures from photographers throughout New Mexico, choosing with difficulty among the many submissions; we thank all who allowed us to review their work.

We have written the guidebook with three groups of people in mind: those who are now traveling in New Mexico, those who plan someday to do so, and those who have toured in our state at some time in the past. Our assumption is that these three kinds of people have one thing in common with each other and with each of us: a desire to know more about New Mexico in order to appreciate it better. We realize that much of our travel, research, and writing has been done in the unspoken faith that when people love the place they live in or visit, they and the world will be better for it.

Like the first editions of the *Guide*, this revision cannot be considered complete. In the course of gathering information, each of us has had to leave out fascinating anecdotes, im-

portant environmental data, and significant historical events. Many of our most important written sources are listed in the bibliography. Sources are not footnoted in the text.

Where material was chosen for inclusion or omission, we have attempted to provide the most pertinent information on attractions the traveler may wish to see. Beyond that, we have concentrated on features that are interesting to us and that we believe will interest the reader, explaining the natural environment when possible and guiding the traveler to further readings. We have found inevitable errors in the information and data supplied in earlier editions; we have undoubtedly contributed errors that we hope our readers will help us to correct before another edition is published. As in earlier editions, individual writers' interests and writing styles determine the emphases and language of each section of the book.

We have several comments for those who would use the guide while traveling. Since 1940, most of the state's major roads have been paved; the reader can assume that roads not indicated as dirt or gravel in the text are fully paved. Distances are given from the beginning of each tour, usually from north to south and from east to west. Because many readers will be using the tours in the opposite direction from that which we have written, we have refrained from giving directions using "left" or "right," instead using "north," "south," "east," and "west." Information on towns and attractions at highway intersections is generally given only once; the traveler should consult the tours crossing the route driven (mentioned in parentheses at the relevant points) to discover information about places that are just off the route of a given tour. In most New Mexico towns, the most interesting, most picturesque streets are not the numbered highways and main thoroughfares. Carol Cooperrider, cartographer, has drawn excellent simplified "strip" maps to accompany each tour, as well as maps of walking tours in some of the major towns and cities, and a map showing life zones of the state (page 60). We thank Jerry Williams for the fine quarter maps of manmade features such as roads, cities, and county lines (pages 191–195). Nevertheless, an up-to-date highway map, obtainable at New Mexico State Highway Department offices, auto clubs, or service stations, is an important complement to this guide. Some information we have felt to be of a transient nature, such as telephone numbers and entrance fees, has not been included. Population figures have been given where available; they are taken from the 1980 census, which did not enumerate the population of small towns separately.

Among those who deserve our gratitude for assistance in producing this revision, we must thank first the many helpful people at the University of New Mexico Press, especially the production department designers, Emmy Ezzell and Barbara Jellow, and our editor, Elizabeth Hadas, who has acted continuously as our advocate and problem-solver since we first approached her with this project more than four years ago. The press has submitted our work to numerous readers for comments: all have been of assistance as we moved through the many drafts of the work. No outside reader has been more helpful than Dave Stuart, a strict and just taskmaster, and Laura de la Torre Bueno was an excellent copy editor. Martha von Briesen served as a discerning proofreader.

Many librarians throughout New Mexico have been extremely helpful, especially those at the Albuquerque Public Library (the librarians who staff the library's information service have been particularly helpful in chasing down some of the myriads of often obscure facts that a book like this requires), and at several libraries at the University of New Mexico (notably Heather Rex in the Map Room and Mary Ann Scholes Spores in the Coronado Room at Zimmerman Library). Octavia Fellin at the Gallup Public Library and Martha Liebert at the Bernalillo Public Library also provided a great deal of assistance.

We are grateful to many others who gave of their time and their knowledge, among whom are Fay Abrams, Tomás Atencio, Mike Barnes, Susan Bennett, Dale Berry, Marsha Bol, Martha von Briesen, Karen Cantrell, Mike Carrigan, Isabel Carroll, Tom Carroll, Genoveva Casaus, Maria Chabot, R. L. and Nora Bella Chilton, Saul Cohen, Charlemaud Curtis, Bill Davis, Mary Davis, John Dickey, Pally and William Ernest Dishman, Eduardo Durán, Martha Egan, Richard Etulain, Bill Fuller, Ken and Mary Frances Fuller, Daniel Gallegos, Felipita and José Manuel García, Jacobo Girón, Ann Gonzáles, Maggie Gould, Ruth Graham, Jack and Betty Greathouse, Roy Harmon, Helen Hobart, Van Dorn Hooker, Jeremiah Johnson, Frances and Paul Judge, Vernon King, Victoria Klemz, the late Joseph Kloeppel, Norman Krekler, Phyllis Mayfield Knox, Albert Kudo, Terry Lamm, Richard Lang, Fern Lyon, Barbara MacPherson, Antonio Márquez, Jesús Márquez, Joe McKinney, the late John B. Minnick, Ignacio Montaño, Jim Moore, Ike Morgan, Effie Mulkey, the late Phillip Neale, Susan Palmer, Regis Pecos, Eugene Perea, Archie and Geraldine Perkins, Arnold Rael, Edward Raventon, David Remley, Michaela Reyes, Joan Roath, John Donald Robb, Allan Savory, Barbara Knott Schwartz, Dan Scurlock, Milton Seligman, Donald Seward, C. L. Sonnichsen, Joseph and Diana Stein, David Steinberg, Mike Swickard, Margaret Szasz, Rose Tafoya, Geoffrey Taylor, Luis Torres, John Truitt, Karin Vallo, Alex and Lucy Vigil, Spencer Wilson, Jeanne Whitehouse, Jerry Williams, Jean Winkless, Joseph Winter, and James Wright. Personnel at the following agencies, among others, were very helpful: the Historical Society of New Mexico, the Los Alamos Historical Society and Museum, the New Mexico State Highway Department, the State Library, the State Record Center and Archives, the State Registry of Historic Places, the University of New Mexico Bureau of Business and Economic Research, and chambers of commerce throughout New Mexico.

The preface to the first edition of this book acknowledged the contributions of numerous "anonymous workers" from throughout New Mexico who contributed to the guide. Although we have not employed "anonymous workers" in producing this edition, we pay tribute to those who gathered the original data for previous editions. The efforts of the three directors of the New Mexico Writers' Program, Ina Sizer Cassidy, Aileen Nusbaum, and Charles Ethrige Minton, must also be recognized; Mrs. Cassidy received no credit in the first edition for her considerable contribution. We hope that our readers will find the labors undertaken by the writers of the Federal Writers' Program and by the present group worthwhile in providing an introduction to the state and its people, and as a necessary

accompaniment during drives and armchair travel along New Mexico's long highways.

The miles we traveled and the hours we spent exploring byways, books, and people have sharpened our sense of what New Mexico was and is, and have left us with a feeling of promise for what the state will be. We hope our readers will share our experiences through this volume. Although we have restrained our enthusiasm for the sake of objectivity, all of us love New Mexico's history, land, and people.

Albuquerque and
Algodones,
New Mexico

LANCE CHILTON
KATHY CHILTON
POLLY ARANGO
JIM DUDLEY
NANCY NEARY
PATRICIA STELZNER

activities and special events

Visitors to New Mexico often remark on the variety of events occurring in a state of only 1.3 million people. Events take advantage of the diversity of peoples, of environments, and of seasons that marks New Mexico. Below are selective lists of activities and specific annual events that take place in the state.

Arts

ART   The art museums of Albuquerque, Santa Fe, Taos, Roswell, Los Alamos, Gallup, and Carlsbad display changing exhibits and permanent collections.

Navajo rug auctions are held several times each year in Crownpoint.

Arts and crafts fairs are plentiful. Notable juried fairs include the New Mexico Arts and Crafts Fair in Albuquerque in late June, the Southwest Arts and Crafts Festival in Albuquerque, the Renaissance Fair in Las Cruces in November, the Eight Northern Pueblos show in July at one of the pueblos, the Feria Artesana in Albuquerque in August, the Spanish Colonial Market in Santa Fe in July, and the Indian Market in Santa Fe in August.

Public libraries throughout the state show local artists' work.

DANCE   Albuquerque, Santa Fe, and Taos have dance troupes which perform regularly, including ballet, ballet *folklórico*, international folk dancing, and modern dance. Towns throughout the state hold square dances. Towns with large concentrations of Indians hold social and competitive powwows.

DRAMA   New Mexico State University in Las Cruces, Eastern New Mexico University in Portales, the University of New Mexico in Albuquerque, and the College of Santa Fe are known for their fine drama departments. Live theater can also be seen at the other colleges in the state.

Professional and amateur theater performances take place in Albuquerque, Corrales, Cedar Crest, Las Vegas, Roswell, Santa Fe, San Jon, Lincoln, and Taos.

Spanish-language theater productions alternate with English-language and bilingual productions staged by La Compañía de Teatro de Alburquerque.

Santa Fe sponsors summer theater festivals and a spring film festival.

MUSIC   Santa Fe, Albuquerque, Taos, Ruidoso, and Madrid host summer music festivals. Madrid's festival is for jazz and bluegrass music.

Fiddling competitions and performances take place frequently throughout the state.

Gallup, Farmington, Roswell, Albuquerque, Taos, and Santa Fe all engage visiting and local musicians to perform in concert series during the fall, winter, and spring.

The Santa Fe Opera is world-renowned, with a season in its outdoor theater each July and August. The Albuquerque Opera Theater and the Four Corners Opera Association in Farmington have winter seasons.

Albuquerque, Farmington, Las Cruces, and Roswell have resident symphony orchestras.

The Chamber Orchestra of Albuquerque and the Orchestra of Santa Fe are smaller groups giving numerous chamber concerts annually.

Singers in Albuquerque, Roswell, and Santa Fe have formed performing choral groups.

Festivals

ETHNIC FESTIVALS   Raton and Farmington host multicultural festivals. Ethnic groups in Albuquerque sponsor events featuring music, dance, arts and crafts, and food. Among them are Scandinavian, Greek, Japanese, and Chinese festivals. At Gran Quivira, Indian artisans demonstrate ancient and modern craft techniques at a festival featuring dancing, music, and food in the ancient ruins. Santa Fe's fiesta and markets celebrate Hispanic and Indian heritages.

OTHER FESTIVALS   Listed in the calendar are the dates and places for such events as the Peanut, Piñata, Rose, and Chile festivals.

Outdoor Activities (*See also Sports.*)

The national parks and monuments have regular schedules of lectures, demonstrations, films, tours, and other activities.

Wildlife refuges feature self-guided driving tours.

La Cienega Picnic Area in the Sandia Mountains and Carolino Canyon in the Manzano Mountains, both in Cibola National Forest, have trails for the handicapped.

Participation Sports

BACKPACKING, HIKING AND CLIMBING
Contact the U.S. Forest Service for maps and information about trails.

BICYCLING   Weekly tours begin in Albuquerque (contact New Mexico Wheelmen or Albuquerque bicycle stores for details). Albuquerque maintains bicycle trails, routes, and lanes within the city; Las Cruces, Los Alamos, and Santa Fe have city street bikeways. Red River and other New Mexico towns sponsor bicycle tours.

CROSS-COUNTRY SKIING   Many forest service roads are closed to all but cross-country skiers and snowshoers in the winter. All mountain areas and all ski areas provide sites for cross-country skiing.

DOGSLEDDING   Clubs in Santa Fe sponsor races. Several forest service roads are open only to dogsledding in the winter.

DOWNHILL SKIING   The skiing season usually extends from December to March or April in the Sandia, Sangre de Cristo, and Jemez ranges in northern New Mexico and on Sierra Blanca and in the Sacramento Mountains in the southern part of the state.

FISHING   State licenses are required in New Mexico except on tribal lands, where a tribal license is needed. Brook, brown, rainbow, cutthroat, and Dolly Varden trout; Kokanee and Coho salmon; black bass; white bass; walleye; crappie; catfish; northern pike; and sunfish can be caught in New Mexico waters. Fishing information may be obtained from the New Mexico Department of Game and Fish, Villagra Building, Santa Fe 87503.

GOLFING   Alamogordo, Albuquerque, Anthony, Carlsbad, Carrizozo, Clayton, Cloudcroft, Clovis, Deming, Eunice, Farmington, Gallup, Jal, Las Cruces, Las Vegas, Lordsburg, Los Alamos, Portales, Raton, Roswell, Ruidoso, Santa Fe, Santa Rosa, Silver City, Truth or Consequences, and Tucumcari maintain municipal courses.

HANG-GLIDING   Albuquerque's Sandia Mountains and foothills are favorite hang-gliding spots.

HORSEBACK RIDING   Albuquerque has a public riding arena. Private stables are located near national forest areas all over the state.

HUNTING   Season dates are set in February for elk, antelope, bighorn and Barbary sheep, oryx, ibex, mountain lion, grouse, and squirrel hunting. In August, season dates are set for dove, pheasant, prairie chicken, lesser sandhill crane, snipe, rail, gallinule, and Pacific Flyway waterfowl hunting. In September, seasons are set for quail and Central Flyway waterfowl hunting. There is also a bow-hunting season. Licenses are required for all hunting. Contact the New Mexico Department of Game and Fish, Villagra Building, Santa Fe 87503, for details.

MOTORBOATING   Motorboating and waterskiing attract visitors to Elephant Butte, Conchas, Bluewater, and Navajo lakes. Heron Lake and Cochiti Lake are restricted to boats that do not leave a wake.

MOTORCYCLING   Off-road motorcycling is limited to designated trails. Contact the National Forest Service for maps.

RIVER RAFTING   During appropriate water-flow seasons, private concerns operate rafting trips on the Rio Chama and the Rio Grande.

RUNNING   Races and marathons are held in several New Mexico towns and cities.

SAILING AND CANOEING   Wind- and human-powered craft can be used at Cochiti, Heron, Bluewater, Elephant Butte, Conchas, and Navajo lakes.

SKATING   Outdoor ice-skating rinks exist at Angel Fire, Hyde Park State Park near Santa

Fe, Los Alamos, Montezuma Castle near Las Vegas, Red River, and Taos. Indoor roller-skating rinks are available in several New Mexico towns; Albuquerque has an indoor ice rink.

SPELUNKING   Many caves are available for exploration in southern New Mexico. Permits are required for caves in Carlsbad Caverns National Park and on Bureau of Land Management–administered areas.

SWIMMING   Towns and cities throughout the state have municipal pools. Lea Lake in Bottomless Lakes State Park near Roswell, Cochiti Lake, and Jal Lake are among the lakes favored by swimmers.

TRAM   Sandia Peak Tram takes passengers up the ten-thousand-foot mountain daily (except Wednesdays).

Spectator Sports

AUTO RACING   Albuquerque has auto race tracks.

COLLEGE AND HIGH SCHOOL SPORTS   Cities and towns throughout the state feature seasonal sports of all kinds.

HORSE RACING   Santa Fe Downs (May to September), Ruidoso Downs (May to September), Raton—La Mesa Park (May to October), Anapra—Sunland Park (October to May), and Albuquerque—the New Mexico State Fair (September) are favorite horse-race sites.

HOT-AIR BALLOONING   Fiestas in Albuquerque, Chama, and Farmington attract hundreds of colorful aerostats and their pilots and admirers.

PROFESSIONAL BASEBALL   The Pacific Coast League (Class AAA) Albuquerque Dukes have an April-to-September season.

RODEOS   Junior, amateur, and professional rodeo competitions take place throughout the state in all seasons and abound in summer.

calendar

Dates may change for any of these events. Please contact chambers of commerce, visitor and convention bureaus, individual pueblo tribal offices, or the Indian Pueblo Cultural Center in Albuquerque for more specific information.

january

1
Taos Pueblo: Buffalo or Deer dance.
Other pueblos: Ceremonial dances.

6
Most pueblos: Installation of new governors.
Taos Pueblo: Buffalo Dance.
San Ildefonso Pueblo: Eagle Dance.
Cochiti, Picuris, Tesuque, San Felipe, San Juan, Santa Clara, Santa Ana, Taos, and Santo Domingo pueblos: Three Kings dances.

7
Many pueblos: Ceremonial dances.

8–10
Laguna Pueblo: Green Corn Dance.

22–23
San Ildefonso Pueblo: San Ildefonso Feast Day: vespers and procession on 22d; fiesta, Buffalo Dance, Comanche Dance, and Deer Dance on 23d.

january *continued*

25
Picuris and *Taos pueblos:* Dances honoring St. Paul.

Dates to be announced:
Santa Fe: Los Tres Reyes Magos ("The Three Wise Kings," a medieval folk play).

february

march

mid-February
Bosque del Apache: Departure of sandhill cranes and their adopted whooping cranes for summer homes in Idaho.
Albuquerque, Las Cruces: Black Heritage Week celebrations.

2
Cochiti, San Felipe, and *Santo Domingo pueblos:* Candlemas Day dances.

18
Belen: Annual Fiesta de San José: Mass, procession, and food at San José Church.

19
Laguna Pueblo: Feast Day of St. Joseph at Old Laguna: Harvest Dance.

Dates to be announced:
Several pueblos: Opening of the irrigation ditches, accompanied by festivities.
Deming: Rock swap: free agates, jaspers, and opals.

april

may

Easter
Ranchos de Taos: Blessing of the animals at St. Francis Church.
Tomé: Religious procession.
Cochiti, San Felipe, Santo Domingo, Santa Ana, San Ildefonso, Jemez, and *Santa Clara pueblos:* Spring Corn Dance, Basket Dance, ceremonial foot races, and pole shinnying.
Santuario de Chimayo: Pilgrimages.

mid-April
Deming: Old-Timers' Celebration.
Farmington: Apple Blossom Festival: dance, parade, and melodrama.
Albuquerque: Rio Grande Valley Bicycle Tour.

Dates to be announced:
Truth or Consequences: Ralph Edwards Fiesta: parades, races, carnival, art show, rodeo, river race, fishing derby, and fiddlers' contest.

early May
La Cienega: El Rancho de las Golondrinas Spring Festival: Spanish colonial arts, food, demonstrations, and entertainment.
Tularosa: Rose Festival: banquet, coronation, parade, carnival, talent show, and food.
Albuquerque: Mother's Day dances at Pueblo Indian Museum.
Albuquerque: Mother's Day concert by New Mexico Symphony Orchestra at Rio Grande Zoo.

mid-May
Española to Pilar: Rio Grande white-water canoe-kayak-raft race.
Tularosa: San Francisco de Paola Festival: Mexcan dances and food.
Farmington: Rodeo.
Deming: Fiddling contest.

late May
Albuquerque: The Great River Race: Park and Recreation Department–sponsored race from Corrales Bridge to San Gabriel Park in anything that floats.
Farmington: Four Corners Hot-Air Balloon Rally: competition, races, and other events.
Santa Rosa: Santa Rosa Day Celebration: parade, barbecue, street dances, arts and crafts show, fishing contest, stock car show.
Albuquerque: Fiesta de San Felipe de Neri in Old Town.

1
San Felipe Pueblo: San Felipe Feast Day: fiesta and spring Corn Dance.

may *continued*

3

Cochiti and *Taos pueblos:* Santa Cruz Day: Corn Dance, ceremonial races, and the blessing of the fields.

5

Albuquerque and *Las Vegas:* Cinco de Mayo (May 5, the day of Mexican independence): celebrations, concerts, and dances.

29

Tesuque Pueblo: Blessing of the fields and Corn Dance.

june

early June

Albuquerque: June Music Festival: chamber music.
Clovis: Pioneer Days and Rodeo: parade, Miss New Mexico Rodeo Pageant, horse sale.
Raton: Rodeo.

mid-June

Farmington: San Juan Sheriff's Posse Rodeo at rodeo grounds.
Fort Sumner: Old Fort Days: parade, barbecue, staged bank robbery, arts and crafts sale, fiddling contest, bluegrass music, and horse show.
Los Cerrillos: Fiesta de la Primavera: art, entertainment, games, food.

late June

Gallup: Indian Capital Amateur Rodeo in Red Rock State Park.
Farmington: Rodeo.
Farmington: Air show.
Pecos National Monument: Trade fair: demonstrations by Indian and Hispanic artisans.
High Rolls: High Rolls cherry festival: cherry cider, cherry butter, jelly, cakes, pies, hay rides, arts and crafts.
Taos: Taos Music Festival.
Tesuque: Opening of Shidoni Gallery outdoor sculpture show, with several acres of sculpture garden.
Albuquerque: New Mexico Cowbelle Cookoff.
Albuquerque: New Mexico Arts and Crafts Fair: exhibits of works by over 200 artisans, entertainment, demonstrations, and lectures, at State Fair Grounds.
Gallup: Lion's Club Rodeo, Red Rock State Park.

june *continued*

july

Albuquerque: Arts in the Parks: dramatic, musical, and variety entertainment in several city parks.

6
Zuni Pueblo: Rain Dance.

12–13
Sandia, San Ildefonso, Santa Clara, and *Taos pueblos:* San Antonio Feast Day: Corn dances.

13
Deming: Santa Ana Fiesta: bazaar, music, dancing, and barbecue at St. Ann's Church.

24
Cochiti, San Juan, and *Taos pueblos:* San Juan Feast Day: Buffalo and Comanche dances, arts and crafts at San Juan, Corn Dance at Taos, Grab Day at Cochiti.

29
Santa Ana, Santo Domingo, San Felipe, and *Acoma pueblos:* San Pedro Feast Day: Corn Dance, Grab Day, and rooster pull.

early July
Santa Fe: opera season begins.
Santa Fe: Rodeo de Santa Fe.
Tucumcari: Piñata Festival: pageant, rodeo, food, bicycle tour, and road races.
Española: Fiesta de Oñate: vespers, torch relay, street dancing, food, parade, entertainment, and fireworks.
Aztec: Fiesta day celebration: pet parade, candlelight parade, burning of Zozobra (Old Man Gloom), coin dig, bicycle race, carnival, and junior rodeo.
Deming: Butterfield Trail Days: parade, fiddling contest, dances, trading post, and barbecue.

mid-July
Raton: Jaycees Rodeo and Parade.
Santa Fe: Santa Fe Chamber Music Festival: concerts, open rehearsals featuring visiting composers.
Farmington: Aquacade at Brookside Pool.
Dulce: Jicarilla Apache Little Beaver Round-up Rodeo.
Magdalena: Old Timers' Reunion: parade, fiddling contest, dancing, hot-air ballooning, rodeo, and barbecue.

late July
Raton: Rodeos.
Santa Clara Pueblo: Puyé Cliffs Ceremonial: dances by various tribes in ancestral cliff-ruins, arts and crafts, food.
A northern pueblo: Eight Northern Pueblos Arts and Crafts Show: traditional and contemporary crafts, dances, and food.
Tucumcari: Rodeo.
Santa Fe: Spanish Market, outside Palace of the Governors.
Eunice: Old-Timers' Fiddling Contest.

Ruidoso: Art Festival.
Estancia: Old-Timers' Day: parade, fiddling contest, junior rodeo, and barbecue at the County Fair Grounds.
Taos: Fiesta: dances and coronation of queen.
Chimayo: Los Moros y Cristianos Pageant: Spanish medieval pageant of Moors and Christians, at the Holy Family Church.
Santa Fe: Festival Theater.

2–4
Grants: Fourth of July Celebration: large parade, arts and crafts show, fiddling contest.

3–6
Mescalero: Mescalero Apache maidens' puberty rites: dances and rodeos.

3–4
Las Vegas: Fourth of July Fiesta: parade, arts and crafts fair, music, food, and fireworks.
Roswell: Country Music Festival: music, fireworks.
Clayton: Fourth of July Rodeo.

4
Silver City: Frontier Days Celebration: parade, dances, and fireworks.
Cimarron: Maverick Rodeo.
Santa Fe: Los Compadres street breakfast.
Nambe Pueblo: Nambe Waterfalls Ceremonial: dances by visiting tribes, arts and crafts, and food.
Albuquerque, Carlsbad, Cimarron, Eunice, Gallup, Lordsburg, Lovington, Moriarty, Santa Fe, Santa Rosa, Socorro, and *Springer:* Evening fireworks.

4–5
Tucumcari: Lions Club Rodeo.

4–6
Red River: Fourth of July Celebration: parade, shoot-out, tug of war, horseshoe-pitching contest, tennis tournament.

5
Roswell: Birthday Shindig: fiddling contest at the County Historical Museum.

5–6
Aztec: Aztec Fiesta Days: parade, mariachi band, carnival, sidewalk sale.

14
Cochiti Pueblo: San Buenaventura Feast Day: Corn Dance.

25
Acoma Pueblo: Santiago Day: rooster pull.
Cochiti, San Felipe, Santa Ana, and *Laguna pueblos:* Santiago Day: Grab Day.

26
Santa Ana and *Taos pueblos:* Santa Ana Feast Day: Corn Dance.
Acoma Pueblo: Santa Ana Feast Day: Grab Day.

Date to be announced:
Galisteo, Silver City, and *Carlsbad:* Rodeos.

early August
Lincoln: Old Lincoln Days: evening re-enactments of Lincoln County War of 1878 to 1881 and the last escape of Billy the Kid, parade, Forty-one-mile Pony Express Run from White Oaks to Lincoln, arts and crafts fair, ghost town tours, fiddling contest.
Pecos National Monument: Pecos feast day and folk mass.
Socorro: Socorro County Fair and Rodeo.
Pie Town: Polo tournament, barbecue, and dance.
Melrose: Old-Timers' Days and Rodeo.

mid-August
Lovington: Lea County Fair and Rodeo: carnival, parade, and horse and livestock shows.
Hillsboro: Black Range Art Exhibit.
Farmington: Connie Mack World Series baseball tournament.
Gallup: Intertribal Indian Ceremonial: parades, dances of many tribes, rodeos, arts and crafts exhibit, and foods, at Red Rock State Park.
Chama: Chama Days: parade, rodeo, arts and crafts, dances, food.
Las Vegas: San Miguel County Fair.
Belen: Our Lady of Belen Fiesta: parade, carnival, dances, arts and crafts fair, burning of the devil.
Bosque Farms: Bosque Farms Fair: parade, fiddling contest, horse show, and dance.
Datil: Rodeo.
Los Alamos: Los Alamos County Fair and Rodeo: parade, exhibits, band concert, rodeo, dance, and ice cream social.
Santa Fe: Indian Market: hundreds of artisans displaying and selling jewelry, pottery, sculpture, weaving, and paintings; dances, food.
Española: Rio Arriba County Fair.

Raton: Street arts and crafts fair.
Albuquerque: La Luz Trail Run, up the Sandia Mountains.
Lovington: Lea County Fair and Rodeo: livestock show, rodeo, carnival, and parade.

late August
Zuni Pueblo: Zuni Fair and Rodeo: arts and crafts, food.
Tucumcari: Quay County Fair.
Capitan: Lincoln County Fair.
Carlsbad: Carlsbad Cavern Bat Flight Breakfast: watching flight of three hundred thousand bats returning to Carlsbad Cavern at dawn.
Clayton: Union County Fair.
Deming: Great American Duck Race: dance, parade, duck costume contest, races.
Las Vegas: Jaycees Rodeo.
Gallup: North American Rodeo Championships: rodeo, dances, fiddling contest, barbecue, and parade, at Red Rock State Park.
Hillsboro: Apple Festival: cider, apples, and pies; arts and crafts, fiddling contest.
Albuquerque: Feria Artesana: Hispanic visual, literary, and performing arts festival.

2
Jemez Pueblo: Old Pecos Bull Dance: celebration of Feast of Our Lady of Angels, patron of abandoned Pecos Pueblo, whose survivors moved to Jemez in 1838, Corn Dance.

4
Santo Domingo Pueblo: Santo Domingo Feast Day: Corn Dance.

4–10
Bloomfield: Salmon Ruins Barbecue, at Salmon Ruins.

8–10
Carrizozo: Santa Rita Fiesta: vespers and dance.
Socorro: Fiesta de San Miguel: coronation, dance, games, food, Mass, and procession, at San Miguel Mission.

9–10
Picuris Pueblo: San Lorenzo Feast Day: sunset dance, foot races, pole climb, Corn Dance.

10
Acoma, Cochiti, and *Laguna pueblos:* San Lorenzo Feast Day: Corn Dance, Grab Day.

11–12
Santa Clara Pueblo: Santa Clara Feast Day: Corn and Harvest dances.

15
Laguna and *Zia pueblos:* San Antonio and Our Lady of the Ascension Feast Days: various dances at Laguna and Corn Dance at Zia.

28
Isleta: San Agustín Fiesta: fiesta, carnival, and concessions.

Dates to be announced:
Chama: Chama Days: parade, rodeo, barbecue.

early September
Grants: Bi-County Fair: rodeo, fiddling contest.
Window Rock, Arizona: Navajo Nation Fair and Rodeo: dance, powwow, arts and crafts, horse races, carnival, food, and rodeo.
Socorro: Socorro County Fair and Rodeo.
Springer: Colfax County Fair: parade, exhibits, livestock show, tractor pull, cow-chip-throwing contest.
Belen: Valencia County Fair: fiddling contest, parade, exhibits, music, rodeo, and carnival.
Fort Sumner: DeBaca County Fair: exhibits, horse and livestock show, barbecue.
Clovis: Curry County Fair: largest county fair in the Southwest.
Alamogordo: Otero County Fair and Rodeo.
Hillsboro: Apple Festival: cider, pie, arts and crafts, and fiddling contest.
Hatch: Chile Festival: queen contest, skeet shoot, horseshoe competition, fiddling contest, art show, dance, chile dish and dinner contest, and *ristra*, wreath, and arrangement contest.
Farmington: Northern Navajo Nation Fair and rodeo: dances, arts and crafts.

mid-September
Santa Fe: Fiesta de Santa Fé: oldest community celebration in the United States, celebrating the 1692–93 reconquest of New Mexico by Don Diego de Vargas; burning of Zozobra (Old Man Gloom), parades, arts and crafts, street singing, dancing, food.
Mesilla: Pan-American Fiesta: parade, folk dancing, frontier ballads, mariachi bands, barbecue.
Las Vegas: Annual People's Fair: arts and crafts, music, puppet and magic shows.
Aztec: Pioneers' Picnic.

mid-September to late September
Albuquerque: New Mexico State Fair: midway, hobbies, crafts, livestock, produce, art, auto shows, model railroads, cooking displays, rodeo, concerts, horse racing, parade, Indian Village, Spanish Village, dances, and food.

late September
Red River: Aspencade: outdoor events, bicycle tour, dances, food, and arts and crafts.
Las Cruces: Vaquero Days, Southern New Mexico State Fair: parade, arts and crafts, hot-air balloons, sports, and food.
Silver City: Cliff-Gila-Grant County Fair.
Ruidoso: Aspencade Festival: parade, motorcycle convention, band concerts, arts and crafts, and mule races.
Silver City: Flaming Foliage Tour.
Red River, Eagle Nest, Ruidoso, Cloudcroft, Albuquerque, Chama, Grants, Los Alamos, Raton, Santa Fe, Silver City, Springer, and *Truth or Consequences:* Fall color tours and celebrations.
Lincoln: Lincoln Apple Festival: apple goods, music, and arts and crafts.
Socorro: San Miguel Feast Day: fiesta and rodeo.

2
Acoma Pueblo: San Esteban Feast Day: fiesta, Corn Dance.

8
Laguna and *San Ildefonso pueblos:* Nativity of the Blessed Virgin Mary Feast Day: dances.

15
Dulce: Jicarilla Apache annual feast, rodeo, foot races, powwows, at Stone Lake.

19
Laguna Pueblo: San José Feast Day: dances, rodeo, barbecue.

25
Laguna Pueblo: St. Elizabeth Feast Day: dances.

29–30
Taos Pueblo: San Gerónimo Feast Day: sundown dance, other dances, races, fair, and pole climb.

october

early October
Taos: Festival of the Arts: art, music, dance.
Deming: Southwestern New Mexico State Fair and Rodeo: parade, exhibits, and livestock judging.
Alamogordo: International Space Hall of Fame Induction and Open House: once-a-year-only tour to Trinity Site, site of first A-bomb explosion.
Farmington: Four Corners Cultural Heritage Festival.
Eagle Nest: Paul Bunyan Days.
La Cienega: El Rancho de las Golondrinas Fall Festival: exhibits, demonstrations, food, and entertainment in museum of Spanish colonial life.
Cloudcroft: Aspencade and Oktoberfest.
Gallup: Heritage Day: celebration for people of various ethnic backgrounds.
Albuquerque: International Hot-Air Balloon Fiesta: races, mass ascensions, parade, food.
Santa Fe: Festival of the Arts: numerous art shows and demonstrations.
Albuquerque: Greek Festival: Greek food, dancing, and church tours at St. George Church.
Shiprock: Northern Navajo Fair.

mid-October
Socorro: Forty-Niners Celebration: mining contests, parade, dances, chile cookoff, fiddling contest, jalapeño-eating contest.
Truth or Consequences: Fiddling contest.
Deming: Klobase Festival: Bohemian sausage barbecue.

late October
Alamogordo: Frontier Fiesta: arts and crafts, fiddling contest.

High Rolls and *Mountain Park:* Apple festival, hay rides, food, and drinks.
Bosque del Apache: Sandhill cranes and a few whooping cranes return to the sanctuary for the winter.
Portales: Peanut Valley Festival: arts and crafts, entertainment, peanut olympics.

3–4
Ranchos de Taos: Fiesta de San Francisco: candlelight procession, fiesta.

4
Nambe Pueblo: San Francisco Feast Day: dances.

12
Albuquerque: Columbus Day Celebration, in Old Town Plaza.

15
Laguna Pueblo: St. Mary Margaret Feast Day: dances.

Dates to be announced:
Las Cruces: Whole Enchilada Festival: food, entertainment, contests, sporting events.

november

december

early November
Las Cruces: Renaissance Arts and Crafts Fair.
Albuquerque: Southwest Arts and Crafts Festival.
Carlsbad: Fall color tours of the Guadalupe Mountains.

late November
Eagle Nest: High Altitude Glider and Soaring Festival.
Roswell: Wool Bowl: national junior college championship football game.
Farmington and *Albuquerque:* Christmas parades.
Zuni Pueblo: Shalako dance (or early December).

1
Taos Pueblo: Dances.

12
Jemez and *Tesuque pueblos:* San Diego Feast Day: early afternoon Corn Dance, all-day trade fair at Jemez; Buffalo, Comanche, Deer, and Flag dances at Tesuque.

early December
Alamogordo, Cloudcroft: Christmas tree–lighting parade.
Tortuga: Our Lady of Guadalupe Fiesta: evening torchlight ascent of Mount Tortuga, fiesta.

mid-December
Raton: City of Bethlehem Christmas exhibit in Climax Canyon.
Las Cruces: Spanish folk drama, *Los Pastores,* in several local churches.
Albuquerque, Ranchos de Taos, Silver City, Santa Fe, and *Artesia:* Spanish folk drama about Mary and Joseph seeking shelter for the birth of Jesus, *Las Posadas.*

11
Taos: Our Lady of Guadalupe candlelight procession.
Jemez Pueblo: Our Lady of Guadalupe Feast Day: Spanish dance and drama, *Los Matachines.*
Nambe Pueblo: Deer Dance.
Pojoaque Pueblo: Bow and Arrow, Buffalo, or Comanche dances.

24
Acoma Pueblo: Christmas celebration, dances.
Ranchos de Taos: Torchlight procession, midnight Mass at St. Francis of Assisi Church.
Albuquerque: City bus tours of *luminarias,* hot-air balloons in Country Club area.
All around the state: Luminaria (farolito) displays.

24–29
Acoma, Cochiti, Isleta, Jemez, Laguna, Picuris, San Felipe, San Ildefonso, San Juan, Santa Ana, Santa Clara, Santo Domingo, Taos, Tesuque, and *Zia pueblos:* Evening Masses, dances; *Los Matachines* at Picuris and San Juan; Turtle Dance at San Juan.

Date to be announced:
Alamogordo: Christmas Fair.
Albuquerque: Fiesta Encantada: Christmas activities and entertainment.

history:
new mexico through its actors

History as we know it is the interaction of people with each other and with their environments. The study of history can focus on individuals, on their motivations, on their environment, and on the popular movements they create. Our account can only hope to provide an impetus for those who wish to look further into the remarkable history of the state of New Mexico. Larger histories begin with Gaspar de Villagrá's long Spanish narrative poem, written after he took part in founding the first European settlement in New Mexico near San Juan Pueblo. Hubert Howe Bancroft's monumental *History of New Mexico and Arizona*, written before the turn of the twentieth century, is still useful. Erna Fergusson wrote a popular history of New Mexico in the middle of the twentieth century, *New Mexico: A Pageant of Three Peoples*. Frank Reeve's *New Mexico, Land of Many Cultures* is another fine history. Innumerable volumes have been written on selected aspects of New Mexico history: local issues, local heroes or anti-heroes, personal reminiscences.

Probably the best short history of the state is Myra Ellen Jenkins and Albert H. Schroe-

der's *A Brief History of New Mexico*, published in 1974. Rather than further abbreviate this excellent summary history, we have chosen to take a biographical approach. We have chosen several of the actors in the state's historical drama to highlight important periods in its evolution. Some spent all their lives in New Mexico; others were influential during a short stay.

The story of the first inhabitants of New Mexico cannot be told biographically, since no individuals from prehistory are known. Indeed, it was not until 1926, when a cowboy, George McJunkin, riding along Dead Horse Gulch, happened to see a distinctively shaped stone arrow point, embedded in a bone, that the world had any idea that men had lived in northeastern New Mexico 10,000 years ago. The people who made this stone point are now known as Folsom men. When they inhabited New Mexico the climate was less arid than it is today. They hunted herds of huge game animals, among them mammoth, bison, mastodon, and antelope. Other people known as Clovis and Sandia men may have lived in New Mexico 1,000 to 2,000 years before the more widespread Folsom group. Links be-

tween Sandia, Clovis, and Folsom civilizations and modern Indian tribes have not been found; skeletal remains of these early men are strangely absent in New Mexico.

Ancestors of the Pueblo Indians almost certainly came from a group of people called the Anasazi (a Navajo word meaning "the old ones"), who built and occupied sites in northwestern New Mexico and throughout the Four Corners area, including such New Mexico locations as Chaco Canyon, Frijoles Canyon (now part of Bandelier National Monument), and Salmon Ruins. The Anasazi constructed remarkable dwellings of intricate masonry, well-exemplified by the 800-room Pueblo Bonito at Chaco Canyon. Chaco was probably the religious or administrative capital of an interdependent network of pueblos; most Anasazi sites in New Mexico were "Chaco outliers." All of these outlying pueblos seem to have been abandoned at about the same time by the fourteenth century, perhaps because of drought, perhaps because of increasing pressure from nomadic tribes. The pueblos' inhabitants settled primarily along the Rio Grande and its tributaries, in countless large and small towns. There the Anasazi took part in a continuing series of creative exchanges with Mogollon people to the south.

The Mogollon tradition had begun considerably earlier than that of the Anasazi. These people developed a magnificent pottery style, arid-land agriculture, pottery, and a clustered arrangement of pit houses in the southern parts of what are now Arizona and New Mex-

ico. During centuries of contact, the Anasazi borrowed crops, agricultural techniques, and pottery styles from their southern neighbors. By the time the great pueblos of Chaco Canyon and Mesa Verde were abandoned, the Pueblo way of life became dominant, although people of the two cultures intermingled along the Rio Grande and east of the Sandia and Manzano mountains, sharing tools, pottery styles, and aspects of social organization.

The origins of the Athapascan tribes, the Navajos and Apaches, are uncertain. The Athapascans share a language similar to those of numerous tribes inhabiting a huge area of northwestern Canada and eastern Alaska; it is likely that the Navajos and Apaches arrived in the Southwest only shortly before the Spanish, sweeping down from the north to hunt large game on the northeastern New Mexico plains and occasionally to parasitize the Pueblos. Settlement of the Athapascan tribes in permanent homes and villages has occurred only in the last two hundred years.

Many anthropologists have contributed to knowledge of the original inhabitants of the Southwest; many continue to sift the sands, trace the ancient roads, and identify the sherds that give hints of the prodigious accomplishments of prehistoric New Mexicans.

The first written accounts of the land and peoples of New Mexico resulted from the sinking of a Spanish ship off the coast of Florida in 1527. Four survivors struggled westward across the continent for nine years until they reached the Gulf of California and then Mexico City. Here they told the viceroy of having heard about the fabled cities of Cibola, already known to the Spaniards through Indian tradition as "seven towns so large that they could be compared in size to Mexico [City] and its suburbs." Silversmiths in these cities were said to occupy whole streets, and houses gleamed with sapphires, turquoise, and gold.

Upon receipt of this news, Viceroy Antonio de Mendoza sent out a small exploring party led by Fray Marcos de Niza, a Franciscan selected because of his previous experiences exploring South and Central America. Mendoza instructed de Niza to carry out his instructions to treat the Indian peoples fairly, to take no slaves, and to observe the land and the mineral resources he was to explore. Esteban, a black slave who was one of the survivors of the shipwreck and nine-year journey, went along as guide. He was to go ahead as scout, with instructions to send back a cross as a sign of his discoveries. If the country was unusually good, Esteban was to send a cross two hands long; if it was as rich as New Spain, a larger cross. Four days later, Esteban sent back four messengers with a cross "as high as a man," an indication of a discovery of major importance. At this point, Esteban was to have waited for de Niza and the rest of the group. Instead, he pushed on alone until he came to Hawikuh, one of the pueblos of the Zunis, where he insulted the Indians and was killed in retaliation.

In the meantime, de Niza, in great excitement, was pressing forward over the deserts of what are now northern Mexico and southeastern Arizona, not stopping even after he learned of Esteban's death. De Niza reached Hawikuh in May 1539 but was not allowed by the Zunis to enter the pueblo. Nevertheless, he took formal possession of the country for Spain, erected a cross on the site, and then returned to Mexico City.

Although de Niza had seen Hawikuh himself, he took back a highly embellished story, recounting tales of great cities, populous nations, and wealthy natives. Mendoza immediately ordered the outfitting of an expedition to conquer the cities. De Niza would guide it; Francisco Vásquez de Coronado was to be its leader.

Coronado and 225 horsemen, 65 foot soldiers, and hundreds of servants headed north from Compostela, New Spain, on February 23, 1540, to search for the seven cities of Cibola. Accompanying the expedition were several clergymen to ensure that the acts of the soldiers toward native populations would be in keeping with their religion, since the saving of souls was as important to the Spanish crown as the procurement of wealth.

On July 7 Coronado, with an advance guard of fifty men, arrived at the first of the cities, Hawikuh. The legendary city was found to be nothing but a village of four-story mud buildings. The Zunis had already experienced the duplicity of the non-Indian in the person of Esteban. They refused to surrender to the Spaniards, who attacked the villages. In the melee, Coronado was knocked off his horse and almost killed. After having won the battle, the Spaniards continued on to the other Zuni pueblos, looting and killing. By this time it was apparent that the Zunis possessed none of the riches sought by the Spaniards. The soldiers grumbled, and de Niza was sent to Mexico City in disgrace.

Hoping for better prospects elsewhere, Coronado split the expedition into four exploratory parties which during the summer and fall reached the Hopi villages and the Grand Canyon of the Colorado, the Rio Grande pueblos as far north as Taos, and the plains to the east, exploring what are now the Texas Panhandle, Oklahoma, and Kansas.

Coronado's main party reached Kuaua, near present-day Bernalillo, in September. Here he established winter headquarters. The Tiguex Indians revolted when Spanish soldiers took their food and assaulted their women. Subjugation of the Indians was accomplished with considerable force, a bitter experience which the Pueblos remembered for generations.

Meanwhile, the party under Hernando de Alvarado had reached the pueblo of Cicuye, or Pecos. Here a captive Pawnee Indian known as El Turco (his appearance suggested that of a Turk) by the Spanish described a fabulous city called Quivira, whose streets were paved with gold. Hearing this, Coronado, still eager for treasure, decided to press on to Quivira as soon as spring came. He left Tiguex with his entire force in April 1541 and marched toward the promised riches.

The Spaniards marched for thirty-seven days. Convinced that the Turk had deliberately given them misleading directions, Coronado picked new guides, sent the main force back to Tiguex, and continued north with a smaller party. Coronado did find the headquarters of the Quiviras or Wichita Indians, but once again the fabled cities turned out not to be golden. Disappointed again, the group headed back to Tiguex, where they wintered before returning to New Spain in the spring of 1542. Three Franciscan friars who had accompanied Coronado, Juan de Padilla, Juan de la Cruz, and Luis de Escalona, remained among the Pueblo Indians as first missionaries. They never returned.

Coronado, recovering from being kicked in the head by a horse, was borne on a litter at the end of the trip. His *entrada* into the new country had been a failure. More accurate than those of his predecessors, Coronado's reports convinced the viceroy that New Mexico was useless to Spain. For many years the region was ignored.

By 1580 the Spanish crown was ready to send another expedition north. This time the focus was to be on missionary work. Agustín Rodríguez, a Franciscan lay brother, having heard stories about the number of Indians living in the northern territories, organized the expedition. Three friars, nine soldiers, and nineteen Indians made up the party under the command of Captain Francisco Chamuscado. The party left Santa Barbara, a border outpost of New Spain in Chihuahua, and pushed north by a new trail, probably reaching Taos and the eastern plains as well as Zuni. The small expedition was able to maintain friendly relations with the Indians, but when Juan de Santa Maria, one of the Franciscans, set off on his own to return home by a different route, he was killed. The two other Franciscans were also killed when they elected to stay to work with the Indians. Captain Chamuscado died on the return trip. However, the rest of the group was able to bring back records, which could be used by later expeditions, of their explorations of the new territory. Following this exploration, the name Nuevo Méjico (New Mexico) was used to designate the country north of the settled Mexican provinces.

Franciscans in New Spain, deeply concerned about their brothers who had remained behind, launched an urgent attempt to rescue them. A wealthy rancher in northern Mexico offered to finance a rescue party. The friars accepted the offer; an expedition was formed under the command of Antonio de Espejo. A party of two friars, fifteen soldiers, and a few Indian servants set out, this time following the Rodríguez-Chamuscado route. By persuading his men to maintain the search for gold, Espejo was able to keep the group intact even after they learned of the deaths of the Franciscans. The group returned along the Rio Grande, with a few men going west through present-day Arizona. Like earlier expeditions, Espejo's found no riches. When he returned home, Espejo also wrote an account of his exploration, exaggerating both the population and the resources of the country, hoping to gain the crown's approval for a more ambitious attempt at exploration and conversion of the Indians.

The crown failed to act on Espejo's information. Not until Don Juan de Oñate's 1595 request to finance a group that would venture north to colonize was the government of New Spain receptive to any further attempts to bring "civilization" to the lands previous explorers had claimed. Earlier, Gaspar Castaño de Sosa had made an unauthorized attempt to colonize New Mexico. After a year, he was arrested and sent back to Mexico City in chains.

Oñate, son of a Spanish pioneer in Mexico, was a wealthy mine owner in Zacatecas. It took three years of political maneuvering and planning for him to ready his expedition. Finally, in January 1598, a large group of soldiers, wagons, cattle, and perhaps four hundred men, women, and children began the slow trek. The party went north along the Rio Grande, following Oñate's advance group. As he moved north, Oñate took possession of the territory in the name of the Spanish king, explaining through interpreters that the King would protect and provide for those who submitted to his rule and attempting to explain the concepts of Christianity.

Oñate established headquarters at Ohke (San Juan Pueblo) in July but soon moved to nearby San Gabriel de Yunque Yunque. From here he and his lieutenants, including his nephews Juan and Vicente Zaldivar, explored much of the rest of New Mexico, seeking gold and the submission of the Indian peoples. The group of colonists quickly became dissatisfied. There was no gold in this desolate land. They had to work hard to wrest a living from the land rather than plucking riches from the ground, as they had been led to believe. The second goal of the colonizing effort—that of Christianizing the Indians—put limits on the harsh treatment of Indians by the colonists, who chafed at being unable to exploit the available free labor. As early as one month after arriving at San Gabriel, several colonists attempted to defect, but they were discovered and forced to remain.

In addition to difficulties with the Spaniards, Oñate had to contend with Indian reaction to his presence. At Acoma when a Spanish party visited, attempting to requisition provisions, the Indians pretended to acquiesce, but then attacked the group. Thirteen Spaniards died, including Juan de Zaldivar, Oñate's trusted lieutenant, nephew, and good friend. Juan's brother Vicente led a detachment of troops bent on revenge that demanded submission of the Acomas and surrender of the responsible Indians. In the bloodbath that followed the Acomas' refusal to submit, the Spanish, who were better armed, defeated thousands of Indians after three days of fierce fighting. The Spanish exacted harsh punishment: they destroyed the pueblo, enslaved the males, cut off warriors' feet, and sent women to Mexico City as slaves.

Oñate described the situation to the viceroy, including details of great wealth ready to be amassed as well as the number of Indians ready to be converted. The good news achieved its desired effect: the Spanish government sent reinforcements to Oñate. Seventy-three soldiers arrived on Christmas Eve, 1599. However, the colonists continued to rebel against the circumstances in which they found themselves, including their futile attempts to obtain food from the Indians and their failure to find gold. Later, while Oñate was on a short expedition to the east, many colonists deserted, leaving only a handful to populate the already exhausted colony. Through the efforts of Vicente de Zaldivar, new missionaries and settlers were recruited to bring new life to the struggling settlement of San Gabriel.

Oñate next headed west, arriving at the Colorado River and then heading south to the Gulf of California, where he arrived on January 25, 1605, again taking possession of the new lands for Spain. On the return trip, Oñate passed by El Morro, leaving his name ("Pasó por aquí", he wrote: "I came this way") on Inscription Rock on April 16, 1605.

Oñate's extensive expeditions, campaigns, and gubernatorial duties had exhausted him and reduced him to poverty, as he had financed much of the colonizing effort from his private fortune. To add to his troubles, when news of the colonists' defections, the lack of success in converting the Indians, and the failure to find gold reached Mexico, the viceroy was horrified. With the concurrence of the king in Madrid, he decided that the colony should be abandoned. However, the problem of what to do with the Christianized Indians prevented this plan from being carried out. Secular and religious authorities decided to keep the new areas as missionary territory and as a buffer to protect New Spain against the anticipated incursion of other European countries.

A new governor was named by the viceroy. In despair, Oñate resigned. The viceroy accepted Oñate's resignation but warned him to remain in his post until further orders arrived. The colonists, defying the will of Spain, rejected the new governor and elected Oñate instead. After the tired Oñate declined the honor, his son, Don Cristóbal, was chosen. However, the viceroy appointed Don Pedro de Peralta as governor, with instructions to found a new capital when he assumed the position.

After Peralta arrived in the spring of 1610, Don Juan and his son were permitted to leave New Mexico. On the way to Mexico City, Don Cristóbal died. Don Juan was charged with a series of crimes, including failure to obey royal decrees, lack of respect for the friars, and mistreatment of the Indians, especially of the Acomas. He was sentenced along with Vicente de Zaldivar and others, fined, and banished perpetually from New Mexico. He may have been pardoned later as records show that in 1624 he still bore the title of *adelantado* (governor), and was named to inspect the mines in Spain.

In retrospect, Don Juan de Oñate is remembered for his extensive exploration of the Southwest, for organizing the first mission system among the Pueblo Indians, and for establishing the first permanent settlement in New Mexico. These accomplishments were heralded in Villagrá's epic poem, *Historia del Nuevo Méjico*, the first poem written about any portion of what is now the United States, published in Spain in 1610.

For the next few years Spain maintained its colony with Don Pedro de Peralta as governor. In 1609 he moved the capital to Santa Fe, a more defensible location. The mission supply service, which had originally been set up to supply only the missions, actually handled all of New Mexico's external commerce during the seventeenth century. The service's heavily laden caravans required six months to journey between Mexico City and Santa Fe, six months to outfit, and six months to return, making the arduous trip every five years.

A lack of agreement between the Spanish government and the Franciscan friars and a festering resentment among the Pueblos toward the Spanish permeated the 1600s in New Mexico, culminating, in August 1680, in what has been described as "perhaps the most successful revolt by natives of the New World." Two strong individuals, aided by allies and by the course of events, played dominant roles in the Pueblo Revolt of 1680. After it was over, one, Popé, sat in triumph in the Palace of the Governors in Santa Fe; the other, Antonio de Otermín, wounded in body and spirit, retreated southward, defeated.

History has, for generations, pointed to Popé, a San Juan Indian, as the sole leader of the 1680 rebellion. While Popé was a key figure in the successful revolt, he was but one of many Pueblo leaders and war chiefs who for perhaps as long as twelve years had been planning to force the departure of the Spanish from this land.

The Pueblos had suffered for almost a century under a government they neither understood nor, in most cases, respected. The Indians resented most the Spanish disregard for the Pueblo religion. The Pueblos were required to work as servants in hacienda and mission gardens, to build churches, and to assume Spanish customs. Perhaps that was endurable. But to give up their religion was not acceptable, for the religion permeated their lives and explained their existence. To convert to Catholicism was more than objectionable. The Pueblos resisted their conversion. They were forced to watch their sacred kivas and ceremonial objects being burned and desecrated by the Spanish. Pueblo religious leaders were persecuted, beaten, tortured, and sometimes hanged.

Popé was one of forty-seven religious leaders flogged in 1676 for practicing witchcraft. He retreated north to Taos, and from there, with other northern medicine men, plotted a revolt. Many of those who worked with Popé were of mixed Pueblo-Spanish blood, familiar not only with the Spanish language, but also with Spanish customs and thought. Meetings among the rebellion leaders were held in secret, often at night after a Pueblo feast day. The planners worked cautiously over the years in laying out their scheme. Timing would be important. It was decided to stage the rebellion just before the arrival of the Spanish caravan, which came every three years. The Pueblo leaders reasoned that the settlers, low on food and supplies, would be most vulnerable then. Strategy also dictated that the capital, Santa Fe, would be cut off from the rest of the colony. Those Spanish living downriver would be advised that the north had been lost.

Popé was instrumental not only in forging the alliances within the Pueblo world, but also in creating the strategy that would make execution of the planned rebellion possible. He and his fellow strategists became increasingly successful in convincing other Pueblo leaders that the Pueblo people could survive only if the Spanish left.

Governor Otermín, who had known for a considerable time of rumblings within the Pueblo world, chose at first to ignore the warnings that were all around him. However, in early August 1680, upon the capture of two Pueblo messengers, Otermín sounded an alarm throughout the region. It was too late. Decades of neglect by the Spanish government in Spain and Mexico had left the little northern colony defenseless. The Pueblos were ready. Runners had notified them of the schedule by means of knotted ropes, each knot representing one day prior to the chosen date, that runners took to all the Pueblo villages. The revolt began, almost in unison, on August 10, the Feast of San Lorenzo. The Indians rose up and killed their missionaries, destroyed their churches, and searched out the countryside for settlers. Entire families were killed and farms were burned. Refugees began to stream into Santa Fe, coming together within the walls of the Palace of the Governors. Surrounded by Indians from all the Pueblos, and by the Apaches, the Spanish were given an ultimatum: either withdraw from New Mexico or suffer the consequences.

For days, the Spanish held out, their water and food supplies cut off. Otermín refused to give in. Battles raged; Santa Fe was burned, homes and churches pillaged. Still the Spanish remained.

Finally, on August 24, with no hope of saving their capital, the Spanish retreated, marching south down the Rio Grande. They were watched in their retreat from mesa tops and from canyons by the triumphant Pueblos, who, true to their plan, did not attack the colonists. The Spanish, continued south, a pitiful column "without a crust of bread or a grain of wheat or maize." They hoped to meet the Spanish lieutenant governor, Alonso de García, and the rest of the settlers at Isleta.

When Governor Otermín and his people came to Isleta, the settlement was deserted; García had taken his survivors and had retreated. South of Socorro, the two groups of refugees met, and together they marched to El Paso. There, despite the desire of many settlers to desert New Mexico, the governor and his colony remained. Otermín, accompanied by a few soldiers, went north in the winter of 1681–82 in an attempt to reconquer the Pueblos. He and his troops burned all that remained of the abandoned Pueblos south of Cochiti, but the reconquest was not successful and they returned to El Paso.

Meanwhile Popé had moved into the Palace of the Governors in Santa Fe. He demanded that all Spanish objects, from churches and statues to grape vines and peach trees, be destroyed. But, while the Pueblo alliance that was forged for the Revolt of 1680 was strong enough to withstand Otermín's reconquest attempt, neither Popé nor the other Pueblo leaders could maintain a permanent Pueblo federation.

Factionalism split the Pueblos. Some had returned to their original homes; others took up residence in the remaining homes and government buildings of Santa Fe. Meanwhile the Spanish were unable to find a governor and lacked the necessary funds for a reconquest. Finally, in 1688, a rich Spaniard undertook to regain the territory at his own expense.

The name alone, Don Diego de Vargas Zapata y Luján Ponce de León y Contreras, speaks for the noble origin of the thirtieth Spanish governor of New Mexico. The reconqueror was born in Spain, studied at the University of Valladolid, and then set sail for New Spain to further his personal and family fortunes. Arriving in the New World as a special courier for the Spanish king, Carlos II, de Vargas advanced through several administrative posts in the Viceroyalty of New Spain (Mexico) between 1672 and 1688.

In 1688, the well-regarded public servant received the King's appointment to the governship of New Mexico, which at that time consisted of a small group of soldiers and settlers living by the Rio Grande at El Paso del Norte, near the Indian allies who had escaped with them from the Pueblo Revolt. Governors of "New Mexico" had not lived in that province since the Revolt, although Otermín and several later governors had attempted unsuccessfully to return. Many of the people who had escaped northern New Mexico in 1680 had abandoned the hardships of El Paso to settle farther south in Mexico, despite orders of the king and viceroy forbidding them to do so.

Arriving in El Paso in February 1691, de Vargas found a dispirited group, fighting against hunger and frequent Indian attacks. The state of the soldiery was precarious: only 300 fighting men, poorly trained and poorly equipped, were available among the 1,000 prospective colonists. De Vargas hoped nevertheless to begin the reconquest immediately.

Delays caused by the need for action against hostile Indians only steeled his determination; finally, de Vargas led a small band of Spanish soldiers and friendly Indians into New Mexico in August 1692.

His march north along the Rio Grande met no resistance. The pueblos along the route, Isleta, Puaray, Sandia, Cochiti, and Santo Domingo, had all been deserted by their inhabitants. A tense confrontation with a large Indian throng at the walls to the city of Santa Fe ended in a bloodless victory for the Spanish. Pueblo leaders in the capital, and later throughout northern New Mexico, pledged their fealty to the king of Spain and to the Catholic Church. Vargas swept through the pueblos on the Rio Grande, then turned west to Zuni and the Moqui (Hopi) villages before going back to El Paso in December 1692 to prepare the settlers for their return.

De Vargas readied the group he would lead to Santa Fe, requisitioning supplies from throughout Mexico. As would occur repeatedly during his governorship, he encountered innumerable delays as settlers and provisions were assembled. Finally, some 800 people, including 18 Franciscans and 100 soldiers, departed from El Paso in mid-October 1693.

The band of Spaniards straggled up the Rio Grande, arriving at the walls of Santa Fe and camping in snow on December 16. On this occasion, the greeting accorded the Spaniards was not friendly. A battle ensued; de Vargas was the victor, and seventy Tano and Tewa Indians were executed. Few of the pueblos welcomed the Spanish; skirmishes were fought at many pueblos, with pitched battles occurring at San Ildefonso and Jemez.

As worrisome as the threat of Indian rebellion remained (and a major revolt was only three years off), an equal concern was the lack of food. Owing to frequent warfare in the first five years after the reconquest, settlers had little protection and little time for the planting of crops. They satisfied their needs at first through forced contributions from the Indians; however, as tribes were pacified, de Vargas would no longer allow the settlers to seize their grain. Food remained scarce, and the settlers had to rely heavily on grain and other supplies sent north from Mexico.

De Vargas's term in office ended in peace between the Spaniards and the Rio Grande pueblos (the Moqui and Zuni were to remain aloof for years). Missionary priests were dispersed among the pueblos once more, and missions were built. Families were recruited from northern Mexico to settle the new colony. De Vargas took responsibility for all these governmental affairs, ruling absolutely, often without consulting the *cabildo,* or council, of Santa Fe as his predecessors had done.

De Vargas's domination of the government proved his undoing when his successor, Don Pedro Rodríguez Cubero, arrived in 1697. As was customary, Cubero conducted an investigation, called a *residencia,* of de Vargas's actions. With the support of the *cabildo,* Cubero prepared a list of charges against de Vargas, keeping the former governor under house arrest for three years while representatives of the warring factions presented their cases to the viceregal court in Mexico City and the king in Madrid.

In the end, de Vargas prevailed. He was reappointed to the governorship of New Mexico to replace Cubero in 1703. Cubero fled the colony by a western route, and de Vargas again assumed the title of governor in Santa Fe. Five months later, while on a campaign against Apaches raiding settlements near Bernalillo, de Vargas died.

Twenty-six governors after de Vargas would represent the Spanish monarchy in Santa Fe before Mexican independence in 1821. Some would be less absolute rulers. Some would be more benevolent toward the Indians entrusted to their care; many others would be much less lenient. Some governors would be more successful than de Vargas in using the governorship of New Mexico as a stepping stone to higher posts in the Spanish empire. All would face the hardships of ruling a poor colony, lacking the riches of other Spanish conquests in the New World—a colony requiring almost constant support from the mother country. All

would have to deal with the raids of nomadic Indian bands, with a presidio and a militia considerably below optimal strength. And all would know the frustrations of slow communications with a corrupt, crumbling empire.

After almost three centuries of colonial rule in the Americas, Spain in the second half of the eighteenth century faced numerous difficulties—shrinking revenues, laxity in both religious and secular colonial administration, and, particularly in the northern provinces, encroachments by the British and the Russians and uprisings by hostile Indians. Hence the Spanish Crown determined to review the management of its American empire. To this end, José de Gálvez was sent to Mexico in 1765, empowered to recommend changes in all aspects of civil, religious, and military life. Among his proposals were the colonization of California and the exploration of land routes linking California with the rest of the empire.

For much of its history, New Mexico had been the most remote Spanish outpost. After several generations, Spanish settlements reached Sonora, California, Arizona, and Texas, but all these colonies were very distant from New Mexico. During the 1760s and 1770s, New Mexicans began the slow process of moving beyond the section of the middle and upper Rio Grande valley, from Taos to Isleta, to which they had retreated after the Pueblo Revolt. Coincidentally, or as a result of these movements into new areas, Apaches and Navajos began raiding Spanish and Pueblo settlements with renewed vigor.

In 1775, acting in the spirit of inquiry that characterized the age, the Franciscan Order sent Father Francisco Atanasio Domínguez, a thirty-five-year-old native of Mexico City, to New Mexico as "Commissary Visitor." He was charged to report in detail on the spiritual and economic condition of the New Mexico missions and to search for new routes to other provinces. Upon reaching El Paso in September 1775, he began his meticulous accounting of what he often described as the deplorable state of the settlement and of the four missions there, as well as that of the three "villas" (Santa Cruz, Santa Fe, and Albuquerque) and the twenty-two pueblos of New Mexico proper. Meanwhile he enlisted the aid of Fray Silvestre Vélez de Escalante in planning a journey to Monterey that, it was hoped, would discover an overland route to California and carry the gospel for the first time to Indians to the north and west of Santa Fe. The party, accompanied by a cartographer and by Laguna Indian guides and interpreters, left Santa Fe in late July 1776 and returned to Zuni in November of the same year. They failed to reach Monterey but did cover some six hundred Spanish leagues (eighteen hundred miles) and peacefully visited and recorded ethnographic information on numerous tribes living in present-day Utah, Nevada, California, and Arizona.

Unfortunately, upon returning to New Mexico, Father Domínguez encountered not a hero's welcome but rather the enmity stirred up against him by people who resented and feared what was contained in his "meddlesome" reports. He resigned his visitorial duties in 1777 and spent the rest of his life at posts assigned by his order in New Mexico and Chihuahua. Records indicate that he died before 1805. His reports were filed away and apparently forgotten until University of New Mexico Professor France V. Scholes rediscovered and published them in the 1920s. Comments in an unknown hand found on Father Domínguez's manuscript note that the report "is intended in part to be a description of New Mexico but its phraseology is obscure, it lacks proportion, and offers little to the discriminating taste." To twentieth-century readers, however, Domínguez's report has provided the most complete account of New Mexican life between the Pueblo Revolt and Mexico's independence from Spain in 1821.

The coming of independence was celebrated in the plaza of Santa Fe, but little change occurred immediately in the structure of the territory's government. Because of continued unrest in Mexico, the neglect to which the northern provinces had been subject also remained unchanged. Military forces were still inadequate for the defense of the settlements, and insufficient funds were available to make up for the New Mexico government's chronic revenue shortfalls. Governors were forced to impose heavy taxes on the goods brought in by trades from the United States. When this source of income proved inadequate as well, the governors forced the wealthy to make loans to enable them to continue government operations, with the loans secured on the basis of future customs receipts. Just as the government became mortgaged to trade with the United States, so did the populace become dependent upon the goods brought in by the American traders.

Ten years after the newly independent Republic of Mexico had opened its northern borders, Josiah Gregg arrived in Santa Fe. Gregg's health, close to the breaking point at home, was restored shortly after the beginning of the arduous journey down the Santa Fe Trail from Independence, Missouri. For at least a century, sufferers from a variety of ailments would continue to come to New Mexico for their health. Some of New Mexico's most celebrated citizens, Gregg among them, came here for a cure.

Santa Fe was by no means a health spa when Gregg first arrived in 1831. His book, *Commerce of the Prairies*, describes Santa Fe as a town of 3,000, "very irregularly laid out," with most of the streets "little better than common highways traversing scattered settlements which are interspersed with corn-fields. . . ."

Gregg was a misfit. He was different from his Missouri schoolmates, different from the people in his wagon train, from those whom he would visit in the East in the early 1840s, and those whom he would guide in California in 1849–50. He showed great promise in science and mathematics as a child, but attempted careers in both medicine and law without success. After his failure at the law had sapped his strength, Gregg entered into the life of a trader on the prairie, initially with his brothers. The Santa Fe Trail required the variety of skills—navigator, linguist, entrepreneur, mechanic, medic—that Gregg possessed. In addition, he was readily accepted, almost with reverence, by the Mexicans both of Santa Fe and later of Saltillo, Mexico, where for a time he was a physician.

Until Mexican independence, Santa Fe was closed to visitors from the north. Captain Zebulon Pike, for example, who had arrived in the province in 1807, was taken prisoner and shipped south to Durango, Mexico. Santa Feans clamored, however, for the goods that American traders began to bring along the Cimarron cut-off of the Santa Fe Trail, which trader William Becknell pioneered in 1821. Becknell and those who would follow could sell their goods for as much as a 1,000 percent profit in the first years of the Santa Fe trade.

Gregg made the journey from the supply point in Independence, Missouri to Santa Fe each year from 1831 until 1840. By that year, American goods had saturated the market; profits were down to 40 percent—inadequate to compensate either for the rigors of the trail, including Indian attacks, or for the exorbitant customs exacted in Santa Fe. Gregg and most other traders abandoned the effort.

The trader went east; he concentrated on writing *Commerce of the Prairies* and selling it. Again dangerously ill in 1846, he attempted to return to New Mexico, but was diverted by the offer of a position as guide to the troops of

General John Ellis Wool, assigned to take Chihuahua in the first phases of the Mexican War. Again he was an unpopular eccentric; leaving the army, he eventually settled in Saltillo to practice medicine. His restlessness prevailed. He studied botany and zoology in central Mexico, and then joined the Gold Rush to California. Despite his excellence as a navigator, his services were not in demand, for he was often unwilling to travel without stopping to collect specimens of new flowers and animals. At the age of 44, in 1850, he died in California of a fall from a horse.

Gregg is remembered for his keen powers of observation and his skill at recording what he saw. He and other traders were important to the inhabitants of New Mexico in bringing a refreshing glimpse of another civilization that had been denied them prior to 1821. These unofficial ambassadors undoubtedly softened the resistance of the populace to eventual American takeover.

Although described by his contemporaries as studious, humorless, and puritanical, Gregg felt at home in the wide-open Santa Fe of the Mexican era. As a place of contact among cultures—the dominant Spanish, the Indian, and the intoxicatingly new American—Santa Fe had many of the characteristics of a frontier boom town. The plaza was ringed by establishments catering to arriving travelers fresh from the rigors of the trail and desirous of entertainment.

María Gertrudis Barcelo, known as La Tules, was the queen of Santa Fe plaza. Her gaming establishment, decorated with the best furnishings that could be brought over the Santa Fe Trail, was the scene of nightly cultural encounters over which she presided at the head of the monte table. La Tules was wealthy—historians are agreed on that—but her shadowy history is otherwise controversial. Gregg wrote contemptuously of her supposed origin as a Taos prostitute. More recent research has established that she probably came from a wealthy Tomé family. We do not know when she left Tomé for Santa Fe nor what became of her marriage to a Señor Sisneros.

La Tules assisted the peaceful American conquest of New Mexico; she is said to have loaned the American army money for provisions to continues its trek down the Rio Grande to Chihuahua. She also played a pivotal role in the Taos rebellion against U.S. Army rule, warning American officers of the coming revolt in time to avert trouble in the capital. The information she provided was presumably gathered from conversations overheard in her fashionable casino.

La Tules' will, written in 1850, listed a large amount of money and property to be divided; among her heirs were two young women from poverty-stricken homes whom she had raised in Santa Fe. Attesting to her station, the will was witnessed by then-governor Donanciano Vigil and by others in the uppermost echelon of Santa Fe society.

Her American contemporaries thought La Tules was the mistress of Mexican Governor Manuel Armijo, by all accounts the most powerful New Mexican of the Mexican period. Recent historians consider this allegation untrue, just as other specifics of La Tules' and Armijo's lives remain in question. Armijo, for example, is said by some to have escaped poverty by sheep rustling, but there appears to be convincing evidence that his parents were members of two of the most prominent families of the middle Rio Grande valley. Armijo and his brothers monopolized the position of alcalde (mayor and magistrate) of Albuquerque in the 1820s, Manuel holding the position in 1825–26. In 1827, Armijo became the fifth Mexican governor of New Mexico. Eighteen months later—months marked by conflict between Armijo, the *jefe político* (political chief), and Antonio Narbona, *jefe militar* (military commander), and by reflections of chaotic conditions in Mexico—Armijo resigned to re-enter private life, if only temporarily.

In 1835, the Republic of Mexico sent Colonel Albino Pérez as governor to Santa Fe with instructions to bolster tax revenues in the territory. Burdened with this charge, Pérez, an aristocrat, was especially unpopular with the poor of New Mexico. The high-handed action of one of Pérez's confidantes, District Judge Abreú, in jailing the alcalde of Santa Cruz in August 1837 provoked rebellion among the northern poor. The governor, marching from the capital, was routed in battle and fled down the Rio Grande.

Upon taking Santa Fe, the rebels installed a new government, electing Taos Indian José González as governor. One of González's first acts was to appoint a three-man deputation to Mexico City to assure the republic of the loyalty of the new regime. Manuel Armijo, included in this group, had hoped to be named governor. Turning his back on his erstwhile allies, he issued a *pronunciamento* stating that he, as prefect in Albuquerque, was the only legal authority remaining in New Mexico. González, not wishing to confront Armijo, departed Santa Fe after a term of less than a month; Armijo took over his position and by mid-October was confirmed again as governor by the relieved Mexican administration. Armijo ordered his former fellow-revolutionaries decapitated.

The Albuquerquean remained governor for all but eighteen months of the remaining nine years of the Mexican regime. He is variously described as a venal and self-seeking coward and as a pragmatic and successful administrator. Armijo's second administration was made especially trying by Mexico's internal problems, which limited the colonists' recourse to the central government. Despite ever more frequent Indian attacks and a Texan invasion attempt, Armijo and New Mexico, largely ignored by Mexico City, were left to fend for themselves. Armijo was nevertheless manifestly successful at mobilizing New Mexicans to defeat the adventurers from Texas in 1841. He also seems to have provided well for himself; it was estimated by American Santa Fe traders of the period that customs revenues were divided equally among the government officials, including the governor, and traders.

Armijo was less successful in meeting the challenge of General Stephen Watts Kearny's carefully designed conquest in 1846, at the beginning of the Mexican War. The U.S. government sent advance agents, including Chihuahua trader James Magoffin, in a successful attempt to avoid a battle in taking Santa Fe. It is clear that Armijo met with Magoffin and U.S. Army Captain Phillip St. George Cooke over dinner on August 12, 1846. On August 16, Armijo massed 6,000 troops at Apache Canyon, fifteen miles east of Santa Fe. He then fled for Chihuahua, and the New Mexicans retired in disarray. Kearny and his Army of the West entered Santa Fe on August 18, taking control of the territory for the United States. Had Armijo been bribed to abandon his people, or had he recognized the superiority of the American forces and retreated to avoid bloodshed? The question has not been satisfactorily answered.

Upon entering the capital, Kearny issued a number of reassurances to Santa Fe's populace: their religion and language would be respected, any provisions requisitioned would be paid for, and they would have a voice in their new government, which would be headed by Taos trader Charles Bent. The Army of the West moved on in two parts, one for California, one to subdue the Navajos, leaving a small garrison behind. President James K. Polk and Congress repudiated some of Kearny's words, stating that New Mexico was still occupied territory during a war, and would be governed by the military. The apparent peacefulness of the conquest was also illusory. Disaffected Spanish and Indians effected a brief revolt in Taos in January 1847; before it was suppressed by American army forces, Governor Bent and several others were killed.

New Mexico was thrown into confusion by events in Washington and in Taos. Not until 1851 did Congress resolve the struggle between proponents of statehood for New Mexico and partisans of territorial status. New Mexico became a United States territory, and boundaries with Texas were established. James S. Calhoun, formerly an Indian agent in New Mexico, was appointed by President Millard Fillmore as the first of eighteen territorial governors.

During the ten years between the attainment of territorial status and the Civil War, New Mexico's government was largely occupied with heading off Indian conflicts and protecting the increasing numbers of immigrants to the lands newly added to the United States. Army forts were constructed throughout the territory, especially in the Apache-dominated Southwest and along the main routes of travel east to west across central New Mexico. Many of the commanding officers would figure in the Civil War, many on the Confederate side.

Although its role is often overlooked because of its isolation and because of the small armies involved, New Mexico was bitterly contested during the Civil War in 1861–62. The battles resembled those fought in the eastern states not just in their ferocity but also in the fact that opposing commanders often were personally acquainted with one another. Two conditions, however, gave the war for New Mexico a character all its own. One was the poverty and inhospitality of the land; the other was the crucial role of Spanish-speaking New Mexicans. Wooed and mistrusted by both sides, these people had been American citizens only fifteen years.

That there was a war at all in New Mexico was largely due to the imagination of Confederate General Henry Hopkins Sibley. Born in Natchitoches, Louisiana, in 1816, and graduated from West Point, he had served in the Seminole Wars in Florida, in the Mexican War, and in the expedition against the Mormons in Utah before assuming command of Fort Union, north of Las Vegas, New Mexico, while fighting the Navajos.

At the time of the secession of the first southern states, Sibley resigned his commission in the U.S. Army to offer his services to the Confederacy. Bold and visionary but inattentive to detail, he persuaded Confederate President Jefferson Davis to approve his scheme of raising an army of volunteers in Texas to conquer New Mexico for the southern

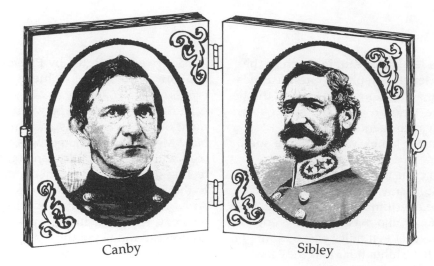

Canby   Sibley

cause. The aim of this campaign would be to
distract Union forces from battles in the east,
and, in its most visionary aspects, to rally
southern sentiment in New Mexico and Colorado and march for California to open the
gold mines and Pacific ports for the Confederacy. Crucial to this romantic gamble would be
the active support of New Mexico's Anglo-
Americans; the acquiescence, at least, of the
Spanish-speaking population, and the ability
of the Texan army to live off the land pending
capture of provisions stored by Union forces.

Major General Edward R. S. Canby assumed command of the federal troops in New
Mexico when the previous commander, Col.
W. W. Loring, joined the Confederacy in 1860.
The task of defending the territory against
Sibley's army became the responsibility of this
prudent and methodical officer. Canby appealed for regular troops from Colorado,
raised and trained New Mexico militia units,
and made plans to protect the forts Sibley
would have to take to carry out his war plans.
Sibley's army of nearly 3,000 reached Fort
Bliss (near El Paso), which was already in
Confederate hands, in July 1861 and marched
toward Fort Craig, twenty miles south of Socorro, meeting little resistance along the way.
The Texans found Fort Craig so heavily defended that they crossed the Rio Grande, com-
pelling Canby's forces to leave the fort in
order to challenge them. The southerners won
the resulting closely contested Battle of Valverde on February 22, 1862. Canby and his

Union soldiers retreated back to Fort Craig,
while Sibley continued north toward Albuquerque and Santa Fe.

Canby's decision not to pursue Sibley but to
remain at Fort Craig to continue training his
troops caused much grumbling throughout the
territory about his timidity. Rumors were circulated that he had declined to fight Sibley because the two were brothers-in-law, a
relationship never verified by historians.

Ironically, the condition of the victorious
Texans was worse than that of the losing
army. Their good fortune at Valverde had
been due in part to the unreliability of the
New Mexico militia units ordered to protect
Union artillery. The Confederate army, however, had so alienated native New Mexicans,
already suspicious of Texans' motives since the
ill-fated Texas–Santa Fe expedition of 1841,
that it could count on no support from the
population, and they could hardly live off the
land in central New Mexico. When Sibley left
the Valverde battlefield, he had only five days'
rations. Canby ordered all provisions and supplies destroyed ahead of the invading army,
whose only realistic hope by then was to capture Fort Union and, with fresh supplies, to
march on beyond this unwelcoming territory.

As the southern army moved up the Rio
Grande, Union forces evacuated Albuquerque
and Santa Fe and gathered for the defense of
Fort Union. When the Confederates left Santa
Fe in early March 1862 en route to the fort, a
sizable detachment of Colorado regulars met

them at Glorieta Pass. Two battles followed, neither decisive. During the second battle, however, a small Union unit guided by Lt. Col. Manuel Chaves scrambled over a mesa, surprised the scantily defended Confederate camp, and destroyed almost any supplies of value.

The Texans, without equipment, ammunition, or food, had no choice but to retreat down the long road to Fort Bliss. Canby then left Fort Craig and challenged the remnant of the invading army at Peralta (near Belen). He decided upon the expedient of "escorting" the Texans out of New Mexico rather than harassing them further. Upon reaching El Paso, Sibley and his remaining troops acquiesced in the disbanding of the Army of New Mexico. Union control over all areas west of the Great Plains was established for the rest of the war.

Shortly after the Confederate Army left New Mexico, the attention of the territorial government returned to a recurring theme: conflict with the Indians. It could be said that the Indian Wars in New Mexico began well before the Spanish arrived in the sixteenth century. There had been conflict between nomadic groups and the more settled Pueblo Indians for generations. However, the introduction of the European element changed the scenario; now there would be other cultures and races fighting for land and power.

With the dawn of the eighteenth century, the pace of the battles between various tribes heightened. In the first part of that century, the Spanish and Pueblo populations were preyed upon by four Indian groups, each raiding in a particular portion of the state. The Jicarilla Apaches raided in the northeast until driven out by the Comanches; the Mescalero Apaches roamed throughout the Rio Grande district; the Gila Apaches considered all of New Mexico south and west of Albuquerque their territory; and the Navajos concentrated their efforts on the mountains and mesas in the western part of the colony. These repeated assaults from all fronts drew the Pueblos and the Spanish together for mutual protection.

In 1786, Governor Juan Bautista de Anza made an artful and lasting peace with the Comanches, and that tribe remained loyal to the Spanish and the Pueblos. However, the Navajos and the Apaches remained tenacious. Their raids on Spanish and Pueblo settlements continued. Geronimo, whose Apache name was Goyakla, meaning "One Who Yawns," was born near the headwaters of the Gila River in about 1829. His lifetime, much of it spent as chief of the Chiricahua Apaches, spanned the era of intense warfare between the nomadic Navajos and Apaches and those, Spanish and Anglo-American, who were present in New Mexico at that time.

Geronimo was on the move throughout his lifetime. From Arizona to Old Mexico and back across the border into New Mexico he ranged, raiding remote ranches or small settlements, declaring always that his motive was vengeance for the murder of his family in Old Mexico in 1850. As the U.S. Cavalry became involved in protecting American forts and settlements in the Southwest, and as ranchers, homesteaders, and miners began to encroach more heavily on Apache territory, especially the area in southwestern New Mexico and eastern Arizona, the warfare with the Apaches intensified. Cavalry units tracked down groups of warriors and captured them. Other Apaches, often led by Geronimo or Cochise, would retaliate. And so the raids and counterraids escalated. Treaties were signed and agreements to establish reservations were made with one Apache band or another. But often the treaties were broken, or the agreements misunderstood.

Finally, after decades of terror and death on both sides, Geronimo, assured of a reservation, surrendered with his warriors at Fort Bowie, Arizona, in 1886. Soon he and his band (including some Apache scouts and a number of wives and children) were put on a train for San Antonio, Texas. The promised reservation did not materialize. Instead, Geronimo and his fellow Apaches were sent on to forts in Florida where many, including women and children, died. Survivors were later

moved to Oklahoma. There Geronimo began his career as an Indian exhibit, first at county fairs, later at expositions throughout the United States. Geronimo never saw his Southwest homeland again, despite repeated entreaties to government officials. He died at Fort Sill, Oklahoma, in 1909. Most of the Apaches later returned to Arizona, settling the San Carlos and White Mountain reservations, although some of Geronimo's descendants are members of the Mescalero Apache tribe of New Mexico.

Meanwhile, the Navajos had made their peace with the United States Government. First, however, they endured the Long Walk from their land in northwestern New Mexico and eastern Arizona to the Bosque Redondo Reservation along the Pecos River in eastern New Mexico. Captured from their remote canyon and high desert homes as part of the American campaign to "concentrate" the Navajos and Apaches, over 8,000 Navajos lived, alongside the Mescalero Apaches, at the Bosque Redondo camp in the mid-1860s. The round-up of both Navajos and Mescaleros was led by Kit Carson.

In 1868 the Navajos signed a final peace treaty in which the United States Government gave them back a portion of their homeland in the Four Corners area. With the surrender of Geronimo eighteen years later, the Indian Wars in New Mexico ended.

Although Indian raids continued at the edges of Anglo and Hispanic settlements, New Mexico continued to attract hardy migrants from the eastern United States. While the Pueblo Indian and Hispanic inhabitants of New Mexico continued, for the most part, their agrarian lifestyle, Anglos moving to the state took up occupations that had not existed prior to the Civil War. A more formal judicial system required lawyers; the beginnings of widely available education attracted teachers at all levels from the primary grades to university; the advent of the railroad in the 1870s not only brought in railroad workers of all sorts but also expanded opportunities in commerce.

While the Spanish and Mexican judicial systems required only that the alcaldes be literate, the American system called for trained attorneys. Anglo lawyers concentrated in Santa Fe; they became involved in the day-to-day legal affairs of the populace, in politics, and in the complicated and protracted land dealings of the period. The Treaty of Guadalupe Hidalgo, which had ended the Mexican War, specified that Spanish and Mexican land grants in the territories acquired by the United States would be respected by the new government. However, uncertainties over titles and use rights resulted in many years of litigation.

A name that figures prominently in accounts of New Mexico's history between 1865 and 1921 is that of Thomas B. Catron, a large man whose personality and presence matched his size. An attorney, Catron was prominent in the areas of land, politics, and the law. Catron moved from Missouri to New Mexico in 1866, became involved almost immediately in local politics, and over the next fifty years first ruled the Republican Party, then, removed from its leadership, served his adopted state by advocating statehood and serving as one of New Mexico's first two senators.

Catron quickly learned Spanish. This knowledge enabled him to amass over a million and a half acres of land grant property over the years. Catron, like many other members of the Santa Fe legal community, was accused of unethical practices in the matter of the land grants, but his defenders have asserted that he collected acreage by legal means. The subject is still controversial.

Catron's activities in the land grant market marked him as a member of the Santa Fe Ring. During the 1860s and 1870s the term *ring* was used to describe a group having common political and economic interests—cattle, public lands, mining, industry, and so forth. Where interests coincided, rings interlocked and were able to wield enormous power. As the exercise of this power inevitably conflicted with the interests of others, the resulting accusations and recriminations found their way into steaming journalistic editorials. The Santa Fe Ring controlled the lesser rings and much of the territory's legislation. Catron was considered its leader, and his name was linked to all its maneuvers. The Santa Fe Ring rose to prominence at a time when the Republican Party was gaining new members among newcomers from the East; the ring was therefore linked to the Republican Party, although ring members belonged to both parties.

The main political efforts of the Santa Fe Ring in the second half of the nineteenth century were directed toward statehood for New Mexico—perhaps because statehood would increase the value of the landholdings of ring members, perhaps because of the political strength statehood would bring them, as they would be likely candidates for state and congressional posts. The territorial delegate to Congress in the 1870s, Stephen B. Elkins, was a close associate of Catron's and a ring member. Elkins came close to success in achieving statehood for New Mexico, but eastern concerns and prejudices kept the territory from becoming a state for another four decades. (See POLITICS AND GOVERNMENT, below, for an account of the continuing debates.)

The 1870s brought violence and lawlessness to parts of New Mexico. This was the era of the Lincoln County and Colfax County wars, where men were murdered and mob violence ruled. Because of Catron's prominence and his involvement in the major political, legal, and business affairs of the territory, his name figured in many of the incidents, making him the target of vituperative attacks in the legislature and the press.

In 1895, the violence over, Catron was elected New Mexico's delegate to Congress, receiving a large majority of the votes cast, especially in the northern, Hispanic counties. He now faced the dilemma of having to espouse the free silver movement supported by many of his constituents, while most conservative Republicans were antisilver. An astute politician, Catron was able to persuade New Mexico Republicans to show moderation on the silver issue so as not to endanger his statehood bill. Despite his tactics, Catron's bills were ignored in Congress, perhaps because of enemies' attacks on his past business dealings.

His adversaries attempted to disbar Catron in 1896 when he became involved in defending a man accused of murder. Catron overcame this attempt, but he lost the election as delegate that year; liberal Democrat Harvey Fergusson was chosen to replace him. This election seemed to signal the demise of the power of the Santa Fe Ring. However, Catron was present in 1910 when President William Howard Taft finally signed the enabling act for statehood for New Mexico.

Anglo-Americans also became involved in the livestock business in New Mexico after the Civil War. The Homestead Act, by which farmers were allotted 160 acres of land on which to settle; the gradual subjugation of nomadic Indians; and the extinction by hide hunters of the bison herds contributed to the popularity of ranching as both a way of life and a business. By the 1880s there had been considerable investment, both foreign and domestic, in ranches all over the territory.

It was against this background that the Morley family came to what was then western Socorro County (now Catron County, named after Thomas B. Catron) and their Datil Mountain ranch. Agnes Morley was born in 1874, in Cimarron, New Mexico, in the historic Maxwell Mansion. Her father was the manager of the two-million-acre Maxwell Land Grant. By trade a railroad construction engineer, he had come from Iowa to supervise the laying of Santa Fe Railroad track over La Veta, Raton, and Glorieta passes. Young Miss Morley had

vivid childhood memories of the exquisite Maxwell Mansion: four pianos placed about the house; two stuffed Bengal tigers guarding the foot of the grand entrance-hall staircase; rooms filled with heavy, ornate furniture that had been shipped across the Santa Fe Trail from the Midwest. She could also recall experiences not quite so elegant. Agnes claimed that her very first memory was of sitting on the steps of the Maxwell Mansion one hot summer day, eating warm bread covered with butter and sugar. Two men rode up on horseback, and one shot the other—dead. The startled child dropped her sweet snack and rushed to cover the face of the dead man. His assailant rode off.

Agnes's father was killed soon afterward by an "unloaded" rifle that accidentally discharged. His family moved west then, in 1886. They traveled by wagon from the eastern plains of New Mexico to their remote cattle ranch in the Datils. There Agnes and her family lived from the last decade of the nineteenth century until well into the Depression Era of the twentieth century.

While Agnes Morley in retrospect marveled at her widowed mother's courage in taking three young children to the ranch, she remembered her childhood there as "one glorious picnic." Her education, although lacking in formal classroom learning (she had brief stays at a Philadelphia boarding school), was filled with the most practical kind of information. She and her siblings often rode, alone, to neighboring ranches or to Magdalena, seventy miles away. They rescued cattle from mud holes, rode and repaired miles of fences, and kept their eyes peeled for calves that, judging by ear markings, might belong to their ranch. They saw the horizon filled with herds of antelope one year, and the next spring would come upon a sea of whitened antelope skeletons after a thaw. The family thought nothing of riding forty miles to a dance that would start at sundown and last until sunrise. Outlaws, who often sought refuge in the desolation of Catron County, were common visitors; one stopped at the ranch houses one day, got a drink of water, and then sat down to play a melody on the family piano. Life was harsh, with weeks of isolation in the winter and unbearable heat in the summer. Children were a vital part of ranch life. They took part in ranch chores, cutting herds at roundup time and running messages between ranching families. They were caught overnight in blizzards, and were confronted, alone, by grizzly bears or fugitives from justice. Girls who grew up on New Mexico ranches were expected to work alongside their brothers. While they might have to ride side-saddle, they could rope, race, and handle emergencies as well as anyone.

Ranching continued to dominate Catron and Socorro counties for decades. While many of the original homesteaders left the area shortly after their arrival, having found 160 acres too meagre a holding to survive on, large ranches thrived. Agnes and her family were able to cling to their ranch until the Great Depression of the 1930s forced them to sell to larger landholders.

Thomas B. Catron and the Morleys lined up on opposite sides in the so-called Colfax County War, which occurred when foreign investors who had bought the huge Maxwell Land Grant from Lucien Maxwell attempted to evict settlers from the land. The territorial governor at the time, S. B. Axtell, was too weak and too closely tied to the Santa Fe Ring to bring an end to the violence in Colfax County or in the Lincoln County War. In September 1878, President Rutherford B. Hayes replaced Axtell with General Lew Wallace, with the charge to Wallace that he put an end to the bloodshed.

Lew Wallace's tenure as territorial governor was only a brief incident in a full life whose principal interests lay far from New Mexico. His birth, in 1827, his marriage, education, admission to the bar, and death, in 1905, all took place in Indiana. He fought in the Mexican War, commanded troops in the Civil War battles of Fort Donelson, Shiloh, and Monocacy, and served in the court martial of the assassins of President Lincoln. In 1870 he ran unsuccessfully for Congress; three years later he published his first novel, *The Fair God*, based on William Prescott's *Conquest of Mexico*. After his tour as governor of New Mexico, he was named minister to Turkey. The most important date of his life, 1880, marked the publication of his novel *Ben Hur: A Tale of the Christ*, for which he is still remembered. The book came out while he was governor of New Mexico, but the novel had nothing to do with New Mexico.

The Lincoln County War, which occupied much of his attention throughout his four years as governor, began as a feud between owners of rival mercantile establishments in the town of Lincoln but quickly involved all the surrounding countryside. A shooting war ensued that included the killing of a sheriff and his deputy (Brady and Hindeman), a pitched battle at Blazer's Mill, countless ambushes and reprisals, and a five-day shootout in Lincoln itself in July 1878. Shortly thereafter Wallace replaced Axtell as governor, imposed martial law, ordered a unit of troops to patrol Lincoln, and proclaimed amnesty to all involved in the war who would lay down their arms, except individuals under indictment. Wallace then had to deal with Billy "the Kid" Bonney, one of the major figures in the conflict. Wallace offered to lessen the charges against Bonney if he would stop his war of revenge. Bonney refused. Later he accused the governor of having gone back on his word, and threatened to kill Wallace. Sheriff Pat Garrett finally ended Bonney's escapades and his life in July 1881, a few months after President

Garfield had accepted Wallace's resignation.

Despite his short stay, Lew Wallace meant a great deal to the people of the territory. The governor was one of a succession of men who have been hailed for bringing progress and enlightenment to New Mexico. A contemporary account describes him as "above reproach, a man of strong principles, and a student of humanity." Another credits him with having smashed the "ring of rascals" who had congregated in Santa Fe to "pluck the taxpayers in every possible way."

The governor befriended other intellectuals in the territory, among them Archbishop Lamy and Adolph Bandelier. He tried to ensure that records of New Mexico's history be properly cared for and made available to researchers. Wallace also took personal interest in the new industries that were transforming the territory. He caught "mining fever" and spent days visiting, among others, the turquoise mines at Cerrillos. Along with most of his contemporaries, he was quite optimistic about the benefits that would come to New Mexico because of the railroad, which reached Lamy and Albuquerque during his tenure. He left New Mexico as one of the territory's most esteemed governors.

Because territorial governors were federal appointees, usually Anglo-Americans to whom political favors were owed, Hispanics were rarely named governor, although they made up a large majority of New Mexico's population and were ascendant in the legislature. In 1897, however, Miguel Otero, a native New Mexican, was appointed governor; he held the position for nine years, the longest of any New Mexico governor in any regime.

The early years of statehood continued to be marked by power struggles between the political parties and among powerful men who would leave their stamp on the new state. Solomon Luna was one of these men, a leader at the 1910 constitutional convention who had long been prominent in politics. Luna was a landholder in the central Rio Grande valley whose vast acreage fed thousands of sheep and required the employment of the largest workforce in the state. Luna operated his holdings in the tradition of the *patrones*, powerful figures who had an almost feudal relationship to the *peones*, or peasants, when New Mexico was a colony of Spain and later of Mexico. The peasants owed everything to the *patrón*, who in turn protected them. Even though peonage was abolished when the Americans took over the territory, the *patrón* system continued in some ways, and was occasionally exploited by both Anglo and Hispano politicians.

In many respects, the *patrón* was like an urban ward heeler. Respected by the locals, to whom he extended a helping hand in time of death or other emergency, he was often able to dispense jobs in return for political support.

Solomon Luna, both a Hispanic leader and a prominent Republican, was in an influential position at the constitutional convention. Once the constitution had been signed and delivered to Congress and to the people of New Mexico, Luna continued to exercise his power, helping to deliver majorities to Republican candidates in the elections of 1911 and 1914.

Octaviano A. Larrazolo succeeded Luna as leader of the Hispanics. Although a Democrat, Larrazolo was supported by northern Republicans of Spanish descent. He accentuated the differences between Anglos and Hispanics, creating strong supporters and many enemies, who defeated him in three elections for statewide office. When Democrats allegedly refused to support the inclusion of protections for Hispanics during the 1910 state constitutional convention, Larrazolo in disgust became a Republican.

An aggressive person and a brilliant speaker, able to command a large following, Larrazolo became governor in 1918, the last Hispanic in this position for more than fifty years. The antagonisms he inflamed in his efforts to concentrate Hispano power played a large role in his defeat in his bid for reelection. In 1924, Larrazolo sought a position on the State Supreme Court, but again the same split—heavy Hispanic support with substantial Anglo opposition from the eastern counties—

defeated him. He was elected U.S. senator in 1928, but died shortly after taking office. During this election, another powerful politician who could also be called a *patrón*, Bronson Cutting, was reelected. Curiously, he too died after election.

Two months after President Taft signed the bill that made New Mexico the forty-seventh state, Thomas Catron and Albert Fall became New Mexico's first senators. These men were strongly opposed by Cutting, leader of New Mexico's progressive Republicans.

Cutting was from a wealthy Long Island, New York, family. The young man attended Groton School in Massachusetts and Harvard University. After graduation, he moved to Santa Fe because he had been diagnosed as having tuberculosis. With family money, he bought the Santa Fe *New Mexican*, which he used to publicize his progressive Republican views.

Cutting's newspaper constantly focused on exposure of corruption in both major parties, and on emphasizing reform movements. Cutting himself constantly challenged the Old Guard of the Republican Party, which he called a gang. He advocated legislation out of line both with his party and with his Hispanic supporters, such as direct primaries and women's suffrage. In 1929 Cutting championed a fair workers' compensation law and an office of state commissioner of labor. The vote over that issue split the Republicans and severely weakened the Old Guard, ending Republican domination of New Mexico politics.

Cutting had the ability to form coalitions among different factions, molding congenial groups of Republicans and Democrats into alignment together. As a Republican, he encouraged voters to elect a Democrat as governor. Although Republicans controlled the legislature, Cutting's followers were able to pass liberal legislation in the 1931 and 1933 sessions by forming a coalition with the Democrats. Cutting supported Franklin D. Roosevelt in 1932, although FDR, a party loyalist, backed Cutting's opponent, Dennis Chavez, in a senatorial campaign in 1934.

Cutting had been appointed to the Senate to fill an unexpired term in 1927, and was elected in his own right the following year. Democrats, then in power and desiring control of Cutting's seat, tried to have him named ambassador to Mexico, but Cutting, preferring to remain a power in New Mexico, refused to go along with their plans. Despite the opposition of the president, Cutting was reelected in 1934, narrowly defeating Chavez. The following year Cutting died in an airplane crash over Missouri, and Chavez became senator, a post he held for eighteen years.

The governor of New Mexico at that time was Clyde Tingley, a colorful politician whose name remains prominent in the state through such projects as Tingley Beach in Albuquerque and the Carrie Tingley Hospital for Crippled Children, named for his wife. Tingley was a native of Ohio who moved to the Southwest with his wife-to-be after she contracted tuberculosis. Carrie had planned to move to Phoenix, but her illness forced her off the train in Albuquerque. Here Tingley started his political life in 1916 as an alderman from the city's Second Ward. He was elected to this position many times. The City Commission usually elected him chairman, which in those days was equivalent to being mayor. From this post, Tingley was able to dispense patronage and decide the course of the city's progress.

Independently wealthy through his wife, Tingley spent his life in politics, serving as alderman, as a district highway engineer, and as governor. He was sworn in as governor in 1935 and again in 1937. He was defeated in a special election to pass a constitutional amendment to permit a third term.

During his four years as governor, Tingley used the powers then inherent in the position to distribute jobs not only in state government but in cities and counties as well. He had a free rein in purchasing and in awarding contracts and was able to bend the legislature to his will. An honest man, Tingley never took any private gain from his machinations.

Tingley had made friends with Franklin Delano Roosevelt before he became governor, carrying on an extensive correspondence with the president. He used this Washington connection to win for New Mexico a disproportionate share of Works Project Administration funds, and badgered federal relief agencies and private enterprises alike to obtain jobs and projects for New Mexico citizens. Tingley pushed hundreds of projects, including Roosevelt and other parks in Albuquerque, Conchas Dam, highways all over the state, a gym for Española, housing construction, and public health and child welfare programs. Tingley returned to local politics, spending many more years as a member of the city commission, where he resumed his post as chairman of the commission and "mayor" of Albuquerque.

New Mexico has experienced explosive growth since World War II. The population tripled between 1940 and 1980 and Tingley's beloved Albuquerque had a tenfold increase. Many factors have contributed to the increase in population; the nationwide movement from the Northeast and the Midwest to the "Sunbelt" has been one cause. New job opportunities in extractive industries and scientific endeavors have also been important. Two "Robert O's", Anderson and Oppenheimer, symbolize these two new attractions to New Mexico.

"There is absolutely no one to compare in excellence with Robert Oppenheimer," a fellow participant in the Los Alamos Manhattan Project said. "He knew what was going on in every nook and cranny of the laboratory." The laboratory, concealed in secrecy throughout its first three years (incoming mail was addressed to Box 1663, Santa Fe; outgoing mail and telephone calls were censored), was charged with racing against German scientists to make a nuclear bomb.

Oppenheimer was at the same time a highly sociable and enigmatic figure. He was esteemed by his students at Berkeley and Cal Tech for his total commitment to their development and welfare. He sparked remarkable loyalty not only among them but also, in later years when he was under heavy fire, among the scientific community. I. I. Rabi described him vividly: "The lanky slouching figure, the reserved air, the penetrating gaze of his blue eyes, and the striking phrases that came out in a soft, yet audible voice, made him a center of attention in almost any company"(quoted in Goodchild, *J. Robert Oppenheimer*).

Oppenheimer was largely responsible for the secret laboratory's location on the Pajarito Plateau. Like so many other prominent New Mexicans, health concerns led to his first visits: his father's worry about Oppenheimer's deepening depression in 1922 and the physicist's 1928 bout with tuberculosis. During that summer and summers to follow, Oppenheimer visited frequently in the state. He spent much of his time on horseback, riding through the Sangre de Cristo Mountains surrounding the family cabin, which he called Perro Caliente (Hot Dog). When he was appointed director of the project in 1942, he toured New Mexico with the project's military commander, General Leslie Groves, before settling on a site close to his family cabin, near transcontinental transportation in Albuquerque, but isolated enough for security.

Most New Mexicans were unaware of the secretive activities at Los Alamos, but many families had been touched by the war. The 200th Coast Artillery, composed largely of New Mexicans, was sent to the Philippines early in the war. This unit was among the 76,000 soldiers under General Douglas MacArthur's command who were ordered to surrender to the Japanese in April 1942. Families of the 1800 members of the 200th heard no

more about their relatives until near the end of the war, when some received postcards bearing the soldiers' signatures, forwarded by the Japanese Imperial Army. Nine hundred New Mexicans from this unit died during the sixty-five-mile Bataan Death March and the following years in prison. Many of the survivors, who had never before been away from the immediate area of their birth, were forced to watch their colleagues shot, abused, starved, or allowed to die of illness. Monuments commemorating their sacrifice appear in cities and towns all over New Mexico.

Originally conceived as a project that could be handled by 100 scientists, Los Alamos rapidly grew to house more than 3,000 people, all engaged in activities that would lead to development of the atomic bomb. Located on the site of the Los Alamos Ranch School, a boarding school for boys, the community in 1943 became a boom town, with boomtown problems such as shoddily constructed housing and recurring supply shortages. The first problem, however, was recruitment. Traveling frantically from coast to coast, Oppenheimer gathered many of the country's best scientists, including Enrico Fermi, Edward Teller, Leo Szilard, George Kistiakowsky, Hans Bethe, and I. I. Rabi; then he returned to assemble them into a team that would produce the weapon.

The scientists were welded into a group by the force of Oppenheimer's personality and by a shared desire to beat the Germans. Soon after their success, however, they began to show differences. Fat Man, the first atomic weapon, exploded in the desert east of Alamogordo on July 16, 1945; Little Boy, the second bomb, exploded over Hiroshima, Japan, three weeks later. Oppenheimer and all of Los Alamos were as jubilant as the rest of the country when Japan's rulers tendered their country's unconditional surrender on August 14. Almost immediately, however, the Los Alamos community began to split; some scientists, with Teller as their spokesman, wanted to proceed to develop the mixed fission-fusion bomb (then called the Super, later the H-bomb), and others, including Oppenheimer, concerned more about the danger of their work to the human race in general than about its deterrence of potential enemies to the United States, wished to limit further research in weaponry.

Oppenheimer and many of the other Manhattan Project scientists left "The Hill" shortly after the end of the war. Rewarded with universal praise for his wartime efforts, Oppenheimer reentered academic life at the California Institute of Technology. Never far from the glare of publicity, he continued as a member of the General Advisory Committee to the newly formed Atomic Energy Commission, and pursued his desire for peace through international agencies and scientific groups.

Oppenheimer had been under close surveillance since his appointment as director of the Los Alamos lab. Like many young professors in the 1930s, he had flirted with communism; unlike most of the others, he was later haunted by this association. Whether or not he joined the Communist Party is disputed, but many of his friends did so. This background was known to those who hired him to run the Los Alamos lab, and, even though fear of the Soviets was not well developed before the end of World War II, Oppenheimer was watched very closely from the time he was made head of the Manhattan Project.

In 1947, headlines trumpeted the news that Oppenheimer's brother Frank had been a Communist Party member and had worked alongside Oppenheimer at Los Alamos. Allegations of Communist infiltration in the Los Alamos project continued and came to be concentrated on Oppenheimer. The former director was first interrogated by the House Un-American Activities Committee in 1949. The continuing investigations culminated in an unprecedented, highly publicized AEC hearing in 1954. Scientists testified both for and against Oppenheimer; Teller incurred the ostracism of his peers by speaking against his former colleague. Oppenheimer was stripped of his security clearance and thus of his advisory posts

in the atomic energy program.

The embittered physicist returned to his teaching post at Princeton's Institute for Advanced Study. He remained a brilliant and stimulating teacher and continued his interest in the philosophy and ethics of science. His three books of essays contain some of his thoughts on the dignity and joy of science.

By 1963, the political climate had changed; McCarthyism had long been discredited and a new administration occupied the White House. Oppenheimer, invited to apply for renewal of his clearance, declined. The Kennedy Administration settled upon the Enrico Fermi Award, the highest AEC honor, as a means of exonerating the scientist. The award, with its $50,000 prize, was presented by President Lyndon Johnson ten days after President Kennedy was shot, and less than four years before Oppenheimer's death.

Oppenheimer spent less than ten years of his life in New Mexico, but, more than any other man, he was responsible for the remarkable growth in the state's scientific community after 1942. Some experimental science had, of course, been done in the state's universities, but none had a strong tradition of scientific expertise.

One of New Mexico's first important scientific projects occurred independently of the state's universities and of the two big national laboratories (Los Alamos and Sandia), although most subsequent work has occurred at one of these institutions. In 1930, Robert Goddard chose the open eastern plains of New Mexico as site for his rocket workshop. His pioneering work in rocketry was funded by the Guggenheim Foundation as he had been unable to interest the U.S. armed forces in his research both during and after World War I. In addition, the Massachusetts fire marshal had reacted to an errant rocket's frightening flight by barring him from launching any of his self-propelled objects within that state's borders. Befriended by Roswell's people, Goddard was loaned a rancher's field, Eden Valley, where he constructed a launching tower and conducted his experiments. Scrimping and saving the remnants of each of his trial rockets, he almost singlehandedly advanced the science of rocketry to a point where, when the Second World War erupted, the military potential of Goddard's flying objects was recognized. Goddard left New Mexico for Annapolis in 1941, ironically the year before science in New Mexico got its big boost by means of the Manhattan Project in Los Alamos.

Goddard struggled for many years to convince the U.S. government of the military potential of his experiments. Much subsequent scientific research in New Mexico has taken the opposite course: the government has created a market (usually military), and scientists have responded. The second major impetus to scientific work has been, according to one observer, the desire of scientists employed in defense work for another outlet for their creative abilities.

One of the few large nonmilitary government-sponsored scientific efforts in New Mexico is the futuristic Very Large Array built on the open Plains of San Agustin west of Socorro. It consists of twenty-seven dish-shaped antennae, each eighty feet in diameter, which can be moved along thirty-seven miles of tracks. The largest radio telescope in the world, the VLA is funded by the National Science Foundation to study radio signals received from heavenly bodies millions of light years away.

Sandia National Laboratories in Albuquerque and Los Alamos Scientific Laboratories (which is overseen by the University of California) are both U.S. Department of Energy installations performing much defense work: Los Alamos provides the theoretical physics and Sandia the packaging for nuclear weapons. Los Alamos has therefore developed considerable expertise in elementary particles, and Sandia Labs has one of the world's most advanced laboratories for the study of materials exposed to extremes of heat, cold, and radioactivity. Spin-offs from these sets of expertise have included Los Alamos Labs' pioneering work in the use of elementary particles for the treatment of diseases, and Sandia Labs' heavy involvement in assuring the safety of nuclear power plants. Related projects have stimulated private industry, especially in the field of laser weaponry, since the armed forces pick up most of the tab.

The debate among scientists involved in nuclear weapons production is probably quieter now than it was in Oppenheimer's time. However, according to one laboratory employee, interest in the controversies surrounding the development and deployment of nuclear weapons remains keen, if muted: lectures on the ethics of nuclear weaponry continue to be well-attended at both laboratories. In addition, scientists at both facilities regularly turn their talents to other fields. The state of affairs has existed for over fifty years; in 1930, Clyde Tombaugh, who later became an employee at the White Sands Missile Proving Range near Las Cruces, discovered the planet Pluto through careful examination of telescopic photographs. More recently, Los Alamos and Sandia Labs' scientists have taken the lead in New Mexico in exploring alternative sources of energy. A small project using geothermal energy in the Jemez Mountains has come from Los Alamos Labs; members of the staffs of both facilities have been heavily involved in the refinement of the use of solar energy. The New Mexico Solar Energy Association has led the way to making solar energy practical for both residential and commercial applications; New Mexico has many solar-supplied houses and the Solar Power Tower on Kirtland Air Force Base in Albuquerque is run by Sandia Labs and consists of acres of mirrors beaming energy to a central collector.

Because New Mexico has little manufacturing and almost no heavy industry, there has been little impetus for research related to commercial products. Recently, however, the state has attracted electronics and computer manufacturing plants, especially in and around Albuquerque, spawning a cry for more research in these "high technology" endeavors. The 1983 New Mexico Legislature enacted a measure calling for "centers of technical excellence," appropriating funds to educational institutions along the "Rio Grande corridor" from Los Alamos to Las Cruces, despite the straitened circumstances forced by recession. Castigated by some as "too little, too late" to capture industrial development for the state, and by others as a meaningless political porkbarrel, the plan nevertheless appropriated needed funds to the state universities in Albuquerque, Socorro, and Las Cruces for development in "high technology" fields.

The future of science in New Mexico will probably continue to show the three influences of weaponry, leisure applications of scientific effort, and industry-related high technology. The balance of these and perhaps other directions will depend in large part on decisions made by the governments in Santa Fe and, to a greater extent, in Washington.

Because of opportunities afforded by the military and by scientific and technical enterprises, much of the growth in New Mexico has occurred along the "Rio Grande corridor." Most rural counties in New Mexico have gained little or no population, and some have experienced a considerable loss in population. The northwest and southeast corners of the state, however, have experienced booms related to energy extraction: natural gas, coal, and uranium in McKinley, San Juan, and Cibola counties in the northwest, and petroleum and gas in the southeast counties of Lea, Chaves, and Eddy.

In New Mexico, uncomfortably situated in the bottom ten states in per capita income, a capitalist with a fortune in eight digits who travels more than 200,000 miles per year in his private jet is not typical. However, Robert O. Anderson has been described as "the most prominent New Mexican" of today; his interests in big business, in ranching, and in the arts bring together some of the diverse strands that characterize New Mexico in the 1980s.

Son of an innovative Chicago banker who made productive loans to oil producers, Anderson came to southern New Mexico in 1942 after his University of Chicago education. He was armed with a $50,000 loan from his father and a fascination with the oil business. With his $50,000 as down payment, he purchased a small but profitable Artesia refinery. Horatio Alger could not have improved on his success. Through product improvement and successful marketing, Anderson increased the value of his holdings in the Hondo Oil Company. In 1965, anxious to devote more time to other pursuits, Anderson sold Hondo to the Atlantic Oil Company for a large block of stock; two years later, he was chairman of its board. Convinced that the future of the United States lay in the West, he engineered a merger in 1966 with Richfield Oil in California, in 1969 with Sinclair Oil, and with Anaconda Copper, a mining concern with a large uranium operation near Grants, in 1977. The resulting corporate giant, ARCO, in 1968 made the century's greatest oil find on the Alaskan North Slope. Anderson, despite his generally pro-environment views, came under great fire from environmental protection groups for his decision to build the Alaska pipeline.

When Anderson sold his New Mexico oil interests, more time became available for other business, principally ranching. He is described as the nation's largest individual landowner, possessing some 1,100,000 acres of land, largely in New Mexico and Texas. His Diamond A Ranching Company, headquartered in Roswell, makes annual sales of $10 million. Anderson still rides each year in the round-up on his Circle Diamond Ranch.

Much of Anderson's travel has had to do with his multitude of other interests; a sampling of these have included his directorship of the Aspen Institute for Humanistic Studies, trusteeship of three universities, membership on the board of the Wolf Trap Farm for the Performing Arts, and ownership of a chain of restaurants renovated tastefully in the style of the Old West. He has not neglected New Mexico institutions: he was the founder and principal benefactor of the Robert O. Anderson School of Management at the University of New Mexico; he has been generous in his support of the Santa Fe Opera; he has acted as chairman of the board of trustees of the Lovelace Medical Center in Albuquerque. "Robert O," as he is known to many, and his seven children have a hand in many New Mexico businesses and an equal number of the state's cultural institutions. One interviewer concluded that "he has tried, consciously or unconsciously, successfully or not, to prove the intrinsic worth of untrammeled capitalism; he wants Big Business to justify itself as public benefactor as well as source of private affluence."

Anderson's activities in New Mexico have involved him in two industries of great importance to the state, ranching and the extraction of oil and gas. New Mexico's dry climate makes agriculture difficult outside the two long valleys of the Pecos and the Rio Grande. The wide-open spaces away from the river valleys are largely devoted to stock raising. When Europeans first came to the Southwest, the plains of eastern and central New Mexico were covered with high grass, grazed by huge herds of bison. Unrestricted hunting brought the bison to the edge of extinction; unlimited grazing and climatic changes destroyed the "sea of grass." Modern-day ranchers must contend with the infestation of mesquite and other brush, as well as the arid conditions that limit the range's carrying capacity to ten to twelve cattle per square mile in most areas.

Rural areas of the state have witnessed steady population declines since 1940. Although the amount of land devoted to ranching has remained about the same during this century, the number of ranches has dropped from over 38,000 in 1935 to only 11,100 in 1980. Modern ranching, as these statistics suggest, is a capital-intensive proposition; huge ranches can be managed with little labor, as at Anderson's New Mexico holdings. Even with the scientific advances that have increased the productivity of the huge ranches, market forces in the 1980s have made the raising of beef marginally profitable, and have driven small landholders to leave the business.

Oil and natural gas have been important to the economy of New Mexico since the early 1920s, when "black gold" was found both in San Juan County, in the northwest, and Eddy County, in the southeast. In the decade of the 1930s, the population of Lea County more than tripled because of the oil boom; before beginning to decline in the 1960s, the county's populace numbered nine times as many souls as inhabited the flat, largely roadless expanse in 1930.

Oil had been discovered in San Juan County as early as 1882; a U.S. Geological Survey report of that year stated that a "flowing oil spring [had been found], but the workmen were driven away by Navajos before they could determine the quantity of oil obtainable." The 1950s were the decade of boom for Farmington and its surrounding communities; despite the early finds, natural gas is more important in northwestern New Mexico than oil, and the demand for gas began to escalate in the 1950s.

The rapid increase in the price of and demand for fossil fuels caused both areas to grow rapidly again in the late 1970s, but the familiar boom-bust cycle brought lean times again in the 1980s with the international oil glut. In San Juan County, the impact was softened by increasing exploitation of large beds of strippable coal.

More than $15 billion worth of oil and gas have been removed from New Mexico since the industry began. Anderson's ARCO has become the state's largest oil producer, seventh largest extractor of natural gas (El Paso Natural

Gas leads in that area). Peak extraction of these substances occurred in 1969; since then, quantities have declined as reserves have been depleted. The year 1982 saw the first decrease in total revenue from oil and gas production; coupled with a virtual end to hard metal mining (principally the copper mines of Grant County), and to uranium mining in McKinley and Cibola counties, this trend wreaked havoc on a state government accustomed to budget surpluses generated by severance taxes. Unless major new reserves of oil, gas, or minerals are discovered in the near future, annual production is certain to decline; oil production in the year 2000 may be as little as 6–18 percent of 1969's peak, according to industry estimates. Not only state government, but also the counties in the corners—Lea and Eddy in the southeast, Grant in the southwest, and San Juan, McKinley, and Sandoval in the northwest—are dependent for jobs and income on mining, oil, and gas; economic hardship seems predestined for the future of these areas.

Solutions for the present and future economic problems of New Mexico vary. The state legislature has accepted the concept of a "high technology corridor" linking Los Alamos, Albuquerque, and Las Cruces. Some would prefer a return to an agrarian society. Robert O. Anderson believes market forces will "adequately regulate the rates at which the United States exploits its oil, gas, and shale reserves." He castigates those who "almost want to close the door behind them and leave the state as it is," believing that "the people who exemplify traditions native to New Mexico feel they can keep their values and respond to changes without any overwhelming problems." Since the door cannot be closed, and local, national, and state change seems preordained, Anderson's views will be frequently tested in the years to come.

Anderson could not be speaking of any group of New Mexicans more precisely than about the state's Indians. As a whole, New Mexico's Indians have maintained their traditions with more integrity than tribes in other parts of the United States. On the other hand, Indians have been increasingly restive as they have come to see themselves as underdeveloped nations within a rich country. Jobs and economic well-being are obviously desired. Several of the tribes have been the beneficiaries of royalties from energy resources found on tribal land: the Navajos have coal and natural gas on their reservation, the Jicarilla Apaches benefit from gas reserves, and uranium has been mined and milled on the Laguna Reservation. Other tribes find varying degrees of economic well-being by other means: Zuni and Santo Domingo pueblos through jewelry making, San Ildefonso and Santa Clara through pottery, Cochiti through long-term land lease, and the Mescalero Apaches by developing their high and beautiful reservation as a vacation spot.

"We want to continue to improve the social, political, economic and educational development of our people while at the same time preserving tribal autonomy." Wendell Chino, chairman of the Mescalero Apache Tribe, made that statement in 1975, but it could have been said by any of his fellow Indian leaders. Those who have been elected tribal leaders in New Mexico during the last half of the twentieth century have had to be politically astute, remaining conscious of their tribe's past and aware of its future.

Wendell Chino, nephew of a famous Apache chief, kin to Geronimo, and a remarkable, if controversial, administrator, illustrates well the traits that seem to mark modern Indian leaders in New Mexico. A graduate of the Santa Fe Indian School and the Western Theological Seminary, Chino came back to the Mescalero Reservation as its first Apache minister. Chino's heritage reflects that of the tribe he now heads; his father was a Chiricahua Apache, his mother a Mescalero. The Mescalero Tribe itself is one-third Chiricahua and two-thirds Mescalero. There are also Lipans, Kiowas, and Comanches on the reservation.

The Mescaleros have been led by Wendell Chino for years. After being a member and then president of the Tribal Business Committee, Chino became tribal chairman. Under his leadership the tribe has lowered its unemployment rate (it was 70 percent in 1970) and has borrowed capital and made business decisions that have resulted in a multi-million-dollar recreational development that rivals any in the state. The Mescaleros' elegant Inn of the Mountain Gods near Ruidoso is the flagship of the tribe's diverse enterprises. Others are a ski area at Sierra Blanca, a timber operation, and a fish hatchery that supplies trout to a number of Pueblo lakes.

Chino's strong personal style of government is not universally popular. He has locked horns with Steve Reynolds, New Mexico's state engineer, over piping water from one part of the reservation to another. He and Toney Anaya, then state attorney general, fought over the issue of liquor licenses for the tribe's recreational developments. The Mescalero Tribe and the Tularosa School Board have disagreed strongly over tribal representation on that board, which oversees a school district with a pupil population that is about 30 percent Mescalero. Yet Chino continues to prevail; his tribe is thriving economically.

Wendell Chino is not the only Indian leader in New Mexico who has successfully brought his tribe into a strong position in this century. Pueblo leaders have formed the All Indian Pueblo Council (AIPC), a body that acts and speaks on behalf of all the pueblos. Delfin Lovato, from San Juan Pueblo, has been chairman of the AIPC for a number of years. Like other Indian leaders, he is courted by national and state politicians. Lovato often explains Pueblo policy to the rest of the world, and supports individual Pueblos when they take a stand that might seem unpopular. Recently, AIPC was involved in an unusual confrontation that included the U.S. Department of Agriculture, the New Mexico Department of Education, individual tribes, and local school districts. The issue, related to free school lunches and longstanding treaties, went into a lengthy court battle. AIPC also acts as a conduit for federal program funds and operates the Indian Pueblo Museum, a repository of Pueblo history and art (see ALBUQUERQUE).

The Navajo Nation has had three especially interesting leaders since the 1960s. Raymond Nakai was tribal chairman twice; he was well known for his public-speaking ability. Nakai was defeated in 1970 by Peter MacDonald, an aerospace engineer who had returned to the reservation from Los Angeles to run the federal poverty program for the Navajos. MacDonald was a thoroughly modern Navajo, a national Indian leader, a seasoned negotiator. He was chairman for twelve years, during which a number of valuable energy leases came up for tribal review and action. Controversy still surrounds some of the decisions that Chairman MacDonald and his advisors made with the energy companies. In 1982, Peterson Zah, a former school teacher from Low Mountain who had run the legal services program on the reservation, defeated MacDonald. Zah, a traditional Navajo, is considered a personable leader (with an "infectious sense of humor," according to a colleague). One of his first actions as chairman was to promise that he and the new Hopi chairman, Ivan Sidney, a friend, would begin to negotiate the longstanding and bitter Hopi-Navajo land dispute.

New Mexico has long led a colonial existence, with decisions made for its people by far-off courtiers and politicians in Madrid, Mexico City, or Washington. Some leaders, such as Diego de Vargas and Clyde Tingley, have been strong enough to bend the policies of the capital to suit their wishes and the needs of New Mexico's people. More recently, influential people like Robert O. Anderson and Wendell Chino have advocated a greater role for New Mexicans in determining their own destiny. Anderson and Chino would agree that continued economic development and maintenance of ethnic traditions should be important components of New Mexico's continuing history.

land:

climate, geology, topography, and paleontology

In geologic terms, the combination of valley, mountain, mesa, and plain that characterizes New Mexico's land represents only the thinnest veneer on the earth's history. To sketch the formation of New Mexico we must look back to the Precambrian Era.

Rock of Precambrian origin covers a relatively small part of New Mexico's surface. The Precambrian gneisses, granites, and quartzites that make up the cores of many of New Mexico's mountain ranges are occasionally exposed, as where erosion has opened the western and southern flanks of the Sandia Mountains, in the Pecos Wilderness in the Sangre de Cristo Range, and in other large mountain chains. Remarkable, rare mineral crystals found near Dixon also date from this period.

At times during the Paleozoic Era (570 to 240 million years ago), New Mexico was a flat, almost featureless plain, largely under water, that teemed with primitive life. For other millennia, much of New Mexico resembled a swamp under a hot sun; during the Pennsylvanian period (330 to 290 million years ago), mighty mountains north of present-day Albuquerque and other north-south ranges divided

shallow seas. The last part of the Paleozoic Era, called the Permian Age, saw most of New Mexico rise above the seas, becoming a tropical desert, except for the Delaware Basin, where sediments laid down at the bottom of the hot, dry, restricted body of water of Paleozoic times became the oil and gas deposits of today.

The mountains of southern New Mexico contain ample fossil evidence of very ancient life. Early marine animals such as brachiopods and trilobites and later sponges, bryozoans, and crinoids can be found in old ocean beds now in high bands on cliffs in the San Andres and Caballo mountains and other southern New Mexico ranges. The largest of the organic reefs built up around Permian seas was the Capitan Reef, which surrounded the huge Delaware Basin, a 10,000-square-mile sea that occupied much of southeastern New Mexico and west Texas.

During the Mesozoic Era (240 to 63 million years ago), a tropical or subtropical climate prevailed over shallow waters and coal-forming swamps. New Mexico rocks from this era, especially from the complex Morrison Formation near Abiquiu, made up of sandstones,

Sheep in Valle Grande, *Harvey Caplin*.

mud, shale, and silt, have yielded numerous remains of dinosaurs, the largest of which was the brachiosaurus, eighty feet long and weighing fifty tons. The varicolored rocks—red, green, gray, and purple—of the Chinle Formation, which can be seen near Laguna and along Interstate 40 in eastern New Mexico, were laid down in Mesozoic times.

Toward the close of the Mesozoic Era, the world's continents and oceans took on roughly their present shape. New Mexico was once again a rolling plain, except for low hills in the northwest corner. The last age of the Mesozoic Era, the Cretaceous (138 to 63 million years ago), was a period of immense change: the lowlands of northern and central New Mexico were riven by erosion, vegetation that would eventually become coal was deposited in the San Juan Basin, and huge volcanoes in the Southwest added volcanic debris to the sediments of ocean bottoms. In late Cretaceous and early Cenozoic times, from about 80 to 55 million years ago, a generalized uplift of what is now the Mountain West occurred; called the Laramide Revolution, this period of monumental change created the Rocky Mountains.

During the first two-thirds of the Cenozoic Era, or from 70 million to about 25 million years ago, much of New Mexico had a lunar aspect, with high, rugged mountains and wide plains strewn with boulders and gravel. The Galisteo Basin south and southwest of Santa Fe was an oasis, however, with wetland plants and animals more characteristic of today's southeastern United States.

The extension of the earth's crust in the late Paleogene period (40 to 25 million years ago) caused the slow sinking of the Rio Grande Rift, a long trough extending from Colorado to Mexico, now occupied by the "Great River," the Rio Grande. The stretching of the crust also thinned it in southwestern New Mexico, resulting in almost constant volcanic eruptions there and along the entire Rio Grande Rift into Colorado. Hot vapors and solutions that extruded from the earth during this period of intense volcanic activity probably led to the

deposition of the mineral riches found in the area today—copper, lead, zinc, and lesser amounts of silver and gold.

There is considerable evidence of geothermal forces in northern New Mexico too. Another possible fracture of the earth's crust, called by geologists a "lineament," extends from the Arizona border near Quemado to the state's northeast corner near Clayton. Volcanic activity has occurred in numerous places along this line. Where it crosses the Rio Grande Rift, the massive volcanic field of the Jemez Mountains grew up, with the huge, twelve-mile-diameter Valle Grande caldera at its center. Capulin Mountain, east of Raton, a geologically recent cinder cone, and dark basalt lava flows near Grants, less than 1,000 years old, also lie along this line. The Jemez Mountains contain the only high-grade geothermal activity in the state, with 500° water temperatures that could be used to generate electricity, though pilot studies have not been encouraging. Geothermal activity elsewhere in the state may be sufficient to provide heat for residential and commercial applications.

Only in Miocene-Pliocene times (10 million years ago) did the open grasslands and the mammal grazers that lived on them begin their dominance here. Evidence of large mammals such as elephants, camels, and horses comes from rocks of the Santa Fe Group found from Española and Santa Fe to Cochiti; earlier mammal remains abound in the thick sedimentary deposits of the Nacimiento Formation in the San Juan Basin. During the last million years (the Pleistocene Age), glaciers have several times extended their icy borders to mountain tops perhaps as far south as Sierra Blanca. Winds blowing gypsum from the evaporating Lake Lucero created the fifty-foot "drifts" called White Sands.

Humans probably came into this region no more than 20,000 years ago, when mountain glaciers still covered many parts of the area, large lakes filled basins near present Estancia and Lordsburg, and the Rio Grande was establishing its present course southward to the Gulf of Mexico. Early Clovis, Sandia, and Folsom people hunted the large mammals driven south by the ice ages. The surprising twentieth-century finds at Blackwater Draw, near Clovis, at Folsom, near Clayton, and at Sandia Cave near Albuquerque have shown not only the tools these hunters used but also the character (and the diet) of the animals they hunted.

The aspect of New Mexico most frequently mentioned in accounts written by early Spanish explorers and missionaries was the coldness of the province and its severe winters. When Anglo-Americans began to comment in the middle of the nineteenth century, they noted principally the region's barrenness, aridity, and inhospitality. Much of the difference in their impressions, of course, is attributable to the fact that the Spanish lived or traveled often in semiarid lands with more moderate temperatures, while most of the Anglo-Americans arrived in New Mexico from the humid eastern half of the United States. Some of the barrenness observed by the Americans may have resulted from the exceptionally dry years of the early 1850s. Despite the differences in perception, both accounts were correct: New Mexico is both dry and cold. Some would add that it gets hot here, too. New Mexico possesses whatever geographic unity it has largely because it regularly freezes everywhere in the state and because no significant portion receives enough precipitation to escape the arid or semiarid classification.

New Mexico's dryness hardly needs documentation. The majority of the state's population—the metropolises of Albuquerque and Las Cruces and the smaller cities of Socorro, Deming, and Farmington—lives in regions that average less than ten inches of annual precipitation. Areas receiving less than fifteen inches include almost all the remainder of the state's population: Santa Fe, Taos, Roswell, Grants, Gallup, Carlsbad, and Alamogordo. Only the eastern plains and high mountain valleys average over fifteen inches per year. Stations recording more than twenty inches

exist only on a few mountain tops. Contributing to the effect of scant rainfall are two factors that hasten evaporation: the high, thin air and the intensity and amount of sunlight. Speaking generally, no matter what direction one travels from New Mexico, into Colorado, the Texas Panhandle, Chihuahua, or into eastern Arizona, it gets wetter.

Some facts about cold in New Mexico: almost every station in the state has recorded temperatures below zero degrees Fahrenheit. Even in the warmest corner (the southeast), nighttime frosts are common during two or three months of the year, and some mountainous areas in the north have only two frost-free months. Average temperatures for January in most of the state are in the thirties. The combination of cold and dryness produces conditions extremely inhospitable to most forms of plant life. Numerous species (cacti and yuccas are best known) have adapted to dryness, but relatively few thrive in both dry and cold conditions. These circumstances also affect the growth and reproductive cycles of the plants that do survive here, since they must wait both for moisture and warmth to produce seed. This explains why August (with the summer rains) usually rivals April in New Mexico as a time of blossoming and new growth and why much of the state experiences two "springs" (April and August), separated often by a hot, dry summer and a cold, dry winter.

Ecologists have been aware for some time that arid lands can deteriorate drastically. The equilibrium achieved among climax flora and fauna is more delicate and more easily upset here than in more humid areas. This fact is underscored by the number of abandoned pueblos, villages, and towns found in every part of the state. People who have been busy making a living have seldom noticed the changes taking place around them that foretell an ecological collapse. For this reason, natural rainfall cycles have been used to explain such occurrences, ancient and modern, as the abandonment of the large pueblos in Chaco, Aztec, and Frijoles canyons, the decrease in the flow of rivers, the loss of native vegetation, and the recent abandonment of dry farming in the central sections of the state. Determining climatic causes for specific historical events, however, can be a confusing undertaking, one that is often misunderstood. The shifts in land use just mentioned probably all have as their primary cause some kind of human activity. The following two examples argue that if the "hand of God" is more evident in New Mexico than in other regions, it can better be traced in the hearts and minds of residents and visitors than simply in rainfall tables and tree-ring widths.

Chaco Canyon is located in northwestern New Mexico in a high plateau region inhabited since the 1770s by Navajo herders. Along an eroded arroyo that now carries large amounts of water only a few times a year stand ruins of a culture that flourished in the canyon from A.D. 900 to 1150. The 800-room, five-story, stone and masonry Pueblo Bonito covered over three acres. Eleven other large pueblos and hundreds of smaller ones occupied the same valley. Archaeologists estimate the population at over 7,000 early in the 1100s. The inhabitants of Chaco constructed complex irrigation systems and an elaborate network of roads. They made beautiful and intricate pottery and jewelry and traded for other goods with distant peoples in present-day Arizona and Mexico.

During the twelfth century, the entire valley was abandoned. Many of the earlier explanations for the relatively sudden end of civilization in Chaco Canyon have stressed climatic factors. The curious fact is that the pueblos in the canyon were built and reached their cultural peak at a time when average rain and snow were probably less than they are today. The pueblos were abandoned, furthermore, during a century when precipitation averages in that area, although variable, were as high as they had been for 1,000 years. Those who have stressed these facts explain that the early settlement of Chaco began when the canyon was well covered with vegetation. Settlers watered their crops from a stream that proba-

bly ran all year because the trees, shrubs, and grass on nearby slopes and mesas helped retain soil moisture. Increasing drought and population pressure led to the refinement of irrigation methods, but farming and woodcutting also caused the surrounding countryside gradually to lose much of its original vegetation. When precipitation increased again during the twelfth century, it eroded the thinly covered slopes and cut a deep arroyo into the canyon, making it impossible for those early farmers to use the stream water because it ran *below* their fields. So they migrated, possibly because of too much rain.

The combination of arroyo cutting, flooding, and droughts probably continued for many years in Chaco Canyon; but during the years of its desertion by Pueblo people and its occupation by Navajo herders, the arroyo gradually silted in, and the stream began to meander across the valley as it had when the Chaco pueblos flourished. The arroyo visible today at the Monument resulted from a repetition of the erosion process that occurred very quickly when the area was overgrazed by domestic livestock at the end of the nineteenth century.

A more recent change actually witnessed by older New Mexicans also suggests strictly climatic influences. Between 1900 and 1940, settlers dry-farmed large areas of the state that are now given over completely to range land. Farming without irrigation, relying on rainfall alone, was always difficult and risky, but abundant crops were harvested, and most of the eastern and central counties then supported populations not equaled since. It is tempting to blame the abandonment of dry farming and the increasing desertification of range lands generally on the drought period that lasted from the late 1940s to the early 1960s. However, there are facts which argue otherwise. Average annual precipitation was declining all during the years of dry farming; many of the farms had already been abandoned before the drought of the late 1940s and 1950s. Precipitation since the 1960s generally has increased to levels above those early in the century. Although local two- and three-year droughts were surely demoralizing, a more plausible explanation for the fact that most of the rural counties have lost population since the 1940s emphasizes the economic and social effects of the Great Depression and World War I, which made jobs available in the cities and raised land and equipment cost.

Topographically, New Mexico can be divided into three zones: the Rocky Mountain zone, a U-shaped section comprising the north central portion of the state; the plains, extending from the eastern border west to the first range of mountains that extends from the Sangre de Cristos south to the Guadalupe mountains; and the intermountain plateau, all the remainder of the state, including the relatively isolated ranges, basins, and valleys of the south, the central portion, and the west.

Mountains are New Mexico's most characteristic natural feature. They are present in or visible from all but a few counties on the extreme eastern border. To a large extent they determine the climate, catch and hold water, and sustain and channel rivers. Above timberline, year-round snow peaks exist in every quadrant of the state, in some places rising an almost vertical 6,000 feet above the surrounding plain. For over a century, from 1680 until the late 1700s, the settled portion of the province of New Mexico retreated entirely to the Rocky Mountain zone—bounded roughly by Taos, Pecos, and Jemez.

First in importance, the Sangre de Cristo Range stretches from central Colorado nearly to Interstate 40 at Clines Corners. Together with the Jemez and Brazos mountains to the west, this region has been the core area of settlement since the Spanish began colonizing in 1598. Although the Rio Grande does not rise in New Mexico, it does receive numerous smaller tributaries and two larger ones, the Chama and Jemez rivers, in northern New Mexico.

A second large, elevated land mass surrounds the Mogollon Range in the southwestern part of the state. This region is the location of the Gila Wilderness, the first designated national wilderness. It spawns three rivers of local importance, the Gila, the San Francisco, and the Mimbres. Although numerous early Indian settlements thrived there

(Mogollon, Mimbres, and Gila are all names for these ancient cultures), Apaches later controlled the area, and neither Spanish- nor English-speaking people had much to do with it until the mining booms of the late nineteenth century.

The San Juan Mountains extend from western Colorado into the northwest corner of New Mexico. The remainder of the state's mountains are either scattered ranges that do not belong to any greater mountain system, or links in a series of relatively thin and sometimes interrupted chains that divide the middle third of the state into long, narrow mountain-flanked valleys. Included in the first category (all in the western part of the state) are the Zuni Mountains, the San Mateos (including Mount Taylor) near Grants, the Datil and Gallinas mountains near Magdalena, and smaller mountains in the extreme southwestern corner. Mountains forming parts of north-south running chains are, beginning on the east, the "front range" that stretches from the Sangre de Cristos through the Gallinas (near Corona), the Jicarilla, Capitan, White, Sacramento, and Guadalupe ranges. These mountains parallel the course of the Pecos River, and their eastern slopes bring many tributaries to the Pecos. A second, shorter chain begins with the Sandias and Manzanos near Albuquerque and proceeds through the Pinos and Oscuras to the San Andres and Organ ranges, the last two forming the western rim of the Tularosa Valley. A short strip consisting of the Fra Cristobal and the Caballo mountains separates the Jornada del Muerto from the Rio Grande valley. Across the Rio Grande, the Magdalena and San Mateo ranges between Socorro and Truth or Consequences form part of the western wall of the river.

Although mountains and rivers give character to the land, plains still cover the largest percentage of the state's topography. The Great Plains proper, their high, western short-grass edges, reach one third of the way across New Mexico. Within that expanse, geographers distinguish two sections, the lava-capped uplands of the northeast corner, and

Jemez River and bluffs, *Steve Bercovitch.*

the Llano Estacado ("staked plains") bounded roughly by Interstate 40, the Pecos River (which cut through the plains' top crust in ages past), and a line joining Roswell and Hobbs. Other areas of plains include the southern desert region extending from Las Cruces to Lordsburg, the northwest plateau area, and various basins (usually called valleys despite their lack of drainage) such as the Tularosa and Estancia valleys and the Plains of San Agustín. Wild herd animals, with their grazing, trampling, and deposition of wastes, actually helped create the native grasses which were thoroughly adapted to arid conditions and able to support the great numbers of bison and antelope that once roamed all the

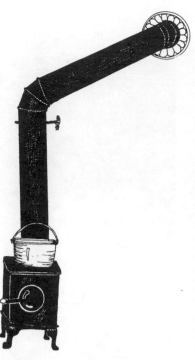

plains. Managed wisely, sheep and cattle establish the same interrelationship with plains grass and represent one of the most ecologically sound and productive uses of the land.

Visitors and newcomers quickly learn that elevation has much to do with rainfall and temperature. The wettest, coldest parts of the state are found at elevations over 7,000 feet. There are important exceptions. The eastern plains receive more precipitation than any areas except the highest peaks. Eastward across the plains, precipitation actually increases with decreasing elevation, because the plains slope downward toward the Gulf of Mexico, the source of most of the moisture. Another exception: the southwestern plains, which average 2,000 feet lower than the San Juan drainage of the northwest plateau region, receive more rainfall. This is due to the "rain shadow" effect of the Mogollon Range, which normally prevents Gulf moisture from moving farther northward. One can also observe that orientation toward the sun affects temperature and humidity significantly. A spot on a south-facing slope, for example, will be warmer, dry out more quickly, and support less vegetation than a spot with comparable elevation and

precipitation situated in a sheltered valley or on a north-facing slope.

New Mexico abounds in extremes. Some weather stations in the state (Red River and Eagle Nest) have recorded years in which no day has been without frost. The twenty-six-degree difference in average temperature between Elizabethtown (near Cimarron) and Malaga (south of Carlsbad) is greater than the difference between Bar Harbor, Maine, and Jacksonville, Florida. Cloudcroft, one of the coolest and wettest places in the state, sits barely twenty-five miles from (but one mile above) Tularosa and Alamogordo, among the hottest and driest. Record low temperatures of twenty to fifty degrees below zero were set in several parts of New Mexico in January 1971. Later that month, record high temperatures in the eighties were recorded in many of the same places.

At the risk of simplification, one can describe the weather of a typical year. In western areas accessible to moist air from the Pacific and on the eastern plains, where cold, wet Canadian air penetrates, January and February can bring a substantial portion of the year's precipitation, in the form of snow. Elsewhere, winters are relatively dry, with only minor peaks of winter rain or snowfall. Spring, beginning from February to May, depending on location, is accompanied by strong westerly or southwesterly winds. Fields irrigated with well or river water turn green, while cottonwoods, willows, and aspens leaf out. Snow melts in the mountains, filling arroyos and rivers. Changes on the grasslands can be less noticeable since there is often little spring rain in these areas. The driest and hottest months over most of the state, in fact, are May and June. Beginning in July at higher elevations, in August at lower ones, the summer rains account for one-third or more of the total precipitation in most areas. In a year with adequate summer rains, August is a month of growth, blooming, and cooler temperatures, when weeds become wildflowers, seasonal lakes appear, and lush grass seems suddenly to cover the plains. Rains extend into October in some parts, especially on the eastern plains. Snows in the mountains begin in November.

Some daily weather cycles also deserve mention. During most of the year, relative humidity rises to a peak at dawn, then descends to its minimum near dusk. Conversely, temperature normally reaches a minimum at dawn and peaks just a few hours before sunset. In many areas, a forty degree difference between the daytime high and the nighttime low is common. Rain, when it comes, often falls in the late afternoon, after huge clouds, which frequently threaten more than they deliver, have gathered for several hours. Residents call the thunderheads that produce only wind and dust "New Mexico rainstorms."

Despite these generalizations, unpredictability is one of the main characteristics of the arid continental climate of most of New Mexico. Yearly fluctuations in both precipitation and temperature are generally greater in arid than in more humid climates. In New Mexico, the weather of successive years is often totally different. A few above-average years can fill up tanks and reservoirs and lull one into forgetting how precious water is. The countryside prospers until a short drought period dries up water reserves, leaving crops withering and ranges overstocked.

The future of agriculture, and indeed of life, in New Mexico is dependent upon better use of the state's most precious commodity, water. New strains of perennial grasses that retain the virtues of native plains grass are being bred to produce grain for human nutrition. These grasses could be dry-farmed in many parts of the state, saving irrigation water, energy, and the damage to arid soil caused by frequent tillage. A grazing method developed by Allan Savory of Albuquerque has already radically changed livestock-raising practices on many of the state's ranches. Savory studied wild herd animals in his native Rhodesia. Observing that large numbers of the animals could graze without damage to the native vegetation, he concluded that heavy periodic grazing with intervals of rest actually benefits native grass. Savory then demonstrated that cattle and sheep can be managed in ways that approximate the habits of wild herds. Since migrating to New Mexico, he has been able to adapt southwestern sheep and cattle ranching by dividing ranges into pie-shaped paddocks, and, depending on rainfall and temperature conditions, rotating the animals frequently among them. The method doubles the yield of meat or wool per unit of land and improves the pasturage at the time. The economic effects of such basic soil and water conservation techniques are far reaching.

The success of agriculture depends both on water and soil. New Mexico soils vary from the moist, acidic, highly developed black earth of the northern mountains to the undeveloped, alkaline sandy river bottom of the Rio Grande. Local factors influencing soil composition and quality include both the natural, such as the grade of a slope, and the man-made, such as the irrigation-induced changes along the middle Rio Grande, which have decreased the once-legendary fertility of farms in the river valley of Bernalillo County.

Water and soil are important to all New Mexicans, not only those who operate farms or ranches. The fragile balance of plant and animal life owing to drought, cold, and unpredictability of weather; the isolation of waterless plains and rugged mountains; and the state's remoteness from ocean or navigable river are the natural features challenging all who have tried to live here. They are the threads that connect the history of the area from early Pueblo times, through Spanish, Mexican, territorial, and modern periods. For several centuries, people not prepared to deal with these realities have sought New Mexico's elusive wealth. Most moved on sooner or later. Some remained and learned to live here, adjusting to the harsh aspects of New Mexico's land and climate to enjoy the beauty hidden within its borders.

flora & fauna

The variety in New Mexico's climate, altitude, and water and soil conditions makes it a suitable home for an enormous variety of plants and animals. Only California and the highlands of Central America have a greater selection of mammals.

There are just seven life zones in the world, and New Mexico has six of them (see the map on page 60). The life zones are classified by vegetation types and vary by altitude and orientation to the sun. The distribution of flora and fauna is determined largely by geography and climate. Animals and plants do not necessarily stay within the boundaries attributed to them by scientists, and adaptation to altered surroundings and expansions of habitat occurs regularly. Migration of some birds, bats, and insects brings representation of the seventh—tropical—life zone into the state as seasonal visitors.

The continually increasing number of humans sharing the New Mexico landscape has sped the pace of change in life forms. People have farmed, hunted, built over, paved, destroyed, preserved, or renewed much of the land, affecting all that live there. Ground sloths, mammoths, and saber-toothed tigers became extinct in the early stages of human occupation of the area. Bison, grizzly bears, and wolves have disappeared in the last century. Many of New Mexico's plants and animals swell the list of endangered species. However, the Barbary sheep, kudu, oryx, and salmon have been introduced here, and the armadillo is taking up residence. More than one-half of the profusion of roadside wildflowers has recently invaded from other areas. Notable newcomers that flourish here include the English sparrow, the Siberian elm, the salt cedar, the tumbleweed, the starling, and the plague bacillus. Some species have been purposely introduced, others accidentally. Several have been disastrous and some highly beneficial to humans and native species.

Rather than enumerate the full range of known inhabitants, we profile here a few representatives of each life zone in order to hint at the variety and complexity of life within the borders of the state of New Mexico.

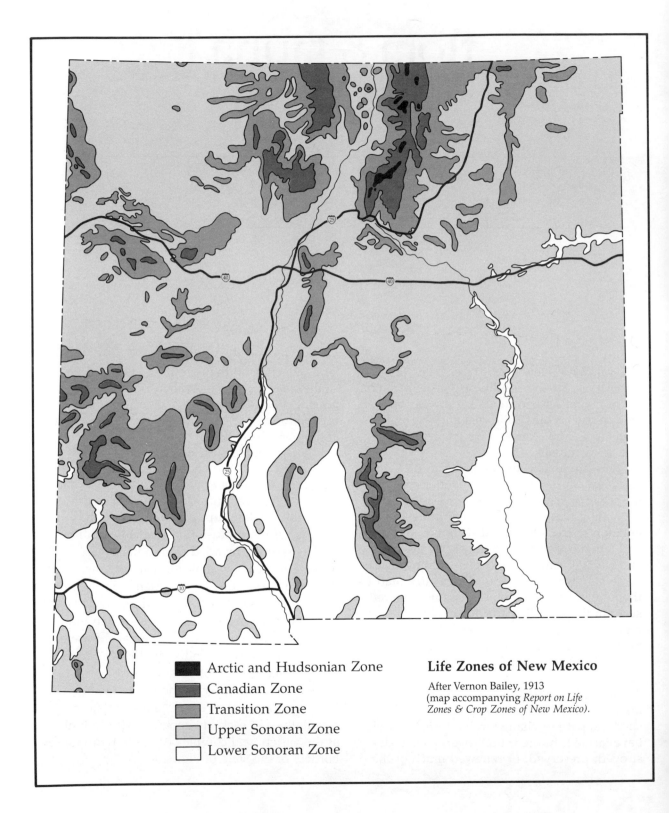

Arctic and Hudsonian Zone
Canadian Zone
Transition Zone
Upper Sonoran Zone
Lower Sonoran Zone

Life Zones of New Mexico

After Vernon Bailey, 1913
(map accompanying *Report on Life
Zones & Crop Zones of New Mexico*).

arctic

A few small areas high in the Sangre de Cristo Mountains can be classified as alpine tundra. The treeless expanse is covered with snow much of the year; the temperature drops below freezing for many more months. Therefore these areas provide only a very short growing season for their sedges, grasses, and flowers. When snows melt and sun hits these areas, plants seem to explode from the rocky soil. The alpine forget-me-not is indeed memorable for its brilliant cushions of flowers with five blue petals and golden pads surrounding the tiny central tube. The blossoms nearly obscure the fuzzy leaves. These hidden leaves, along with grasses and other leaves, are harvested by the diminutive member of the lagomorph (rabbit and hare) family, the pika.

The pika is a daytime creature who uses the sun to dry the bits of plant material it has cut and spread out upon flat rocks. Then it gathers up the cured "hay," stashing it in its rockpile or talus-slope home. Thus the vegetarian creature is prepared to survive the winter. The pika droppings provide for the tundra one of the few links between plant and soil, since by the end of the growing season much of the plant life is frozen, or at least refrigerated, slowing or denying the possibility of decay. The pika, however, converts some of the plant nutrients into excrement, which rapidly becomes part of the soil, ready to nourish other plants.

New Mexico is the southernmost range of the pika, a seven-inch-long mammal that is covered with fur from its head to its foot. The fur protects its short ears and the pads of its feet and is arranged in three layers on its body: first, a dense underfur of short, fine hairs; next longer, coarser hairs with tips that enclose the underfur; and then thicker, longer hairs that enclose the middle layer. These thermal layers allow the pika to nap comfortably on the snow, to shun hibernation, and to inhabit zones as high as any mammal in the world. Because of its harsh environment, the pika is endangered by few predators. When a hawk or a human appears, the community of pikas bark or whistle warning signals and scurry into their homes in the interstices of the rock piles.

In the Sangre de Cristo tundra, the pika is a light gray to cinnamon color, but in its small range in the volcanic rock of the Jemez Mountains, it has nearly black fur. This demonstrates its adaptation to its surroundings.

Plants with extremely rapid growth and prolific mammals such as the pika and the marmot demonstrate two ways to survive a short growing season: swift development and quantity of reproduction. The bristle-cone pine,

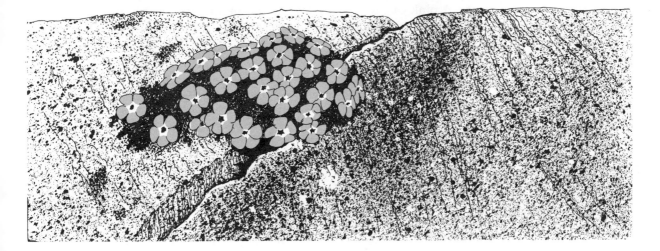

whose few specimens in New Mexico show extremely slow growth and infrequent reproduction, has made an opposite but effective accommodation to the brief summer. One of these short, gnarled trees may grow for centuries along the edges of the tundra zones, demanding little nourishment and few rootholds. The tenacity of the Alpine Zone species belies the fragility of their habitat. However, their adaptation to severe climate does not imply adaptation to heavy foot or horse traffic.

hudsonian

The Hudsonian Zone is primarily an area of spruce and fir forests, which exist in New Mexico at elevations of between ninety-five hundred and twelve thousand feet. Meadows here are overgrown with luxuriant stands of grass and wildflowers during the short summer. The relatively generous supply of moisture encourages the emergence of a variety of fungi; some large animals (elk, mountain goats, and bighorn sheep) and many small rodents (such as marmots, chipmunks, and pikas) inhabit the rocky slopes; songbirds, soaring raptors, and insects occupy the cool air. Livestock and some humans are summer visitors to this small, high area of the state.

Just below the tundra, patches of snow may linger through the summer. A pink cast to some of these patches is watermelon snow, a red alga that survives on and beneath the crust of old snow. The minuscule algae are cryophiles (cold lovers) that favor the thirty-two-degree temperature of melt water. The minerals needed for the plants' growth come from windborne soil particles. The usual green color of chlorophyll, which makes nutrients accessible to plants, is masked in this alga by a red substance that smells and tastes like watermelon. The material acts as a laxative for humans, but the algae are the staple diet for millions of minute, black, jumping insects called springtails or snow fleas.

Some fungi flourish at the edges of these grainy snow patches. The fly amanita is one that arises from the forest floor. Its brilliant red cap is dotted by white tissue patches of the universal veil, the egg-like enclosure from which it emerged. Another remnant of the veil forms a skirt around the two- to seven-inch white stalk. The amanita's frequent growth under spruce trees suggests a symbiotic relationship between the mushroom and the roots of the tree. The beauty of its appearance disguises its toxicity—poisonous chemicals contained in the mushroom can cause profuse sweating, delirium, and death.

Near the edge of a summer snowbank one may also see the compact grass-and-moss nest of the small water pipit. The male and female birds are similarly plain brown, but have a bright song and a wheeling flight. After a summer of living on insects on the treeless New Mexico mountaintops, the pipits leave the state for the winter, to return in mid-March.

One of the larger animals taking advantage of melting snow and the absence of many predators at high elevations is the bighorn sheep. It was once abundant in the rough, rocky heights of New Mexico's mountains. By 1927 scarcity of browse plants, indiscriminate hunting, and disease had reduced the population to very small ranges in the Hatchet, San Andres, and Guadalupe mountains. A few desert bighorns remain in these ranges and in the Peloncillo Mountains today. Rocky Mountain bighorn sheep have recently been reintro-

duced into the northern and central mountains and are faring well.

Coronado, in 1540, described sheep as big as horses, with large horns and short tails. He wrote of the bighorn. Both the large (two- to three-hundred-pound) male and the smaller female have horns; the ewe's spikes are slender and curved slightly backwards; the ram's are the true big horns. The permanent horn growth can extend to thirty-three inches, wrapped in a complete, tight circle starting at a broad base above the ears, sweeping back out and coming forward in an upward coil. The massive horns serve the male in battle with other rams, fought to win three or four ewes. These tourneys, which follow a definite pattern, begin in the rutting season of November and December. Two combatant rams' seeming indifference to each other is interrupted by snorting and pacing. When they are at a distance of about thirty feet from one another, each rears up on its hind legs, advances, drops down with head lowered, and lunges at the other ram. The two collide with a loud and accurate impact and then back

away. The dramatic battle may continue, with these actions repeated, for several hours, until one ram wanders off. The victorious animal stays in the flock with its mates through the winter and then joins a group of rams or travels alone in the spring.

By late May or early June, each of the pregnant ewes finds an isolated spot in which to give birth to one or sometimes two lambs. The newborn is covered with dark brown fuzz, which will become a coat of brown hair with a white rump, muzzle, and belly. A bighorn lamb can nurse within hours of birth and can eat solid food within a week. The playful lambs and their mothers soon rejoin the flock. They will begin browsing every day at dawn, rest and ruminate before noon, graze, and rest again. After eating once more in the evening, each bighorn sheep returns to its own habitual bed at night. Bighorns can browse along steep inclines or travel easily among lichen-covered boulders because of their unique hooves. The hard outer edges surround a concave, spongy pad, which maintains good traction on slick surfaces.

canadian

The Canadian Zone (eighty-five hundred to ninety-five hundred feet) covers only two percent of the state, but contains the autumn splendor of golden aspen for which New Mexico is renowned. Mixed conifer stands of deep green accent the color of the gold aspen leaves. The aspen's beauty is notable in other

seasons: the ivory and black trunks repeat shade patterns on winter snow; the light green of early leaves announces spring; and summer breezes give voice to the shimmering of the aspen leaves. The leaves' trembling in the slightest breeze is made possible because the flat leafstalk is attached at right angles to

the blade of the leaf, allowing a whisper of wind to catch and flutter the broad vertical surface of the leaf.

The tree is attractive to animals of the Canadian Zone largely for gastronomic rather than esthetic reasons. The saplings and trees provide cover for deer and elk, which also use the trunks as rubbing posts for their antlers. Squirrels eat the small, cottony seeds, and beaver cut and store aspen logs in their ponds for a winter supply of nutritious bark. Borers, aphids, and tent caterpillars feed freely on the trees. Elk and deer not only devour the young shoots and low leaves, but also gnaw on the bark. The black healing scars from elk and deer bites create a pattern on the lower trunk of the creamy-colored trees. Humans also have been tempted by the papery smoothness of the undisturbed bark to carve pictures, initials, and dates. Although it is interesting to find the markings of early travelers and high-country Basque and Spanish shepherds, the practice of bark carving can be harmful or fatal to the aspen.

Other human uses of the tree range from medicinal use of the bark's salicin (similar to aspirin) by Indian groups for the reduction of fever and inflammation to use by industry for coffin padding material. Since the lightweight wood is taste- and odor-free, it is the wood of choice for honeycomb boxes. New Mexicans use the smooth branches for *latillas* (small ceiling slats), for elegant wood carvings, and for the excelsior pads in their evaporative air coolers.

The aspen survives its heavy use by rapid, typically vegetative reproduction, by infrequent wind-borne seed and root sprouting, and by quick growth. Its requirements of full sun and open, bare soil make the tree one of the first to grow in burned areas. Its shade nurses the conifers that eventually replace it.

Even before the aspens sprout in a burned area, two tiny fungi, the pink burn cup and the ocher cup, grow in concave masses on the scorched ground. They grow nowhere else: heated or sterilized soil is necessary for these species to appear. Fireweed is another early arrival after fire in the Canadian Zone. Its purple summer blossoms cluster along a straight stem that reaches from one and one-half to eight feet in height. Young roots, leaves, and flowers have been valued for wild salads, dried older leaves for use as tea, and the stem pith as a thickener in soups.

Back within the cover of mature aspens, an occasional, rare yellow lady's-slipper may be seen blooming in the early summer. The delicate individual blossom attracts insects into its pouch, from which the only exit is past the stigma. There the pollen from a previously visited flower is brushed off. The insect must then proceed under an anther, where new pollen is picked up, thus reducing the chance of self-fertilization and increasing the probability of pollination from another flower.

transitional

Most of the New Mexican mountain area is covered with the Ponderosa pine of the Transition Zone (sixty-five hundred to eighty-five hundred feet). The Ponderosa pine is a valuable commercial tree, especially for lumber made from its uniformly grained wood. The tree provides cover for a large number of animals. Elk, deer, and Barbary sheep eat the young trees, and bears claw at and devour the bark of the stately pine.

Merriam's turkeys, an indigenous species, are highly prized game birds that were once abundant in the Ponderosa forests. The turkey depends on the Ponderosa for shelter, for roosting, and for part of its food. It eats beetles and other forest tree pests and their larvae, the destruction of which is essential to the growth of the Ponderosa. The remainder of the turkey's diet is made up of piñon nuts, acorns, juniper berries, and grass seeds. The bird has been affected by the scarcity of these plants in the lower levels of its range, where it is often in competition with livestock. The State Game Department now provides supplemental feedings to the turkeys in such ranges. A turkey that is unable to find sufficient vegetable matter in the winter is easy prey for bobcats, foxes, and coyotes.

The large and handsome turkey protects itself and its young by camouflage and by the placement of its meager nests near canyon or mountain edges for easy, unobtrusive escape by flight. The hens' consolidation of their broods provides more adult lookouts against danger.

High in the branches of the Ponderosa, the Abert, or tassel-eared squirrel, builds a nest of twigs, grass, and pine needles for itself and its annual litter of three or four young, and for numerous other relatives. The large nest is often mistaken for the hideout of the porcupine, which also prefers this habitat close to its bark food source. Pine seeds, mushrooms, birds' eggs, and nestlings are the squirrel's summer fare. In the process of finding and

eating the pine seeds, the squirrels accommodate the Ponderosa pine by inadvertently planting many seeds. The mature pines in turn serve the jaunty squirrels by providing homesites and winter food, the vanilla-perfumed inner bark of the tree.

It is in the fall that the squirrel's tassels begin to appear, with black hairs growing on the tips of the ears to a midwinter length of one and one-half inches. The color fades and the hairs thin in the spring; the tufts are gone by July.

The mushrooms eaten by the little rodents might be one member of the abundant *Russula* genus. Bite marks around the edges of the brittle cap give evidence of the squirrel's taste for these gilled forest-floor fungi. Where the pine needle duff is deep, few other plants can grow.

The cold-blooded Douglas horned toad, actually a wide-bodied lizard, has adapted to the cold of the Ponderosa-clad heights by giving birth to live young rather than allowing its reptilian eggs to freeze. This lizard is protected by the magnificent camouflage of its gravelly, multicolored skin. Its width provides a large surface area for solar heating in the winter. In summer heat the lizard finds shade or rests with its narrow side pointed toward the sun.

upper sonoran

Three-quarters of New Mexico lies within the Upper Sonoran Life Zone (four thousand to seventy-five hundred feet). Part of that area is made up of piñon and juniper woodlands, and part is extensive grasslands.

Artists and writers referring to the New Mexican scene often include images of piñon-studded hills. The piñon pine thrives in the vast Upper Sonoran region, varying from sparse growth of low, round-crowned trees to dense forests of pines up to seventy-five feet high. The "Colorado piñon," New Mexico's state tree, is a hardy, slow-growing tree with ancestors from the tropics. Its contorted branches bear thousands of clusters usually of two evergreen needles, bound by the bundle sheath and punctuated by woody cones. The cone has a spiral formation of scales, which open after three year's maturation to spill out pairs of edible nuts. The delicious piñon nuts and the importance of the wood for fuel make the tree a favorite of New Mexicans in spite of its clumsy shape and scrubby appearance. Indeed, the piñon's nut and wood probably made human habitation of the area possible. Evidence of man's use of the tree in the Southwest dates from 4000 B.C. Among the Navajos, it is said that piñon nuts were the basic food of the early Diné (Navajo people); Pueblo legend tells of the piñon providing *to,* the oldest food. The nuts are still a significant cash crop for the Navajos, who gather as many as one million pounds a year. The people rake and sift the groundfall, shake the laden branches over a blanket, or find and rob a pack rat's nest. The roasted nut commands high prices in Eastern markets and is a favorite snack of New Mexicans.

In the recent past, piñon pitch was boiled by Navajos with sheep and goat hooves to make a strong glue. Pitch was also used for natural dyes, for the waterproofing of baskets, for dressing wounds, and for an early version of nonstick-cookware coating. Piñon plays an important role in various Navajo, Apache, and Pueblo religious ceremonies. The twisted gray branches of weathered piñon provide hot, crackling fires for many New Mexicans, who are reluctant to classify its fragrant smoke as smog.

From the branches of the piñon comes the laughing call of crowds of grayish-blue birds demonstrating at once their propensity for flocking and their association with the piñon tree. The piñon jays may migrate out of piñon woodlands, but the jay's bulky nest is found with other nests of its colony in scrub growth of oaks or piñon. Usually four bluish-white and lightly spotted eggs fill the nest in the early spring. The young are fed insects, berries, and seeds by both parents, but leave the nest in the fall and join their elders in the collection of nut morsels. As many as twenty nuts can be carried in the long, heavy bills and esophagus of this relative of the crow. It discriminatingly picks the dark-coated nuts rather than the tan ones, which are self-pollinated or not pollinated and therefore undeveloped. The piñon jay buries some of its treasure in clear areas in or near the woodland floor for its winter supply. The jay's excessive preparation for famine and its poor memory account for the expansion and thickening of piñon stands. The piñon seed must be buried to germinate well, and the jay unwittingly obliges.

The wood rat or pack rat scurries beneath the piñon. This hoarding rodent amasses a huge number of piñon needles and other flora as well as small metal objects and similar bits of human litter, collected from within a hundred yards of its den, in order to build a large, bark-lined nest. Only one portion of the home, the midden, is used for urinating and defecating. This area becomes compacted and, when built in caves or overhangs, preserved. Middens that have survived in fossil form have given scientists clues about the growth and range of the piñon and other flora of the ancient past.

With a nest that serves as an insulated shelter and with nocturnal habits, the pack rat avoids desert heat. Succulent plants provide food and water for the rat, which nibbles between the spines of cacti, especially on the joints of the cholla. The cholla also provides a

favored shelter for the pack rat's nest.

The same life zone in the eastern part of the state is widely covered with grama grasses, combined with galleta, mesquite, and buffalo grass, the most extensive vegetation type in New Mexico. The grassland is described as a climax, or stable, ecological community, in which simple communities of plants and animals were replaced by more complex ones of great diversity that tend to perpetuate themselves unless severely disturbed by manmade or natural convulsions. The grassland's wide range belies the intense changes in the grasses' growth in the past century. Both natural and manmade disturbances have been considerable. The drought of the 1930s abruptly reduced the health and thickness of the stands of grass. Most farming land was once grama grassland vegetation. That grassland which remains has, in many areas, been so unsparingly overgrazed that other, invasive vegetal types have moved in, and the grama has been degraded.

The foot-high stalks of blue grama bear highly nutritive grains in a purple spikelet

that, when dry, curls into small gray or gold crescents and wreaths. The grass is relished by all livestock and is therefore easily overgrazed. The perennial bunch grass is itself an indicator of heavy grazing, as it tends to increase in number of plants with corresponding decreases in the number of edible grains and in soil-protecting ability. It serves livestock well in a mix with galleta, an excellent erosion-con-

trol grass that has tough rootstocks but is of nutritive value only in summer, and with the buffalo grass, a short, creeping grass that is also drought-resistant and a provider of good forage. Vast herds of bison and pronghorn antelope ate the grass of the eastern plains. Now the area supports some antelope and many more cattle and sheep, which reciprocate by fertilizing the soil.

lower sonoran

At least three different vegetation types are easily recognizable in the Lower Sonoran Life Zone (under forty-five hundred feet). The gravelly alluvial fans that cover the desert floor at the mouths of canyons support the growth of creosote bush, fourwing saltbush, Mormon tea, and yucca. In the sandy areas grow mesquite, acacia, and cholla. These thorny plants are replaced by grasses, aquatic plants, reeds, cottonwood, salt cedar, and Russian olive trees in the river valleys. Each of these types of vegetation hosts different forms of animal life.

The southwest corner of the state is especially rich in its variety of butterflies, plants, reptiles, and mammals, and is the home of

one of New Mexico's most unusual mammals, the javelina. Although the animal resembles a hairy pig, it is as closely related to the hippopotamus as to the pig. Herds of eight to twelve javelinas travel together in the mesquite savannahs, their range limited to warm regions primarily by their fur, which is inadequate for protection against cold, and by their short legs, which would not allow them to forage in heavy snow. The javelina, or collared peccary, depends upon the herd for toothy defense and for a greater chance of detecting threats from predators. The javelina's vision is poor but its sense of smell excellent. Its own odor, exuding from a flesh fold on its back, is not strong enough to keep enemies away, but

is sufficient to help the javelina keep track of its musky companions. The coarse-haired, malodorous, graceless, long-snouted mammal is a favorite of hunters.

In spite of the impression given by their sharp teeth and tusks, javelinas are not ferocious meat-eaters, but are quite tolerant of humans' company and eat the succulent plants of the desert, including the spiny pads of the prickly pear and roots and tubers growing in their thorn forest habitat.

Many types of cactus, legumes such as mesquite, and other thorny plants grow in scattered bunches around which blown sand collects in drifts. Between the sparse clumps of vegetation, the seemingly ubiquitous black pinacate beetle leaves a delicate track. The Aztecs named it *pinacatl*; the Spanish changed that to *piñacate*, and used the name as a mild insult to someone who acts in a presumptuous way. In English its common name is stinkbug. Though it is not a bug, it does stink. When disturbed, it stops, raises its rear end, and emits a foul-smelling black oil. The Navajos, knowing it is a beetle, call it *k'ineedlishii* and give the same name to a small Volkswagen.

Its long hind legs and short front ones force the stinkbug into an ungainly walk but serve it well when the early morning dew collects in a droplet on its back that rolls into its mouth, thus assuring it a portion of the desert's meager water supply. The inch-long, wingless beetle and its larvae are scavengers that do not attack living plants but feed on decaying organic matter, thus speeding the turnover of nutrients otherwise locked in by the lack of moisture. About one hundred species of stinkbug live in New Mexico at a wide variety of altitudes.

Another insect of the Lower Sonoran region is the tegeticula moth, a creature vital to the yucca plant, which in turn has been essential to the human inhabitants here. Since the configuration of stamen and pistil inside the creamy yucca blossoms prohibits self-pollination, the plant must depend upon insects for this function. The pollen is too sticky, however, to be brushed into the pistil by visiting insects. The female tegeticula solves the problem by collecting the sticky pollen from the anthers with unique curved tentacles. The moth than kneads the pollen into a large ball, transports the mass to another yucca (sometimes over great distances), injects the base of the pistil of a new blossom with her eggs, and then rams the pollen down the top of the pistil with her head. When the larvae hatch a week later, they feed for a month on a small portion of the yucca seeds produced. The yucca pods are still green and fleshy when the mature larvae bore holes to the outside, drop to the ground, and begin to hibernate in silky cocoons under the ground. The metamorphosis is completed a few days before the spikes of the yuccas burst into fragrant bloom the following spring and the mating, egg-laying cycle is repeated.

Indians have valued the yucca for the fibers along the edge of the leaves and for the leaves themselves, both used in weaving. Paint brushes are still made from the fibrous ends of the leaves, chewed to an appropriate softness. Yucca roots are mashed and mixed with water for soap and shampoo, an ancient idea recently adopted by beauty products corporations. The lather combined with the oxygen in pools of water, thereby aiding early peoples in catching fish by depriving them of oxygen.

The fish would rise to the surface and were netted. The cascade of bell-shaped blossoms of the yucca has become the state flower.

Many of the dramas of life in the arid Lower Sonoran region are enacted in water. The streams, rivers, and sinkholes of the dry land nurture a variety of native gars, trout, suckers, minnows, and killifish that have been joined by transplanted fishes. Amphibians, reptiles, crayfish, and insects also inhabit the water and provide some food for the vast numbers of birds that winter in the Lower Sonoran Zone of New Mexico.

One fish, whose fin outlines its dorsal and ventral sides, resembles a snake and swims in the waters of the Pecos River and the Rio Grande. The large dam on the Rio Grande at Elephant Butte stops the northward migration of the female American eel. Prior to the dam's construction, the long brown fish would swim as far as southern Colorado in the Rio Grande, probably bypassing lesser dams by its habit of feeding and traveling in damp areas. The truncated journey of the slender eel is still extraordinary, as it begins near Bermuda, where eggs have been deposited in deep water (in the same location as the European species' eggs). The transparent, ribbon-like young eat plankton in the sea, change from larvae to elvers with tiny scales at about one year of age, and then begin to emigrate. Upon reaching the Texas coast, the eel develops its olive-brown top and yellow-white bottom coloration. The adult male remains near the ocean, but the female travels and resides inland for four to twenty years before it stops eating, turns silver, and returns to Bermuda to breed and spawn. While in fresh water, its nocturnal feedings consist of frogs, insects, fish, worms, crayfish, and other dead or live animal material. The oily flesh of the eel is considered a delicacy by some people and birds.

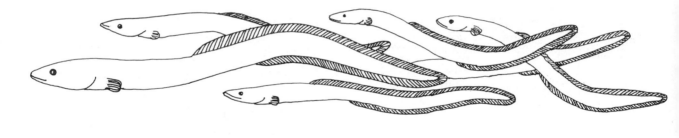

The traveler can find numerous guides to the state's flora and fauna, including fossil guides, in bookstores and libraries. The Museum of Natural History on Mountain Road in Albuquerque is a valuable resource for persons interested in New Mexico's plants and animals, past and present. Hunting and fishing information can be found in the Activities and Special Events section of this guide, on pages 6–7. Many species of both plants and animals are protected by law, and others are essential to their ecosystems. It behooves us not to pick, transplant, transport, or kill them, but to enjoy their color and action where they are found.

people

New Mexicans pride themselves on the mixture of cultures and races that is such a prominent part of the state. The three groups into which New Mexicans usually divide themselves—Indians, Hispanics, and Anglos—differ from each other in tradition, history, customs, and racial characteristics. But it should be remembered that from the earliest European intrusion into this land of desert, mountain, valley, and plain, there have been intermarriage, friendship, exchange, and respect among its peoples. And even before the Spaniards appeared in the sixteenth century, the resident Indians (Pueblos, Navajos, Apaches, and to an extent Utes and Comanches), while often at war with each other, also traded among themselves, in some cases intermarried, and even were known to live peacefully side-by-side. So while it is convenient to retain the image of a state with three cultures, in reality the people of New Mexico are as varied as the wildflowers on a New Mexico ditch bank in summer, yet as interdependent and interrelated as the sturdy, colorful plants are to each other, to the water that flows in the ditch, and to the sun that shines from above.

INDIANS

The first New Mexicans were the Indians, whose place in history goes back into the far reaches of time and whose continual habitation in the Southwest is itself almost timeless. Traces of Southwestern prehistory reach back thousands of years. In New Mexico, archaeologists study petroglyphs, arrowheads, potsherds, and other remnants of ancient civilizations all over the state, from the Folsom Site in northwestern Union County to Burro Cienega No. 9 down in the state's far southwestern corner. The existence of Paleo-Indian and newer sites is of itself not unusual. Many states in all parts of the North American continent contain significant archaeological ruins. What is unique about New Mexico is that perhaps some of the descendants of the region's earliest dwellers survive today close to the places where their ancestors made their homes.

Three major groups of Indians now live in New Mexico: Pueblos, Navajos, and Apaches. There are nineteen Pueblo villages, most of them strung along or west of the Rio Grande

The Pueblos

Petroglyph State Park, *Daniel Gibson*.

The Pueblo Indians are descended primarily from the Anasazi, a Navajo term that means "the ancient ones." New Mexico's other ancient village dwellers were the Mimbres, a branch of the Mogollons who lived in the southwestern quarter of the state along the Gila River. By A.D. 1100 they had been integrated into the more northern Pueblo people. The pottery of the present-day Pueblos can be traced back, in some instances, to the exquisite wares created by the Mimbres. The Anasazi lived in the dry desert areas of the Southwest for thousands of years. In about 2000 B.C. they were primarily hunters and gatherers, living on nuts, berries, and the fruit of the cactus, and hunting for the meat of desert- and mountain-dwelling animals like deer, antelope, and elk, and for turkeys and other birds. This way of life continued almost unchanged for more than two thousand years. The Anasazi gradually began to farm, in some cases planting corn in varied sites and waiting until fall to see if sufficient rain had fallen to grow a crop. Later on they created dams, irrigation ditches, and other devices to ensure that whatever water fell over the summer reached their plantings. By the time they were living in Chaco Canyon, the Anasazi had begun to refine their farming and irrigation techniques, building storage areas for food they had grown or gathered and constructing massive dwellings.

For hundreds of years the Anasazi lived in villages in the western part of New Mexico, in eastern Arizona, and in southern Colorado. As climatic and other factors (exactly what some of these were is debated to this day) began to dictate a move away from the Four Corners area in about A.D. 1300, the Anasazi migrated eastward, settling along rivers like the Frijoles and the Chama and eventually concentrating in the Rio Grande area where Coronado and his troops found them living in 1540. Some of the pueblos that Coronado's expedition visited exist now only as ruins. However, up and down the broad Rio Grande valley and west

valley, near where they have been since before the Spanish conquest. The Navajo population is concentrated in the western part of New Mexico, on the Navajo Reservation straddling the state's border with Arizona, home of most of the Navajo Nation; a few isolated bands of Navajos dwell in the west-central part of the state. The Jicarilla Apaches live in rugged mountains in New Mexico's northern tier; they were placed there by the United States government in 1887. The other Apache group in New Mexico, the Mescaleros, has carved out a healthy tribal economy from its almost five hundred thousand acres in the Sierra Blanca in the southern part of the state.

of that river toward Jemez, as well as in Zuni, Acoma, and Laguna, descendants of those who first greeted Coronado continue their Pueblo traditions today.

The Pueblo languages of New Mexico—Zuni, Keresan, and Kiowa-Tanoan (including Tiwa, Tewa, and Towa)—remain distinct. In some cases, two Pueblos (San Juan and Taos, for example) will speak different dialects (Tewa and Tiwa) of the same language.

From north to south, the pueblos close to the Rio Grande are: Taos, Picuris, San Juan, Santa Clara, San Ildefonso, Pojoaque, Nambe, Tesuque, Cochiti, Santo Domingo, San Felipe, Santa Ana, Sandia, Isleta. The Jemez River, a tributary of the Rio Grande, runs through the pueblos of Jemez and Zia, and the ancient home of the Santa Anas. To the west are Laguna, Acoma, and Zuni. There are more than thirty thousand Pueblo Indians in New Mexico today.

While outwardly many of the Pueblo villages seem much as they were almost four hundred years ago—low brown clusters of houses huddled alongside the rivers that are the lifeblood of New Mexico—there have been many changes within the pueblos as a result of the arrival of the Spaniards and later the Anglo-Americans. The coming of the Spaniards signaled devastation, disease, and for some of the pueblos (Pecos and Galisteo, for example) doom. The Pueblo population was decimated by European-introduced diseases and by other factors, and dropped from more than twenty thousand in 1680 to fewer than nine thousand a century later. Life for the Pueblos of New Mexico had been irrevocably altered.

A major change was wrought by the importation of the Catholic faith; missionaries, mission churches, and Catholic precepts were added to Pueblo life. Past Pueblo methods of securing land by either claiming it or fighting for it also changed; henceforth reservation land would be set aside for Pueblo use by treaty. The Pueblos also had to learn to deal with another culture and another government. After hundreds of years of frustration, a solution was attempted in 1934, when the Indian Reorganization Act exhorted tribes to organize themselves into self-governing bodies, patterned after western democracies. Therefore, while within the Pueblos there remain the hierarchies of religious and social organization, there has also been created another hierarchy, the tribal council, which devotes itself to interacting with those entities—school boards, county commissions, state agencies, private corporations that do business on reservation land—whose actions affect the lives of Pueblo members. Some contend that vital tribal energies are being spent on off-reservation matters at the cost of the heart of the Pueblo, its religion. Other Pueblo people will argue that it is a healthy separation, and a vital one, to keep the business of the Pueblo in one sphere and its ceremonial life in another.

To the observer, Pueblo life seems to be vibrant and adaptable. While the trappings may have changed—for example, men now drive in pickup trucks to the annual spring ritual of cleaning the ditches—the essence of Pueblo life seems to survive. Pueblo ceremonies, public or private, take precedence over all other activities, and local employers and school systems have learned to accustom themselves to periodic absences. In fact, some school districts include Pueblo feast days in their calendars of school holidays.

Many young Indians, educated locally, go away to college, but they often return to their villages. "I knew when I went away to college that I would come back here," says a man in his twenties. He attended an Ivy League school, then returned to his home above the Rio Grande to take part in Pueblo life and to become active in local politics and national Indian causes. "My father and my grandfather told me that it would be important for me to receive a good education so that I could come back here and serve my people. They said that changes would be coming for the Pueblos, and that some of us would have to know how to react to those changes so that our people would survive. There was never any doubt in my mind that I would return."

Taos man, *Ferdinand Joesten.*

It also should be noted that many Pueblo youths have not been able to adjust to the conflicting mixture of the Indian world and contemporary U.S. society. Individual tribes view the high alcoholism and suicide rates among their young as disturbing and have initiated mental health and other programs to deal with the problem.

The Athapascans

The Navajos and Apaches who live in New Mexico share a common lineage. Both are descendants of the southern Athapascans, some of whom, according to a widely accepted theory, traveled down to the Southwest from the northern plains of Canada hundreds of years ago. The southern Athapascans probably arrived in the region sometime before the sixteenth century, when the Spaniards first mentioned groups of raiding Indians, the Teyas and the Querechos, who attacked Pueblo and Hispanic settlements alike.

The Apaches and Navajos also share a common linguistic heritage. The Mescalero Apaches and the Navajos both speak an Athapascan language known as Western Apache. The Apaches and Navajos also trace their origins to a place in the north, acknowledging a mutual underworld source from which they emerged. Both peoples also share a belief in a powerful woman figure who, after merging with the sun (*Yusn* to the Apaches), gives birth to twin sons who become the tribe's war gods. The coyote, the curse of western farmers and ranchers, takes on a mythical shape for the Athapascans' descendants; the coyote figure often represents man's excesses, weaknesses, and propensities for comedy. Even the elaborate curing ceremonies presided over by medicine men, or shamans, are similar in both Apache and Navajo tradition. And both groups faced the horror and sadness of the Long Walk and internment by U.S. forces at Fort Sumner in the 1860s. Now the Apaches and Navajos live on separate and distant reservations. The two groups have adapted to their places in New Mexico, both economically and socially, in different ways.

The Navajos

The Spaniards first mentioned the Navajos, or the Diné ("the people") in the sixteenth century, finding them on the plains east of the Pecos River. By the 1700s the nomadic tribe of hunters and gatherers, some now also raising corn, squash, and beans, had begun to move westward into what is now eastern Arizona and western New Mexico. Over the next century, as living patterns among the various tribes shifted to accommodate each other and the white man, the Navajo people often found themselves locked in battle with the Pueblos, the Spaniards, and then the Anglo-Americans. Yet the Navajos often came to the aid of the more western Pueblos at the time of the Spanish conquest; to this day there are strong ties between the Navajos and the Jemez, for instance, with Navajo pickup trucks a fixture at many Jemez dances.

In the canyon-studded, barren land they called home, the Navajos herded sheep; foraged for fruits, vegetables, and berries; and created a rich ceremonial life that integrated the land where they lived with both tribal origins and their wandering way of life. The Navajos never stayed in one place long, each family walking from place to place depending on the season and the task at hand. But land pressures from both Hispanic and Anglo settlers were mounting; the Navajos (and the

Apaches) stepped up their raids on livestock and settlements. By the time the United States government conquered New Mexico in 1846, it was felt that the wandering tribes, the Apaches and Navajos, should be centralized. Because of their sheer numbers—there were an estimated thirteen thousand of them in the Southwest in 1860—the Navajos became prime targets. Colonel Kit Carson and his troops delivered an ultimatum to the Navajos: either they were to relocate to near Fort Sumner in eastern New Mexico on the Pecos River, or the women and children would be captured and the men killed. Carson emphasized his determination by building Fort Wingate at the southern edge of the Navajo homeland. Aided by volunteers from the Ute tribe, Carson began his sweep of the vast region. He burned everything in sight, from hogans to herds of sheep. Soon the Long Walk began. By the summer of 1864, there were eighty-five hundred Navajos trying to exist along the Pecos River in a land they were unused to, alongside Apaches they had grown to dislike, and with little food, water, or clothing. The federal government had planned to use this massive encampment, called the Bosque Redondo Reservation, to teach the Indians the ways of the United States: how to read and write, grow crops, and raise cattle. A year later, it was clear to everyone that the relocation attempt was a failure. The Navajos retraced the Long Walk back to their land. Many of them had died in internment. In 1868 the United States and the Navajos signed a treaty giving the Navajo Nation legal possession of part of the land that had been theirs for generations.

The Navajo Reservation encompasses 14,450,369 acres (twenty-five thousand square miles), 3.5 million of which are in New Mexico; the rest is in Arizona and a small portion of southern Utah. Most reservation Navajos continue to live rural, isolated lives. Many of the one hundred forty-six thousand Navajos live in hogans or modern versions of the ancient house form. Many still herd sheep; women and children can be seen following their woolly charges in and out of *arroyos* and alongside lonely highways. Those women who weave can make a living from the prized blankets sold in reservation trading posts, in shops throughout Arizona and New Mexico, and at the Crownpoint rug auctions. Men are the jewelers of the tribe. Their work in silver and turquoise, while prey to the whim of fashion, is sought-after all over the world. Sheepherding, weaving, and the making of jewelry are occupations that the Navajos can practice in their isolation. Artisans and herders can follow the old custom of wintering in one place and spending the summer in a cooler, shadier spot.

Nevertheless, there are changes taking place within the Navajo Nation. Window Rock, the tribe's headquarters just over the border in Arizona, not only houses the tribal government but is also the business and tourist center for the Navajo. Tribal energy leases for the coal, gas, uranium, and other minerals on the reservation are managed from Window Rock. Tribal enterprises are varied, from lumber mills to the Navajo Community College to shopping centers, recreational developments, a zoo, and a museum and gift shop. While the Navajo Nation receives revenue from the many leases and businesses active on the reservation, per capita income is low. It is hard to earn a decent wage so far from urban areas and transportation systems, and the Navajo unemployment level is high.

Navajo cultural and religious tradition is rich and alive, especially for those who can remain on the reservation. The landscape and the land itself are life-giving and provide a vital part of Navajo ritual. Ceremonies, some lasting for days, remain a major source of strength and social activity for tribal members. Yet many of the medicine men who preside over curing or preventative rites are old now, their ways likely to be lost as young people leave the isolation and poverty of the reservation. However, efforts are being made to teach young men and women the Blessing Way and other ceremonies. Non-Indian medical professionals now often call in medicine men to help cure Navajo patients hospitalized in Gallup or Albuquerque. In many ways, the Navajos are keeping their traditions intact and revered by taking what is necessary from the Anglo-American world and merging it with what is strong within the Navajo Nation.

The Apaches

There are many fewer Apaches than Navajos in New Mexico. In all, they number less than four thousand, but the Apaches' impact on the area in which they live is great, and their presence and cultural traditions add to the richness of the state.

Coronado's expedition saw what were probably Apaches around the Texas Panhandle in the middle of the sixteenth century. By the time of Spanish colonization efforts, the Apaches were notorious for their ability to successfully raid any Pueblo, village, or farm against all but the strongest defense. They usually took only food or animals, although human captives were sometimes seized. The Apaches did not spend the majority of their time in such pursuits, however. They were hunters and gatherers who later became farmers. Apache sites in northeastern New Mexico include the ruins of small villages with a variety of house styles and small, irrigated fields. The Jicarillas seemed to adjust best to a sedentary way of living, and they slowly moved west from the eastern plains to valleys in the mountains of northern New Mexico. The Mescaleros moved south, continuing their nomadic lifestyle, usually staying to the east of the Rio Grande and persisting in their hunting pattern.

When the United States took over New Mexico in 1846, the presence of these roving bands of Indians became an irritant to the new government and to the settlers who followed. Raids and counterattacks raged all over the state between nomadic Indians and contingents of U.S. soldiers. Both sides suffered. The Jicarillas were pushed further and further to the west and often were forced off their small farms when Anglo settlers discovered that the

Jonathan Meyers © 1979

Indians were living on arable land. As larger numbers of people came into the state from the east, the situation of the Apaches and other nomadic Indians became more desperate. By the 1860s, U.S. policy was clear: Indians would be settled in areas designated by the U.S. and guarded by newly built and garrisoned forts. The plan did not succeed, and thus began the internment of both Navajo and Apache people at Fort Sumner in the 1860s.

When conditions at Fort Sumner became intolerable, the Mescaleros were the first to leave. They just disappeared one night in 1865, and were soon followed by other Apaches and the Navajos. The Mescaleros scattered, then went south; the Jicarillas fled to the north. Ranchers in the area of Fort Sumner were glad to see them go; the Indians

had been placed on almost forty square miles of good grazing land, and settlers eagerly claimed it. Within a decade most of the Apache people had been rounded up and given reservation land. The Navajos and Apaches signed treaties with the American government, and both sides hoped that peace would prevail.

It took many years for the Apaches to become used to living in one place and raising stock and food, following the pattern of the Anglo-American settlers. The Jicarillas, who had begun to ranch and farm when they lived close to the Rio Grande in the Taos area, raised sheep and cattle on their new reservation in the mountains of northwestern New Mexico. The Mescaleros, on the other hand, were forced to give up many aspects of their hunting way of life when, in 1873, they were placed on their reservation in the Sierra Blanca. Both groups slowly adjusted, changing their dress from a leather and buckskin wardrobe to jeans and shirts for the men and voluminous skirts and colorful blouses for the women. Apaches today dress in the casual attire common to the Southwest. Life continues to revolve around the family, with ceremonies a time for socializing as well as for keeping up tribal religious traditions.

The Apaches, like the Navajos and the Pueblos, must live in both the Indian and the non-Indian world. Apaches fought in World War II and, like the Navajos, served as code-senders to prevent Japanese interception of official United States communications. Ironically, no Indian, even one who had defended his country, could vote in either New Mexico or Arizona until 1948.

The Mescaleros (so named by the Spaniards because of their affinity for the edible portion of the mescal, or century plant, a major part of the diet of the southern Apaches) have created a successful recreation complex on their reservation high in New Mexico's southern mountains. The Mescalero-run Sierra Blanca Ski Area and nearby Inn of the Mountain Gods have become an exemplary tribal enterprise and favorite vacation spot for New Mexicans and Texans. Tribal lumber and forestry businesses also provide jobs. The Mescaleros send their Red Hats, professionally trained, highly skilled firefighters, all over the United States to combat forest fires.

The Jicarillas also run a recreational complex, but Stonelake Lodge, in its spectacular setting in the northern mountains, is more isolated than the Mescalero's enterprise and is therefore on a smaller scale. Much of the Jicarilla tribal income results from revenues from gas and oil leases on the energy-rich reservation.

The Genízaros

Around 1700 a new population was apparent in New Mexico. These were the *genízaros*,

referred to officially by that name until 1822. The *genízaros* were people of mixed tribal backgrounds who carried Spanish surnames. In many cases they were Plains Indian women and children who had been captured by other tribes and then ransomed to Hispanic families, where they became laborers or servants.

In 1776 there were three predominantly *genízaro* communities in New Mexico: Analco, in Santa Fe; Abiquiu, in present-day Rio Arriba County above Española; and Los Jarales, near Belen. Residents of Analco eventually left Santa Fe and went east to San Miguel del Vado and San Jose del Vado toward the end of the eighteenth century. Some of the *genízaros* also married Pueblo or Hispanic families and were absorbed into the dominant culture.

When Mexico became independent of Spain, the Mexican government issued a decree that forbade the use of the term *genízaro* on official documents. Henceforth all those within the province of New Mexico were to be referred to as Mexican citizens, whatever their origins. Informally, children of Indian and Hispanic unions were still referred to as *coyotes*, *lobos* ("wolves"), *mestizos*, or *mulatos*. Today parents of children with mixed backgrounds (generally Anglo and Hispanic) will jokingly call their offspring "little coyotes."

HISPANICS

New Mexico's Hispanic population began to trickle into the state at the very end of the sixteenth century; for the next three hundred fifty years, Spanish customs prevailed in New Mexico. Various expeditions had come north from Mexico in the sixteenth century, always seeking the illusive Seven Cities of Cibola. Not until 1598 did any real settlement efforts take place. But once the first hacienda had been built and scraggly peach trees planted, it was Spanish religion, Spanish customs, Spanish language, and Spanish politics that ruled New Mexico. Not until the middle of this century could it be argued that New Mexico might no longer be a predominantly Hispanic state.

There are many today who still debate that point.

In 1598 Juan de Oñate and his several hundred soldiers, settlers, and friars entered New Mexico to plant the Spanish flag and the seeds of both Spanish culture and the Catholic religion. The expedition was accompanied by Gaspar Pérez de Villagrá, who was not only a soldier but a poet and a chronicler as well. He was the first of many poet-soldiers who came to New Mexico and recorded for posterity their experiences in this place so far from the homeland. The first settlers made homes for themselves north of Española at Yunque Yunque, along the banks of the Rio Grande. They brought with them domestic animals, vegetable and flower seeds and plants, household items, and religious ornaments. Those who followed them over the next centuries also carried important items from home, creating for themselves islands of Spain in the midst of Indian pueblos and in the isolation of high deserts and mountains. The missionaries who accompanied the settlers also were responsible for transplanting the Spanish culture to New Mexico; they cultivated the land near their Indian missions with fruits and vegetables whose seeds and seedlings they had cherished throughout the long journey from Mexico or Spain to their new home. The crafts of spinning, tanning, carpentry, adobe brick making, and building in the Spanish style were taught by the friars to the Indians, this despite the fact that the ancestors of the Indians had centuries before proved their construction skills at Chaco Canyon. The Indians were not only required to learn these new trades, but had to work at the missions and often at the neighboring haciendas.

The Pueblo Revolt of 1680 began more than a dozen years of Indian dominance in New Mexico. However, when de Vargas and his troops re-entered the state in 1692, they met with little Pueblo resistance. A year later, Spanish colonists again appeared in the Rio Grande valley. Some descendants of those who had come with the first wave of settlers the century before chose not to return to New Mexico, but many whose families had arrived in the area with Oñate came back to reclaim their haciendas or to start anew. Even the statue of the Virgin saved by the fleeing colonists as they left Santa Fe in 1680 was brought back to the capital in triumph; her name was changed from Our Lady of the Assumption to La Conquistadora ("the conqueror"), and she still enjoys a warm place in the hearts of New Mexico's Hispanics.

New Mexico has never been a rich state. During its centuries of Spanish control, and even into the nineteenth century under Mexican rule, its people lived simple, rural lives, with few trappings of wealth or ostentation. Houses, even those of wealthier landowners, were plain adobe structures, blending architectural elements borrowed from the Pueblos with Spanish and Moorish designs. Floors were dried adobe, often painted with ox blood and polished to a rich glow. Few homes had windows until glass was introduced into the state in the nineteenth century, although some featured thin mica sheets that covered window-like openings. Clothes, hand-woven and handmade, hung from rods in bedrooms. Later, in the eighteenth and nineteenth centuries, artisans nameless to this day built ample wardrobes, desks, and other pieces of furniture, often carving fanciful designs to lighten the massiveness and simplicity of their work. Family heirlooms, many of which were carried lovingly across the ocean and up the rugged Camino Real to New Mexico, were treasured and handed down from generation to generation. Thus small elements of a European tradition took root in New Mexico's soul. The traditions and strengths of Hispanic culture seemed to thrive here.

It was their families and their Catholic faith that gave the Spanish colonists strength as they struggled against poverty, extremes of weather, loneliness, and a land that could be inhospitable to attempts at agricultural enterprise. Life revolved around home; births, deaths, and marriages were commemorated with large gatherings and long days and nights of celebration or consolation. The visit of the priest or the passing of an itinerant peddler broke the monotony of the days along the Rio Grande valley, the region of initial colonization. Food on such occasions was simple but abundant: beef or pork simmered in rich chile sauce, blue corn tortillas, peas and beans, squash and melons, frequently served with homemade wine or rich, warm cocoa. The wealthier landowners often had Indian slaves, but the majority of the settlers produced large families and worked themselves and their children from dawn to dusk.

Life along the Rio Grande and its tributaries was pastoral. Most families grazed sheep on common lands and raised food crops on the land they held individually. The Spanish and, later on, the Mexican method of allotting land made such agricultural activity possible. Under the land grant system, acreage was given to a grantee, often composed of a group of families or relatives. In the early days, the Spanish Crown sometimes chose land grant sites based upon the need for frontier outposts and protection of larger populations by several outlying, fortified settlements. Besides sharing community lands, each family owned a small plot of its own. Thus the land grant system fostered a pastoral economy and lifestyle. This was the land ownership system until 1846, when the United States took over control of New Mexico.

The 1848 Treaty of Guadalupe Hidalgo, which stated that property held under Mexican law was to be respected by the United States, was written to solidify Hispanic claims to lands that by then had been in many families for generations. However, by the time of the U.S. takeover, much of the land grant system was in chaos: grants, whose boundaries were often described in terms of *arroyos* and trees, frequently overlapped each other; in many cases families had lost their papers proving ownership; and sometimes a number of people claimed a single parcel of land. As new settlers arrived with the new government, the competition for arable land grew fierce. In 1854 U.S. officials surveyed the grants, and much of the land held in common

(a concept never fully understood by these officials and surveyors) was partitioned.

By 1903 most of the communal property held by villages and small communities had been lost to outsiders, the public domain, or the federal government. Some communities were able to hold onto their lands well into the twentieth century, only to lose them because they could not pay the taxes. In some cases, villagers who themselves could not raise sufficient cash to pay the taxes due on their land would assign that job to their *patrón* (the village boss, or leading political figure), who would accept chickens, sacks of pinto beans, or labor in lieu of actual money from his neighbors. In exchange he was to pay the taxes on the grazing land. Sometimes he did, but frequently he did not. The *patrón* then often bought the land when it was put on the block for back taxes. Many families in northern and central New Mexico thereby lost acreage that was essential to their main economic activity, the raising of sheep. Whole villages were almost abandoned throughout the twentieth century as the loss of communal lands, coupled with expensive and complicated water-rights issues, forced small farmers off their land.

Other changes also came to New Mexico with the arrival of the Anglo-Americans in 1846. The Easterners brought with them a different language, English (thus the term *Anglo*), which is now the dominant language in New Mexico. The state is still officially bilingual, however, with translators present during some court procedures, ballots printed in Spanish and English, and bilingual programs an integral part of some school systems. The Anglo-Americans also brought Christian religions other than Catholicism, and missionary efforts from a number of Protestant faiths spread throughout the state. Such proselytizing endeavors were sometimes more effective with the Hispanic population than among the Pueblos, whose Catholicism was often used as a shield against missionaries of other faiths.

In New Mexico today, the family, often a large, extended one ("We'll have 180 people,

Jonathan Meyers © 1983

Jonathan Meyers © 1979

all my cousins, for Easter today," announced a child who lives along the Rio Grande between Albuquerque and Santa Fe), forms the heart of Hispanic life. Even in the larger metropolitan areas, family occasions, from baptisms to high school graduations and weddings, bring together family members from all over the state (and from other states, especially California) to trade stories, drink coffee and beer, eat chile and *posole*, and bask in the warmth of kinship. The Spanish language will still be spoken by most of the older members of the families, with many Spanish words and phrases interjected into everyday English conversations by both Spanish- and non-Spanish-speakers.

Many people in present-day New Mexico who do not carry Hispanic surnames are Hispanic in background and culture. As the state grew, and as unmarried soldiers and bold entrepreneurs came to New Mexico, many young women of Hispanic background married young men with Irish, or Lebanese, or

German last names. The families they raised, though surnamed perhaps McBride or Smith, would be Hispanic in tradition and language. There are also New Mexicans today who neither look nor speak Spanish but can trace their roots back to those who left their signatures on El Morro rock, the autograph book of New Mexico. And there are others with Hispanic surnames and traditions who carry the blue eyes and blonde hair of Anglo grandparents. At almost any gathering in Hispanic New Mexico (and that includes about half of the state's population) there will be a rich mixture of languages, foods, physical features, and surnames.

ANGLOS

Anglos are those New Mexicans who are neither Indian nor Hispanic. Another definition of an Anglo is one who speaks only English. In the New Mexican lexicon, therefore, an Anglo is a white Anglo-Saxon Protestant, a black, a Jew, a person of Oriental background, or anyone without roots in either the Hispanic or the Indian culture. Any outsider or newcomer to New Mexico without Spanish or Indian blood is an Anglo. The term can be and is used in a derogatory fashion, but more than anything else Anglos are the third cultural force in this tricultural (many would argue multicultural) state.

If an Anglo is anyone who is neither Hispanic nor Indian, then perhaps the first known Anglo to enter New Mexico was Esteban, the explorer who came to the Southwest with Cabeza de Vaca in 1536. Esteban was a black, a Moorish slave who was killed in 1539 in an expedition to Hawikuh, or Zuni.

New Mexico saw no significant Anglo influx until the dawn of the nineteenth century, when trappers and traders first trickled through the northern mountains. These mountain men and wandering peddlers posed no immediate threat to what had been for more than two hundred years a bicultural state. The opening of the Santa Fe Trail in 1821, however, signaled the beginning of an intrusion upon the Mexican colony that would change it forever. By 1846, when General Stephen Kearny's troops conquered New Mexico, there were Anglo traders, trappers, farmers, housewives, and children living here.

As New Mexico became a prime route to the gold fields of California and for the transportation of goods across the country and down into Mexico, the United States built forts to protect the stage lines that crossed in the middle of the Rio Grande valley. Anglos defended these forts and fought the nomadic Indians, who often found the stages and wagon trains easy prey. The soldiers' influence on the state was not great, but their presence was symbolic of the new Anglo rule that was here to stay.

Another, primarily Texan, influence swept into New Mexico after the Civil War. The green valleys of the western half of the state and the high plains on the east side were soon enveloped by herds of cattle—grazing, being driven to markets, and competing with the native sheep of the Hispanic population. Large- and small-scale wars between the ranchers (predominantly Anglo) and farmers/ herders (mainly Hispanic) developed and were resolved only after bitter conflict and actual battles. In some parts of New Mexico, such conflicts over grazing or water rights continue, the identities of antagonists unchanged. When Anglo farmers came to New Mexico to homestead in the latter part of the nineteenth century, another element was injected into the land disputes. However, the homesteaders found that their 160-acre tracts of dry, barren land were far from adequate to support a farm or range cattle, and so they often lost or sold their claims.

In the last quarter of the nineteenth century, prospectors and miners, followed by colorful attendant enterprises, began to populate isolated niches in the state. From Shakespeare and Pinos Altos in the south to Elizabethtown in the north, a mining boom was on. Wooden-walked, saloon-filled towns, plopped down along mountain streams, came and went. Their populations were transient but left a permanent mark on the character of New Mexico.

Business in New Mexico had been small in scale, limited to individual tradesmen and peddlers prior to 1846, but the change in government also saw a revolution in business practices. A new kind of merchant, one who had received his training in the mercantile centers of Europe or along the East Coast, came to Las Vegas, Santa Fe, Bernalillo, and other towns, and not only presented customers with a wider selection of goods, but extended credit, built up inventories, and changed the face of many small towns. Some of the first merchants were German or Russian Jews or were of Lebanese extraction. They came alone and soon married into old Hispanic families; a number of their traditions— food, religion, a business sense—sometimes survived intact, but their languages and other elements of the different civilization that they had come from were lost as they were absorbed into the dominant Hispanic culture.

The coming of the railroads in the 1870s played a significant role in the importation of many new ideas, cultures, and people to New Mexico. The railroads, one-third of which were built in two years, between 1879 and 1881, linked remote parts of the state and solidified mining and cattle enterprises; provided transportation for people, goods, and cattle through the state and to the rest of the country; and brought to the railroad towns solid Midwestern folks. From the towns and cities they had left, the newcomers brought with them new ideas about architecture, opinions on public schooling and government, and a wide range of backgrounds, surnames, and traditions. They were responsible for the construction of many "new towns," sections of New Mexico cities that would resemble as much as possible the tree-lined, grid-patterned Midwestern places they had left.

By the beginning of the twentieth century, whole sections of central and eastern New Mexico were dominated by Anglo populations. The arrival of tubercular patients, for whom large hospitals, nursing homes, and sanatoriums were built in Albuquerque, Las Vegas, and other towns, assured the emergence of a new majority. To this mixture of citizens were added the soldiers and scientists of the 1940s and 1950s in places like Alamogordo, Clovis, Albuquerque, and the new town of Los Alamos. Service industries followed, and universities and school systems developed and grew to serve the burgeoning population. Later a new kind of refugee began to arrive, fleeing from the two coasts, from blighted cities and months of snowdrifts. Retirees moved to Roswell and Truth or Consequences where housing was reasonable and winters warm. Hippies, living in tepees, garishly painted buses, and geodesic domes, peopled remote canyons, the valleys around Taos, and university ghettoes; some stayed to take on lives as "straights" or to remain counterculture in a state that would absorb them.

And New Mexico's artists, present since the first petroglyph was carved and the first clay

bowl painted upon, hold a special place in the tradition of the state. From all cultures and places, they perform an important function by preserving their images of New Mexico in clay, on canvas, or within the pages of books for the descendants of today's population to ponder over and enjoy.

New Mexico is also a western state, heir to cowboy legends and country drawls. When the homesteading effort on the east side of the state proved a failure, Texans, both oilmen and sheep and cattle ranchers, bought the land. Their comfortable down-home culture now predominates in the small cities and towns that range up and down the eastern quarter of New Mexico. But Western accents and cowboy folkways are not limited to the state's border with Texas. There are ranches all over the state, and cattle raising remains an important, and colorful, part of the economy. In any small town in New Mexico, the cafe conversation usually revolves around cattle prices, the cost of farm equipment and bank loans, and perhaps the local rodeo. In fact, rodeos, whether the gigantic state fair event held each September in Albuquerque or the many weekly rodeos that take place at county sheriffs' posse grounds, are picturesque pieces of New Mexico tradition. Predominantly Anglo in heritage, rodeo is now enjoyed as a sport by all segments of the population. Indian cowboys, for instance, are often ranked nationally in rodeo competitions, and local Indian rodeos are as exciting and dusty as their better-known Anglo counterparts.

In many ways, for many people, the real heroes of New Mexico's past are the women who came, often not of their own volition, as immigrants to this land. Whether Hispanic or Anglo, they endured long, dry journeys over nonexistent roads. They implanted their own culture through their children, and they buried those offspring who could not survive. Women of all backgrounds and of varying educational and economic levels learned to make do in the sod houses of the eastern prairies; they cultivated and cooked new varieties of food; and like the Pueblo women who preceded them, they plastered adobe homes. New Mexico's women worked to ensure schooling and culture for their children, and in many cases kept alive both the language and the traditions of a faraway home.

New Mexico's journey into a multicultural twentieth century has been neither easy nor altogether peaceful. As English became the dominant language in an officially bilingual state, those who grew up speaking either Spanish or one of the Indian languages often suffered discrimination when they entered school. Many Hispanic and Indian adults can remember the shame they were made to feel when they spoke their mother tongue in the classroom or on the playground. In one of the ironies of education, some of those same adults now are bilingual teachers, much sought-after for their skills in imparting information in a language other than English. The entrance of a number of different religions into a state predominantly Catholic also was not without its difficulties; Hispanics who left the Catholic faith were often ostracized by their friends and neighbors. As Anglos began to control much of the business, political, and educational worlds, discrimination against New Mexico's long-time, deeply rooted citizens became evident. Hispanics and Indians had to fight long, bitter battles to gain positions above the blue-collar level at New Mexico's many defense bases, for example. Not until 1954 did it become clear in some areas of the state that the existence of two school systems, one for Anglos, the other for Hispanics, was illegal. Indians and Hispanics were not the only ones to suffer the outrages of prejudice; New Mexico's blacks also had to fight both in and out of courtrooms to receive equal education and job opportunities.

New Mexico's population includes a greater percentage of minorities than any other state in the union. While by many reckonings Indians and Hispanics still do not hold as many positions of leadership as their numbers warrant, most New Mexicans would agree that the state does provide opportunities for advancement in all areas. As the educational system has opened up, more and more members of minority groups have taken on powerful roles at the state's universities, within state government, and in industry. There are now Indians on school boards and county commissions, Hispanics chairing important university committees and state agencies, and blacks named to head medical societies and government bodies. New Mexico has had two Hispanic governors since the mid-1970s. Residents of the state are so conscious of the multicultural aspects of New Mexico that any savvy Hispanic politician names an Anglo to run his campaign, and vice-versa.

Within the easily defined tricultural pattern in New Mexico are obvious exceptions. Chinese, Italians, blacks, Jews, and Lebanese come to mind as ethnic groups that continue to contribute greatly to the rich fabric of New Mexico life. Many such groups retain strong identities, celebrating their feast days (the Greek festival, held in Albuquerque each fall, has introduced much of central New Mexico to the joys of Greek cuisine, for instance) and respecting their distinctive pasts. These minorities, counted in population figures as members of the state's Anglo majority, are well-integrated into New Mexico life in some parts of the state and remain as pockets of diversity in other areas.

Those who live in New Mexico view their state as unique, not only for its sweeping landscapes, multihued sunsets, and clear, brilliant sky, but because of its remarkable and rich variety of people. The pride of New Mexico is its people, of all colors, languages, traditions, and backgrounds. Like the wildflowers on the ditchbanks, they draw strength from their environment, and they thrive in the company of their neighbors.

food

New Mexico's traditional food is as colorful as its landscape, as rich as its multicultural heritage. Often misnamed "Mexican food," the bowls of red or green chile, plates of pinto beans, and the entire array of other gastronomic delights cooked and eaten in almost every kitchen of the state are proudly and decidedly New Mexican by cultivation and heritage. Experts agree that no other state in the union, except perhaps Louisiana, enjoys a cuisine as singular or as pervasive as that of New Mexico.

Because New Mexico's food traditions are, for the most part, the fruits of generations of inventive, intuitive cooks, recipes and analyses can seldom convey the subtleties of this unique cuisine. However, it is worthwhile to focus on three key ingredients: corn, beans, and chile. Almost every dish that falls within the definition of traditional New Mexican food will contain at least one of these components. And in tracing the roots of corn, beans, and chile and their paths into New Mexican recipes, one soon finds that the many facets of the state's cuisine reflect the history and the heritage of the people who live here.

Corn, whence come tortillas, *posole,* and

tamales, originated in Mexico. Since about 2500 B.C., those who have dwelt in what is now New Mexico and in other parts of the high Southwestern deserts have nurtured corn, recognizing its food value and adaptability by honoring it as a religious symbol of life and fertility. For New Mexico's first settlers, the Indians, corn is related to tribal origins, and the plant is revered in Pueblo ceremonies that precede planting time or anticipate the harvest.

When Coronado and his men happened upon Zuni in 1540, they were served delicious corn cakes by the women of that Pueblo. Other Spanish explorers through the centuries noted the Pueblo *hornos* (beehive-shaped ovens) in which all manner of pleasing corn breads and dishes were cooked. An American anthropologist, Frank Cushing, lived at Zuni in the late nineteenth century and delighted in chronicling his culinary discoveries, listing, for example, a typical Zuni feast replete with corn in many forms: blue corn dumpling soup, corn on the cob, red corn tamales, meat and hominy soup, loaves of skinned-corn paste, and *piki,* which Cushing believed was "the most perfect of all known corn-foods." *Piki,* a

Horno, Taos Pueblo, *Jean Blackmon.*

blue, paper-thin bread that comes from the Hopi of Arizona and is also enjoyed by the more western Pueblos, is one of the most ancient forms of edible corn. For centuries Hopi and Pueblo women have prepared the bread by laying a thin film of liquid blue cornmeal on a hot stone. Cooks also use blue corn, its kernels almost navy in color, for the tortilla base in blue corn enchiladas and in a thin gruel called *atole*. The flavor of blue corn seems almost nuttier and more cornlike than that of its yellow counterparts, and *piki* bread, cooked over wood fires, delivers an unusual, smoky flavor.

In most parts of the United States, corn is yellow, perhaps white. But corn in New Mexico, especially if it is cultivated in Pueblo or Navajo gardens and fields, is of many colors, with blue favored for *piki, atole,* and other treats. Most of the traditional corn dishes in New Mexico now are made from white or yellow corn. These include *posole,* a hearty pork, chile, and hominy stew served especially at Christmas time; tamales, chile-laced meat stuffed into a corn dough and wrapped in a cornhusk; a variety of corn breads, some incorporating chile; and *chauquehue,* a thick corn pudding similar to polenta.

Pinto beans originated in the New World, and by the time the Spaniards arrived in New Mexico in the sixteenth century they had long been a staple in the Indian diet. The Spaniards brought with them their own beans, including the fava. But as the years passed and as generations of New Mexicans planted, cooked, and tasted, the pinto beans became the favored bean. Other beans have been used in New Mexican cooking—especially the *bolita*, a small, hard, light-brown legume—but pinto beans (*frijoles* in Spanish), pink and faintly speckled, reign in today's kitchens. At one time the Estancia Valley boasted that it was the Pinto Bean Capital of the World, but that title now belongs to the high valleys of southern Colorado. Still, pinto beans, rich in protein and enjoyed in many forms, retain an important role in New Mexican cooking. They are served with tacos and enchiladas in restaurant "combination plates"; in green chile stew; mashed and refried in dips at cocktail parties; wrapped inside steaming burritos; and in a bowl by themselves, perhaps topped with a dollop of red or green chile.

Those who know beans argue about who cooks them best: Indian women who simmer them inside hornos; Hispanic cooks who keep huge pots of *frijoles* gently boiling atop the stove; or the "cookies" on ranches who throw beans, water, salt, pepper, a ham hock or bacon, and a chile pod into an iron kettle where it cooks over a fire on the open range. But prepared by any of these methods, the bean always tastes good.

In fact, pinto beans can be used in unusual ways. Those who lived out the Great Depression on New Mexico's farms and ranches remember the many uses their mothers found for beans. Some recipes have survived into the next generation, including bean pie, a rich, heavy dish. Recently, a recipe for pinto bean fudge made the rounds of county extension offices.

Chile, whether spelled *chili* (a Mexican Nahuatl word) or *chile* (a Spanish word) is the soul of New Mexican cooking. Its fiery antecedents were cultivated as early as 4000 B.C.

by the Indians of the Andean highlands, where it is called *ají*. The plant, a member of the nightshade family and a relative of potatoes and tomatoes, moved slowly northward to Mexico, where it was further refined and came to be known as chili. In 1493 Columbus brought home to Europe a "pepper more pungent than that from the Caucasus," and in the sixteenth century Spanish explorers found chile being cultivated in New Mexico.

Now more acres of chile are farmed in New Mexico than in any other state. The flat, narrow fruits grow on sturdy plants in neat home gardens in the state's valley areas, both rural and urban. Many gardeners save the seeds from year to year, cultivating varieties that have no name but are tailored to the tastes of each family. By late summer the plants are laden with bright green pods. Perhaps half the fruits are picked then and skinned. Peeling green chiles is a skill that requires considerable practice. Most gardeners now prefer to blister their chiles over outside barbeque grills, plunging them into cold water or wrapping them in damp towels before they are skinned, seeded, and frozen. The peeling of chiles is almost an autumn ritual, with entire families set up in lawn chairs around a grill, the air filled with pungent smoke. Those chiles not picked green are left to turn red on the plants. Then another skill comes into play, the making of *ristras*, or strings of red chiles. City-dwellers

from Hatch to the Mexican border. New Mexico State University in Las Cruces now studies and cultivates thirty of the two hundred known varieties of capsicum peppers. Dr. Roy Nakayama, a professor of horticulture at the university, is the acknowledged authority on chile. He and his staff research the varieties, creating new hybrids that are milder and therefore more acceptable to Eastern palates.

As might be expected, New Mexicans consume more chile per capita than residents of any other state. Aficionados who find themselves in places foreign to the pepper speak of cravings for "a bowl of green," and studies now indicate that an element in chile, capsaicin, may actually be addictive. Travelers who come to New Mexico sometimes look in disbelief at a plate whose offerings have been smothered in red chile sauce, but true New Mexicans lace breakfast eggs, mashed potatoes, quiche, and many other dishes with red or green chile. Newcomers often wonder which is hotter, red or green chile. Remember that both are different stages of the same plant, harvested at different times and prepared in different ways, so there is no reliable answer—only taste can tell.

Not only is chile high in vitamins A and C, it also dilates the blood vessels, thus cooling the body, according to Dr. Nakayama. It is a folk remedy in New Mexico and in other parts of the world: eating chile can soothe the effects of arthritis or cure ulcers, it is said. For some, chile actually symbolizes the state of New Mexico. Colorful *ristras* are now depicted on tee shirts and Christmas cards. And the New Mexico State Legislature has declared chile the official vegetable of New Mexico, even though technically it is a fruit.

New Mexicans do not limit their consumption of traditional foods to corn, beans, and chile. Any dinner table often includes freshly made white flour tortillas wrapped in a warm tea towel, round loaves of Indian bread, or golden ovals of Navajo fry bread. Squash, like chile, corn, and beans of New World origin, was cultivated by New Mexico's prehistoric inhabitants and remains a prime ingredient in

purchase chile *ristras* for decorative purposes; serious chile gardeners create them because they are the most effective way to dry the pods. Throughout the state, as the days grow short and the nights cold, entire sides of houses will be enveloped by rows of bright red *ristras*. Later the chiles will be brought inside and hung in pantries or kitchens. When the cook needs to make chile sauce or chile powder, she or he will cut the pods from the *ristras*, remove seeds and veins, and whirl the chiles in a blender.

Chile growing is a big business in New Mexico. In 1981, 15,300 acres of chile were cultivated in the Las Cruces area alone. Fields of the leafy green plants straddle the Rio Grande

many local dishes, including *calabacitas* (summer squash, green chile, cheese, and sometimes corn). Wild greens (*quelites* and *verdolagas*) are often served with meats raised or hunted by members of a household.

The *matanza*, a tradition that includes the slaughter and butchering of an animal, takes place in many of New Mexico's villages and on its farms and ranches as soon as the weather gets cold. Clusters of men gather at dawn to kill a pig or cow, and then teams of relatives take on carving duties. The men stay outside around the fire, the women remain in the house, cooking a meal that might be accompanied by homemade wine. At the end of the day, everyone will take home some meat, or at least some *chicharrón* (pig skin, or cracklings). Another *matanza*, at another house in the village, will occur the next weekend, and so it will go throughout the winter. Families also enjoy venison, elk, and other wild game hunted each year in the mountains and on the high plains of the state.

Traditional New Mexican desserts tend to be very sweet. The most popular seem to be hot *sopaipillas*, squares of puffy deep-fried bread, their interiors smothered in honey. In many homes, however, *sopaipillas* are not dessert but rather the bread served with the main course. The dessert might then be *enmeladas*, a kind of *sopaipilla* that is dipped in sticky syrup. *Sopa*, which usually means soup, is another favorite for large gatherings. It is made with bread cubes, condensed milk, raisins, cheese, and sugar. At Christmas many households bake batch upon batch of *biscochitos*, light sugar cookies with a hint of anise and a sprinkling of cinnamon. But just as every cook makes a unique chile stew, so *biscochito* recipes differ from family to family and village to village. Other desserts include Indian pies, flat and cookielike and filled with raisins, apricots, or other fruit; they fill tables at Pueblo homes during feast days. Restaurants often feature desserts that incorporate piñon nuts, the small, hard-shelled pine nuts or pignolias gathered each autumn from the piñon trees that stud New Mexico's hillsides.

Pueblo woman, *Barry Frankel*.

Many of the ingredients of traditional New Mexican cooking also find their way into folk medicines and remedies. *Curanderas* (healers) still practice their art, creating potions and poultices either from plants that grow wild or from herbs found in kitchen gardens. Both European and Indian cultures have contributed herbs and formulas to folk medicine, the two ways now blended into practices that differ little. Remedies range from *agua de sandía* (watermelon juice) for the eyes to *ajo* (garlic) for stomach and high blood pressure problems to *manzanilla* (chamomile), a favorite for infant stomach disorders. *Yerba buena* (mint) is an all-purpose plant, a favorite tea, a powder for wounds, and a poultice. New Mexicans can find their favorite medicinal herbs packaged and labeled for use at local pharmacies and grocery stores. Folklorists write books listing

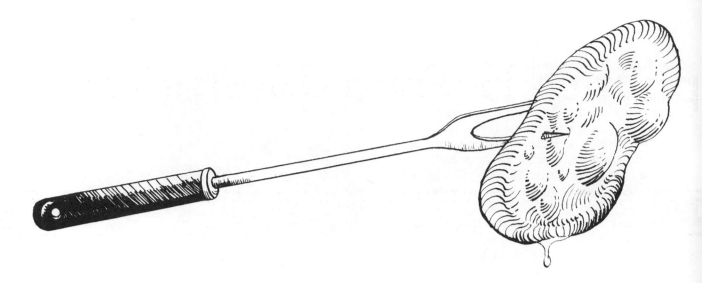

remedies for every kind of ailment from dog bites to anxiety attacks.

The food of New Mexico has always been simple, multipurpose, and plentiful. Its ingredients come from kitchen gardens and local fields. While tastes and recipes—handed down through generations or adapted by newly arrived New Yorkers—may vary by household, village, and culture, the food on the table at a wedding feast in Portales, a high school graduation in Jemez, a bar mitzvah in Albuquerque, or a weeknight supper in Silver City will be similar, unpretentious, delicious, and decidedly New Mexican.

Because New Mexico is blessed with a cosmopolitan population, it offers every kind of restaurant imaginable, from a little French bistro in Santa Fe to a Chinese kitchen in Gallup. Yet visitors to the state will find traditional menus in towns and cities all over New Mexico. There are large restaurants that cater to tourists and small family operations that serve meals based on family recipes. At the Pueblos and on the Navajo Reservation, visitors can purchase Indian breads, pastries, and other specialties. Local fiestas held throughout the state present the best opportunities for sampling New Mexico's splendid, and special, food.

politics, law, and government

While both Indian and European settlements in New Mexico are among the oldest in the United States, the state's electoral politics is among the newest. New Mexico was governed for more than three centuries as a colony, headed by an appointed official—first of Spain, then of Mexico, then of the United States, with a very brief Confederate interlude. Only beginning in 1912 have the people of the state had the right to choose their own governor and voting representatives in the United States Congress.

The Spanish governors of New Mexico held absolute power over civil and military affairs. Prospective appointees received the five-year term as governor of the isolated province from the king of Spain with some misgiving; the poverty of the Rio Grande settlements, the haphazard support in manpower, supplies, and money provided by the Spanish Crown, and the constant danger of Indian attack all made the assignment to Santa Fe an uncertain reward. As a result, the quality of the governors varied from embittered, rapacious grandees to vigorous, just officials.

During many gubernatorial terms in office, a major and recurrent concern of the office-holder was the protection of the scattered pueblos and Spanish settlements from the depredations of Comanches, Apaches, Utes, and Navajos. The governor, as captain-general, was responsible for the training, equipping, and deployment of the small force of professional soldiers and the citizens' militia. The governor also regulated the location of settlements in order to prevent the establishment of small, indefensible haciendas and towns. With the same reasoning in mind, small pueblos were consolidated into larger, more easily protected units. Administration of the rudimentary judicial system, collection of the meager tax revenues, and supervision of the missionary church in New Mexico also fell within his purview.

Local administration was carried out by *alcaldes mayores* in each of the eight jurisdictions, or *alcaldias*, in New Mexico. The *alcaldes mayores*, required to be "honorable citizens capable of reading and writing," were appointed by the governor, usually serving for life unless they incurred the displeasure of a governor under whom they held office. Only the town of Santa Fe elected a council, or *cabildo*, and its own *alcalde* (mayor). Not paid for their services, the *alcaldes* earned a living by levying small fines and often by exploiting the Indians within their domains. The *alcaldes* both enforced and adjudged the law, submitting their decisions to the governor for review.

Legal codes for the Spanish empire in the New World existed, but subordinate officials received little legal training and were expected to judge matters according to "principles of natural right and justice." All, including the governors, were held accountable for their actions. Each newly arrived governor served as judge of his predecessor in a formal proceeding called the *residencia*. More than one departing governor was found to have violated the strict laws protecting Indian vassals of the king. It became standard practice to withhold a portion of the governor's salary to pay fines assessed during the *residencia*, though direct payments from old governor to new often assured a favorable judgment. *Alcaldes mayores* were frequently more difficult to bring to justice, although many were guilty of maliciousness or simply of turning their jurisdiction over the Indians to their private profit, because the pool of literate colonists from which replacements could be drawn was very small.

The short period of Mexican rule (1821 to 1846) gave New Mexicans a brief taste of representative government. Political boundaries within the newly independent republic changed several times during the period, New Mexico at first being classified as part of the huge Estado Interno del Norte ("internal state of the north") and later as a territory. New Mexico sent a representative to the Mexican Congress, elected a provincial assembly, and had at least a voice in the choice of the provincial governor. During the Mexican interlude an attempt, largely unsuccessful, was made to provide public schooling. Reversing Spanish precedent, Mexico finally opened the borders of the province to trade and immigration from the United States.

The conquest of New Mexico early in the Mexican War left it an occupied territory under the United States Army's military rule for the years 1846 to 1850, while Congress in Washington and rival factions in New Mexico debated whether statehood or territorial status should be accorded the newly acquired area. Perhaps the most important stumbling block to early statehood for New Mexico was the question of slavery, a debate applied to all territories seeking admission to the Union in the mid-nineteenth century. In addition the borders of the territory were uncertain, as the republic of Texas's claims extended as far west as the Rio Grande. While these concerns dominated discussion in Washington, politically active New Mexicans squared off into a battle between advocates of statehood, led by former army paymaster Richard H. Weightman and by Manuel Alvarez, U.S. commercial agent in Santa Fe, and partisans of territorial status, headed by Judge Joab Houghton.

While controversy swirled, the commanders of American troops in Santa Fe ruled as military governors of the newly conquered territory. At the time of General Stephen Watts Kearny's peaceful conquest of Santa Fe in 1846, he had proclaimed that New Mexicans were to be given the right to elect a governor and a territorial legislature like those of the United States. Charles Bent, a long-time trader and Taos resident, and Donanciano Vigil, who had participated in military affairs and in the Mexican government of New Mexico, were appointed by Kearny as governor and secretary, respectively. Leaving a garrison in Santa Fe, Kearny then departed with the remainder of his troops for California. In Washington, however, President Polk disavowed Kearny's generous actions, stating that New Mexico would have to be considered conquered territory and that, in any case, the granting of territorial status and a form of government was a privilege reserved to Congress.

As news of these events traveled slowly back and forth across the plains, New Mexico's government was thrown into confusion. At the time, Diego Archuleta, a former aide to the last Mexican governor, Manuel Armijo, plotted insurrection because of anger over broken promises. On January 19, 1847, a group of rebels from Taos Pueblo and the surrounding Hispanic settlements broke into Governor Bent's house, killing him and several other

Americans. The American military response was prompt and decisive, establishing its pre-eminent role in governing New Mexico. Dona-ciano Vigil, who became governor, took his cues from the military commander.

Maneuverings of the rival factions in Santa Fe continued until, in 1850, Colonel John Munroe, military and *de facto* civil governor, called for an election to a constitutional convention. The document resulting from the convention took several strong stands: it claimed large parts of what are now Texas, Oklahoma, Kansas, Colorado, Utah, and Arizona; emphatically rejected slavery; and defined the position of the Catholic church and clergy. Less than a month after the convention closed, its results were overwhelmingly endorsed by the electorate (8,731 to 39), and a slate of officers was elected. However, Munroe did not step aside to allow the new civilian government to function. While the newly elected "governor," Dr. Henry Connelly, traveled in the eastern U.S., "lieutenant governor" Manuel Alvarez established a government, appointing judges and executive officers and calling the legislature into session. Munroe's response was to order his subordinates in Santa Fe and throughout the domain to ignore Alvarez's actions.

At the same time Zachary Taylor had taken office as president of the United States. The victorious Mexican War general strongly supported statehood for New Mexico, using his power of appointment to send the area an Indian agent, James Calhoun, and an Army officer, George McCall, to press secretly for statehood. Advocates of statehood were encouraged by the highly placed support, but when Taylor died of cholera in July 1850, their hopes ended. The new president, Millard Fillmore, was less firmly committed to statehood; only staunch support could have overcome the roadblock of the slavery issue. A committee led by Henry Clay established an eastern border of New Mexico, offering monetary compensation to Texas. This cleared the way for a compromise, which gave New Mexico territorial status on September 9, 1850. The In-dian agent and provocateur James S. Calhoun was named by Fillmore as first territorial governor, with Weightman to be the first nonvoting delegate to Congress.

The issue of slavery had long been moot when New Mexico was finally granted statehood in 1912. Much political activity, many constitutional conventions, and many congressional hearings took place over the sixty-two years that elapsed between New Mexico's attainment of territorial status and its statehood. During the remainder of the 1850s and into the 1860s the nation was preoccupied by the increasingly strident controversy over the abolition of slavery. Statehood advocates began their movement again in 1872. Putting aside an almost comic partisan battle in its halls, the state legislature drafted a new constitution with at least some bipartisan cooperation. That the constitution was defeated in a confused referendum did not end the movement toward statehood. Coupled bills for Colorado and New Mexico statehood progressed through Congress in its 1876 session. Parliamentary tactics left both bills on the Speaker's table in the House on the last day of the session. Each required a two-thirds vote to be considered. The Colorado bill, taken up first, carried by a margin of four votes. The vote on New Mexico was in favor, 154 to 87, but failed by seven votes, a bitter defeat for New Mexico's delegate, Stephen B. Elkins. In postmortem discussion, the luckless Elkins, who had pushed hard and effectively for New Mexico, took some of the blame for the defeat. In a story first publicly told twenty-five years later, he was said to have gained the enmity of a group of Southern congressmen. Entering the House during an impassioned speech by Michigan representative Julius Caesar Burrows, Elkins was carried away by the orator's force and eloquence, rushing up to be the first to shake his hand at the conclusion of his speech. Burrows's oratory had been severely critical of the south; in retaliation for Elkins's untimely support, it is said, New Mexico lost crucial votes.

Statehood for New Mexico was delayed for

years after this defeat. In 1889 another constitution was written, but as the constitutional convention's delegates had been elected from Republican-gerrymandered districts, even Democratic congressional delegate Antonio Joseph opposed the constitution's passage, and New Mexico's voters sent the document to a resounding defeat.

Between 1872 and 1912, New Mexico's elected delegates in Washington, including a number of forceful, eloquent men, made little progress toward statehood. Many of the delegates were members of the "Santa Fe Ring," a group that controlled much of the trade in land grant titles as well as a substantial share of the commercial activity of the territory. Elkins and another Missouri-born attorney, Thomas Catron, were prominent both in the activities of the ring and in the partly self-serving push for statehood: large landowners believed that land values would increase markedly with attainment of the sought-for status. The ring was largely made up of lawyers (it was said that one of every ten Anglos living in Santa Fe at the time was an attorney), but it included enough Democrats and native New Mexicans to make it appear representative. Antonio Joseph, for example, was a ring member and a Hispanic Democrat, and like his Republican, Anglo colleagues, a strong proponent of statehood. The group allied itself, usually in the Republican party, with the Spanish *patrones* (members of rich, politically active families) of the mid–Rio Grande settlements. These included important families such as the Oteros and Solomon Luna of Valencia County and Pedro Perea of Bernalillo County, who also served as congressional delegate from 1898 to 1900. The *patrones,* operating in the semifeudal system prevalent in central New Mexico at the time, supplied credit and other services to the *peones,* their poorer countrymen, requiring in exchange their loyalty at the polls.

Although peonage was outlawed by an 1867 congressional action specifically applying to New Mexico, continued economic ties and the widespread and almost open practice of vote-buying continued to enable the wealthy *patrones* to deliver large blocks of votes regularly. Latter-day politicians have maintained electoral support through careful attention to constituent needs and to the distribution of patronage. The *patrones* of the past were frequently accused not only of voting their *peones* but even of voting their sheep.

Throughout the pre-statehood period and until the New Deal wrought marked changes in New Mexico's political landscape, the coalition of usually Republican Hispanic voters and wealthy Anglos centered in the Rio Grande counties left the state dominated by the Republican party. Considerable growth in the population of heavily Democratic southeastern New Mexico made many of the elections close, occasionally resulting in Democrats in high offices, though the territorial and then state legislature was dominated by Republicans.

Meanwhile, efforts for statehood continued. In 1906 influential members of Congress urged the territories of Arizona and New Mexico to apply for statehood as a single entity. There were at least two reasons behind the request for jointure: Eastern states' political power would be diluted less, and Arizona's predominantly Anglo population would balance New Mexico's largely Catholic, Spanish-speaking populace, which was viewed with suspicion by Eastern politicians. However, Arizona voters decisively rejected the proposal. Finally, in 1910, President Taft lent his prestige to the issue and succeeded in overcoming House-Senate differences, resulting in enabling acts for the separate territories. A Republican-dominated constitutional convention was elected and within two months had approved a constitution over the objections of progressives, who were angered by the constitution's omission of such progressive rallying points as the initiative, recall, and referendum. The constitution was endorsed by 70.3 percent of the electorate. One more hurdle remained. On August 21, 1911, President Taft signed a resolution promising statehood to Arizona and New Mexico if each slightly amended its con-

stitution. On November 7, New Mexico voters approved this requirement, which made the state's constitution easier to amend, and elected the first state governor and two representatives to Congress. The Republican party, divided over whether to support the constitutional amendment, lost most of the top positions, but having apportioned the seats in the legislature carefully it won a two-thirds majority in each house. On January 6, 1912, with New Mexico's congressman-elect in attendance, President Taft signed the declaration that began the state's existence.

That first state constitution, which, much amended, still governs New Mexico, was an essentially conservative document, written to provide a healthy climate for investment and to preserve Republican majorities. It was unexceptional except insofar as it protected the rights of Spanish-speaking citizens and firmly established the Spanish language as equal to English in both public education and legal discourse. A bill of rights was incorporated, similar to that in the federal constitution except that it also provided that those aspects of the 1848 Treaty of Guadalupe Hidalgo which guaranteed rights to New Mexicans formerly citizens of Mexico be respected. Despite liberalization of the amendment process, several portions of the constitution dealing with the rights of Spanish-speakers were left virtually inviolable. To safeguard the Republican legislative majority, a complicated system of overlapping districts was created to give as much representation as possible to such Republican strongholds as Santa Fe and Las Vegas.

New Mexico politics since statehood has reflected a balance between the predominantly Hispanic counties of the North and the Rio Grande valley and the "Little Texas" of the South and East. For the Hispanic counties, Re-

publicanism fostered by the *patrón* system came to an abrupt end with the New Deal; those counties have provided increasing Democratic majorities since then. The "Little Texas" counties, on the other hand, were heavily Democratic at statehood, reflecting the politics of the large neighboring state. By the late 1970s, again mirroring changes seen in the conservative South, much of "Little Texas" returned Republican majorities for national and statewide offices. The electoral importance of Bernalillo County, containing as it does one-third of New Mexico's population, has grown along with its proportion of the state's electorate. Its political inclination has also changed; when Bernalillo County was largely a fiefdom of the Perea family in the middle of the nineteenth century, it was strongly Republican. Like other Hispanic-dominated counties, Bernalillo became strongly Democratic in 1932. However, Albuquerque's post–World War II population growth has consisted largely of Anglos, who have made political battles in the county, and thus in the state, very close and unpredictable. In 1982 voter registration in New Mexico gave the Democrats a 2.3-to-1 advantage, and Democrats won the governorship and control of the State Senate. Nevertheless, three of the five members of New Mexico's congressional delegation were Republicans, and the state House of Representatives was in the hands of a Republican–conservative Democratic coalition.

New Mexico has never provided a comfortable home for third-party politics, instead accommodating diversity within its two dominant parties. A Populist Party candidate for territorial delegate drew 5 percent of the vote in 1894. At that time, as well as in 1912 and 1924, third-party activity was centered at the northeast corner of the state. That four-county area gave one-third of its presidential vote to candidates from the Progressive and Socialist parties in 1912 and contributed strongly to Wisconsin Progressive candidate Robert LaFollette's statewide tally in 1924. Radical Chicano activity began with Reies Tijerina's land grant advocacy in the middle 1960s and the takeover of the Rio Arriba County courthouse by his followers of the Alianza de los Pueblos Libres ("alliance of the free towns," formerly the Alianza Federal de Mercedes) in 1969. Many of his followers were among those who organized a political party, La Raza Unida, that has sponsored gubernatorial candidates and candidates for local races in the northern counties, but has not carried any of these elections.

As have many other areas where one party has maintained its ascendancy for a prolonged period, New Mexico has seen factionalism develop in its dominant political parties. The Republican Party of early statehood days had been divided among the old guard conservatives, such as Thomas Catron and Miguel Otero, and the progressive wing, led by Bronson Cutting. Similarly, the Democratic Party, after forty years of dominance in the state government, began showing cracks. Liberal Democrats, led by Walter Martínez of Grants, ruled over the legislature from 1971 to 1979, often riding roughshod over the aspirations of more conservative party members from southern and eastern New Mexico. This ruling group, dubbed the "Mama Lucy Gang" after the owner of a restaurant where they gathered in Las Vegas, New Mexico, suffered a rude and unprecedented defeat in 1979. The more conservative wing of the Democratic Party formed a strong coalition with Republicans from throughout the state to elect Democrat Gene Samberson, from Lea County in the southeast corner, as speaker of the house, dumping Martínez and consigning the Mama Lucy Gang to the less important committees. Throughout the next three legislative sessions, this unique "Cowboy Coalition" (or "unholy alliance," as it was described by one political writer) held together, making traditional party labels meaningless. The 1982 legislature, called to Santa Fe early for a special session on reapportionment of the legislature and of the state's congressional districts to account for the state's newly added Third Congressional District, met to the accompaniment of great interest. Would the Cowboy Coalition hold up, or would reapportionment lead to a reunion of Democrats in the two wings of the party? With surprisingly little controversy, the state senate and house were reapportioned in the short session. The senate bill was passed on a straight party line vote, with the Democrats winning over the Republicans. In the House, members of the Cowboy Coalition were victorious, routing the small group of liberal Democrats in a bill thought to favor conservative members of the lower chamber. However, as the legislature had used a votes-cast formula rather than population figures in this reapportionment plan, the entire plan was scuttled by the courts, throwing primary elections into disarray. Another legislative session was required and a separate primary was held solely for legislative seats.

By 1980 the New Mexico constitution had been amended almost one hundred times, as voters approved nearly half of the 205 amendments submitted to them. This piecemeal approach to constitutional reform seems well-established; a 1969 constitutional convention wrote a new document, with many of its innovations traceable to a "Little Hoover Commission" appointed by Governor Mechem in 1950. The new constitution was rejected by a small majority of an apparently apathetic electorate. Since that time the process of amending the 1910 enactment has continued at an accelerating pace.

The constitution provides for the usual executive, legislative, and judicial branches of government. Voters elect seven executive officers, ranging from governor to state auditor; elected separately, these officials may or may not have similar political philosophies. Governors and other state executive officers are elected to four-year terms, increased in 1970 from two years, without the right to succeed themselves. The governor appoints a cabinet of secretaries of the major departments and is responsible for the appointment of hundreds of administrative officers and board members. As in many states, the governor is permitted to veto portions of appropriations bills presented to him (the "line veto"). He is also empowered to call special sessions of the legislature and to develop the "call," or list of matters (other than appropriations) that can be taken up by the legislature during its short, thirty-day sessions in even-numbered years. (During odd-numbered years the sessions last for sixty days.) The other elected state officers generally are given little exposure, although state attorneys general have recently taken a more activist role in consumer protection and environmental regulation.

The legislature consists of a forty-two-member senate and a seventy-member house, elected respectively for four and two years. The legislature was empowered by the 1910 constitution to reapportion itself after each decennial census. No action, however, was taken until a 1962 U.S. Supreme Court decision in a Tennessee case led to a New Mexico suit that overturned the method previously used for apportionment, which, in New Mexico as in Tennessee, favored sparsely settled rural areas. Since 1972 House and Senate seats have been allotted to districts of relatively equal population.

Much of the legislature's business is done in committees. Senators are appointed to these by a committee on committees that includes the chamber's minority and majority leaders. This committee's function in the House is performed by the Speaker, elected by the entire House. Between sessions a series of interim committees carries on important continuing functions. Of highest importance are the Legislative Council, with eight members each from the House and the Senate who provide direction to the legislature as a whole and appoint other interim committees, and the Legislative Finance Committee, which develops budgetary recommendations for approaching legislative sessions.

The judicial system in New Mexico differs little from those in most other states. Judges of district courts, which serve one to four counties each, and of a statewide court of appeals and a supreme court are all elected by the general public. All face partisan elections; as codes of legal ethics forbid judges and prospective judges to run on their judicial records or philosophies, the elections are often sterile affairs. Between 1965 and 1967, voters approved a number of changes in the judicial system. Measures included the establishment of a court of appeals, the replacement of justices of the peace with magistrate courts, and the establishment of a judicial standards commission. This commission, composed of judges, lawyers, and private persons, is appointed by the governor to oversee the activities of the state's judges and to recommend their dismissal when indicated. In 1980 another constitutional amendment created for Bernalillo County (and for other counties, should they reach a population of 200,000) a metropolitan court that consolidates the functions that magistrate, municipal, and small claims courts serve elsewhere.

The law adjudicated by New Mexico courts is in most ways similar to that of other states. Perhaps its most outstanding provisions reflect the state's Spanish heritage. Spanish and English are considered equally as official languages of the courts, a stipulation that results in the provision of Spanish interpreters at state expense when requested. As required by the terms of the Treaty of Guadalupe Hidalgo, the New Mexico constitution and the law recognize Spanish land grants made to groups, a provision foreign to English common law. Like several other Western states, New Mexico is a "community property state," meaning that most property acquired during marriage belongs equally to husband and wife. Also in common with Western states, New Mexico's laws regarding the rights to water are highly specific, recognizing among other things the prior rights of the Pueblo Indians and the existence of local water systems. These systems range in size from the huge Mid–Rio Grande Conservancy District to small, local *acequia* (irrigation ditch) associations. The importance of water in New Mexico is such that in many areas the *mayordomo*, or chief, of the *acequia* is one of the area's most feared and respected citizens.

Local government in New Mexico is also similar to that of other states. Thirty-three counties are governed by commissions, usually composed of three members (five in Bernalillo County). Voters elect the commissioners; a sheriff responsible for law enforcement, usually only outside the county's municipalities; and various other county officials. The ninety-three municipalities, villages, towns, and cities each elect a council, which in some cases exists alongside an elected mayor and in others appoints a city manager.

Federal constitutional law specifies Indian tribal government as a form separate from and not subject to the state government. In some senses the tribes are sovereign nations within the state; tribal constitutions or customs specify their own taxes, law enforcement, and courts; fish and game laws; and many other forms of regulation. The tribes' governments operate subject to the federal constitution for the most part, although a separate bill of rights for the tribal governments was enacted by Congress as the Indian Civil Rights Act of 1968. In most respects this document is similar to the first ten amendments to the Constitution, but an interesting difference concerns religion: although freedom of religion is prescribed, tribes are left free to establish a religion, traditional, Christian, or both.

Each of the nineteen pueblos has a separate tribal government, headed by a *cacique*, or religious leader, or by a lay governor, elected by the pueblo's populace for a one-year term. Symbols of the governors' power and prestige are the silver-headed canes bestowed upon each pueblo's governor by Abraham Lincoln. A form of tribal council in each pueblo performs legislative functions. A confederation of pueblo governments, the All-Indian Pueblo Council, with offices in Albuquerque, has several functions in which all pueblos have joint interests.

The Athapascan tribes—Navajo, Jicarilla Apache, and Mescalero Apache—each elect a tribal council and a chief executive. Tribal governments, especially those of the Navajos and Apaches, have been heavily involved in making decisions on elements of "progress" and of exploitation of mineral and energy resources. The U.S. Bureau of Indian Affairs, which is to act as trustee for the Indian tribes and their lands, has usually encouraged the tribes along the lines of increasing development, sometimes at the expense of tradition and religion. Thus the BIA approved the controversial leasing by Cochiti Pueblo of a large tract of tribal land to non-Indian developers, a decision that led to a deep schism within the Pueblo.

As in most parts of the United States, New Mexico's citizenry is subject to a confusing welter of governing bodies: city, county, and state governments, school boards, water conservancy and soil conservation districts, municipal, district, and state courts, and in the case of Indians, tribal governments and the Bureau of Indian Affairs. New Mexico's law and governmental forms are entirely American in nature; few remnants remain of the Spanish and Mexican forms of government that prevailed here for almost two hundred fifty years.

economy

Visitors to New Mexico often ask, "How do people make a living here?" A local politician once answered the question this way: "Everyone takes in everyone else's laundry."

He was not far from wrong. Because of the nature of the state, particularly its scarcity of arable land and water resources, New Mexico has no large manufacturing cities, no industrial corridors, none of the usual indicators of an economic base. So other kinds of economic activity take up the slack. For instance, the trades and services sector of the New Mexico economy employs about 40 percent of the state's work force. Combine trades and services with government employment, and almost 70 percent of New Mexicans are engaged in nonfarm, nonmanufacturing activity.

The services and trades sector in New Mexico includes not only those who work in the state's laundries, but also those who sell merchandise and real estate, run hotels and restaurants in the tourist industry, and provide educational and medical services to the state's citizens. It has been said that trade has flourished in New Mexico since its earliest days, that the inhabitants of Chaco Canyon exchanged goods for beads and feathers in the

twelfth century. A form of barter has existed in New Mexico ever since. When the Pueblo Indians were settled along the Rio Grande and its tributaries prior to Spanish entrance into New Mexico, they often traded with the Plains Indians who lived to the east. The Taos trade fairs, begun as an informal mingling of various Indian tribes, became an annual event and symbolized the importance of trade to the people, Indian and Hispanic, who lived in New Mexico in its colonial days. The fair went on for days, with livestock, skins, beads, food, tools, and even slaves being exchanged. It was a wild, colorful event.

In the seventeenth and eighteenth centuries, pack trains plied the fifteen hundred miles between Durango, Mexico, and Santa Fe, bringing New Mexico settlers cherished foodstuffs, dry goods, and implements three times a year. The nineteenth century saw the growth of other trade routes as New Mexico's borders opened up and all manner of entrepreneurs poured into or at least passed through the state. American merchants arrived here in the middle of the nineteenth century, as did itinerant peddlers, many from Europe and the Middle East. Descendants of some of the earli-

est merchants still practice their trades in New Mexico, although many of the original mercantile establishments have long since been absorbed by large companies.

Today real estate and tourism also play important roles in the state's economy. While the real estate boom of the 1950s and 1960s has leveled off, a sizable number of people buy, sell, design, and build homes, office buildings, and shopping centers in New Mexico's metropolitan areas. Tourism and its allied businesses—gas stations, hotels, ski areas, and the like—account for an increasingly large share of the state's income. Most tourists visit the state's national parks and monuments (almost two million visitors were counted in 1977), attend annual events like the Balloon Fiesta in Albuquerque, the Indian Ceremonial in Gallup, and the opera in Santa Fe, or come to hunt, fish, camp, and ski in New Mexico's mountains.

Educational and medical services account for a large share of the state's services industry. Thousands of New Mexicans teach and work in the state's schools, colleges, and universities. Many of New Mexico's best-educated workers are employed by its large medical establishments. Albuquerque, the center for the state's medical services, has a number of major hospitals staffed by highly trained personnel and equipped with sophisticated machines and instruments. As a regional medical center, Albuquerque's hospitals serve not only New Mexicans but also residents of bordering states. Satellites of Albuquerque's larger hospitals can be found all over the state.

Although their numbers are small, bankers, whose industry began in New Mexico as an informal credit system extended from merchant to customer, have always had a great deal of influence in the state. New Mexico's first bank was chartered in Santa Fe by Lucien Maxwell in 1870. Maxwell's picture, complete with cigar in mouth, was featured on the original stock certificates of the First National Bank of Santa Fe. In the state's early days, banks, often set up in mining towns, rose and fell with the fortunes of their clientele. Today many New Mexico banks belong to statewide holding companies, and banking is no longer a colorful occupation or a dramatic one.

Thirty percent of New Mexico's work force is employed by government entities; one-quarter of the state's income is derived from government activity. Government, whether at the federal, state, or local level, ranks second only to trades and services in economic importance in the state. Almost fifty-three thousand New Mexicans work for the federal government, many of them on military bases in Albuquerque and Clovis, and near Alamogordo. Others who work for the federal government are employed by agencies that oversee the one-third of New Mexico's land that is owned and administered by the federal government. The Bureau of Land Management (BLM), for instance, manages acreage all over the state, leasing much of it to private farmers and ranchers and building campgrounds and recreation sites in attractive areas. Other federal employees include those who manage New Mexico's five national forests and staff the Bureau of Indian Affairs (BIA) and similar agencies.

Even more New Mexicans are employed by state and local government than by the federal government. At the end of the 1970s, close to eighty-five thousand residents worked in state government offices, in county courthouses, and for municipalities. The majority of state workers, however, were employed by local school districts and the state's colleges and universities. In many small towns and rural counties, entire families depend on the county government or the local schools for jobs as bus drivers, road crew members, maintenance personnel, teachers, and administrators. Such jobs are often awarded on the basis of kinship and political ties.

Like trade, mining can trace its roots in New Mexico back thousands of years. The earliest mining was probably for silica, from which arrowheads and scrapers could be carved. Early Indians also mined turquoise, especially in the Cerrillos area south of Santa Fe. Not until the nineteenth century, however, did mining become a major enterprise in New Mexico. Precious metals, especially gold and silver, were mined in the state's mountains. There were two gold rushes in New Mexico prior to the 1840s and later gold strikes in the 1880s. Gold brought to life places like Elizabethtown in the North and White Oaks in the South. Silver, also a sought-after commodity, created such boom towns as Shakespeare, Black Hawk, and Georgetown, all in the South. The gold-mining industry in New Mexico was affected by the discovery of gold in California in 1848; by the end of the century, few mines were active, and abandoned towns were all that was left from New Mexico's gold- and silver-mining era.

The kind of enterprise that now ranks New Mexico eighth nationally in mining activity includes metals and minerals that have neither the glamor nor the value of gold and silver. The mining of copper, discovered near Silver City in 1800, remains an important extractive industry in New Mexico. Large open-pit and surface mines are located in the southwestern corner of the state at Santa Rita and Big Burro. Uranium, long used as a dye in glass and ceramic ware, has experienced two major periods of growth in New Mexico, particularly in the Grants area. The first great demand for uranium, an element crucial to the nuclear process, occurred in the 1950s. A downswing followed in the 1960s. The 1970s again saw Grants growing, its labor force swelling as residents and others rushed to its surface and

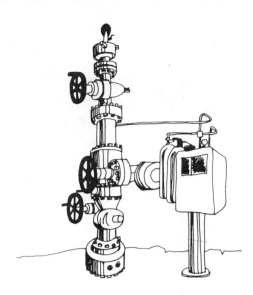

subsurface mines. In the 1980s, with the demand for nuclear-powered generating plants less than had been predicted, the mines at Grants again slowed their activity or closed altogether.

Other materials, coal and potash, for example, are also mined in New Mexico. Coal, strip-mined in the state's northwestern corner, provides energy to local and regional generating plants. High-quality coal, important in the processing of steel, is mined near Raton and shipped by rail to steel plants in California. All mining activity, of course, rises and falls with industrial demand. Thus during the recession of the late 1970s and the early 1980s, the demand for copper fell off, and Silver City, like its uranium-rich counterpart, Grants, suffered high unemployment rates as its mines and mills shut down. Even the coal industry experienced setbacks; the York Canyon mine near Raton saw its output limited considerably as the steel industry curbed its own production. Potash, mined near Carlsbad and used in the fertilizer and chemical industries, seems to fluctuate less in the marketplace. Other metals and minerals mined in New Mexico include lead, molybdenum, and vanadium.

The other major product extracted in New Mexico is petroleum. New Mexico ranks fourth in the United States in gas production and seventh in oil. Gas and oil are found in the extreme corners of the state, gas in the San Juan Basin in the northwest and both gas and oil in the southeast in the Permian Basin.

Sheep shearing, *Joan Larson*.

Gas-pumping stations are a common sight throughout the dry scrubland of the San Juan Basin, where, in the first part of this century, natural gas was used to generate electricity in some of the area's towns. Now 47 percent of the state's natural gas comes from the area, much of it shipped through pipelines to other parts of the United States. There is also natural gas in the Permian Basin, but the region is best-known for its oil production. Oil was first discovered in Lea and Eddy counties in the 1920s, and the Permian Basin now accounts for more than 90 percent of the oil produced in New Mexico. Large and small refineries give the southeastern corner of the state an industrial aura lacking elsewhere in New Mexico. Fortunes have been made in the petroleum business in New Mexico. The industry seems to reward self-made men and has produced a number of millionaires, some

of whom, including the Runnels family of Lovington and the Yates family of Artesia, have spawned succeeding generations of entrepreneurs.

The state of New Mexico depends upon its extractive industries for severance taxes that pay for the running of state government and provide revenue for public schools. When mining and petroleum production fall off, so do revenues, necessitating a tightening of state budgets and capital expenditures.

New Mexico is a Western state, and although ranching is no longer king (despite the fact that a rancher named King has twice been governor), agriculture, including farming and ranching, retains a symbolic prominence in the state that transcends its economic importance. In 1975 only 2 percent of the state's workers were engaged in agricultural activity. Some counties, however, particularly those on the eastern side of New Mexico, depend heavily on farming and ranching. Chaves County leads the state in the value of its farm products, with livestock the single most important commodity. Curry County ranks second, again with livestock of prime importance, and Doña Ana County, the nation's leading producer of pecans, is third. Other major agricultural products in New Mexico include chile, peanuts (from the Portales area in Roosevelt County), cotton, and sorghum.

State-wide, ranching accounts for an overwhelming portion of agricultural income, and a large portion of the state's "Western" lore. Often romanticized in Western novels and movies, the introduction of large-scale cattle ranching in the mid-1800s brought about basic changes in New Mexico life.

The earliest Hispanic settlers drove sheep and goats with them into New Mexico. Raising these animals for their wool, meat, and milk continued throughout the colonial and early territorial periods as part of a rural economy that combined farming in the irrigated valleys with sheepherding on nearby mesas and mountains. A large number of sheep could be tended by a single person, often a child, who knew their habits and could anticipate their movements. Since sheep require few keepers but constant attention, sheepherding has long been a dull and lonely but exacting job. Wool, the major product of sheep raising, is easily stored and transported.

Cattle were first brought to New Mexico in large numbers with the approach of the railroad; their advent wrought many changes, both economic and cultural. Cattle normally are not controlled by a single person but need not be protected so carefully from heat, thirst, or poor forage. Left to themselves for long periods, they are then rounded up to be branded or shipped, events that require dozens of hands for brief periods.

Cattle raising, in short, requires different habits and values from sheep raising; this fact probably accounts for the storied antagonism between keepers of the two kinds of livestock. Cattle raising is a modern industry, requiring quick and dependable storage and transport to get its principal product, meat, to market. Cattle have almost completely supplanted sheep on New Mexico's vast rangelands, ending a way of life—*patrones*, *peones*, and *pastores*—brought by the first Spanish colonists.

Like ranching, the railroad industry in New Mexico has great historical and less current importance. The coming of the railroads brought tremendous changes to New Mexico within a relatively short period. The steam engine introduced a new economy to the territory and vastly accelerated movement into formerly unoccupied regions.

All the major railroad line construction took place within a span of thirty years. The Santa Fe Railroad, connecting Kansas City with Los Angeles, missed Santa Fe but created New Las Vegas, New Albuquerque, and railroad Socorro. The Southern Pacific built across the southern counties via the new town of Deming. Smaller companies, which would be absorbed by the Southern Pacific, built north from El Paso, bypassing Tularosa, White Oaks, and Puerto de Luna, but connecting with the Rock Island Line at the railroad town of Santa Rosa. The Pecos Valley Railroad created Portales and Carlsbad, bringing hopeful farmers

Chile truck, *Jean Blackmon*.

and homesteaders to the eastern plains and the lower Pecos Valley.

By 1907, when the last major line was completed, virtually all of New Mexico was inhabited. Railroads promoted agricultural settlement under the Homestead Act and pursued irrigation schemes to attract farmers. Access to markets stimulated ranching and mining.

Railroad building and maintenance themselves created thousands of jobs in the railroads' heyday. Many northern New Mexico villagers and immigrants from Europe, Asia, and Mexico got their first jobs making roadbeds, cutting tie lumber, or laying track. After the trains were rolling, they needed to be watered, supplied with coal, and kept in repair. Locomotives required water every 20 miles and an engine shop every 90–100 miles.

Railroad jobs brought new prosperity to many but ended a self-sufficient way of life that had characterized New Mexico for generations. In addition, increased lumbering, dry farming, ranching, and mining, made possible by the railroads, was often done thoughtlessly, without consideration for the degradation of New Mexico's fragile soil resources.

Manufacturing, the bedrock of the industrial northeastern United States, is of little importance to the overall economy of New Mexico. Less than 10 percent of the state's labor force is engaged in manufacturing, most of which takes place in Bernalillo County, where a number of high-technology firms have located. Anxious for more of this clean industry, the New Mexico legislature, with the cooperation of the governor, key state agencies, selected universities, and the technological community, decided in the early 1980s to devote a significant amount of capital and expertise to the development of a "high-technology corridor." The corridor is to run through the state, tying together scientific communities from Los Alamos to Las Cruces. The hope is that this "high-tech" area will act as a magnet to draw more such industries to the state.

A major source of New Mexico's income already comes from its three centers of nuclear research and development, the laboratories at Los Alamos and at Sandia Base and Kirtland Air Force Base in Albuquerque. Working with the United States departments of defense and energy, in concert with the universities of California and New Mexico and with private contractors, the three laboratories employ thousands of scientists and skilled workers in the design and testing of nuclear weapons. Researchers also work on alternative sources of energy, peaceful applications for the nuclear process, and other endeavors. Sandia National Laboratories, for instance, has created a $21 million solar tower, a veritable sea of solar collectors. Scientists at Los Alamos National Laboratories engage in cancer research projects and geothermal experiments. Unlike Boston or California, New Mexico has seen relatively little private development of local enterprises related to the work of its scientific laboratories.

There is another form of manufacturing in New Mexico that is as ancient as the state. The Indian arts, including jewelry making, weaving, and pottery making, contribute to the economy and to the charm of the state. While their output is not massive, those who create and sell the small masterpieces of this historic art can maintain a steady income. Most Indian art, which must bear a mark indicating its Indian origin, is sold in New Mexico's tourist centers.

While New Mexico continues to be, in many ways, a poor state, things are changing. Per capita income rose from $4,785 in 1975 to $8,529 in 1981. In 1975 the state ranked forty-fourth nationally in per capita income; by 1981 it had risen to forty-second. There has been greater diversification of labor within the state recently, with an increase in the number of people employed in the trades and services sector and a decrease in the number of workers who must depend upon the government for jobs. And, while New Mexico generally does not prosper with the same degree of intensity as most other states, neither does it react as deeply to national recessions. In its own way, New Mexico's economy reflects the state's unique blend of landscape, resources, and people.

education

The early Indian peoples of New Mexico evolved their own system of education by which they passed on to their offspring their values, their culture, and their knowledge of things spiritual and natural. Elders taught children the meaning of tribal dances and legends, the making of pottery, the construction of dwelling places, the preparation of food and herbs, and the conversion of pelts and hides into clothing. As an integral part of this learning, the children learned how they fit into society as a whole and into their natural environment.

After the coming of the Spaniards—and with them the Franciscans, who had as their mission the conversion of the Indians—a different kind of education was imposed on those Pueblo Indians whom the friars gathered under their supervision at the missions. The Spaniards did not place much value on the Pueblo way of life, and it was left up to Indian families and leaders to pass on the learning of their ancestors. Instead the Franciscans taught the Spanish language, European-style agriculture, carpentry, blacksmithing, masonry, spinning, and weaving.

The Spanish Crown ordered public schooling for the children of colonists in 1721; this decree had little effect, however, since there was no money to keep the schools open. Thus the church continued to educate both Spaniards and Indians, giving them rudimentary teachings based on European principles. Those who could afford it sent their children to Mexico for secondary schooling.

After Mexico won its independence from Spain, the new government launched a movement toward general education for the common people. In response, the provincial deputation in New Mexico passed a law to establish public schools in the territory. Funds for the schools were to come from voluntary contributions and, among other schemes, fees from dance halls. Unpersuaded of the benefits to be gained from schooling, the residents of the territory resisted collection of these monies and between 1827 and 1832 the number of schools declined from seventeen to six. In 1836 Governor Albino Pérez proclaimed officially the institution of a public school system. Ironically, by this time there were no schools left in the territory, and no new ones resulted from the proclamation.

When the United States annexed the territory, the Americans were appalled at the state of education among its Spanish and Indian

residents. Illiteracy was commonplace. Concerned people like Father Antonio Martínez had tried to keep some spark alive: he opened his own school in 1835, teaching religious and civil law and other subjects. Padre Martínez issued textbooks, tracts, and even a Bible on his printing press. Since the departure of the Spanish friars in the 1820s, however, what schools existed in the pueblos and *villas* had generally been neglected. The few priests who were left had been hard-pressed to care for souls; book learning took second place. The extreme isolation of the communities from centers of learning only made the situation worse.

When Archbishop Lamy arrived in Santa Fe, he determined to change these conditions. He encouraged teaching priests and nuns to come to the new territory to open schools where students would learn English and be instructed in American ways. In 1852 the Sisters of Loretto opened a boarding school for girls, Loretto Academy, in Santa Fe, and in 1859 the Christian Brothers established a similar institution for boys, St. Michael's College. The sisters also administered the only school in Albuquerque, known as Sister Blandina's School and located in Old Town. Archbishop Lamy concentrated on the Spanish population and opened schools in Taos, Mora, Las Vegas, Las Cruces, and Bernalillo. During this period schools in the pueblos were neglected.

In 1856 another public school law was passed in the territory. Schools were to be funded by property taxes, except in five counties whose representatives had persuaded the legislature to allow property owners to decide by popular vote whether they wished to be part of the system. They didn't. After ten

months the law was repealed by majority vote.

In 1860 and 1863 the legislature once again ordered the establishment of community schools and created a board of education and an office of territorial superintendent. However, there was still no financial support for public schools. Since property owners continued to resist taxation, laws passed in 1872 required schools to be funded by fines imposed on citizens for such transgressions as burying the dead on Sunday, cockfighting on the Sabbath, and marrying a first cousin. Also in 1872, county commissioners were authorized to act as county school committees and to use public funds for educating youth. In Albuquerque the funds were paid to religious orders and churches to staff and run the free schools; in other parts of the state the laws had little result. During these decades the churches continued to build schools for children and adults.

The Jesuits opened Holy Family College, a grammar school, in Albuquerque in 1870, and later in Las Vegas they founded the state's first institution for higher education. The order also ran free schools for Bernalillo County, while the Sisters of Loretto moved their school to Las Cruces. St. Vincent Academy in Albuquerque boarded daughters of the wealthy and provided free schooling for all children in the north end of town. As Protestant churches moved into the territory they also opened schools, recognizing education as a primary need of New Mexicans and as a powerful tool in winning converts. The Congregationalists opened Albuquerque Academy in the New Town and contracted with the county commissioners to conduct free schools to the south of town. The Methodist church opened Albuquerque College and later its Harwood schools for boys and girls. In 1882 the Presbyterians founded Santa Fe Academy. The churches also sponsored schools in adjacent villages for the "Mexican" population, operated schools on the reservations, and by the 1890s had opened schools in a few pueblos. Presbyterian "plaza" schools in the rural northwestern sector of the state for years were the only local schools and exerted a tremendous influence on those communities. They not only educated children in the three R's and religion, but instructed adults in home economics and agriculture as well. Students were encouraged to continue their education in Santa Fe and Albuquerque. With U.S. government help, the Presbyterian church also opened a school for Pueblo children near Old Town in Albuquerque. It was later moved to the site of the Albuquerque Indian School, and Pueblo children were sent there to be educated along with Utes, Apaches, and Navajos.

At this time the federal government was opening several similar boarding schools for Indian children all over the country. Since 1869 the government had had schools on reservations. Public protest against federal aid to sectarian schools had persuaded the government to open its own schools, but separate mission schools remained on the reservations.

Indian students from reservations were sent to boarding schools to be taught to become "Americans." This meant uprooting children from their homes, sending them long distances away, forbidding them to speak their language, and teaching them subjects that would enable them to be assimilated into the majority culture. Although these practices may seem harsh, it must be remembered that those who advocated them did so for what they thought was a good reason: the Americanizing and assimilating of a people until recently subject to annihilation.

In Albuquerque the Presbyterian church wished to teach with more focus on religious principles and so withdrew from the government-assisted Indian School and opened Menaul School across the road. Menaul was closed for a few years in the 1890s but reopened as a boarding school for Hispanic boys. It continues today as a boarding and day school for boys and girls.

Church schools were dependent on contributions from their members; when there were few donations, schools had to close. Many rural areas remained without any schools. In this respect New Mexico's experience was like that of the rest of the country, where public schools were struggling to become established.

In 1877 citizens of Grant County in the southwestern part of the state voted to join Arizona, in part because of the lack of a decent school system and the feeling that Arizona would meet this need. When the territorial legislature realized that they were serious about becoming part of another state, it passed a bill incorporating the main town of Silver City, thus allowing it to collect taxes. These monies helped establish the first independent school district in the territory; in 1878 the first public school in New Mexico was completed in Silver City.

Only in 1891, when the legislature established common school systems and named Amado Chávez territorial superintendent, was some progress made in establishing a statewide system of education. With the passage of the bill, the Protestant majority in Albuquerque voted for the establishment of Eastern-style schools, administered by public employees, as did other Easterners in railway towns all over the state. Hiram Hadley, school superintendent from 1905 to 1907, is credited with having initiated the present system of education.

Opposition to public education still came from several sources. Often the Spanish population was suspicious of schools where "gringo" ideas and culture would be taught. Taxes on property were abhorrent to landowners large and small alike. The big businesses like the railroads resisted paying taxes for education; they were interested in New Mexico strictly as a passage to the coast. The general population saw public schools as part of the political patronage system, with its attendant abuses. Some writers cite this lack of support for public education as a major factor in the delay New Mexico experienced in gaining statehood.

By the time the territory did become a state in 1912, both school buildings and the system itself were in disrepair. John Conway, the superintendent who made the first statewide survey of schools, found deplorable conditions existing in most rural facilities. However, legislatures continued to allot very little funding for schools, and in 1930 New Mexico ranked among the lowest states in literacy. Although tax revenues from 12.1 million acres were alloted to support public schools and the constitution of the new state devoted several statutes to education, including financial subsidies from the state to local districts, local interest in schools still was not very strong.

This changed in the 1920s when a new school code was written that covered all aspects of education. Teachers were to be properly certified and a specific curriculum was to be followed, with approved textbooks and local budgets fixed by special budget commissioners. Public schooling improved, although it retained distinctive practices; for example, until 1951 Catholic nuns taught in public schools.

The famous case of *Zeller* v. *Huff* changed this practice. In the little northern New Mexico town of Dixon, public school students went to classes in a poor adobe building. The Catholic church had opened a new school on church property and invited the public school students to use it. Parents, unhappy with this situation and supported by the local Presbyterian minister, founded the Free Schools Committee, which traveled through the state to find out whether similar situations existed in other small communities. The committee found 145 nuns teaching in public schools; they were qualified teachers but were nonetheless violating church-state separation principles. The committee brought suit, and the district court barred nuns from teaching in public schools. The decision was appealed all the way to the Supreme Court. In 1951 the archbishop recalled all the nuns from the schools. Although opposed on constitutional grounds, the teaching sisters were recognized for their educational contributions to rural counties, where often they were the only teachers.

Public schooling in the state improved for several reasons. The growing population provided a better tax base for better schools. Education advocates pushed for more equitable funding of school districts, important in a state like New Mexico where many of the districts lie in sparsely populated areas. Since 1974 schools have been funded by a combination of property, sales, and other taxes, with a high percentage of state funds going for education. The state allots an equal amount for each pupil and then adds to that figure if bilingual teaching or special education is necessary. This method of funding, which is recognized nationally as a model for equal treatment of students, has protected the state from lawsuits like those filed in Texas and California protesting unequal funding of school districts. As isolated communities were linked to larger centers, schools built in the smallest of towns were able to hire better teachers.

Public school education in New Mexico has become a priority in state goverment. Candidates for the governor's position traditionally devote a lot of rhetoric to schools. Administrators seek top funding for their students and try to keep up with trends such as computer education, cultural pluralism, career education, and special programs for children with handicaps and for the gifted. Although New Mexico is the only state in the union which has elected not to receive federal funds for special education, the state is committed to quality programs for the handicapped.

Abuses that existed in the earlier days of the public school system are now gone. Segregation was never an official policy of the state, but at least one school system assigned black students to a separate facility, and many schools were segregated *de facto,* with Anglo children attending one school and Hispanic another. When large numbers of Spanish-speaking students entered the schools, the educational thought of the day was that the best way to learn to speak English was to speak only English. Spanish-speaking students were therefore strictly forbidden to speak their first language in the school. Many New Mexicans remember being punished for breaking this rule, and the threat hung over every playground. While controversy still exists over the best way to assimilate numbers of non-English-speaking students into an English-language system, the consensus is against such a ban, which not only frightens young children but denigrates their whole cultural background.

Indian children suffered similarly. In off-reservation boarding schools run by the federal government, they were forbidden to speak their languages. Later, when reservation boarding and day schools were built as alternatives to the far-off central boarding schools, Indian languages were forbidden there, too. This policy was only one of several, including subsistence diet and mandatory labor, that seriously hindered the progress of children in these schools.

Nowadays Navajo, Apache, and Pueblo Indian children attend a variety of schools, depending on where they live: community day schools, mission schools, and local public schools. Students on the Jicarilla Reservation attending public school there can live in a dormitory if their homes are too far away. The community day schools are elementary schools. They emphasize the cultural background of their students and stress community values, for example, the importance of working for the good of the group rather than for individual achievement. These schools involve parents and local residents at all levels of planning and administration. Nearly all the pueblos and reservations have day schools.

Indian students who attend public schools sometimes travel forty miles or more to their classes. Some schools have special "pull out" programs to help them adjust to their new environment. In others the Indian students are

totally assimilated into the mainstream system, with no concessions made for their different background.

New Mexico receives federal funds for educating Indian children. One source of funding is the Johnson-O'Malley Act, passed in 1934. Before this the federal goverment would pay school districts that educated significant numbers of Indian students. This complex system of payment meant negotiating thousands of contracts with individual school districts. With the passage of "J-O'M," the secretary of the interior was able to contract directly with the state departments of education. New Mexico was one of the last states to sign a contract with the federal government.

Another source of funds resulted from "federally impacted area" legislation of 1950, which provided monies to school districts burdened by federal activities in the area. In 1953 these funds became available to schools serving children whose parents lived on reservations. This bill, Public Law 874, has since become the basic support for Indian children, while Johnson-O'Malley, and later Title I funding from the Elementary and Secondary Education Act, became supplementary sources of support to the state. These funds were often used for the benefit of whole schools instead of just Indian students. Influenced by increasingly activist Indian leadership in the mid-1960s, parents and community members demanded more participation in budget planning and in serving on boards of directors. The Indian Education Act of 1972 made parental and community participation in federal impact aid programs mandatory and encouraged community-run schools. Title VII of the ESEA was amended to emphasize cultural and bilingual curricula. Adult education was also stressed, with Indian tribes and organizations responsible for drawing up proposals for projects. All of these factors have made schools more accountable for spending funds directly on Indian students and their special needs.

Children in pueblos sometimes have a choice between attending elementary schools in their pueblo or the local public school. The Albuquerque Indian School, a boarding school, has closed, and its students have been transferred to the Santa Fe Indian School, a high school that until recently housed the Institute of American Indian Art. Indian high school students from all over the country attended this school, well-known for its focus on the arts. The institute has moved across the road to the College of Santa Fe but remains under Bureau of Indian Affairs control.

Churches continue to educate many New Mexican children. Existing alongside state public schools are parochial schools of the various churches—Catholic, Baptist, Lutheran, Christian Reformed—as well as the Sikh school in Española and the Baha'i school in Las Vegas. Albuquerque Academy is a private school run like college preparatory academies in the East. Other private schools throughout the state attract students to their various programs.

The state maintains many special schools:
one for the visually handicapped in Alamogordo; the Los Lunas Training School for the mentally retarded; the New Mexico Industrial School for Boys in Springer; a children's psychiatric center in Albuquerque; and a diagnostic school in Albuquerque for teenagers with problems.

As interest in educating the territory's residents increased, the territorial legislature passed a bill in 1889 providing for the location of a university in Albuquerque, a school of mines at Socorro, and an agricultural college at Las Cruces. The University of New Mexico opened its doors on June 15, 1892. Following the land grant tradition, in which the federal goverment set aside public lands for the benefit of postsecondary institutions, Congress granted 111,080 acres of land to the university on June 21, 1898, and later granted it a further 200,000 acres from the total provided by the enabling act for the territory. Revenue derived from timber sales and from oil, gas, and other mineral leases goes to the support of the University of New Mexico. Enrollment in 1981 was 22,092. Satellite campuses in Los Alamos, Gallup, Los Lunas, and Santa Fe bring graduate and undergraduate courses to scattered communities.

Land grants for revenue for the New Mexico State University, at University Park, near Las Cruces, total two hundred fifty thousand acres. No longer strictly an "aggie" school, NMSU attracts some twelve thousand students looking for a smaller campus than UNM's. The state university also has branches in Alamogordo, Carlsbad, and Grants, where students can get an associate of arts degree. The other universities in the state system are Western at Silver City, with sixteen hundred students; Eastern at Portales and Roswell, with thirty-eight hundred students; and Highlands in Las Vegas, with twenty-two hundred students. These universities are small in student population but important to the areas in which they are situated. They not only offer their students the advantages of small classes, but also make cultural programs and athletic events available to the general public.

Courses at the New Mexico Institute of Mining and Technology, opened in 1892, include mining, metallurgical, and geological engineering and general courses. New Mexico Tech, as it is known, derives revenue from two hundred thousand acres apportioned to the school from federal land grants. Its location in Socorro lends itself to the study of field geology and mine surveying.

Northern New Mexico Community College in El Rito was originally founded to train teachers to work in rural, Spanish-speaking communities. The modern campus now serves a varied student population. The New Mexico Military Institute, in Roswell, which opened in September 1898, was established as a junior college in 1914, with one hundred fifty thousand acres of public land allotted to it. It is now a preparatory school as well as a coeducational junior college. In Farmington, the two-year institution once associated with New Mexico State is now locally controlled. The College of the Southwest in Hobbs, once Baptist, is an independent junior college. Hobbs is also home to New Mexico Junior College. Technical-Vocational Institute in Albuquerque, nationally recognized, serves students from all over the state. A smaller technical institution, Vo-Tech, exists in Las Vegas.

The University of Albuquerque was founded in 1920 by the Sisters of St. Francis. It is a four-year liberal arts institution with a strong emphasis also on two-year programs not offered in other colleges. In 1947 the Christian Brothers obtained a portion of the Bruns Hospital site in Santa Fe and established St. Michael's College as a four-year institution of higher learning for men. Today the college is known as the College of Santa Fe and enrolls both men and women. Its Greer Garson Theater is named after the well-known resident of Santa Fe and offers innovative theater programs. Southwestern Indian Polytechnic Institute, on Albuquerque's West Mesa, has fought for years to continue its existence. Run by the Bureau of Indian Affairs, it depends on the Interior Department and congressional funding to survive. There are no colleges on New Mexico reservations or pueblo lands, but tribal and pueblo governments maintain educational funds to provide scholarships to members wishing to attend postsecondary institutions.

New Mexico today sees education for its citizens as a means to making the state a true participant in the age of technology. At the same time, educators recognize the richness of the state's ancient civilizations and seek to weave that culture into the preparation of students for the modern world.

religion

When the Franciscan friars planted crosses on New Mexican soil, they were bringing a new religion to a land already inhabited by a religious people, although the friars did not recognize the Indian religions. Many years later, the Catholic church learned to function side-by-side with Indian beliefs, and other churches sent missionaries to spread their creeds. New Mexicans today accept Sikhs and Moslems as part of the religious mosaic of their state.

There is no word for religion in the Indian languages, and it is difficult to separate religion from the daily lives of the Indian people. The tenets of Indian religions are not contained in a holy bible; Indian religion is not celebrated in a certain place on an appointed day. Rather Indian religion is a way of ordering life; it directs every aspect of the everyday life of every Indian.

The Southwestern Indians' religion traditionally has dominated their lives from birth to death, celebrating an arrival into this world or the age of maturity, healing a sick person, calling for precious rain, appeasing the spirits, readying the councils for war or for a hunt. Their religion teaches the Indians—Pueblos, Navajos, and Apaches—the importance of keeping their lives in harmony with the natural world, other humans, and the supernatural.

New Mexico Indians share a creation story, which scholars and Pueblo Indians argue originated with the Pueblos. It relates how the ancestors came from a series of lower worlds to this one, which is bounded by four sacred mountains and in which four sacred colors—coral, black, turquoise, and yellow or white—predominate. No single "Great Spirit" rules over this world, but rather it is directed by a variety of spiritual personages, male and female, some more benevolent and others less so, each with realms of power and special functions. Their struggles affect the physical earth and the lives of the people on it. The Indians maintain contact with the spirits through their medicine men, by chants, prayers, and other rituals.

According to anthropologists, society for the Pueblo Indians has followed a preordained plan over time. The origin myths taught specific procedures for carrying out ordinary functions as well as for sacred rituals. The priests and leaders of the people interpreted the myths to ensure that these procedures would be performed properly. The *cacique*, or

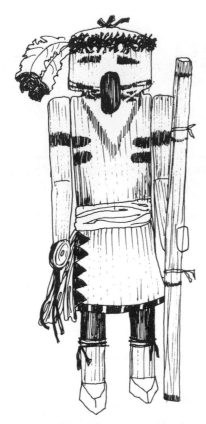

others. Sandia, for example, has retained most of its religious heritage and allows no information about its practices out of the pueblo. Taos Pueblo's deeply held belief in the sacredness of Blue Lake, high in the Sangre de Cristo Mountains, encouraged it to struggle for years to retain control of the precious site rather than cede it to the federal government, even though this meant revealing aspects of its religion to outsiders. Within the pueblos themselves, differences of opinion over the role of religions have often caused factions to develop. In Laguna these disagreements were so divisive in the 1850s that one conservative faction broke away and founded the new village of Mesita. Picuris is an example of a more secular society, with dances and rituals retaining importance for their cultural more than their religious significance.

Differences among the pueblos also show up in the variations of the creation stories that have been handed down by the elders. All the stories share a common theme, emergence from a lower world through a hole, the *sipapu*, but different pueblos emphasize particular themes or personalities.

The Eastern Tewa pueblos of the Rio Grande valley believe that men, gods, and animals all lived together in a world below where life began. At that time the upper world was "unripe," formed of mist and haze. As this world began to harden, the inhabitants of the lower sphere emerged into it. Two men were chosen as leaders, one for the Summer people, one for the Winter. The Summer people went south on the west side of the Rio Grande, the Winter people went on the east. The two groups met at Ojo Caliente and founded the five Tewa villages of San Juan, Santa Clara, San Ildefonso, Nambe, and Tesuque.

Santo Domingo and other Keresan communities emphasize the position of Iyatiko or "Bringing to Life," the Corn Mother. Iyatiko remains at the *sipapu* or emergence place but is represented at ceremonies by a perfect ear of corn, the symbol of fertility. At Zia and Cochiti, Spider Woman or Thinking Woman holds a more central place. The sun is also re-

priest, still holds an important position in most pueblos. Many Pueblo Indians practice Catholicism; they attend Mass, receive the sacraments, and hold *velorios*, or wakes for the dead. At the same time, the Pueblos observe the old forms in their kivas, ceremonial chambers where rituals have traditionally been held. During the early years of this century, the importance of the ceremonies diminished in some pueblos, but today they are an integral part of the Pueblo calendar, both for cultural and for spiritual reasons. The two religions, traditional and Catholic, coexist in a process described as compartmentalization, in which each religion has kept its own forms and the people observe the practices of both.

Change does not come easily to the Pueblos; rather, proposals for change are weighed against past experience. The tried and true way usually wins. This resistance to change has carried through in the religious as well as in the economic and social spheres. Some pueblos have resisted change more than

vered; he is the father of the twin war gods who taught the ancestors how to function in the world. The *kachinas*, gods with human forms, helped the ancestors with their crops; today they are represented in ceremonies by masked men who belong to the individual *kachina* societies. The Koshare and Quirina are also gods, messengers between the living and the ancestors. The Koshare perform the roles of clowns at ceremonies. Besides amusing their people, they scold and cajole in order to preserve certain standards of behavior.

In the Zuni world the most important personages are the Sun Father and Moonlight-Giving Mother. Their sons guard Zuni from six sacred directions. Rain priests, water priests, bow or warrior priests, and beast priests each perform a particular function in the Zuni world. *Kachinas* possess medicines, and from the bottom of a lake not far from Zuni pray for rain and good crops. The *kachinas'* home is called Kachina Village and is ordered like a Zuni community, with a hierarchy ranging from the chief and his couriers (the Shalako) to the house chiefs (the Koyemshi or Mudheads) and the ordinary folk, including the clumsy and the lazy.

The elders of San Felipe explain their history by recalling how the ancient people emerged into this world feeling a great reverence and love for what was left behind and a great fear and respect for what they were about to encounter in the new world. The spirits guided the people southward and saw that each group settled in a different place. Within the communities the people were reminded of their shared past and told how they were to work together in the future for the good of the community. Their *cacique* would give them the laws, and they were to obey him. Obedience to the prescribed behav-

ior enables the community to keep the necessary harmony with the universe. Actions that disturb the balance bring illness or some other evil.

To maintain not only the internal cooperation of the community but harmony with the universe, the Pueblo people developed their complex ceremonial system. The priests direct the ceremonials, and the people of each moiety or *kachina* cult or society take charge of carrying them out properly for six months at a time. Some pueblos are divided into two moieties, the Summer (Squash) and Winter (Turquoise) people. Some rituals take place in the kivas, the usually round buildings symbolizing *sipapu*, the exit from the underworld, or the womb of the Earth Mother. The ladder leading from the roof of the kiva to the inside reminds one of the climb from the lower world. Pueblos often have two kivas, the Winter people's kiva to the north end of the plaza and the Summer people's to the south.

Water has always played a central part in Pueblo life. The villages, built up along or not far from the Rio Grande and smaller rivers, depend upon good rains to keep the waters high and crops rich. Pueblos like Acoma, built high off the plain, are even more dependent upon the rain. Thus water-giving rites induct the infants of San Juan into the tribe; San Juan's creation story tells of the people emerging from the *sipapu* by way of a lake; many of its ceremonies focus on the production of rain and the subsequent fertility of crops, especially corn, symbol of all that is life-giving.

Ceremonies in the kivas or in the home of a member of the society that controls the particular ritual are private. Participants in the ceremonies fast and abstain from food and drink. A purification rite and continence are important to the rituals. The holy men offer the

However, other ceremonies follow a calendar dictated by the planting season.

The Indian new year begins after harvest in October, and major rites are held at the winter solstice or the "turning-back-of-the-sun." At the spring equinox, the Summer moiety takes over. From this time to the harvest, the ceremonies held are prayers for growth, fertility, and rain.

Of the winter dances the best-known is Shalako at Zuni in late November or early December. Other winter dances are prayers for abundant game and the success of the hunters. These include the Deer Dance at Taos and the Buffalo Dance at San Felipe. Individual pueblos hold onto traditional dances unique to their communities; for example, the Bull Dance at Jemez Pueblo, brought there by the people of Pecos when they abandoned their village in 1838. The Matachines Dance, adapted from the Spanish and accompanied by a fiddle, is also performed at Jemez and other pueblos.

In more traditional pueblos like Santo Domingo, dances and other rites take place in accordance with the requirements of the traditional religion; an example is the cleansing ceremony, in which the medicine or curing societies cleanse the village of evil spirits before spring planting.

As Protestant missionaries moved into New Mexico in the 1850s following the American conquest of the territory, they tried to establish missions in the pueblos. With the exception of the Presbyterians in Laguna, however, the influence of Protestant churches upon Pueblo life has been minimal, most of these churches preferring to work with Anglo and Hispanic congregations. In 1907 the peyote religion of the Plains Indians of Oklahoma, formalized as the Native American Church, was introduced in Taos. This religion centers around peyote, a cactus bud with hallucinogenic effects, which is eaten as a sacrament. Peyotists believe that power is found in peyote and in water, plants, and earth. The powers of God and peyote come to worshippers through prayer and song and through smok-

deity a prayer stick, smoothed and pointed, adorned with feathers, and placed before a shrine in the kiva or buried in the plaza. Cornmeal and pollen are other sacred symbols used in ceremonies. The public part of the ritual unfolds in the plaza with rhythmic dances which sometimes include most of the pueblo's population, chants, and often the clowning of the Koshare. Although called public, these dances are often open only to pueblo inhabitants. (The general public is welcome at all announced dances.) The dances function as prayers for an orderly life, good crops, game, protection; they are a form of worship as well as entertainment. Some dancers wear masks, a sign of the deity to whom the prayers are being offered. Spruce or fir branches, symbolizing freshness or fertility, adorn the dancers and shrines.

When the Catholic friars first attempted to convert the Pueblo people, they thought they could do so by rooting out all aspects of the native religion. They ordered religious objects to be burned, forbade ceremonies, and had the religious leaders beaten, enslaved, or hanged. After the Pueblo Revolt of 1680 and the subsequent reconquest of New Mexico by the Spanish (1692–93), the church became more tolerant of native practices, with the result that ceremonies are often held on the feast day of the patron saint of a pueblo or on Christian holy days like Christmas and Easter.

ing and eating peyote. A "roadman" conducts the rituals called meetings. Taos Pueblo elders rejected the practices of the Native American Church, mainly the use of the hallucinogenic peyote in rituals, as foreign to traditional Pueblo beliefs. Some pueblo members nevertheless continue to participate in peyote ceremonies.

Navajo religion as practiced today contains elements of Plains Indian and Pueblo beliefs superimposed upon ancient Navajo teachings. Whereas the Pueblo religion emphasizes the community, the Navajo religion focuses on the individual and his personal relationship to the supernatural. The most important feature of Navajo religion is neither the external ceremonies nor the beings who people the spiritual world, but a value system that stresses harmony with nature, society, and the supernatural world.

The Navajo people, the Diné, have been told for generations by their medicine men that they are the descendants of earlier folk who emerged into this world from a series of four lower worlds. The Diné were then plants and animals with human characteristics. Threatened by a great flood, the people rose through successive worlds until they emerged to this one through a central hole somewhere in southern Colorado. Along the way, the primordial beings progressed from the darkness toward the light. In this world of sunlight and understanding, men and women were given the shapes they now possess. Another version of the creation myth describes how in the Fourth World the people met Pueblo Indians, who shared with them their crops and knowledge of irrigation. Coyote was also created in the Fourth World. He is the instigator of mischief and chief antagonist in many Navajo folktales.

First Man and First Woman are the prototypes of humans, created before the Emergence. First Man found a baby and took her to First Woman, who adopted her. The baby grew up to be Changing Woman, so-called because she changes aspects with the seasons, or White Shell Woman, the most powerful su-

pernatural being of the Navajos, symbol of fertility and regeneration. Other supernatural beings are the Yei, or gods, who are strong influences in Navajo life. Changing Woman mated with the sun and bore the hero twins, Monster Slayer and Child of the Waters. The hero twins slayed the enemy monsters and made earth safe for the Diné.

Earth is limited, for the Navajos, by four sacred mountains, one for each direction of the compass. Holy people live in the sacred mountains and in eight other holy mountains and protect the Diné from harm. Once in this world, the Diné were taught by their medicine men the right way to build a house, to hunt, to manage personal needs, to act toward others, and to adapt to their environment. Acting in the wrong way causes disharmony and ultimately bad luck, accidents, and sickness. Other forces outside a person can also cause disharmony: a powerful animal like a coyote, or a force in nature like a cyclone.

Navajo witches can also cause evil by sprinkling corpse powder on a person. (The powder is obtained from the skin of a dead person; Navajos fear the bodies of the dead and will close up a hogan in which a person has died.) In order to be less visible, witches roam in the skins of powerful animals when they are seeking victims. Sorcerers can also affect a person by casting spells from a long distance, using the victim's clothing or a piece of hair or nail as a substitute for the physical presence.

To re-establish harmony, the medicine men, called singers, perform intricate ceremonials. They learn the chants and movements of the ceremonies during an apprenticeship in which they follow the older practitioners. Before the apprentice can himself practice a ritual, he must have someone perform one on him, and he must pay the older practitioner for the service. Women can also be singers.

Medicine men use diagnosticians like "hand tremblers" or stargazers to help them determine the afflicted's specific ailment. The hand trembler observes the shaking of his hand as it points to different parts of the body where

illness may lie. The stargazer consults the night sky in his diagnosis.

Once an illness is diagnosed, the medicine man performs the proper ceremony, one based on a specific chant or sing. Medicine men use only about ten chants today, far fewer than the thirty-five (plus variations) from which singers of fifty years ago had to choose. Each sing or chant has a name, such as Beauty Way, Enemy Way, or Night Way. The medicine man chooses the correct chant by comparing the complaints of the patient with those of the hero or heroine of a chant. For example, Beauty Way can be sung for someone with swollen joints because its heroine suffered from similar symptoms.

The chant or sing is made up of specific songs, prayers, ritual acts, and sand or dry paintings, all of which have been determined in ages past to be restorative for this ill. The medicine man takes pulverized sandstone of different colors—the sacred coral, yellow or white, black, and blue-gray—and on a smooth bed of sand he dribbles the sandstone to make the shapes and diagrams that tell a story. Like the songs, the painting tells of the hero's journey to the supernatural to attain the power described in the chant.

One of the more frequently conducted ceremonies is the Blessing Way; it corrects the mistakes made in past ceremonies, removes fear of a bad omen, protects flocks, and ensures a harmonious life. Blessing Way is also the easiest sing; the complete versions of some of the most complex sings last up to nine days.

All of the chants go through several stages, starting with the purification of the afflicted and ending with the transfer of vital power from the figure in the sandpainting to the patient. This transfer the medicine man accomplishes by pressing his damp hands against the colored sand and onto the patient's body. Any remaining evil is neutralized, and the harmony that had been disturbed is restored. Modern medical practitioners and therapists recognize the real benefit of sings to those who are sick, theorizing that belief in the cure can effect a healing.

Although parts of the sing are private, the end is a public sharing of the cure. For the longer ceremonies, Navajos gather from afar to cook, to eat, to dance, and to celebrate a friend's release from illness.

The early missionaries' attempts to stamp out traditional Indian ceremonies and to denigrate long-held beliefs contributed to their lack of success in converting Navajos, who were not attracted to churches that deplored their ways. In the early 1900s Father Berard Haile and the other priests at the St. Michael's Mission in Arizona, through their deep interest in and study of Navajo ethnology and anthropology, came to realize the worth of Navajo beliefs. By the 1930s the government policy toward Navajos and other Indians was to preserve Indian religious life and expression, counseling that "the cultural history of Indians is in all respects equal to that of any non-Indian group." Most Protestant churches did not heed this admonition, and into the 1950s there were only a few Protestant missions. Since then missionary activity on the Navajo Reservation has increased, especially among new Pentecostal and independent churches, probably a result more of the Indians' changing way of life than of a changed attitude on the part of these churches, which still urge their members to throw away their traditions.

Christian and traditional Navajos also attend meetings of the Native American Church, although both groups viewed peyotism with alarm as it began to grow in influence on the reservation. In 1940 the Navajo Tribal Council prohibited the use of peyote on the reservation, but in 1967 it amended the ban, allowing it to be used in connection with the practices of the Native American Church. Christian churches and the Mormons still decry its use and do not allow their members to be peyotists, but it is estimated that as many as 40 to 50 percent of the Navajo people are members of the Native American Church.

Apaches and Navajos share common ancestors. Both tribes came from the Athapascan group that emigrated to the Southwest some five hundred years ago. Since the two tribes have common roots, it is not surprising that the religion of the Apaches is close in form and belief to that of the Navajos. The two groups of Apaches in New Mexico live at opposite ends of the state, the Jicarillas close to Colorado in the north and the Mescaleros near the southern border. Both hold the same basic philosophy, but they emphasize different ceremonies.

Apache religion is rich with myths, spirits, and ghosts. Yusn, the Giver of Life and Source of Power, and White Painted Woman, who corresponds to the Changing Woman of the Navajo, share this world with other beings, each with his or her own power. The Controller of Water brings rain, while Water Monster causes drownings. Other spirits who live in the mountains, the Gan, or Gahan, can help or harm people and must be placated. Apache myths feature Coyote, source of many human troubles but also bringer of fire to men.

The medicine man or shaman remains influential. He receives his power through certain birds, snakes, or forces of nature. In turn he can pass this power on to others, but only after the applicant has spent years from adolescence on learning the chants and rituals. Like Navajo medicine men, Apache shamans diagnose and cure illness, psychological and physical. They seek lost objects and pray for a person's success. Women can also be sha-

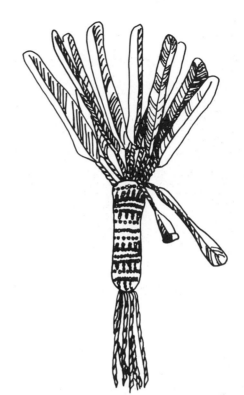

mans; some have been powerful influences in the community, while others take part only in minor ceremonies.

The shaman divines illness either as due to evil intent of witches or sorcerers or as stemming from contact with a ghost or from violation of a taboo. Then he holds a sing, usually not as elaborate as the Navajo sings. The ceremony follows precise procedures; for example, the rituals begin from the east and continue sunwise, ending up to the north. Apaches use the same sacred colors as the Navajos and Pueblos, but they are associated with different directions, black representing east, for example, instead of north. Special powers are attributed to the number four. Many ceremonies last four days or nights, and the rituals within the ceremonies are performed in sets of four. The medicine ceremony of the Jicarillas lasts four nights. During the puberty ritual of the Mescaleros, the men representing the Gan or Mountain Spirits arrive in fours, and the girls are grouped in fours.

The Apache girls' rites of womanhood highlight the religious calendar of the Mescaleros. White Painted Woman began this ceremony, and it has been performed annually except

Mountain Spirit Dancers, *Harvey Caplin.*

perhaps during the times when the U.S. government forbade it. Not only are the young girls received by the tribe as women, but they are able to bestow upon the whole tribe power from the rites, the gift of fertility that makes all things grow.

The girls are secluded in a tepee built especially for them. The tepee, adapted from the Plains Indians, is assembled under the direction of the shamans, who bless participants and materials and raise the poles in a ritual order. They set up four evergreens near the opening and wreathe the tepee in greens. The maidens, dressed in yellow buckskin to represent the sacred pollen, kneel on four blankets to receive a blessing at nightfall. They then dance in a single step through the night. Four male singers provide the music. Although this part of the ceremony takes place inside the tepee, it is not private; however, visitors must leave at night.

Outside, the Mountain Spirits have arrived and blessed the bonfire that lights the plaza. A clown accompanies each group of Gan; these beings play, while the Gan dance aggressively around the fire to the rhythms of the singers and drummers. At times a file of women circles between the singers and the spirits. The Mountain Spirits' power heals the tribe.

At one time the ritual of the Gan was performed apart from the puberty rite, but the Mescaleros joined the two after the federal government gave permission to perform them only during the Fourth of July period. The daytime part of the ceremonies, a rodeo and tourist-oriented Plains dances, is kept separate from the nightly religious rites.

The Grizzly Bear Dance of the Jicarillas demonstrates the respect the Apaches have for that powerful animal, whose body is said to be inhabited by the spirits of bad people. Other Apache ceremonies center around the planting and harvesting of crops.

The Christian churches have had a long although not always fruitful relationship with the Apaches, which began when the early Franciscans tried to convert them. In 1628 Fray Alonso de Benavides assigned a missionary to the Gila Apaches and claimed the conversion of that tribe and other bands. However, any conversions were fleeting; the nomadic ways of the Apaches and the actions of the Spanish slavers made Christianizing these Indians impossible. The Franciscans moved back to the Jicarilla reservation in 1915. Catholic priests began visiting the Mescaleros in 1869. By 1902 a priest came for monthly Mass, and in 1916 Father Albert Brown was assigned to the reservation and began a long and loving mission there. Today the Catholic church continues its mission on the Mescalero Reservation in a building that combines symbols of that faith with those of the native religion. The Dutch Reformed church built up active missions at Dulce (Jicarilla) and Mescalero, providing schools and medical attention as well. Baptists, Mormons, and Apache Reformed churches also minister to the Apaches.

The Spanish explorers brought Catholicism to New Mexico. When Cabeza de Baca, Esteban, and their companions stumbled into Mexico City after a harrowing journey across unexplored territory, their stories of the potential of that vast and rugged land and of the Indian tribes that peopled it persuaded the viceroy to send an expedition to the region. Perhaps thinking that religious men would be cheaper to outfit and less threatening to the Indians than soldiers, the viceroy named Marcos de Niza, a Franciscan priest, to head the group, stating that he sought only the services of Our Lord and the good of the Indian, in accord with the intent of the Spanish Crown to convert the natives of the New World to Catholicism.

Although this first venture into what later became New Mexico ended in Esteban's death, Fray de Niza had seen the Indian villages of Hawikuh and Hakona, and he encouraged other, better protected expeditions. Several of the monks and priests accompanying these expeditions remained to live with the Indians; Juan de Padilla, Juan de la Cruz, and Luis Escalona became the first martyrs, dying at the hands of hostile Indians. Don Juan de Oñate's group of colonizers included eight Franciscan priests and two brothers who planted the cross near the Rio Grande at a pueblo they called Puaray, halfway between modern Alameda and Sandia. The group did not linger among the Indians there but moved north where Oñate established his colony at San Gabriel de Yunque Yunque, near modern San Juan. One of the first things the colonists did was build their church, finished in two weeks, a large wooden structure named after St. John the Baptist.

The new country was made a missionary province of the Franciscan order, and divided into seven districts. Friars were assigned to different pueblos, each missionary concentrating on first building a place of worship, dedicated to the saints who would protect them: St. Anthony at Quarai, St. Dominic in Santo Domingo, and St. Lorenzo at Picuris. By 1608, the friars claimed to have baptized 8,000 souls.

In 1610 the colony moved to Santa Fe, which then became the only Spanish town in the new land. By 1617, three years before the English landing at Plymouth Rock, eleven churches had been built in the pueblos, some in "appalling wilderness," according to commentators, "with neither civil nor military assistance, but only the labor of the Indians." Soon there were forty-six "Christian" pueblos;

however, seven of these, including Quarai, Abo, and Humanas, known today as Gran Quivira, were destroyed by Apaches. The pueblos with resident priests were *doctrinas* or parishes; lesser towns that were only served periodically by missionaries were called *visitas*.

These missions were under the direction of Mexico City until 1626, when a separate *custodia* was created, called the Conversion of St. Paul, under the care of Alonso de Benavides. The *custodia* denotes a territorial grouping of Franciscan missionaries. (According to Fray Angelico Chavez, the old Spanish word means "jail." The *custodia* or *custos* was the guard; this was St. Francis's way of humbling his followers.) In his first report on the state of the missions, his famous *Memorial* on New Mexico, Fray Alonso noted that there were *conventos* as well as churches in many of the principal pueblos. Here *convento* signified the house of the resident missionary, and not the residence of nuns. Benavides also reassembled several groups of Pueblos who had been scattered by attacks of enemy tribes and reestablished missions to them. By the time he left New Mexico, there were thirty-three *conventos* and 150 churches and chapels. Fray Alonso found that numbers of Indians wanted to be baptized through the visitations of a "lady in blue," a Franciscan nun who actually lived in Spain. When the friar returned to Spain, he sought out the nun, a Sister Maria. She told him that she had visited the Indians, flying 20,000 miles to accomplish the conversions.

Benavides also noted that although the people of Taos were all baptized, they were wavering in the faith because the Catholic doctrine on marriage was opposed to Indian custom. In Zuni, he said, 10,000 souls were already converted; however, the religious "suffered too much from the mischief and opposition of sorcerers." These comments hinted at the opposition of the Indians as well as the disdain the Spanish had for Indian religion, which conflict contributed to the revolt of 1680. The Franciscans also worked among the Apaches and Navajos. Fray Alonso wrote of a peace treaty negotiated between the Navajos and Christian

tribes so that a mission could be built in Santa Clara, at that time adjoining Navajo territory.

As a result of his trip to New Mexico, Benavides recruited thirty Franciscans and sent them into neglected pueblos. The missionaries' first priority was the spiritual welfare of the Indians. They would go into pueblos by themselves with the "naked cross," kneel and cross themselves, and invite the Indians to do the same; they would show paintings of religious scenes and sing. Later, as they learned the language, the missionaries were supposed to instruct in it; however, few priests actually mastered Indian languages, in contrast to priests in Mexico, whose knowledge of local idioms undoubtedly contributed to their effectiveness. The priests would also direct the Indians to build a church. Where Indians were scattered, the Franciscans encouraged them to live together in a single pueblo in order to minister to them better.

Besides spiritual work, the missionaries tended to the sick, established schools, and taught the Indians how to grow European crops and build in the European style. The Franciscans believed that work was good for the soul and therefore emphasized labor. This emphasis and the use of corporal punishment for breaking the rules of the church too often led to abuse of the Indians, although official Spanish policy was against harsh treatment and punishment.

Serious conflicts arose between the Spanish governors and the Franciscans, the latter accused of using their extraordinary powers as ecclesiastical judges and officials of the Inquisition in a vindictive manner. The Inquisition was a centuries-old institution used to root out heresy among the Catholics and had no jurisdiction over non-Christians such as Moors, Jews, and, in America, Indians who retained their Indian identity. Although its influence had declined in the rest of Europe in the fifteenth century, it became a powerful instrument in Spain and its new territories, where the Franciscans were accused of using its courts against Spanish officials, including governors, with whom they disagreed.

There were also conflicts over the resettlement of Indians. As Pueblo populations declined owing to disease and abuse, church and colonists competed for increasingly scarce labor. The missionaries wanted their flocks settled close together near the churches, which meant that the Indians would be further under the control of the *encomenderos*. The *encomienda* system allowed favored subjects to exact tribute from Indians, in either goods or forced labor. Such employment of mission Indians caused dissension, the friars feeling that Indian labor should be used only for the work of God. The governors often backed up the *encomenderos*.

Later, after the revolt of 1680, Indians explained the rebellion as due in large part to the exactions of work and produce from them by the Spanish, both lay and religious. The fathers viewed the Indian religion as idolatry, and the Indians were not allowed to practice their customs or obey their own priests. Worse, the fathers ordered the sacred kivas to be destroyed. Thus when the Indians rebelled, among the first to be killed were eighteen priests and brothers.

When Don Diego de Vargas returned to Santa Fe in 1692, three missionaries came with him and immediately began baptizing the Indian children. Rumblings of discontent were still heard, however, and in 1696 there was a small revolt in which several priests and brothers were killed and churches and religious objects destroyed. A few years later a *custos* making his rounds noted that the missionaries had succeeded in "suppressing abuses, superstitions and idolatry as well as scalp dances and estufas (kivas)." However, the hold of the church on the Indians was still tenuous.

In 1696 Santa Cruz, to the north of Santa Fe, became the second settlement to be accorded the honorable title of *villa*, with a parish of its own. In Albuquerque, the third *villa*, the settlers erected San Felipe de Neri Church in 1706.

Thus re-established, the church continued its mission work, not only to the Indian pueb-

Pueblo church bell, *Harvey Caplin.*

los, but also to the Spanish villages that were growing up near the main towns along the Rio Grande. The village chapels were called *visitas* and each was under the direction of a nearby Indian mission. For example, the Spanish settlement of Alcalde was a *visita* of San Juan Pueblo.

However, there was conflict between the Franciscans and church officials in Mexico over the amount of authority the missionaries possessed in the reconquered territory and the way they ran the missions. These issues, along with the opposition of civil officials and the continued unwillingness of the Indians to abandon their practices for the civilization and Christianization of Spain, slowed the growth of Indian missions during the eighteenth century. There was a shortage of priests, vestments, bells, and even candles and wine for

Mass. Smallpox in the 1780s killed a fifth of the population, forcing the consolidation of missions. In 1793 the viceroy wrote that after 200 years the Indians were as ignorant of the Faith and religion as if they were starting catechism; the religious customs of the Spanish settlers were not much better.

New Mexico suffered repercussions from Mexico's political struggles for independence in the early nineteenth century. When Mexico became a republic in 1821 there was a move to lessen the influence of Spain; all Spaniards who refused the oath of allegiance to the new nation were ordered home. Many of the Franciscans, already diminished in numbers because of a sharp decline in vocations and almost all Spanish, left New Mexico. "Secular" priests from Mexico, belonging to no one order, replaced them. These priests served the mostly Spanish townspeople, whose numbers were growing, while the Pueblo missions with declining populations were neglected. The few remaining friars were unable to serve all the missions. Soon the Pueblos had begun to observe their ancient ceremonies in public. The new Mexican government became less tolerant of religion and in 1833 abolished *conventos* and limited the activities of the clergy. Even the parish church in Santa Fe, once the pride of its parishioners, fell into disrepair.

After General Kearny's takeover in New Mexico for the United States, the Catholic church continued its work under a new bishop. Because the church tends to draw its administrative lines according to civil government boundaries, it was appropriate for it to change its seat of government to U.S. territory. The heads of the American church asked the Pope to institute a new "vicariate apostolic" in the New Mexico Territory, including present-day Arizona, Colorado, and Utah. This title designated an incipient diocese headed by its own bishop. Pope Pius IX agreed to this, and in July 1850 formed the new vicariate with Father Jean Baptiste Lamy as bishop.

Bishop Lamy was a Frenchman who had answered the call for missionaries to the young church in the United States and had worked zealously in Ohio and Kentucky before being named New Mexico's bishop. He arrived in Santa Fe after an arduous trip, which included a shipwreck in Galveston. Although earlier writers on his reception have commented that the priests in New Mexico had no notice of his arrival and would not accept his authority, the new bishop was in fact well received. Father Macheboeuf, his good friend and co-religionist, gave a sermon in the Santa Fe church that might have put a damper on the bishop's welcome. Father Macheboeuf's French accent perplexed the parishioners, who, suspicious of the American newcomers, questioned whether he was even Catholic.

Bishop Lamy soon went to Durango, Mexico, probably to clarify his position as lawful bishop. He was received graciously by the bishop of Durango, who acknowledged Lamy's position and sent word that he must be obeyed in accordance with his office.

The new bishop found that although the Spanish settlers had kept their faith and some religious customs, both clergy and laity were lax in following church rules. All were lacking education. Therefore, he made the building of schools one of his main preoccupations and recruited to staff them the Sisters of Loretto, the Sisters of Charity, and, from Europe, the Christian Brothers.

There were few Mexican or New Mexican priests in the territory, and Bishop Lamy did not place much confidence in them. One of his celebrated battles, fictionalized in Willa Cather's *Death Comes for the Archbishop*, was with Father Antonio José Martínez, who himself had worked very hard to educate his parishioners and had even run a preparatory school for the seminary in Durango. He fought Bishop Lamy on the subjects of tithes, fees for services, Spanish *santos* (which the bishop deemed crude and not worthy to be placed in houses of religion), the appointment of priests, and pastoral letters. Bishop Lamy eventually excommunicated him. Father Martínez continued to say Mass and give sacraments. Martínez, while not the ignorant priest blindly fighting change, had faults, among them arrogance and an inflated sense of his own learning. These led to the unfortunate clash that overshadowed many of his accomplishments. The new bishop, coming from the formal and reform-minded French church, also had differences with other native clergy, whose background he never fully understood.

The mission territory became a regular diocese in 1853, extending over Utah, Colorado, and Arizona, and the bishop not only traveled extensively himself but also had to try to supply priests for the whole area. Bishop Lamy therefore made several trips to Europe to encourage priests and nuns there to come and work in New Mexico and the other territories. Assignment to New Mexico was difficult; several clergy died of disease and some left, overwhelmed by the empty and strange land. Others stayed, most for the rest of their lives.

During one of his European visits, the bishop persuaded five Italian Jesuits to return with him. They first went to Bernalillo, but soon moved to Albuquerque to the parish of San Felipe de Neri. From San Felipe the Jesuits were able to exert considerable influence in New Mexico and southern Colorado through their schools and their parish work. They also started a newspaper in Las Vegas, New Mexico.

Bishop Lamy had old churches repaired and built eighty-five new ones, including the impressive Cathedral of St. Francis of Assisi in Santa Fe, started in 1860. The cathedral was built over the old *parroquia* or parish church put up during the first days of the town and rebuilt in the early eighteenth century.

Since 1798 San Miguel del Vado, built with a fort for protection on the edge of the plains, had been the only settlement on the eastern side of the state. Now, as the American cavalry pacified the Indian tribes on the eastern plains and the Navajos and Apaches to the west, settlements grew up far from the Rio Grande, each with a parish church or chapel. The parish priest would travel out to the chapels on a regular basis. Most of the Anglo pioneers to the Great Plains were Protestants,

Ranchos de Taos Church, *Jean Blackmon.*

but there were enough Catholics among them, as well as pockets of Hispanic settlement, to warrant the activity.

Bishop Lamy and his successor, Archbishop Salpointe, made a concerted effort to extinguish a group known as Los Hermanos Penitentes, viewed by the authorities as a secret society whose penitential practices were excessive and abusive. After the reconquest, the Franciscan clergy had introduced the Third Order of Penance of St. Francis into New Mexico, building chapels in Santa Cruz and Santa Fe. The Third Order was an institution of lay members, male and female, governed by a Franciscan priest, who held daily prayers and other Franciscan devotions. As the Franciscan fathers left the territory and were not replaced, the lay group's ties to the order became more tenuous. Between 1780 and 1820 another lay group composed of men only, the

Confraternity of Our Father Jesus the Nazarene, grew up around Santa Cruz. Some historians believe that the newer group had its roots in Spanish confraternities that may have come by way of Mexico. Others say it is a native New Mexican organization, born of the need of the time. In any case, this later group was probably tolerated by the official church as long as there were no abuses related to the flagellations and mock crucifixions that were part of the rites of penance. The group had gained strength in the vacuum left by the departure of the Franciscans and other clergy. Its members not only conducted religious services focusing on penance and the Passion of Christ, but they provided other support to their isolated communities. Known as the Cofradía or brotherhood, the group ensured that knowledge and practice of the Catholic faith did not disappear. The brotherhood was very strong in the northern, mountainous regions.

When Bishop Lamy arrived, however, he viewed the group's practices with horror. As Archbishop Salpointe noted, to the clergy in Santa Fe the brotherhood was "an anomalous body of simple credulous men who retreated to the remote areas where they would have the darkness of woods to add to the mystery of their performances." Such condemnation was disregarded by its members and their followers, who saw their movement for atonement of sin through suffering as a genuine expression of religion. Both the attempts of the church to control them and the curiosity of nonbelievers drove the *hermanos* to hide themselves completely from the public and take on the air of mystery long associated with the group.

Official condemnation of the brotherhood remained until 1947 when the archbishop publicly accepted it as part of the church as long as the penances did not cause physical harm, deliberate abuse of the body being considered sinful. At that time the church recognized the accomplishments of the *hermanos* in keeping alive the Catholic faith during difficult times and sanctioned the aim of the group to do corporal and spiritual works as a worthy one. The archbishop also forbade the curious to spy on Penitente services.

The *hermanos* divide themselves into Hermanos de Luz (Brothers of Light) and Hermanos de Sangre (Brothers of Blood). The Brothers of Light are the organizers and the readers, while the Brothers of Blood, men in their first years of membership, perform the penances.

The *moradas*, or chapels, of the Penitentes are low, long buildings, dimly lit. During Holy Week, there are processions from each *morada* to the village church and then to the Calvario, a hilly place near the *morada* symbolizing Mount Calvary. The Brothers of Light sing *alabados*, traditional hymns whose melancholy tunes have overtones of Moorish influence from medieval Spain. The *alabados* are accompanied by the plaintive wailings of a *pito* (flute). *Matracas* (wooden noisemakers, which make whirring sounds) and "clackers" are the only instruments used in ceremonies and processions.

The Brothers of Blood, dressed in white cotton trousers and black hoods so that others will not know who is performing penance, a private act, also walk in the procession, scourging themselves with the *disciplina* or whip. During one of the processions on Good Friday, El Encuentro ("the encounter"), a simulation of the meeting of Christ and his mother on the way to Calvary, takes place. At the end of the final procession of Holy Week, the brothers re-enact the Crucifixion. Although in the past incidents were reported of actual crucifixions, this part of Christ's suffering is symbolized by tying one brother, chosen to represent Jesus, to a large cross. The cross is raised for a short time before the brother is taken down and all participants return to the *morada*. Other rites of Holy Week include a supper on Holy Thursday and Los Tinieblas or Tenebras services held in darkness in the *morada*. Women are not members of the *cofradía* but attend services and are honored to provide food for the supper as well as meals for the other days, traditional Lenten foods like *panocha*, a sweet dish made from sprouted wheat flour and *capirotada*, bread pudding.

The Catholic church in New Mexico expresses itself today in different ways. Two Benedictine monasteries that invite visitors to share in two different experiences are examples of this diversity. The Benedictine Abbey of Pecos is a center for the charismatic movement, while the Monastery of Christ in the Desert near Abiquiu is a quiet retreat where visitors can join the monks in their prayers and work.

Although sharing its territory with many denominations, the Catholic church remains strong in New Mexico. Three religious congregations were founded in New Mexico: the Little Brothers of the Good Shepherd, who care for homeless men, and the Servants of the Paraclete and the Handmaidens of the Precious Blood in Jemez Springs. Two new dioceses have been created, one in Las Cruces, the other in Gallup. Archbishop Robert Sánchez of Santa Fe is the first native New Mexican bishop; he was born in Socorro.

After the American occupation, Protestant missionaries found their way to the territory. In spite of the difficult going at first, the missionaries overcame the natural barriers of language and customs and made some progress with the native population. The building of railroads into New Mexico caused an influx of Easterners, mostly Anglo-Americans, who added to the growth of Protestant denominations.

The Reverend Hiram W. Read was ap-
pointed to the New Mexico Mission by the American Baptist Home Mission Society (Northern Division) and arrived in 1849, the first of the evangelical Protestant missionaries to reach this part of the country. He and his wife were on their way to California, but, drawn by the challenge of New Mexico, he remained in Santa Fe as chaplain of Fort Marcy and later as a "visitor" to outlying areas, including the growing cities of Albuquerque and Socorro. Aged thirty when he arrived here, the Reverend Read died at seventy-five after years of work for the New Mexico, Arizona, and Texas conventions. Other well-known Baptists were the Lewis Smiths, who conducted the first revival in New Mexico; the Samuel Gormans, the first missionaries to the Indians; and the James Shaws of Albuquerque and Socorro, who influenced Blas Chávez, himself an indefatigable missionary, to become the first Hispanic convert. The Shaws also introduced the gospel to the Navajos but for financial reasons had to stop working with them in 1855. In 1853 a Baptist church was formed in Albuquerque which counted among its members Blas Chávez and John Sena, an Indian convert.

The early proselytizing efforts of Baptists sometimes brought them into conflict with the Catholic priests, who eyed their inroads with alarm. The clash led to at least two lawsuits. The Baptists soon withdrew from the territory owing to the financial drain upon the Home Society's resources, the division caused by the Civil War, and the harassment of native Baptist leaders. Before they left, they turned over all their property to other Protestant denominations.

Seventeen years later the Baptists returned to make a completely new start in Las Vegas, soon extending their efforts to Raton, Socorro (which still had a Baptist congregation), and Albuquerque, and then turning to rural areas like Roswell, Peñasco, and Loving. Their energy was spent in establishing churches rather than schools, hospitals, or assemblies.

A result of this second start was a renewed effort at converting Indians. Baptists took over the work of the Women's National Indian

Association, an interdenominational organization, at Two Gray Hills on the Navajo Reservation, but the missionaries' tour of duty was up in 1905 and the mission was not kept up. Baptists also had missions to the Pueblos, but let most of these lapse as they concentrated on gaining strength among the Anglo-American population.

In 1900 the New Mexico Baptists formed a convention or union to promote cooperation in advancing the missions. Because of the shifts in population and the turnover in ministers, it has been difficult to keep up a concerted effort in this area, but since the turn of the century the Baptist church has been a force, especially in the southern part of the state and on the reservations. Churches may belong to either the southern or the northern convention or may exist independently. Today, Baptist schools are listed in towns all over the state.

The Baptist Assembly at Glorieta is well-known throughout the country. The state mission board purchased the Breede Ranch near Glorieta for its assembly, and in 1949 the national Southern Baptist Convention recommended that a western assembly be held there. That year, 100 years of Baptist missionary work were celebrated at Glorieta. Other groups since then have enjoyed Glorieta's facilities.

The Presbyterian church sent its first missionary to New Mexico in 1849. The Reverend W. T. Kephart soon became caught up in the American Anti-Slavery Society and gave up preaching to edit an abolitionist newspaper. The Civil War put a damper on Protestant missionary activity, but as soon as that conflict was over, enthusiastic ministers of the gospel moved into the state. Among them was the Reverend David McFarland, who is recognized as having begun the permanent work of the Presbyterian Synod in New Mexico. He started the first church in the living room of the governor's wife and later opened parochial schools in the capital city. His efforts to distribute Bibles in Santa Fe and the nearby areas were opposed by parish priests, who dis-

trusted the Protestant idea of laymen reading and interpreting the word of God for themselves—and from a Protestant Bible.

Besides founding schools in Santa Fe, the church also made inroads among the small villages and towns of northern New Mexico, opening schools and churches. At "plaza schools" the Presbyterians offered community services as well as school lessons. Agricultural education, home improvement, and health for adults were emphasized. These schools closed permanently in 1958 as a result of improved and accessible public school education even in remote areas once served only by the missionaries. The influence of the Presbyterian church throughout northern New Mexico remains strong.

Presbyterians were also active for a time among the Navajos at Jewett and Fort Defiance, Arizona. The U.S. government encouraged churches to serve the Indian reservations and invited the Presbyterian and later Christian Reformed churches to the New Mexico reservation. The federal government funded the schools and contracted with the churches to provide the teachers. In 1868 a government-appointed "Peace Committee" pricked the collective conscience of churches by comparing the amount of money and number of people sent overseas with the little expended on Native Americans. President Grant formulated a "Peace Policy" through which missionary societies were to nominate and supervise Indian agents and expand their own work on reservations, thus injecting a spiritual force into the government's work. Theoretically this placed a lot of power in the hands of the missionaries, but in actuality the missionaries did not serve on the committees that oversaw Indian affairs. The government also allotted lands to various missionary societies, although it could not award title.

When the Presbyterians closed their mission in Fort Defiance in 1872, the pastor, Dr. John Menaul, and his wife, Charity Gaston, an early worker among the Indians, moved to Laguna Pueblo and there established a church. Dr. Menaul also built a school and operated a printing press, which published in both English and Keres, the Laguna language. He and his wife are legendary in both Presbyterian and New Mexico annals. Menaul School in Albuquerque carries their name today. Three small churches now serve Laguna and its villages. Other efforts, for example those at Jemez and Zuni, were not as durable.

Besides the ministers of established churches in rural New Mexico, "Sunday school" missionaries traveled from place to place by horse and later by motorcar, preaching on Sundays to whatever group they could assemble. Ralph Hill was one of these missionaries to ranchers and cowboys at scattered homes on the plains. He established "camp meetings" where groups came to stay in a camp setting for worship services, song, and prayer. These meetings were often shared with other Christian denominations.

The Presbyterian church also established a network of medical services, not only through its tuberculosis hospital in Albuquerque but also with its small clinic near Embudo, which served area residents for years. Today Albuquerque's Presbyterian Hospital is part of the widespread Southwest Community Health Services, operated independently of the church.

Methodists did not come to stay in New Mexico until 1853, when one Reverend Nicholson arrived in the company of Benigno Cardenas, the first Spanish-American missionary in the area. The Reverend Nicholson soon returned to his base in Missouri with discouraging reports about the possibilities of proselytizing in the territory. Nothing daunted, however, the Reverend T. Harwood and his wife moved to Watrous in 1869, where they built a school and established a Sunday school. Dr. Harwood's orders from his presiding elder about the extent of his field reveal the zeal of missionaries in those days:

> Get your pony shod, and then start
> out northward via Ft. Union, Ocate,
> Elizabethtown, Cimarron, Vermejo
> and Red River until you meet a Meth-
> odist preacher coming this way, then

> come back on some other road and
> rest up a little; thence go south via
> Las Vegas, etc. until you meet an-
> other Methodist preacher coming this
> way; thence go home and rest a little;
> thence westward and eastward until
> you meet other Methodist preachers
> coming this way. All this will be your
> work.

Dr. Harwood did indeed travel throughout the state and beyond, and later became superintendent of the Methodists. He also edited a newspaper called *El Abogado* ("the advocate"). Schools in Albuquerque for boys and girls were named for him. The Reverend and Mrs. Harwood joined other Protestant groups and the Women's Christian Temperance Union in their fight against alcohol, an effort that was to culminate in 1917 with the state's vote to prohibit the sale of liquor.

During their early missionary efforts, the Methodists and Presbyterians, in order not to duplicate efforts in areas where they would be competing for souls, tacitly agreed to divide the state into north and south, with the Presbyterians focusing on the north and Methodists concentrating on the southern regions. The Methodist church also felt it should have a presence among the Indians. Protestant missionary activity among the Navajos had practically ceased around 1870, and the Methodists were the first to return to the Navajo Reservation, which they did in 1890 with a mission at Fort Defiance. Between 1890 and 1897 the Methodists were the principal Christian representatives on the reservation. After the end of the contract-school system, when the government decided to staff and operate its own schools, the Methodists tried to expand their work, but after 1912 their efforts among the Navajos ceased.

The lack of schools in New Mexico brought the Congregationalists to Albuquerque. The American College and Education Society created by Eastern Congregationalists was eager to meet the challenge of making converts among the "Spanish-speaking Romanists" and

Indians of New Mexico. One way to accomplish this was through Christian academies for boys. Thus the Albuquerque Academy (no relation to the present academy) was founded in 1879. At the same time the First Congregational Church of Albuquerque opened with three members guided by the Reverend Jacob Mills Ashley, a minister from Kansas whose son was ill with tuberculosis.

Early members of the Congregational church included several representatives of the New Town of Albuquerque's business community as well as Charles Hodgin, well-known among early educators in New Mexico. He left his post as principal of the academy to become the first superintendent of education in Albuquerque, then moved to the University of New Mexico as a professor.

Between 1900 and 1917 the Congregational church advocated social gospel through progressive reforms. Recognizing problems inherent in the new industrialism, the national church sought to reach workers through social services such as employment agencies and legal aid. Albuquerque in the 1890s was a hard-living town. The Albuquerque Congregationalists concentrated on eliminating liquor through prohibition; they saw their efforts approved by the voters in 1917.

The Congregational church also opened small schools in outlying areas. Like other Protestant churches, it established missions to Spanish-speaking congregations. In conjunction with other churches it also held revivals, two-week meetings in central locations where ministers from several churches preached.

Also establishing roots in Albuquerque's New Town was the Grant African Methodist Episcopal Church, which opened in 1882. The church had its beginnings in New Mexico in 1851 and received a lot of its own when the New Town was laid out. Since then the Grant AME has been a force in the black community.

During the summer of 1863 the Right Reverend J. L. Talbot, missionary bishop, held the first service of the Episcopal church at Santa Fe, but a regular Episcopal organization was not established until 1880, with a church built in Albuquerque. The Episcopal church joined other Protestant denominations in missionary activity, beginning in 1894 with a hospital in Ft. Defiance. Later its missionary work was expanded to the Farmington area, and at the same time churches were established in the larger towns of New Mexico.

The Christian Reformed church in New Mexico is known for its work among the Navajos. The church took over Methodist land in 1891 and set up a mission at the Indian agency at Ft. Defiance and later at Tohatchi; it subsequently also took over the Methodist mission at San Juan. In 1905 the church moved from Ft. Defiance to a piece of land near Gallup which it christened Rehoboth ("the Lord hath made room") in reference to what it felt was an escape from the limitations of government. It started a boarding school for Indian children which became one of the most successful schools for the Navajos. Christian Reformed missionaries also established a church at Zuni and translated hymns and prayers into the Zuni language. Today a glance through the telephone directory of any New Mexico town will reveal a number of other Protestant denominations that find the state hospitable and tolerant.

Mormons arrived in New Mexico during the last quarter of the nineteenth century. A group of families set out from Utah in the winter of 1877–78 under the leadership of Luther C. Burnham. Traveling in covered wagons, some drawn by oxen, these religious pioneers took three months to make the difficult and hazardous journey. The group settled in Ramah, south of Gallup; the little town and surrounding area remain a Mormon settlement today. Later Burnham moved to the Fruitland Mesa on the San Juan River, where he and nearly all the settlers there lived in a long, fort-like commune for protection against the tribes whose territory it was. Burnham became the first Mormon bishop in the territory, which was known as Burnham's Ward.

The Mormon church or Church of Jesus Christ of Latter-day Saints has a particular mission to convert Indian people, and it has been active among the Navajos for years. Mormons settled in Kirtland, Bluewater, Virden, Luna, and other western towns, where their knowledge of water control in desert areas was most important. Mormon communities, rural and urban, maintain their religion and traditions. Among these is the obligation to proselytize. Young Mormons, neatly dressed and traveling in pairs, carry out their missionary duty today throughout New Mexico.

Jews have been mentioned as part of New Mexico's history since the 1500s when a Spanish Jew named Carvajal governed New Spain, which included New Mexico. Other Jewish names crop up in New Spain from time to time, but because of the temper of the times, Jews did not practice their religion openly. Until the arrival of European Jews via the Santa Fe Trail in the nineteenth century, there was no organized Jewish religious community in New Mexico. The first formal gathering took place in Las Vegas in 1844 as Congregation Montefiore, a Reform group that remained active until 1931.

Because Jewish traders were drawn to Santa Fe as the crossroads of commercial activity in the territory, by 1860 there were several Jewish families living in Santa Fe who observed Yom Kippur together. After the first formal bar mitzvah in 1876, the families recognized the need for a school and synagogue in the capital. Although over the years the community held many meetings for religious observances and discussions, Temple Beth Shalom was incorporated only in 1946 and its building was not completed until 1953. Because the community was so small, it wasn't served by a full-time rabbi until recently. In Albuquerque, Jewish families formed their own congregation, completing their temple in 1897 and naming it Temple Albert after the father of a founding member.

Communes bound together by a shared philosophy have been settling in New Mexico at least since 1894, when the Faithists established their community, Shalam, near Las Cruces. The Faithists believed in the word of God as revealed to their founder in the Osaphe Bible. The main purpose of the community was to purify a degenerate society by raising children according to the principles in their bible. The Faithists therefore took in orphans and foundlings of all races and gave them both spiritual and agrarian training.

Shalam raised its own produce and divided the profits from its endeavors among the whole community. Men and women sat on the council that decided all questions concerning the community's fortunes. The colony was successful for a time, receiving the approval of its neighbors for its hard work and initially for its moral ways. In the end Shalam failed because its agricultural experiments, though forward-looking, were too expensive, the settlement was too isolated, and not enough responsible people were attracted to it. Of those who did come to Shalam, many were adventurers.

Besides the European religions, other groups have settled in New Mexico. A community or *ashram* of Sikhs lives near Española. The Sikhs, a religious group founded in India in the fifteenth century, practice a monotheistic religion that combines some teachings of Hinduism and Islam with its own customs. Reading the words of the Sikh holy book helps the Sikhs to attain a balance of spirit, body, and mind. In New Mexico the group is distinguished by its costume, usually white cotton, with tight trousers called *puttees* and long shirts for the men, long dresses for the women. All wear high white turbans to keep their hair tidy, since the Sikh religion mandates long hair. Recently a mosque was built near Abiquiu for a planned community of Moslems in the area. The Baha'i Faith also has several congregations in the state, with the national center of the orthodox Baha'i in Las Vegas.

Religion continues to play a vital role in New Mexican life, from the traditional philosophy of the Indian peoples to the more recent expressions of spiritual thought.

arts

New Mexico has a greater proportion of artists among its residents than any other state. The Roswell-Taos axis is third only to the East and West coasts in volume of art sales. In all parts of the state, visitors may readily see works of arts. The enormous quantity of art reflects both the expression of the artistic spirit of New Mexico's people and the appreciation of that expression.

There are at least three reasons for this artistic wealth. The first is related to the nature of the state. Simple land forms, a variety of plant and animal life, the quality of light, and the richness of color have inspired inhabitants and visitors, many of whom express that inspiration in art. The painter Marsden Hartley called New Mexico "the only place in America where true color exists. . . ."

A second influence on the quality and quantity of art here has been the intermixture of cultures. Each of the state's many cultures has rich artistic traditions. Exchange between cultures has occurred repeatedly though not always intentionally. Trade, warfare, and intermarriage brought new design elements to inhabitants. The Navajos learned weaving from the Pueblos; all of the Indian tribes learned metalwork from the Spaniards, who in turn had learned it from the Old-World Moors; beadwork was learned from the Plains tribes.

Each culture has been the patron of other cultures' work. The early Spaniards used Navajo blankets; the Anglo traders on the reservations bought and sold weaving, jewelry, and pottery; Pueblos wear Navajo bracelets; Navajos use ceremonial baskets woven by Paiutes and wear blankets manufactured by the Pendleton Company in Oregon; corporations hire Navajos to weave company logos into rug patterns; and Pueblo women wear Czech shawls.

One group, having a fascination with another, has often portrayed other groups in its own medium. The Navajos drew pictographs of the Spanish clergy; the painters of Eastern and European traditions who sought exotic subject matter came to New Mexico in this century to paint Indians; Cochiti pottery figures have been modeled after camera-toting Anglo tourists; and Mickey Mouse is an occasional image in Zuni mosaic jewelry.

With intercultural encounters, new perspectives were gained and ingenious ways to use materials developed. Artists have made coins into buttons, set pieces of 78 r.p.m. records

and toothbrush handles into jewelry mosaics, formed local clays into abstract sculpture, carved modern designs into adobe, and worked plant fibers into fabrics and handmade papers.

A third factor encouraging artists and craftspersons in New Mexico lies in the culture climate, in the form of support given by the general populace as well as by museums, schools, churches, periodicals, business, and government. It is said that the world's finest saddlemaker, automobile designer, knife maker, and bird carver reside here, in addition to glassworkers of consummate skill, superb violin makers, scribes, carousel carvers, and quiltmakers. These craftspersons, along with the creators of traditional New Mexican crafts, come to or stay in this state because of an exceptional appreciation of handwork by the state's populace.

Objects made by people here from prehistoric times to the present have been fashioned to go beyond strict utility, to delight the eye. Folk art still flourishes in all parts of the state. Oil pump jacks whimsically painted, decorative shrines made of stone and plumbing fixtures, farm implements fashioned into sculpture, and homes decorated with carved wood are examples of unpretentious and ingenious manipulation of existing materials.

The space and pace of New Mexican lifestyles have also been attractive to artists. Rejecting the expensive New York life, many artists now make their homes in rural New Mexico. The fact that one might live simply and cheaply here brought Eastern painters to

Taos and Santa Fe beginning in the 1910s and 1920s. Some, like Stuart Davis, George Bellows, Edward Hopper, John Marin, John Sloan, and Eric Sloane, had brief "New Mexico periods," while others stayed to form art colonies in those towns.

In 1917, at the insistence of painter John Sloan, the Museum of Fine Arts in Santa Fe began an open door policy under which it would exhibit any artist's work. This practice was responsible for the discovery of many fine artists. Quantity precluded the continuation of the policy, but the museum, handsomely restored in 1982, still plays an important role in fostering both traditional and nontraditional art on the local level. The Museum of International Folk Art, housing the extensive and exciting collection of the Girard Foundation, has been a valuable resource for art historians and artists seeking more information or training. The dramatic entry to the Girard exhibits is lined with toy theaters of paper and cardboard. In the main hall, a festival of color surrounds folk art figures that are grouped with common themes such as a parade, a banquet, or heaven and hell.

Government support of the arts has been largely indirect: through the museum system, the university system, the Institute of American Indian Art, libraries, and the Artist in the Schools program. The University of New Mexico has been relatively independent from and less conservative than the art community at large. It has brought well-known artists to the state to train others. Its programs in photography and lithography have been exceptional. The notable Tamarind Institute at the university has done much to advance the art of printmaking. Other state universities have also given rich and varied art experiences to their students.

"The Studio," established in 1932 by Dorothy Dunn to encourage Indian students in painting and the study of traditional arts, was the precursor to the Institute of American Indian Art, where native American art has been invigorated. The state adoption of the "one percent for the arts" law, which provides funds for artworks as part of construction allotments for public buildings, is the most direct government support of the arts.

Religion continues to play a major role in the state, providing both subject matter and sponsorship of major works in wood, glass, and embroidery. Ceremonial art such as sandpainting and fetish carving is of itself part of native American religion.

Support from the private sector has come in several ways: from galleries (some of which have been especially innovative), from the New Mexico Arts and Crafts Fair (a juried summer fair run by volunteer efforts that has consistently introduced good new talent and has spawned numerous other quality fairs), and Roswell's unique Artist in Residence Program, a year's stipend that is restriction-free for talented working artists.

Weaving, pottery, jewelry, sculpture, and two-dimensional art in New Mexico are described below in a historic and cultural perspective. Some of these art forms have rare continuity over several centuries; others show remarkable variation in use of the same medium by varied individuals or cultures.

weaving

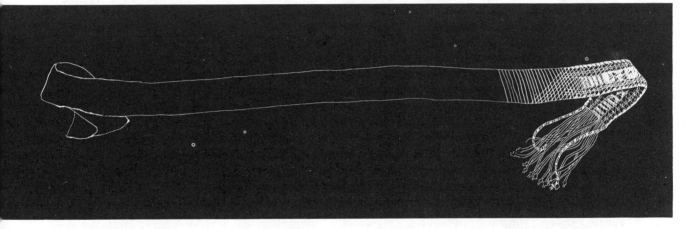

The Basketmakers, ancestors of the Pueblo people, were, as the name implies, weavers of baskets. They plaited, twined, and coiled plant fibers into useful items of apparel and into simple baskets. Plant fibers were employed in the creation of mats and sandals; later dog hair, fur, and feathers were used for the making of sashes and loincloths. Cotton was introduced to them around A.D. 700 by trade from other southwestern people, via Mexico, and by A.D. 1300 the Pueblo people of northern New Mexico were cultivating it. The white fibers refined the nature and expanded the extent of their weaving. Finger-weaving skills were finely developed and then were applied to the backstrap loom when Pueblos imported it from Mexican Indian groups after A.D. 1000.

In most pueblos weaving was an activity for men, the Zuni tribe being an exception. Religious and social gatherings of men in the kiva provided them time but little space in which to weave; it is believed that the limited floor space of the kiva gave rise to the development of an upright form of loom. The cotton was spun on the disc whorl spindle.

Decorative wefts of elegant complexity were woven with the cotton fibers. Plain and tapestry weaves; herringbone, diamond, and diagonal twills; and delicate open weaves were fashioned into *mantas* (dresses), shoulder blankets, shirts, kilts, and belts.

The period of classic Pueblo weaving was disrupted by the Spaniards in the seventeenth century, with a resultant simplification of

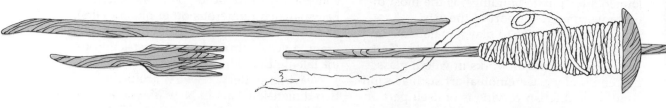

weaving techniques and designs. The plain tapestry technique, in which the vertical warp threads are entirely covered by beating down the entwined wefts to compress them, was dominant when Pueblo refugees of the Spanish reconquest in 1692 began teaching the craft to their Navajo hosts and, in some cases, their Navajo wives. The Navajo women learned weaving well, and it soon became an essential part of every girl's and woman's life, while gradually fewer and fewer Pueblo men devoted their time to weaving.

Contact with the Spaniards brought to the Indians a change in fiber use, and it also had an effect on design through the influence of the zigzag, or serrate, figures of the Mexican Saltillo *serape.* However, the loom and the basic technique of weaving remained unchanged. The *churro* sheep brought by the Spaniards to the Southwest provided meat and wool to the tribes. (The occasional four-horned sheep found on the Navajo Reservation today are descendants of the first *churro* sheep.) The *churro's* long wool was carded with toothed paddles, spun on the easily transported disc whorl spindle, and woven on the upright loom built to the future size of each blanket. The Navajo blankets were woven with a wool warp and a selvage edge along all four sides in the natural colors of the wool, and sometimes also with wool dyed indigo blue. These characteristics of Navajo weaving continue today, with an extensively expanded repertoire of colors (from both commercial aniline dyes and numerous vegetal or plant dyes) and greatly refined technique. The technical skill of many weavers is exemplified by Two Grey Hills weaver Daisy Tauglechee, who spins and weaves wool blankets with a

thread count finer than that of some cotton percale, 125 threads per inch.

Originally the Navajo weavings were used as dresses by women, wraps by men, saddle blankets for horses, and as door hangings and blankets. Weaving was not a profession but a part of being a woman in the Navajo culture. Designs were built upon the basic format of stripes that accentuated the spine and arm lines of the wearer. As commercially woven fabric replaced the hand-loomed wool for clothing in the nineteenth century, weaving became more decorative, with the creation of handsome patterns and eye-dazzling textiles using English baize and other unraveled wool in bright red and an explosion of various other colors from commercial dyes. Indians of many tribes purchased Navajo weaving until the 1880s, when a flood of manufactured goods came to New Mexico by train from the East. Traders then tried to create a tourist market for the textiles among non-Navajos, often offering the Indian blankets as sturdy floor rugs. Entrepreneurs presented weavers with designs to emulate that were thought to look Indian or Oriental, and hence were more salable. In the 1890s, under the traders' influence, regional styles of rugs became discernible.

Eventually blankets were sold by weight, which did little to encourage fine weaving. Quantity superseded quality in many cases. In the 1920s some post traders provided Navajo women with both encouragement and instruction in color and design; superlative weaving began again. Research by a Navajo teacher in the 1930s increased the use of a myriad of subtle, natural dyes made from berries, bark, roots, and flowers. Freedom of individual

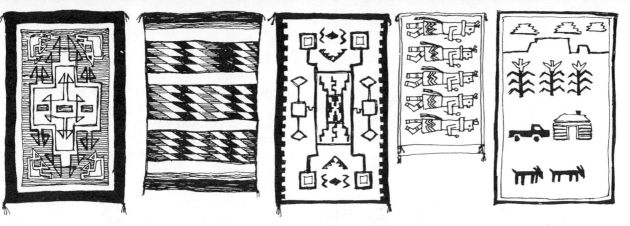

expression within the traditional format has brought modern Navajo weaving to the level of fine art.

Navajo weavers do not use a preliminary sketch; the upward growth of the design is a visual echo of that in the mind of its creator. Although there are many fewer weavers now than at any time since the tradition began, the quality of texture and design is extremely high.

Within New Mexico there are several regional styles, but weavers are not bound to them. The Shiprock area is known for designs of Yei, rectangular god figures, and Yeibichei, human dancers dressed as Yei. Teec Nos Pos designs tend to be busy and brightly colored. Great complexity is seen in the weaving of the Two Grey Hills region, with intertwining geometric patterns woven in natural wool colors embraced by a dyed black border. The most practical blankets come from the Gallup area, where small throws of heavy weave and angular motifs are made for use as rugs or saddle blankets. Twills, double-weaves, and the whimsical, dramatic, or patriotic pictorial weaves that may portray pickup trucks, cows, Coke signs, mesa patterns, or flags have no geographic limitations.

Many Navajo blankets that have borders include a *chinde* (spirit trail), a single strand of a color from an interior design leading to the outside. This spirit thread allows the good spirits of the blanket to escape, permitting the weaver to make another good blanket. Navajo legend relates that Spider Woman taught the people how to weave using sky, earth, sun rays, crystal, and lightning as raw materials.

The Pueblo Indians, once the Navajos' instructors, now do little weaving, making only simple black wool *mantas* and white kilts with exquisite embroidery of red, green, and white that replaces the woven border designs of earlier times. Some cotton is still finely woven into ceremonial sashes or knitted into leggings.

While the Navajos developed their skill at weaving textiles, the other Athapascan tribe of the Southwest, the Apaches, became proficient basket makers. Plaiting yucca leaves into ring baskets is an ancient skill still practiced in Jemez Pueblo; openwork wicker bowls of simple design are made today in Zuni and San Juan pueblos; a very few Navajos continue to make coiled tray baskets. But the masterpieces of form and pattern are Apache works. In their rod-bundle construction, stem or branch coils are wrapped by sewing sumac and willow strands in a continuous spiral, binding the coils together. Within the regular coils of the finest baskets intricate patterns of people, animals, or geometric figures ring the bowl or burden basket. The Jicarilla ("little basket") Apache tribe, named by the Spaniards for their basket-making skill, developed this art continuously until the 1900s, when tuberculosis struck the tribe severely, many children went away to boarding school, and the skills were largely lost. Recent revival attempts have been successful in teaching young Apaches their handwork heritage, and some simple but handsome baskets again can be found.

The Hispanics had weaving traditions of their own. Men and women participated in shearing, carding, spinning, and weaving on horizontal treadle looms in New Mexico beginning in the mid-seventeenth century. The Rio Abajo was an area of sheep raising and wool production in the 1700s. In Albuquerque

in 1790, one-third of the heads of households were recorded as being weavers.

In Spanish colonial New Mexico, weaving provided a broad range of household goods: *sabanilla* ("homespun") yardage to make clothing, *fresadas* ("blankets"), and checkered *jergas* ("carpets"). Because of the narrow loom, most Rio Grande blankets were made in two widths which were then sewn together, a technique that required great skill for the two sides to match. While these essential household items had their esthetic aspects, well-to-do women developed the purely decorative technique of *colcha* embroidery, long, parallel stitches tacked down by short cross-stitches. Flowers, leaves, or animals of thread covered the background *jergas* and commercial cotton fabrics. A small pocket of *colcha* embroiderers now works in Taos County.

After the arrival of the railroads, the textile crafts waned as purchased goods met the needs of the area residents. The Spanish Colonial Arts Society, established in the 1920s, helped revive weaving. A renewal of the tradi-

tion of fine stitchery has occurred at Villanueva, south of Las Vegas, where the church interior is decorated with festive and colorful embroidery panels made by townswomen in the 1970s. The town of Chimayo, home of many generations of professional weavers, remains the heart of Spanish blanket weaving. The products of the loom here are primarily blankets of banded designs in natural colors or brilliant, multihued patterns of birds or serrated diamonds. Some retain recognizable elements of the Mexican *saltillo* style.

Hand spinning and dying are the most important links between contemporary weaving in the state and the Indian and Spanish textile traditions. Spinning alone is practiced by many New Mexico craftspersons; others combine their skill in spinning with weaving, creating textiles that evoke earlier eras. An appreciation for and knowledge of natural dyes remains strong among fiber artisans. Chamisa, mistletoe, walnut, and cedar bark dyes penetrate fibers in shades of yellow, green, brown, and red. The combination of colors used, reflecting local vegetal and mineral hues, combined with the influence of the sometimes bizarre tones of the surrounding landscape, is characteristic of weaving here.

Within the general framework of local color and texture, contemporary weaving design has taken many nontraditional directions. Pictorial representations in tapestries are common in the Española-Taos area; sculptural weaving is an innovation in the Santa Fe area; and clothing, including yardage for apparel, is woven in Albuquerque. Fiber arts have expanded to include batik, stitchery, knitting, and crocheting.

Weaving remains a solitary art. A great number of looms are worked at remote Navajo chapter houses, under branch sun shades, in small Spanish village workshops, or in the homes of independent contemporary artisans far from urban settlements.

pottery

The earth beneath the feet of the prehistoric Pueblo people took shape in their hands as clay vessels. Coils of wet clay were spiraled up and smoothed with the fingers, then with stones; the pots dried and were fired in a crude outdoor kiln. The relative permanence of ancient pots, made in southern New Mexico beginning about A.D. 200, has given archaeologists clues to the old civilizations and has allowed insight into peoples who have consistently fashioned utilitarian objects into things of beauty.

Some of the earliest pottery bowls were shaped within baskets, leaving impressions of weaving on their bases. The woven imprint pattern was copied with paint on some bowls indicating that the geometric tradition in Southwestern pottery decoration was preceded by textile patterns. The simple, center-oriented decorations on common pottery of the Mogollon people gave way in the eleventh century to the vibrant, dark-and-light designs of the classic Mimbres period (A.D. 1000–1150). Artisans produced the painted geometric and life-form abstractions to fit the shape and spirit of the pot. Painting leapt beyond the design limitations inherent in the earlier craft of weaving. The common vocabulary of painted spirals, checkerboarding, crosshatching, circles, squares, and stars was used in highly individualistic ways on Mimbres pottery. Designs on the vessels of this culture often depicted naturalistic or mythic images, which have been informative to students of the Mimbres way of life. Unremarkable clay shapes display extraordinarily fine painting encircled with geometric borders; the whimsy of the images is probably in the eyes of present-day observers. The current popularity of this elegant prehistoric pottery has led to massive thefts, the use of bulldozers to unearth burials, and tragic plundering of archaeological sites in the southwestern part of New Mexico, ancient home of the Mimbres people.

The line of influence in Pueblo pottery design is not direct. Some scholars believe the Mimbres people left their valley and foothills in the early 1100s. The relationship of other, later black-and-white pottery to the Mimbres tradition is unclear. Although there had been trade between groups, prehistoric Hohokam and Anasazi peoples had developed their own styles and variations of pottery. Their modern counterparts in the Hopi, Zuni, and Rio Grande valley pueblos have developed regional styles of high quality and utility.

Craftsmanship waxed and waned several times, to be revived once more at the beginning of the twentieth century by individual artists, notably the Hopis Nampeyo and Lesou and the San Ildefonsans María and Julián Martínez, all of whom studied the designs on potsherds left behind by their ancestors. Other Pueblo artists readily accepted the innovations in form and style of these pioneers and others in Rio Grande valley pueblos, but technical tools such as potters' wheels, electric or gas kilns, and new clays and glazes have been repeatedly rejected by all Pueblo potters.

The arrival of the railroad in 1880 opened tourist markets to Pueblo potters as it did to weavers. Quality vessels were still made, but a plethora of gaudily painted pots for curio shops also appeared. Day-glow pots and ashtrays are now generally relegated to shelves alongside balsa tomahawks and dolls in plastic fringe.

Fine craftsmanship is important at each stage in the construction of traditional Pueblo pottery: selection of the clay, aging and tempering of the material, coiling and smoothing, application of slip, burnishing, painting,

Pueblo potter, *Harvey Caplin*.

incising, inlaying or texturing, and firing. Sure hands are necessary, for no sketching, erasure, or reassembly is possible.

The clays used at each pueblo are local ones, and they affect the color, thickness, porosity, and texture of a completed pot. The micaceous clay near Taos and San Juan glistens on the surface of simple Taos and Picuris ware and the decorative, incised pottery of San Juan Pueblo. White kaolin clay, employed as a slip in prehistoric times, is used for pots in Acoma, Laguna, Isleta, and Zuni. Such pieces are usually decorated with black and ocher painting on the thin, water-proof shapes. The few remaining Zuni potters often make owl effigy jars or pots bearing the design of deer with red arrow hearts. Of the southern pueblos, Acoma is the richest in pottery and skilled potters. Delicately lined geometrics, birds, and flowers or modern echoes of the Mimbres past proliferate on the exteriors of most Acoma pots.

It is significant that in the production of pottery family groups comprise informal schools of art with recognizable stylistic variations on traditional themes. The Lucy Lewis family of

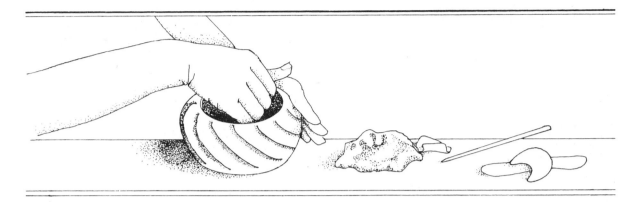

Acoma is credited with the reintroduction of Mimbres and Hohokam designs. Five generations of the Tafoya family of Santa Clara Pueblo and four generations of the Martínez family of San Ildefonso are revered for their pottery making, especially the blackware produced with the technique rediscovered by María and Julián Martínez. The Martínez method of covering a pot with powdered dung during the firing blocks the entry of oxygen around the pot so that the clay is impregnated with black soot. The same piece fired with a surrounding of broken pots, wire mesh, or sheet metal would be red. The amount of iron content in the clay also determines color. Clay with a large amount of iron is red, while decreasing amounts of the mineral result in orange-, yellow-, buff-, and cream-colored vessels.

The use of matte painting on polished pottery was an invention of Julián Martínez in 1919 and soon became characteristic of pottery from the entire San Ildefonso Pueblo. Circles of feathers and water serpents are favored motifs on the red or black ceramics. Nearby Santa Clara also uses this technique, as well as deeply incised patterns or sgraffito (scratched) work, which have become trademarks of excellent Santa Clara pottery.

Zia pots have retained their highly traditional character; stylized black birds and flowers grace the tan *ollas* (water pots). Jemez pots also display black designs on tan or rust backgrounds. In Jemez, the geometric decorations are often applied with paint rather than with a clay slip. Bold geometric patterns decorate Santo Domingo and Cochiti bowls. The long tradition of figurine making in Cochiti was infused with new strength in the 1960s by the appealing work of Helen Cordero. Her grandfather, Santiago Quintana, had been the village storyteller, entrancing Cochiti children with tales of great silver birds, child-eating giants, and animal adventures. Helen Cordero modeled clay to fit her memory of her grandfather, his eyes closed as he spins out another tale. Many children scamper over the seated figure. The "Storyteller" and the Cordero nativity scene began a new figurine art developed in many pueblos according to each group's style and individual vision.

The small Pueblos of Tesuque, Nambe, and Pojoaque have very few potters and no classifiable style, although some artists do work in these pueblos. No potter is restricted to the style of his or her pueblo, and exciting individual efforts in polychrome painted work, multifired color blending, inlay with stone and silver, corrugated texture, and sgraffito of extraordinary skill come from the hands of Pueblo potters.

The Spaniards served the Pueblo potters as patrons but brought to New Mexico no custom of ceramic making. Among the vast number of contemporary craftspersons living in New Mexico are many superb potters, using local clays and slips as well as commercial clays and glazes to form useful or ornamental pieces.

jewelry

People of the Mogollon and Anasazi cultures made and wore jewelry of mica, turquoise, jet, shell, bone, and stone. More than a thousand years later, their descendants, the Pueblo people, and the Pueblos' neighbors, the Navajos, have become world-renowned for their jewelry made with the same materials, often in combination with metals. Since the beginning of the craft here, elaborate personal adornment has fulfilled both ritual and esthetic functions and has been a means of holding or showing wealth.

Metalworking was introduced to the Pueblos by the conquistadors, but metals were not worked by the Indians until the 1800s. Copper, brass, and iron work, learned by observation of Hispanic New Mexican smiths, usually preceded work with silver, the metal of Pueblo and Navajo masterpieces. A Navajo iron worker, Atsídí Sani, is said to have been the first Navajo silversmith. He learned to use iron in about 1850 from a Hispanic smith near Mount Taylor. Atsídí Sani then taught the skill to other Navajos during the forced residence at Fort Sumner from 1863 to 1868. There, many Navajos learned and invented ways to work with copper, making decorative twisted or stamped bracelets. After the Indians returned from Fort Sumner, trading posts on the Navajo Reservation carried copper and brass, which the Navajos worked into rings, buttons, earrings, and belts of metal disks strung on leather. These were the first of the Navajo *concha* (shell) belts, high fashion around the world today. Silver work also began shortly after the Long Walk to Fort Sumner and quickly became the ornamentation of choice among the Diné (people). Spanish *plateros* (silversmiths) had been roaming the reservation freely and influenced the novices among the Indians. They taught the Navajos scratching, filing, and engraving, but punching and stamping were probably Navajo innovations adapted from Mexican leather tooling. By the 1880s many Navajo men were consummate silversmiths.

Great ingenuity went into the creation of silversmithing tools. Using crude, found implements, the Navajos crafted radiant works of art. The kinds of jewelry that became and remain distinctly Navajo include the oval *concha* medallions; the pendant *naja* ornament (a reflection of the Moorish crescent, a design passed on by the Moors to the Spaniards and then brought to the New World and the Navajos); hollow beads; *ketohs* (leather bow guards mounted with silver and worn as bracelets); large stones set in silver; symmetrical cast-silver ornaments; wrought and cast buttons; *jato* (earrings); squash blossom necklaces; and dress ornaments. Characteristic of all of these pieces is the sculptural weight and three-dimensional strength, symmetry, and simplicity of large areas of pure stone or pure silver.

Commercialism, beginning about 1900, triggered the creation of a glut of lightweight Navajo curios patterned with arrows and thunderbirds. Eventually the recognition of superior workmanship, along with better monetary rewards, fostered the continuation of the craft and its growth to its present high level of quality. The popularity of Navajo silver, however, has opened the door to stock, repetitious work, imitations, and machine-made "flimsies," or manufactured items, some of which are stamped "Reservation-made" but actually come from a place in Japan renamed Reservation. Sham items with plastic turquoise still surface frequently, but it is difficult for the fakes to approach the handsomeness of

the genuine article. Both Navajo men and women now make jewelry, struggling with the inconsistency of the silver market and the dictates of fashion. Silversmiths frequently join together in organizations such as the Navajo Arts and Crafts Guild to further their art and market their wares.

The original Zuni ornaments were strings of turquoise and shell beads. This tribe also pounded brass, copper, and occasionally tin cans into jewelry beginning in the 1830s, and so had some metalworking experience before the silversmithing instruction received from Atsídí Chon, a Navajo smith, in 1872. Early Zuni pieces resembled Navajo work, but Zuni smiths soon devised a way to set stone in silver, a skill which the Navajos then appropriated. Since turquoise already had an important place in Zuni religion and mythology, the incorporation of the stone into silver jewelry was eagerly advanced. Zuni masterwork with stones is manifested in inlay or mosaic representational designs pieced with jet, coral, turquoise, or shell and the delicate cabachon needlepoint in which minute silver crowns encircle identically shaped bits of polished turquoise. Heishi (circular, flat beads) strands with finely carved animal fetishes and channelwork that gives the appearance of cloissonné are also characteristic of Zuni jewelry. The making of jewelry is an important part of modern Zuni's economy and artistic expression.

Coin silver was converted into jewelry in Acoma and Laguna in the 1870s, but smithing did not survive as a craft there. A few smiths have come from each pueblo over the years. Santo Domingo, located near the turquoise mines of Los Cerrillos, has for centuries used turquoise and shell for bead necklaces. The heishi were drilled and polished with hand tools; some are still made in this way. Electric tools have made possible the almost incomprehensible slenderness of some of today's "liquid silver" and "liquid stone" strands. Earth colors and sky turquoise are often integrated along the filaments of the heishi necklaces. In 1983 many Santo Domingans produced jewelry. In keeping with their long-standing reputation as skilled traders, the Santo Domingans are in the majority among the venders a tourist meets in the plazas of Santa Fe and Albuquerque, and a large annual crafts fair is held at their pueblo.

Few Spanish artisans now use the old filigree style of the *plateros*, but Hispanic and other contemporary smiths and stoneworkers from all backgrounds make jewelry in New Mexico. Some of the current works resemble the bold and simple Anasazi ornaments, while other jewelry displays a complexity made possible by modern tools, study, and imagination.

sculpture

Sculpted forms of bone, wood, and stone have been shaped by people in this area for thousands of years. Early New Mexicans applied decorative detailing to utilitarian items such as arrows and arrow points, and later to planting sticks and awls. They shaped stone by pecking and grinding to make *metates* and *manos* (milling tools) or by chipping and flaking to make arrow points and knives.

The transience of prehistoric desert people made it necessary that decorative objects be created in portable forms. Small animal figures and human shapes, from abstractions to what may be portraits, were made of clay, sandstone, lava, limestone, or wood by peoples of this region from 1000 B.C. into the Anasazi and Pueblo periods. Adornments of shell beads or mosaics, feathers, and fiber aprons dressed some of these sculpted figures. The consistent economy of line in the figures is highly appealing to most modern observers. Limbs and appendages were often merely suggested; the slightest eye detail on an invitingly smooth shape portrayed the essence of a frog. The reason for the making of figurines in the past is not understood, but one can surmise that they were related to modern fetishes and *kachinas*.

Fetishes are usually made as magical or ritual objects to help in curing ceremonies, to bring good fortune in hunting, to ensure fertility, or to ward off evil. Zuni people excel in the creation of stone animal fetishes in small to miniscule sizes. Navajo fetishes are very personal items of stone or wood carried for protection or curing. Apache fetishes have a Plains Indian influence and are of beaded or painted leather.

In Albuquerque shopping centers today, toy promoters add the label "educational toy" to colorful boxes. A short distance across the high desert, carvers create truly sophisticated and colorful educational toys. Present-day *kachina* dolls have no specific ritual function, but elders use them to teach children the attributes of the real *kachinas* or gods. The Hopis of Arizona make the most elaborate, highly realistic *kachinas*. In New Mexico, the Acoma and Laguna tribes make some simple, flat or oval *kachina* figures, and the Zunis carve cottonwood into elongated figures with articulate arms and real miniature clothing. This art form is seldom for sale, as many of the Hopi *kachinas* are.

The ritual equipment of all the New Mexico Indians is made only for intratribal use. *Kachina* masks, *tablitas* (dance headpieces), feathered ruffs, finely beaded peyote fans and rattles, Navajo and Pueblo altars, and Apache headgear are usually exquisitely made, and the fortunate outsider may be able to view them in use during those ceremonies open to the public.

Portability and religious significance, important features of the Indian sculptural tradition, were also characteristic of the sculptural art of the first Spaniards exploring and settling here. Religious images, carved of wood, covered with a white, chalky substance (gesso or *yeso*), and painted, were made in Spain and transported to the New World. The same methods were then used in the colony. In Spain a member of a different guild would carry out each phase—one carving, a second sizing, and a third painting—but in New Mexico usually only one artisan performed all of the steps. Expertise in each area may have been lost, but a sense of the completeness and integrity of the whole was gained by this necessity. A regional style was developed by local artists in their interpretation of European models.

The Hispanics in New Mexico practiced their strong Catholic religion, carried their own religious art on their journeys, and set

aside a place in their homes for worship. Small wooden altars and rosaries were essential traveling equipment; carved wood saints were popular travel companions.

The *santeros* (saint makers) themselves were travelers in the late eighteenth and nineteenth centuries, carrying tools and carving the favorite saint of families or villages along their circuitous routes through northern New Mexico. A preferred saint in the territory was Santa Rita of Cascia, to whom prayers were addressed requesting accomplishments of the impossible.

Some few Franciscan priests made images or *bultos* (carved saints) for their own missions. Laymen took over this task with more vigorous and theatrical renditions of the holy figures. Native carvers of the eighteenth and nineteenth centuries had little training and limited materials but gained inspiration from their religion, from examples by Spanish-born woodcarvers such as Miera y Pacheco (a military cartographer) and Fray García (a priest), and from models such as the handsome stone *reredos* (altar screen) now in Cristo Rey Church in Santa Fe.

Hand-prepared egg tempera paints over gesso made of local gypsum and animal glue were the materials used by the *santeros* until the railroad brought commercial paints after 1880. With the arrival of new materials the art of the *santero* faded, and *bultos* were often replaced by painted plaster or zinc saints portrayed with an unchanging sweetness.

The Penitente Brotherhood played a major role in the preservation of this colorful and vibrant art form, both by housing *santos* of the past in respect for tradition and by commissioning *santeros* to make those figures which would not be available commercially. One of these could have been the figure of Christ with an emphasis on his tortured condition or his pendant heart, tempered by decoratively stylized blood and wounds and by a serene face.

Another specialized carved figure has been Doña Sebastiana or La Muerte (Lady Death). Nazario López of Cordova was said to have made the first such figure in New Mexico around 1850. This angel of death was used as an image in those *moradas* (Penitente chapels) which did not display a human skull—perhaps as a substitute for that potent furnishing. The macabre female skeleton, riding in a village wood-hauling cart, derives from fifteenth-century European processions based on Petrarch's allegories of the victories of death over chastity and fame over death. These triumphal processions have for centuries been portrayed on sets of tarot fortunetelling cards, some of which arrived in New Mexico with the Spaniards. Card number thirteen shows a mummified corpse or skeleton with bow and arrow in its bony hand, a model for New Mexican *santeros*' carvings of La Muerte. A barefoot member of the Penitentes pulled

Doña Sebastiana in her cart during Holy Week celebrations. Morbid stories of her supernatural power have surrounded her, and evidence of her influence is seen in her many superb and grotesque representations.

The son of Nazario López, José Dolores López, was a master carpenter who made utilitarian objects such as chests, doors, *vigas* (roof beams), and corbels until his son went away to World War I. Moved by his child's departure, he turned, in the last decade of his life, to the making of *santos* and other figures in a new way. These light, smooth cottonwood figures were not painted, but intricately carved details softened the severe stylizations. Adam and Eve and the flight into Egypt were favorite subjects. López, a carpenter himself, portrayed Joseph carrying a box of woodworking tools on his back; he also carved raw wood shelves, chests, toys, and his own grave marker. His work marked the beginning of a new carving style, carried on by his three sons, by other villagers in Cordova, and by artisans in various other New Mexican villages. With the popular acceptance of this art form have come some return of the *santeros'* work and an expansion of skill and carvers' repertoires, to include animals, trees in full leaf, elaborate creches, and furniture.

Spanish settlers rarely brought furniture to New Mexico, and the resident tribes had no tradition of furniture making. By 1600 Spanish colonists began making some pieces of furniture. Of the woods available for furniture making, cottonwood was too irregular and brittle; pine, clear and soft, was easily handled but weak, splintery, and prone to warping. Carpenters usually chose pine to form heavy, angular pieces that had a simplicity dictated by crude tools. The furniture was visually lightened by shallow surface carving and decorative cut-out patterns.

Characteristic pieces included the *trastero* (dish cupboard), the chest, the low bench with a decorative back, and great chairs of Gothic proportions and design. Few of the pieces were painted except for the colorful chests, the most common pieces of furniture. Each rectangular box was different from all others in its decoration of carved rosettes or animals, painted flowers or scenes, gesso relief, or iron hardware. Mortise and tenon and pegged joints held these indispensable storage boxes together.

A furniture maker's skills were apparent in the creation of the *trastero*. Decoration was concentrated on the upper panels of the cabinet doors, usually in the form of a serrated wooden grill or cut-out Maltese crosses; the *trastero* was crowned with a carved cornice. New Mexican versions of European baroque and rococo designs were simplified and reworked to fit the soft pine wood.

Some *trastero* panels were decorated with straw mosaics. The pine panels to be decorated were smeared with dark pitch and set with contrasting golden segments of split wheat or oats. The delicate appearance of geometric or floral mosaic inlay also covered picture frames and crosses. The craft nearly disappeared around 1850, re-emerged with WPA encouragement, and continues today in the hands of a few skilled artists, including several members of the Rio Grande Pueblo tribes.

Cabinetry, like other handicrafts, was affected greatly by the railroad's introduction of manufactured goods, furniture, and machined nails, screws, and tools. A revival of the old Spanish way of furniture making was fostered in the 1930s by a WPA program. The simplicity, utility, and honesty of Spanish colonial furniture is appealing to many modern home-makers, and the cabinetry is now hand-worked again.

In the 1970s and 1980s many young artisans began to work within the local tradition of making doors and furniture by hand. The great variety of woods and the styles used are not based upon the old ways. The sculptural pieces are highly individualistic, skilled works that have gained national renown for their makers.

New Mexico did not produce iron, so quantities of pig iron were first brought to the state by Santa Fe Trail traders. What little iron was here before 1820 was sparingly used and reworked when possible. Blacksmiths working in recent times have used models that come from Mexico and Spain for architectural grills, fences, and gates. Santa Fe is the center for the current resurgence of skilled blacksmithing and the development of new art forms in iron.

The working of tin is a craft brought to New Mexico in the early nineteenth century by itinerant smiths. The influences of Pennsylvania Dutch and New England styles (borrowed in turn from North African and Welsh tinwork) can be seen in the punched and pierced rosettes, stars, scallops, and dotted lines in tin *trastero* panels; in tin surrounding paintings and mirrors; and covering tin crosses. The reverse side of century-old tin ware may well carry the design of the vegetable canning company that distributed the original tin. Decoration was concentrated on the tops and corners of pieces to mask unfinished joints. A very few talented tinsmiths shape and decorate tin today.

A form of present-day Hispanic metal smithing that transforms an ordinary, utilitarian object into an extraordinary one is the work applied to the lowrider car. The reshaping of body parts, the use of small chain-link steering wheels, the relocation of bumpers, and al-

terations on the frame create a shiny, slow-moving sculpture. Luminous paint jobs, ingenious hydraulic lift systems, and luxurious interior upholstery complete the sleek, contemporary transformation of some old and new American automobiles. The owner (often a father whose entire family works on the car) sometimes dedicates his creation to a favorite local saint. The Española, Santa Cruz, Chimayo, Albuquerque, and Mesilla valleys seem to produce the greatest number of lowrider clubs and fanciful vehicles.

Sculpture for pure esthetics, without a basis in utility, is a twentieth-century phenomenon in New Mexico, with the few exceptions of such earlier work as Frederic Remington bronzes. Hispanic woodcarvers and Indian potters have recently turned to the elegantly simple lines of carved or shaped animals and human figures appropriate to their respective media. New Mexico has several foundries specializing in bronze work of both the Western representational school and other contemporary styles. The Shidoni Foundry in Tesuque has regularly sponsored an influential summer sculpture show covering eight acres of scrub land. Monumental stationary works are arranged among kinesthetic sculptures and earthworks. Slick, electrified fiberglass and smooth stone forms are intermingled with rough woodcarving and textured bronze, indicative of the range of three-dimensional works being made in New Mexico.

musical instruments

A type of sculpture that has been created for regular use but is not truly utilitarian is that which makes music. Kokopelli (the humped-back flute player) is a figure which often appears in paintings and on pottery of the prehistoric era. The early Pueblo people linked the beauty of sound with fanciful carving by making creative wood, reed, and bone flutes. Decorative conch-shell trumpets, clay and copper bells, bullroarers, rattles, tinklers, and rasps have been found in prehistoric sites.

Drums have been crafted in New Mexico for centuries from dry, hollowed aspen logs and prepared hides. The Cochiti tribe has earned a reputation for superior drums. A few fine wood flutes are still made in Taos Pueblo, and rattles are made by craftspersons of all tribes. The appearance of many contemporary peyote rattles seems to contradict their aural simplicity with a complexity of bead and feather work designs.

The Spanish colonists of New Mexico had to make their own musical instruments out of wood. Painted drums of wood slats laced together with thongs and homemade violins provided the music for fiestas and Masses in colonial times. Hand-carved *matracas* (wooden rattles) were whirled to simulate hailstorms as part of the Penitente Good Friday services; songs in other Penitente services were accompanied by wood and brass *pitos* (flutes) until this century. In the twentieth century the Hispanic tradition of musical instrument production is best represented by the Pimentel family of guitar makers. Seasoned rosewood, cyprus, cedar, mahogany, and ebony are combined in guitars that are sought after the world over for their superior sound and for their exquisitely detailed woodwork.

two-dimensional art

Two-dimensional works of art created in New Mexico over the past two thousand years are disparate in character but contain two commonalities: the fascination with light and the use of color. Painter John Marin said, "If you think you know what light is, then go to New Mexico and you'll find a quality of light many times more intense than anything you get in New York or Maine or the White Mountains." Indian, Spanish, and Anglo painting has moved over the centuries from anonymous community works to individual expression through the use of light and color.

Although there is much still to be learned about Indian petroglyphs (carved rock designs) and pictographs (painted rock designs), it appears that some of them were created for purely artistic reasons; others conveyed messages; some represented aspects of the practiced religion; others may have been pictorial representations of a hand sign language; and some few were simply doodles. Light played a part in the expressive power of the petroglyphs, both in the play of sun and shadow on the textured surfaces of the rock and in its role as marker on stone measures of cycles of the sun and the moon, most notably on Fajada Butte in Chaco Canyon.

In petroglyphs, the rock surface provides the dominant color for realistic or abstract human figures, animals, spirals, circles, and stars. Water stains and lichen growth add their own hues. Pecking or chipping away the surface of stone exposes a variant color in the de-

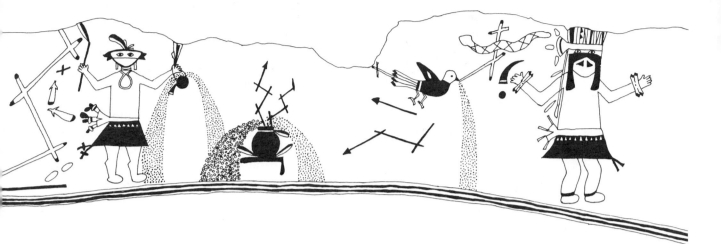

sign. Eventually the exposed rock surfaces develop a patina, which might again be chipped in another layer of petroglyphs. These subtle color variations aid in the rough dating of the designs, most of which are from two thousand to one hundred years old. Carved, chipped, or spray-painted modern graffiti that have no religious or astronomic significance are vandals' disturbingly frequent overlay on New Mexico's ancient writings.

Pictographs are painted on rock surfaces in pigments made from soot or powdered local minerals. The common hand motif and other designs were often painted with a technique of paint splattered around a stencil. Many of the petroglyph and pictograph sites found all over the state are rock surfaces that display a collection of designs created by many individuals, sometimes from different tribes or from different centuries—an intriguing interplay of messages.

Wall paintings made by one tribal group at one specific time have been found on kiva walls in several Pueblo ruins. Large, varicolored and stylized birds, animals, and humans are portrayed on interior walls. The best-preserved frescoes are found at Coronado State Monument near Bernalillo. Beginning about A.D. 1300, seventeen layers of frescoes ultimately lined the kiva walls of the now abandoned pueblo of Kuaua. All active kivas are closed to the public.

The painting of rock walls and adobe surfaces by Native Americans has a more recent counterpart in New Mexico in the form of murals. The strong Latin American tradition of mural painting has come north from Mexico with large and colorful political and religious statements in paint. Walls of some houses and businesses in Santa Fe and Albuquerque provide the surfaces for expression of Chicano ideals in brilliant hues and massive forms.

Murals often reflect, in a monumental way, a specific place or heritage. After having met the famous Mexican muralist Diego Rivera in the 1930s, New Mexican Peter Hurd painted the walls of the old Alamogordo Post Office, now the federal building, as part of a WPA project. Hurd used the dirt of the area to make his fresco colors as he depicted local landscapes and people.

Muralists have traced local histories along the buildings of the Heritage Walkway of Artesia, a wall in San Jon, a water tank in Las Cruces, and the New Mexico State Archives in Santa Fe. Artists Harrison Begay, Alan Houser, and Pablita Velarde have become well-known for their murals of tribal ceremonies and events. Students of the New Mexico School for the Visually Handicapped in Alamogordo have formed a textured mural of clay, and students at the Institute of American Indian Arts in Santa Fe have coated the walls of their school with decorative murals.

Quah Ah

The Navajo practice of creating designs—sandpaintings—with powdered minerals, pollen, crushed petals, charcoal, and cornmeal is centuries old, but each creation is ephemeral. As a part of a curing ceremony, a medicine man may direct up to six other Navajo men for several hours in the dropping of colored powders from between their thumbs and flexed fingers to form a pattern as large as six feet across on a sand floor surface. More than six hundred complex designs of events, holy people, the elements, and animals are recorded only in the memory of the Navajos. Numbers, colors, and directions are all important aspects of these healing sandpaintings, which may be the temporary residences of divinities. As in Navajo homes, there is an opening in the designs to the east, allowing the exchange of good and evil.

The pattern of the true sandpainting is destroyed during and after the ceremony; the re-maining colors are dispersed far from the ceremonial hogan. In recent years, some sandpaintings with designs modified to avoid sacrilege are preserved with glue on pressboard. Some New Mexicans use the medium to draw pictures of people and places as a tourist sale item.

In the twentieth century the individualism of Indian artists became established; previously their work had been part of a communal whole. Paper and opaque watercolor paint became the new medium for young artists' expression. Dr. Edgar Hewett and others on the staff of the School of American Research in Santa Fe gave moral and financial support to young Indian painters. By 1932 Dorothy Dunn had established "The Studio" in Santa Fe, where students responded to exposure to the best of past and present Indian art and to Dunn's encouragement of their own work by producing technically refined paintings of people, ceremonies, and animals. Students Pablita Velarde, Quah Ah, Fred Kabotie, Vilino Herrera, and several others began showing their fine work in New Mexico and around the world.

Much of the Indian painting in subsequent decades followed the pattern of precisely outlined figures with decorative detail presented on a solid-colored background. A similar figure-ground format, used in pastel or lithograph by R. C. Gorman and Dan Namingha and in oil and acrylic by Fritz Scholder and Kevin Red Star, is one common feature of their diverse styles. The texture and strength of their bold, contemporary work allow it to break out of the classification of "Indian art," although their works may have Indian themes.

European and American-style painting in New Mexico has moved in several directions from the time of its introduction to the present. Colonists brought statues and prints of high quality from Spain to the area that is now New Mexico. Using these models, local artists carved and painted *bultos* (sculptures of saints) and painted *santos* (portaits of saints) on wooden slabs or occasionally on leather.

The artists used adzes to prepare the surfaces of seasoned pine or cottonwood slabs, covered them with gesso for a smooth white plane, and painted them with tempera. They used plentiful local materials to meet the demand for *retablos* (panels).

There was a gradual loss of the third dimension in local paintings; the devices used to show perspective in the models became decorative patterns on one plane in the interpretations by New Mexican painters. Outlines of the figures were generally drawn in black or brown and filled in with solid shades of warm colors. The Catholic church dictated the characteristics of the saints, but embellishments of the portraits were areas of free and lively expression for the artists. A standard vocabulary of oval faces, almond eyes, and single strokes for noses, eyes, and kneecaps was enriched with decorative curtains, Christian symbols, and borders. The lunette on top of the *retablo,* derived from the fluted shell above European statue niches, was carved or raised in relief with gesso.

Few of the artists signed their work or were known by name. One may recognize the work of Molleno, "the chile painter," by his red wedge chile trademark or that of "the calligraphic *santero*" by his fine lines and complex patterns. José Aragón and José Rafael Aragón represent the classical period (the 1820s and 1830s) of New Mexican *retablo* painting. Their simple and intense paintings and those of the other *santeros* were important in the daily lives of Catholic New Mexicans and in the development of art in the state.

Although some *santeros* work at their craft today, Hispanic artists have developed modern idioms in which to express both political and apolitical work through murals, sculpture, and painting.

It is said that a broken wagon wheel kept traveling companions Ernest Blumenschein and Bert Phillips in Taos. There they found a sympathetic fellow artist, Joseph Henry Sharp, and a beautiful location where the existing cultures revered nature. This attitude was one that early Taos artists tried to reflect

in their own painting. In spite of the eventual repair of the wheel, the artists stayed on in Taos. Blumenschein and Phillips later joined other artists to form the Taos Society of Artists. The society members had similar, rather romantic emotions that found different expressions in the palettes and brushwork of members Kenneth Adams, Oscar Berninghaus, Blumenschein, E. Irving Couse, W. Herbert Dunton, E. Martin Henning, Victor Higgins, Phillips, Sharp, and Walter Ufer. They did not create a regional style but a critical and productive society primarily for purposes of promotion outside New Mexico.

Five young men, Jozef Bakos, Freemont Ellis, Walter Mruk, Willard Nash, and Will Shuster, came to the Southwest to paint the countryside and the people. They met each other in Santa Fe and formed Los Cinco Pintores (the five painters). Their goal "to bring art to the people" was soon met in their first exhibit at the Museum of Fine Arts in 1921 and in subsequent exhibits throughout the country. The friends built their own adobe homes along Camino del Monte Sol. The group's importance lay not only in the artists' painted representations of the area but also in their creation of an art colony in Santa Fe.

Many other artists came to New Mexico in the 1920s for a variety of reasons. An era of increasing tourism brought some painters who decided to stay, and ill health brought a steady stream of artists for recuperation. Others arrived at the request of controversial patroness Mabel Dodge Luhan. Cubist painter Andrew Dasburg and author D. H. Lawrence were among her guests. Painter Robert Henri also invited talented artists to visit his summer home in northern New Mexico.

Soon the Santa Fe–to–Taos area became renowned for the number and quality of artists who made the region their home, at least temporarily. They included John Sloan, painter and etcher; Gerald Cassidy, lithographer and painter of the murals in Santa Fe's La Fonda Hotel; Gustave Baumann, master of the woodcut and creator of whimsical carved marionettes. Leon Gaspard and Nicolai Fechin independently left Russia to study art in western Europe and finally to settle in Taos. Frank Applegate, author, builder, and painter; Marsden Hartley, expressionist painter, lithographer, and poet; B. J. O. Nordfeldt, painter of Cézanne-like depictions of New Mexico; and Olive Rush, fresco artist, took up residence in the area. John Marin painted with both hands at once to facilitate the precision timing important for his watercolors. Also living in the state were Emil Bisttram, painter and teacher; Maynard Dixon, muralist and social commentator; Randall Davey, painter of portraits and horse racing scenes; and Raymond Jonson, of the transcendental school. The influences of the color and brushwork of Cézanne, the philosophy of Kandinsky, the daring of the artists of the 1913 New York Armory Show, and a respect for nature are evident in the work of various members of the art colonies.

The Transcendental Painting Group was founded in Taos in 1938, its stated purpose "to carry painting beyond the appearance of the physical world, through new concepts of space, color, light, and design, to imaginative realms that are idealistic and spiritual." Founder Raymond Jonson's home, studio, and gallery on the University of New Mexico campus in Albuquerque served to house his own immaculately crafted works and to host shows of

dedicated nonobjective artists from 1947 to his death in 1982. The building continues to be a university gallery. Jonson was an innovator with the airbrush and acrylic paints and an experimenter with lighting, and is considered a dominant force for the growth of modern art in New Mexico.

Not all New Mexico painters have resided within the Albuquerque–to–Taos region. Peter Hurd, a representational artist of extraordinary ability, comes from the southeastern part of New Mexico. After attending West Point, Hurd studied with illustrator N. C. Wyeth in Pennsylvania and later married Wyeth's daughter, Henriette, also an accomplished painter. Hurd later taught his brother-in-law Andrew Wyeth and father-in-law N. C. Wyeth the essentials of tempera painting, which was to be the younger Wyeth's forte. Peter Hurd has used primarily egg tempera on gesso as a medium for his landscapes and portraits, a technique suited to the luminous character of his paintings of the hills, people, and ranches of the area around his San Patricio home.

Painter Georgia O'Keeffe's home is in Abiquiu, a barren land of severe beauty. She had experienced and felt comfortable with the vast emptiness of space around Amarillo, Texas, where she took a two-year job as a public school art teacher in 1912. Artist-photographer Alfred Stieglitz received some of O'Keeffe's drawings from Texas and hung them in his gallery "291" in New York City without her permission. Her arrival at the gallery to complain sparked the relationship with Stieglitz that resulted in their marriage in 1924. The open spaces appealed to the painter again during her visits to New Mexico from her New York home. Mabel Dodge Luhan influenced Georgia O'Keeffe to come regularly after a visit in 1929. O'Keeffe's annual summer sojourns here eventually stretched into fall and spring, and in 1940 she bought a house in Abiquiu. Stieglitz, who never came along to New Mexico, died in 1946. After settling his estate in 1949, O'Keeffe moved to Abiquiu permanently. The place, her person, and her work have a stark beauty in common.

O'Keeffe has said, "All the earth colors of the painter's palette are out there in the many miles of bad lands. The light Naples yellow through the ochres—orange and red and purple earth—even the soft earth greens."

Stones, bones, and flowers of the desert have been frequent subjects of O'Keeffe's austere yet sensuous paintings. Magnification and simplification of a cross, the Ranchos de Taos church, a pelvic bone, or a jimson flower fill large canvases with abstract images from organic models. Georgia O'Keeffe's exhibitions are the best-attended of any American artist's save those of Andrew Wyeth.

The drama of confrontation between cowboy or cavalry and Indian, the labor of the cowhand, and the color of Indian life are some of the subjects portrayed in the canvases of Western artists. Some, like R. H. Kern and George Catlin, were brought on military and explorative expeditions to New Mexico in the nineteenth century to record places and events; Charles Russell and Frederic Remington passed through New Mexico. Their documentary paintings of the American West were the beginning of a tradition of depiction, in oil and watercolor, of ranch landscape and of cowboy and Indian scenes. The organization Cowboy Artists of America is represented by New Mexico artists Wilson Hurley, Morris Rippel, Gordon Snidow, and Bettina Steinke.

photography

Since the 1840s the brilliant light of New Mexico has passed through the lenses of cameras to register images. In the early days fixing agents applied to metal plates or sensitized paper within the cameras made the images endure. Photography in New Mexico has had a history parallel to that of photography in general. The highly photogenic landscape, weather, and mixture of cultures have brought the world's finest photographers to the area.

The controversial Father Antonio José Martínez, founder of the first coeducational school in the state and operator of a printing press and newspaper, was the subject of the earliest surviving daguerreotype (a direct positive on a metal plate) in the state, printed in 1847. During subsequent decades some itinerant daguerreotypers created portaits of New Mexicans, while other photographers journeyed with survey teams to document the land and cultures of the area. They used wet collodion photography, a process in which glass negatives dampened with silver iodide in suspension were exposed, then developed immediately in a dark tent that was often mounted on a pack animal or wagon. The required quantity of chemicals, glass, and other equipment and the rapidity necessary for the technique made this process especially difficult in the arid land. The photos that remain are, however, of consistently good quality because the determined photographers had the finished print within moments of the shot, knew whether a retake would be necessary, and could choose to keep only the successful photos. Alexander Gardner (who had worked for Mathew Brady during the Civil War), Timothy O'Sullivan, and William Henry Jackson used the collodion medium for their documentary work.

The railroad's arrival here in 1879 coincided with the increasing popularity of the dual-image stereograph and with the availability of the hand-held camera. Tourists took home their own snapshots and sets of paired photos of Taos Pueblo, mesas, donkeys, prospectors, and Indian children printed on cardboard for their stereopticons. The stereograph photos had been taken with an eye for near, middle, and far distant objects to obtain the best three-dimensional effects.

Tourist, portrait, and documentary photos were complemented by subjective fine art prints. Ben Wittick placed Indian subjects in front of painted scenery backdrops that were suspended from tree branches. He took many Indian portraits before his death by snakebite in 1903. Edward Curtis often used a soft-focus lens in his endeavor to record a representative of each of the tribes of the United States.

Paul Strand, one of Mabel Dodge Luhan's guests in Taos in the 1930s, was able to bring together the traditions of art photography and documentary photography. He generally chose sky or buildings as his subjects, rather than Indians and their homes, in order to record the elements and the erosion of time.

In the same period, Dorothea Lange and Russell Lee were among the photographers sent to New Mexico by the Farm Security Administration to document the plight of people displaced by drought. Their sensitive portrayals are of lasting artistic and human value. Pie Town, on U.S. 60, was the focus of a sympathetic series by Lee. Community sings, picnics, square dances, and construction work shared by neighbors have been shown to the world through the photographs taken by Lee,

who also worked in the northern part of the state.

Ansel Adams, Edward Weston, Henri Cartier-Bresson, and Robert Frank all brought their cameras here. Adams's tranquil *Moonrise, Hernández, New Mexico,* (taken near Española), has become his best-known work. Some fine photographers have stayed in New Mexico: Ernest Knee and Harvey Caplin have depicted the landscape and people, Laura Gilpin created a remarkable visual chronicle of the Navajos, and Eliot Porter has sensitively recorded birds and other wildlife subjects, using the dye-transfer process to produce vivid color prints.

The University of New Mexico's support of photographic art has been strong as a result of the work of photographer-historians Beaumont Newhall and Van Deren Coke. The energetic program in photography at the university has launched many young photographers with cool and precise visions and with a wide range of philosophic and artistic orientations.

Artistic talent has become a major resource of New Mexico. Yet many of the state's inhabitants have been reluctant to accept the most avant-garde art. For this reason, perhaps, many of New Mexico's nontraditional artists may be better known beyond the borders of the state than within them. Paintings by Agnes Martin and Forrest Moses and glass

artwork created by Larry Bell are among works most frequently shown out-of-state, but they suggest the quality of light of their birthplace. Unusual color, light, a sense of open space, and respect for tradition continue to shape the work from the hands of New Mexican artists, whether they are painters, potters, silversmiths, or sculptors.

performing arts

Memories of visits to New Mexico embrace much of the dance, music, and drama of the state's peoples. A spectacular ceremonial by costumed dancers accompanied by the beat of a cottonwood-log drum on a dusty plaza; the song of a *trovador* at a traditional New Mexico village wedding; an internationally known diva singing an aria from *The Magic Flute* as lightning flashes in the Santa Fe skies—these are integral to the life and landscape of the state. To New Mexico's Indians, music, dance, and drama combine in traditional religious ceremonies. Many of the Spanish songs, dances, and theatrical works also serve a religious function; others celebrate the common and not-so-common aspects of life in the Spanish towns and villages. Anglos in New Mexico use music in religious observances as well, though church music, like that heard at the Santa Fe Opera or the New Mexico Jazz Workshop, is rarely of local origin. Some of New Mexico's cowboy music, however, is locally generated, acknowledging roots in Texas and Mexico.

It is difficult to separate the Indian and Spanish performing arts into categories of music, dance, and theater; elements of each are included when any is performed. New Mexico now does have well-developed companies specializing in each of the performing arts. Musical groups are especially numerous and well-supported, but theater, dance, and the less common arts of the storyteller, juggler, magician, mime artist, and puppeteer can also find a public in New Mexico.

Indian Music, Ceremonial Songs, and Dancing

Indian tribes' ancient ceremonials include music and dance as central parts of decidedly theatrical and deeply meaningful events. The seeming changelessness of the shuffling dance steps and repetitive chanting, accompanied by the steady beat of a drum, hides variations that bring up-to-date, topical elements to the ceremonies. (Spanish music, too, has a timeless air, although it too changes.)

Ethnomusicologists active in the Southwest state that new elements appear constantly in the music and dance of the Pueblos and the Athapascan (Apache and Navajo) tribes and that over the past twenty years there has been increasing evidence of careful preparation and

Dancer, *Barry Frankel.*

practice for the ceremonials. Loss of Indian cultural traditions is less likely in New Mexico than it is among other Native American groups throughout the United States.

Marcia Herndon, perhaps the first Native American to study Indian music in an academic sense, states that the purpose and meaning of music to the Indian are so different from those of European music that it is difficult for a non-Indian to understand Native American music. The music, she explains, attempts a unity between that which is performed and danced and the forces of nature that are evoked or subjected to ceremonial entreaty. This she contrasts to the decorative aspects of European music. In addition, Indian music represents an essential part of the Indian's way of life, a group phenomenon divorced of the individual virtuosity of composer and artist in the European tradition.

To the non-Indian spectator at a ceremonial, the music may seem to be a monotony to be endured while enjoying the spectacle of the dances. In addition, it is often difficult for the outsider to differentiate among the songs or musical ceremonies of tribes from different parts of the United States. Songs of one tribe differ from those of another in various ways, as the native folk music of Europe differs among the nations. Not only do the melodic style and rhythmic composition vary, but the manner of execution may also be vastly different. The Pueblo songs are pitched in medium and low voice, while those of the Navajos are often high, being sung in falsetto. Both the Athapascan and Pueblo tribes use simple rhythms, though their music differs in other respects. Navajo and Apache music usually contains only two durational values, such as quarter and eighth notes, while Pueblo music uses more variable note durations. In Athapascan music, large jumps in pitch are heard, while Pueblo music generally contains progressively descending tones. Expert musicologists and participants can pinpoint the origin of the music they hear, although the differences among the music of tribes within the two major groups are subtle.

Types of songs may bear a tribal identity. The Eagle, Deer, Buffalo, Corn, Basket, and Turtle dance music belongs to the Pueblos. Plains Indian songs adopted by the Pueblo Indians differ greatly from their own in tempo and melody. The Navajos sing round or circle dance songs as well as their healing songs in the Night and Mountain chants. The Apache, in addition to their distinctive Devil and Bear dance songs, enjoy back-and-forth circle songs.

Visitors are welcome at most of New Mexico's traditional Indian dances. D. H. Lawrence described a Taos Indian dance in these words, quoted in *New Mexico: A Guide to the Coloful State:*

> The Indian singing, sings without words or vision. Face lifted and sightless, eyes half closed and visionless, mouth open and speechless, the sounds arise from the chest. He will tell you it is a song of a man coming home from the bear-hunt: or a song to make rain: or a song to make the corn grow: or even, quite modern, the song of the church bell on Sunday morning. . . .
>
> The dark faces stoop forward in a strange race-darkness. The eyelashes droop a little with insistent thuds. And the spirits of the men go out in the ether, vibrating in waves from the hot, dark, intentional blood, seeking the creative presence that hovers forever in the ether, seeking identification, following on down the mysterious rhythms of the creative pulse, on and on into the germinating quick of the maize that lies under the ground, there, with the throbbing, pulsing, clapping rhythm that comes from the dark, creative blood in man, to stimulate the tremulous, pulsating protoplasm in the seed germ, till it throws forth its rhythms of creative energy into the rising blades of leaf and stem.

For every occasion there is a song and a dance; the Indian repertoire is as extensive as that of the white man. In some ceremonies lasting several days, definite groups of songs are sung, with only rare instances of repetition. Among these are the Shalako of the Zuni, the Yeibichai of the Navajo, and the Corn Dance of the Santo Domingo Pueblo, where as many as six hundred performers synchronize their movements in a superb pageant.

The percussion accompaniment varies with the tribal ceremonies. Rattles are used for the Navajo Night and Mountain chants and some of the Pueblo ceremonies, while the drum is used by the Pueblos in the Corn and most other dances. Apaches use the drum also, preferring soft-toned instruments similar to the water drum of the Indians of the Atlantic seaboard. More recently, the Apaches have used drums made of lard buckets in preference to the Pueblo wooden drum, for these carry a louder, more resonant tone.

Pueblo ceremonials, carefully orchestrated pageants of song and dance, usually occur at times specified by a calendar (the calendar in this book lists some): tribal feast days or the day of the Pueblo's patron saint, time for planting, time for hunting, or time when rain should come. On the other hand, many of the Navajo ceremonials are held for the purpose of curing physical or mental illness, determined by individual need. The family of the sick person hires a medicine man, who becomes responsible both for the execution of the exquisite, highly stylized sandpaintings and for the performance of the chants and sings learned from long apprenticeship to another Navajo healer.

The Apache puberty ceremony is another rite depending upon an individual's need, in this case the need to usher a child into womanhood. Ethnomusicologist David McAllester describes this ceremony:

> This is a time of celebration and blessing for the whole community. The girl dances for hours and observes ritual taboos that indicate the sacred forces now inherent in her body; for example, she must drink through a tube, because the touch of her lips would have a powerful effect on all water and make it unsafe for others to drink. Gifts and food are exchanged, symbolic of the wealth and happiness implied by the fertility celebrated in the ceremony. The girl runs in the four directions as an earnest of her future energy and physical well-being, and a beautiful woman molds her body to ensure symmetry and perfection. ("Indian Music in the Southwest")

Instruments, music, costumes, dance steps, and formations of the ceremonials form an integral whole. Dancers are often divided into groups that alternate on the dusty plazas of the Rio Grande pueblos. Some dances require only men or only women; others include both, as well as children of all ages. Dance formations are in part dependent on available space: San Felipe's almost square plaza lends itself well to circles, while line formations fit better into the long, narrow Santo Domingo plaza. Formations may, however, change during the course of one dance. In some dances, such as the Zuni Shalako, there will be many differently costumed participants, each with a separate role. In Santo Domingo's Corn Dance, on the other hand, almost all of the dancers are dressed alike—the exceptions are the clowns, or Koshare. Dance steps are usually simple, slow, and repetitive, although in some of the showpiece dances, many of which have been borrowed from Plains tribes, the footwork may be complicated and frenzied.

Ceremonials include much evidence of humor; many include clowns of various sorts: Pueblo tribes often have a "Navajo" clown, and Navajos at their ceremonials often include a *bilagaana*, or white man, in each case making the clown the butt of jokes. But, as a whole, the ceremonial satisfies serious purposes.

A form of music with similar serious intent is the peyote music of the Native American

Church, which takes its inspirations from Navajo, Apache, and Plains Indian music but has elements all its own. A Native American Church meeting includes the consumption of the hallucinogenic peyote cactus button to the accompaniment of almost continuous song. Each male in the group sings a series of four songs of his own choosing, each taking a turn with the water drum and a rattle. The beat, maintained by drum and rattle, is very rapid, more so than in most Indian music.

Variations of ceremonial music, less serious in intent, have appeared. The Navajo social song is an example: sounding to the untutored ear like any other Navajo chant, it nevertheless sets to music classic themes of love and death as well as commentary on current events. Further alteration of Indian musical material is also more controversial. This includes the compositions of Louis Ballard, a Plains Indian Cherokee living in Santa Fe, who modifies traditional music in his works; and the appropriation of Indian musical themes by Indian rock groups such as Red Bone and Exit.

At any Indian ceremonial in New Mexico, a portion of the audience is certain to be made up of Indians from other tribes. The circuit of powwows throughout Indian country and in some of the larger cities to which Indians have migrated also allows the mingling of traditions and exposes Indians to other tribes' music and dance, usually nonreligious in nature. The powwow is in many ways antithetical to the principle of Indian music as integral to a religious observance or to a prayer for rain, for the hunt, for the crops. While the group is the important element in the Indians' ritual observances, at a powwow individual virtuosity is rewarded, often with monetary prizes. Rewards are also presented to spur the dancers to greater showmanship at the annual Gallup Intertribal Ceremonial, held each August for more than fifty years.

The traditional folk music of New Mexico's Indians has been extensively studied and recorded. The Wheelwright Museum in Santa Fe and the John Donald Robb Archive of South-western Music at the University of New Mexico are among important repositories of this tradition, which had hitherto passed only from mouth to ear.

Spanish Music and Drama

The Robb Archive also preserves a great deal of the Spanish music of New Mexico. J. D. Robb, former dean of the College of Fine Arts at the University of New Mexico, is preeminent in a group of musicologists who have recorded, translated, and analyzed the songs of New Mexico Spanish villagers and shepherds; Robb has been doing this for more than forty years. New Mexico's Spanish-language music can now be divided into several distinct types. Both the traditional music of the old northern New Mexico villages and the popular songs of the towns and barrios, heavily influenced by Mexican and Caribbean music, are alive in the state today. In addition, Spanish flamenco dancing and music have established a foothold in New Mexico as nowhere else in the United States.

Spanish music was first introduced into the New World when Cortez came to the American continent in 1519, bringing with him the folk songs of the mother country. In Spain, *trovadores* and *juglares* had been composing and singing romances and ballads for centuries, built around the lives of their heroes or dealing with the subjects of love, religion, or war.

The Spanish ballad of the sixteenth century used sixteen syllables to a verse and was usually assonated instead of rhymed. The sixteen-syllable verses were unpliable, so they were eventually broken down into octosyllabic meter, which, with greater variety of themes, was employed in a subsequent composition known as the *décima*. The *décima* consisted of forty-four lines, a four-line introduction followed by four stanzas of ten lines each, with the first line of the introduction becoming the last line of the first stanza, the second line of the introduction becoming the last line of the second stanza, and so on. This stanzaic form was first used by Lope de Vega in Spain and is still recited in New Mexico as poetry, though rarely sung.

The first colonizing expedition of Juan de Oñate in 1598 brought Spanish music to the churches, pueblos, and village homes of New Mexico. Since the Spanish expeditions were made for the glory of God as well as for the acquisition of land and wealth for the Crown, Franciscan missionaries were a vital part—and in some instances the dominating force—of each expedition. Among these missionaries, some of whom had been well trained in letters and in the arts, were found musicians of ability, and it is to them that partial credit for the introduction of European music into the New World must be given.

With each of the pack trains that traversed the miles of desert between Durango, Chihuahua, and Santa Fe could usually be found a resourceful *trovador* and his guitar, responsible for the entertainment of the troops and drovers of the pack train. The most spectacular evening entertainments occurred when two pack trains met, resulting in two rival *trovadores* pitting their talents against one another. *Décimas* and *romances* would fill the early evening; later, when these had been exhausted, the *trovos* would begin. Starting with an exchange of musical taunts, the rivals would take turns improvising verses to a long-continued song, with listeners vigilant for the appearance of advantage to one of the two.

The *trovadores'* florid verbal engagements are said to have stemmed from medieval singing contests sponsored—and often judged—by the kings of Spain and Portugal. The *trovadores'* spiritual descendants, the singers and folk poets of northern New Mexico, continue to hold forth in the mountain and Rio Grande villages. Often lacking in formal musical training, the modern-day performer commits long works to memory or to precious, well-thumbed notebooks that are handed down from generation to generation. Today's *trovador*, usually an elderly village resident, is in great demand. *Velorios* (wakes), marriages,

even traditional engagement ceremonies all require his presence, usually to sing a part of his large repertoire or occasionally to perform a *corrido* or *canción* composed for the occasion. Spanish folk music is not the sole property of the village singer; it is widely sung by others throughout the Spanish settlements for entertainment or as an accompaniment to work.

Of the traditional forms, the *corrido* and *canción* are now most popular in New Mexico. Both are composed of an indeterminate number of rhymed or assonated *coplas,* four-line stanzas with eight syllables in each line. The *corrido* is a narrative ballad about an ordinary person (as compared with the *romance,* an older form celebrating someone famous), often dealing with death. Very precise in its details, it often begins with specification of the date and location of the events described. *Canciones* are happier and more melodic, usually concerning affairs of the heart. *Inditas* are still heard on occasion. Also composed of stanzas, often with a refrain or *estribillo, inditas* often describe a beautiful Indian maiden. Usually sung by one voice or occasionally by several in unison, the music is often accompanied by the singer's guitar.

The *alabado,* a religious ballad related to Gregorian chant, was prevalent in New Mexico at the time when Fray Cristóbal de Quiñones brought the first organ to the area in about 1600. Sung without accompaniment or with the *pito,* a clay flute, the *alabado* remains an important part of Penitente services. The melody is somber, with a wavering, keening note.

The Spanish dance to their music as well, usually to guitar or violin, rarely to vocal music. Like the Indians, they have several ritual folk dances or ceremonials. The most important of these, still frequently performed, is the Matachines Dance. Probably related to dances performed all over Europe symbolizing battles between Moors and Christians, the Matachines Dance in New Mexico follows a set pattern, with a melody endlessly repeated on violin or violin and guitar. As in the Indian ceremonials, music, costuming, dance steps, humor, and caricature unite to create an impressive performance. The main characters are La Malinche, a little girl dressed in white, and El Monarca, the leader of the dancers, who at one point in the dance protects La Malinche from the clown-like Toro (the bull). At the end of each dance, El Polverero (the powder carrier) fires a shotgun as a sign to the Virgin Mary.

Many of the Pueblos perform versions of the Matachines Dance, often hiring Spanish fiddlers and guitarists to accompany the dancers. At Jemez Pueblo, the yearly Matachines Dance alternates Indians in costumes resembling those used for the dance in the Spanish settlements with Indians in more traditional dress dancing to Indian voices and the drum.

The ancient forms of Spanish folk music described to this point have been largely pushed into the northern mountain and middle Rio Grande villages. In Santa Fe, Las Vegas, Albuquerque, Las Cruces, and Española, radio stations and popular bands play what has been described as "Latin American jazz." This music takes some of its themes from New Mexican sources but is heavily influenced by the popular music of Mexico, Cuba, and Puerto Rico and, increasingly, by American rock music. Catchy melodies and a danceable beat mark this popular form.

Spanish flamenco music is much more restricted in its audience but continues to offer fine performances to its aficionados. New Mexico's leading flamenco dancer, María Benítez, performs the sensual dances, accompanied by other dancers and the florid music of a guitarist and a *cantear* (singer), often imported from Spain. Flamenco music can be heard from time to time in Taos, Santa Fe, and Albuquerque.

The best-known Spanish theatrical works, still frequently performed, are the religious plays *Los Pastores* ("the shepherds") and *Las Posadas* ("the inns"). Both combine music with biblical references to the Nativity, and the two are often performed together, usually on Christmas Eve. In *Las Posadas*, participants playing the parts of Joseph and Mary visit each of eight houses asking shelter. At each

The Monarcas, Matachines Dance, Bernalillo, *Phyllis Mayfield Knox.*

home they are told in song by the owners, dressed as Spanish grandees, that there is no place for them. The pair is followed by a procession of villagers, singing traditional and modern folk songs. Finally, at the ninth house, the Holy Couple is welcomed and a celebration ensues. *Los Pastores* tells the story of the Magi. Interwoven into the tale of the journey are encounters between Lucifer and the angel Michael, defender of the Christ Child, and the humor of the lazy shepherd, Bartolo, who sings that he is "violent only in eating."

These two religious spectacles represent almost all that remains of the few plays of pre-American days. Despite the richness of Spanish theater in Mexico, little found its way to the solitude of New Mexico. Villagra's chronicle of Oñate's first colonizing expedition refers to plays written by the colonists, but these no longer exist. Two theatrical works consisting largely of mock battles and speeches by commanders on horseback are still extant: *Los Moros y Los Cristianos* and *Los Comanches*. *Los Comanches* was until recently one of very few Spanish-language plays that dealt with New

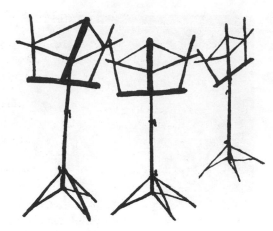

Mexican subjects; in it, Comanche raiders carry off the Christ Child from a village, are converted by hearing the child's story, and return him to the village with their gifts and offerings. Recently bilingual theater groups in Albuquerque and Portales have begun to feature works of young New Mexico playwrights writing in the Spanish language.

Music, Dance, and Theater of the American Era

Anglos in the Southwest are spectators at Indian and Spanish folk music and dance ceremonials and performances, produce and watch programs of all types of music from opera to jazz to rock, and have developed a small body of folk music of their own. The original New Mexican music is the major subject of this essay.

The music of the Anglo cowboys is still popular in many areas. "All lonely people sing," says Margaret Larkin in *Singing Cowboy*, "and much of the cowboy's work is done in solitude. Singing relieves the monotony of the night watch, or the day's ride on the range." After the Civil War, men and boys came to the new frontier of the West from Kentucky, Illinois, Louisiana, and Ohio. With them they brought their folk tunes: English and Scottish ballads, Irish reels, Negro spirituals, and sentimental songs of the day, and to these they

added words that told of their experiences in cow camp and cattle range. Miss Larkin states,

> There always were one or two fellows in an outfit who were said to have a voice, and they sang the solo stanzas while the rest of the group joined in with Whoopee ti yo yo, or the yell that took the place of a chorus. If there was any accompaniment, it was the guitar, supplemented by the fiddle and an accordion at dances. Fiddling and singing were highly regarded accomplishments, and the cowboy who could do either was in demand at frontier celebrations.

The songs of the range are usually melodic and sentimental, often incorporating references to the work of the cowboy, to the land, and to loneliness and death. Typical is the last stanza of a popular cowboy song, "When the Work's All Done This Fall":

> Poor Charlie was buried at sunrise,
>   no tombstone at his head,
> Just a little slab-board, and this is
>   what it read,
> Charlie died at daybreak, he died
>   from a fall,
> And the boy won't see his mother
>   when the work's all done this fall.

Fancy fiddling has been enjoying a renaissance in New Mexico since the 1970s. Young and old perform the hornpipes, jigs, and reels of the British Isles, spiced with Mexican and New Mexican touches, but have little to do with the cowboy songs.

Although the sum of Anglo indigenous music is less massive than those of the Spanish and Indian peoples, the great contributions of Anglos to New Mexican music have been in the areas of musical education and preservation of the local musical tradition. From the many individual classical music teachers in studios and in schools (Albuquerque's Youth Symphony, under Dale Kempter's direction, has been especially notable) to Will Erwin's concert fiddling association to K. L. Higgins's busy Hummingbird Music Camp to the strong apprenticeship program for promising singers at the Santa Fe Opera, music instructors have improved the quality of all forms of music in New Mexico. Adding to New Mexicans' musical education have been the many musical programs, originating both within and outside of the state, broadcast by the public television station, KNME, and by Albuquerque radio stations KUNM and KHFM.

The performance of music takes many forms throughout New Mexico. The internationally renowned Santa Fe Opera currently stages five different operas during its annual two-month-long summer season in its spectacular open-air opera house north of the capital. Under the vigorous direction of John Crosby, the Santa Fe Opera yearly performs several old favorites and at least one modern work. The cast includes some soloists who have graduated from the apprenticeship program and some who frequently appear with larger companies in New York, Chicago, and San Francisco. Smaller, more locally oriented opera companies are found elsewhere in the state, notably in Albuquerque and Farmington.

The New Mexico Symphony Orchestra, headquartered in Albuquerque but playing annual concerts in many other parts of the state, is New Mexico's longest-established performing arts organization; it celebrated its fiftieth season in 1981–82. The Orchestra of Santa Fe and the Chamber Orchestra of Albuquerque

are adventurous smaller ensembles with annual concert series. These and other groups in all corners of New Mexico draw on a cadre of professional musicians in Albuquerque and Santa Fe and from the state's university faculties and student bodies.

The University of New Mexico's music faculty annually produces a series of chamber music concerts in Keller Hall at the university's Fine Arts Center. Yearly chamber music festivals in Albuquerque, Taos, and Santa Fe bring world-renowned musicians to the state.

Among its composers of classical music, New Mexico claims two of special note, Michael Mauldin and John Donald Robb. Mauldin, a native of Santa Fe, has written many modern works on New Mexico themes. Perhaps best-known and most frequently performed is his *Three New Mexico Landscapes* for clarinet and piano, first performed at Washington's Kennedy Center as part of the nation's Bicentennial celebration in 1976.

Robb, a prolific composer, music educator, folk song collector, and former lawyer, has written works in all idioms, from electronic music to settings of folk tunes. Robb's widely performed Third Symphony, commissioned by the Saint Louis Symphony, is of more modern tonality than the lyrical works he has recently written for chamber groups. *Little Jo*, Robb's opera based on Robert Bright's novel *The Life and Death of Little Jo*, incorporates the composer's modifications of several of the Spanish folk songs in his collection.

The New Mexico Jazz Workshop has been prominent in organizing the state's small corps of jazz artists. Local and imported jazz groups play in Albuquerque's renovated KiMo Theater and other locations under workshop sponsorship. The ghost town of Madrid hosts weekly jazz performances under its auspices. In summer these concerts are held in the stands of the town's old stone ballpark.

Local modern dance and ballet groups have generally not attracted large audiences in New Mexico. Professional companies of dancers, even in the cities of Santa Fe and Albuquerque have usually led short, difficult existences, although the Southwest Ballet is showing promise of stability. New Mexicans' appetites for the dance have been whetted by televised performances and well-attended performances by visiting troupes.

Like the dance groups and like dramatic groups in other parts of the United States, most of New Mexico's privately organized theater companies have been short-lived. Only the Albuquerque Little Theater, founded in 1930 by the well-known actress Katherine O'Connor, has remained vital for a long period with professional staff and actors. Housed near Old Town in a theater built with the help of the Works Progress Administration during the Depression, the group has been successful in offering annual subscription series of light dramas to Albuquerque patrons, using local talent supplemented for most plays by a nationally known star.

Many smaller theater groups in Albuquerque, Santa Fe, Los Alamos, and other towns provide theatrical performances ranging from farce and melodrama to serious repertory. Their efforts are supplemented by touring theater, including Broadway musicals, dance groups, and classical plays brought to the University of New Mexico's Popejoy Hall as part of a widely acclaimed series of visiting performers that also includes other events such as opera, symphony orchestras, folk dancing, and ballet.

Each of New Mexico's universities has a strong theater program. The University of New Mexico Theater Arts Department produces many plays annually in its Rodey and Experimental theaters, including an annual festival of locally written drama. The College of Santa Fe's fine drama department is housed in the well-appointed Greer Garson Theater. The famous actress may often be seen there, instructing students in the art of acting. Tony Award–winning playwright Mark Medoff presides over New Mexico State University's new theater complex in Las Cruces. The plays staged by Medoff's students often include a professional star who also becomes an instructor for the cast otherwise made up of students.

Medoff's 1980 Tony was given him for *Children of a Lesser God* during its highly successful Broadway run; its first production had been in the theater at NMSU. Medoff first tasted success with his play *When You Comin' Back, Red Ryder?*, a nightmarish spectacle of unprovoked savagery and puerile accommodation set in a diner at a highway crossing "somewhere between Deming and Lordsburg."

Unlike Medoff, who adopted New Mexico after a childhood in Florida, playwright Preston Jones was born in Albuquerque and spent many years in the state before finishing his career at the Dallas Theater Center. Jones's best-known work is *The Texas Trilogy*, three works written about the seamy side of life in a small West Texas town. His *Santa Fe Sunshine*, filled with hyperbole, pokes fun at the trendy art set in New Mexico's capital.

New Mexico's unique setting has proven an inspiration to composers and playwrights, just as it has to artists, craftsmen, and writers. In addition, it has been said that nowhere in the United States are the indigenous folk arts better preserved and performed for their original purposes, rather than being kept solely as museum pieces.

architecture

Civilizations leave marks on the earth by which they are known and judged. In large measure the nature of their immortality is gauged by how well their builders made peace with the environment.

—Nathaniel Alexander Owings

Visual continuity and physical transience are both characteristics of architecture in New Mexico. The continuity over nearly nineteen centuries of building in the area has been enhanced by the use of indigenous materials (earth, stone, and wood) and a basic style that has been dictated in part by those materials. Modular units of flat-roofed, earth-brown dwellings are gathered together in rows and stacks in Indian pueblos, are collected around plazas in Hispanic villages, are isolated on yards in urban communities or in rural settings, and are clustered in modern townhouse complexes or hotels. Some buildings or portions of buildings remain from each of the successive periods of New Mexican history that are related to the *entradas* (entrances) of cultures into the area, but most of the early buildings have been buried, burned, washed away, remodeled, or replaced. Yet there is a lasting architectural heritage from each era.

The first of these periods is the prehistoric or pre-Columbian era, extending to the exploration by Coronado in 1540. This was followed by the Spanish era, which began with the conquest of New Mexico and extended through three centuries, including the period under Mexican administration, until the American occupation in 1846. The last period, beginning with the United States' annexation of the territory and extending to the present, may be subdivided into two parts: the territorial, which lasted until statehood came in 1912, and the modern, reflecting the many changes brought by improved technology.

Archaeologists believe that the earliest habitations in the area were caves used about ten thousand years ago. Pit houses, built by Basketmaker people outside of cave dwellings, probably date from A.D. 100. These subterranean structures began as pits dug out of the earth. Four logs placed upright at intervals in the pit supported roof beams level with or slightly above the ground. Smaller poles and brush covered the beams and were then packed with earth. Early pit houses were en-

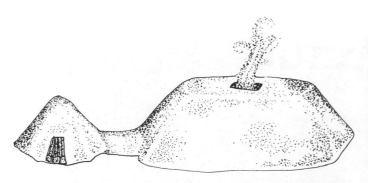

tered by tunnel passageways; later they were entered by ladders placed in the roof holes.

The above-ground successors to pit houses, built around A.D. 700, were single-unit dwellings, the first of the modular units characteristic of Southwestern architecture. Later the units were built in contiguous series that formed windbreaks on the northern and western sides of a communal area or plaza. Constructions of the pit house type were used as ceremonial chambers, the antecedents of Pueblo kivas.

Pueblo Indians added upper stories to these clustered community dwellings beginning about A.D. 900. The rooms on the lower level, which at that time had no windows, became storerooms, and upper and outer rooms were used as living space. While there were many variations, a multiple dwelling of a particular style emerged in the classic period of Pueblo culture (A.D. 1100 to 1300). The basic unit of these structures was the rectangle, a shape that permitted the greatest number of rooms within a given area. The buildings' width was determined by the length of the roof timbers available. The units were arranged in terraces four or five stories high facing a central court. On the inner side, facing this plaza, each tier receded the depth of one room, while out-facing walls were kept flush. Eliminating large openings in the walls on the ground floor enabled the inhabitants easily to convert the structures into strongholds by withdrawing the ladders that provided access to the upper terraces.

Walls were built of stone or mud, depending on the availability of materials. The Spanish term *adobe* stems from *atob*, an Arab word,

meaning sun-dried brick, that had been brought to Spain by the Moors. The technique of forming bricks of mud had come to the Arab world via many cultures from Mesopotamia, where adobe bricks were employed in construction some ten thousand years ago. The word "adobe" is now used to describe both dry earth bricks and the combination, wet or dry, of clay and sand mixed together in a proportion that minimizes cracking and maximizes hardness. This is used as mortar, as plaster, or as cement, or is formed into bricks.

Pueblo Bonito at Chaco Canyon is a multiple dwelling of the Pueblo classic period, said to have housed twelve hundred people at one time. It is a magnificent example of Pueblo stonemasons' art. Chaco masons used tabular stone slabs, which were readily obtainable from nearby ledges. These were laid in adobe and fitted with such care that little mortar was needed, especially when the builders filled the joints with a mosaic of stone chips, leaving hardly a chink between the stones.

When adobe was used as the primary construction material, it was cast or puddled into place along the walls in stratified layers; each layer was allowed to dry for several months before the addition of the next. A smooth coating of adobe finished the walls. The interiors of the rooms were also coated with white gypsum or a light-colored clay and then decorated with a contrasting color, with especially fine decoration in ceremonial rooms.

Roofs were formed by placing round logs six to eight inches in diameter at regular intervals across two opposite walls. Small, peeled poles were placed across these beams and then covered with long grasses, rushes, and small branches. Finally, adobe was spread over the entire roof. These roof surfaces also served as floor for the rooms above. The roofs sloped gradually toward openings in the side walls, through which water spouts extended to carry off rainwater.

The supporting beams were cut and trimmed laboriously with stone axes. Because of the work involved, carpenters reused old timbers whenever possible. When a beam was too long for its new position, it was not shortened but allowed to protrude beyond the exterior wall, thus producing a characteristic feature of Pueblo architecture. In New Mexico today, roof beams, small ceiling poles, and water spouts are still very much used and are referred to by their Spanish names: *vigas, latillas,* and *canales,* respectively.

Blankets or hides rather than wooden doors probably covered the small openings to the rooms. Trap doors in the roofs provided access to rooms on the ground floor. The upper floors were reached by ladders or masonry steps on the building's exterior. Windows were simply small holes, used principally to let smoke out and air in.

The extensive ruins at Chaco Canyon National Monument, Aztec Ruins National Monument, and Salmon Ruins hint at the magnificence of the multiple dwellings of the era. These edifices may be said to be American, and their influence can still be felt in contemporary American architecture.

Rectangular or circular kivas (ceremonial chambers), usually below the ground, often featured highly complicated ventilating flues, repeating the pattern of the entryways to earlier pit houses. The great kivas of prehistoric times stood apart from other buildings and projected above ground only enough to ensure drainage. Their roofs were either flat or cribbed, resting on pillars that rose at intervals from a continuous bench around the wall within, and were pierced with a hatchway entrance.

Today's kivas do not deviate from this traditional plan. Excellent examples of the old circular types, built partly above ground, are found in the living pueblos of San Ildefonso, Nambe, Santo Domingo, and Cochiti. The kivas at San Juan, Santa Clara, and Tesuque pueblos have rectangular exteriors and are attached to other buildings. Fine examples of the prehistoric kiva are present at the Bandelier National Monument and at Chetro Ketl ruins in Chaco Canyon National Monument. Kivas at Aztec National Monument and Co-

Terrones, *Harvey Caplin.*

ronado State Monument have been restored and may be entered by visitors. Kivas are of interest culturally, but have not influenced subsequent architecture to the same extent as have the great pueblos.

When the Spanish colonists and priests arrived in New Mexico in 1598, important architectural changes occurred. These were due only to the Spaniards' different floor plans, tools, and methods of construction; building materials remained the same until the mid-1800s. The continued use of adobe and wood accounts for the harmonious blending of the old and the new.

The Spanish priests exerted a great architectural influence, building many fine churches despite conditions that were adverse both to themselves and to their Indian forced laborers. The newcomers adopted the plans of European Christian churches, usually coffin-shaped or cruciform. They used adobe in a way that was new to the Indians, first mixing mud with

Pecos National Monument, *Dave Wilson.*

straw, then forming bricks and drying them in the sun. This became the standard method; the former practice of puddling was gradually abandoned. Turtlebacks (mounds of dried adobe) and *terrones* (mud bricks cut from flood plains, dried, and held together by the plant root systems they contained) were also used. Church walls were thick, in contrast to the rather thin walls of earlier buildings. Heavy timbers were hauled great distances to allow increased roof spans so that the churches could accommodate large congregations.

With the Spanish iron axes and adzes, carpenters could expand their work with wood. *Vigas* were cut into sections, squared off, and carved. Artisans shaped decorative corbels (capitals) to crown the pillars or columns that supported the roof beams. Finally, doors, windows, and frames of wood could now be constructed.

A typical mission church was characterized by massive dignity and simplicity, relieved by decorative details of grace and charm. The nave was lit by rectangular windows placed high in the walls on one side. The walls of the sanctuary were usually higher than those of the nave, creating a clerestory opening above and in front of the altar so that it was illuminated by light from an invisible source. This effect was designed to produce a feeling of awe in the beholder. The interior walls were plastered smooth and whitened with gypsum. Artists painted them with colored earth in a pattern of dadoes or bands topped with traditional Indian designs. The *vigas,* corbels, and *portales* (porches) were richly carved with designs more reminiscent of Moorish Spain than of the Indian world. The great church and adjacent monastery at Acoma and missions at Laguna, San Felipe, and Isleta pueblos are especially noteworthy. These structures are still used as models for monumental buildings in the Spanish-Pueblo style.

A Spanish house plan was suitable for use in New Mexico because of the similarity of the two regions' climates. A house on a large hacienda or within a settlement was often built around a patio with *portales* facing a planted enclosure, an arrangment that provided shelter from wind and sun and also a measure of defense. Most Spanish colonial communities were fortified and built in contiguous units around a plaza. The Indians used plazas as social gathering places and communal work areas, but to the Spanish settlers plazas were first a means of defense and only secondarily social spaces. Ranchos de Taos, Taos, Dixon, and Trampas were built in this manner to withstand Indian raids.

The houses were rarely built more than one or two rooms wide because of the limitation imposed by the length of the roof beams. Interior doors allowed communication from room to room. Small windows facing the plazas were not glazed in the early days and were barred with wooden grills and shutters that could be closed at night. Shutters and doors were sometimes paneled and beautifully carved, but more often they were simple, hand-hewn planks held together with crossbars. They were not hinged, as iron was scarce, but instead were secured to their frames by pivots made by extending the stile into pockets in the frame. Floors were of packed earth mixed with animal blood and

ashes. Corner fireplaces came into general use. High-walled corrals for the safekeeping of livestock were usually attached to the houses.

There were many variations in these early Spanish buildings, but certain features that were also evident in their Indian predecessors were common to all: the uneven contours of earthen walls; rectangular masses; flat roofs; wood ceilings; and white interior walls. Erosion by the elements, destruction by rebelling Indians, and remodeling have eliminated all complete examples of Spanish homes predating the 1692 reconquest of New Mexico, but some fragments remain.

Homes of the wealthy *hacendados* or *ricos* up and down the Rio Grande valley were finer than those of the poor people, but the difference was a matter of size and detail only. As communication with Mexico became more regular, the availability of iron, tin, glass, and other refinements led to slight modifications of buildings.

The Spanish Crown recommended the building of *torreones* (round towers) to be used as watchtowers along all trade routes, but only the one in Talpa remains. Reconstructions of *torreones* exist in Lincoln and Los Golondrinas; the ruins of two *torreones* linger in Dixon. Like the round kivas of the Indians, these structures did not influence the main current of architectural development.

Native Americans developed another style of house using wood and adobe, the *jacal.* Horizontal rails or woven willow branches held small timbers in a vertical position and mud was packed between these uprights. The Anasazi used the *jacal;* the Spanish adopted it in the villages east of the Manzano Mountains; and Pueblo tribes built *jacales* in the Rio Grande valley.

A distinctive architectural style was developed over several centuries by the Navajo tribe. "Hogan" ("dwelling") has come to mean any round or polygonal home, usually with one room. Probably the earliest hogans were conical, forked-pole structures similar to the ones made by other tribes of the Athapascan group in Canada. One forked pole held up two other principal poles. Smaller poles and brush were placed on these supports, and the surface was covered with packed earth. A variant of the early hogan form has a separate support for a roof, with vertical walls leaning against it. Logs notched and stacked as in frontier log cabins or toy Lincoln logs have been used in hogan construction for at least the past one hundred fifty years. Frequently the roofs are also of cribbed log construction, covered with fragrant brush and earth. In areas where stone is available, masonry hogans have been built using mud mortar. One hogan near Gallup was constructed with stones of many colors collected from each Navajo chapter (political land division).

Adobe, cinder block, and frame-stucco hogans have also found a place among the sandstone, pine forest, or desert scrub surroundings of the Navajo Reservation. Navajo Forest Products Industry attempted recently to market prefabricated hogans, but with little success. The handsome cribbed-log remains the most common and popular form, though most Navajo families now live in suburban-style frame houses. Many maintain traditional hogans in which to hold ceremonies.

In many of the hogans in use today, the oil-drum stove has been replaced with the more efficient cast iron stove, and some hogans have such amenities as polyurethane insulation, shag carpeting, sliding glass doors, and, in at least one instance, a bomb shelter.

Most Apaches, Athapascan relatives of the Navajos, now live in rectangular houses no different from those in most cities and towns in New Mexico. A few canvas or hide tepees and wood-pole wickiups can still be seen on the Apache reservations, however.

The raising of the American flag in 1846 signaled the onset of profound changes in the architecture of New Mexico. These changes were slow at first, keyed to the tempo of the caravans crossing from the United States into the new territory. As the Santa Fe Trail became safer for travel, increasing numbers of Anglo-Americans began to arrive, bringing with them new materials and architectural ideas based on those of the communities from which they had come.

Anglo settlers imported millwork and brick and lime plasters from Saint Louis and Kansas City. Adobe walls were then capped with protective cornices of brick in ornamental patterns, and walls were coated with lime stucco. The small, grilled, glassless windows of the Spaniards' homes were replaced by double-hung, glazed sashes, often with slatted shutters on the outsides. Slender, squared columns replaced the heavy hewn ones. *Portales,* doors, and windows were ornamented with white-painted wood trim that recalled Eastern precedents. Hispanic Catholics preferred the blue oil paint that was brought over the trail, their window and door trim displaying the color associated with the Virgin and with a supposed power to ward off witches. In 1983 local paint manufacturers still offer blue tints labeled Taos, Laguna, or Madonna.

The new territorial style using these refinements became very popular. In some parts of the state, such as the eastern slopes of the Sangre de Cristos and Manzanos, many such houses still stand, sometimes modified by wood, shingle, or corrugated tin roofs that can readily shed a build-up of snow. The territorial style fell from favor in the cities around the turn of the century but remained the mode in isolated villages until the 1930s, at which time a revival returned the style to the cities. It is commonly used for contemporary homes. Original examples of the territorial style are present in Santa Fe, notably in Sena Plaza and in houses near the intersection of Canyon Road and Camino del Monte Sol. In its revival form the style can be seen in the state government buildings and in homes throughout New Mexico.

The advent of the railroad in 1879 influenced two factors that until then had dictated the architecture of New Mexico. Imported supplies replaced local building materials, and new designs supplanted the native architectural tradition. As a result, buildings of a great variety of styles and construction methods were erected, and the newer towns began to resemble the Midwest and the East. The Italianate style, with ornamented brackets; the irregular, turreted, multitextured Queen Anne style; Richardson Romanesque, with stone arches; and the neoclassical style, with fluted white columns— all these arrived in New Mexico by the trainload, and they lingered here long after their popularity had waned in the East. Las Vegas resembled a catalogue of varying architectural styles. Victorian buildings such as the Veeder building, the Carnegie Library, the Masonic Temple, the Presbyterian Church, and the Ilfeld Auditorium still stand there. The Bursum house in Socorro and the Armijo house in Las Cruces display examples of exceptional architectural millwork.

The venerable Palacio Real, or Palace of the Governors, in Santa Fe did not escape remodeling with millwork ornamentation brought by the railroad. This building is so old that some of its walls are constructed of puddled adobe, the technique typical of the pre-Columbian era, although most of the walls were probably built by Indians after the Pueblo Revolt of 1680 and were subject to frequent remodeling through the next three centuries. The palace was trimmed and "modernized" in the 1880s to include a delicate Victorian balustrade along the entire facade.

During the first decade of the twentieth century, a reaction to architectural imports set in. Some residents began to realize that New Mexico's ancient forms not only had aesthetic value but were admirably adapted to the climatic conditions of the state. At that time, while the rest of the country was trying out a fanciful period revival and dramatic, austere international styles, New Mexicans turned to their own architectural heritage. Among the first buildings to reflect this reaction was the Palace of the Governors. Under the direction of archaeologists, the structure was brought back to what was thought to be its original state, based upon a plan found on an old map in the British Musuem. Its interior has been extensively remodeled twice since then.

The architect John Gaw Meem was a central figure in the restoration and construction of buildings in the Spanish-Pueblo style. Examples of the revival of interest in Spanish-Pueblo forms include the New Mexico Museum of Fine Arts, the Laboratory of Anthropology, the headquarters of the National Park Service's Southwest Region, and the Cristo Rey Church, all in Santa Fe. The University of New Mexico buildings in Albuquerque, especially the Zimmerman Library, and the Eddy County Courthouse in Carlsbad are also examples of the style.

Both changing fashion and the changing needs of their inhabitants have brought about alterations in the physical character of existing buildings. By the late nineteenth century, pueblos no longer needed to limit access to their interiors for defense reasons. The adobe walls were opened up to make additional doors and windows in all the living pueblo buildings. When wagon trains and railroads brought to New Mexico styles that were popular elsewhere, some features of those fashions were attached to existing buildings. Wooden "folk Gothic" towers were added to the adobe of San Felipe de Neri Church in Albuquerque and to the churches of Las Trampas and Bernalillo. Adobe houses scorned by Anglo newcomers were resurfaced to resemble stone, brick, or wood. In the 1970s and 1980s, adobe homes were again in vogue, and wood-frame and cement-block structures were built with intentional surface irregularities, clipped corners, and adobe-colored stucco exteriors.

Adobe is still used to a large extent because of its economy, heat retention, insulation from noise, flexibility, and appropriateness to the Southwestern setting. Adobe has, however, a fugitive nature. Structures with exterior adobe plaster need to be replastered annually. It is estimated that weeds, wind, and water can return an unmaintained adobe building to the surrounding earth within twenty years.

New Mexico now has a little of every style of modern architecture, including Bauhaus, Brutalism, prairie, California ranch house, and franchise styles. All of these are external to the state. Influences from within the area that affect contemporary architecture beyond New Mexico's borders are the Spanish-Pueblo style and the construction of energy-efficient buildings, particularly solar-heated structures.

The orientation toward the sun of most prehistoric cave dwellings and multiple dwellings shows an early knowledge of passive solar heating fundamentals. Some Spanish colonial buildings in Albuquerque, Santa Fe, Las Vegas, and Mora were built according to a solar plan. More recently, pioneers of modern solar design have taken advantage of New Mexico's almost omnipresent sunshine to build experimental structures here. The majority of solar homes built in the 1960s and 1970s were standard constructions fitted with solar appliances

that resemble the handiwork of orthodontists. Many solar fixtures are now less obtrusive in appearance, and passive solar devices for heat storage include materials such as water, adobe, brick, and rock. In 1982, according to the New Mexico Public Service Company, more solar-heated buildings existed in New Mexico than in the rest of the world combined. The number of langleys (units of measure of solar energy) is reported daily in New Mexico newspapers, an indication of local interest in solar heating.

Another type of energy-efficient architecture, underground houses, also has many local precedents. Economy of construction, necessitated by the simple tools they possessed, was the reason for early Indian peoples' building of pit houses. The scarcity of building materials necessitated the digging of underground homes on the eastern plains during the nineteenth century. Civil defense consciousness in the 1950s led to the construction of Abo Elementary School in Artesia below ground and of bomb shelters under many homes. High energy costs in the 1980s have sent many New Mexicans under ground again, into ingenious solar-heated homes built into hillsides.

The wind is often taken into consideration when homes are built in this state. The early Pueblo community houses were constructed as windbreaks; so also solid walls and fences are built on the west sides of modern structures for protection from the occasionally fierce, usually westerly wind. Working windmills have pierced the horizon of the plains for the past century, and the community of Clayton has put the winds to work turning the giant windmill (turbine) that supplies part of the local electrical power.

The odd appearance of many of the experimental, energy-efficient houses is itself a characteristic of some local architecture. The state has an extensive collection of eccentric or individually styled buildings. New Mexicans pride themselves on doing things by themselves; many buildings reflect that staunch individualism.

On a small scale, New Mexicans assert their individuality in wood or adobe houses with elaborate, hand-worked decorative details, in geodesic domes, and in vintage trailer homes embellished with adobe annexes (shiny mobile homes are now a ubiquitous addition to the New Mexico landscape).

On a grand scale, several buildings referred to as castles have deviated from the local architectural norm. The Montezuma Castle outside of Las Vegas, a majestic red sandstone constructed in a turreted Queen Anne style, was a favorite tourist spa beginning in 1880. The once-lavish resort now houses an international college dedicated by Great Britain's Prince Charles in 1982.

The Museum of New Mexico has acquired another architectural oddity, the Dorsey Mansion east of Springer. Stephen Wallace Dorsey, a controversial politician and cattle baron, built an expertly joined log house in 1878. A portion of the log house was removed to make way for an addition; Dorsey constructed a stone castle with a crenelated tower and carved gargoyles representing President Chester A. Arthur, animals, and personal enemies. The interior boasted a billiard room decorated with suits of armor, a collection of Parisian art, a menagerie of animal trophies, a dining room that seated fifty, a parlor with a curved cherry-wood staircase, and twenty-seven other rooms. All of this was surrounded by a white picket fence and a lush garden standing in the dry prairie. Dorsey's fortunes rose and then fell; after he left the state under the taint of scandal, the mansion was used as a tuberculosis sanatorium, a resort, a home, and a popular site for wedding photos; it is now a museum property.

In Albuquerque another castle took five years to build in the 1880s and was demolished in one month in 1955. The Huning Castle had five-foot-thick adobe walls that were covered with wood brought from Illinois, painted to look like the stonework of an ornate Italian villa. Also in Albuquerque, a Norwegian-style villa built of heavy logs in 1903 crowns a small hill near I-25, while a pseudo-Mediterranean villa on San Rafael Avenue, S.E., and Tudor-style mansions on Rio Grande Boulevard, N.W., could be the modern counterparts of the earlier castles.

The use of a common material in an unusual way has made several New Mexican buildings remarkable. Among them are free-form adobe homes, an old home and hotel in Mountainair decorated with whimsical wooden gingerbread, and several absurdly eclectic homes in Taos. Also in Taos are artist Nicolai Fechin's home, a masterpiece of carved wood details, and the home of his fellow Russian painter Leon Gaspard. The Gaspard house is a combination of Byzantine opulence and pink adobe, with arched windows and elaborate woodwork. Adobe has been formed into multiple domes and pointed arches for the new mosque of the Dar Al-Islam community near Abiquiu. (The only early uses of the arch in adobe construction in the state occurred in the seventeenth-century mission church of Pecos and in the common *hornos* [beehive-shaped ovens] found outside many Pueblo and Hispanic homes.)

Buildings made of unusual materials also stand out in the New Mexico landscape. Conspicuous examples are the creek-cobble buildings near Embudo, the munitions-crate houses outside Gallup, and a collection of homes made of aluminum cans near Taos. In Albuquerque, the handsome white tile Occidental Insurance Company Building, water pillars in buildings by Antoine Predock, and the glass ark and globe additions to two adobe homes by architect Bart Prince are examples of intriguing materials usage.

New Mexico's unique architectural heritage has been increasingly appreciated by the state's citizens. At the same time, an influx of immigrants to the Sun Belt hastens change of the architectural profile. Building a New Mexico that is at peace with the environment remains a challenge for the future.

literature

Legends, Cuentos, Chronicles

A sense of mystery and of magic and a deep appreciation of the bounty of nature permeate much of the literature of New Mexico, especially that of the state's Indians. Without a written language, early Indian literature could be passed from generation to generation only through the media of storytellers and medicine men. In many Southwestern tribes, both groups were revered by their society as preservers of their literary tradition.

Since the beginning of the twentieth century, missionaries and linguists have made progress in recording Indian languages in Roman orthography. With this aid, recording of the oral tradition is now possible in the original languages. However, as relatively few, Anglos or Indians, can read the newly developed orthographies, the most accessible forms of Indian literature are those in English translation. Because the English and Indian languages differ so greatly in their structure, the reader must be cautioned that the resulting translations are at best approximations of the originals.

The Navajo Curriculum Center at Rough Rock, Arizona, has pioneered in the production of side-by-side English and Navajo versions of folk tales, Navajo biographies, and other materials. *Coyote Stories* (1968), a compilation of animal tales with morals for the young, is among the most intriguing.

Navajo religious and curing ceremonies provide visual as well as spoken and sung imagery. These poetic masterpieces, often requiring days for their performance, are maintained in the custody of the medicine men, whose preparation requires years of apprenticeship. Segments of the songs and chants included in the ceremonies have appeared in English, recorded by writers and ethnologists such as Washington Matthews, G. W. Cronyn, Father Berard Haile, and Mary Austin. Franc Johnson Newcomb describes the training and life events of a well-known medicine man in *Hosteen Klah, Navajo Medicine Man and Sandpainter* (1964).

Pueblo Indian legends, too, have been recorded. Charles Lummis presents vivid translations of a number of legends in *Pueblo Indian Folkstories* (1910). Further treasuries of folk tales were recorded by Frank Cushing and Frank Applegate in the early twentieth century. In *Masked Gods* (1950), Frank Waters presents some of the mysticism and symbolism of both Pueblo and Navajo ceremonies, with interpretation born of years of studying and living with Indians of the Southwest. Erna Fergusson, in *Dancing Gods* (1931), describes Pueblo ceremonial dances and adds a spirited commentary.

The Spaniards, the first non-Indians in the Southwest, possessed the means of recording their stories and their impressions of the new land in a written language. This difference between them and the Indians was more apparent than real, however; schools were nearly nonexistent until after the arrival of Archbishop Lamy in 1850, and there were few who could read the precious books transported fifteen hundred miles up the mule trail from Durango, Mexico. The first printing press in what is now New Mexico did not arrive until the middle of the nineteenth century.

Like the Indians, then, the Spanish settlers developed a lively oral tradition. In story, song, and dramatic productions, the people of Santa Fe and the sequestered mountain villages found creative outlet and entertainment. The stories or *cuentos*, with their embodiment of the wit and wisdom of New Mexico's first Europeans, combine the customs and ideals of Spain and Mexico with the landscape and realities of life in the north. They have been collected, transcribed, and translated by several modern authors, including Lorin W. Brown of the Federal Writers' Project in *Hispano Folklife of New Mexico* (1978), Sabine Ulibarri, in *Tierra Amarilla: Stories of New Mexico* (1971), and José Griego y Maestas and Rudolfo Anaya in *Cuentos: Tales from the Hispanic Southwest* (1980).

Chronicles of travel and conquest by the explorers and governors of Spanish New Mexico form a priceless archive of the life of the period. The remarkable journey of Alvar Núñez Cabeza de Vaca from Florida to the Gulf Coast of Texas and then to the Gulf of California in northern Mexico, whether he passed through New Mexico or not, is a fascinating story retold by numerous authors. The faith that sustained Cabeza de Vaca and his companion,

Esteban, shines forth in the former's brief report to the Spanish monarch. Haniel Long's equally short and equally eloquent *Interlinear to Cabeza de Baca* (1936) (republished later as *The Power Within Us*) interprets Cabeza de Vaca's writings in the light of the wanderer's reliance upon his beliefs and his growing humility.

Archives and journals of the early explorers, the first Spanish governors of the province, and the first priests exist but are often difficult to find. Many priceless volumes were burned during the Pueblo Revolt of 1680. A definitive translation of the journals of Don Diego de Vargas is in preparation. In his own words de Vargas tells the story of the self-possessed, pious grandee who led the reconquest of New Mexico in 1692, became governor, and was then a reviled prisoner in the Palace of the Governors, only to be released to eventual acclaim. The finest chronicle of the early Spanish period is undoubtedly Gaspár de Villagrá's *History of New Mexico* (1610). Villagrá was a member of the first group of Spaniards to settle in New Mexico, under the leadership of Don Juan de Oñate, and he recounted in his poetic version the hardships and glories of the Oñate expedition. The author's personal role in the events described culminated in his involvement in the Battle of Acoma of 1599. The work, published in Spain and addressed to King Phillip III, has been translated into English prose by Gilberto Espinosa (1933).

Trappers, traders, and other wanderers were the first Anglo-Americans to reach the Rio Grande valley in the early nineteenth century. Lieutenant Zebulon Pike, surveying for the U.S. Army, was among the first to reach Santa Fe by a route other than the Camino Real from Durango. Pike's *Journal of a Tour Through the Interior Parts of New Spain* (1810) covers his arrest and forced march from the upper Rio Grande in what is now southern Colorado through Santa Fe and on to Chihuahua, Mexico, before his release in 1807. Pike gives intimate and vivid accounts of the manners and customs of the New Mexican people and of their villages and settlements from the

point of view of an unwilling but interested visitor. The trapper James O. Pattie in *The Personal Narrative of James O. Pattie* (1831) wrote of his days of hunting and trading in northern New Mexico's mountains and towns.

By all accounts the great narrative of the Santa Fe Trail days is Josiah Gregg's *The Commerce of the Prairies* (1844). Gregg, a trader in Kansas, Santa Fe, Chihuahua, and the vast stretches in between, offers an illuminating portrayal of the perils of travel along the trail and the life he observed along his way. The diaries of Susan Magoffin, first published in 1926 as *Down the Santa Fe Trail and into Mexico*, describe the author's involvement in the intrigue and high-stakes commerce of a Santa Fe in transition between Mexican and U.S. rule in 1846 and 1847. The young bride and members of her family were intimately involved in the negotiations that culminated in the surrender of Santa Fe and the territory of New Mexico to General Stephen Watts Kearny. From the same period came *Wah-To-Yah and the Taos Trail* (1850), Lewis Garrard's account of his adventures as a seventeen-year-old traveler with a Santa Fe–bound caravan.

The first travel books on New Mexico and the southwest were made available by a number of European travelers in the middle of the nineteenth century. The best known of these, from the period surrounding the Mexican War, are the books of George Frederick Ruxton, a young Englishman who journeyed up the Rio Grande in 1846. His *Life in the Far West* (1847) and *Adventures in New Mexico and the Rocky Mountains* (1848) give his firsthand impressions of New Mexican life in the earliest American days.

Immediately after the American occupation, U.S. Army officers and mapmakers assigned to the vast New Mexico Territory began to write another class of travel literature, sometimes technical, often of great interest. The works of Emory, Marcy, Cooke, Johnston, and Sitgreaves, published as U.S. Senate Executive documents, make fasinating reading. Of the same era is *El Gringo, or New Mexico and Her People* (1854) by W. W. H. Davis, written while the author was U.S. attorney in Santa Fe during the early territorial days. His book describes contemporary New Mexico in close detail.

In any account of writers of New Mexico and on any tour of Santa Fe, the name of General Lew Wallace is certain to rise. Wallace is said to have completed his novel *Ben Hur* in the Palace of the Governors in Santa Fe in 1880, having divided his time as territorial governor between the affairs of Christian gladiators in Rome and those of Billy the Kid in Lincoln County. While the governor wrote of events distant in time and space, his wife, Susan E. Wallace, recorded her interesting and lively impressions of the local scene in letters to an Eastern newspaper, later collected in a book entitled *The Land of the Pueblos* (1888).

The first of a flood of Billy the Kid books began to appear soon after the notorious desperado died "with his boots on." Sheriff Pat E. Garrett, responsible for his "capture by killing," began the torrent with *The Authentic Life of Billy the Kid* (1882). Since then, the Lincoln County War has been continuously waged in print. Amelia Bean, in *Time for Outrage* (1967), presents what may be the most readable and balanced account, not only of the short life of Billy, but also of the warring factions and their motives in the conflict. Other famous gunmen of New Mexico have been celebrated in subsequent frontier narratives, but the literary battles surrounding the Lincoln County War and Billy the Kid continue to be fought.

Fiction on New Mexico themes written since the Civil War can be divided into groups according to the ethnic origins of the stories' protagonists. Novels on Indian subjects are now very common. Like much other good fiction, the best of these books teach a great deal about their subjects, in this case about Indian life and customs. First among these are Adolph Bandelier's *The Delight Makers* (1890). The famous Swiss archaeologist's novel describes his appraisal of the life of the cliffdwellers by the Rito Frijoles, near which he worked, spiced by speculative fiction regarding the religious orientations and the events that led to the abandonment of the Pueblo of Tyuonyi.

Oliver La Farge's *Laughing Boy* won its author the Pultizer Prize in 1929. In this book and in *The Enemy Gods* (1937), La Farge tells of the encounters of Navajo youth with Western culture and the peace that came to them from a return to traditional ways. The inner calm of La Farge's characters contrasts with the restlessness of Mangas Coloradas, a great chief of the Apaches who ranged though southern New Mexico and Arizona and northern Mexico in the nineteenth century and is described in Will Levington Comfort's novel *Apache* (1931). Making virtues of brevity and the picaresque, Mary Austin, in *One Smoke Stories* (1934), tells tales of New Mexico's Indians and their contacts with Anglos and Spanish-Americans.

Frank Waters became deeply involved in attempting to understand and portray Indian ceremonialism. Waters wrote *The Man Who Killed the Deer* (1942), which followed La Farge's lead in telling of New Mexico's Indians caught between Indian and Anglo cultures. Leslie Marmon Silko, a Laguna Indian, uses the same theme, one central to present-day native American existence, in *Ceremony* (1977). She tells the story of the painful readjustment of a Laguna tribesman returning from his wrenching experiences during the Second World War. N. Scott Momaday's novel *House Made of Dawn* (1968) treats the same subject, in this case through the experiences of a Jemez Indian whose drunken degeneration follows his return from World War II. Like Silko's hero, Abel, the protagonist, finds part of the way back to serenity through the traditions and mysticism of his people.

Mystery novels are not always considered fit subjects for review, let alone sources of substantive information. Tony Hillerman's engrossing thrillers, among them *The Blessing Way* (1970), *Dance Hall of the Dead* (1973), and *Listening Woman* (1975), can be read as escape literature or can be sifted for much carefully gleaned information about Zuni and Navajo ceremonialism.

The Spanish settlers of New Mexico have

also been the subjects of a considerable volume of literature. Many of these stories treat the conflicts and accommodation between Spanish-Americans and Anglos. Others, less numerous, have dealt with life in wholly Spanish towns and villages, or with conflict between Indians and Spaniards before the arrival of the Anglos. Eugene Manlove Rhodes, better-known for his cowboy novels and short stories, wrote in *Penalosa* (1934) of Don Diego de Penalosa, governor of New Mexico from 1661 to 1664, as one who opposed the gathering storm of the Inquisition. He saved the San Juan Pueblo leader, Popé, from punishment at the hands of the Inquisitors. Despite the reprieve, the embittered Popé returned to his people to organize and lead the Pueblo Revolt of 1680. Popé and the Pueblo Revolt are central to Irwin Blacker's *Taos* (1959), a fictionalized account of the rebellion presented on a grand scale. Despite the fact that the validity of the portrayal cannot be proved, Blacker's long work presents a great number of characters—Indians, Spanish common soldiers, priests, and grandees—in credible, three-dimensional form, avoiding many of the black-or-white characterizations that defile much of the Southwest's regional literature.

Nonfictional works descriptive of life in the Spanish villages of northern New Mexico include Fray Angelico Chavez's *La Conquistadora* (1954) and *The Lady from Toledo* (1960), both of which deal with the Spanish reconquest of New Mexico in 1692 and the reverence attached to the statue of the Virgin Mary given credit by the returning settlers for the success of their quest. Marta Weigle's *Brothers of Light, Brothers of Blood* (1976) is a careful portrayal of another form of religious observance, that of the Penitente sects of the mountain villages. Robert Coles's *The Old Ones of New Mexico* (1973) is based on interviews conducted by the author, a Harvard psychiatrist. The book depicts the way of life the old Spanish-Americans have left behind as younger villagers leave the mountains for the jobs and faster-paced society of Española, Santa Fe, or Albuquerque. Fabiola Cabeza de Baca's *We Fed*

Them Cactus (1954) reminisces about another Spanish-American lifestyle, ranching on the eastern New Mexico plains, the Llano Estacado.

Twentieth-Century Fiction

A large proportion of twentieth-century fiction based in New Mexico brings the Anglo and Spanish-American cultures into contact, contrast, and often conflict. There are, however, a limited number of volumes that consider life in the Spanish *villas* before, or divorced from, the impact of the later arrivals. The world of the migrating Spanish shepherd in the mountains and *arroyos* of New Mexico (or Arizona—the location is not specified) is described with calm and sympathetic feeling by Jack Schaefer in *Old Ramon* (1960). Rudolfo Anaya's *Bless Me, Ultima* (1972) describes life in a small town on the eastern plains with a dollop of humor and a touch of the supernatural.

Of the novels relating to contacts between Spanish-Americans and Anglo-Americans, two by Harvey Fergusson deserve first mention as classics. *Grant of Kingdom* (1950) begins as the story of an omnipotent Taos trapper and mountaineer, Jean Ballard. The hero, closely patterned after Lucien Beaubien Maxwell, meets and is captivated by the daughter of a Spanish *patrón* of Taos, marries her, and receives as dowry a huge, undeveloped tract of land identifiable as the Maxwell Land Grant on the east side of the Sangre de Cristo Mountains. Ballard's open-handed generosity toward Spaniard and Texan alike and his overextension in all directions lead to his eventual loss of the land. Leo Mendes, principal character of Fergusson's *The Conquest of Don Pedro* (1954), similarly succeeds in all that he attempts. However, at the end of the book he loses his wife to a friend and leaves the sleepy southern New Mexico town of Don Pedro, which he had conquered from its Spanish *patrón,* to wander again. The parallels between Ballard, the pioneer-turned-landed-gentleman, and Mendes, the itinerant Jewish peddler-turned-aristocrat, are many; among them are their successfully concluded, muted conflicts with the Spanish establishment.

Far less muted are the conflicts related in a number of other novels. The antagonisms between Anglo and Hispanic are relatively innocent, if intense, in Richard Bradford's *Red Sky at Morning* (1968), which tells of an adolescent's awakening in a small town in northern New Mexico, probably a caricature of Santa Fe. The story is usually humorous, usually believable, and sympathetic to each of the groups portrayed. Bradford's *So Far from Heaven* (1973), though in parts as amusing as the author's first book, presents Anglo-Chicano conflict in a sharper focus.

From an earlier era come the historical facts behind Harvey Fergusson's *Wolf Song* (1927), a story of the individualistic, iconoclastic American mountain men, the first arrivals from the north and east into New Mexico. The interactions of Indian, Spanish, and American groups are presented as a sympathetic commentary on the differences among cultures. *Wolf Song* is the first volume of a trilogy, *Followers of the Sun* (1936), in which Fergusson traces the history of conflict between the races in New Mexico. Ruth Laughlin's *The Wind Leaves No Shadow* (1948) is centered around a depiction of Doña María Gertrudis Barcelo, "La Tules." The book brings to life the intrigue and the maneuvering that took place in Santa Fe in the years surrounding the U.S.–Mexican War, as Americans, following the mountain men's advance guard, flooded into the capital. La Tules, a famous figure in the gambling dens of the Santa Fe plaza, played an important part in the tactical negotiations between Mexicans and Americans.

Willa Cather's *Death Comes for the Archbishop* (1927) is deservedly the best-known novel of the Southwest. It follows the life of a young French priest, Father Latour, from his native land to frontier Ohio and then to Santa Fe as the Southwest's first Catholic bishop and its first non-Spanish priest. It is no secret that Latour is a thinly disguised Jean Baptiste Lamy, first bishop of New Mexico. Like the actual bishop, Latour combats what he perceives to be the slothful apostasy of the Spanish clergy of New Mexico, earning the lasting enmity of the priests and some of their followers. The calm drive that animated the priest illuminates this beautifully written historical novel.

Calm is not a word that can be used in describing the works of John Nichols about life in northern New Mexico. The frenetic activity of *The Milagro Beanfield War* (1974) and *The Magic Journey* (1978) centers on the attempts of Spanish villagers in the Sangre de Cristos to maintain their traditions, their land, and their livelihoods in the face of Anglo-led conspiracies. The conspirators, in Nichols' view, are ably abetted by government agents and by certain high-flying Spanish turncoats in the pillage and destruction of the beautiful mountain valleys. Both novels display much authentic detail but tend toward excess in portraying the rapacity of the plotters. An earlier story with a very similar theme is Frank Waters's *People of the Valley* (1941), also set in the Sangre de Cristo Mountains. More mystical and literary in style, it nevertheless also describes the destruction of a valley and a village by an Anglo dam-building scheme. The people of the valley are led to a new life in a hidden paradise by a legendary, aging goatherd, considered by her people both as leader and as *bruja*, or witch. Its excesses are less bothersome than those of Nichols.

Norman Zollinger's *Riders to Cibola* (1977) combines Hispanic-Anglo encounters with a chronicle encompassing the rise and fall of ranching as a way of life in south central New Mexico. The hero, a Mexican *vaquero* of remarkable skill and accomplishment, is followed through a life filled with exaggerated virtue and unexcelled villainy. The story is nonetheless gripping and revealing of its late-nineteenth-century milieu. Set in another ranching area west across the Rio Grande, Conrad Richter's *The Sea of Grass* (1937) similarly catalogues the slow decline of a wealthy ranching family. The enmity between rancher and homesteading farmer is one major theme; the other involves the lovely, elegant Lutie

North Valley, *Mike Gallegos.*

Brewton, true mistress of the ranch and of her husband, the dour rancher on the grass-covered plain.

Richter's and Zollinger's novels are part of the often-maligned rancher-cowboy genre. The ill repute of the mass-produced formula "Western" of such writers as Zane Grey and Louis L'Amour need not taint all novels on "Western" subjects. New Mexico has produced several writers who brought talent and knowledge to books of this class. Eugene Manlove Rhodes, who rode the range of the Bar Cross Ranch along the Jornada del Muerto as a young man, later turned his experiences into a great many short stories and several novels. In all, Rhodes's wit and clear style are apparent, as is his recognition of the cattleman's ideals of independence and open-handedness.

Emerson Hough, who practiced law in the boom town of White Oaks and dabbled there in journalism, wrote of other parts of the United States as well, but his *Heart's Desire* (1903) remains among New Mexico's best Westerns. Even though written at an early date, *Heart's Desire* takes up a theme often discussed in later literature, the tendency of

Anglo-Americans to overcivilize the wilderness and fence in its mystery. The book describes conflict between lovers of the beauty of New Mexico's plains and an Eastern syndicate that would exploit its mineral wealth.

From his log cabin in a sweeping valley north of Cuba, New Mexico, William Eastlake wrote novels that were at times Westerns, at times commentary on Indian-Anglo relationships. *The Bronc People* (1958) and *Go in Beauty* (1956) are among Eastlake's best treatments of conflict and its resolution in the Checkerboard area of northwestern New Mexico.

Two of the novels of Edward Abbey, perhaps best known for his anarchical *Monkey Wrench Gang* (1975), are set in New Mexico. Both *The Brave Cowboy* (1956) and *Fire on the Mountain* (1962), like the *Monkey Wrench Gang*, Eastlake's *Dancers in the Scalp House* (1975) and Hough's *Heart's Desire*, concern attempts of individuals to stand up against the juggernaut of "progress," law, and big government. Both novels are set in a cowboy-ranching context, and both share in a wealth of detail and humor and not a little bitterness.

Less glamorous than the cattleman or cowboy, the New Mexico farmer has less often been the subject of fiction. John L. Sinclair's *In Time of Harvest* (1943) treats of dryland bean farming in the Estancia Valley in the lean years between the world wars. Paul Horgan, in *Mainline West* (1936) and *Far From Cibola* (1938), has written of the intermittent hopefulness and pathos of the same area at about the same time, an era when farming the broad valley, always difficult, became impossible. Horgan's considerable fictional output also includes several books centered around life in early-twentieth-century Albuquerque. *The Common Heart* (1942) and *The Thin Mountain Air* (1977) both display the city at the time of its rapid expansion as a health- and breath-giving oasis in the desert.

A very different sort of book about New Mexico life is that found in the series of novels by Lars Lawrence, a pseudonym for Phillip Stevenson. The four novels, of which *Morning, Noon and Night* (1954) is best-known, have a muckraking sarcasm about them. Reata, a thinly disguised Gallup, is home of the action, which consists of gun battles and legal battles between members of the corrupt, incestuous establishment and the heroic but undermanned group of poor, striking miners. Like Upton Sinclair, Lawrence/Stevenson uses hyperbole to expose the venality of the uncaring town structure. Also like Sinclair, he is given to overstatement that stretches credulity.

A miscellany of other works describes life in nineteenth- and early twentieth-century New Mexico, portraying Anglo pioneers who made their way by other means than farming, stockraising, or city occupations. Among these, Paul Horgan's *A Distant Trumpet* (1960), while set primarily in Arizona, describes in considerable detail life in the forts of southern Arizona and New Mexico, which existed to control the raiding Apaches.

Edith Warner is the subject both of fiction, in Frank Waters' *The Woman at Otowi Crossing* (1966), and documentary, in Peggy Pond Church's *The House at Otowi Bridge.* In both, the disparate worlds of San Ildefonso Pueblo and Los Alamos's wartime Manhattan Project meet in the remarkable teahouse owner in her spot of calm and comfort between the two.

D. H. Lawrence, perhaps the best-known writer to be associated with New Mexico, lived near Taos for several years but did not use the state as a backdrop for any of his novels. He commented, however, in essay and in letter, that the experience of New Mexico "liberated me from the present era of civilization, the great era of material and mechanical development," freeing him to write. And Conrad Richter, reporting on the forces of the Southwest that encouraged him and others to write of the region, stated:

> In my own case, the most helpful thing I found in writing of the Southwest was the Southwest itself, its brilliant light, wide spaces, mountains and deserts, particularly its great sky and finer air, which lift a man into a more rarefied and stimulating world

Rio Grande at Otowi Crossing, *Betty Lilienthal.*

of life and thought, inhabited by certain lesser gods called Southwesterners, a portion of which world filters through the porous human mind to come out scattered through a mortal's manuscript.

As long as New Mexico and the Southwest retain their uniqueness, the regional fiction of the area will remain as rich and varied as it has become.

Nonfiction About New Mexico

Unlike the novel, which aims first to entertain and perhaps offers information in the process, nonfiction generally shifts the balance in the opposite direction. The overweening importance in fiction of writing style and storytelling excellence may be subjugated in some forms of nonfiction, especially nonfiction of the informative sort that is found on other lists of references within this book. However, many works of nonfiction are genuine literature and belong in this discussion. New Mexico has, for example, stimulated numerous authors to make personal statements and interpretations of New Mexico's history, its cultures, and its landscape. Some of the earliest interpretive histories and descriptive works have been described, those of Cabeza de Baca, of Villagrá, of Pike, and of Magoffin, to name a few.

The late nineteenth and the first half of the twentieth century brought many writers to join the artists' colonies of Santa Fe and Taos or to strike out on their own. Charles F. Lummis and Mary Austin both arrived in New Mexico from the East in the late 1880s, primed to experience and describe all that the territory had to offer. Lummis wrote personal impressions that welded history with descriptive prose. *Mesa, Canyon and Pueblo* (1925) and *The Land of Poco Tiempo* (1893) have been most popular, the latter recently reprinted and frequently cited. A similar book, also intensely personal, is Austin's *Land of Little Rain* (1903), a romantic description of the land and people of New Mexico. In her autobiography, *Earth Horizon* (1932), Austin describes herself as a philosopher and mystic, one who could equally well describe the essence of a people, of a tree, or of a poem.

Mabel Dodge Luhan, Oliver La Farge, and Harvey Fergusson are three other writers whose autobiographies tell much about their surroundings as well as about themselves. Luhan was a central figure in the artists' Taos of the 1920s; her memoir *Edge of the Taos Desert* (1932) describes the aesthetes following their muses and D. H. Lawrence in and about Taos. La Farge's *Raw Material* (1945) comments on the author's awakening to the realities of the American Indian, a realization not present at the time he wrote his first novel, *Laughing Boy*, in 1929. Harvey Fergusson's autobiography, *Home in the West: An Inquiry into My Origins* (1944), recounts his life as a child and young man in growing Albuquerque. In addition to this work and his numerous novels, Fergusson wrote *Rio Grande* (1933), a vividly expressed personal statement regarding the conflict between the modern and the aboriginal, displayed nowhere better than in the crucible of the valley of the great river.

Erna Fergusson, sister of Harvey, devoted her considerable chronicling skills to the description of the land of her origin. Her *Albuquerque* (1947) is made to appear a place of many fascinations, though the town described bears little resemblance to the present-day city. Fergusson's *New Mexico: A Pageant of Three Peoples* (1964) is a selective history, brightly written. *Murder and Mystery in New Mexico* (1948) claims neither to be complete nor objective, but presents gripping glimpses of violence in the author's native state.

Libraries specializing in the Southwest (such as the Gallup and Albuquerque city libraries and the Anderson and Coronado rooms of the Zimmerman Library at the University of New Mexico) contain numerous monographs of regional New Mexico history, usually written by residents of the areas described. Well-documented histories of towns as dissimilar as Jal, Madrid, and Los Alamos are on the shelves.

As well-written history, the works of two non–New Mexicans, Hubert Howe Bancroft and Herbert E. Bolton, are of considerable importance. Bancroft's *History of New Mexico and Arizona* (1889) is still a valuable reference source. Bolton, whose articulate books describe many parts of the United States, brings his careful scholarship to bear on New Mexico in *Spanish Exploration in the Southwest* (1916) and *Coronado, Knight of Pueblo and Plains* (1949). More recent historian-writers have produced a number of New Mexico histories of literary note. Cleve Hallenbeck's *Land of the Conquistadores* (1950) and Marc Simmons's *New Mexico* (1977) are two engrossing, highly readable single-volume histories of the Land of Enchantment. Frank D. Reeve's *New Mexico, Land of Many Cultures* (1969) is another closely written introductory narrative.

C. L. Sonnichsen specializes in nonfictional works about the plains country of New Mexico and Texas, written in exciting prose. *Alias Billy the Kid* (1955) and *Tularosa: Last of the Frontier West* (1960) are accounts of feuds and cattle wars in central New Mexico; *Cowboys and Cattle Kings* (1950) is a more sober description and history of cattle ranching on the high plains. The same lifestyle is documented in a different literary form, that of recorded interviews with an elderly rancher, Joe Pankey, in Jack Parsons and Michael Earney's *Land and Cattle* (1978). The narrative is accompanied by a spectacular collection of old and new photographs depicting aspects of ranching. As armed conflict plays a part in these accounts of life on the plains, so it also takes an important role in William Keleher's well-written *Maxwell Land Grant* (1942) and *Turmoil in New Mexico* (1951). The former describes the same huge grant of beautiful land in northeastern New Mexico as that portrayed in Harvey Fergusson's *Grant of Kingdom; Turmoil* focuses on periods, such as the Mexican War and the Civil War, when events in New Mexico became more tumultous than usual.

Marc Simmons has written a number of carefully researched historical works about parts of New Mexico; *Spanish Government in New Mexico* (1968) is a scholarly work, contrasting with the leisurely descriptions and evocative photographs of the peoples of New Mexico in his *People of the Sun* (1979). Simmons's definitive history of Albuquerque, profusely illustrated and well-written, appeared in 1982. John Kessell is another scholar. His books *Kiva, Cross and Crown* (1979) and *The Missions of New Mexico Since 1776* (1979), written for the occasion of the United States bicentennial, are goldmines of information about the long period of Spanish rule.

Known equally for his novels and for his historical works about the Southwest, Paul Horgan has won two Pulitzer Prizes for history. The two award-winning books are *Great River: The Rio Grande in North American History* (1954), a gripping account of events that have taken place along the river's course and determined the history of New Mexico and Texas, and *Lamy of Santa Fe* (1975), which traces the life of the pioneering, strong-willed cleric from his native Auvergne to and through his many eventful years in Santa Fe. Also worthy of note as works of history are Horgan's *The Centuries of Santa Fe* (1956) and *Conquistadores in North American History* (1963).

Like Horgan's *Great River*, Laura Gilpin's *The Rio Grande, River of Destiny* (1949) follows the course of the life-giving stream from its Colorado sources to its Texas delta. The book is, however, description rather than history, woven around the author's unexcelled photographs. An earlier alliance of beautiful photography and well-written narrative is Edgar L. Hewett's and Wayne L. Mauzy's *Landmarks of*

New Mexico (1940), while a more modern combination, this time in vivid color, is *New Mexico* (1974) by David Muench and Tony Hillerman.

A different sort of description is found in Ross Calvin's *Sky Determines* (1934, revised in 1965). Calvin catalogues many interesting facts in support of his contention that sky (or climate, or water) determines the history and destiny of New Mexico. W. Eugene Hollon develops a similar thesis for a wider area of the dry Southwest in *The Great American Desert, Then and Now* (1966).

Bibliographic Works

Books about Indian life, plants, birds, music, and New Mexico geology, among other subjects, are listed elsewhere in this volume, but books about books must be mentioned here. Although there are no bibliographic works dealing solely with New Mexico, there are several that catalogue the literature of the Southwest. *Southwest Heritage* by Mabel Major and T. M. Pearce, the latter an emeritus professor of English at the University of New Mexico, is an exhaustive yet highly readable bibliography in the form of written narrative divided by subject matter. It covers a Southwest defined as Arkansas, Texas, Oklahoma, New Mexico, and Arizona. Other bibliographers define the Southwest differently and offer more personal, less thoroughgoing lists and narratives. Walter S. Campbell's *The Book*

Lover's Southwest (1955) is a categorized list with brief annotations. Lawrence Clark Powell's *Southwest Book Trails* (1963) and *Tales from the Heartland* (1974) make excellent reading, with longer descriptions of the books and their effects on the author of the compilations. J. Frank Dobie's *Guide to Life and Literature of the Southwest* (1952) is also a subjective look at those regional books that have captivated the author, who has also published many books of nonfiction largely about Texan subjects.

Poetry

New Mexico's poetry, like other literary genres, reflects the character of the people who inhabit this state and the experiences that have shaped their lives and the life of New Mexico. New Mexican poetry reflects the character of the land whose geography and climate, variable, sometimes harsh, always dramatic, have so powerfully affected the people living here. Each of the major groups inhabiting the state has contributed to the body of poetry created here, although with significant differences among the types of poetry created by them.

In its oldest and most universal form, poetry is an oral phenomenon, articulating in pure sound and rhythm the images, myths, and experiences of a community. The religious ceremonies and songs of the Indian tribes of New Mexico represent this oral tradition of poetry as a vital contemporary manifestation of community life. In a real sense, they also resemble modern poetry in its quintessential form: pure images, phrased in sequence to suggest relationships of idea or emotion. Likewise, the traditional songs of the Hispanic New Mexican community embody the universal emotions, experiences, and beliefs of its people. Couched in the more familiar rhymes and rhythms of conventional musical form, these songs are integral expressions of the life of Hispanic New Mexico, at once creating and created by its community.

Much of New Mexico's written poetry has been produced in the twentieth century by settlers or visitors to the state, rather than by natives. However, the state's body of written poetry continues to reflect the concerns and lifestyle of the area. Poetry written during the first half of the century, in keeping with the oral poetic tradition of the state, articulates a preoccupation with the land and community life of the people who inhabit it. John Gould Fletcher, Alice Corbin Henderson, and Witter Bynner are poets whose work, although not exclusively New Mexican in origin or subject matter, deals to some extent with life in New Mexico. Furthermore, the work of several major poets of the early twentieth century responds to their experiences in the state. D. H. Lawrence, the sometime resident of Taos, is the most notable of these. Other important poets who visited and wrote about New Mexico during this period are Carl Sandburg, Vachel Lindsay, Edna St. Vincent Millay, and Robinson Jeffers.

More recent New Mexican poetry, although continuing to evoke the community and regional aspects of its earlier verse, manifests an increasingly modern preoccupation with the personal, psychological experiences of the writer. Such poetry may use the land or culture of the region as a metaphor for the experience or emotion that is the true subject matter of the poem. Verse forms are increasingly, although not universally, based on images and the organic rhythms of language.

Fray Angelico Chavez, Rudolfo A. Anaya, and Jimmie Santiago Baca are Hispanic writers of New Mexican poetry. Among the numerous Indian writers currently acclaimed as poets, the best known New Mexicans are probably Simon Ortiz and Leslie Marmon Silko. Winfield Townley Scott and Keith Wilson are Anglo poets who have written in New Mexico during this half of the century. Robert Creeley, a major American poet who has spent much of his writing life in New Mexico, writes introspective, personal poetry that evokes the feelings of a particularized, fleeting moment in experience.

Creeley's poetry itself is a major indication of the expansion of New Mexico's poetic vision. Since the late 1960s, the state has attracted a group of sophisticated, experimental poets who have settled, written, read, and taught here. The continued presence of such poets as Larry Goodell and Gene Frumkin marks the extension of the state's written poetic voice beyond the parochial aspects of regionalism to the universal community.

Children's Books

While New Mexico often appears foreign to adults from other parts of the United States, the state can be still more fascinating to their children, since many of its characteristics are outside of their experience. Thus books for children on New Mexico's unique features have been many. Animals, often popular with children, have figured prominently in New Mexico's juvenile books. Indians too seem to be perennially popular and so are heavily represented as subjects of many types of young people's literature.

Several stories of prehistoric Indians expose children to the wondrous accomplishments of the Anasazi (a Navajo word meaning "the old ones") of northwestern New Mexico. R. B. Marcus's and Mary Elting's *The Secret Story of Tse Bonito* (1968) gives a great deal of information in highly readable form about the well-developed society of Chaco Canyon. Lucille Mulcahy's *Natoto* (1960) is also set in Chaco's ancient apartment complexes; unlike *The Secret Story*, it is a novel, concerning romance and conflict with an invading tribe of nomadic Indians. A similar story line appears in Mulcahy's *Dark Arrow* (1953), but it is set in cliffdwellings like those in present-day Bandelier National Monument.

In children's literature the distinctions between fact and fiction are often blurred. Many works of fiction aim to instruct through the painting of well-designed background; much children's history and biography is fictionalized to the extent of inventing enlivening dialogue. This is certainly the case with books describing the way of life of Southwest Indian tribes. One of the first descriptions of Indian

life by an Indian is *I Am a Pueblo Indian Girl* by E-Yeh-Shure, better-known as the famous Santa Clara potter Blue Corn. Her simple prose is accompanied by beautiful drawings by Indian artists. Ann Nolan Clark, a prolific writer of children's books and teacher and companion of Pueblo children for many years, describes the cycle of time in Pueblo ceremonial and secular life in *Circle of the Seasons* (1970). Her earlier work, *In My Mother's House* (1941), describes Pueblo life from the vantage point of an Indian child.

Ann Nolan Clark has also written of Navajo customs in *Little Navajo Bluebird* (1943). This book and Natachee Scott Momaday's *Owl in the Cedar Tree* (1965) are novels with extensive action, but both give careful details of Navajo hogan living, ceremonials, and ambivalent relationships with Anglos, and both portray the fear of Navajo families for the authorities who come to drag away their children to government boarding schools. The ambivalence is omitted from Flora Hood's book for younger readers, *Living in Navajoland* (1970). The simple, poetic nature of the work is seen in the closing lines, "Navajoland is a picture book land. The sky is wide and high and blue. Mountains look like monuments of purple and gold in the sun, sometimes red as blood." The monuments, the sky, Navajo hogans, and Navajo dress shine in magnificent color photographs in Jack Crowder's *Stephannie and the Coyote* (1970), which features an uncomplicated English text accompanied by its Navajo translation.

Indian life is portrayed in several novels for older readers. Scott O'Dell, a well-known children's author, has absorbed and portrayed much of Navajo life of the last century in *Sing Down the Moon* (1970), a story of the Navajos' capture in the Canyon de Chelly in 1864 and of the harrowing Long Walk through central New Mexico that followed. Lucille Mulcahy's *Magic Fingers* (1958) combines the mystery of a missing governor's cane with the story of a young Isleta Pueblo girl learning the art of pottery making. Lois Duncan has written several novels set in Albuquerque. Her *Season of the Two-Heart* (1964) unites modern teenage romance with a consideration of the differences separating Pueblo Indians and Anglo-Americans.

Several biographies of Indian leaders have appeared. Geronimo, warrior chief of the hard-pressed Apaches of the 1880s, is described in biographical works for children by Edgar Wyatt (1952) and Ralph Moody (1958). A series, *The Story of an American Indian*, consisting of monographs describing important Indian figures from throughout the United States has included several works on New Mexicans. Annie Wauneka, Navajo leader in the movement to obtain better health care for her people, is described in one volume (1972). Four Pueblo Indian artists are subjects of other volumes in the series—María Martínez, San Ildefonso potter; Pablita Velarde, painter, and Michael Naranjo, sculptor, both of Santa Clara Pueblo; and Daisy Hooee Nampeyo, Hopi potter living in Zuni (1973–77). The biographies are well-told and are couched in a comprehensive discussion of the tribes from which each subject comes. Another fine biography of María Martínez, that by Alice Marriott (1948), makes pleasant reading for older children or adults.

Tales of the origin of humanity and of man's relationship with nature and instructive homilies for children are all parts of the folklore of the Southwest, both Indian and Spanish. Among writers who have recorded Indian folk tales for children, Elizabeth Willis DeHuff was an early collector who published *Taytay's Tales* in 1922. More recent collections include the multi-authored *Grandfather Stories of the Navajo* and *Coyote Tales*, already mentioned. Gerald McDermott's *Arrow to the Sun* (1974) is a beautiful book, combining striking drawings with the retelling of a single Pueblo myth. Advocacy of Taos Pueblo's claim to Blue Lake (a claim finally recognized by Congress in 1970) is a major theme of Nancy Wood's *Hollering Sun* (1972). After an introductory history of the Taos people and their appeal for the restoration of their sacred lands, the remainder of the book presents short segments of Taos philosophy, accompanied by fine photography of the Taos Reservation and its people.

Spanish folklore has been less commonly recorded for children. Camilla Campbell's *Star Mountain* (1946) retells Mexican and New Mexican folk stories. Proverbs and nursery rhymes collected among the Spanish-speaking populace of the Rio Grande valley have been assembled with attractive line drawings as *Mother Goose on the Rio Grande* (1973) by Frances Alexander. The short selections are presented in Spanish with approximate, rhyming English translations. Also in both Spanish and English, Dolores Gonzáles's *Canciones y Juegos de Nuevo México* (1974) incorporates a Federal Writers' Project collection of children's songs and games, originally published in Spanish.

Appealing to children's love of adventure, a number of books have been written about the early Spanish exploration of the Southwest. Betty Baker, in *Walk in the World's Rim* (1965), invents an Indian boy who accompanies Cabeza de Vaca and his black slave, Esteban, on their monumental journey. The boy idolizes the slave, learning of the Moor's longing for freedom. John Upton Terrell's *Search for the Seven Cities* (1970) carries the story further, from the first reports of gold in the north through Coronado's vain search for Cibola to the arrival in New Mexico of the first Spanish colonists under Oñate. A good biography of the gentleman conquistador Don Diego de Vargas is that of Rosemary Buchanan (1963).

Spanish village life in New Mexico, foreign

to most American children, is well-described in a number of stories. Flora Hood's *One Luminaria for Antonio* (1966) is a charming Christmas story telling of a poor child's earnest preparations to properly receive the Christ Child in the traditional Spanish village manner. Peggy Pond Church's *The Burro of Angelitos* (1936), also for young children, is a child-and-animal story set in a mountain village in northern New Mexico. Ann Nolan Clark also writes of village customs in her story of the adoption of a small French boy by a young Spanish couple in her *Paco's Miracle* (1962). For older children, Lucille Mulcahy's *Pita* (1954) and *The Blue Marshmallow Mountains* (1959) combine description of mountain life and problems with the more universal theme of adolescent romance. Another popular theme of adolescence, coming of age in an adult society, is dealt with in Joseph Krumgold's classic *And Now Miguel*, the story of a teenager attaining adult status in a Spanish sheep-raising community.

The last of the three groups to arrive in the Southwest, the Anglo-Americans have fewer dissimilarities to others in the American mainstream than the Spanish and Indians. Perhaps for this reason, fewer books have been written about New Mexico's Anglos. Holling C. Holling's *A Tree in the Trail* (1942) employs the unusual literary device of following the occurrences that accompany the birth, growth, and senescence of a majestic cottonwood growing along the Santa Fe Trail, beginning in Indian times and continuing into the days of heavy Anglo use of the trail. Beautiful color drawings and short explantory notes on equipment and utensils of the times and on history make this a unique book. It must be noted that the tree grew in Kansas, but the events described did not respect state lines.

The cowboy has long been a children's favorite. *Cimarron Kid* (1973) by Paul Conklin describes in words and fine photographs the life of a child growing up on a cattle spread in the eastern foothills of the Sangre de Cristos. An informal style like the drawl of a cowboy sets the tone for Glen Rounds's informative *The Cowboy Trade* (1972). Lela and Rufus Waltrip's collection of brief biographies *Cowboys and Cattlemen* (1967) begins with "the first cowboy," a *vaquero* who accompanied Coronado's expedition, and includes some other New Mexicans, such as Lincoln's John S. Chisum and the cowboy-author Gene Rhodes.

Animals are, of course, central to the life of the cowboy, and are also of great importance to many children. Many of the books already described concern children's affectionate regard for animals. Several writers, such as Ernest Thompson Seton in *Wild Animals I Have Known* (1898), Mary Austin in *The Trail Book* (1918), and Lloyd Tireman in his Mesaland Series (1943–47), have essentially written careful children's biographies of animals living in the Southwest. *Hawk, I'm Your Brother* (1976), the story of a boy's admiration for the power and freedom of the hawk, is very different; as in her many other children's books, the author, Byrd Baylor, creates a poetic vision of the Southwest.

For general information on New Mexico, a child can refer to George and Mildred Fitzpatrick's *New Mexico for Young People* (1965), a very inclusive yet readable introduction to the state. Jack Schaefer, in *New Mexico* (1967), injects more of his personality into describing what he finds unique and exciting about New Mexico. The book, less inclusive of detail than the Fitzpatricks' but more enjoyable to read, concentrates many of its chapters on the people of the state and their history.

It is clear that, like literature written for adults, children's literature about New Mexico is remarkable for its richness. While much of the adult fiction and nonfiction is concerned with relationships among the races, most of the juvenile books restrict themselves to description rather than analysis of interracial contact. In either case, the unique heritage of the Land of Enchantment and its people has been the material for exploitation by writers since long before New Mexico became a state.

tours

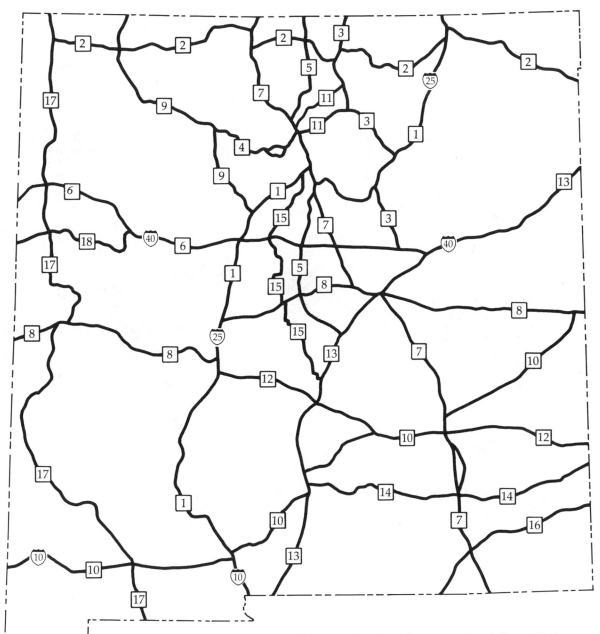

The numbers on this map are those assigned to the tours that follow. Highway numbers and other features are shown on the maps preceding each tour, and detailed maps of each quadrant of the state appear on the following pages. The north-south tours are odd-numbered; the east-west tours are even-numbered.

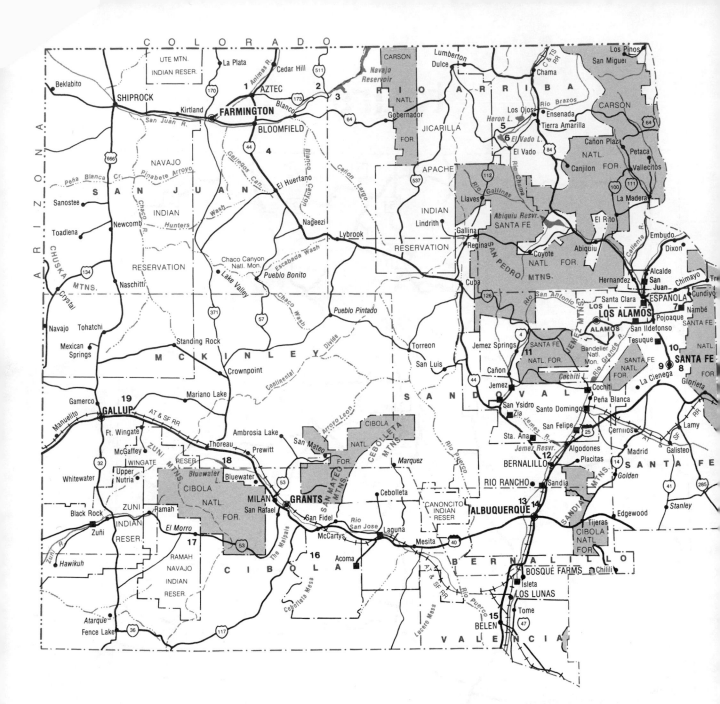

Names of Abandoned Towns Given in Italics.

■ Pueblo Settlement

1. Aztec Ruins National Monument
2. Navajo Lake (Pine) State Park
3. Navajo Lake (Sims) State Park
4. Angel Peak National Recreation Site
5. Heron Lake State Park
6. El Vado Lake State Park
7. Santa Cruz Lake National Recreation Site
8. Old Palace of the Governors State Monument
9. Santa Fe River State Park
10. Hyde Memorial State Park
11. Jemez State Monument
12. Coronado State Monument and Park
13. Indian Petroglyph State Park
14. Rio Grande Nature Center State Park
15. Belen Valley State Park
16. El Malpais National Recreation Site
17. El Morro National Monument
18. Bluewater Lake State Park
19. Red Rock State Park

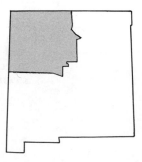

192

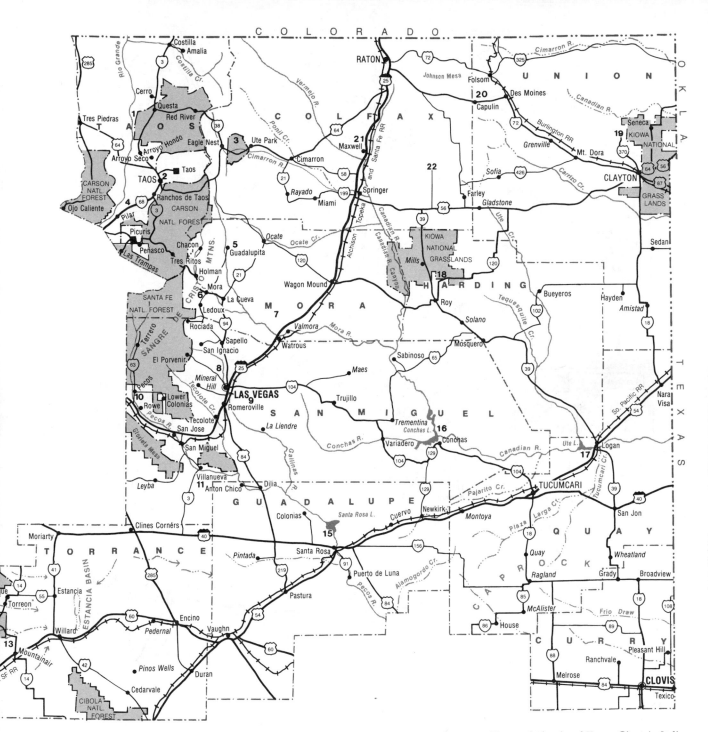

■ Pueblo Settlement

Names of Abandoned Towns Given in Italics.

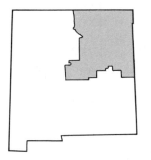

1. Rio Grande Gorge National Recreation Site
2. Kit Carson State Park
3. Cimarron Canyon State Park
4. Rio Grande Gorge State Park
5. Coyote Creek State Park
6. Morphy Lake State Park
7. Fort Union National Monument
8. Storrie Lake State Park
9. Las Vegas National Wildlife Refuge

10. Pecos National Monument
11. Villanueva State Park
12. Manzano Mountain State Park
13. Quarai at Salinas National Monument
14. Abo at Salinas National Monument
15. Santa Rosa Lake State Park
16. Conchas Lake State Park
17. Ute Lake State Park
18. Chicosa Lake State Park
19. Clayton Lake State Park

20. Capulin Mountain National Monument
21. Maxwell National Wildlife Refuge
22. Dorsey Mansion State Monument

193

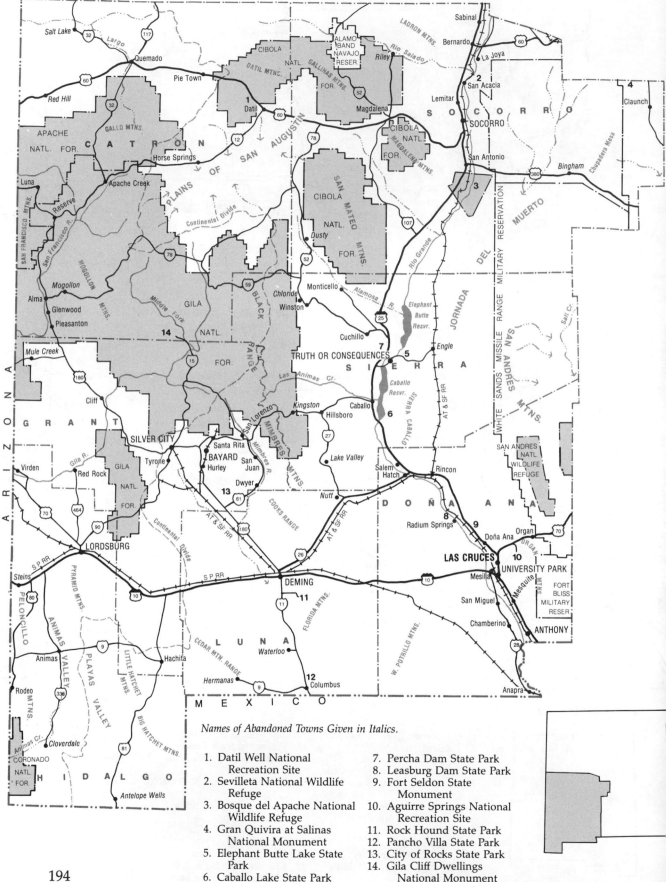

Names of Abandoned Towns Given in Italics.

1. Datil Well National Recreation Site
2. Sevilleta National Wildlife Refuge
3. Bosque del Apache National Wildlife Refuge
4. Gran Quivira at Salinas National Monument
5. Elephant Butte Lake State Park
6. Caballo Lake State Park
7. Percha Dam State Park
8. Leasburg Dam State Park
9. Fort Seldon State Monument
10. Aguirre Springs National Recreation Site
11. Rock Hound State Park
12. Pancho Villa State Park
13. City of Rocks State Park
14. Gila Cliff Dwellings National Monument

194

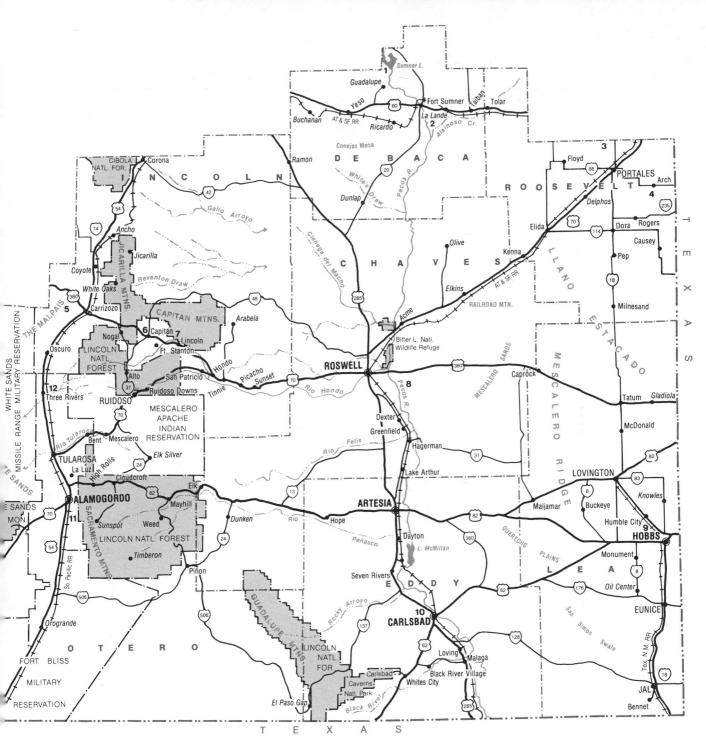

Names of Abandoned Towns Given in Italics.

1. Sumner Lake State Park
2. Fort Sumner State Monument
3. Oasis State Park
4. Grulla National Wildlife Refuge
5. Valley of Fires State Park
6. Smokey Bear State Park
7. Lincoln State Monument
8. Bottomless Lakes State Park
9. Harry McAdams State Park
10. Living Desert State Park
11. Oliver Lee State Park
12. Three Rivers Petroglyph National Recreation Site

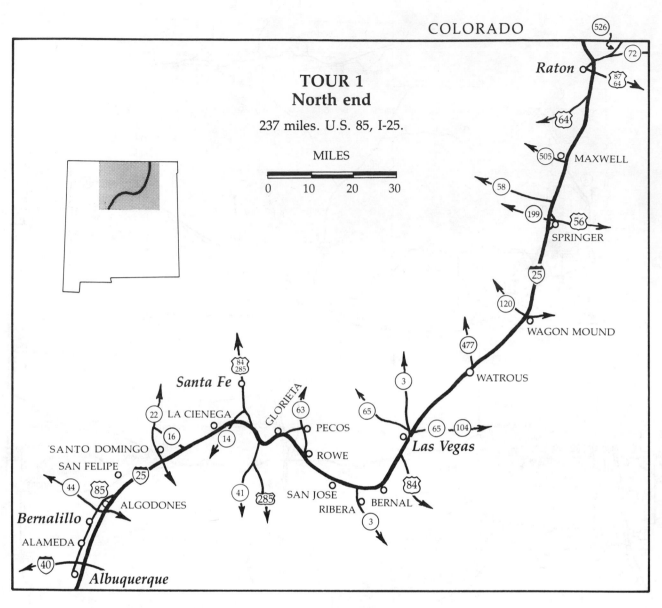

COLORADO

TOUR 1
North end

237 miles. U.S. 85, I-25.

MILES

0   10   20   30

Raton

526

72

87
64

64

505   MAXWELL

58

199   56

SPRINGER

25

120

WAGON MOUND

477

3   WATROUS

Santa Fe

84
285

22   LA CIENEGA

16

14

SANTO DOMINGO

SAN FELIPE

44   85

25

ALGODONES

Bernalillo

ALAMEDA

40

Albuquerque

GLORIETA

63

PECOS

ROWE

41   285

SAN JOSE

RIBERA

BERNAL

84

3

65

65   104

Las Vegas

See page 260 for southern half of tour one.

tour one

Colorado Border • **Raton** • **Las Vegas** • **Santa Fe** • **Albuquerque** • **Socorro** •
Las Cruces • *Texas Border*

To travelers familiar with the Rocky Mountain states, the path I-25 follows is a sensible and natural one, linking El Paso (and central Mexico), Albuquerque, and Santa Fe with Denver, Cheyenne, and intermediate cities. Old U.S. 85 used this path and, at least in New Mexico, so did the Santa Fe Railroad. For most of New Mexico's history, however, the route of Tour 1 was actually two very different roads; and although both had Santa Fe as their destination, the purposes and characters of the two had little in common. and, since one road led to Mexico and the other to the United States, were often antagonistic.

The ancient trail from Mexico City to Santa Fe, called the Camino Real (meaning "royal road," or, in effect, a road that Santa Fe officials paid some attention to) or the Chihuahua Trail, had been New Mexico's link with the glory and authority of Mexico City (and Spain, and the outside world) since the Rodríguez-Chamuscado Expedition of 1581. These sixteen-hundred-odd miles were intimately connected with the hopes and fears of the inhabitants of New Mexico, of all Spain's provinces in the New World the most remote and difficult of access. Except for the cutoff across the Jornada del Muerto and the last stretch between Santo Domingo and Santa Fe, the New Mexico part of this trail was a river road that stayed as close as possible to the towns and pueblos along the Rio Grande.

Running northeast from Santa Fe, the Santa Fe Trail, on the other hand, connected New Mexico with the United States. It began to be used in the 1820s and was improved for freight caravans in the 1860s. Traders of French, American, and other nationalities endured the hardships and dangers of the trip from Independence, Missouri, via Council Bluffs, Iowa, and Fort Dodge, Kansas, to Santa Fe in pursuit of the enormous profits that U.S. merchandise could bring. The Mexican government discouraged this trade from time to time, and in 1844 prohibited it altogether. When the trade became legal again after the U.S.-Mexican War in 1846, working on the huge wagon trains was a way for New Mexicans of all ages to get their first experience of city lights and spending money, and their first look at the railroads moving west.

The Santa Fe Railroad secured its right of way over Raton Pass in 1878 and in three years united the two old trails, making both obsolete. The tracks followed the Santa Fe Trail, but in a sense never quite reached their destination. On account of steep grades, Santa Fe was left off the main line, connected by an eighteen-mile shuttle to Lamy. Cities like Las Vegas, Belen, and San Marcial came to be as crucial to the railroad as the territorial capital. The new line immediately became not only the principal north-south route but also—since the point of the Santa Fe's coming through New Mexico in the first place was to reach California—an important east-west route as well.

Today, I-25 has taken over from old U.S. 85 and enters New Mexico north of Raton. Lava caps the Raton Mountains, as it does many of the volcanic cones and mesas that can be seen from RATON PASS, 2 mi. Travelers have taken advantage of this pass since prehistoric times. Its modern history began when William Becknell crossed it in 1821 on his trip that inaugurated the Santa Fe Trail. U.S. forces under Stephen Kearny marched through the pass in 1846. After the American occupation, "Uncle" Dick Wootton received authorization to operate a toll road and blasted twenty-seven miles of wagon road across the mountains. He built a ranch house with a tollgate at the pass and let wagons proceed after receiving $1.50 from each driver. The Barlow, Sanderson, and Company Stagecoach Line then began using the toll road. The first locomotive entered New Mexico along essentially the same route in December 1878. The 7,622-foot elevation of Raton Pass is the highest point on the Santa Fe Railroad.

Eight miles south of the pass, stages stopped for water and feed at the Willow Springs Ranch. Otero, the railroad's construction camp, sprang up five miles south of Willow Springs. When the Santa Fe decided to locate a division point in 1880, it changed the site's name from Willow Springs to Raton ("mouse"), moved buildings from Otero, and created a town of three thousand souls. With the railroad shops and nearby coal fields, RATON, 5 mi. (alt. 6,600, pop. 8,242), called itself "the Pittsburgh of the West." Stores, restaurants, hotels, and a newspaper appeared. Brick and stone buildings gradually replaced flimsy wooden ones. The importance of coal and the railroad to the city's economy declined greatly in the mid-twentieth century, but the town then began to benefit from skiing, sightseeing, hunting, fishing, and camping in the surrounding mountains.

Raton itself hosts annual rodeos, arts and crafts fairs, and ethnic fairs and offers horse racing at La Mesa Park on weekends and holidays, May through September. Popular side trips from Raton include Sugarite Ski Basin, Sugarite Canyon (hiking, camping, and picnicking), and Lake Maloya, all northeast via N.M. 526; Johnson Mesa and Folsom State Monument, east via N.M. 72; Capulin Mountain National Monument (described in Tour 2) east on U.S. 64/87; and the Maxwell National Wildlife Refuge and Philmont Scout Ranch, southwest via U.S. 64.

The Raton Downtown Historical District consists of five blocks just west of the railroad tracks along First, Second, and Third streets. Included within the district are several buildings dating from early railroad days: the Gambles Department Store, once Louis Blair's Home Ranch Saloon; the Fred Bruggeman Building, previously Marchiondo's Store; and the Gem Saloon, the Roth Building, and the sandstone Palace Hotel, built in 1896 and now restored and operated by the Tinnie Mercantile Company as a restaurant.

The tour then proceeds south on I-25 and intersects U.S. 64/87 East, 6 mi., the highway to Capulin Mountain and Clayton (on Tour 2). At ten miles, U.S. 64 branches off to the southwest towards Cimarron and Taos and across the Rio Grande Gorge to Farmington.

MAXWELL, 30 mi. (founded in the late 1880s), was the shipping center for the Maxwell Land and Irrigation Company. In 1841, Governor Manuel Armijo issued a huge grant of land to Charles Beaubien, a French trapper, and Guadalupe Miranda of Taos. The property then passed to Lucien Maxwell, Beaubien's son-in-law, and became known as the Maxwell

Land Grant. The largest single landholding in the Western Hemisphere, the grant contained 1.7 million acres of minerals, timber, pasture, and great natural beauty. Maxwell oversaw the cattle and sheep operations on his estate and also introduced extensive beet cultivation. After Maxwell's death, this wealth passed among a series of Eastern, British, and Dutch speculative companies. Although the grant was approved by the U.S. Congress and later confirmed by the Supreme Court, its validity has long been a subject of controversy.

SPRINGER, 44 mi. (alt. 5,891, pop. 1,361), originated in 1879 with the coming of the railroad. It took its name from two Springer brothers: Charles, a rancher near Cimarron, and Frank, a lawyer for the Maxwell Land Grant. Since Springer had its railroad before the eastern plains and Texas Panhandle regions, it served for a decade as a railhead for cattle driven from over a wide area. The Colfax County seat was located here until 1897, when Springer lost out to Raton in a bitter political fight over the issue.

Springer continues to host the Colfax County Fair and Rodeo, an event held in early September in which tugs of war, tractor pulling, cow-chip-throwing contests, and one- to six-mile foot races have been attractions. An old church houses the Santa Fe Trail Museum, which features a livery stable in addition to many other reminders of methods and conditions of travel in the past century. U.S. 56, from Clayton and the Oklahoma Panhandle, ends here. It skirts the Kiowa National Grasslands and provides indirect access to the Dorsey Mansion (on Tour 2), Chicosa Lake State Park (off N.M. 39), and Mills Canyon of the Canadian River.

Melvin Mills, Mills Canyon's most re-nowned inhabitant, seems to have been personally involved in every business venture, political feud, and financial intrigue in northeastern New Mexico almost from his birth in 1845 to his death as a broken old man in Springer. One of his more admirable achievements was the ten-mile-long, fourteen-thousand-tree fruit empire he created in the canyon of the Canadian River, twenty-five miles southeast of Springer. In the section of the canyon now named for him, where the ancient river had cut a gorge a thousand feet into the red sandstone, he blasted underground irrigation channels; built cisterns, bunkhouses, a cider press, and a stone mansion; set out orchards of peaches (with fruit the size of large grapefruit), apples, pears, cherries, plums, apricots, walnuts, almonds, and chestnuts; and cultivated grapes, tomatoes, cantaloupes, cabbages, and other vegetables besides. Most of the produce was hauled up to Springer and shipped to the Harvey Houses all along the Santa Fe Railroad. A diastrous flood in 1904 ruined this enterprise. Over the years, Mills practiced law in Elizabethtown, ran a stage line between Kansas and Fort Union, served in the territorial legislature, and figured in the Colfax County War as an attorney for the Maxwell Land Grant interests. During that war he was implicated in the murder of Thomas Tolby, a Methodist circuit preacher who sided with a group of small landholders against the land grant corporation. He also built a three-story, thirty-two-room mansion on the banks of the Cimarron River in Springer, became district attorney for north-central and northeastern New Mexico, opposed New Mexico statehood in favor of his plan for a separate state with a capital in Raton that would be free of "Mexican domina-

Fort Union, *Harvey Caplin.*

tion," acquired farms, ranches, feedlots, and stores, and served as legal representative for the Santa Fe Railroad. But by the time of his death in 1925, his one-time partner, Thomas B. Catron, had foreclosed on his mansion in Springer. The man feared in several counties, whose stationery had been inscribed "District Attorney, Etc.," begged to be allowed to die on a cot in his beloved old home.

WAGON MOUND, 69 mi., occupies a spot noted for the intermingling and clashing of plains and mountain Indians, Santa Fe Trail travelers, dry farmers, and cattle and sheep ranchers. Here the Cimarron Cutoff rejoined the main Santa Fe Trail. Traders willing to face a drier crossing and greater danger of hostilities with Comanches and Apaches turned south at Fort Dodge, Kansas, and used the route that present U.S. 56 approximates, crossing the Canadian River just above Mills

Canyon. This way they often beat traders following the main mountain route via Bent's Fort and Trinidad, in Colorado, and Raton.

During the Taos Rebellion (1847), Spanish-speaking farmers in this area allied with Apache, Ute, and Cheyenne people against the newly established Americans and attacked wagon trains here on the Santa Fe Trail. Originally both the town and nearby hill were named for Santa Clara. This village shipped farm and orchard products from the nearby Canadian valley over the Santa Fe Trail. The rock formation resembling a covered wagon suggested a new name, Wagon Mound, adopted in 1859. Flooding in the valley killed the fruit industry, but Wagon Mound continued for some time as a corn and bean farming center. One local merchant did a brisk business setting up beginners in sheep ranching and then foreclosing when the market slumped. Although beans are no longer raised here, Wagon Mound still celebrates its annual Labor Day event, Bean Day.

At Wagon Mound the tour intersects N.M. 120, a partly paved road that wanders like a sleepwalker over the northeastern plains from Grenville to Black Lake.

Samuel B. Watrous maintained a trading station just to the north of the present town of WATROUS, 90 mi. (alt. 6,185, pop. 416). He helped supply Fort Union's needs, and his place served as a rendezvous for soldiers stationed there. From the junction of N.M. 477 it is an eight-mile drive up to Fort Union National Monument. Established in 1851 to guard both forks of the Santa Fe Trail, Fort Union gained importance when Colonel E. V. Sumner moved army headquarters here from Fort Marcy in Santa Fe. Its soldiers participated in the open war with the Jicarilla Apaches in 1854. In 1862, General Sibley, former commander of the post, led a Confederate army north from El Paso to capture Fort Union. He was defeated by Colorado regulars and New Mexico volunteers in battles at Pigeon's Creek and Apache Canyon in Glorieta Pass near Santa Fe (see pages 34–35). With the increased traffic after the Civil War, the fort became the principal supply depot for other posts and the largest military bastion in the Southwest, employing some four hundred civilians in addition to the troops it headquartered. The railroad ended wagon train travel, the fort's reason for existence, and the army abandoned it in 1890.

A national monument since 1956, Fort Union has undergone stabilization and restoration efforts in order to preserve something of its original form. Markers and charts within the ruin locate and explain the various components of the old fort and give some idea of what daily life here must have been like.

The railroad town of Watrous inherited its location at the junction of the Sapello and Mora rivers from an older Hispanic settlement called Rio La Junta. Nearby Anasazi masonry ruins date from the 1200s, while some of the early Sapello sites indicate habitation nine thousand years ago. Farming, ranching, lumbering, and rail shipping have been the businesses of Watrous for over a century.

From Watrous to Las Vegas, a distance of twenty-one miles, I-25 continues to parallel the Santa Fe Trail, picking up the historic path again at the outskirts of Las Vegas.

LAS VEGAS, ("the meadows"), 111 mi. (alt. 6,391, pop. 14,278), sits at the edge of the eastern plains, the green slopes of the Sangre de Cristo ("blood of Christ") Mountains at its back and the Gallinas River running through its center. Las Vegas has long been a town of contrasts: a Hispanic stronghold since its nineteenth-century founding; a wild frontier outpost; an important way station on both the Santa Fe Trail and the Santa Fe Railroad; and, at the turn of the century, one of the most important trading and financial centers in New Mexico.

For decades Las Vegas was actually two cities, East Las Vegas and West Las Vegas. An aging Spanish plaza anchored the west side of the community, while sturdy Midwestern-style buildings and a proper town square gave focus to the east side. Las Vegas is now primarily a service town, the county seat of San Miguel County, home of New Mexico State

Hospital and New Mexico Highlands University, and the center for regional shopping and business activities. New Mexico history and architecture enthusiasts have long considered the town a remarkable repository of the state's past; within its environs are several state cultural districts and many national designated historic districts.

The plains around Las Vegas were home for many centuries to nomadic Indians, especially the Comanches, who considered the grassy land their hunting domain long after Hispanic settlers entered the area in the early 1800s to establish farms and ranches. In 1821, Luis Maria C de Baca petitioned the Mexican government for a grant along the Gallinas River for himself and his seventeen sons, but repeated Indian attacks and other problems prevented the C de Baca men from ever occupying the land. In 1835, thirty-five settlers came from a village to the west, San Miguel del Vado, and established the Las Vegas Land Grant where the present town of Las Vegas now stands. Meanwhile, William Becknell had brought the first packtrain from Missouri to Santa Fe in 1821, opening up United States–Mexican trade and pioneering the Santa Fe Trail. Las Vegas soon became the Mexican port-of-entry on the historic thoroughfare.

As a condition of their grant, the original thirty-five settlers had been directed by the Mexican governor to construct a plaza, and it quickly became the center of life in Nuestra Señora de los Dolores de Las Vegas ("our lady of sorrows of the meadows"), as the town was first called. The plaza was a meeting and marketplace and the loading area for the caravans that plied the Santa Fe Trail, crossing the Gallinas River on Bridge Street as they passed through town. Las Vegas was a thriving trading center. It served the hundreds of stagecoaches and wagon trains that rumbled across the prairies and mountains to link Missouri with Santa Fe, Mexico, and California. Ruts of the trail were still visible south of town in the 1970s, more than one hundred years after the last wagon train had passed by.

It was in the Las Vegas plaza that General

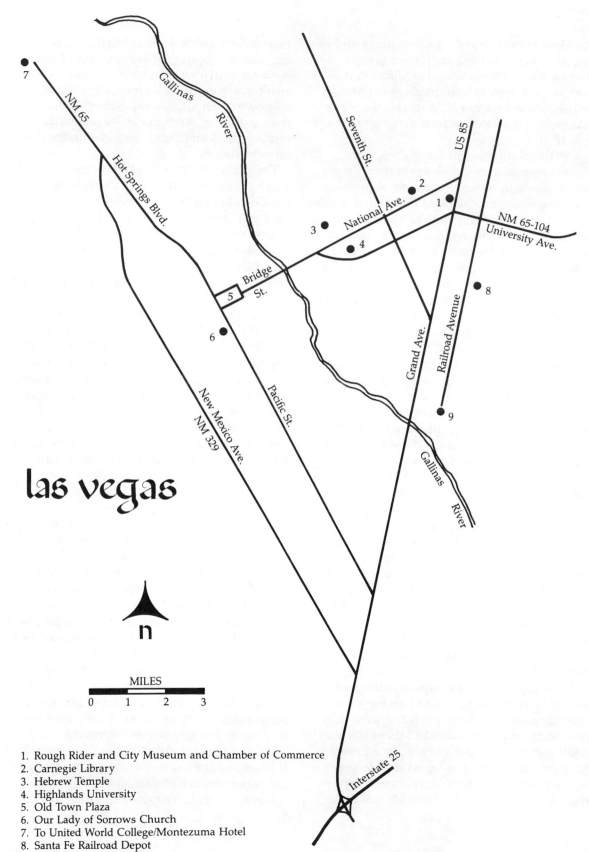

las vegas

MILES

0   1   2   3

1. Rough Rider and City Museum and Chamber of Commerce
2. Carnegie Library
3. Hebrew Temple
4. Highlands University
5. Old Town Plaza
6. Our Lady of Sorrows Church
7. To United World College/Montezuma Hotel
8. Santa Fe Railroad Depot
9. Old Santa Fe RR Roundhouse

Stephen Watts Kearny read his proclamation when he claimed New Mexico as United States territory in 1846, declaring, "We are your protectors, not your conquerors." Research has established that Kearny read the document from the rooftop of 210–218 Plaza, now a private residence facing Old Town Plaza. Until Fort Union was built in 1851 to protect the Santa Fe Trail from Indian raids, Las Vegas was the seat of military operations for the region.

The town played a minor role in the Civil War in New Mexico. In early 1862, Union governor Henry Connelly moved his territorial headquarters from Santa Fe to Las Vegas. Federal troops from Fort Union, meanwhile, were moving through Las Vegas to meet Confederate forces advancing from Santa Fe, which they had occupied. The two sides met in battle near Glorieta Pass in March 1862.

Many consider that the prime of Las Vegas's one-hundred-fifty-year history comprised the decades during which it was a stopping place and staging area for the Santa Fe Trail. Others contend that the arrival of the Santa Fe Railroad in the 1870s began a boom era for the prairie-mountain town, a period that lasted well into the twentieth century. More than one million dollars per year were pumped into the Las Vegas region by the railroad and its attendant businesses. Construction, which had earlier been limited to simple adobe buildings, became grander as the railroad ferried in materials from the East familiar to the region's newcomers. Although frequent fires destroyed many of the railroad age's first buildings, a number of brick, stone, and adobe territorial masterpieces have survived.

Many of Las Vegas's architectural jewels, some in disrepair, others renovated and on national and state historic preservation lists, are located close to the Gallinas River. Interesting buildings in the Old Town Plaza area just west of the river include many adobe structures which predate the railroad's arrival. Some of the adobe compounds could have been lifted out of any colonial neighborhood in Latin America. Their fronts are close to the

streets, but the doors and windows are locked and silent. Family activity is centered around interior courtyards hidden from passers-by. While a number of private residences have fallen into ruin, a few public buildings remain used and cherished. Some are anonymous but others better known. Casa Redonda on Pacific Street was a boys' school, founded by the Jesuits in 1874. The Jesuits also started a college nearby that later moved to Colorado to become Regis College. Another mission school, founded by the Presbyterians in the 1870s, began life next door to the lovely old Presbyterian Mission on Chavez Street and later relocated to Albuquerque as the Menaul School. Our Lady of Sorrows Catholic Church on National Avenue was completed in 1880 and once housed an organ considered the "best in the West" at its inaugural concert.

Close by the old New Mexico–style neighborhoods are buildings of solid brick, stone, and adobe whose antecedents came straight from the Midwest. Around Old Town Plaza are the renovated Plaza Hotel, erected in 1881–82 as a retreat for consumptives (it was the leading hotel in Las Vegas until the Castañeda was built next to the railroad station in 1898); the sandstone First National Bank, which served the community from 1888 to 1922; and the stone Charles Ilfeld Company headquarters, built in 1882 and 1890. A gem of a building, the Louis C. Ilfeld Law Office at 220 North Plaza, was erected in 1921, serving as a law office and general headquarters for Ilfeld until his death in 1950. The handsome red brick building was the first landmark in the plaza area to be restored to its original state. It now houses a bookstore specializing in Western literature. On the other side of the river, the Carnegie Library, the Newman Club (in a building that was the first synagogue in New Mexico), and St. Paul's Episcopal Church are among the many Las Vegas buildings considered worthy of historic preservation.

The prosperity of the railroad era of the 1880s was not confined to the town of Las Vegas. Accounts of the day report wagon trains stretching from Las Vegas to Romeroville, al-

As a railroad shipping point and trade center, Las Vegas also became headquarters for a number of famous New Mexico business firms. The Charles Ilfeld Company, founded in 1867, had branches throughout the region and became one of the leading retail establishments in the New Mexico Territory. The Ilfeld family was powerful; some say that the railroad was built east of town because Ilfeld, who owned property close to the center of the old part of Las Vegas, had asked so exorbitant a sum for his land that Santa Fe officials were forced to build on the outskirts.

In 1900 Las Vegas was the largest town in New Mexico, with a colorful population that included Hispanics, Italians, Chinese, Russians, and Germans. Broadway casts played in the stone opera house, built in 1896 and since destroyed. Teddy Roosevelt's Roughriders, forty percent of whom were from New Mexico, made Las Vegas their headquarters, and the famous Roughrider himself appeared in town for their 1899 reunion. The year 1912 saw the world championship Jack Johnson–Jim Flynn heavyweight bout staged in Las Vegas. A few years later, Tom Mix and other cinema stars made motion pictures in a studio located at the south end of town. In 1917 the Santa Fe Railroad built one of Las Vegas's landmarks, a thirty-four-stall roundhouse in which, during three eight-hour daily shifts, 380 mechanics worked on the line's steam locomotives. The roundhouse, located at the southern outskirts of town, is presently abandoned and dilapidated.

Its heydays behind it, Las Vegas is now a solid, quiet community, although ethnic and racial problems occasionally surface. Its major employer is New Mexico Highlands University, created by the territorial legislature in 1893 as New Mexico Normal University. When it chose the nation's first Hispanic college president in 1971, Highlands carved a special niche for itself in the academic world. The small, two-thousand-student university now has a reputation for building strong programs in the area of minority (especially Hispanic) education. Highlands also provides cultural

most five miles away. The Baca brothers were said to be running half a million sheep in the area. The largest wool-shipping point around, Las Vegas kept its three scouring mills busy. Fifty wagons a day waited outside the flour mills to have wheat ground. From Anton Chico to Mora, wagons filled the old trails and hauled goods to and from the bustling train depot.

While the 1870s signaled boom times for Las Vegas, they also ushered in more than a decade of violence and bloodshed. Bandits and cutthroats with names like Scarface Charlie and Web-fingered Billy roamed the streets. Frontier legends on both sides of the law— Billy the Kid, Doc Holliday, Bat Masterson, and Wyatt Earp—passed through town. Vigilantes patrolled Las Vegas, taking the law into their own hands at night by hanging outlaws, as many as three at a time, on the windmill derrick that stood on the plaza. The Gorras Blancas ("white hoods") first made their appearance in 1889 to protest, with wirecutters and matches, the fencing of community lands on the Las Vegas Grant. The Gorras Blancas, a primarily Hispanic organization, has reappeared in the area periodically, especially in times of interethnic strife.

and sports events for Las Vegans, and fielded nationally ranked football teams in the 1960s. Las Vegas's other major institution, New Mexico State Hospital, began life in 1897 as St. Anthony's Hospital, a tuberculosis sanatorium run by the Sisters of Charity.

Travelers who come to Las Vegas via railroad, I-25, or any of the many roads that lead into the community will find tourist accommodations along the major thoroughfares on the outskirts of town. The Chamber of Commerce offers detailed brochures as well as a self-guided historic tour of Las Vegas and the surrounding area. The Roughriders Memorial and City Museum, housed next to the Chamber of Commerce on Grand Avenue, contains displays of the Cuban Campaign and pioneer artifacts.

Hot Springs outside Las Vegas, *Mike Gallegos.*

Any visit to Las Vegas should include the five-mile trip to the old Montezuma Hotel. Hot Springs Boulevard (N.M. 65) first passes the state hospital and then the turnoff to Camp Luna, the World War II training camp for the 200th Coastal Artillery, many of whose members died on Bataan. Camp Luna now houses a technical school and various federally sponsored programs. The road passes a string of old villages and reaches the community of Montezuma, long overshadowed by the Montezuma Hotel and Las Vegas Hot Springs across the river.

Members of the earliest of the Pecos Pueblos came to these thermal springs as early as A.D. 800. They shared the spot with neighboring Pueblos, each group taking a turn at soaking in the water that is 110 to 140 degrees in temperature. Later, the early Hispanic settlers journeyed out from Las Vegas and the small communities around it to cure their illnesses, to bathe, and to bury themselves up to their necks in the warm mud. When New Mexico became a U.S. territory in 1846, federal military authorities chose the site for a military hospital. Wagon trains on the Santa Fe Trail often detoured to Las Vegas Hot Springs to give their passengers a chance for a warm soak.

In 1879, the Santa Fe Railroad bought the hot springs property, constructed a hotel and bath house, and connected the spa it called Montezuma to Las Vegas with a spur line up the canyon. The hotel burned down in 1880, so the Santa Fe built another, even grander structure, complete with chandeliers and the first electric lights in New Mexico. When it burned, the Santa Fe went to work again and in 1888 created the multistoried, turreted, balconied, 343-room castle dubbed the Phoenix but always known as the Montezuma. It is that massive building, on every state and historic landmark list, that visitors see today.

For many years, the Montezuma was the crown jewel of the Santa Fe system. Its guests included presidents Theodore Roosevelt, Ulysses S Grant, and Rutherford Hayes. Kaiser Wilhelm and Japan's emperor Hirohito also slept there, as did moneyed Easterners, army generals, and

thousands of train travelers. Guests rode horses in the surrounding mountains, fished for trout, gambled in the casino or in the oak-paneled card rooms, and enjoyed the rituals of the thermal baths. As many as a thousand bathers per day could be accommodated in the various pools and tubs containing mineral-laden water or oozing black mud.

The Montezuma's decline began with the opening of the El Tovar Hotel at the Grand Canyon. The Santa Fe Railroad closed the Montezuma in 1903, donating the abandoned property to the YMCA in 1912. In 1920, New Mexico Baptists bought the Montezuma and began their struggle to create Montezuma College. Its first class graduated in 1925, but the Baptists never succeeded in winning the battle to establish the college as a financially secure institution. The New Mexico Baptists lost over three hundred thousand dollars in the venture before selling the property to the Archdiocese of Santa Fe in 1937 for less than twenty thousand dollars. The diocese ran a seminary here for Mexican priests until 1972. For the next decade, the Montezuma was abandoned, left to crumble and decay.

In 1981, the Armand Hammer Foundation purchased the historic 110-acre site from the archdiocese for ten million dollars. The foundation spent millions more renovating both the Montezuma castle and the adjacent, smaller Stone Hotel for use as the American branch of the United World College, an international system of secondary and postsecondary schools.

Beyond the Montezuma complex, N.M. 65 follows the Gallinas River to a large pond formed by a dam. Here Las Vegans fish and picnic in the summer and ice-skate in the winter. Steep palisades on either side of the river become more spectacular as the road climbs along the mountainside. Sheer cliffs, some with caves carved into their sides, sport fir trees on their ledges. The road drops quickly into the village of Gallinas, now primarily a summer resort. Vacation cabins, resorts, youth camps, and dude ranches have replaced many of the working ranches and small farms that once filled the canyon floors. A few miles beyond Gallinas, at El Porvenir ("the future"), the road ends at the base of Hermit's Peak.

El Porvenir was established by Margarito Baca in 1905. A four-mile trail to the summit of Hermit's Peak begins here. At the top of the high mesa, hikers may find the remains of Penitente crosses and the spring which the hermit, it is said, caused to flow. The nearby mountains and forests are now part of Santa Fe National Forest, and numerous campgrounds have been built in the canyons and on the mesas. Some are accessible by car and offer camping facilities; others are more primitive. All are open only from late spring through early fall. Signs on N.M. 65 direct the traveler to them.

I-25 departs from Las Vegas in a direct manner, bypassing much of the city's commercial center. The road passes swiftly through the outskirts of Las Vegas, shunning even historic Romeroville (Tour 3) and remnants of the Santa Fe Trail.

The trip from Las Vegas to Santa Fe via I-25 (or the old highway, U.S. 85, which parallels the interstate much of the way) is about sixty miles long and follows almost exactly the paths of both the old Santa Fe Trail and the Santa Fe Railroad. Historic crossings, monuments, and battlefields are accessible either from the main highway or from the many side roads which intersect it. The scenery changes gradually, beginning with the flat, high plains around Las Vegas and moving into mesas, canyons, and the foothills of the Sangre de Cristos. Glorieta Mesa, a high, wide tableland covered with dark fir trees, hovers above the road for nearly half its distance. The highway follows the Pecos River from San Miguel del Vado to the Pecos exit. Soon after the mountains and the mesa have closed in on the highway, the road cuts through Glorieta Pass, and Santa Fe appears.

TECOLOTE, 120 mi., takes its name from the Mexican Nahuatl word for owl. Another in the chain of Hispanic settlements that thrived during the decades of the Santa Fe Trail, Tecolote was established in 1824 by Salvador Montoya. It served as a U.S. Army supply post during the Indian Wars from 1850 to 1860. Close by the highway, which bypasses Tecolote's small white church and its plaza, ruts from the Santa Fe Trail are sometimes visible.

West of Tecolote, just before the turnoff to Bernal, travelers can see Starvation Peak, at whose summit, it is said, one hundred twenty Spanish colonists sought refuge from attacking Indians. The colonists, men, women, and children, starved to death. A Penitente cross long marked the site.

BERNAL, 126 mi., is named for the Bernal family whose ancestors included Juan Griego, a Spaniard who came to New Mexico with Oñate in 1598. Griego married Pascuala Bernal, and their sons chose either the Bernal or the Griego name. Bernal was the first stage stop on the route between Las Vegas and Santa Fe. Its stone and adobe church, the Capilla de Santa Rita de Casia, was built in 1916. It has three belfries and one wonderful old bell.

SIDE TOUR

About seven miles west of Bernal, I-25 crosses the Pecos River, 132 mi. A small road, N.M. 3, comes up from the south, following the Pecos as explorers—Coronado, Espejo, Castaño de Sosa, and many others—did for centuries. Travelers can take N.M. 3 to visit two interesting towns, San Miguel del Vado and Villanueva. There is also a state park about thirteen miles to the south.

N.M. 3 crosses the Santa Fe Railroad tracks at RIBERA ("shore, banks"), a small settlement established by the Ribera family of Santa Fe. The Riberas (often spelled "Riveras") were also among the founders of SAN MIGUEL DEL VADO or BADO, three miles down the road. The wagon trains of the Santa Fe Trail crossed the Pecos River here, making it one of the most important sites on the historic path.

San Miguel, a national historic district, is another New Mexico village whose prominence is now attested chiefly in history books. One remaining link to its important past is its church, an immense, handsome, twin-towered edifice with rock walls three feet thick and twenty feet high. Built in 1805–6, it displays silver donated by parishioners. The church and its missions up and down the Pecos River valley were served for more than thirty years by Padre José Leyba, who is buried, along with other prominent citizens, beneath the church's floor.

Among those who populated the village were *genízaros*, Indians from various tribal

backgrounds who had assumed Catholicism and Spanish names and customs. They mixed with Hispanics, who formally founded the village in 1794 with a grant made by Governor Fernando de Chacón to Lorenzo Márquez and his fifty-one followers. By 1830 the village was a customs-collecting point on the Santa Fe Trail. In 1835, with their *alcalde*'s (mayor's) blessing, a group of thirty-five San Miguel residents trekked north and founded Las Vegas. Texans who unsuccessfully raided New Mexico in 1841 were jailed in the village for a time. The namesake of San Miguel County, it once boasted a courthouse. At its peak, when the Santa Fe Trail was a busy highway and wagons splashed across the Pecos here, the town had a population of a thousand people. The importance of San Miguel del Vado diminished with the arrival of the Santa Fe Railroad in the late 1870s; as traffic on the wagon trail slowed, so did the pace of life in San Miguel.

N.M. 3 is a narrow, winding road as it follows the Pecos River southward. Hillsides crowd its two lanes, and curves should be met cautiously. About twelve miles from the interstate, travelers will come to VILLANUEVA. This is a hilltop town with shining, peaked tin roofs and sturdy stone walls that twist and wind along the bluffs above the Pecos.

Mariano Baros and José Felipe Madrid founded Villanueva at the dawn of the nineteenth century. They called their village Cuesta ("hilltop"), but when the U.S. Post Office came to town in 1890, it be-

came Villanueva, for more Villanuevas than Aragóns had signed the name-change petition.

In the middle of the town is a modest stone church that dates back to 1818. Village women have embroidered a splendid 265-foot tapestry that circles the interior walls of the church, telling the history of the community. It depicts the Indians who first lived here and Coronado and the other explorers who marched through the valley hundreds of years ago seeking gold and souls. There are scenes of a priest who was killed, of nuns arriving to teach school, of the construction of the church and the paving of the road. When the hanging was officially installed in 1976, the governor and the archbishop were brought to town in buggies and buckboards. The archbishop celebrated a folk mass in the church to dedicate the tapestry, and the whole town took part in a memorable fiesta with the honored guests. The church is often open. If not, a resident priest is usually available in the rectory next door; he will proudly show off his parishioners' work.

Just below town VILLANUEVA STATE PARK has been created along the steep cliffs and wide banks of the Pecos. It is a quiet park, with hiking and fishing the main activities offered. Camping accommodations are simple but sheltered and adequate. Food and gas are available in the village. The twenty-five-mile section of N.M. 3 leading south from the park to La Palma and I-40 is paved.

The mountains on the north and Glorieta Mesa on the south draw closer to each other and to I-25 as the Pecos River, which has paralleled the interstate since the N.M. 3 intersection, bears north toward its source in the mountains. N.M. 63 intersects I-25 at 148 mi., leading north to Pecos National Monument, the town of Pecos, and eventually to the Pecos Wilderness Area. To the left at the junction is ROWE, named in 1876 for a contractor on the Santa Fe Railroad. Rowe is noted as much for the gigantic stacks of firewood next to its homes as for the steep, high mesa which looms over the little settlement.

PECOS NATIONAL MONUMENT is about four miles from I-25 on N.M. 63. Most of the land between the interstate and the monument belongs to Forked Lightning Ranch, owned by Greer Garson, the actress. At the monument, visitors will see the ruins of a large eighteenth-century church and its adjacent *convento* (convent or priest's quarters). But this was also the home, from 1450 or earlier to 1838, of an important Towa-speaking pueblo, a group of skilled hunters, farmers, and builders.

The original Pecos settlers came to this valley from the north and west; they were joined by some Jemez Indians (also Towa-speaking) and other groups. A scattering of archaeological sites in the area indicates that once there were many outlying settlements. However, in the 1200s residents began to consolidate into large communities, so that by 1450 there was a large, multilevel village at Pecos. Apartments were four and five stories high. There were 660 rooms and twenty-two kivas. Villagers farmed (corn, squash, beans), foraged for wild plants, and hunted. They were also excellent traders, taking advantage of their location to exchange goods with the Pueblo Indians to the west and the Plains Indians to the east. They were small people—the women were under five feet tall—who dressed simply, the men wearing cotton blankets and skins, the women in one-shouldered dresses, turkey feather robes, and "many curious things," according to an early chronicler.

In 1540, Pecos tribal leaders went west to meet Coronado. They later brought part of his expedition to the plains in search of the illusive Quivira. Other Spanish explorers, including Espejo and Castaño de Sosa, also visited Pecos. Castaño de Sosa was met with hostility here, and although outnumbered five hundred to thirty-seven, he defeated the Indians, who then left the pueblo for a time. Castaño's descriptions of Pecos are excellent. He carefully detailed the apartmentlike dwellings, noting that there were no outside entrances on the ground floors. He was at pains to observe how rooms were entered—via ladders through hatches. He mentioned the bathing areas on either side of the complex and took note of the low wall that enclosed the compound, remarking on its simplicity.

Franciscan friars came to Pecos in the 1620s, building (with Indian labor) the 170-foot-long, 90-foot-wide Misión de Nuestra Señora de los Angeles de Porciuncula. Within the self-contained mission, the Franciscans nurtured gardens of flowers, fruit trees, and vegetables. There were weaving rooms, tanneries, classrooms, and a carpentery shop. They made wheat bread and kept goats, cows, horses, and sheep. The friars introduced metal implements and the method of making adobe bricks. They were not only going to convert the Indians to Catholicism, but to the Spanish way of life as well. The Indians were required to be-

SIDE TOUR

come baptized and to pay tributes of food, supplies, and labor.

In the 1680 Pueblo Revolt, the Pecos burned their mission church and joined in the attack on Santa Fe. They were reconquered quietly twelve years later, and built a new, smaller church. The 1700s saw the Pecos attacked repeatedly by the Comanches. Their Apache allies, the Jicarillas, who had lived close to the Pecos and had often left their women and children at the Pueblo during extended hunting trips, moved north. Continuing Comanche raids, the loss of their Apache friends, and smallpox epidemics and other diseases decimated the Pecos. By the end of the eighteenth century, Pecos Pueblo was so small that it was only a *visita* (mission), with no resident priest. Some of those who had learned Spanish crafts and had been baptized moved to the nearby villages of San Jose and San Miguel del Vado. The last baptism was held at Pecos in 1828. Ten years later the remaining residents, perhaps as few as seventeen in number, left the pueblo and joined their Towa-speaking brethren at Jemez Pueblo, where some Pecos traditions, including the Buffalo Dance, have survived.

Excavation of the Pecos ruins began in 1915. One of the early excavators at Pecos, Alfred V. Kidder, used his experiences there between 1914 and 1929 to demonstrate the continuity that cultures show through time. In 1965 the pueblo became a national monument. Archaeologists had puzzled for years over seventeenth-century accounts of the Pecos church. It was described by writers of the day as large, splendid, and unusual. The ruins the archaeologists were finding, however, were more modest. Experts theorized that those who wrote so grandly of the simple church were perhaps seeking to embellish their own importance. In 1967, however, extensive digging revealed the foundations of the original 1620 mission, described by a chronicler as a magnificent structure. The antecedents of the earlier mission, over which the later building had been placed, were more French than Spanish and fit the florid seventeenth-century descriptions.

Pecos National Monument is small and easier to explore than many Southwestern ruins. Visitors are given self-guiding brochures at the entrance. National Park personnel are also available to provide information and answer questions. There are no camping facilities at the monument, but a small, shaded picnic ground is located just outside the ruin walls. The monument is isolated and, on a typical day, quiet. The Pecos Mountains hunker behind it, their colors changing from deep green to blue to dark purple. The silver of a passenger train flashes in the distance. Its effect is jarring.

The village of PECOS is located less than two miles up N.M. 63 from the monument. Founded about 1700, and known as Levy until 1883, Pecos is a small Hispanic mountain village with a good school system and a respect for traditions; it is also the gateway to the Pecos portion of the Sangre de Cristos. A large church, St. Anthony's, sits in the middle of town, its back turned to the road, its front facing the river. An elaborate steeple tops its pitched tin roof. Visitors will find overnight accommodations, groceries, gas, and other amenities in Pecos and its environs. The Pecos ranger station, located on the highway, provides information about the mountains, camping facilities, and the wilderness area ahead. Those planning to enter the mountains should obtain permits at the station.

The mountains within this southern finger of the Sangre de Cristos have peaks as high as thirteen thousand feet. Hundreds of millions of years ago, the peaks were islands in an immense sea. As the sea subsided and various layers of deposits were laid down, the stage was set for the gradual movement of strata, creating

Lower Colonias, Pine, *Jeanne House.*

faults and uplifts and bringing rocks from different geologic ages to the surface, making uneven, canyon-studded mountains. Twelve thousand years ago, when much of the North American continent was under ice, the upper Pecos was covered by glaciers. The jagged peaks apparent now were formed by the constant scraping and moving of the glaciers. Visitors will notice a number of bare spots on the mountains. Some of these were caused by recent forest fires. The worst local blaze occurred in 1887, raging across the mountains from north of Santa Fe almost to Wagon Mound over a two-month period.

N.M. 63 goes north right up the Pecos valley, though in a curving path, passing small villages, resorts, summer camps, and campgrounds. The trails leading into the wilderness area, where motor travel is forbidden, begin about twenty miles north of the town of Pecos.

Campers and hikers will enjoy the trails leading to the tops of some of New Mexico's most famous peaks: Pecos Baldy, Truchas Peak, and Santa Fe Baldy. There are mountain lakes, meadows of wildflowers, abandoned mines and logging camps, waterfalls, and the headwaters of a number of rivers, including the Pecos and the Mora. Hikers should carry their own food and water, remembering to pack warm, all-weather clothing.

Continuing west on I-25, following the historic path used by Indians, trappers, traders, and wagon trains, the traveler will soon come to Glorieta Pass and Apache Canyon. It was near Apache Canyon in 1846 that Governor Manuel Armijo was to have defended his Mexican colony against U.S. forces led by General Stephen Kearny, who had already claimed the Pecos and Mora valleys and Las Vegas as American territory. Armijo, in a controversial decision, chose not to fight, fled south with his troops, and left New Mexico to the Americans.

During the Civil War, Glorieta Pass and Apache Canyon were the sites of a historic battle, "the Gettysburg of the West," which took place in late March 1862. Loyalist troops, composed of volunteers from Colorado and New Mexico and regulars from Fort Union, marched south from above Las Vegas. Confederate forces led by Brigadier General H. H. Sibley had set out from Fort Bliss, Texas, and had already defeated the North at Valverde the month before. Sibley and his men then marched through Albuquerque and on up to Santa Fe. Pushing east from Santa Fe, they met Union troops near Glorieta Pass. The first day's battle came to a draw. On the second day, however, a Colorado volunteer, Major John Chivington, and a New Mexican, Colonel Manuel Chaves, climbed the mountainside above the battle, entered the canyon, and burned Sibley's supplies. The Confederates could not fight without equipment, and so they fled south.

Glorieta Pass forms a wide, gradual path through the mountains. Its elevation, 7,400 feet, is lower than those of most comparable passes, making it a less hazardous route than many. A small village, GLORIETA ("bower" or "arbor"), 156 mi., sits off the road, overshadowed now by the large interstate highway and the Glorieta Baptist Conference Center. There are many ranches and outdoor recreation areas in the vicinity. U.S. 285, 165 mi., joins I-25 from the south here (Tour 5).

As the canyon opens up, revealing the broad Santa Fe Plateau below, the city of Santa Fe can be seen in the distance. Its suburbs begin as small farms and rural compounds, increasing in density and urbanity as the capital city nears. (See Tour 11 for Santa Fe.) I-25 bends south toward Albuquerque.

From Santa Fe, Tour 1 passes mountains, plains, farms, grazing land, and here and there a stream bed, usually dry. There are Indian pueblos to the southwest along the Rio Grande, interspersed with small Hispanic villages whose antecedents were, in some cases, stage-coach stops along the historic Camino Real between Santa Fe and Mexico.

I-25 follows the Rio Grande Valley from here south to the Texas border, below Las Cruces. Travelers will sometimes glimpse the river itself, but more often they can sense its presence by the curving stands of cottonwood and tamarisk trees that flank the historic waterway. The Rio Grande is now controlled to a large extent by a series of dams along its course through the state. However, even twentieth-century technology has not tamed the river, once also called El Rio Bravo Del Norte ("the wild, swollen, or imposing river of the north"). Spring runoffs can bring threats of floods along its banks, and those who have lived in the flood plain know just how angry, high, and dangerous the usually somnolent river can become.

Southwest of Santa Fe, I-25 crosses the Santa Fe Plateau. To the south are the Cerrillos hills, outlined against the larger Ortiz Mountains; both sets of mountains were once part of a north-south belt of volcanic centers. The Sandia ("watermelon") Mountains loom farther along the southern horizon, only a portion of their mass visible. Detached buttes stud the lava-capped mesas which slope toward the valley below. There are strips of fields all along the river here; most of them are now planted in alfalfa, although corn,

pinto beans, and chile and a wide variety of other vegetables are also grown for home and market consumption. Old apple orchards can also be seen tucked between the fields.

Shortly after leaving the southern limits of Santa Fe, I-25 reaches more open land, although housing and commercial developments seem inevitable along this heavily traveled highway. A racetrack, open in the warmer months of the year, can be seen on the west. The exit to the racetrack also provides a means for reaching the small village of La Cienega ("the marshland"), home of many New Mexico artists and site of El Rancho De Las Golondrinas ("the ranch of the swallows"), a living museum of Spanish colonial life.

The village of La Cienega sits along a narrow river valley and is actually divided into Upper La Cienega and Lower La Cienega. Homes and small farms perch along the road or nestle in the rough hillsides. The studios of potters, glassblowers, painters, and other artists have signs which indicate their hours of business. Most of them welcome visitors and have work for sale on their premises. There is a cooperative open house in La Cienega each year near Christmas.

As the dusty road dips and weaves back and forth across the little river, signs point the way to El Rancho de las Golondrinas. The historic ranch was the first stop south of Santa Fe along the Camino Real for eighteenth- and nineteenth-century travelers from Santa Fe. As the road ran then, it was fifteen miles south of the capital city, just a day's journey by horse.

For those coming up from the south, the large hacienda was their last stop en route, a place to spend the night before reaching Santa Fe. The ranch, owned by the Baca family for two hundred years, prospered as an hacienda and a *paraje* (inn, or place to rest) for much of that time.

Today El Rancho de las Golondrinas is leased by its present owners, the Paloheimo family, to the Colonial New Mexico Historical Foundation. The foundation runs spring and fall open houses that celebrate hacienda life as it was lived two hundred years ago in New Mexico. Not only have the original ranch buildings been restored, but the Paloheimos spent decades searching for chapels, irrigation devices, grist mills, tools, looms, and other colonial items, large and small, with which to recreate a New Mexico village.

Las Golondrinas, *Jeanette Williams.*

Acres of rolling land, divided by a small stream, have been planted in crops common in the late eighteenth century. During the open houses held at planting and harvest times, men and boys dressed in period clothing work the fields with horses and antique farm tools.

Scattered up and down the ranch's hills are the structures necessary to hacienda life: a village store; a chapel; a *torreón* (watchtower); sheep sheds; a molasses press; barns; wheelwright and blacksmith shops; two small, water-driven mills; even a winery. Little gardens and orchards, watered by an irrigation system that includes log flumes, are placed throughout the ranch. During the fall and spring open houses, all the parts of the ranch are working: an older woman tends a dye pot, a blacksmith shoes horses, a youngster works on a nineteenth-century loom. Visitors may sometimes purchase articles at the ranch. The atmosphere is one of fiesta, with dancing, singing, processions, and food. The ranch is open by reservation during other times of the year. There is an entrance fee. Those planning to visit the ranch can write to the State Tourist Office or the Colonial New Mexico Historical Foundation in Santa Fe for more information.

After the La Cienega exit, I-25 begins to climb, passing a large rest area on the east. The nearby Waldo exit leads only to the rest area. The exit was built, it is said, to serve a large land development which never came to fruition. A town of Waldo did exist once a few miles to the east; it was a watering stop along the Santa Fe Railroad tracks and also boasted a chemical plant that served the mines in nearby Cerrillos.

Shortly after the Waldo exit, the basalt-capped Santa Fe Plateau begins a sharp descent down LA BAJADA ("the descent"), 188 mi., the bane of travelers since the earliest days. Even today, if snow has recently fallen, care must be taken in ascending or descending the grade. The geologic formation of La Bajada is an interesting one. Lime soils and gravels top the black basalt volcanic flow on the crest of the hill. Highway cuts reveal various layers of rock that change color with each stratification; some of the layers date back to the Jurassic Age, one hundred forty-five million years ago.

About midway down La Bajada's incline is the N.M. 16 turnoff leading west to Cochiti Lake and Dam, the town of Cochiti Lake, and Cochiti Pueblo. A small village, now largely deserted, is hidden beneath the looming presence of the hill. This is the village of La Bajada; a sign along N.M. 16 points to the almost-forgotten scatter of adobe buildings. La Bajada was once a freight depot and trading center, and is a *visita* of the church in Peña Blanca.

N.M. 16 was recently built to provide access to the interstate for residents of the communities to the west. An earlier road, used for a number of years, was abruptly closed by Santo Domingo Pueblo because it traversed sacred ground. The highway department quickly negotiated for and built the present road.

Cochiti Dam, which can be seen from La Bajada as a long black strip against the brown and purple hues to the west, is a water storage and flood control project of the Corps of Engineers. The enormous earthen dam holds Rio Grande water, Cochiti Lake's level rising at peak flood time in the late spring. As summer progresses, water is released for agricultural and urban uses downstream. The construction of Cochiti Dam and Lake, which are on Cochiti Pueblo land, provided this region of New Mexico with a recreational resource. Fishermen and swimmers come from miles around to enjoy the lake, designated "no-wake," with marine speed limits enforced. Sailboats, from homemade kits to sleek catamarans, race across the choppy waters throughout the summer, their colorful sails a strange sight in this land of little water. A public camping and picnic area sits just above the lake.

The town of Cochiti Lake was built on land leased to developers by Cochiti Pueblo for ninety-nine years and is primarily a retirement and vacation commu-

nity. A golf course has recently been added to the existing recreational facilities. There is a small shopping center near the town.

Although most of the land in this area, aside from the housing development, is either reservation land or the property of the federal government, there are a few private landholdings. Jim Young, the founder of a well-known New York advertising agency, moved to Santa Fe in the 1930s and then started an apple farm in a sheltered canyon of the nearby Jemez Mountains. His apples, patented red and golden delicious varieties, are famous throughout the state. For years it has been an autumn ritual in central New Mexico to make the journey past Cochiti Lake, following the apple signs to the ranch, now run by the Dixon family. There, next to a small river, buyers and visitors wander around the busy packing shed, munching on crisp apples, sipping fresh cider, and buying bags of apples to take home.

In the area of Cochiti Lake and Cochiti Pueblo, a number of forest roads lead to campgrounds, hiking trails, and in some cases across the eastern slopes of the Jemez Mountains to N.M. 4 on the other side. Extreme care should be taken in traversing these unimproved dirt roads; they are bumpy and narrow at all times of the year, and especially hazardous any time that rain or snow has fallen. However, they also wind and dip through spectacular scenery—streams, meadows, Ponderosa pine trees, hidden hiking paths, and ghost towns. Trails off the roads are marked, as are some areas set aside for camping.

COCHITI PUEBLO, a Keresan-speaking pueblo, lies about one and one-half miles south of Cochiti Dam on N.M. 22, a paved road. From the highway a visitor first sees Cochiti's neighborhood of new homes sitting atop high scrubland overlooking the Rio Grande and pueblo fields below. The Sandia Mountains are to the south, the Sangre de Cristos to the north, and the foothills of the Jemez Mountains rise to the immediate west. Enormous water tanks at the edge of town have been painted like the drums for which Cochiti craftsmen are famous.

Cochiti's Spanish land grant of 1689 was confirmed by the United States government in 1858, surveyed for more than twenty-four thousand acres in 1859, and patented in 1864. Acreage was added in the 1930s by the Indian Lands Commission, and the present holdings of the Pueblo, including the land leased for the dam and lake project, are now over twenty-six thousand acres. These people have been living on their present site for over four hundred years. In 1598, Oñate gave them the name Cochiti, perhaps basing it on his perception of their Keresan name. Shortly after Oñate's visit, a mission church, San Buenaventura de Cochiti, was established, with Fray Juan de Rosas in charge. Little is known of the earliest mission history of Cochiti.

Even before the 1680 Pueblo Revolt, Cochiti resisted Spanish rule. In 1650 Cochiti and Jemez pueblos conspired with the Apaches to drive the Spanish intruders out. However, the plot was discovered by the Spanish governor, Hernando de Ugarte y La Concha, who hanged some of the leaders and placed others in slavery. When a successful revolt occurred in 1680, the Cochitis took part, although they did not kill their resident priest. Legend says that the priest was warned by an Indian sacristan and was able to flee the rebellion. Governor Antonio de Otermín tried to retake New Mexico in 1681, but Cochiti residents, along with their neighbors from Santo Domingo Pueblo and San Felipe Pueblo, fled the Spanish soldiers. They took refuge for a few years at Potrero Viejo, a massive rock that rises above the Rio Grande north of the pueblos. Cochiti residents again retreated to Potrero Viejo when de Vargas reconquered the area in 1692, building a stronghold on the rock's summit. De Vargas visited them there and successfully persuaded the Pueblos to return home. However, the Cochitis retreated to the rock again, to be finally driven out in 1694 by de Vargas and a small army of soldiers and allies from San Felipe and Santa Ana pueblos. Not only were the Cochitis forced to leave their refuge, but the fortifications they had built were destroyed, their winter corn supply was stolen, and one hundred fifty of the women were captured. Cochiti soldiers later freed the women.

A Franciscan, Fray Antonio Carbonel, took charge of Cochiti Pueblo after their tribe's final return to the present site. Carbonel rebuilt the Church of San Buenaventura and attempted to mend relations between the Spanish and Cochitis. The church was reconstructed on its original ground in 1694, and still stands today. Close to it is the large, dusty plaza. Generations of Cochitis have danced here

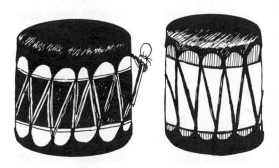

during the ceremonials which highlight the pueblo's year.

The Church of San Buenaventura is a simple structure, though large. It measures one hundred feet long and thirty-four feet wide, and is a fine example of early Spanish-Indian architecture and building. At the beginning of this century, the original roof and facade of the church were changed; the roof was pitched and covered with tin, and a pointed steeple was placed atop it. Even the outside balcony was removed, and the main entrance was enclosed by an adobe porch with three arches. Recently, San Buenaventura has been restored and looks today probably much as it did almost three hundred years ago. The following description of San Buenaventura Church is from the original WPA guide:

"... the interior is still typical of the early Indian mission. Old tin candle-sticks brought from Chihuahua, Mexico long before New Mexico was part of the United States, still firmly hold lighted tapers. Above the altar a large painting of San Buenaventura adorns the center of the wall, while the Nativity, the Transfiguration, the Last Supper, and three scenes of the Crucifixion are on the *reredos*. The ceiling of the chancel is decorated with moons, horses and other figures which the Cochiti executed in yellow, black, and red. Thirty-eight great *vi-gas* [beams], most of them with Indian carving, support the roof. The church possesses three wooden statues representing San Buenaventura, the patron saint of the Pueblo. The largest of these statues is of French workmanship, the next in size was done by a Mexican Indian, and the smallest and most revered is an antique. In their pottery the Cochiti confined themselves to black-on-white ware until the recent revival of Pueblo arts, when they included some reds. The designs representing rain, planting, growing, and harvesting frequently appear all over the vessels." (p. 245).

The mission church, served by a Franciscan friar stationed at Peña Blanca, becomes the focal point for Cochiti's largest Roman Catholic celebration, the Feast of San Buenaventura on July 14. An elaborate Mass precedes a long day of dancing and feasting. The Pueblo's turquoise and pumpkin clans, their male members painted in representative colors, perform. Cochiti's population of eight hundred is joined by guests and friends coming together from great distances for the celebration.

Cochiti Pueblo is renowned not only for its elaborate ceremonies, open attitude to outsiders, and unique drums, but also for the quality of its pottery. A number of Cochiti women, kneading, shaping, firing,

nor's office located near the church. Tribal officials can give directions to the homes and showrooms of the artists.

While the Cochitis have traditionally been an agricultural tribe, less than one-half of their irrigable acreage is presently tilled. Residents now work in Santa Fe, Bernalillo, or Albuquerque, commuting to their distant jobs because they value living in their ancestral home.

Leaving Cochiti, venturesome travelers can drive south through Pueblo land along the Rio Grande. The road, about fifteen miles long and almost all dirt or sand, is known as Alternate or Tribal 85. It connects Cochiti, Santo Domingo, and San Felipe pueblos. There are no road markers, and other dirt roads often cross it, so the traveler must often stop and guess which is the main route. However, the spectacular views across the flood plain, into the cottonwood-rich riverbed, and on up through the high desert to the Sandia Mountains are well worth the many pauses at the forks in the middle of the road. The drive is slow, ruts are often deep, and the road can be impassable in any but perfect weather. The most interesting segment of Alternate 85 is the nine-mile stretch linking Santo Domingo and San Felipe.

If the traveler follows Alternate 85, the first settlement reached will not be an Indian pueblo, but the small Spanish village of SILE. A Hispanic anomaly between two pueblos, Sile was founded in the early 1800s by Antonio de Síle, who was given a land grant of about four square miles by the Spanish governor. Down through the years, the land was divided among Síle's heirs, who were bought out in the first part of the twentieth century by Marcos Baca. He then parceled out most of Sile to his own descendants. Much of the original grant has thus changed hands a number of times. In the 1930s some of Sile was purchased by the federal government to be given to the neighboring pueblos,

and painting at their homes, create pottery figures acclaimed throughout the world. The large and small pieces are well made, whimsical interpretations of the life and legends of the Pueblo. Helen Cordero first popularized the Pueblo's most famous ceramic figure, a venerable grandmother or grandfather sort, seated with children climbing and crying and clinging and laughing up and down the body. The figure is called the Storyteller. It is dressed in traditional clothing, the details painted in red and black. The Storytellers of Helen Cordero and others are for sale in Santa Fe and Albuquerque, and are on display in museums of the region.

Visitors who are interested in purchasing pottery or drums can visit the gover-

reducing the grant's area considerably.

About forty-five families or one hundred twenty people live in Sile now. The small homes at the north end of the village were built originally to house the hired help—household and field workers—who were brought in by larger landowners. The Church of Santa Barbara, off the main road but visible from it, was built in the 1920s. The saint's feast day, December 4, is a time for the annual fiesta in Sile, presided over by the *mayordomos* (caretakers) chosen by the mission priest at Peña Blanca. Traditional roots run deep in Sile. The *mayordomos* are not only responsible for caring for the church, but during their tenure they also became the leaders of the community. An old Spanish tradition, the *mayordomo* role in most New Mexican villages today is restricted to church functions.

The land around Sile is fertile, and most of its residents farm, if only part-time. The majority work in the county seat, Bernalillo, or in Albuquerque or Santa Fe.

Most of the land traversed south of Sile belongs to Santo Domingo Pueblo. Skirting irrigation ditches, the road meanders through the sandy scrub, reaching an intersection with the road to Santo Domingo village approximately three miles south of Sile. To enter the village, a visitor turns left at the intersection, crosses the Rio Grande, and remains on the road that hugs the north side of the community.

If the traveler wishes to continue on to San Felipe Pueblo, about nine miles south, the task is the same as that of the previous three miles: stay on what seems the main route, watching for the most-traveled ruts and taking them. Miles of fields planted in alfalfa and corn line the sandy path. Crooked fences march symmetrically almost to the river's edge. Horses wander, grazing in the hardy grasses, their corrals empty much of the time. The road seldom comes close to the

Rio Grande itself; instead, it wanders around the low sand hills, sometimes winding down into a portion of the flood plain. As San Felipe Pueblo draws near, the dark Santa Ana Mesa looms closer. The road soon follows the base of the rocky hills and inches nearer to the river. Alternate 85 ends at the outskirts of San Felipe village. The bridge across the Rio Grande leads to I-25.

Those who do not plan to take Alternate 85 after touring Cochiti Pueblo can turn back, heading north toward Cochiti Dam and N.M. 22, following 22 south to Peña Blanca, a distance of about six miles. PEÑA BLANCA is in many ways only a shadow of its former self. Once it was the county seat for Santa Ana County, one of the state's original counties and the forerunner of Sandoval County. Peña Blanca was also the cradle of the Montoya family, a powerful political force in New Mexico for decades. The late Senator Joseph Montoya, born in Peña Blanca, held a stepladder pattern of elected offices on the local, county, and state levels before reaching the U.S. Senate. His brothers became school board presidents, state representatives and senators, and county commissioners. His cousins were county sheriffs, school board members, and political appointees. For years, it is said, nothing happened in Sandoval County, or even in the northern part of the state, that did not have Montoya family approval. By the end of the 1970s, most of the politically active generation of the Montoya clan had died.

Peña Blanca was originally part of the Juan Montes Vigil Grant, awarded in 1745. The area was always a bone of contention between the two nearby pueblos, Cochiti and Santo Domingo, both of which claimed it as their own. Long, complicated court cases have resulted from boundary disagreements; the king of Spain intervened in the controversy at one point. In 1758 Montes Vigil sold his grant for 500 pesos to José Miguel de la Peña, a descendant of colonists who came to New Mexico with de Vargas in the 1690s. De la Peña founded his ranch in 1770, and that date is generally accepted for the founding of Peña Blanca. Eight years later, Luis María Cabeza de Baca married into the Peña family, and it was under his stewardship that the ranch expanded and prospered. From the ranch a village grew, never a bustling one but certainly a hardy farming settlement. When Adolph Bandelier was studying the neighboring pueblos in the 1880s, he made Peña Blanca his headquarters, noting the simple prosperity of the families, the abundance of plain but good food, the irrigation system, and the serious droughts which, along with flooding, have always been a fact of life in Peña Blanca. The population of the small village reached its peak in 1910, when 789 people were counted; Bandelier guessed that there were one hundred families there when he was in residence. Many expected that the building of Cochiti Dam, with its attendant recreation facilities, would bring a faster pace to Peña Blanca. There are now more general stores; some houses were sold and their faces lifted; traffic to the lake is heavy on summer weekends—but most of the time Peña Blanca is quiet and unchanged.

Midway through the village, on the east side of the road, dwarfed by large trees, stands the Church of Nuestra Señora de Guadalupe. Next to the church is the residence of the Franciscan priest who tends not only his Peña Blanca flock but also the missions in the outlying Spanish villages of Sile, La Bajada, and Domingo, and the churches at Santo Domingo, Cochiti, and San Felipe pueblos.

The Franciscans accompanied the earliest Spanish explorers into New Mexico and stayed to serve the pueblos and missions they had established up and down the Rio Grande valley. However, in 1835,

the Franciscans were replaced by Jesuits, who remained for almost seventy-five years. In 1910 a group of Franciscans returned, and Peña Blanca has been their headquarters since then. To the south of the church sits a large, gray house, the home of an order of Catholic nuns who teach religion in the missions run by the friars.

The Church of Nuesta Señora de Guadalupe is usually open to visitors. It was recently restored, and an interesting mural was added to its interior. Fray Angelico Chavez served for many years in Peña Blanca. Although better known as a respected author, Fray Angelico is also an artist. He painted the Stations of the Cross, but not in the usual way. Those who know Peña Blanca well can see the faces of their friends and neighbors in the colorfully depicted narrative that flows across the walls of the church.

Many of the homes and farms that make up Peña Blanca are scattered on either side of N.M. 22. Once most farming activity took place to the west along the river. Land to the east, part of the immense La Majada Grant, was reserved for grazing. Although many who remain in Peña Blanca are employed elsewhere, the agricultural tradition of the valley has been retained. Residents keep sheep, grow alfalfa, and tend vegetable gardens.

A few miles beyond Peña Blanca, N.M. 22, which has undulated through the grazing land of Santo Domingo Pueblo, reaches a Santa Fe Railroad overpass. I-25 is about three miles straight ahead. Travelers to either the Pueblo of Santo Domingo or the settlement of Domingo will turn east on N.M. 184 just before the overpass.

DOMINGO, 196 mi., lies east just down the road. Also known as Domingo Junction, it contains little more than a railroad depot and a run-down but gaudy trading post boasting of its role in movies past. Once, however, Domingo was called Thornton, and it was an important trad-

Corn Dancers, *Harvey Caplin.*

ing center for the surrounding pueblos. A branch of the Bernalillo Mercantile Company was located here in the early part of this century. Santa Fe Railroad trains used to stop here daily. Now Amtrak passenger trains and Santa Fe freight trains hurry through the small settlement.

Those wishing to visit SANTO DOMINGO PUEBLO will also turn east before the overpass. Instead of continuing east to Domingo, however, they will soon bear westward and travel a paved road that soon arrives at one of the largest Indian villages in New Mexico. Santo Domingo is a Keresan-speaking nation. Its reservation includes more than seventy-four thousand acres.

During the seventeenth and eighteenth centuries, tribe members took part in the sporadic revolts and retreats that marked the Pueblo relationship with the conquering Spaniards. After the 1680 revolt, a number of Santo Domingos fled to the Jemez Mountains, building fortified villages on high mesas and living with the Towa-speaking Jemez. Other Santo Domingos went further west and stayed with the Acoma people. It was important to the Santo Domingos to protect themselves and their traditions from invaders, whether nomadic Apaches and Utes or pale Spaniards. Now, hundreds of years later, Santo Domingo thrives on the banks of the Rio Grande. The tribe's population is growing, and its traditions remain intact. In fact, the more than two thousand

Santo Domingos are today considered among the strongest and most conservative of all the Pueblo people. The tribal council, selected each winter, carefully monitors the encroachment of the outside world on the pueblo. Land claims and old contracts between the tribe and private and governmental bodies are now being scrutinized; in some cases, the tribe has reworked past documents that had not benefited the Pueblo. Tribe members adhere strictly to the dictates of their governor.

The village of Santo Domingo is modest, brown, and laid out in narrow, east-west rows on the east side of the Rio Grande. In other times, the settlement lay to the west of the muddy river. Tribal offices and a community center are located near the eastern entrance to the village. If visitors wish to wander through the village or stop at the church, they should first ask permission at the governor's office in the community center. Those who plan to cross the Rio Grande at Santo Domingo in order to take Alternate 85 to San Felipe should watch for the post office on the right shortly after entering the village. A narrow dirt road leads from the post office along the northern edge of the village into open farmland and across the river.

One of the highlights of the Santo Domingo year, and a celebration for which it is world-renowned, is the Green Corn Dance held each year on August 4, the feast day of St. Dominic, patron saint of the Pueblo. The ceremony honors both St. Dominic and Iyatiko, the tribe's mother figure, symbolized often by corn. The celebration is a fine blend of Catholic religion and Pueblo tradition, the older belief system colorfully dominating the day.

For weeks and months Santo Domingo prepares for its Green Corn Dance. The *cacique,* a revered senior member of the tribe who will preside over the ceremo-

nies, has been fasting and meditating in preparation for this day since spring. Dancers and chanters have been practicing nightly, making sure that the complex rhythms and steps, passed down through the clans for longer than anyone can remember, are performed correctly and with dignity. Women have been shopping and cooking throughout the days preceding the dances. Stacks of pies and sweet breads, mounds of Indian bread, and cupboards and refrigerators full of pastries and other foods await the feast. Cartons of soda pop line the floors of the small brown houses along the plaza. And everyone will have enough chile to last them for a long time. Houses are cleaned and yards are raked, all in preparation for the special day. By early morning on August 4, excitement has been transmitted up and down this part of the Rio Grande valley. Friends and neighbors from nearby villages and pueblos are filling the dusty streets with all manner of pickup trucks. Tour buses from Santa Fe and Albuquerque line the road. Sometimes traffic is backed up beyond the overpass. However, everyone fits into the village, and the ceremony seldom starts until all visitors have found a viewing spot around the enormous dirt plaza.

By late morning, smoke strays from the kivas located at the north and south ends of the village.Soon the Koshare ("delight-makers," or clowns) appear in gray paint with black stripes. They are ugly creatures, whose role now is to warn the Pueblo that attackers are on their way. Having cautioned the village, the Koshare pantomime the battle waged, the victory won against the invaders. Throughout the day, the Koshare will mingle with the dancers to see that everyone is performing correctly. After their pantomime, the Koshare leave and then reappear as escorts for the two lines of dancers, male and female, who have come up from the kivas. The squash clan dances in from the

south, the turquoise from the north. A bearer leads the two groups, his swaying pole dangling shells, beads, feathers, and a fox tail. The dancers pause and dance for a moment in front of the church.

Soon the drums can be heard closer to the plaza, and bobbing feathers and headpieces herald the arrival of the dancers. Dancers from each clan will perform four times during the day. The lines of dancers look similar, despite their being from different clans. However, although the women of both clans dress essentially the same way, the bodies of the men are washed with different colors. Men from the squash clan are tinted a warm orange-tan for the day; the bodies of the turquoise clan are painted blue.

The clothing of the dancers has varied little in the past one hundred years. Women wear a black, one-shouldered dress (*manta*), with a stiff board (*tablita*) on their heads. The *tablita* is painted with sun, moon, and cloud symbols. Everyone wears their finest silver and turquoise jewelry and carries an evergreen sprig. Men dancers are bare-chested, wearing kilts with a foxtail attached at the waist. A special belt falls down one leg, and skunk skins are wrapped around each ankle. In his hair each man will have parrot and ea-

gle feathers. Seashells, spruce twigs, gourds, and turtle shells are also part of the costume.

Drums thunder, singers chant, and the ritual dances go on until noon. An enormous group dance often anticipates the midday rest and feasting. After everyone has eaten and drunk to capacity, dances continue until the afternoon sun has reached the Jemez Mountains to the west.

There are other feast days at Santo Domingo, but none is celebrated with the public display that characterizes the Green Corn Dance. Many ceremonies at Santo Domingo are closed to outsiders; often tribal officials place guards at the entrance to the village during the private celebrations. Dances at Christmas time are usually open to the public, and for many residents of Santa Fe and Albuquerque, Christmas day includes a trip to Santo Domingo.

Santo Domingo is known for more than its dances. Many fine jewelers, who often specialize in shell or heishi work, come from the pueblo. Santo Domingo vendors display their wares beneath the portal at the Palace of the Governors in Santa Fe and around the plaza in Albuquerque's Old Town. Others sell their jewelry in shops or at the pueblo itself.

After a visit to Santo Domingo, a traveler can return to I-25 by following the road from the pueblo back to N.M. 22, which then intersects the freeway. Turn south for Albuquerque. Between Santo Domingo and San Felipe pueblos there is little but grazing land on either side of the highway. However, a wide spot in the road called Budagher's is of note because of the family that settled there.

The population of Sandoval County, through which I-25 now passes, is a diverse one. Until the recent growth of its large southern towns, Corrales and Rio Rancho, Sandoval County was rural and predominantly Indian and Hispanic in character. Within its 3,714 square miles are seven Indian pueblos and parts of the Navajo (Cañoncito) and Jicarilla Apache reservations. For years, the political structure of the county has been dominated by Hispanics, although that is changing with the influx of Anglos to the area. Among the Hispanics are descendants of a number of leading trading families, the patriarchs of whom were often German, Russian, or Lebanese. Through intermarriage many of the non-Hispanic names and traditions have been lost, but the Budagher name remains a powerful one in the county.

Saith Budagher came to New Mexico from Lebanon by way of Cuba and Mexico. By the turn of the twentieth century, he was working in Jemez Springs with a cousin, Moses Abousleman, who had a variety of enterprises there. Soon Saith moved to Algodones, where he maintained a slaughterhouse and a barber shop. A few years later he moved north to Peña Blanca. There he married, opened a general store and trading post, and set up similar operations nearby in Domingo and at Santo Domingo Pueblo. Budagher's relations with the Pueblos were excellent, and his businesses thrived. When the Depression came in the 1930s, some poor business decisions spelled financial ruin for the entrepreneur, so he left Domingo and, with his growing family, homesteaded about six hundred acres between Santo Domingo and San Felipe. Members of his family still live in scattered houses on that land, now bisected by I-25. The Budagher name has long been influential in county politics: there was a Budagher on the school board, a Budagher was county sheriff, and a descendant now sits in the state legislature.

SAN FELIPE PUEBLO can be seen huddled beneath high, dark mesas to the west along the Rio Grande, about ten miles south of Budagher's. I-25 has dipped and climbed into and out of the arroyos and hills that line this stretch of road. The turnoff to the west for San Felipe is well-marked. The old village of San Felipe lies across the Rio Grande, brown houses hugging the riverbanks.

The Rio Grande is very much a presence at San Felipe. In the spring it seems to climb daily, its muddy water surging close to the bottom of the bridge, grabbing at the brush and small trees that grow along its banks. Flooding is often a possibility in spring and early summer. By late June, however, when the days are hot and lazy, the river seems to slow down. San Felipe children have special, quiet swimming holes in the river at the foot of the village. Those who come to San Felipe for the Christmas Eve dances see a cold, silent river when they cross the Rio Grande to reach the church at the edge of the village.

San Felipe, like its Pueblo neighbors, is Keresan-speaking. It is probable that ancestors of the present population migrated south and east from the Chaco Canyon area in the late thirteenth century. The pueblo was mentioned in European sources as early as 1700. The Church of San Felipe, a wonderful twin-belfried structure with a gaily painted balcony, was built about two hundred years ago.

The village of San Felipe is a busy one. More than eighteen hundred people live

San Felipe Pueblo, *Harvey Caplin*.

in adobe houses along the crooked streets beneath Santa Ana Mesa. There is a large day school east of the river. A new governor's office has been built from which tribal officials oversee various Pueblo activities, ranging from health and education projects to economic development programs. Visitors should ask permission in the governor's office before walking through the village.

San Felipe usually resembles any other small New Mexico town. Most residents commute to jobs in Bernalillo and Albuquerque; others tend fields that stretch out from the river along the length of the pueblo's forty-eight thousand acres. However, two feast days find the village pulsing with excitement and activity. During the Christmas season and on May 1, cars, buses, and pickup trucks jam the small community. The enormous plaza is ringed by a colorful collection of neighboring Indians, Hispanic friends, anthropologists, school children on field trips, and spectators from every corner of New Mexico.

The public festivities at Christmas begin with a traditional Christmas Eve Mass in the old church along the river. Pueblo residents and visitors crowd the thick-walled structure, standing on its dirt floor for hours, awaiting with patience the Mass that will be celebrated by the Franciscan missionary assigned to the parish. Often a San Felipe couple will be married during the service. Like all Christmas Masses, this one celebrates the birth of the Christ Child. At San Felipe, his arrival is announced by a surprising chorus of bird warbles. All the youngsters who have been crowded in the choir loft all night long let loose with chirps and songs and bird whistles, acting out an ancient legend that says that all the birds of the earth began to sing when the baby was born.

When the Mass has been completed and while the birds are still warbling, the Indian part of the celebration begins as it has for centuries. Drums sound from far away, slowly coming closer. The congregation backs up against the high adobe walls of the church and forms a wide aisle for the dancers. Soon the drummer appears, followed by a male dancer who leads a long line of women into the church. Costumes are colorful and replete with ancient symbols: shells, feathers, sprigs of spruce, and masses of turquoise. As the dancers perform, the earth floor throbs with the beat of the drum and the pounding feet. After the women exit, deer dancers enter, their heads topped with

antlers, their canes representing prancing hoofs. Throughout the long night, the two sets of dancers take turns. They end the ceremony just before dawn.

Christmas day brings more dances, and the festivities will continue into the next week. Some of the ceremonies are limited to San Felipe residents; a guard is usually posted at the outskirts of the village to advise visitors of this fact. Holiday dances at San Felipe culminate near the first of the year when new tribal officials are installed in ceremonies on the plaza.

San Felipe's Green Corn Dance is held on May 1, which is also the feast day for St. Phillip, the pueblo's patron saint. As at other pueblos, preparations begin weeks ahead, with special private ceremonies in the kivas and with fasting and meditation. Families lay in enormous stores of food; each home will be open to friends, and no one will leave hungry on May 1. Dancing begins around noon and continues on into the late afternoon. Long rows of richly costumed dancers file into the plaza, dancing before the statue of St. Phillip that is now flanked by elders of the tribe. When the hours of dancing cease the feasting begins, lasting far into the night. By sunset, the leaden skies, which have threatened all day, often open up, pelting the pueblo with a cold spring rain.

After leaving San Felipe, one can return to I-25 and drive south to Albuquerque, a distance of about twenty-five miles. Or the traveler can take U.S. 85 (often referred to as "Old Highway 85") and follow the river valley into the heart of Albuquerque. Old Highway 85 is marked, pointing the way to Algodones and Bernalillo.

ALGODONES, 208 mi., is a small Hispanic settlement just south of San Felipe Pueblo. The name comes from its many cottonwood trees, *alamos*, that shower the village with cot-

ton, *algodón*, in the late spring. Its modest homes and small farms straddle U.S. 85. Once a local trading center, Algodones has now slipped into a quieter role. Many of the extended families who live in Algodones are direct descendants of the original settlers of this part of the Rio Grande valley. Names like C de Baca, Archibeque, and García still grace the rolls at the village school, and roots and traditions run deep.

The mission Church of San José, which sits in the middle of the village, is the center of

community life. Algodones honors its patron, St. Joseph, on June 19 rather than on March 19, the traditional feast day, so that an outdoor procession can give the saint his full due. Late in the mid-June afternoon, a float is prepared in the church parking lot. On it little girls in First Communion dresses and boys in acolyte vestments surround the statue of St. Joseph. The procession winds down U.S. 85, picking up residents as it stops at each home to sing. The little parade continues along the road to Las Colonias, the oldest neighborhood in Algodones, and then arrives back at the church where bells are rung and the Mass is said. A potluck supper at the school or a lively dance at a nearby hall usually follows.

Much of Algodones was formed from two Spanish land grants. Land claims were an issue here from early in the nineteenth century until a federal board settled them in the 1930s. Within the boundaries of Algodones there are still patches of Pueblo land.

Travelers who passed through Algodones in the eighteenth and nineteenth centuries often remarked on the fertility and lushness of the fields and orchards that lined the Camino Real. Apples, peaches, even grapes were grown, along with corn, chiles, and beans. Most of the orchards have now been replaced by alfalfa fields, but small vegetable gardens with neat, irrigated rows of traditional crops are still a part of each homestead. In the fall, the green chile pods are left to turn red on the withering plants, and the deep burgundy peppers are then strung into *ristras* (garlands) and hung from rooftops and clotheslines to dry.

Visitors and soldiers who passed through Algodones long ago mentioned not only the agricultural vitality of the area, but also the warmth and friendliness of the people. Wil-

liam Carr Lane, the second American governor of the New Mexico Territory, often traveled through Algodones on his trips between Santa Fe and Albuquerque. On a rainy summer night in 1853, he stopped in Bernalillo at the hacienda of Don José Leandro Perea, a wealthy landowner, and asked for lodging for the night. Perea told Lane, "It is not a proper night to take travelers in," and refused the governor shelter. Lane rode north another six miles through rain and mud and was taken into the home of Don Ignacio Miera in Algodones. The governor never forgot Miera's kindness or Perea's snub.

The high hills east of Algodones are studded with juniper bushes, old wagon trails, and ruins. It is clear that the little valley and surrounding hillsides have been hospitable dwelling places for a long time.

Algodones offers little in the way of roadside attractions. There are several bars and a grocery store in the village; along the interstate a few tourist services cater to travelers.

South of Algodones, old U.S. 85 passes through Santa Ana Pueblo lands, 213 mi. This section of the pueblo, which extends across the Rio Grande and many miles to the west, is known as Santa Ana Number Two, or Ranchitos. It is the modern housing area for Santa Ana Pueblo. (See Tour 9 for information about Santa Ana Pueblo.)

The town of Bernalillo, the seat of Sandoval County, begins south of Ranchitos, its boundary marked by a collection of once-independent rural neighborhoods. At the intersection of U.S. 85 and N.M. 44, travelers may turn west to go to the Jemez area or Cuba (Tour 9). A turn to the east brings the visitor to I-25 or, farther east, to Placitas and the Sandia Mountains.

PLACITAS ("little plazas" or "little towns"), a small village about six miles east of Bernalillo, is tucked into the foothills of the Sandia Mountains. N.M. 44 begins its ascent to the western slope of the Sandias by passing through Placitas, which is really a cluster of small eighteenth-century villages.

Most of Placitas was formed from the San Antonio de las Huertas Grant, given in 1745 to twenty-one families who promised to build a fortified village to protect themselves and other nearby settlers from Apache attacks. A number of Placitas families are directly descended from those who first built their homes along Las Huertas Creek to the north of the present community; a few crumbling walls and some recent archaeological finds indicate the original settlement. The Las Huertas Grant, composed of descendants of the original grantees, remains an active organization today.

Because petroglyphs and Indian ruins exist within the Placitas region, it is certain that man inhabited this hilly country long before the Spanish settled the Las Huertas Grant. It should be noted that these sites are protected by law from random exploration.

The first Hispanic residents of the Placitas area were farmers. They were followed in the nineteenth century by more small farmers and ranchers, and by miners drawn by stories of gold strikes to the east of the village. Coal and iron were mined in Placitas in the 1800s, but no one has yet uncovered the fabled Montezuma gold mine said to have been worked by Indians who covered it over at the time of the 1680 revolt. Some modern villagers point to a mine shaft east of Placitas near the old settlement of Ojo de la Casa ("the spring near the house") and call it the Montezuma mine of legend. Stagecoaches used to bump their way through Placitas on route to Santa Fe or across the mountains east to Tijeras. A favorite Placitas story tells of Union forces, accompanied by Indians, passing through the village during the Civil War.

Besides Las Huertas and Ojo de la Casa, today's Placitas also encompasses the old villages of Tecolote and Tejon. Each of these early settlements was established near a water source. To this day the reservoirs behind Placitas, fed from mountain springs and runoffs, provide most of the town's water, as they have for centuries.

The heart of Placitas sits above N.M. 44. Houses are perched on the mountain slopes along winding dirt and asphalt roads, some of the older structures dating back to the eighteeenth century. New homes, some heated only by the sun, have now been built above and within the village. In the small canyons and valleys below Placitas proper, modest farms and ranches continue the area's agricultural tradition. Fruit orchards are common in the valleys and within the village itself. West of town, modern housing developments creep over the hills and along the *arroyos*.

The population of Placitas is now a mixture of old Hispanic families and Anglo newcomers. They meet each other at the large, brown Presbyterian church in the village, at Catholic services, at the elementary school, or at the numerous local events which draw residents from each of Placitas's communities, new and old.

As N.M. 44 winds into Las Huertas Canyon, it passes Sandia Man Cave. A group of Boy Scouts explored the cave in 1927. Almost ten years later, a student from the University of New Mexico came upon it and brought it to the attention of his professor, Dr. Frank Hibben. Hibben's students excavated the area, and the theory of Sandia Man emerged. While no actual skeletons were found, prehistoric artifacts (points and scrapers) were discovered here. Visitors can climb up to the well-marked cave, imagining for themselves what life was like in this rocky place long ago.

SIDE TOUR

BERNALILLO, 215 mi. (alt. 5,084, pop. 2,721), holds a venerable place in New Mexico history. For hundreds of years predating the European discovery of the Southwest, Bernalillo was the site of a number of Tiguex pueblos. Pottery dating from before the thirteenth century is still occasionally dug up around town, and recent excavations behind the Catholic church have revealed extensive Pueblo dwellings, as well as one of the largest kivas ever discovered in this part of the Rio Grande valley.

When Coronado and his troops first made their way into New Mexico in 1540, they spent the winter across the river from Bernalillo at one of the Tiguex villages. It is said that the Indians abandoned the pueblo of Coofor (or Alcanfor) for Coronado and his men to use. The village was large, containing at least twelve hundred rooms and several hundred people. Its inhabitants were probably among the ancestors of the present southern Tiwas, the Sandias and Isletas. Coronado Monument (Tour 9) marks the spot of this Tiguex pueblo and Coronado's encampment.

By 1674, according to Fray Francisco de Ayeta, quartermaster for the Franciscans, there were a number of large haciendas along the Rio Grande. The hacienda of the Gonzales-Bernal family was one of the largest, and perhaps de Vargas later named the settlement after a member of that family. The Spanish living around Bernalillo fled the area during the Pueblo Revolt of 1680, but as soon as they re-turned in 1692, the haciendas along the riverbanks flourished again.

Don Diego de Vargas, accompanied by troops and a handful of settlers, stayed in Bernalillo at the time of the reconquest, founding the town in 1695. He died there in 1704, either from wounds he had received in a campaign against Indians in the mountains or from having eaten spoiled eggs. De Vargas is buried in Santa Fe.

Bernalillo became an important trading center almost from its inception. Its location at the northern end of the Sandia Mountains, close to the confluence of the Jemez River and the Rio Grande, made it a natural point of departure, rest spot, and business center for early settlers. In the nineteenth century, Bernalillo was the commercial seat of Sandoval County. Miners, ranchers, and lumbermen throughout the region traded at a branch of the Bernalillo Mercantile Company founded by Nathan Bibo in 1871 with headquarters on Bernalillo's main street. The "Merc" was the base of operations for a far-flung commercial empire. There were stores in the lumber town of Porter, the gold-mining village of Bland, and the train stop called Thornton. Thornton was named after one of the Seligmans, a pioneer New Mexico family that bought the "Merc" from Bibo and ran it until the late 1970s.

An inventory list from the early days of the Bernalillo Mercantile Company includes coffins, harnesses, overalls, tractors, Studebaker wagons, brass bells, feathers, beads, spit-

A monarca dancing with La Malinche, Matachines Dance, *Phyllis Mayfield Knox.*

toons, coal buckets, loggers' hooks, nails, cook stoves, horseshoes, fringe and ticking for shawls, shells for heishi, blue cornmeal, native herbs, hides, pelts, bolts of cloth, and dolls. Customers could rent rooms at the "Merc" while they made their purchases, had their wheat ground, or sold their sheep. Bernalillo Mercantile, its name and structure modernized, is now a grocery and hardware store.

When the Santa Fe Railroad came to New Mexico in the middle of the nineteenth century, it laid its track through Bernalillo. If Don José Leandro Perea, a powerful local figure, had not chosen otherwise, the Santa Fe would also have placed its yards and shops in the sleepy village. However, Señor Perea, the owner of most of the land in the Bernalillo

area, is said to have liked his village just the way it was. So when Santa Fe officials came to him to negotiate the purchase of land for their operations, Perea asked such a high price for his property that the railroad turned him down. The Santa Fe went twenty miles south and built its train barns and switchyards in Albuquerque. Bernalillo became a brief stop on the route and remained a sleepy village.

The history and traditions of Bernalillo are Hispanic. The town reflects its heritage in a variety of ways. The Fiesta of San Lorenzo, which probably dates back to the seventeenth century, is held each year on August 10. Los Matachines, a dance-drama traced to medieval Europe, is an integral part of the three-day festival. Rehearsals for Los Matachines begin in Bernalillo in early summer. By August, the whole town is caught up in the centuries-old ritual, which tells the story of Montezuma, Cortéz, and Malinche, a young girl of noble lineage who was given in slavery to the Spanish. Malinche, portrayed each year by a girl dressed in white, is often considered a link between the Spanish and Mexican Indian forces. Other characters in the drama are usually a bull, a clown, and an old man. The Matachines, accompanied by more dancers, singers, and musicians, dance in a procession through the main street of Bernalillo. Other community members walk with them, some having made a private vow to participate in the rigorous dances. The *mayordomos* for the year are responsible for providing a haven for the *santos* (statues of the saints that belong to the parish) that are carried in the procession. The *mayordomos* also provide food and sponsor a dance on the fiesta's last night.

Since Bernalillo's settlement by the Spanish in the seventeenth century, its religious, social, and political organizations have been dominated by Hispanic families. Although a succession of German, Irish, French, Lebanese, and other non-Spanish-surnamed people made Bernalillo their home, their marriages into the large Spanish families of the area integrated them swiftly into the Hispanic culture. Today Spanish conventions, some dating back two hundred years, are still observed in Bernalillo. The Spanish language is used as often as English in social and business conversations.

Bernalillo's main street, El Camino del Pueblo, was once lined with handsome adobe houses and commercial buildings. Some were two-story edifices with shuttered windows and elaborate porches. Many of those buildings have now either been destroyed or hidden beneath a veneer of brick or siding. At the far northern end of Camino del Pueblo, however, a National Historic District preserves the work of a local craftsman, Abenicio Salazar, who built hundreds of sturdy adobe structures in Sandoval County in the early twentieth century. One of Salazar's remaining buildings,

the old Our Lady of Sorrows High School, has been restored (with plaster work by Salazar's son, grandson, and great-grandson) and is now the cornerstone of the preservation district. To the north of the old high school building is the rambling adobe convent that once housed the Sisters of Loretto who taught in Bernalillo.

Across the street from these two restored buildings, behind the modern red brick Catholic Church, sits the twin-spired Our Lady of Sorrows church, erected in 1857 and abandoned in 1971. Said to have been at one time the only consecrated adobe structure in New Mexico, the church is considered one of the most significant architectural remainders of the Bishop Lamy period, the second half of the nineteenth century. However, the local parish and the Archdiocese of Santa Fe have agreed that the historic structure will be left to deteriorate. Its interior was stripped of its oak floor long ago; its altar (donated by Perea), its wooden pews, and anything else of value have now been removed or vandalized. Some local residents attempted to save the church from neglect, but renovation efforts failed, and the structure continues to decline.

At the south end of Bernalillo, just west of its main street, is a collection of crumbling adobe houses called Las Cocinitas ("little kitchens"). These were the homes of the workers and cooks in the kitchens of the haciendas of the region. The buildings in the Las Cocinitas district are modest, humble reminders of Bernalillo's varied and historic past.

As Bernalillo ends, the Sandia Reservation begins, taking the traveler along U.S. 85 to the Bernalillo County line and the outskirts of Alameda.

SANDIA PUEBLO, 218 mi., is one of the smallest (about two hundred fifty people live there) and least studied of the New Mexico pueblos. Its popular name is derived from the Spanish name for the mountains to the east, the Sandia ("watermelon") Mountains. Sandia's twenty-four thousand acres extend from the Rio Grande on the west to the Sandia Mountains on the east, and from Bernalillo on the

north to Alameda (an Albuquerque suburb) on the south. Much of the land belonging to the Sandias was in dispute for decades; a vestige of the bitter land quarrels remains alive in the sometimes-volatile relations between Bernalillo and the pueblo. The center of Sandia Pueblo is its village, located a few miles south of Bernalillo.

The recorded history of Sandia Pueblo is scant and the Sandia Pueblo people are close-mouthed about many of their traditions and rituals. Because the present site, probably occupied intermittently since the 1300s, was abandoned after the 1680 revolt and was not settled again for almost half a century, it is speculated that some Sandia traditions were lost in the fifty-year interval.

When Coronado and his troops passed through this part of the Rio Grande valley in 1540 they visited Tiwa villagers, whose descendants may now live at Sandia Pueblo. Sandia was first mentioned in European documents in 1617, when it became the mission seat for the surrounding area. In the 1680s, during the Pueblo Rebellion, the Spanish burned and destroyed Sandia many times in attempts at reconquest. History has long asserted that the Sandia fled west to the Hopis during the rebellion. There, it is said, they built the pueblo of Payupki on Second Mesa. Although there are some Hopi words in the Tiwa language spoken at Sandia, both Pueblo tradition and historical research indicate that, while some Sandias may have sought refuge in Hopi, the majority of the three thousand Sandias resident at the pueblo in the 1680s probably dispersed themselves among other neighboring pueblos. However, when the present village was re-established in 1748, it is

likely that two distinct communities were formed. The first was Hopi and has since disappeared. The other village, composed of refugees from various pueblos, was the precursor of the present Sandia Pueblo. Sandia thus is one of only two (the other is Isleta) Tiwa pueblos that survived the Spanish conquest.

Despite its small size and its location between two non-Indian communities, Sandia has kept much of its culture and traditions intact. Led by a *cacique* who chooses the governor and other tribal officials, the Pueblo settles its problems internally and celebrates its feasts as the seasons change and as Catholic holidays are observed. The nuclear family is a key to Sandia's survival, as are the many ceremonial and religious groups to which all members belong.

Sandia has taken advantage of its location near Albuquerque to bring employment and revenue to the Pueblo. A number of tribal enterprises have been established which serve the metropolitan area while also benefiting the tribe. Sandia's youngsters attend Bernalillo public schools, and many go on to colleges and universities. Most Sandias work in Albuquerque, leaving agricultural activities to weekend farmers. Traditional crafts (basketry, pottery, and the making of moccasins) are seldom practiced now at Sandia, which moved faster than most pueblos into the money economy of the twentieth century.

A visitor to Sandia will notice that while some residents still live in the old village, where new tribal buildings have been constructed, many families have moved into modern homes on the sandy hills to the east. Kivas and other ceremonial structures remain in the historic center of Sandia. There, traditions of the Pueblo, nurtured for centuries, are still revered and practiced.

Going south on Old Highway 85, the traveler reaches the outskirts of Albuquerque soon after passing through Sandia pueblo land. Corrales Road, 224 mi., intersects Fourth Street (Old Highway 85) at the north end of Albuquerque, within the village of Alameda. Two distinct municipalities, Rio Rancho and Corrales, can be reached by taking Corrales road west across the Rio Grande to Coors Boulevard, a distance of less than two miles.

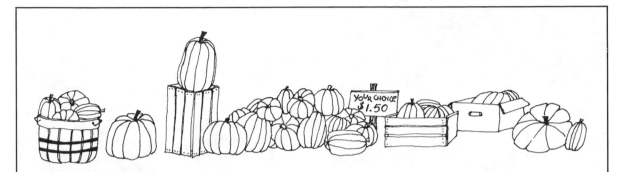

At the Coors intersection, N.M. 46 veers north to Corrales (see below), while N.M. 528 leads straight ahead and up the mesa to Rio Rancho.

RIO RANCHO (alt. 5,290, pop. 10,200) began life in the early 1960s as a land development project of AMREP Corporation, a New York–based firm. Originally this city at the southernmost tip of Sandoval County was open grazing land, much of it part of the Thompson Ranch that had been carved from the eighteenth-century Alameda Land Grant. In the 1960s, AMREP held numerous East Coast dinner parties and slide shows in an effort to persuade customers to fly out to New Mexico to tour its empty developments. Soon busloads of visitors tramped the platted desert, many purchasing a lot or two and some eventually moving here. Rio Rancho's first residents, drawn mainly from the New York area, found themselves living in the middle of a windy, sage-dotted ninety-thousand-acre tract of land with few neighbors other than wandering cattle and rattlesnakes. They later lived in isolated suburban-style neighborhoods, shoveling sand instead of snow from their yards. Slowly shopping centers, schools, and churches were established to serve the growing population. By the time of its incorporation in 1980, over ten thousand people lived in neat Rio Rancho bungalows and townhouses, their streets paved, their children swimming in municipal swimming pools, their dogs and cats counted and regulated by one of the strictest animal control ordinances in New Mexico. Predictions in 1980 foresaw Rio Rancho, already one of the state's fastest-growing communities, as the second largest city in New Mexico by the year 2000.

Visitors to Rio Rancho will find a well-ordered city. There are shopping and tourist facilities, a motel, a country club, many churches and schools, an industrial park, amd magnificent views across the Rio Grande to the Sandia Mountains.

CORRALES ("corrals") (alt. 5,100, pop. 2,885), begins at the Corrales Road/Coors Boulevard intersection and stretches north for almost six miles. The village's population is strung north along Corrales Road (N.M. 46) as it traverses the bottomland of the Rio Grande.

SIDE TOUR

Corrales, *Harvey Caplin.*

Corrales was once part of the Alameda Land Grant, given by the king of Spain to Francisco Montes y Vigil in 1710. The grant of 106,274 acres extended west from the present village of Alameda to the Ceja del Rio Puerco, the ridge which separates the Rio Puerco basin from the rest of Sandoval County.

Vigil planned to settle his grant, but instead sold it for the equivalent of two hundred dollars to Captain Juan Gonzales in 1712. Gonzales was a powerful figure in the Albuquerque, Alameda, and Cor-

rales communities, all of which at that time were on the west side of the river. He and his relatives settled the southern or Rancho del Abajo part of the grant, the Montoya family took over the northern end, and a Martínez group settled the middle section. Descendants of all three families still live in the Rio Grande valley, many of them in Corrales.

In the eighteenth century Corrales was probably composed of small groupings of homes, each cluster built around a little plaza with corrals near by. Settlers kept sheep, raised fruits and vegetables, and planted vineyards. They endured floods and droughts, Indian raids, and isolation from familiar amenities. Eighteenth- and nineteenth-century Corrales was Hispanic, agricultural, and, for the most part, poor. It is certain, however, that there were at least three large haciendas in the Corrales area in the 1700s, one of which has now been restored to its eighteenth- and nineteenth-century appearance. Casa San Ysidro is the home of its owners-restorers, but the rambling house, built around a garden courtyard, is also a private museum, visited by scholars from all over the world. Its rooms have been furnished and rebuilt to mirror life as it was lived by the large landowners in eighteenth-century New Mexico. Casa San Ysidro is not open to the general public.

The old San Ysidro Church, maintained by the Corrales Historical Society and home of the Adobe Theater, is another Corrales landmark. The tin-roofed, twin-steepled adobe building constructed in the 1860s is on the National Registry of Historic Places. It is located about a mile north of the village proper to the west of Corrales Road. Adobe Theater signs point the way.

Among the first non-Hispanics to settle in Corrales were the French, who came shortly after the American occupation of New Mexico in the 1850s. They were followed by a number of Italian families. Soon large vineyards and extensive vegetable farms were flourishing. Produce was hauled by wagon into Albuquerque, a distance of almost ten miles, which necessitated fording the Rio Grande at specific points to avoid high water and danger spots; a bridge connecting the two banks of the river was not built until well into this century. Visitors to Corrales in the nineteenth century spoke of the fine wines, delicious fruits, and wide variety of foods served in local homes. The combination of Spanish, French, and Italian customs was reflected most obviously in the agricultural style of the valley. Vineyards and truck farms filled the bottomlands. In fact, until the late 1920s, when a number of factors—Prohibition, the rising water table, the Depression, and competition from California—worked together to end Corrales's wine industry, this part of the Rio Grande valley depended heavily on its vineyards for revenue. Wine is still produced in Corrales, but on a small, private scale.

Many farms still line Corrales Road as it runs the length of the village. Albuquerque residents visit Corrales in the spring to see the fruit trees in blossom and in the fall to buy corn, pumpkins, apples, and other fresh produce.

Although Corrales is now a mixture of old Spanish homesteads and commuter-owned solar adobe homes, its urge to remain a quiet, pastoral village has been strong. Residents have fought to keep their rural lanes unpaved, their street corners unfettered by big shopping centers. They maintain large vegetable gardens, keep farm animals, and serve as volunteer firemen and village officials. Villagers worked together to build their own library, each family donating construction materials, plumbing expertise, or hours of adobe-laying. No outside funding was solicited for the handsome structure to which all Corraleños point with pride.

Those who drive down Corrales Road will find a homey mix of restaurants, art galleries, small shopping centers, new and old homes, and churches and schools. Once a Spanish farming village, now an affluent suburb that respects its past, Corrales has survived intact. Its residents expect that it will continue to do so.

N.M. 46 curves westward at the end of Corrales and climbs to meet N.M. 528.

SIDE TOUR

ALAMEDA, 224 mi., is the northernmost town in Bernalillo County. Once, near the Rio Grande, a Tiwa pueblo stood here. Spanish colonists first settled this rich agricultural area in 1696. Although commercial establishments line both sides of U.S. 85 (Fourth Street), side roads to the west and east lead to truck farms, alfalfa fields, and the groves of cottonwoods for which the town was named.

Travelers can enter the city of Albuquerque either on Rio Grande Boulevard, which leads to "Old Town," the earliest settled part of the city, or by continuing on U.S. 85 (Fourth Street), which enters "New Town," Albuquerque's downtown area, 232 mi. To reach Rio Grande Boulevard, from U.S. 85, turn west on Corrales Road—now a busy thoroughfare linking the rapidly growing West Mesa on the far side of the river with the rest of Albuquerque—in Alameda, and turn south again on Rio Grande Boulevard, the last street before crossing the river.

The southern limit of Alameda is not discernible as one passes successively through the communities of Los Ranchos, Los Griegos, Los Candelarias, and Los Duranes and on into Albuquerque. Los Ranchos, an independently incorporated village, contains many fine adobe buildings, some of considerable antiquity and others more recent. A detour along Rio Grande Boulevard, parallel to U.S. 85 and one mile west of it, brings into view many beautiful, low homes in the territorial and Spanish-Pueblo styles. Large fields of alfalfa and grapes can be seen, and horses abound. Children and a group of bison stare at each other through a fence at a sharp bend in the road. The John Gaw Meem–designed Los Poblanos ranch house and La Quinta "sports house" are encountered just beyond the bisons' pasture. These beautiful territorial-style structures were constructed in the 1930s for Congressman (later Governor) Albert Simms and his heiress wife, Ruth McCormick Simms, who had previously also been in Congress. La Quinta, which sits back from the road behind fields and orchards, has long been used for public functions.

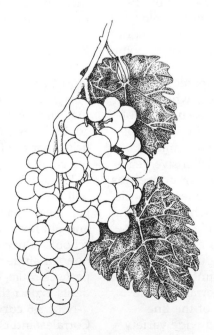

albuquerque

Transportation

Transportation within Albuquerque: municipal bus service (Suntran), taxis, and rental cars. To or from the city: many major airlines to the Albuquerque Sunport/International Airport. Greyhound and Trailways bus service in all directions at Albuquerque Bus Depot, 300 Second Street, S.W. Amtrak passenger trains east to Raton, Kansas City, and Chicago and west to Gallup, Flagstaff, and Los Angeles at Amtrak Passenger Station, 314 First Street, S.W.

Accommodations

Many hotels and motels throughout the city, clustering along the freeways (I-40 and I-25) and along the old east-west highway, U.S. 66, or Central Avenue. Private campgrounds at the east and west boundaries of the city.

Entertainment

Movie theaters and numerous small theater groups, especially near the University of New Mexico. Classical and popular music concerts in several locations, but particularly in Popejoy and Keller halls in the Fine Arts Center at the university, where the New Mexico Symphony Orchestra and the Albuquerque Civic Light Opera have annual series. Annual June Music Festival of chamber music in Woodward Hall at the University of New Mexico. New Mexico Jazz Workshop and Albuquerque Opera Theater productions, as well as other events at the KiMo Theater downtown. Bilingual theater from the Compañía de Teatro de Alburquerque.

Sporting events at the University of New Mexico for men and women. Albuquerque Dukes Triple-A baseball at the Albuquerque Sports Stadium. Horse racing and a variety of other events at the New Mexico State Fair each September.

City and university libraries, museums, tennis courts, golf courses, and swimming pools. Indian Pueblo Cultural Center.

Mountain trails in nearby Sandia and Manzano mountains, including those accessible from the Sandia Tram to the crest of the "watermelon mountains."

Information Services

Albuquerque Chamber of Commerce in the Civic Center, 401 Second Street, N.W. Information booth on west side of Old Town Plaza.

Universities

University of New Mexico. University of Albuquerque.

Annual Events

June Music Festival, chamber music; Feria Artesana, a display and sale of works of Hispanic artists and craftspeople, August; State Fair with rodeo and horse racing, September; International Balloon Fiesta, October; Greek Festival, October; *Las Posadas* and *luminaria* displays, December.

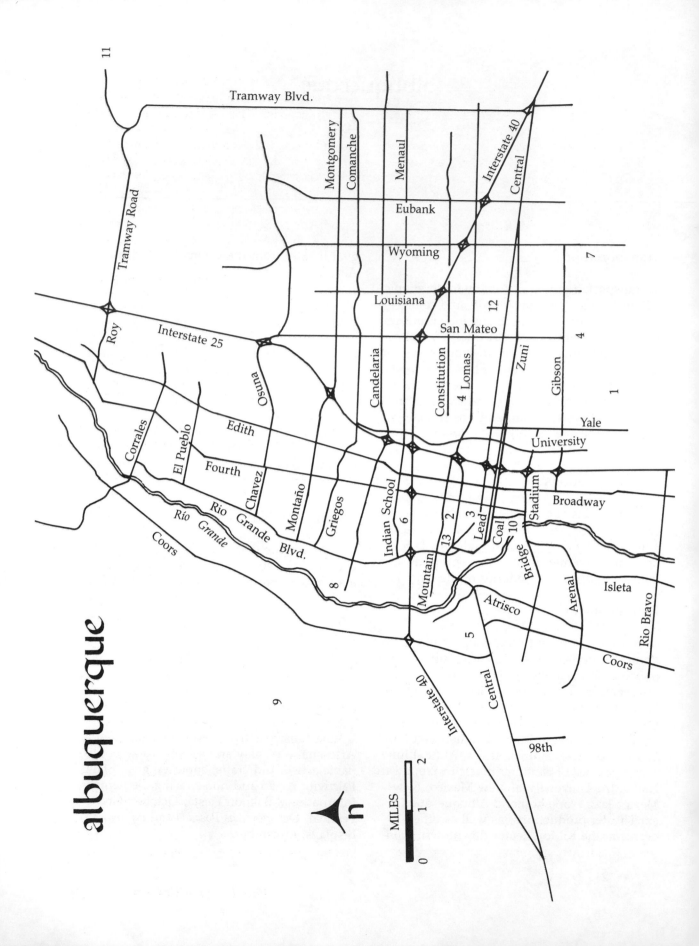

ALBUQUERQUE (alt. 4,950, pop. 328,829), contains about one-third of New Mexico's people in a sprawling city of surprising contrasts. It is easy to dismiss the "Duke City" for its ugly fast-food-restaurant-and-car-lot-lined arterials, for its freeway- and automobile-dominated society, and for its failure to plan its burgeoning residential areas. It is also easy to love it for its history and its peoples, for its art and music, for its architecturally unique university, and for the proximity of its chile fields and its skyscrapers. Albuquerque now has groups working to preserve its historical landmarks and neighborhoods and to bring some order to its growth. The city has exploded in size since World War II, when it was a town of forty thousand. Growth has been a boon to some and anathema to others, but most agree that it needs to be controlled.

Albuquerque's setting is impressive. Visible from all parts of the city are the mountains to the east, the Sandias and Manzanos, with their peaks rising a steep five thousand feet above the city. The parallel strata of the Sandias' Crest, alternately light and dark, were deposited beneath the ocean two hundred fifty million years ago. Movement along a great fault at the west base of the mountains thrust the area east of the rift higher and higher, while the valley to the west gradually settled. Though they are impressive now, it is estimated from the present location of strata that the mountains were once three times as high as at present and were worn away by erosion. Erosion is responsible, too, for the spires and crags visible near the horizontal crest of the range. Sixty miles to the west, a higher peak can be seen from anywhere in eastern Albuquerque. This peak was named Mount Taylor by Anglo-Americans after Zachary Taylor, twelfth president of the United States, but was known to Spanish settlers as Cebolleta ("little onion"). To the Navajos it was Dził Dotł'izi ("turquoise mountain"), one of the four sacred mountains that border their domain. Five extinct volcanoes, surrounded by basaltic lava deposits, mark Albuquerque's western border.

The trough of the Rio Grande around Albuquerque was formed by a slow fall of some three miles in the ground level. In pursuing its course from north to south through this trough, the river has deposited clay and gravel along the way, but the course it has cut cannot really be considered a valley. The part of the city now called "the Valley" represents the flood plain of the Rio Grande, which has eroded several channels across the land in past centuries. Ruins of the Pueblo of Alameda, for example, are more than a mile west of the river; when visited by Coronado in 1540, the pueblo was on the east bank.

The river is currently believed to be under control, with an extensive series of levees, channels, and ditches holding the water to its present banks. Despite this, flooding occurs in certain areas after heavy rains. However, the massive flooding of the past (Albuquerque had a major inundation covering the downtown areas as recently as 1955) should not occur again.

Flow in the "great river" has dropped more than fifty percent in the last one hundred years, largely as a result of heavy agricultural use all along its course. Partly as a consequence of the decreased flow and partly because of Albuquerque's insatiable demand for building space, the amount of land in the Valley used for food crops has decreased; the vineyards and orchards of the past have yielded to housing developments and alfalfa fields. Water is easily available only in some areas in the Rio Grande valley; many small truck farms, interspersed with housing, still exist in these regions.

There is evidence that Indian settlements in the Albuquerque area date back thousands of years. Hundreds of sites have been discovered, corresponding to all major epochs of Indian development, from the Paleo-Indian hunters and gatherers who killed mammoths and bison near the modern suburb of Rio Rancho to major late-Pueblo complexes found in Alameda. Pueblo remains have been found throughout the Rio Grande valley in Albuquerque; in 1980, residents of Los Ranchos, an enclave surrounded by the city in the North Valley, unearthed a large archaeological site when digging a swimming pool. For this family, as for many other Southwesterners, excavation and preservation of the site became a passion.

The latest Indian groups to occupy the Albuquerque area were Tiwa Indians, who founded numerous pueblos in the valley in the fourteenth century. These pueblos were abandoned at about the same time that Spanish settlers, lured by the fertile valley, first came to the region. No town was established until 1706, when acting governor Francisco Cuervo y Valdés moved thirty families from Bernalillo and several more from Zacatecas, Mexico, to the location of today's Old Town. There in the bend of the river a villa was planned, named after the Duke of Alburquerque, viceroy of New Spain, with a church, a plaza, and a ring of adobe houses. Cuervo y Valdés proposed these accoutrements in order to be accorded the honor of having founded a town; the actual Villa de San Felipe de Alburquerque remained less grand than his description for some time.

Designed to withstand Indian attacks, the villa rapidly attracted settlers, who numbered about eleven hundred in 1800. Part of the protection offered by the Villa de San Felipe de Alburquerque resulted from its position as a military post, which it maintained during Spanish, Mexican, and American days. The plaza, scene of communal life, marketing, and fiestas, became after U.S. annexation a drill ground for troops.

Albuquerque was still an isolated frontier town during the Civil War, and the sympathies of its residents fluctuated. Several skirmishes occurred in the vicinity, and the post was alternately occupied by Union and Confederate forces, with only a few shots fired. In 1862, Captain Enos, with a small Union command, was informed of the approach of Confederate General Hopkins Sibley and a large force. Realizing that defense was impossible, Enos loaded all available wagons and set out in them for Santa Fe, setting fire to the army storage houses to destroy remaining supplies. After his departure, Southern sympathizers

extinguished the blazes and saved many of the provisions, which they turned over to Sibley. He occupied the post without opposition for two months, but on learning that strong Union forces under Colonel R. S. Canby were advancing from the north to take the town, Sibley hastily evacuated, burying eight heavy howitzers, or Napoleon guns, which he had previously captured from Union forces. Two of these cannons were later unearthed and have now been placed on display at the Albuquerque Museum; replicas are on the plaza in Old Town.

The town itself remained centered around the old plaza until the 1880s, when the hub of commercial activity shifted east to meet the railroad. The obstinacy of a landowner near Old Town and the desire for a railroad secure from flooding made it necessary to route the tracks two miles east of the plaza. As often happened in the West, a new town grew up along the tracks. New Albuquerque, as the settlement was called, was surveyed and platted in 1880 under direction of a railroad subsidiary. Following the usual procedure on the frontier, the first lots were sold from a railroad flatcar. Reflecting the origins of their owners, many of the houses constructed near the railroad station were gabled replicas of Midwestern town dwellings. With the coming of the railroad and better transportation in 1880, Albuquerque changed rapidly. The wool and cattle industries prospered; horse-drawn streetcars appeared; and new housing was built, usually of local materials, adobe and brick, dressed with imported decorative luxuries. The showpiece of the period was the Huning "Castle," built with five-foot-thick *terrone* (sod) walls but finished on the outside with wooden paneling incised to resemble the stonework of the castles of merchant Franz Huning's native Germany. The castle was torn down in 1955, in one of the city's fitful periods of destroying its past.

Albuquerque's early days, like those of many Western towns, were colorful and unruly. Catering to ranchers, cowhands, and miners from the surrounding countryside, its

amusement facilities ran the gamut from saloons and burlesqueries to opera houses. Albuquerque had three of the latter in the 1800s. Such notables as Nordica, Pavlova, and Paderewski visited their stages. Saloons, gleaming with glassware and polished bars, served as meeting places, casinos, and occasional sites of violence.

Albuquerque did not have public schools until 1884. The Albuquerque Academy, a private school, was begun in 1878 in Old Town. (It had no connection with present Albuquerque Academy, founded in 1955 in the northeast section of the city.) Parochial schools were opened and closed several times in Old Town, becoming a permanent fixture with the opening of St. Vincent's Academy in 1885. Higher education in Albuquerque had its start in 1889 with the establishment of the University of New Mexico on a campus then two miles beyond the eastern edge of town. The university's rapid growth during the twentieth century has been witnessed by citizens of Albuquerque as the town grew around the campus and beyond it. The Sisters of Saint Francis opened Saint Joseph's College in 1920. It has since moved twice, presently occupying a campus on the West Mesa with a spectacular view of the valley and the mountains beyond, and is now known as the University of Albuquerque.

Albuquerque's growth has occurred for numerous, unrelated reasons. The town's population quadrupled shortly after the arrival of the railroad in 1880. The railroad has remained an important employer, with active repair shops in the city, but other industries now employ greater numbers of Albuquerqueans. The livestock and wool businesses were of great importance in bringing Easterners to the area and stimulating growth in the city in the late 1800s. Health became a major industry around the turn of the century; as the city crept up the hill toward its fledgling university, both sides of Central Avenue were lined with the screened porches of homes and sanatoriums for tuberculosis victims. Physicians in the East sent their consumptive patients, including some of New Mexico's most illustrious citizens of the early twentieth century, to Albuquerque (and to Las Vegas and Santa Fe), either to die or to assume new, healthier lives in the thin mountain air. Hospitals have continued to be major employers.

The Second World War brought two of the city's largest employers to Albuquerque: a large air force base and the Sandia National Laboratories, formed during the war for munitions development. Sandia Labs has since branched out into many areas of research in such diverse fields as ceramics and solar energy use. Electronics and clothing manufacture are among the newer industries responsible for the rapid growth of the city in the 1960s and 1970s. As the major city of the state, Albuquerque attracts residents of smaller towns from a radius of two hundred miles to its shopping centers and entertainment facilities, much as it did in the earlier days, making these industries also major sources of employment for Albuquerqueans.

Since World War II, freeways and shopping centers have drained Albuquerque's downtown area of commercial establishments. Just as the railroad moved the commercial center of the city east in the 1880s, the freeways have shifted it in the 1960s and 1970s still farther toward the mountains, where that center can be found in an amorphous sprawl of low buildings, large signs, and huge parking lots. The downtown area has been refurbished,

with a fine new plaza, modernized structures along Central Avenue, and handsome new buildings serving the banking, legal, and utility communities. However, the city's attempt at commercial renewal in the area in the late 1970s was a notable failure. "Renovation," "renewal," and "restoration" of old buildings are new words in Albuquerque, where magnificent old edifices have more frequently been destroyed; Huning's Castle and the Alvarado Hotel are only the best examples of what has been lost. Several older buildings along Central Avenue have now been refitted, and there is increasing movement of young families into old homes in the downtown communities. Most of what makes Albuquerque different from Fresno, Indianapolis, or Atlanta remains west of the railroad tracks, just as it was in 1706, 1880, and 1945.

A vestige of the character of Hispanic villages remains in the Rio Grande valley section of Albuquerque. Some of the old villages, no longer recognizable or now absorbed into the city, were built around plazas, lost today under asphalt and new buildings. Martineztown and Santa Barbara, enveloped by urban redevelopment, maintain a close relationship with the Church of San Ignacio. Craftsmen of the neighborhood poured and laid over five thousand adobe bricks used in the construction of the church in 1916. Other neighborhoods come together at Christmas to celebrate *Las Posadas* (a re-enactment of Mary and Joseph's search for shelter) or to outline their homes and walkways with *luminarias*, paper bags weighted with sand and glowing with the light of the votive candles inside. Also centered around the church, at least one neighborhood in the South Valley maintains its Penitente *morada*, while another on the West Mesa is completing the construction of a *santuario* (healing church). Neighborhoods identify themselves by association with a family grocery store, a church, or perhaps a ditch-cleaning group, and they are often held together by a common language or an elementary school. Many neighbors have the same last name in such family neighborhoods as Los Duranes, Los Griegos, Los Padillas, and Los Anayas.

The area around South Broadway has long been a black neighborhood, and its public library is the city's media center for black studies. Much of Albuquerque's early black community settled here and north of Central

Avenue on Arno Street while working for the Santa Fe Railroad.

At the turn of the century, members of some of the city's richly varied ethnic groups lived in close proximity to their fellows, including the Italians, many of whom had been neighbors in Lucca in northern Italy. The early Chinese population, half of whom were launderers in 1900, lived in a small Chinatown near the railroad station. In the 1980s, members of an ethnic community will meet to enjoy food, religious services, dances, or speaking together, but they now live in all parts of the city.

It is largely an interest in the renewal of quiet, tree-lined areas and their homes' architecture that holds together many of the other defined neighborhoods, such as Downtown, Huning-Highland, Silver Hill, and the Country Club area. Griegos, Downtown, Martinez-town–Santa Barbara, and Huning Highland residents have devised walking tours of their respective areas. The Chamber of Commerce or the Historic Landmarks Survey of Albuquerque can supply information about these tours.

Albuquerqueans amuse themselves in a variety of ways, some of which are familiar to citizens of other parts of the country: cruising in the exquisitely fitted and custom-decorated lowrider cars on Central Avenue (see section on Española, Tour 11); riding spirited horses among the cottonwoods and elms along the irrigation ditches of the Rio Grande valley; riding bicycles along one of the city's many bike trails; and screaming at a University of New Mexico basketball game, an auto race track (Al and Bobby Unser are homegrown heroes), or Triple-A Albuquerque Dukes baseball contest. More unusual are various types of escapes: to one of Albuquerque's many art galleries clustered around the university and around Old Town; to the Sandias for hiking, picnicking, or skiing; or to the open air, in a balloon. Albuquerque has become an international center for hot-air balloonists. Early risers on weekends at almost any time of the year will see the magnificent, parti-colored, silky envelopes and their wicker gondolas drifting over the city, for area residents own many of these showpieces. Record-setting transoceanic balloonists Maxie Anderson, Larry Newman, and Ben Abruzzo were all Albuquerque residents. (Anderson died in a ballooning accident in 1983.) After an earlier attempt to cross the Atlantic Ocean ended off the coast of Iceland,

Balloon Fiesta, *Steve Bercovitch.*

the three aeronauts crossed successfully from Presque Isle, Maine, to Miserey, France, in six days in August 1978. In commemoration of the first balloon flight across the Atlantic, their craft, the Double Eagle II, now rests on exhibit in the Smithsonian Institution in Washington.

Each October, balloon fever reaches a climax in the International Ballon Fiesta. In 1983, more than four hundred balloons and their owners came from all over the world for a week of daily ascents and games and nightly rounds of parties and celebrations. A tradition of the festival is a closing-day mass ascension, when the sky is crowded with a great many of the spectacular craft.

POINTS OF INTEREST

Albuquerque's many attractions include the following. They are numbered to correspond to their locations on the overall map of Albuquerque (page 238).

1. ALBUQUERQUE INTERNATIONAL AIRPORT (Yale Boulevard south of Gibson Boulevard, S.E.). Both the old airport, now a meeting hall, and the bustling "new" airport building, dating from 1954, are among the few in the world that are distinguishable from those in Cedar Rapids, Eureka, or Marseilles. The old building has huge beams supporting *latilla* ceilings and carved woodwork; the new one

Balloon Fiesta, *Harvey Caplin.*

includes high ceilings with carved beams and Indian-inspired mosaics among many New Mexican touches.

2. ALBUQUERQUE MUSEUM (2000 Mountain Road, N.W.)   In 1979 the Albuquerque Museum moved from pleasingly decorated but cramped quarters in the old air terminal to a bright building near Old Town. The new museum, constructed over the shell of a truck terminal, has space for several large exhibits at once, a courtyard for outdoor displays, and back gates through which guides lead architectural tours into some of the back streets of Old Town. In the first year after its moving, the museum showed internationally and region-ally inspired temporary exhibits—including one on innovative energy uses in New Mexico, a display of the arts of each of the state's peoples, an exhibit of Japanese art, a show on railroad days in Albuquerque, and a display of antique automobiles—typifying the museum's imaginative exhibit design. Extensive photo archives and taped memoirs of old-timers are maintained at the museum.

3. DOWNTOWN PLAZA (Fourth Street between Tijeras and Marquette streets, N.W.).   The large downtown plaza was part of a mid-1970s effort to revitalize the downtown area, which was decaying after businesses left for the northeast's shopping

centers. A fine, large fountain is a cool playground for children in the summer, and many
events and entertainments are held on the
raised stage at the west edge of the plaza.
Nearby are large new buildings, including a
well-designed city library, and some refurbished older buildings such as the KiMo Theater, a 1927 Art Deco movie palace, attesting to
Albuquerque's attempted downtown renaissance. The old city library, at Edith Street and
Central Avenue, is a handsomely restored and
refitted adobe, with comfortable rooms and
fireplaces, housing some of the library's special collections and the Center for the Book.

Each summer and fall, truck farmers sell
their fresh produce along a closed street near
the plaza several mornings a week. At the
southwest corner of the plaza, the Telephone
Pioneers run a small museum of old telephone
equipment.

4. HOSPITALS. Medical care has been a major industry in Albuquerque since the days of
the tuberculosis sanitoriums along Central Avenue. Four hospitals are of some special interest for varied reasons: the Veterans
Administration Hospital (Ridgecrest Drive
south of Gibson Boulevard, S.E.) is a cluster of
large buildings, the exteriors of which are

faithful to the Spanish-Pueblo style of architecture. Lovelace-Bataan Medical Center (across
Ridgecrest Drive from the V.A. Hospital) is
notable for its collection of Western art. It has
served as a referral hospital for many patients
from throughout New Mexico since it was
founded by Dr. W. R. Lovelace in 1947. The
Albuquerque Indian Health Service Hospital
(Lomas Boulevard and Vassar Drive, N.E.) is
designed in an Art Deco style, similar to hospitals in Washington, Alaska, and other places
fortunate enough to have had W.P.A. projects
during the Depression. The University of New
Mexico Hospital, alongside the Indian Hospital, is the teaching hospital for the university's
medical school.

5. HURLEY PARK (Yucca Drive and Bluewater
Road, N.W.) typifies much of the good and
the awful of New Mexico's big city. Perched
on the West Mesa above the Rio Grande, the
small park provides a superb view of the valley below and the mountains beyond the city.
Luscious grass, watered by Albuquerque's
plentiful underground supplies, belies the
city's edge-of-desert location. However, the
park is itself at times inundated with the tide
of litter that is the shame of many parts of the
city. Albuquerque has a great many small and

medium-sized parks, carefully manicured by the city and all abuzz with the activities of thousands of adults and children playing soccer, football, softball, and other sports, or resting under the trees. Among the most used are Roosevelt Park, a dark and grassy glade offering cool beauty on the hottest days of summer (Coal Avenue just east of I-25) and Tingley Park, another favored spot for picnics, just north of the Rio Grande Zoo.

6. INDIAN PUEBLO CULTURAL CENTER (Twelfth Street and Indian School Road, N.W.). Located across the street from the former Albuquerque Indian School, the IPCC, run by the All-Indian Pueblo Council, is housed in a modernistic structure built in 1976. The cultural center contains two levels of museum displays surrounding a large central courtyard where Pueblo dances are held on many weekends and holidays throughout the year. The walls of the courtyard display large murals, painted by some of the best-known Pueblo painters. In 1981 a controversial action of the council dictated that some of the murals be painted over, as they were considered to portray sensitive religious material. The permanent exhibits of pottery, photographs, and other artifacts on the upper level and dioramas of Pueblo life on the lower level portray something of the art and culture of the Pueblos. Frequently changing temporary exhibits of Pueblo crafts fill other rooms.

7. NATIONAL ATOMIC MUSEUM (on Kirtland Air Force Base on Wyoming Boulevard south of Gibson Boulevard, S.E.) represents New Mexico's important role in the creation of nuclear weapons at the Los Alamos Scientific Laboratories, the Trinity Test Site near White Sands, and the Sandia Laboratories surrounding this museum. Displays of nuclear weapons are impressive and frightening; the collection of nuclear weapons is touted as "the world's most complete." Exhibits having to do with energy research into both production and conservation are recent additions. A large experimental solar collector made of hundreds of

mirrors focused on a collecting tower can also be viewed by the public. This impressive construction of steel and glass is seven miles south of the National Atomic Museum and is open for display on weekdays only.

8. RIO GRANDE NATURE CENTER (Candelaria Road, N.W., at the Rio Grande). Pheasants, roadrunners, toads, beavers, and skunks, which inhabit the Rio Grande Bosque area (the woods on the river's banks), are joined in May and October by migrating Canada and snow geese, perhaps some of the sandhill cranes, and an occasional whooping crane as the Candelaria Farms Nature Center becomes established as a refuge for the large birds on their way between summer quarters in Idaho, Montana, and western Canada and winter habitats at the Bosque del Apache and La Joya wildlife refuges south along the Rio Grande. Cultivated seed crops and an artificial pond attract many other types of birds. The area, characterized by a cottonwood woodland with Russian olive understory and meadowlands, has been seasonal home to more than thirty-six species of songbirds. The nature center's building, placed partially underground so as to intrude as little as possible in the natural setting, is set next to the artificial pond and is designed for close observation both above the water and below, with a periscope through which to observe plant and animal life in the pond. Visitors may tour the center's excellent natural history exhibits, which explain the ecology of the area, or may walk along the nature trails.

The wooded area of the bosque along the river near the nature center has long been used as a destination of weekend boating and hiking groups, a site for birdwatching, and, unfortunately, a dumping ground for assorted trash. The City of Albuquerque, along with other agencies, has a master plan to develop the bosque within the city both for improvement of public access and for protection of its natural features. Extension of the bicycle path along the river, construction of bridle paths and pedestrian ditch crossings, and development of a system of parks along both sides of

Sandia Tram, *Harvey Caplin*.

the river are envisioned as means of exploiting and preserving the wild beauty of New Mexico's most important river.

9. PETROGLYPH STATE PARK (Atrisco Road, N.W., northwest of the Coors exit from I-40). This small state park on volcanic rubble preserves drawings made by Pueblo tribesmen in centuries past. The simple, whimsical faces, snakes, men, and other figures are etched on the black lava. The petroglyphs are found along both sides of a trail to the top of a volcanic mound. This mound and the park that

surrounds it lie along a line of several other small volcanic cones, long dormant, which form the western edge of the city.

10. RIO GRANDE ZOO (Atlantic and Tenth streets, S.W.). A pleasant, medium-sized facility which has largely done away with the crowded wire cages of previous years, the zoo displays several unusual buildings, including a tropical aviary and a reptile house. Of more local import, a large prairie dog village attracts onlookers of all ages as the centerpiece of a children's zoo. The zoo is adjacent to several

parks where one can eat a quiet lunch or watch a lively softball game. West of the zoo is a long artificial pond, filled with water from the neighboring Rio Grande. Photographs from the 1930s, labeling the pond the "municipal bathing beach," show Albuquerqueans lolling on sand or swimming in clear water. Symptomatic perhaps of the city center's move to the east, the pond has become fit only for ducks and fish, and sometimes not even for them—several outbreaks of botulism decimated the flocks in the 1970s. The area is now called Tingley Beach, after the benevolent despot who acted as mayor of Albuquerque in the Depression years. An attempt to restore some of the pond's former beauty began in 1980.

11. SANDIA TRAM (west side of the Sandias, off Tramway Boulevard, N.E.). Called the "world's longest," the tram gives magnificent views of the rugged west side of the Sandias. It climbs 3,819 feet and has only two supporting towers along its 2.7-mile course. Passengers on the eighteen-minute ride sometimes see eagles, mountain sheep, and other wildlife. One is equally likely to see a human soaring past the tram car, as the Sandia Crest is a favorite spot for experienced hang-glider pilots. The upper end of the tram is at the top of the ski lifts on the east side; Alpine and cross-country skiing or hiking along the Crest, which reaches 10,610 feet at its highest point (also accessible by road from the east; see Tour 15), are favorite activities of Albuquerqueans and visitors.

12. STATE FAIRGROUNDS (between Lomas Boulevard and Central Avenue, San Pedro Drive and Louisiana Boulevard, N.E.). The state fair, held in September, is an old-fashioned event, with prize pigs and pickles, concho belts and crowing roosters, a midway and an art exhibit, which annually draws a crowd surpassing the state's population of 1.3 million. A rodeo and horse racing are featured attractions that, along with the many small dramas of competitions in Indian crafts, hobbies, horseshoe throwing, and rabbit raising, are major magnets that drain other areas of the state for two weeks each fall. At other times during the year the fairgrounds play host to such diverse activities as the New Mexico Arts and Crafts Fair, a 4-H fair, an Arabian Horse show, dog shows, ice shows in Tingley Coliseum, flower shows, and a huge outdoor flea market held each weekend except during the state fair.

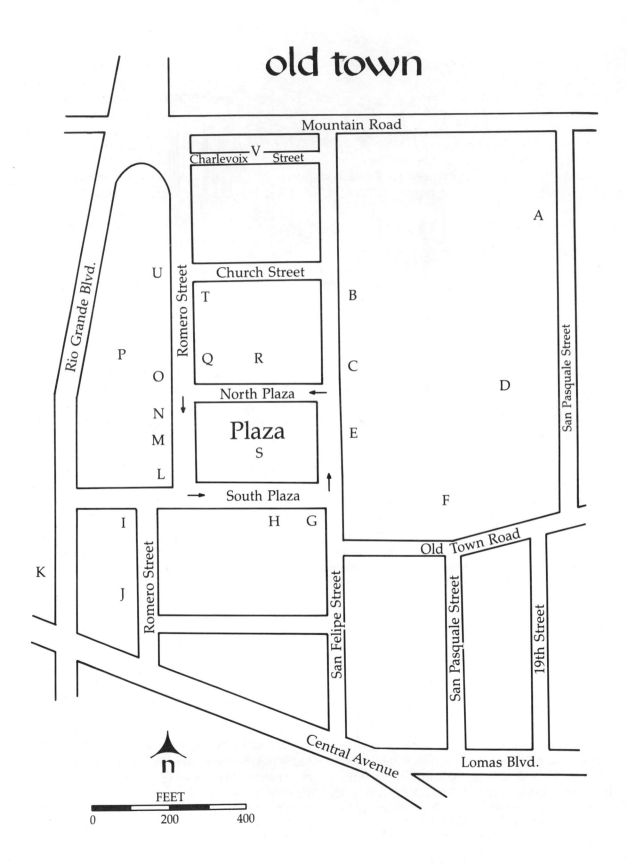

old town

Mountain Road

Charlevoix V Street

Rio Grande Blvd.

Romero Street

Church Street

North Plaza

Plaza

South Plaza

Old Town Road

San Pasquale Street

San Pasquale Street

San Felipe Street

Romero Street

19th Street

Central Avenue

Lomas Blvd.

A

B

C

D

E

F

G

H

I

J

K

L

M

N

O

P

Q

R

S

T

U

V

n

FEET

0   200   400

13. OLD TOWN (near Central Avenue and Rio Grande Boulevard, N.W.). Migratory hunters and gatherers were the first people to camp in the Old Town area, but the original settlers, who came in about A.D. 500, are thought to have been pithouse dwellers. Tiwa-speaking Indians had built villages in the spot by about 1300. They were peaceful farmers who lived in villages along the river. Encounters with the Spanish explorers from the mid- to late sixteenth century were often devastating for the local Pueblo people and their farms. Raids by nomadic tribes and abuses by some Spanish settlers further beset the Pueblos in the early 1600s. These difficulties and attempts by Franciscan priests to centralize the population caused the number of Tiwas in the area to decrease greatly between 1630 and 1680. A Spanish settler, Diego de Trujillo, is thought to have built his home directly on the site of Old Town in 1632. All of the *estancias* along the river were destroyed during the Pueblo Revolt of 1680, and the pueblos were deserted. In 1693, after de Vargas had reoccupied Santa Fe and Taos, Spanish settlers moved back into the region. Francisco Cuervo y Valdés was made interim governor upon the death of de Vargas. He established a villa named after the viceroy of New Spain, who was the duke of Alburquerque. Although Cuervo had not fulfilled the requirements for a villa, settlers did move to the area, and a church was begun in 1706. The Villa de San Felipe de Alburquerque was a collection of isolated and vulnerable farms and ranches in the years betwen 1706 and 1779. Then authorities in Santa Fe ordered settlers to build and live around defensible plazas to decrease the possibility of success for Indian raiders. It was this order that brought permanent residents to the plaza around the church.

Trade, except for that with official Spanish caravans, was illegal until 1821. Trade with the Republic of Mexico and with the United States then began with a brief flurry, bringing Albuquerque lasting importance as a main stop on the trail to Chihuahua. The standard of living rose dramatically. General Stephen Watts Kearny marched into Old Town and pro-claimed it to be a part of the United States in 1846. The establishment of a U.S. military garrison increased the population and provided it with added protection. For two confusing weeks in 1862, Albuquerque was a part of the Confederacy, but the Confederate forces retreated without fighting any battle in the town. The military post was withdrawn in 1867, causing the economy to flounder briefly. The railroad arrived in 1880, its straight course bypassing Old Town, which then lost its previous role as a market area and became a church center and Spanish residential neighborhood for New Town. The territorial fair was held just outside of Old Town, keeping it lively for part of the year, and gradually shops opened to serve tourists. Artists, many of whom lived west of Rio Grande Boulevard, sold their works in galleries there. Shop owners and residents have been alternately friendly and at odds as they work together on zoning, fiestas, and remodeling. Past events and past styles have left their mark on the restaurants, shops, and homes of today's Old Town.

Side streets, hidden patios, the smells of roasting chile and burning piñon, a street musician, or an elaborate wedding party emerging from San Felipe Church may delight the visitor. Surprises are part of Old Town's charm. In digging foundations for new construction, people have found arrowheads left by early Indian hunters, bits of armor, Spanish colonial housewares and grave goods, Civil War cannons and shot, and old coins.

A walking tour may acquaint the visitor with the flavor of Old Town. The tour begins at the Museum of Albuquerque which also offers guided tours during the warm seasons. (See the Old Town map, p. 250, for details of the tour.) Across the street from the museum entrance is Tiguex Park, with a popular small playground and welcoming thick grass covering what not long ago was a productive truck farm. It has been the site of museum festivals, political rallies, and Civil War re-enactments. North of the park is the location of the Natural History Museum, designed to house some of the skeletons and fossils of New Mexico's

many dinosaurs and other paleontological finds and to describe New Mexico's six natural life zones. The wiry dinosaur coelophysis is the museum's mascot.

To the south of the park, along Old Town Road, are some of the few remaining examples of straw- and mud-plastered houses in the city of Albuquerque. North of the museum, a large hotel covers what until very recently was farmland that grew vegetables.

An exit from the museum courtyard (A) leads directly into one of Old Town's alleyways. The shop and gallery buildings along the alley are new and, in accordance with historic zone rulings, conform to surrounding styles. The alley emerges on San Felipe Street, the west side of which had been a residential area since 1750 and now houses shops and studios under its portals.

The house at 306 San Felipe Street (B), built in the 1890s, had an adobe exterior shaped to look like clay-fired brick. That surface is now covered with stucco made to look like adobe. Changing fashion has dictated adobe homes all over the valley made to look like brick, stone, or wood, and wooden frame houses given the contour, color, and texture of adobe.

On the northeast corner of San Felipe Street and North Plaza (C), the Albuquerque Academy had its beginning in an old adobe building in 1878. At this location (302 San Felipe), the Herman Blueher home was built in 1898. The large Italianate brick house is now the core of a neo-Pueblo style restaurant. Blueher came to Albuquerque as a hired hand but soon amassed a small fortune, kept nearby vegetable farms, tried growing tobacco, owned a farm equipment store, and brought the first draft horses to Albuquerque.

Walking east into the Plaza Hacienda (D), one sees a long row of shops fitted into what once were stables and servants' quarters.

Back on San Felipe Street, the old Armijo home (the 200 block of San Felipe), built in 1880, faces the plaza. Its original wooden false front has been replaced by the present facade and the portal (arcade) that shelters jewelry and pottery vendors, most of whom come from Santo Domingo Pueblo to spend their days selling crafts and watching tourists. It is said that the spirit of a girl who died in a servant's room in the house haunts the building and calls out the names of employees of the restaurant which now occupies the premises. In the 1970s and early 1980s, a long-brewing controversy over the restaurant's request for a beer and wine license divided the Old Town community. The battle was fought in the courts and on the plaza; San Felipe church members were prominent in the fight, at one point using the weapon of prohibiting visitors from entering the church except during Mass.

An alleyway south of the Armijo house leads to the sealed wishing well (F), more shops, and the favorite territory of the local cat population within another and much older Armijo home. The *placita* (little plaza) style of house was developed not only for defense purposes but also as a way to accommodate several generations of the same family in different wings of a single dwelling. South of this building, Casa Armijo, the forty-room hacienda of former governor Manuel Armijo, stood until 1909.

Still another Armijo house, the home of Cristóbal Armijo (G), dating from 1880, stands at the corner of South Plaza and San Felipe Street (2004 South Plaza). Cristóbal Armijo was a town alderman, county commissioner, and merchant.

Adjacent buildings (H) are said to have

housed the town's first barber-dentist-surgeon, a restaurant, a hide and wool store, a saloon, and the first drugstore. On the plaza's southeast corner (2036 South Plaza) the brick Springer house, its Queen Anne–style decorations and bay windows now obscured by a newer facade, was grocer Manuel Springer's home until his death in 1917. Old Town residents say that the house was a brothel and speakeasy during Prohibition. The corner building across Romero Street (121 Romero) (I) was the location of a bank established in 1878 that was later replaced by the Romero grocery store. Its wooden floors, tin ceiling, and adobe walls now surround gifts rather than vegetables, but the structure remains in much the same condition as when it was built in the 1890s.

South on Romero Street, shops cluster along both the street and another *placita*, the Pass of the Bells, on the west side (J).

Going west on South Plaza, one is confronted with the traffic of Rio Grande Boulevard, formerly known as Main Street, which delimits what is now Old Town. What was once the U.S. military post corral is still a parking lot, now for a shopping center (K). South of this lot was the town jail that held criminals serving their sentences or waiting to be hanged. On small, quiet streets heading west from Rio Grande Boulevard are the cottages of artists, who developed a nonconforming colony here in the 1930s. The colony soon faded, as have the little pastel and earth-toned houses.

El Parrillán ("open-air market") is the name given the building at the northwest corner of the plaza (201 Romero) (L). A shop, a tavern, a barbershop, and a home have occupied the building; the site was probably used as a market before the present building went up about 1898. A romantic legend about the spot tells of a young army colonel and future bride. Col. William McGuiness lived in a house on this corner at the time of the Civil War skirmish near the plaza. He saw a child leave her family's departing wagon and race back to her home on the plaza through the gunfire to rescue her beloved doll. Years later, McGuiness met and married the brave girl.

The Romero house (205 Romero) was built in prairie and Mediterranean styles in 1915 and stands unchanged behind its tiny, grassy yard (M).

Part of the original San Felipe Church lies under the brick store at 301 Romero (N). This brick-trimmed former post office still has a mailbox in front of it.

A visitor information center and public rest rooms face the plaza on Romero Street (O).

Behind the parking area, former postmaster Charlie Mann had a barn for his truck farm early in this century. The simple adobe structure is now filled with pottery and gifts instead of farm machinery and produce (P).

On North Plaza is the entrance to Sister Blandina Convent (Q), built in 1881 as a dormitory for nuns who came to teach in the nearby school.

The entrance to the Church of San Felipe de Neri is centered between the two "folk Gothic" towers (R). This building was begun in a cruciform plan in 1793, after the small adobe church west of the plaza disintegrated. Architectural changes on the exterior of the structure have been made frequently, so that today the church is a pleasing mixture of Spanish colonial, Gothic, Pueblo revival, and modern Albuquerque styles. Visitors are welcome to attend church services.

The plaza itself (S) is still the tranquil center of neighborhood activity. Elderly gentlemen

Luminarias in Old Town Plaza, *Hugh Atwell*.

chat on the benches, musicians and dancers perform on or near the bandstand, and climbing children inadvertently polish the brass on the replicas of Civil War cannons. The plaza was enclosed at various times by white picket fencing and a hideous, WPA-built stone wall. In spring the plaza perimeter is lined with yellow daffodils, and on Christmas Eve the golden glow of *luminarias* outlines all of its walkways.

A small bell tower on the roof of the building at 409 Romero Street (T) is now without the bell that called children to Our Lady of the Angels Schools in 1881. The building served brief stints as the town hall and as a museum,

and it now houses several shops. It has been altered very little since its construction; one should note its weathered but finely carved doorway and Corinthian columns.

The Vigil house at 413 Romero Street (U) is built of double-thick *terrones* (sod bricks). The *terrones* are similar in size and shape to adobes but are cut from riverbed mud, thick with root systems that strengthen the bricks. Remodelers, in an attempt to make the building look more "Pueblo," added false *vigas* (extended, rough-cut roof beams) on both the south and east exterior walls, giving the impression that the beams crisscross inside.

Charlevoix Alley (V) takes the visitor just

south of what is falsely rumored to have been a red-light district. (The real red-light area stretched along Central Avenue south of the plaza until about 1930.) South on San Felipe Street one finds an alleyway leading to a small chapel, open to visitors (W), with many fine handworked details.

The next alley leads back to the Albuquerque Museum.

14. UNIVERSITY OF NEW MEXICO. Occupying a large block of land east of the downtown area between Central Avenue and Lomas Boulevard and between University and Girard boulevards, the University of New Mexico is of interest for the beauty of its architecture and landscaping as well as for its museums, libraries, and cultural events.

An act of the New Mexico Territorial Legislature created the university in 1889. Initially it rented rooms in a preparatory school, but in 1892 the first permanent building, Hodgin Hall, was created on a campus beyond the eastern edge of the city. This three-storied, red brick Victorian-style edifice still exists, carefully hidden in the stucco Pueblo-style shell which made it the first of numerous campus buildings to be styled after the Rio Grande pueblos. Hodgin Hall is the only remnant of the University's Victorian Gothic period. The present face of the campus was determined by the policies of Dr. William Tight, a geologist who became president of the university in 1901. An enthusiastic student of Pueblo architecture, Tight decreed that all future buildings be designed in what is now called Spanish-Pueblo style. His recommendation was adopted much later—in 1927—after considerable dissent, and Tight lost his job amidst criticism of the university's architecture. Continuation of his policy, however, has led to a campus more homogeneous in appearance than most in this country.

Each Arbor Day, Tight led students into the mountains, and an evergreen was brought back to campus. This tradition, practiced throughout his tenure as president, resulted in the now-stately Tight Grove at the campus's southwest corner. The tremendous expansion of the student body, from 99 in 1912 to 21,400 in 1980, has been accommodated through several stages of growth. Purchases and gifts of land on the desertlike East Mesa continued through the early years of the twentieth century. Student enrollment reached 1,000 in 1930. In 1933 the university's regents first retained Santa Fe architect John Gaw Meem, who designed the unique and stately Zimmerman Library, the administration building, Scholes Hall, and many other structures over the next thirty years.

During World War II, Meem's magnificent designs were surrounded by long, low, gunmetal gray temporary buildings and quonset huts, used initially in officer training. Between 1945 and 1950, student enrollment spurted from eighteen hundred to five thousand, increasing the need for space. By 1960 Meem and later San Francisco architect John Warnicke had developed plans for a permanent campus to serve twenty-five thousand students. This plan has guided further development of buildings and landscaping and resulted in the creation of an automobile-free central campus, with a large plaza and a grass-bordered lake.

University policy dictates that each building retain ties to the theme of the Spanish-Pueblo revival, but allows creativity within modern idioms. The first building to be permitted a freer interpretation of the style was the College of Education, in 1963, which sparked a controversy similar in intensity to those of the Tight era, but with dissidents taking the opposite view to the one they had held in the twenties. Construction was especially active during the late 1960s, but the last temporary World War II building was not removed until 1978, to be replaced by the modern, solar-powered Mechanical Engineering Building.

Expansion of the campus to the south for new sports facilities and to the north around a new medical school and relocated law, pharmacy, and nursing schools was rapid in the late 1960s and 1970s. The stark concrete buildings of the North Campus surround a large

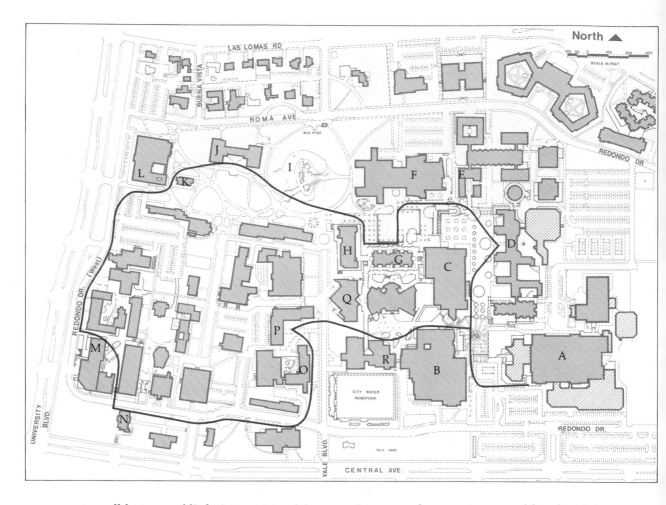

concrete mall but are of little interest to visitors, with the exception of the Medical Center Library, the Children's Psychiatric Center, and the Law School building, Bratton Hall. The medical library's commanding view of the Sandia Mountains through a three-story glass wall facing northeast lures students from all over the campus. The Children's Psychiatric Center, completed in 1980, is a treatment facility for children from the entire state, housed in beautiful small "cottages" on a campus of its own. Both the law and medical schools are known for affording "hands-on" experience to their students. The law school requires practical experience in supplying legal care to disadvantaged clients; the medical school has developed a nontraditional approach to teaching that trains some students in basic medical

sciences such as anatomy and biochemistry through contact with patient problems and a preceptorship with a physician in a smaller New Mexico town.

The university has strengths in many areas but is especially well-known for the quality of its anthropology and music departments. Capitalizing on its proximity to Mexico and its high proportion of Spanish-speaking students, the university has also developed specialties in Latin American culture, history, and politics.

A walking tour of the main campus begins in the large parking lot at Stanford Drive and Central Avenue, shown on the accompanying map. It will take the visitor to the sites that follow, keyed by letter to the map.

Johnson Gym (A), now used for recreation, was replaced as a center for intercollegiate athletics by the University Arena, known locally as "The Pit," south of the main campus at University and Stadium boulevards. The gym boasts three fine swimming pools. A statue of the New Mexico *lobo,* or wolf, by former faculty member John Tatschl, stands in front of the building.

The Fine Arts Center (B), including Popejoy Hall, is certainly the performing arts center of Albuquerque. Popejoy Hall and two smaller theaters in the Fine Arts Center present varied cultural programs, including opera, chamber music, dance, drama, symphonic music, and touring performers of all kinds. Music students and faculty find the center an ample showcase for their talents. The U.N.M. Art Gallery presents exhibits gathered from its extensive collections, including an exceptional collection of photographs, as well as touring shows. Art and music libraries are located within this building. The John Robb Archive of Southwestern Music contains extensive collections of the folk music of New Mexico, much of which was collected by Dean Robb, a lawyer turned composer, musicologist, and music collector. This collection, staffed by knowledgeable musicians, is available to all. Information on the diverse cultural events taking place in the Fine Arts Center may be found at the box offices on the east face of the building and on kiosks throughout the campus.

The Student Union Building (C) contains meeting rooms and student services. Mesa Vista Hall (D) is now a rambling office building. Designed by John Gaw Meem, the structure was once the men's dormitory.

The Education Complex (E) consists of six interconnected buildings that house the College of Education's many areas of study, which range from early childhood to industrial education. Its west wall consists of a large stained-glass mural, designed by John Tatschl, spectacular in the afternoon sun.

Zimmerman Library (F), the main university library, presents fascinating contrasts. The soft curves designed by John Gaw Meem in the original structure of 1937 meet the angular contours of the additions of the 1960s and

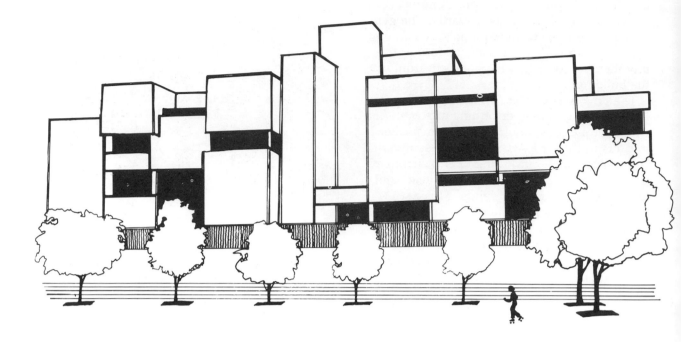

1970s. The high beam-and-*latilla* ceilings of the building's west end contrast with the cramped quarters of the tower bookstacks. Tremendous carved and decorated beams, desks, and corbels in the old section emit a peacefulness that contrasts with the jangling, wall-sized messages of the newer part. The old section of the library, west of the entrance, is a gem of Spanish-Pueblo architecture, and is now used for reading rooms and special collections. These include the well-stocked map room; the Coronado Room for Southwestern materials; the John Gaw Meem Room, honoring the architect with a collection of architectural materials including Mr. Meem's drawings; and the Clinton P. Anderson Room of Western Americana, where one may read books pertaining to the region in comfortable chairs in a beautiful setting resembling the library of a grandee. The newer section of the library, to the east, is spacious and comfortable. A multistory mural decorating the stairwell depicts the history of the alphabet. The east wing contains the library's general collections, which are especially strong in anthropology and Latin American studies, and various services for users.

Humanities (G), described as a "cubist's pueblo," and Ortega Hall (H), which complete the set of buildings surrounding the large Sherman Smith Plaza, are modernistic constructions housing liberal arts departments and classrooms. The plaza contains several kiosks on which notices of cars for sale and rides wanted vie with announcements of all that is happening in Albuquerque. The Duck Pond (I), completed in 1978, must be one of the few existing examples of pleasant natural landscaping replacing a road and parking lot.

Scholes Hall (J), the main administration building, was designed by John Gaw Meem and built by the Public Works Administration in 1936. The building is named for France Scholes, distinguished historian of Mexico and New Mexico in the period prior to the Pueblo Revolt of 1680, a former academic vice-president of the university. Meem designed the twin towers of the exterior to suggest the mission church at Acoma. Details inside and out reflect both Spanish and Indian influences.

The Alumni Memorial Chapel (K), dedicated in 1960 to honor university war dead, was designed by Meem and his associates. The outside resembles a Pueblo mission church, with massive stucco walls and twin bell towers. The interior features carved and painted corbels and square beams, with a large, serene *reredos* designed by the architect.

The Anthropology Building (L), once the Works Projects Administration–built student union, houses the Maxwell Museum of Anthropology, which contains as a permanent exhibit the story of man in the Southwest and offers impressive changing exhibitions of folk art and anthropological research from cultures throughout the world. The Department of Anthropology, occupying the balance of the building, has taken advantage of New Mexico's many archaeological sites in establishing a worldwide reputation, which now extends to anthropological and archaeological work throughout the world. Among the department's activities have been the unveiling and restoration of the ruins of Sapawe, a Tewa pueblo near El Rito, north of Española. New York's American Museum of Natural History and the National Park Service (which has offices for scientific study in this building) have joined the anthropology department in investigating the pueblos at Chaco Canyon and describing the remarkable irrigation systems, road and trade networks, and astronomical knowledge displayed by that civilization. Ongoing projects include further excavation at Gran Quivira, to the south, and at the pueblo ruin of Paa-ko, northeast of Albuquerque.

The Mechanical Engineering Building (M), one of several buildings housing engineering and applied technology, uses exclusively solar energy for heating and cooling. The sophisticated equipment for capturing the sun's energy, state-of-the-art for 1980 and very costly, can be viewed by the public, along with related exhibits. The building itself provides training opportunities for engineering and architecture students in the field of solar energy,

where New Mexico has played a leading role.

Hodgin Hall (N), described above, has recently been restored by university alumni as a campus showplace. To its west is the Tight Grove.

Castetter Hall (O), the biology building, has a 1960s addition, including a two-story-high atrium containing a large botanical collection. This is both a teaching collection, designed to show students and visitors examples of sixty-seven plant families, and a general-purpose exhibit of plants thought to be of interest. The spectacular collection is open to the public.

Northrop Hall (P) contains the Geology Department and its museum. The museum itself has an excellent collection of fossils, complemented by many examples of modern shells like those seen in the fossil record. Minerals from throughout the world are exhibited according to a scientific classification system, with New Mexico's minerals given special attention. There is a small display of photoluminescent rocks. The halls of the museum hold many showcases of geologic displays. Similar showcases, exhibiting work relevant to other areas of study, are found in many of the other buildings on the campus.

Walking between the bookstore (Q) and the Art Building (R) and past the Fine Arts Center (B), one returns to the parking lot where the tour began.

Tour 1: ALBUQUERQUE   259

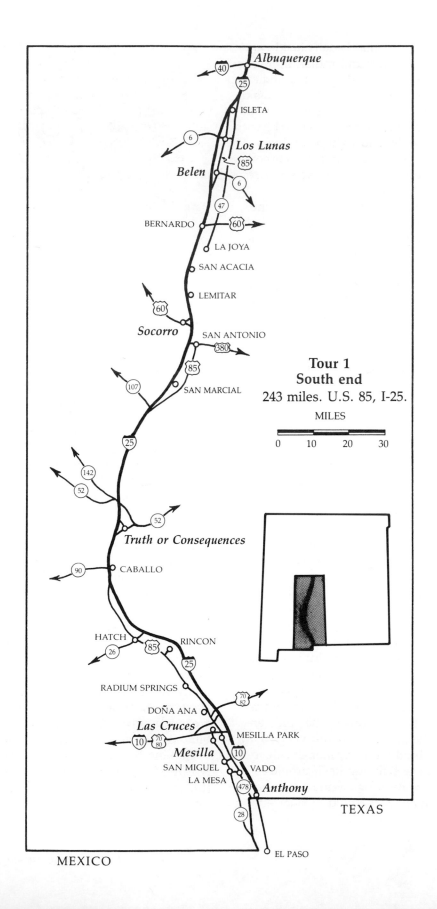

Tour 1
South end
243 miles. U.S. 85, I-25.

MILES

0   10   20   30

Leaving Albuquerque on old U.S. 85, Fourth Street passes through the barrio of Barelas. The highway crosses the Rio Grande on Bridge Street and immediately turns south on Isleta Boulevard. On Isleta, one traverses the South Valley, the result of the growth of the communities of Atrisco, Pajarito, and Los Padillas toward one another until they merged.

All of these villages began as Spanish land grants, a few of many made under the Spanish and later the Mexican governments. There were two major categories of land grants, those to communities and those to individuals. Land might have been granted to a homesteading individual or family, to an *empresario* (contractor) to promote settlement of an area, or to someone who had offered a government official personal or political favors. The granting of land stopped when the United States assumed control of New Mexico in 1846, although later homesteading was to some extent comparable. However, well into the twentieth century, agitation over the sale and alienation of land grants boiled over in many parts of New Mexico.

The Atrisco Land Grant's fractious history is typical in many respects. The king of Spain issued the grant to an early settler, Don Fernando Durán y Chávez, upon the Spanish reconquest of New Mexico in 1692. At that time the grant consisted of some forty-one thousand acres on the west side of the Rio Grande, south of the present site of Albuquerque. Three-quarters of a century later, descendants of the grantee petitioned the governor for more land, as they needed a place to gather firewood. They requested and received twenty-five thousand adjacent acres. At the time when Fray Francisco Atanasio Domínguez made his journey through the Southwest in 1776, he found 288 people (fifty-two families) living in Atlixco, near what is now the Westgate Heights subdivision.

As in most grants held by more than one individual, each family was accorded a *sitio*, or plot, for farming and for a dwelling near the water supply (in this case, the Rio Grande). In some grants, such as that at Carnuel in Tijeras

Canyon east of Albuquerque, the *sitio* consisted of a narrow strip of land that stretched from one canyon wall to the other, allowing each family to have a piece of each type of available land. In Atrisco, as in many grants, the livestock were grazed on the *ejidos*, common land held by all of the villagers. In part because of this provision for common land ownership, which is foreign to Anglo-American law, vast numbers of suits and countersuits have tied up title to many of the lands in the northern part of the state for years. Some of the quarrels generated are still unsettled, erupting periodically in violence.

The 1848 Treaty of Guadalupe Hidalgo, ending the Mexican-American War, specified that the United States was to respect the Spanish land grants. Because many of the grants had been imperfectly patented, or their boundaries had been vague or had shifted (as in the case of the Rio Grande, the east boundary of the Alameda Grant north of Albuquerque), problems with conflicting and questionable claims immediately ensued.

In 1854 the federal government sent Surveyor-General William Pelham to New Mexico to recommend on the adjudication of claims. Pelham began his enormous task by sorting through some one hundred sixty-eight thousand items of Spanish and Mexican archives, locating 1,715 that dealt with land grant questions. The surveyor-general recommended the confirmation of grants to the Pueblos, and Congress by 1860 had approved these, in addition to several individual and community grants. The work slowed, however; by 1886, when the Atrisco Grant was finally confirmed by Congress, only forty-six of the 205 claims that had been submitted to Pelham and his successors had been confirmed. Finally, in 1891, Congress established the Court of Private Land Claims to adjudicate the remaining disputed claims. The court considered 282 parcels containing almost thirty-five million acres. Many of the claims were fraudulent, some spectacularly so. By the end of its work, in the twentieth century, the court had allowed seventy-five grants in addition to eight Pueblo grants. Many of the parcels confirmed were markedly reduced in size compared to the areas originally claimed; in the end, some one million nine hundred thousand acres, or 6 percent of the total initially claimed, had been confirmed.

The history of the Atrisco Grant since its confirmation is similar to that of many others, embroiled as they have been in almost constant litigation. There have been numerous attempts to sell or divide part of the land, which has become valuable as Albuquerque's boundaries have stretched. An attempt to partition a large part of the grant into five-acre plots for the descendants of the grantees and several tries at selling land to outsiders at prices so low that intrigue was suggested have been rejected by New Mexico district courts. Finally, in a bitterly contested fight among descendants of the grantees, Westland Development Corporation was set up to develop common land remaining. Descendants were given shares in the corporation, but they have realized little profit from their ownership.

In the 1950s and 1960s, land grant activists such as Reies López Tijerina attempted to regain grant land lost through tax sales and U.S. Forest Service takeovers. Tijerina's Alianza Federal de los Mercedes (Federal Alliance for Land Grants) attempted legal action at first. Realizing that this recourse was both time-consuming and exceedingly expensive, the alliance turned to civil disobedience. Their efforts, which culminated in a raid on the Tierra Amarilla courthouse (see page 415) and included occupation of Echo Amphitheater Campground and the burning of some Forest Service signs, netted little more than prison terms for some of the leaders.

Mainly Hispanic, the South Valley has traditionally treasured its independence from the larger, urban, predominately Anglo-American Albuquerque. The area has been largely responsible for the defeat of several initiatives aimed at annexation of the Valley by the city or at consolidation of county and city governments. Their treasured independence has permitted the inhabitants freedom to burn trash and keep animals, but also has left the South Valley with poor police protection, roads, water supplies, and sewers, and virtually no park land.

The Hubbell house is one of many fine buildings interspersed among fast-food outlets and feed stores along busy Isleta Boulevard. James L. (Santiago) Hubbell bought and added to the house shortly after his arrival with Kearny's troops during the Mexican War. One of Santiago's sons, John Lorenzo Hubbell, founded a well-known trading post at Ganado, Arizona, on the Navajo Reservation, where he stimulated a renaissance in the Navajo crafts of weaving and jewelry making. Others of Hubbell's descendants were important in the early political life in Albuquerque. Santiago Hubbell's house at 6029 Isleta Boulevard, S.W., and John Lorenzo's trading post in Ganado look alike in many ways: both contained living quarters and retail establishments in similar long, low buildings.

ISLETA PUEBLO, 245 mi., lies along the Rio Grande, although pueblo lands stretch from the crest of the Manzano Mountains to beyond the Rio Puerco. It is reached either by continuing south on Isleta Boulevard (U.S. 85) or by taking the Isleta Pueblo exit from I-25.

Isleta is now one of the largest pueblos in existence, with a population of three thousand. Isleta and Sandia are the only remaining Tiwa-speaking pueblos of a string of some fifteen that once occupied the middle Rio Grande valley. Isletans' ancestors came from at least six settlements surrounding the present large pueblo, as well as from Portezuelo in Tijeras Canyon, east of Albuquerque. In addition, following a religious schism at Laguna Pueblo in 1881, Laguna religious leaders and some of their followers walked to the Rio Grande, where Isleta officials invited them to stay. Most eventually returned to Mesita on the Laguna homeland, but some stayed to care for their ritual Kachina masks, which are to remain in Isleta.

Isleta's large mission church named for Anthony of Padua, built in 1629 on the north edge of the main plaza and restored after its destruction in the Pueblo Revolt, serves as the village's focal point. Its massive walls have frequently been depicted by artists. The church contains many relics, among them several large and ancient paintings of saints important to the village. According to tradition, the church is the resting place of Fray Juan de Padilla, one of two Franciscans to have remained behind because of their missionary zeal when Coronado's expedition returned to Mexico in 1542. Padilla is said to have left the valley of the Rio Grande shortly thereafter, intending to convert the Indians of the ephemeral Quivira. Legend states that he was killed along the way and that his body was mysteriously transported to Isleta, where it was buried in the church in a cottonwood coffin. Even now, so the story goes, the body of the venerated priest can be counted upon to rise periodically to perform miracles.

Isleta Pueblo played an important part in the events of the Pueblo Revolt. Alonzo García, lieutenant governor of New Mexico in 1680, was in Isleta when the revolt broke out. Fearing from reports of events in Santa Fe that Governor Otermín and the entire northern colony had been exterminated, he fled south to El Paso del Norte in August 1680, taking with him the Spanish settlers of the southern part of New Mexico, most of the Isleta tribe, and remnants of the Piro tribe, which had been living near present-day Socorro. Otermín and the survivors of Santa Fe arrived in Isleta to find the pueblo virtually deserted. When Otermín attempted reconquest in 1681, many of the erstwhile inhabitants of Isleta accompanied him, only to discover that the pueblo had been occupied by Indians from other pueblos. With the failure of this mission, the Christianized Indians returned with Otermín to El Paso. Near that town they built a pueblo

Irrigation Ditch, *Jackie Fuqua.*

Isleta Window View, *Dave Wilson.*

which still exists as Ysleta del Sur, though only recently has an effort been made to revive traditions lost through three centuries of acculturation.

In 1692 the new governor, de Vargas, peaceably subdued the occupants of the old pueblo, making it his headquarters as he prepared for the reconquest of the northern pueblos and Santa Fe. Since that time, the inhabitants of Isleta have been at peace. Most now work in Albuquerque or in their fields along the Rio Grande. Although the trees are not as productive as in former years, Isletans still tend orchards especially known in the past for their fine peaches. Some jewelry and pottery are also made in the village.

Los Lunas, 252 mi. (alt. 4,841, pop. 3,531), was named for the Luna family, which began a sheep-ranching operation centered here in 1808. A small colony of sheepherders and other functionaries in the large ranching business grew up in the town. Solomon Luna, son of the ranch's founder, was well-known as one of the principal political chieftains of New Mexico at the time it became a territory of the United States in 1846. He and his successors controlled the political destiny of Valencia County until the Roosevelt New Deal wrested it from the Republican Party supported by the Luna family. Luna often controlled more than the votes; old-timers claim that all articles of the constitution drafted before statehood were either written by or cleared with the *jefe* (chief or boss). Luna insisted that provisions be written into the constitution to protect the rights of the Spanish inhabitants under the American government. But business came first; to Luna is attributed the statement, *Educar un muchacho es perder un buen pastor* ("To educate a boy is to lose a good shepherd").

The Luna mansion has been restored to its former glory and is now a restaurant on N.M. 6 just west of U.S. 85. Many of its former furnishings and architectural details dating from the early twentieth century, which were once scattered throughout the state, have been reinstated.

Several small farming villages stand on both sides of the Rio Grande between Los Lunas and the next large town, Belen. Tomé, the first of the small towns established on the east bank, was almost wiped out by a Comanche raid in 1776 and was subjected to frequent raids by Comanches and Apaches throughout its early years. Tomé is now a quiet town, best known for its impressive Easter sunrise procession to the top of Tomé Hill.

BELEN (formerly Belem, or Bethlehem), 262 mi., on U.S. 85 (alt. 4,794, pop. 5,607), is known as the "Hub City" for its prominence as a railroad center. A community grant of the land on which Belen was founded was made by the Spanish governor of Santa Fe in 1740 to twenty-four families, probably from settlements farther north along the river. Six years later, members of a group known as *genízaros*, Indians separated from their tribes and living as Hispanics, appealed to the viceroy in Mexico City with the claim that they had settled on the land granted to the Spanish years before the arrival of the Europeans. The protest was disallowed, but the *genízaros* continued to live in the area, using the rich river-bottom lands along with the Spanish settlers.

Belen's prosperous merchants contributed heavily to the building of the railroad, assuring that it would pass through their town. The arrival of the railroad from the east spurred Belen's growth, and it came to depend upon the railroad and upon trade with the surrounding agricultural region. Freight trains bound from Denver to El Paso or from Chicago to Los Angeles and passenger trains taking the original route through Lamy and Albuquerque all converge on the large rail yards in Belen. The coming of the freeway in the 1960s brought Albuquerque within reach of many living in what had been Belen's trading area, leaving some of the main street's storefronts unoccupied.

From Belen, N.M. 6 roughly parallels the "Belen cutoff," the railroad line southeast to Abo Pass, where the road meets U.S. 60. At a point six miles southeast of Belen on N.M. 6, a graveled road leads almost due east to John F. Kennedy Campground, the only Forest Service campground on the west side of the Manzanos or Sandias. From the campground a trail leads to the crest of the Manzanos, a network of trails along the top, and the towns and campgrounds of the east side.

Also near the foot of the west wall of the Manzanos is the partially excavated Comanche Springs site, which gives evidence of occupation dating back at least three thousand years. The discovery in the ruins of bison bones west of the previously accepted range of the animal surprised archaeologists; Spanish majolica pottery sherds indicate that Hispanic settlers of 1600 to 1700 followed the archaic hunters, the basketmakers, and the Anasazi at this location.

SIDE TOUR

Midway store, Jarales, *Paul Murphy.*

Leaving Belen, the traveler has a choice of routes: across the mesas west of the Rio Grande on I-25, or the older way south along the valley floor on N.M. 116. Between Belen and Bernardo, N.M. 116 uses the old U.S. 85 roadbed, passing towns made indistinct by the spread-out suburban lifestyle of the mid-twentieth century. The San Juan Baptista Mission, whose history and exact location are unclear, apparently occupied a site near SABINAL, 274 mi. Franciscan fathers, along with their Piro (or Tiwa) converts, had abandoned the mission by 1626. Over one hundred fifty years later, Apaches settled here after signing a peace treaty with the Spanish Crown. The Apaches did not remain long, but during the first half of the nineteenth century Sabinal was resettled as part of the colonization process that eventually repopulated the entire Rio Grande valley to El Paso.

The de Veitia family, of Basque origin, came to New Mexico after the 1692 reconquest and lived near Santa Cruz, north of Santa Fe. Their descendants became part of the colonization of the Rio Abajo ("downriver region") when they founded Los Abeytas, 276 mi., in the late 1700s.

BERNARDO's store and gas station, 279 mi., mark the intersection with U.S. 60 east and Tour 8. Between Bernardo and Socorro, U.S. 60, the first transcontinental automobile route, shares the roadway with I-25. The mountains just to the west are the Ladrones ('thieves"), named for Navajos, Apaches, and their later Anglo-American counterparts who stole horses from Rio Grande towns and hid out there. The mountains look bare from the interstate, but an early Spanish mission and sheep-raising town did exist on their western side, first as Santa Rita, later as Riley. Today Riley is one of New Mexico's dozens of abandoned towns, beautiful and frightening, and quite distinct from the places that are being repopulated and commercialized as "ghost towns."

Just south of Bernardo, the Rio Puerco enters the Rio Grande. (*Puerco* means "pig," in the sense of "dirty"; the name refers both to the river's silty water and to its ugly, crumbling banks. There are three rivers in the state with this name.) This river rises north of Cuba and flows nearly straight south, making a sharp V with the Rio Grande. Over the 145 miles between Cuba and Bernardo, the Rio Puerco sustains no living town. At the turn of the century, developers predicted that its entire valley would be settled and would rival the Rio Grande's, but evidently few were lured to the "green banks" of the Rio Puerco.

Beyond the Rio Puerco bridge the interstate leaves the Rio Grande and, for the twelve miles before it crosses the Rio Salado ("salty river"), passes virtually no sign of human habitation. This is also the only stretch of I-25 between Albuquerque and El Paso not paralleled by an older, alternate route. Curiously, this area once supported numerous settlements. During the formative era of Pueblo development, it was the beneficiary of cross-fertilization between the Mogollon culture to the south and west and the Anasazi culture to the north. Anthropologists recognize the resulting "Jornada" culture by its pit houses, aboveground pueblos, and black-on-white and brown pottery, found in the valleys of the Rio Grande and such tributaries as the Rio Puerco

and the Rio Salado here. Later, during the Pueblo period proper, this area belonged to the Piros. At the time of contact with the Spanish, Piros inhabited twenty-two pueblos, of which thirteen fronted the Rio Grande, stretching from Sabinal to towns now covered by Elephant Butte Lake. There were at least forty-five settlements, representing an estimated population of over twelve thousand, just prior to the coming of the Spanish, when the Piros lived in smaller villages for more efficient use of resources. Early explorers described eight Rio Grande Piro pueblos, all of which received the attention of mission fathers. By the later 1670s there were only three left. During the 1680 Pueblo Revolt, the majority of the Piros retreated with the Spanish to the El Paso area. Their towns were burned, either by the victorious northern Pueblo Indians or by Spanish expeditions attempting reconquest. None were reoccupied, and the Rio Abajo ("lower river") remained uninhabited for a century and a half. The Piros as a people disappeared, although some residents of the Tortugas settlement southeast of Las Cruces claim to be their descendants.

One of the most important Piro pueblos for the Spanish, and the northernmost Piro town about which much is known, was SEVILLETA ("little Seville"), located ten miles south of Ber-

nardo on the east bank of the Rio Grande where the village of La Joya now stands. There were originally two towns. Both were deserted early in the 1600s, and one was reclaimed in 1628 when Franciscan fathers supervised the building of the San Luis Obispo Mission. After increased hostilities with the Apaches, Sevilleta was "congregated" with Alamillo in 1660 and abandoned after 1680. People from Chimayo recolonized the old pueblo in 1800. Zebulon Pike, an American soldier who made his way into New Mexico and was accused of being a spy and escorted down the Rio Grande by authorities of New Spain, passed through Sevilleta in 1807. He described it in his journal as a well-laid-out little town, neat and prosperous. (The main trail through New Mexico, the Camino Real, stayed on the east bank of the river from the time of the Pueblo Revolt until the early 1800s.) Sometime during the nineteenth century, the village's name changed to La Joya de Sevilleta and, finally, to La Joya ("the jewel"). Since the 1970s, former residents have been moving back to their town, approachable by paved road only via N.M. 47 from Bernardo.

Public agencies protect the land and wildlife on both sides of the river here. On the west side, Exit 169, 285 mi., provides access to the La Joya State Game Refuge. In 1973 the Na-

Sand Dunes, *Ed Tilgner.*

ture Conservancy bought much of the old Sevilleta Grant east of the river and turned it over to the U.S. Fish and Wildlife Service, which administers it as the Sevilleta National Wildlife Refuge, reached via La Joya.

The Shifting Sands rest area, 288 mi., has been a stopping point since the early days of automobile travel. A few miles after crossing the Rio Salado, I-25 suddenly drops into a part of the valley that, until this century, supplied bread and wine to large areas of New Mexico and beyond. Irrigated fields still produce alfalfa, chile, and corn. The superhighway exit

at 292 mi. serves two towns. To the right is the church and village of Alamillo (a diminutive of *alamo*, "cottonwood"), a Hispanic descendant of the ancient Piro pueblo. In March 1800, as part of the government-sponsored resettlement, sixty-two families arrived at Alamillo, supplied with farm equipment and provisions to last until the first harvest. The newer town of San Acacia sits between the interstate and the river and is named for a favorite saint of the *santeros* (saint carvers), who is traditionally dressed in Spanish military uniform. The Middle Rio Grande Conservancy

Church at San Acacia, *Paul Murphy.*

District constructed a floating dam here in 1934 for irrigation and flood control.

LEMITAR, now the largest of the valley towns north of Socorro, was long believed to be near the old pueblo of Teypama. Coronado camped at Teypama in 1541; Oñate received corn there in 1598 for his starving troops and named it Socorro ("help"). In 1981 archaeologists from the University of New Mexico excavated the old pueblo at a site south of Socorro quite a distance from Lemitar. From the interstate exit at 298 miles (opposite Polvadera Mountain to the west), one can visit Lemitar and then turn either north on the old road to Polvadera ("dusty") or south to Escondida ("hidden"). San Lorenzo Arroyo waters Polvadera when the village's saint, San Lorenzo, "who always brings rain," cooperates. From Escondida south to Socorro one must take the freeway (I-25).

The history of SOCORRO, 305 mi. (alt. 4,519, pop, 7,008), may be better understood by imagining that, but for a few minor quirks, the city could have been the capital of New Mexico. Situated in a wide, fertile valley amid thriving pueblos, watered by mountain springs, and surrounded by mineral wealth, it certainly possessed advantages. During the 1880s and early 1890s it was the largest city in the territory, shipping silver, cattle, flour, wine, and hides all over the country. The main defect in this picture is the fact that Socorro had lain abandoned for over one hundred thirty-five years, from the Pueblo Revolt to the resettlement period early in the nineteenth century.

Franciscan fathers Antonio de Arteaga and García de Zúñiga established the San Miguel Mission at the Piro Pueblo of Pilabo in 1628. Here, on a "secondary bottom" of the Rio

San Miguel Church, Socorro, *Paul Murphy.*

Grande, two hundred feet above the marshy lower bed, they planted the first grapes in New Mexico, instructed Pueblo adults and children, and coordinated mission churches and schools up and down the river. Siding with the Spanish soon proved a mixed blessing for the Pueblo people. Probably because the Spanish military presence upset whatever balance the Pueblos had achieved among themselves and with the nomadic tribes, Apache raids became increasingly frequent and destructive beginning around 1630. Since they were left out of the uneasy Spanish-Pueblo alliance, Apaches helped foment and, some believe, even coordinate the Pueblo Revolt. By the 1670s all the Piro towns had been raided, many repeatedly. Only Sevilleta, Alamillo, and Socorro survived until 1680, and when the two thousand refugees from the revolt in the north reached here that August, inhabitants of those towns joined the retreat to El Paso. From that time until the resettlement period and intermittently into American territorial years, the Apaches controlled the lower half of the Rio Grande in New Mexico.

In 1816 the Socorro Grant from the Spanish Crown awarded twenty-one families land extending north to San Lorenzo Arroyo, east to the summit of the Oscura ("dark") Mountains, south to the Bosque del Apache meadow, and west to the summit of the Magdalena Mountains. By 1821 these families had completed the rebuilding of San Miguel Church on its original site and were living in a series of *placitas*, clusters of adobe houses facing a central courtyard. The old town was built and remains today in an "organic" arrangement, a term architectural historians use to describe an irregular, nonrectangular street pattern. A visitor in the 1850s reported that Socorro then consisted of three plateaus. The lowest, a meadow too wet to cultivate, was used for livestock pasture. Fields of wheat and corn, vineyards, and orchards surrounded the six plazas on the second plateau. From the third plateau, the grama-grass-covered slopes along the base of Socorro Mountain, warm and cold springs flowed, used by the people for irrigation and bathing.

The building of Fort Craig, some twenty miles south, brought to Socorro the first of many changes during the second half of the nineteenth century. In the 1850s the town became a trading center and rendezvous for the fort. Army-related traffic increased greatly during the Civil War and continued throughout the later Apache campaigns. In 1867, prospectors discovered silver in the Magdalena Mountains. The Santa Fe Railroad arrived in 1880, and soon thereafter the Billings Smelter began a unique new process of refining the silver ore. By the early 1890s the triple impetus of mining, railroading, and smelting, added to farming, ranching, and trapping in the area, pushed the population to over five thousand.

Eugene Manlove Rhodes describes the Socorro of those years (his fictitious "Saragossa") in "Hit the Line Hard" as a series of steps:

> The first step is Venice, in the lush green of the valley—railroad buildings, coal chute, ferryman, warehouse, two *n*th-class hotels, a few farmhouses, all on stilts, being a few feet above the Rio Grande at low water and a few feet under it at high water. Whence the name, Venice.
>
> On the first rising ground to the westward is the business quarter, as close to the railroad as safety permits.

A step up comes to a sheltered, sunny terrace and to the Old Town—the Mexican village dating back to before the great uprising of 1680. Another, a steep and high step, rose to the residence section, on a strip of yellow mesa; for Saragossa has water piped from the high hills, so please you, and is not confined to the lowlands, like most of her New Mexico sisters. Still above, on the fifth and last step, smelter and mining town clung to a yellow-brown slope reached by a spur of railroad looping in a long bow-knot from the valley below.

> Above all, sheer and steep, circling about, sheltering, brooding, hung Saragossa Mountain, rose and gold in midday or morning sun; blue and rose-edged when the long shadows thrust eastward stealthily, steadily— crept like kittens at play, or like them fell off, down those old, old steps. (pp. 359–60)

A well-known figure of those days was Elfego Baca, community leader, sheriff, and hero for standing off eighty-odd armed Texas cowboys at a shootout in Reserve, then part of Socorro County. In the story just quoted, Rhodes portrayed Baca in something less than heroic proportions. Elfego promised, in jest or in earnest, to kill the writer if he ever returned to the county. Records show that both men died of natural causes.

Events beginning in the 1890s brought a series of reverses to Socorro that continued for forty years. In 1893, the U.S. Congress demonitized silver, causing its price to drop sharply. On July 30, 1895, the *arroyo* in Blue Canyon flooded and destroyed the lower town. In 1896 the smelter was shut down. Socorro continued as an agricultural center, but flooding and droughts in the 1920s and 1930s ruined successive wheat crops, and the Golden Crown Flour Mill, known throughout the state, closed its doors.

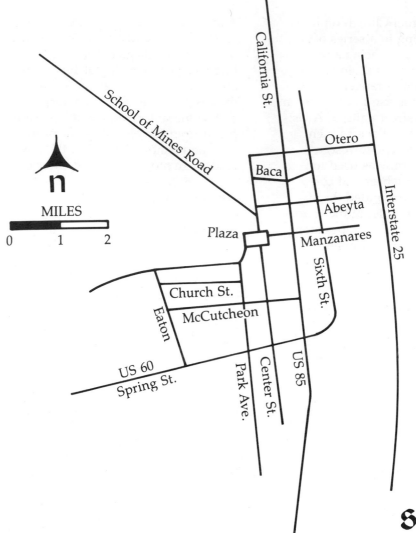

socorro

Because of its successive bursts of growth and prosperity, but also because there was often wealth enough to build and redecorate but not enough to tear everything down and start over, Socorro is a paradise for people interested in New Mexico architecture. It is also a place to wonder, in darker moods, at human vanity. A wealthy family builds an ostentatious home, falls on difficult times, perhaps leaves town. A second wealthy family buys the house and conspicuously redecorates the entire home in the latest style. The economy slumps again, and a third family buys the

place, tearing off and adding according to "good taste." Finally a fourth or fifth owner tries, by spending lots of money, to restore the house to its original form. Roughly speaking, the resettlement period brought adobe; the Fort Craig/Civil War/Indian campaign period introduced the territorial style; Victorian- and Queen Anne–style red brick came with the mines and railroads of the 1880s and 1890s; the early twentieth century saw some mission-style building; and the restoration period continues today.

But few people let such somber considera-

tions dampen their interest in Socorro's history or diminish their enjoyment of the many living old houses and buildings. Socorro is still small enough to be covered on foot. Two walking tours of architectural styles can begin at the plaza, one block west of California Street (the main street) on Manzanares Street. During the course of Socorro's history, its plaza has drifted southward. Into the twentieth century the plaza occupied a block just north of the present one. The old *camino* from Chihuahua entered from the southwest and exited along the street that older residents still call the Camino, which heads straight north from the middle of the present plaza. U.S. 60, the "Ocean-to-Ocean Highway," entered the older plaza from the north via the old *camino* and turned west at the plaza, passing the Ocean to Ocean Garage on its way to Magdalena and the Continental Divide.

The first walking tour proceeds north from the present plaza along the old *camino*, which begins as a double street. At the corner of Abeyta Avenue stands the Juan N. García house, an adobe structure with a *placita* floor plan. The interior courtyards of this type of house contained space for livestock, fruit trees, and often a well or cistern for protection and self-sufficiency in times of danger. North across the street is the J. J. Baca house, another adobe, with a pitched roof and elaborate territorial-style scroll-cut brackets added. Both the García and Baca houses once faced the older Socorro plaza. One half-block east (right) on Abeyta Avenue is the García Opera House, a State and National Historic Site, constructed

in 1886. It has been the scene, if not of opera, of concerts, masked balls, school programs, theater performances, and even college basketball games. Returning to the J. N. García house and proceeding north, one sees adobe houses of the *placita* type as well as those that began as one room and were added onto, room by room, either in an L shape or in a straight line. Adobe houses of both basic floor plans continued to be built after other architectural styles were introduced.

Socorro's church is *not* located on the present-day plaza, but was built on the site of the original seventeenth-century mission, three blocks north. Legends say that a silver communion rail was buried here at the beginning of the Pueblo Revolt. Another legend (or the same one) claims that another silver communion rail (or the same one) was buried when the Anglos came in the 1840s. Treasure hunters have searched in vain for both rails. The church that we see today was completed in 1821; a second wing was added in 1853. Among its parishioners, San Miguel Church can boast Roberto Sánchez, archbishop of Santa Fe.

Leaving the church, the walker can turn east (right) down Otero Avenue or Baca Avenue to Sixth Street. Three blocks north of Baca is the Illinois Brewery, the first and, until passage of the Volstead Act in 1919, largest brewery and ice plant in New Mexico. Built partly of stone and now remodeled, it is a registered State and National Historic Site. Turning south (right) on Sixth Street, one passes the length of the Valverde Hotel before reaching its entrance on Manzanares Street. This hotel opened in 1919 to accommodate automobile travelers on the Ocean-to-Ocean Highway as well as Santa Fe Railroad passengers. It gave impetus to a California mission revival style, visible also in a number of buildings in the 100 block of Plaza Street, just south of the plaza. All but abandoned in the 1960s, the Valverde is now being reclaimed and restored. Going west (right) on Manzanares Street towards the plaza again, one passes three structures belonging to a generation of brick commercial buildings of the 1890s: the Torres Block (brick over adobe) near California Street, the Rio Grande Supply at Manzanares and California streets, and the Abeyta Block (solid brick) facing the plaza.

For a tour of more brick and territorial-style gems, one can walk south off the plaza on Park Street, turning right (west) on Church Avenue. Near the end of a long block are the Chambon and Bursum houses (the latter a State and National Historic Site), both exhibiting some of the finest Queen Anne details in the state. With the coming of the railroad in 1880, milled lumber, brick, tin and terneplate roofing and catalogue-ordered, prefabricated architectural elements arrived by train, quickly transforming the face of Socorro.

Rounding the corner on Eaton Avenue (left), proceed back east along McCutcheon Street. Arched windows, bay windows, and columns characterize the Italianate and Queen Anne influences in the brick cottages that line the north side of the street. After the 1906 earthquake, some of these cottages employed tie-rod construction for greater stability. On the northwest corner of Paul and McCutcheon streets is the famous "El Torreón," an adobe house with towers added at both ends of the U-shaped building. South along Park Street a few houses, one recognizes the equally famous Queen Anne–style Casa de Flecha ("house of the arrow") by its weathervane-topped turret. The light and spacious Socorro Library, in an old house that has undergone considerable renovation, is located between the Casa de Flecha and El Torreón. Return

north (left) on Park Street to the plaza, keeping in mind that many of the structures one passes are adobe at their core.

Not included on a walking tour is the Crown Mill, a three-story brick structure clearly visible from I-25, located on the old railroad spur to Magdalena. Night and day the Crown Mill ground wheat brought from as far north as Isleta.

A newer road angling northwest from near the plaza leads to the New Mexico Institute of Mining and Technology. The college opened as the New Mexico School of Mines in 1893, when the region was one of the richest mining districts in the country. It all but shut down for academic purposes when it was used as army barracks during the Second World War. The school recovered its students and became an institute in 1951. Newer buildings imitated the red tile roofs and whitewashed walls of the original structures. "Tech" now attracts students from many states and countries to its campus on one of the higher "steps" under Socorro Mountain. One of the school's special divisions is the Petroleum Recovery Research Center, housed in a new, solar-heated building on the upper edge of the campus. In March 1982, New Mexico Tech, Socorro, and supporters from around the state dedicated the new Macey Convention Center. Designed by John McHugh, architect also of the Santa Fe Opera pavillion and the Caprock Amphitheatre, the theater seats 666 people and is equipped for a wide variety of dramatic and musical performances.

At the southern end of Socorro, U.S. 60 branches off west to Magdalena and Quemado (on Tour 8) and Springerville, Arizona.

From Socorro south to El Paso, Texas, the traveler has the choice of taking I-25 or the old route (U.S. 85), which runs closer to farms and towns but is sometimes difficult to follow.

SAN ANTONIO, 315 mi., onetime crossroads and garden spot of New Mexico, birthplace of Conrad Hilton, and home of the Owl Bar, sits a mile east of I-25 at 315 mi. Walnut Canyon, a gorge a thousand feet deep in places, emerges here from the Magdalena Mountains (west).

Crystal Palace, San Antonio, *Paul Murphy.*

Its underflow has watered the many towns that have occupied this site. San Antonio has been confused with San Antonio de Senecu, a large Piro pueblo located where San Marcial later stood, twenty miles south. When Spanish-speaking settlers from the Rio Arriba reoccupied this part of the valley around 1820, they named their new town after the old San Antonio, so the confusion is understandable. The uncertainty in locating abandoned pueblos can be better appreciated when we realize that living pueblos like Isleta have changed locations in historic times, and even in the twentieth century whole towns have disappeared with hardly a trace. There almost certainly was a Piro pueblo of some size here. After centuries of floods and shifts of the river, pot hunting by treasure seekers, and honest use of materials by later settlers, antiquarians find it difficult to say exactly where a pueblo mentioned in the accounts of early explorers might be found.

The settlers of San Antonio cultivated grain, beans, chile, onions, and grapes. In the early 1800s traffic between Chihuahua and Santa Fe began using the west side of the river, stopping at San Antonio. General Estanislado Montoya distinguished himself in the Civil War and returned home to operate a mercantile store. His son Eutemio opened coal mines across the Rio Grande and built coke ovens to process the coal. Meanwhile, Augustus Hilton arrived, built another store, traded with miners and trappers, and established a stage line to White Oaks, eighty miles east, connecting the mining towns of Nogal, Carthage, and

Geese at Bosque del Apache, *Penni Adrian.*

Bosque del Apache, *E. A. Scholer.*

Magdalena. They called Hilton the "merchant king of San Antonio." His son Conrad was born in 1887 and educated by the Sisters of Loretto in Socorro. During the Panic of 1907, Gus Hilton converted part of his store into hotel rooms. This apparently gave Conrad the inspiration to begin building hotels in nearly every major city in the world.

When the railroad arrived, it advertised forty thousand irrigable acres within six miles of San Antonio and platted a town just north of the older one. Soon the Santa Fe was hauling one hundred carloads of alfalfa and two hundred fifty barrels of native wine annually, plus tons of coke and coal, over a spur that extended east to the Carthage and Tokay coalfields.

The coal, wine, and wheat are mostly gone, but much of old San Antonio remains. The Owl Bar serves both as a stopover for travelers on the superhighway and as a gathering place

for townspeople. The bar itself, on the State Historical and Cultural Properties List, was moved from the old Crystal Palace Bar. The Crystal Palace, run for many years by the Miera family, still stands on South Main Street, but it is no longer open to the public. Ruins of the Hilton place can be seen nearby at Sixth and Main streets. The San Antonio Church, also on South Main Street, was moved from an earlier location (on Church Street) a few blocks to the northeast. One's imagination must fill in the park, railway depot, and stores now gone but remembered by older residents.

Tour 12 ends at the intersection of U.S. 380 and I-25. Travelers going to the Bosque del Apache National Wildlife Refuge (323 mi.) will take old U.S. 85 south of San Antonio. The U.S. Fish and Wildlife Service established the refuge in 1939, mainly in order to preserve the whooping crane, then threatened with extinc-

Bosque del Apache, *Dave Wilson*.

tion. It includes fifty-seven thousand acres of the 1845 Bosque del Apache Land Grant; fifteen hundred of these acres are used to grow corn, sorghum, winter wheat, and millet for the wintering birds. October through January (especially in the evenings) are the best months to see the migratory birds, but visits at any time of year can inspire delight and wonder. In addition to the sojourning cranes, herons, and geese, many other species, including eagles, coyotes, deer, and ducks make the bosque their home, permanently or occasionally. A self-guiding automobile tour takes about an hour and a half. No camping or fires are permitted, but hunting and fishing are allowed, subject, of course, to state game and fish laws.

The favorite success story of the refuge is the sandhill-whooping crane crossfostering program. The whooping crane, tallest bird in North America (four and one-half feet high), with a wingspan of up to seven feet, had dwindled in number to seventeen by the early 1940s. Biologists studying the bird then discovered that few of the young could survive the long and difficult migration route from northern British Columbia to the Texas Gulf Coast. They experimented with placing whooping crane eggs in sandhill cranes' nests to see if the sandhills would accept their foster chicks. They did. The sandhills have a shorter, safer migration path from Grays Lake in southeastern Idaho to central New Mexico's

Bosque del Apache. These birds have raised many whoopers now and have helped assure the future of the whooping crane. New Mexicans along the Rio Grande count on seeing both types of cranes in November and March, flying to and from their winter home in the bosque.

The site of SAN MARCIAL, 330 mi., three miles off the interstate, may be symbolic to readers and travelers of the fact that this entire valley has more past than it has present. Torrents of water carved this course over millennia amid rising mountains and erupting volcanoes, but now there is often only a trickle in the former river's course. Hundreds of prehistoric sites indicate relatively dense habitation and advanced cultures; the historical period has witnessed the growth and decline of towns and small cities. At this point on the river near the black mesa, Spanish explorers found the large Piro pueblo of Senecu, close to the southern end of the Piros' domain. Soon Fray Alonso Benavides, "apostle to the Piros," built the San Antonio mission at Senecu and established a *reducido*—a "conversion school" with workshops, dorms, crafts, cooking, music, and catechism. He learned the Piros' language, a variant of Tanoan. After he died, two other Franciscans, Antonio de Arteaga and García de San Francisco, continued his work. Fray García was buried here. Apaches attacked Senecu in January 1675, causing many deaths and much destruction. By the time of the 1680

revolt, the Pueblo had retreated to Socorro. Most of the town's survivors then accompanied the Spanish south to El Paso, where they established Senecu del Sur downriver from the mission there.

Sometime after the resettlement of Socorro, a group of colonists ventured near the old pueblo here and established Paraje ("stopping place") across the river. Each settlement farther south made the lonely and dangerous trek from El Paso a little shorter. By 1848 the colony called itself La Mesa de San Marcial. After serious flooding in 1866, the town moved over to the west bank of the Rio Grande. The Santa Fe Railroad reached San Marcial in 1880, ever more eager for a transcontinental rail link. Entrepreneurs set up temporary stage coach service to transport California-bound train travelers to the Southern Pacific tracks at Rio Mimbres (now Deming). The railroad caught its breath here before pushing on to Rincon and El Paso, built a roundhouse and repair shops, established a small city of a thousand people, and contemplated a crossing of the Rio Grande.

Although there are those who belittle New Mexico's major river, bridge builders who have expected their structures to survive them have respected the Rio Grande. Despite the fact that numerous bridges had been built (several each at El Paso, Albuquerque, and Española), at the time of the American occupation (1846) not a single one spanned the river.

This might seem unimportant during dry times, but anyone familiar with the amount of water that the river still often carries, as well as its marshes, quicksand, and rapids, can appreciate the importance of permanent crossings. The railroad built for keeps and maintained a respectful distance from the river. It crossed to the west bank at Isleta to reach Belen and Socorro, and at San Marcial intended to cross back in order to parallel the caravan track cutoff across the Jornada del Muerto. So that both ends might be anchored in rocks, railroad engineers selected the spot here where an ancient lava flow had once boiled into the Rio Grande's path and had been cut through by the determined water. Once across the river, the tracks made a beeline towards Las Cruces over seventy-five miles of the Jornada, rejoining the valley at Rincon.

In the 1920s San Marcial was a thriving ranching, farming, and railroad center, with hotels, a Fred Harvey restaurant (among other eateries), repair shops, and a population of several thousand. The Rio Grande flooded, burying locomotives, cars, and the first floors of many buildings in silt; but the people dug out and apparently went on enjoying life here. In September 1929, however, they received warnings of another flood and evacuated shortly before a torrent of muddy water completely destroyed the city. The traveler who wants to drive around and get an idea of what San Marcial was like will look in vain. *Nothing* remains except a crumbling corner of the roundhouse. One can follow the tracks to the railroad bridge and get a look at the four-hundred-foot-high black wall and the growth along the river, imagining oneself a Senecu child, a San Marcial kid, or perhaps a Santa Fe Railroad traveler prior to the discontinuation of passenger service on this line in the 1960s.

San Pascual Hill, the volcanic cone responsible for San Marcial's mesa, is easily visible east of the interstate. Many mesas in the state have been called Black Mesa, but this one has had another name as well: Mesa Contadera ("counting mesa"). The term derives from the

early practice of driving livestock up the old east-side trail and forcing the animals into the narrow passage between the steep mesa walls and the marshes of the Rio Grande. Here herders could count their animals, thus learning how many had survived the Jornada crossing.

At the Fort Craig rest area, 337 mi., a historical marker tells some of the story of this member of a string of forts (the others were Forts McRae, Thorne, Selden, and Fillmore) in the Apache-controlled stretch between Socorro and Las Cruces. Its establishment in 1854 and continued use during the Civil War and in later campaigns against the Apaches stimulated the growth of Socorro in the 1850s and 1860s. Early in 1862, an army of Texans under General Sibley moved up the Rio Grande from Mesilla (just south of Las Cruces), the newly designated capital of the Confederate Territory of Arizona. General Canby left Fort Craig and crossed the river with thirty-eight hundred Union troops to block the Texans' advance, and the two armies met at Valverde. The Confederates won the ensuing battle and moved north, occupying Albuquerque and Santa Fe and continuing towards Colorado, where they would have posed a serious threat to Union forces. Since the (eventual) victors write the history, it is usually mentioned that, a few weeks later, Sibley's army was defeated at Apache Canyon near Glorieta Pass, and that the territory of New Mexico and all the West remained in Union hands for the rest of the war. In 1981 the family corporation that had owned the ruins of Fort Craig and of the nearby Piro pueblo of San Felipe donated them to the Archaeological Conservancy. The public will soon be welcome to visit both the fort, the largest in southern New Mexico, and the pueblo, the spot where the Rodríguez-Chamuscado Expedition claimed New Mexico for Spain in August 1581.

Travelers bound in three directions use the exit to N.M. 107 (340 mi.). For northbound travelers it provides the most direct paved route to the Bosque del Apache National Wildlife Refuge via old U.S. 85. Southbound traffic headed for recreation sites in the San Mateo

Bosque del Apache, *Dave Wilson*.

Mountains will exit here to follow old U.S. 85 south (go back under the freeway, then turn right). N.M. 107 itself, unpaved, parallels Mulligan Gulch northwest up between the San Mateo and Magdalena mountains to the town of Magdalena (on Tour 8). East of this point (no road), Elephant Butte Resevoir begins, stretching forty-five miles south to its dam near Truth or Consequences. Its waters have covered Paraje de Fra Cristobal, the village at the northern end of the Jornada cutoff.

In order to avoid the marshes and rough, steep walls and canyons of the bend in the Rio Grande valley, travelers bound for Santa Fe from the earliest days left the river near the site of Fort Selden and crossed ninety miles of an intermountain basin called the Jornada del Muerto ("journey of the dead one") to rejoin the valley here at Fra Cristobal. The advantage of this cutoff was that it saved several days' travel. Disadvantages were the scarcity of water and greater danger from hostile Indians. Springs on the eastern slopes of the Fra Cristobal and Caballo ranges and a lake out on the Jornada supplied water for travelers. Water was hauled to four stations on the road used by the freight caravans. Arriving back at the river at Fra Cristobal must have been an occasion for thanksgiving and rejoicing. In the late nineteenth century, the Santa Fe Railroad used substantially the same Jornada cutoff, except that the tracks left the valley further upriver at Rincon and rejoined it at San Marcial.

Although the Rio Grande has been a major

trade and travel route for centuries, as a consequence of the alternate Jornada route discussed above, the bulk of north-south traffic has used *this* particular part of the valley (between the N.M. 107 junction and Hatch) only in the twentieth century. Fairly high above river level at this point, one sees the Fra Cristobal Range to the east, partly hiding both the Sierra Caballo and the San Andres Mountains, not included within the White Sands Missile Range. Nearby, on the west side, the Magdalena and San Mateo mountains form the only "chain" comparable to those east of the river that divide the middle third of the state into a series of long valleys and intermountain basins separated by mountain ranges. West of the San Mateos, the Bear, Datil, Gallinas, and Mangas mountains, plus those of the Gila country, seem to be scattered in haphazard and bewildering fashion. Right along the highway, the Chihuahuan desert extends in a long narrow arm up the valley as far north as Albuquerque. In this area it is characterized by a gravelly soil that favors the creosote bush, a small, green-leafed shrub with a sharp smell. All vegetation here guards its space, its "water rights," conspicuously. This is also a good place to observe the difference between north- and south-facing hillsides. The south-facing slopes get more light and heat from the sun, and thus lose more moisture. For this reason, north-facing slopes usually support more and larger vegetation.

At 365 mi., the highway swoops down into Cañada Alamosa, the first of three large, inhabited canyons in this section of the trip. The Alamosa River flows southeasterly around the San Mateo Mountains, emptying into Elephant Butte Lake a few miles east of the highway. In 1874 the government established the Ojo Caliente ("warm springs") Indian Agency a little way upstream. The short-lived agency counted among its reluctant "boarders" both Geronimo and Chief Victorio, until they were transferred in 1877 to the San Carlos Reservation in Arizona. Two mining towns, Monticello and Placita, grew up near the old Indian agency. Monticello has recently become a

(part-time) mining town again with the increase in the price of silver. N.M. 52 west, 368 mi., provides paved access both to Monticello and Placita and to the Black Range towns of Winston and Chloride. Harry Pye, freighting supplies to military forts, struck silver at Chloride (named for the character of the ore) in 1879. Pye was soon killed by Apaches, but others cashed in on his find. Winston boomed as "Fairview" until it was renamed for its mercantile store, owned by Frank Winston, a member of the territorial legislature.

N.M. 52 east, 370 mi., is the turnoff for Elephant Butte State Park, the Elephant Butte Dam, and the abandoned Jornada town of Engle. The state park, completed in 1965 and the best-attended of the state's parks ever since, includes playground, picnic, camping, and boat launching facilities. New Mexico's largest lake offers fishing (white and black bass and perch are stocked), power boating, and sailing. The concrete dam a few miles to the southeast measures 306 feet high, 1,674 feet long, 16 feet wide at the top, and 205 feet wide at the bottom. The resulting forty-five-mile lake has two hundred miles of shoreline and a capacity of 2.2 million acre feet of water. Its irrigation district covers eighty-eight thousand acres in New Mexico and sixty-seven thousand acres in Texas. The building of the dam during the years of 1911–16 created a sizable construction camp and aided the growth of Hot Springs (later Truth or Consequences) five miles to the southwest.

The traveler who proceeds the nineteen miles up N.M. 52 to ENGLE will get one of the few remaining views of the Jornada del Muerto not fenced off by the White Sands Missile Range, but will see little evidence of the place that three times became a boom town and three times a ghost town in the space of forty years. Santa Fe Railroad surveyors located seven sidetracks for watering stations across the Jornada. There were seven surveyors: Pope, Morley, Crocker, Engle, Cutter, Upham, and Grama. With one exception, each put himself on the map by giving his name to one of the sidetracks; Morley, father of Agnes Morley Cleveland, modestly named his track Lava. Few would suppose that any of the seven were immortalized; but for a while Engle did have its day, and the name just missed joining Grand Coulee, Hoover, and others in the list of well-known dams.

In 1880, the railroad pumped water to Engle for its locomotives and workers, and the new town, as the nearest rail shipping point, immediately became a base of supplies for the Black Range mining boom towns to the west. With two stage lines, two general stores, various hotels, and an all-night restaurant, Engle proclaimed itself capital of the Jornada. Within three years, the miners had all the equipment they could use (or afford),

trade withered, and Engle dried up about as quickly as it had bloomed. Then, in 1886, cattlemen from the Lincoln area discovered they could drive their herds across the Jornada to the railroad in the wet season. The huge Bar Cross Ranch set up headquarters near Engle, and for fifteen years the town again became a bustling shipping center, this time for cattle driven from the White, Capitan, and Sacramento mountains to the east, and from Black Range pastures to the west. By 1901, newer, closer railheads took over most of the livestock shipping, and the Bar Cross disbanded because dry years and overgrazing had ruined the Jornada ranges. For a second time Engle lay abandoned.

When engineers chose the site for a dam at Engle ford, where the Rio Grande plunges into the Caballo Mountains and veers sharply to the west, both Engle and its neighbor Cutter stood to prosper. Engle's road down to Hot Springs was improved, and the town again supplied construction materials brought by rail to the project. The town of Cutter also blasted a road through the Caballo Mountains and shared some of the traffic. Engle, once more a lively little city, portrayed itself as "the best town in New Mexico by a dam site." By 1920, alas, it was all over for the third, and apparently the last, time. The dam that it helped build took its name for a short while, misspelling it "Eagle"; but the name of the landmark, Elephant Butte (whose trunk now hung under reservoir water), soon won out. Freight trains still pass, but they rarely stop. Four buildings remain to mark the old town.

The area around TRUTH OR CONSEQUENCES, 374 mi. (alt 4,269, pop, 5,223), had been known for its hot springs long before the construction of Elephant Butte Dam. For centuries nomadic Indians visited it as a neutral resting and healing place. In 1860 the García and Tafoya families founded the town of Palomas Ojo Caliente, now under Caballo Lake. The town lay opposite Palomas ("doves") Gap in the Caballo Mountains and on the trail from the Santa Rita copper mines near Silver City. Cowboys from the Bar Cross and John Cross ranches built the first adobe bathhouse at the springs near Engle ferry. This place was called Paloma Springs. At the time of the dam's completion the baths were still free, and the town changed its name to Hot Springs. The Rio Grande originally ran down present Main Street, but by filling in marshes and swamps, workers changed its course. Soon there were numerous hotels for people seeking cures at the springs or just enjoying the usually pleasant climate. Other commercial and residential buildings were moved down from the dam construction camp. Most of the stores and houses on the south side of the 400 block of Main Street date from the early months of Hot Springs. By the 1930s, with easier automobile travel, Hot Springs had become a small resort city, strung between the river and the hills that supply its springs. In 1936, the seat of Sierra County moved here from Hillsboro, some thirty miles to the southwest.

Towns all over the country have used promotional schemes to attract the people and wealth they want. In 1950 the citizens of Hot Springs elected to accept the offer of a national television program for free publicity and an annual fiesta with Hollywood celebrities to any town that would change its name to "Truth or Consequences." Some thought the name change plain foolish. Others feared it made the love of money and the adoration of show-business stars a little too visible for comfort. But in a series of elections challenging the name change, opponents of the scheme of the TV show's host, Ralph Edwards, failed each time to gain a majority. The fact is that, despite the curious name, Truth or Consequences remains a friendly resort town, with the nostalgic air of a place where people of ordinary means come to enjoy the simple pleasures of hot mineral water and one another's company.

The Sierra County Historical Society maintains Gerónimo Springs Museum on the main southbound street, near the center of town. Besides the springs, the museum offers exhibits of Mimbres pottery and culture, the Apache way of life, the mining, sheep, cattle, and goat industries, and the building of Elephant Butte Dam, plus a gallery of fine regional artwork. Along the river, usually running clear and green from under the dam, Ralph Edwards Park provides picnicking and playing areas. At the southern edge of town stands the WPA-built, state-owned building that from 1937 to 1981 housed the Carrie Tingley Hospital for Crippled Children. This hospital is the setting of *Tortugas* ("turtles"), a novel by New Mexico author Rudolfo Anaya. An imaginative eye can discover the shape of a turtle in the mountains opposite.

Two events highlight Truth or Consequences's calendar: the Ralph Edwards Fiesta in early May and the Fiddle Contest in early October that picks the national champions in the various classes of fiddle-playing.

Just south of Truth or Consequences the hamlet of Williamsburg, 379 mi., also boasts hot springs. Las Palomas, 382 mi., settled in the 1860s, was covered by Caballo Lake in the late 1930s and moved to higher ground. The valley of the Palomas River here is the second large inhabited canyon traversed by I-25.

CABALLO, 389 mi. (named for the lake, named for the mountains, named because of the likeness of a horse's head on their northern end), has grown up as a town of people who want to live by the lake and people who serve them.

N.M. 90 turns off I-25 near Caballo, climbing up from the Rio Grande valley and across the Black Range, past the open-pit copper mine at Santa Rita to Silver City (Tour 18). The trip takes in picturesque Victorian towns, remains of once-noisy mining camps, and the mountains and forests of the Black Range.

From its junction with I-25 at Caballo, where the state has built a park around the reservoir, N.M. 90 runs seventeen miles west over a barren stretch to HILLSBORO (alt. 5,180) set in the Percha Creek valley. This little town was once the center of a rich mining district that stretched out through the area to Lake Valley in the south, Winston and Chloride in the north, and Georgetown in the west. In 1877, two prospectors found signs of gold on Percha Creek and started a rush. Gold and silver mines with names like Bonanza, Ready Roy, and Snake Son reached out from the town and yielded millions of dollars. Miners built homes and gave their settlement a respectable name.

Hillsboro became the seat of Sierra County as well as a bustling town that served the miners, gamblers, and soldiers, the latter stationed there to protect settlers against Apache attacks. The courthouse, an imposing brick structure, and the jail were built above Main Street. Hotels, stores, and saloons served the population; one hotel was run by Madame Sadie Orchard, who first came from London in 1886 to open a brothel on Shady Lane. Sadie remained a fixture in the area until her death in 1943, running a more respectable hotel and boarding house in her later years.

When the mines closed, cattle ranching became important. The excitement brought on by quick riches died down, and Hillsboro's population became more settled. Today it is a gentle and pretty town, a seat of artists, writers, and people who like the peace of the area. Adobe and frame houses have flower-filled yards, and the main street is still lined with shady cottonwoods. Some of the old stores have been taken over by craftspeople whose wares line the streets during summer fairs, like the Apple Festival on Labor Day weekend, that strain Hillsboro's resources but remain a popular attraction for visitors.

The county seat moved to Truth or Consequences in 1938, and the courthouse and jail fell into ruins, only brick walls remaining. In earlier days the courthouse was the scene of the notorious Lee-Gilliland trial of 1898 (see Tour 10). Eugene Manlove Rhodes's short novel, *The Proud Sheriff*, one of his few works that portrays the upholders of "law and morality" in a favorable light, takes place in Hillsboro at the turn of the century, and describes the town and the surrounding countryside with remarkable clarity. The old Catholic church, destroyed in a flood in 1972 and since rebuilt, still overlooks the town. It stands next to the imposing home of Sir Victor Sasson, an English banker who once lived here. The Black Range Museum is housed in Sadie Orchard's old Ocean Grove Hotel; it is worth a stop to view the exhibits of life in the old mining towns and to swap stories with the curators. Grocery stores and a hotel still function, and antique shops flourish in old residences.

Outside the town stretch apple orchards and the large spreads which gradually took over the smaller cattle concerns. Some mining has been revived.

South of Hillsboro, N.M. 27 leads to Lake Valley and on to Nutt, where N.M. 26 branches off east and west. The west fork runs into I-10 at Deming.

Lake Valley produced silver ore of a fabulous richness. However, for a long time prospecting in the area was dangerous because the Apache chieftains Victorio, Loco, and Nana roamed the region. The Apaches resented bitterly their forced removal from the Warm Springs reservation in the Black Range foothills. Most refused to leave and fought the settlers during the 1870s and 1880s. In 1878 two determined prospectors saw a pure silver sample from the area and searched until they found its source, but then had to wait until they could get more funds and Victorio had settled down. Eventually they sold their strike for $100,000. Two days later the new owners worked their way into a subterranean room, christened the "bridal chamber" for the richness and purity of its silver. The chamber eventually produced some $3 million worth of horn, or pure silver, one of the richest single silver deposits in the world. Workers ran a spur from the railroad right into the chamber to load the silver; it was so pure that there was no need to smelt it.

Traffic between Hillsboro, Kingston, and Lake Valley was brisk. Sadie Orchard and her husband owned the coach line that served the route. Sadie boasted of being one of the best drivers on the route, but she probably never actually took the reins herself.

The town that sprang up around these riches flourished until 1893, when the mines were closed. A resurgence in mining was followed by further depressions in the industry, until today only a few determined people are left. Some false-front buildings, a school, and a church bake below the dusty hills. Much of the remaining property is privately owned; check before exploring. Monthly squaredances are still held in the old schoolhouse here, attended by people from miles around.

To reach KINGSTON, 26 mi, N.M. 90 squeezes through the Box Canyon of Percha Creek, whose narrow passage gave attacking Apaches an advantage over the vulnerable travelers who took the stagecoach between Hillsboro and Kingston.

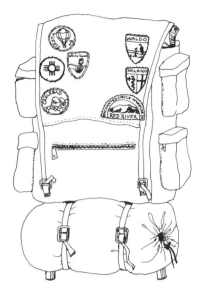

The road into Kingston branches right off N.M. 90, so the modern-day traveler must take a short detour to get the flavor of the town. In an era of hard-drinking, hard-working, and hard-playing mining towns, Kingston had the reputation of being the hardest. Today few buildings remain of the one-time boom town, but the sturdy old stone Percha Bank still stands. The old Kingston Brewery across the road used to ship beer all over the Southwest. Former territorial governor George Curry lived down the street while he was state historian. However, you cannot walk through the old casino or saloon, or the church built with funds donated by the ladies of the night (some of whom worked for Sadie Orchard and plied their trade along "Virtue Avenue," which paralleled Main Street). The Victorio Hotel, three stories high and a landmark in its day, was named after the Apache chieftain whom the citizens were able to keep out of their town. It is only a shell now. A few of the old houses also remain, used now by artists. The twenty-two saloons, the dance halls, and the theater at which Lillian Russell's troupe once played are memories. The old fire bell still hangs from its supports on Main Street, where it summoned volunteer firefighters or 1ater notified residents that the mail had arrived from Hillsboro. The Spit and Whittle Club still meets here. One of its charter

SIDE TOUR

members was Sheba Hurst, so famous for his tall tales that he was featured in Mark Twain's *Roughing It.*

The mines of Kingston were called the Bullion, the Comstock, and the Miner's Dream. The "dream" was that of Edward Doheny, partner of Albert Fall, also once a Kingston resident and later a key figure in the Teapot Dome Scandal. Some $10 million in silver and other ores was removed from the mines, and Kingston grew to a population of seven thousand by 1885. After the mines gave out, cattlemen moved into the area, but their business was not enough. Outside of town the old graveyard is the resting place of many of the citizens of Kingston, prominent among them Sheba Hurst and Tom Ying, who died at 104 after many years as Sadie Orchard's cook and owner of his own cafe.

West of Kingston, N.M. 90, which has been climbing since Hillsboro, gradually ascends the east slope of the Black Range. This range stretches north and south for sixty-five miles, its dark contours rising to about ten thousand feet. Stands of pine, fir, oak, and other growth give the range its somber colors and protect the game—deer, bear, and wild turkey—that lives there. Part of the Black Range has been set aside as a primitive area where motor vehicles are not allowed. There are 240

miles of trails in the area, and streams drain into three major rivers: the Rio Grande, the Gila, and the Mimbres. Day hikers, backpackers, and horseback riders are invited to try the trails, some rugged, some traversing gentle alpine meadows. For those passing through the Black Range on wheels, there are wide views of the mountains and the plains below.

The highway crosses Emory Pass (8,178 feet) at 25 mi. During the summer months there is a good hike or horseback ride from here up to the Hillsboro Peak Lookout. N.M. 90 leaves the Gila National Forest at 45 mi. and drops down into the Mimbres valley to cross the Mimbres River. The Mimbres ("willow") culture flourished in this area between the tenth and twelfth centuries, an outgrowth of the Mogollon period. The Mimbres people are best known for their classic black-on-white pottery. A group of Apaches that later roamed the area in the 1800s also took its name from the valley.

San Lorenzo, a small trading center, is reached at 52 mi. N.M. 35 turns right here, to the Gila Cliffs National Monument (Tour 17). To the left N.M. 61 bypasses an old health resort, Mimbres Hot Springs, and leads to the City of Rocks Park (Tour 17) and U.S. 180. From San Lorenzo, N.M. 90 passes Santa Rita and Central on the way to Silver City (Tour 17).

Following the old road (N.M. 85) south here, one gets a close look at the rich farming area of the southern New Mexico Rio Grande valley. The section is famous for its chile, and produces a large percentage of the nation's green and red chile peppers. The road passes between fields, crosses sandy ridges, then descends to the farmland again. Grown here in addition to chile are cotton, lettuce, onions, and alfalfa. Travelers can see the plants at various stages of maturity and witness bed preparation, irrigation, or harvesting, depending on

the season. Unseen but ever present in fertile agricultural regions such as this one are the moral and economic issues of fair payment for farm workers and conservation of the land and water for future generations. Arrey, Derry, Garfield, and Salem (named for Salem, Massachusetts), four Rio Grande farming towns in the distant shadow of the Caballo Mountains, all date from around the turn of the century.

Most of New Mexico's visitors and residents think of the Rio Grande as flowing nearly straight south down the middle of the state. The truth is that, even at Albuquerque, the river is almost twice as far from the eastern border as from the western, and that, since entering the state near Costilla, it has been flowing slightly southwesterly. South of San Antonio the river turns more sharply toward the west, heading for the Continental Divide. Its elevation here, about forty-two hundred feet, is within a few hundred feet of that of the Continental Divide, a short distance to the southwest. The great river, however, meets a finger of rock that forces its course east into the Gulf of Mexico, preventing it from taking the more obvious path to the Pacific Ocean. The old highway crossed and recrossed the Rio Grande to avoid that nameless rock, easily visible opposite Derry at 405 mi.

HATCH, 417 mi., "Chile Capital of the World," began as a stop on the Santa Fe Railroad's diagonal between Rincon and Deming. The railroad first called it Hatch's Station, after General Edward Hatch, commander of old Fort Thorne a few miles to the northwest. At the time when settlers arrived in Hatch (1880), at least three outer villages existed in the immediate area. They were Colorado, later called Rodey, to the southeast, Santa Barbara (old Fort Thorne) to the northwest, and Santa Teresa, or Placitas, at the western end of present-day Hatch. All three had been farming communities that depended upon irrigation ditches transporting water from the Rio Grande, and they were at the mercy of periodic floods. In 1886 the river washed away the buildings and covered the farmlands of Santa Barbara. The refugees moved into Santa Teresa, and thereafter the people of the three towns cooperated in maintaining a single irrigation ditch. For a while Rodey became infamous as the headquarters of the John Kinney horse-stealing ring.

For thirty years Rincon remained the main trading and business center for railroad shipping, but by the end of the First World War Hatch had grown into a small town. A flash flood caused by a cloudburst up the Santa Teresa *arroyo* destroyed the town in August 1921.

Chile pile, *Harvey Caplin*.

Although several families and businesses moved to Las Cruces, Elephant Butte and Caballo dams on the Rio Grande and Soil Conservation Service projects on the Santa Teresa and Springs Canyon *arroyos* offered relatively good protection from further flooding, and Hatch began to grow again. Farming on the rich, irrigated bottomland around the town (cut off from the larger Mesilla Valley by a narrow neck of the valley) enabled banks, retail stores, hotels, and restaurants to prosper. Hatch has shipped farm products and livestock ever since, by both rail and truck.

The White Sands Missile Range took over most of the territory east of Hatch in 1948, and soon became the town's largest employer. New Mexicans, however, still know Hatch primarily for the quality and quantity of its famous vegetables. Chile is New Mexico's top cash crop, and Doña Ana leads the state's twelve chile-producing counties. New Mexico ranks first in chile produced and acreage planted, with more than double the acreage of its closest competitor, California. Hatch celebrates its Chile Festival the Saturday and Sunday before Labor Day. Held at the municipal airport, the festival includes a chile cook-off, a parade, a senior citizens' race, fiddling contests, and two days of watermelon eating, carstuffing competitions, and hay rides.

RINCON, 423 mi., takes shelter at the bottom of a third deep canyon that is crossed by I-25. *Rincon* means "corner" or "intersection"; it was here that the Santa Fe Railroad tracks coming off the Jornada forked, one line proceeding to Deming, the other to El Paso. Travelers have a clear view of the schoolhouse from the highway. The old railroad center itself consists of several fine stone stores and residences, all bounded by the tracks, which leave Rincon in three directions.

Between Rincon and Fort Selden, one gets some idea of what it must have been like for early travelers to leave the Rio Grande and strike out across the Jornada del Muerto. The ruins of FORT SELDEN, 440 mi., mark the spot where the freight caravans usually rejoined the river (or left it depending on their direc-

tion), beginning or finishing ninety miles of desert travel. The fort here, one of a string built to protect travelers during the American territorial period, dates from the end of the Civil War. During the twenty-five years of its existence, Fort Selden saw little action from the Apache it was to defend against, but it was the home for a while of young Douglas MacArthur, son of the post commander. The fort also played a role in heliography, a system of communication using the sun and mirrors that was then being tried by the army. Soldiers built heliograph stations atop mountains along the Rio Grande to send messages between Fort Bliss, near El Paso, and Fort McRae, near present-day Truth or Consequences. One station was located on Robledo Mountain, just opposite old Fort Selden here. By 1891 the new railroad had been built and had taken over most of the traffic up and down the river and the need for the heliograph system. The army abandoned Fort Selden and consolidated at Fort Bliss. In 1972 the state opened Fort Selden and an accompanying museum to the public. These ruins offer some of the best evidence in New Mexico of what life in a nineteenth-century military outpost must have been like. The Fort Selden State Monument has no facilities for travelers, but nearby Leesburg State Park offers picknicking and hiking along the river.

RADIUM SPRINGS, on old U.S. 85 across the river from Fort Selden, has been a well-known resort, a women's prison, and lately a budding art center.

At DOÑA ANA, 449 mi., we enter the second largest metropolitan area of New Mexico in one of the oldest and biggest agricultural regions, the Mesilla Valley. The name Doña Ana ("Lady Ann") refers either to a legendary Doña Ana Robledo, a woman of noteworthy kindness and charity who lived here in the seventeenth century, or to an inscription on a child's grave, dated 1798. Some settlement undoubtedly existed here prior to the Pueblo Revolt. Early reports even mention pueblos along this part of the Rio Grande, but the re-

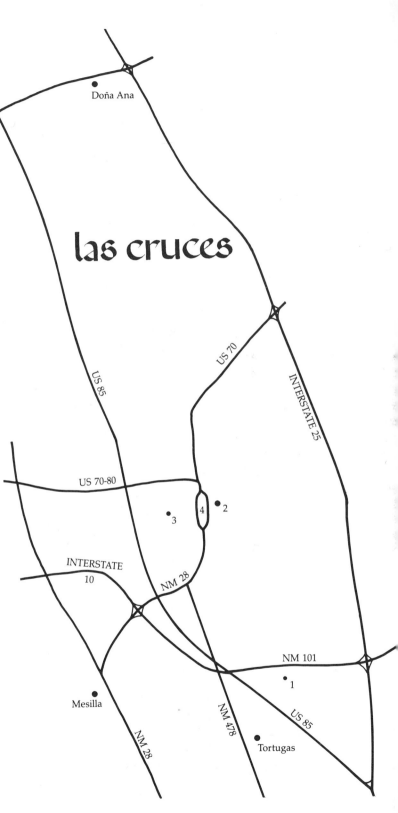

las cruces

1. New Mexico State University
2. Original Townsite
3. Alameda Depot
4. Downtown Mall

gion was evacuated in 1680. During the long century of the 1700s the Spanish could maintain no settlement here, and the entire stretch south of Belen lay abandoned except for the irregular passing of caravans until the "resettlement" period of the early nineteenth century. In 1839, the governor of Chihuahua granted El Ancon de Doña Ana ("the Doña Ana bend") to José María Costales and 116 others. They established the town on a hill north of the present site. At the time of the American occupation of New Mexico in 1846, many Hispanic dissenters moved south to Mesilla ("little hill"), then still part of Mexico. In 1852, Doña Ana became, briefly, the seat of one of the original nine huge counties created by the territorial legislature. A wagon road through San Agustin Pass connected the new town with Tularosa and Lincoln (then called Rio Bonito).

Doña Ana soon lost out as the metropolis of the Mesilla Valley to LAS CRUCES, 455 mi (alt. 3,900, pop. 44,902), a town created in the territorial period. In 1598 Don Juan de Oñate passed here on his way to establish the province and the capital of New Mexico. Las Cruces's site had been a camping area and stopping place for centuries. Early Spanish accounts name it Estero Largo ("long estuary"). The Robledo Mountains just to the north, the landmark for travelers returning over the Jornada route, were named for Pedro Robledo, a soldier whom Oñate buried here. On at least two occasions Apaches surprised and killed

traveling parties in this area: in 1787, travelers found the bodies of oxcart caravan drivers and erected crosses on the spot; a group of forty travelers from Taos met the same fate in 1830. The area became known as La Placita de las Cruces ("the place of the crosses").

After the 1848 Treaty of Guadalupe Hidalgo, which ended the U.S.–Mexican War, sovereignty over the land at present-day Las Cruces remained in doubt. Before the Gadsden Purchase in 1853, the Mesilla Valley was split between the two countries, the town of Mesilla on the west bank of the Rio Grande being in Mexico, and Las Cruces on the east bank presumably in the United States. When U.S. control became evident, the army made a survey, and prospective settlers drew lots for land sites. The original Las Cruces town site still exists, centering on Mesquite Street in the eastern part of town. In 1852 Las Cruces became seat of Doña Ana County, which extended from Texas to Arizona. A sore point during the early years were the so-called Texas Head Rights—land grants made by the republic of Texas (which had claimed this area) that appeared to predate and nullify the original settlers' rights to their land. This was not the first clash, nor would it be the last, between people of the two states over land and water.

In 1859 Father Manuel Chávez directed the building of Las Cruces's first chapel. The St. Genevieve Church was completed in 1879 and served the needs of its parish until it was demolished in 1977. With the advantages of the railroad, irrigated farming, and ranching on nearby slopes and mesas, the new city grew rapidly. Building boomed in the territorial and Victorian styles then popular. Jacob Schaublin established El Molino, Las Cruces's flour mill. A College of Las Cruces opened in 1880, and within a decade the legislature authorized the founding of the New Mexico College of Agriculture and Mechanic Arts, which eventually would become New Mexico State University (NMSU).

Located in the sharp V formed by the intersection of interstates 25 and 10, NMSU claims to have the world's largest campus, 6,250 acres. Here the university boasts one of the three full-time planetary observatories in the nation. It also has one of the largest computer centers in the Southwest and the state's first student-operated AM radio station (plus student-operated FM and TV stations), and it ranks among the top one hundred universities in the country in federal research and development funds, grants devoted in large part to weapons research. The New Mexico Department of Agriculture building on campus has the largest integrated solar heating and cooling system ever used. Tile-roofed stucco buildings, both old and new, unify the spacious campus. A favorite place for children is the fish pond on the northern edge of the campus near University Avenue. Ongoing attractions at the university include the University Museum and numerous theater, music, and sporting events.

Las Cruces offers many places of interest to travelers. The city takes pride in the Downtown Mall, the city hall, and the new Branigan Memorial Library. Municipal recreation sites include Apodaca Park (Madrid Street at Solano Drive) with a public swimming pool, Young Park (on Nevada Avenue) with a stocked lake, and the eight-acre Burn Lake (on West Amador Avenue). Las Cruces contains two historic districts. The original town site district extends north and a little south of Amador Avenue along Mesquite and San Pedro streets, and surrounds Klein Park. The Alameda Depot district begins just west of the city and county buildings on Amador Street and extends north beyond the old depot (still in use for freight handling) on Mesilla Street at Las Cruces Avenue. Here the various architectural styles of a one-hundred-year period have been preserved. Noteworthy old buildings include the Amador Hotel (Water and Amador streets), built in the 1850s and now open as a museum *and* as the Citizens Bank, and the American Victorian-style Armijo House, built in 1877 on the north side of Loretto Mall.

The Southern New Mexico State Fair is held early each October at the fairgrounds west of the city. In mid-October aficionados of chile cook off in the New Mexico State Chile Championships. Tour 10 provides information about places west along I-10 and east on U.S. 70/82.

When the Spanish and Pueblo people retreated down the Rio Grande at the time of the Pueblo Revolt, the old and weak supposedly stayed behind at Tortugas. Present-day TORTUGAS is located on territory of the old Tewa resettlement pueblos of Guadalupe and San Juan, now a part of southeastern Las Cruces. Tortugas commemorates the three appearances of Mexico's patron saint, Our Lady of Guadalupe, to Juan Diego, an Indian, on a hill outside Mexico City on December 10–12, 1531, by holding a three-day fiesta and a climb up Mount Tortugas. The celebration, originally a Pueblo ceremony brought from Nuestra Señora de Guadalupe Church in old El Paso, begins at dusk on December 10. Fiddlers, dancers, trumpeters, choirs, priests, and people young and old take part in the fiesta that culminates in the torchlight procession up the mountain (heralded by shotgun blasts), followed by a Mass by firelight on top.

The village of MESILLA, also now included within the Las Cruces metropolitan area, has a history of its own. It can claim to have been the largest city west of San Antonio, Texas; "capital" of the Gadsden Purchase; capital of

the Confederate Territory of Arizona; and the scene of Billy the Kid's trial. Oñate referred to it as Trenequel ("dyke") de la Mesilla. The present town, situated on the slight rise for which it is named, was begun in 1850. Half the population of Doña Ana moved here the following year, intending to remain on Mexican soil after the occupation of the east bank by American forces. The Mexican government approved a land grant for the new town in 1853. However, in the same year it agreed to the sale of Mesilla and nearly thirty thousand square miles to the west (the Gadsden Purchase) to the United States. American possession was celebrated in the plaza on July 4, 1854, but some of the original settlers missed the event because they had moved south once more to remain in Mexico. The Rio Grande flowed between Mesilla and Las Cruces at first, and a ferry connected the two cities. A flood in 1863 cut a second channel west of Mesilla, leaving it on a malaria-infested island. In 1885 the river chose the western course, where it flows today. Mesilla's plaza was the scene in late 1871 of a bloody political riot between rival Democratic and Republican rallies. Its years as an important territorial city ended when the Santa Fe Railroad left it out of its plans in 1881, selecting a route via Las Cruces instead.

La Posta, visible from N.M. 28 entering old Mesilla, is a 175-year-old building that served as a way station on the Butterfield Overland Mail route. Employing over seven hundred fifty people, the Butterfield stages ran the "oxbow" route, twenty-eight hundred miles from Tipton, Missouri, to San Francisco, normally in twenty-five days. The stages swooped down into Arkansas and Texas and entered New Mexico from the south, turning west at Mesilla on a trail north of present-day I-10. They stopped every nine miles to change horses and mules. The company set up stations every 110 miles for food, overnight lodging, and care of the draft animals. La Posta is the only Overland Mail way station still used by tourists, serving food and drink in several dining rooms that display items from the past.

Mesilla Plaza, *John Waszak.*

On the old plaza itself, San Albino Church dates from March 1, 1851, St. Alban's day and the day water first ran in the newly dug irrigation ditches. Father Ramón Ortiz had supervised the construction of the adobe church when immigrants from Doña Ana arrived, assuming Mesilla would remain part of Mexico. A new brick church was built on the same foundations in 1906.

Around the plaza one finds numerous original buildings still in use. The Old Tortilla Factory is now a gift shop. One of Mesilla's noteworthy early citizens was Colonel Albert Jennings Fountain (some of whose life and death Tour 10 describes), a force in territorial politics. The Fountain Theater, established in

1905, contains a mural painted by A. J. Fountain, the colonel's son. The Las Cruces Community Theater used the building from 1961 to 1976. Since then it has hosted films, chamber music, and live theater. El Patio Lounge and Restaurant was established in 1935 by a great-grandson of the original Fountain, in a building dating from the 1860s. This building also housed offices of the *Mesilla Valley Independent.* The Old Courthouse Building was for a time the seat of Doña Ana County while the courthouse in Las Cruces was being completed. Billy the Kid was tried here in 1880 and sentenced to be hanged. The courthouse has also been used as a school and a jail.

Just off the main plaza, the Gadsden Museum displays relics and artifacts as well as articles donated by the Fountain family. Next door, the Museum of the American Vaquero has put together a collection of cowboy gear and tack that is probably unmatched in the country. Exhibits of saddles, stirrups, lariats, and clothing, from North Africa, Spain, central Mexico, Sonora, Baja California, and California trace the origins of styles that became popular in New Mexico.

Between Las Cruces and El Paso, travelers have three choices of route: I-10 or N.M. 478 on the east side of the river, or N.M. 28, which crosses over to the west side at Santo Tomas. From the interstate one gets a view of several large dairies; dairying has become a major industry here because of the dry, healthful climate and the availability of feed and cheap labor. Both state roads pass through the pecan orchards and onion, lettuce, and chile fields of the Mesilla Valley, the richest farming section of the state before deep-well pumping began on the eastern plains after World War II. In recent years, two struggles (besides the everlasting one of winning food from the soil) have been going on here: the battle between New Mexico and Texas (Mesilla Valley farmers versus the City of El Paso) over water, and the movement of farmworkers, many of them Mexican citizens, to gain a more just share of the fruits of the harvest.

N.M. 478 connects the farming towns of Mesquite, Vado ("ford"), and Berino, crossing into Texas at the bistate town of Anthony. The only battle of the U.S.–Mexican War fought in New Mexico took place one mile west of old FORT FILLMORE (460 mi.), active from 1857 to 1862. Here, on Christmas afternoon 1846, Colonel Alexander Doniphan's Missouri Regulars defeated Mexican forces under General Trías at an ancient camping spot called La Salineta. Three days later, the Americans encountered no resistance in occupying El Paso.

Opposite MESQUITE, 466 mi., bones of ancient sloths, camels, and cave bears have been found in Conklin Cave, located in Bishop's Cap, a park in the southern end of the Organ

Mountains. ANTHONY, 480 mi., is a cotton-growing and -processing center whose railroad name of La Tuna (the fruit of the prickly pear cactus) was rejected by an elderly lady. The station was on the Texas side; she lived on the New Mexico side and insisted the town take the name of her patron, St. Anthony.

Travelers using N.M. 28 pass through the west bank farming communities of San Miguel, La Mesa, Chamberino, and La Union (twenty-six miles south of Las Cruces). Chamberino began as a refuge for New Mexicans who, according to the 1848 Treaty of Guadalupe Hidalgo, could choose between Mexico and the United States. Many chose Mexican citizenship and moved south of the supposed boundary line. The nationality of this section remained in doubt, however, until the Gadsden Purchase and subsequent surveys set the international border at its present location. Beyond La Union, N.M. 273 continues sixteen miles south to the triple intersection of New Mexico, Texas, and Mexico. Sunland Park Race Track has taken advantage of the fact that New Mexico allows parimutuel betting and Texas does not. The popular horse races take place on a piece of land on the El Paso side of the river which, because of a sudden change in the Rio Grande's course after the border was fixed, remained part of New Mexico. State leaders of New Mexico and Chihuahua have spoken in favor of a direct Mexico–New Mexico border crossing near the old village of Anapra. Many people in both countries hope that the proposed new crossing soon becomes a reality.

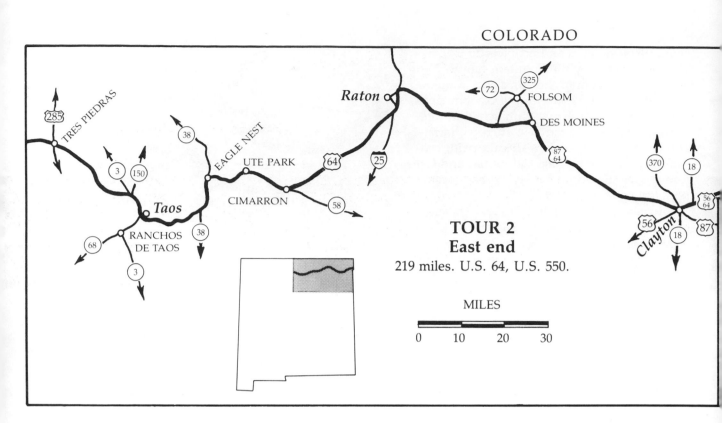

See page 309 for western half of tour two.

tour two

Texas Border • **Clayton** • *Raton* • *Taos* • **Chama** • **Farmington** • **Shiprock**

Westbound travelers can enter Clayton from either of two directions and leave in one of two directions. U.S. 56 closely approximates the path of the Cimarron Cutoff of the Santa Fe Trail—the southern fork, more dangerous but often faster than the main trail that entered New Mexico via Raton Pass. The Cimarron Cutoff branched off at Fort Dodge, Kansas, crossed the plains of the Oklahoma Panhandle and eastern New Mexico, and rejoined the main trail in the Wagon Mound/Fort Union area. A second route, U.S. 87, used the right of way adjacent to the Colorado and Southern, a division of the Denver and Fort Worth Railroad. This line, completed in 1888, followed paths opened by cattle drivers on their way to railheads at Springer, New Mexico, and Granada, Colorado. U.S. 64 enters Clayton with U.S. 56 but joins U.S. 87 from here to Raton. Between Raton and Taos, U.S. 64 follows still another Santa Fe Trail alternate, the occasionally used Taos Branch that *crossed* (instead of going around) the Sangre de Cristo Range, and descended the Rio Grande to Santa Fe. It was not until the 1970s that sections of U.S. 64 were opened west of Taos, across the Rio Grande Gorge High Bridge and

through the Brazos Mountains, completing the first highway across northern New Mexico. U.S. 64 then used existing state routes that connected Dulce, the Jicarilla Apache Reservation capital, with the coal and oil boom town of Farmington.

Tour 2 follows U.S. 64 its entire length to Farmington, and continues on across the northeastern corner of the Navajo Reservation (via U.S. 550) to Shiprock. Its indirect and curvy path is an indication of the ruggedness and beauty of the terrain. Travelers are advised of the hazards of winter driving (the highway between Tres Piedras and Tierra Amarilla is often closed during winter months) and of the lack of tourist facilities over long stretches of the route.

The Colorado and Southern Railroad established CLAYTON, 11 mi. (alt. 5,054, pop. 2,981), in 1887 on a campground used by drovers and herds from the Texas plains. Its boom times as a railroad cattle-shipping station were marred by a killer blizzard in October and November 1889 that left twenty-five inches of snow (with seven-foot drifts); thousands of dead cattle, sheep, and horses; and several lost cowhands and shepherds. Trains were held up for two weeks, and livestock shipping on the railroad took a year to recover.

The early history of Clayton is associated with two personalities whose deeds were suspicious enough (in the case of Senator Dorsey) and notorious enough (in the case of Black Jack Ketchum) to hold the interest of later generations. Stephen Dorsey served a term as United States senator from Arkansas during the 1870s. After coming to New Mexico, he figured in bringing the railroad to Clayton, established a trading post here, and with his lawyer partner, Bob Ingersoll, acquired the Triangle Dot Ranch in Union and Colfax counties. On this ranch, fifty miles west of Clayton, he built a spacious and lonely mansion. Dorsey was also involved (but eventually acquitted, with Ingersoll's help) in a mail fraud case in which monthly mail deliveries were provided to people who believed they had purchased daily service. The senator named Clayton after his son and the mountain and town of Mount Dora to the west after his sister-in-law.

Thomas "Black Jack" Ketchum was born in Texas in 1860 and robbed his first train in 1891 on the Dawson coal line north of Tucumcari. His exploits included holdups in Texas, Arizona, and Sonora, Mexico, and reached a climax with his unassisted heist of a train in Turkey Creek Canyon in Colfax County, New Mexico. Wounded during a holdup attempt in August 1899, he eventually turned himself in at Clayton to Sheriff Saturnino Pinard. Ketchum was executed and buried (off by himself) here in 1901, humorous and defiant to the end.

By 1895, when Clayton won the designation as seat of Union County (named for the spirit of union felt by settlers), several fine buildings that stand today had been erected. One of the most notable of these is the Ecklund Hotel, built in 1892 by John C. Hill, range manager for Dorsey. The story goes that Carl Ecklund won a bar in a poker game in Folsom and used the proceeds to buy Hill's two-story sandstone hotel in Clayton and to add two more stories onto the eastern end. To the rest of the building Ecklund later added a third floor and opera balcony with a view of Clayton. The Ecklund Hotel, considerably neglected, was rescued in 1977 by John Chilcote, who began work to restore the place to the style of the 1890s, when the Ecklund advertised its reputation as "the only first-class hotel between Trinidad and Fort Worth." An elegantly furnished dining room that seats ninety now serves meals Wednesdays through Sundays. The Ecklund, on the main highway through town, is often filled on Wednesdays, when the weekly livestock auction draws ranchers from five states to Clayton. Among the area's seasonal attractions are the Union County Fair in September, the Arts and Crafts Festival in late October, and the Western dancing tradition during the end-of-year holiday season.

Cattle ranching is still big here, and limited irrigated farming has been successful. The Bravo Dome carbon dioxide gas field, however, figures importantly in Clayton's near future. An estimated ten trillion cubic feet of the gas lie under the 1.2 million-acre dome, where there are plans to drill one thousand wells. The carbon dioxide may be piped to Texas and southeastern New Mexico oil fields to be used in the tertiary recovery of oil pools not accessible by other methods. The gas boom promises to double Clayton's population. Developers claim that damage to grazing lands will be minimal. People all over the northeast plains region wait to see how Clayton emerges from the sudden growth (and probable later decline) that has characterized the history of so many New Mexico cities and towns.

Deer and antelope, as well as fossils, dinosaur bones, and petroglyphs, are hunted in the countryside around Clayton. Twelve miles northwest of town on N.M. 370, the 170-acre Clayton Lake offers camping, fishing, a playground area, and boating at trolling speed during the April-through-October fishing season. (Boating is prohibited during the winter months because of the numerous waterfowl that visit here.) On the way to Clayton Lake,

Seneca Post Office, *Toby Smith.*

the road crosses Rabbit Ears Creek, and Rabbit Ears Mountain is visible to the east. This was a major landmark on the Santa Fe Trail, and its curious shape became the symbol of the Cimarron Cutoff. For four days of travel, traders kept an eye on Rabbit Ears and, because good water, wood, and grass were plentiful, often lay over for a day of rest here, sending runners ahead to Las Vegas to make arrangements with Mexican customs officials. After Rabbit Ears, the long wagon trains passed to the north of Round Mountain (also called Mount Clayton), reached Point of Rocks and the Canadian River crossing, and then turned south to Wagon Mound.

The state's extreme eastern highway, N.M. 18, proceeds south from Clayton across the high plains to Tucumcari. West of Clayton, U.S. 56 branches off to Springer. Travelers who enjoy making choices are reminded that the distance to Cimarron and Taos is virtually the same via Springer as it is via Raton. An

attraction on U.S. 56, fifty-seven miles west of Clayton, is the Dorsey Mansion, located at the base of low, rocky hills twelve miles north of the highway. Stephen Dorsey bought a 1.5-million-acre land grant in 1877, but could make it profitable only by buying up the water holes of the homesteaders whose property surrounded his. Dorsey's mansion began as a log house in 1880, but by its completion in 1886 it had become a thirty-six-room palace, with hardwood floors, Italian marble fireplaces, brass carbon arc fixtures, a hand-carved, solid cherry staircase, and a dining room that seated sixty people. The fate of the disintegrating mansion was not known at this writing.

Proceeding on U.S. 64/U.S. 87 some distance west of Clayton, with a view of several mountains of volcanic origin, one gets a feel for how these lava-capped uplands differ from other parts of New Mexico's high plains. Black-topped mesas, volcanic craters and remnants of craters, and a more varied landscape with considerable surface water characterize the *altiplano* (high plains) region between Clayton and Raton. Rabbit Ears Mountain, rising six hundred feet above the plain northeast of Clayton, is one of a series of vents in this area from which lava flows have issued.

Although DES MOINES, 56 mi., was given its name (to honor the Iowa city) in 1888, when the Colorado and Southern came through, the actual town at the foot of Sierra Grande ("big mountain") dates from 1907. It grew to a

good-sized community during the next twenty years, slumped with the Depression, and prospered again for a while with the dry ice industry that resulted from tapping a rich carbon dioxide deposit in the mid-1930s.

The traveler will have little trouble recognizing Capulin Mountain, north of the highway. One turns on N.M. 325, 65 mi., to visit the 8,215-foot volcanic cone, a national monument since 1916. From the parking area at the top of the crater's west rim, one can see five states, wagon ruts of military supply trains, the older volcanic peak of Sierra Grande ten miles to the southwest, and black-rock-capped Barela, Johnson, and Raton mesas to the northwest. Geologists estimate that Capulin Mountain is seven thousand years old, dating from the last stages of a period of volcanic activity along the fault lines of western North and South America. The cinder cone, one of the most nearly perfect in shape anywhere, rises a thousand feet above the plain. The crater measures one mile in circumference and 415 feet in depth. From the parking lot, one can walk the Crater Rim Trail (one mile) and/or the .2-mile trail that leads to the bottom of the crater. Many species of plant life thrive within the crater, including the chokecherry (Spanish *capulín*) for which the mountain is named. From the north side of the rim, there is a view of the Folsom area, where a cowboy found a spear point that led to a dig that changed our conception of early life on this continent (see below).

Capulin, *Harvey Caplin*.

Continuing north on N.M. 325 (or following N.M. 72 from Des Moines) the traveler reaches FOLSOM, on the southern slopes of the Raton Mountains. The town, named for Grover Cleveland's wife, Frances Folsom, shared in the growth that the cattle industry brought to the region at the turn of the century. A summer hotel here once provided accommodations for tourists on the spectacular railroad between Clayton and Trinidad, Colorado.

The Folsom Museum, formerly Doherty's Mercantile, now attracts four thousand visitors each summer. For many years the town's best story has been that of the chipped stone darts, found among bones of extinct animals, that indicated a hunting culture here twelve thousand years ago. One of the principals in the tale is George McJunkin, the black cowhand on Lige Johnson's Crowfoot Ranch who brought the bones and weapons to the world's attention. Not only was McJunkin curious and observant, he was persistent enough to keep telling people about his find until the Denver Museum of Natural History began the "Folsom dig" in 1926.

The state of New Mexico, impressed with the archaeological significance of the region, eventually created the Folsom Man State Monument just west of town.

―――――――――― SIDE TOUR ――――――――――

Follow either N.M. 72 or U.S. 64/87 to RATON, 93 mi., where Tour 2 intersects Tour 1; Tour 1 describes that coal, railroad, and recreation center. Tour 2 then proceeds south on I-25 to Exit 446, 98 mi., where U.S. 64 branches off to the southwest.

The junction at 107 mi. once was called Santa Fe Forks because the Santa Fe Trail forked here, with the main branch going south via Las Vegas and the other proceeding via Taos and the Rio Grande. The old U.S. highways also split here when the spot was called Hoxie's Junction: U.S. 85 continued south, and U.S. 64 went westward, as it does today.

The Vermejo River crossing at 120 mi. is a reminder of the powerful Maxwell Land Grant interests that once dominated this corner of the state and of their successor, the remote and beautiful Vermejo ("auburn") Ranch. Early in this century Charles B. Eddy built a coal railway from Tucumcari to the coal fields at Dawson and York Canyon, northwest of this point. This line followed the Vermejo River upstream to the mines to haul out thousands of tons of fuel for the expanding railroad industry. The Dawson settlement had begun when John B. Dawson bought what he thought was one thousand acres from the Maxwell Land Grant Company in 1869. Later surveys turned his thousand acres into twenty thousand, on sections of which Dawson discovered coal. Eddy built his 144-mile spur up from Tucumcari after the coal mined at Capitan proved to be of low quality. The Phelps Dodge Corporation then bought the Dawson mine and established the "model community" of Dawson which at times numbered nine thousand people, with a hospital, a swimming pool, and a mercantile store. It was a city of immigrant miners, who came from Italy, Poland, Greece, the Balkans, Mexico, Great Britain, Finland, Sweden, and Germany. A mine explosion killed 263 men in 1913; another in 1923 killed 120 more. The mines finally closed in 1950, and the town has been deserted since.

Another old-time source of energy also tapped in the mountainous region north of U.S. 64 was charcoal. In the 1890s twenty-five beehive-shaped brick ovens, twenty-eight feet high and twenty-eight feet in diameter, were built in the sawmill town of Catskill to convert pine logs into charcoal. The process took ten to twelve days, and the resulting product was then shipped via a Union Pacific Railroad spur for use in refining metals in Pueblo and Denver, Colorado.

CIMARRON, 133 mi. (alt. 6,385, pop. 892), was a principal stop on the Taos branch of the Santa Fe Trail. It dates from 1841, the year of the huge Beaubien-Miranda Land Grant. The town became a gathering place for ranchers and miners from a wide area and was headquarters and post office for the organization that took over the Beaubien-Miranda Grant, the Maxwell Land Grant Company. *Cimarrón* means "wild" and refers to wild sheep or horses in the region. The Cimarron River flows through a magnificent canyon west of town and then continues southeasterly to join the Canadian River near Springer. Some confusion is understandable: *another* Cimarron River (usually called the Dry Cimarron) rises in Colfax County near Folsom and flows all the way across Oklahoma as the Cimarron River, joining the Arkansas River and, again, the Canadian River near Tulsa.

The holdings that Lucien Maxwell inherited from his father-in-law, Charles Beaubien, or purchased from other partners amounted to 1,714,765 acres. That equals 2,679 square miles, three times the area of Rhode Island. His land included the towns of Springer, Maxwell, French, Raton, Vermejo Park, Ute Park, and Elizabethtown, plus a large area in Colorado. Although Maxwell had mediocre success in mining and banking, sales of beef to army posts and to the Ute Indian Agency kept the money flowing in Cimarron, where, as an extravagant gambler and entertainer, he employed some four hundred people. In 1864 he built a block-long house with gambling rooms, a billiard room, and a dance hall. In the early 1860s Lucien Maxwell and "Buffalo Bill" Cody became business partners. Cody later staged his Wild West shows at Cimarron and took particular interest in a special Christmas program for children held at the St. James Hotel.

From 1872 to 1882 Cimarron, "cowboy capital of northern New Mexico," was also the seat of Colfax County. The building on the northeast corner of the old square dates from 1848 and served as the Ute Indian Agency Headquarters, later housing the Cimarron *News and Press*, which began publishing in English and Spanish in 1875. An outraged Clay Allison, cowboy, gunfighter, and sometime challenger to Maxwell Land Grant Company interests, once threw the paper's press into the Cimarron River.

Henry Lambert built the forty-room St. James Hotel across the street from the Maxwell House. Legend has it that the St. James (later known as the Don Diego) was the scene of twenty-six murders. Three other hotels and fifteen saloons rounded out the business section of Cimarron. The town could boast the first public library in the territory, founded in 1881 by Frank Sherwin, manager of the Maxwell Land Grant Company.

When Raton became a railroad metropolis in the 1880s, Cimarron declined in influence and population. However, mining and lumbering continued to be important industries. In 1905 the Saint Louis, Rocky Mountain, and Pacific

Dawson 1921

Railroad (later taken over by the Santa Fe) built a branch to Cimarron and Ute Park and established a new town on the north side of the river. A fire destroyed five business blocks of the new town in the early 1930s. The polo field and racehorse stables inside the village limits date from 1933.

Five miles west of Cimarron, the tour enters the narrow, twisting gorge of Cimarron Canyon. In places here, the sandstone walls come down to the edge of the road, once the path of Santa Fe Trail traders and of the railroad branch to Ute Park.

UTE PARK, 146 mi., is named after the Ute Indians who lived on the eastern slope of nearby Mount Baldy. The Utes resisted white domination even after an Indian agency and a military force were established in nearby Cimarron. The tribe was eventually moved to a reservation in southern Colorado and Utah. Ute Park was also the terminus of an Atchison, Topeka, and Santa Fe Railroad branch from which freight was distributed for the

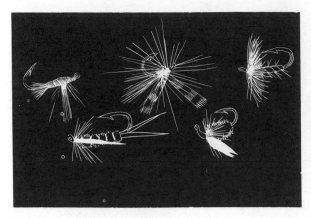

Moreno Valley, Red River, and Taos.

EAGLE NEST, 157 mi. (alt. 8,200, pop. 201), is the name of both the small village and the private lake which sit, ringed by mountains, at the bottom of the Moreno Valley. Charles Springer, a prominent cattleman, merchant, engineer, and banker, designed and built Eagle Nest Dam at the head of Cimarron Canyon in 1919. Part of the Maxwell Land Grant, the five-mile-long lake that resulted is an irrigation source for the valley. It is also a favorite fishing spot, with permits available. Straight ahead across the horizon rise some of New

Mexico's highest peaks, among them Touch Me Not (12,045 feet), Baldy (12,441 feet), and Wheeler, New Mexico's highest mountain (13,160 feet).

The village of Eagle Nest was founded in 1920, shortly after the dam was built. It was first called Therma, but the presence of golden eagles in the surrounding mountains prompted citizens to rename the small town Eagle Nest in 1935. A row of tourist cabins, motels, bait and tackle shops, and small grocery stores lines U.S. 64 here. For many years Eagle Nest was the largest settlement in the Moreno Valley, but the recent arrival of recreational developments has lessened its importance as a trading center for ranchers and supply spot for fishermen. Most stores and restaurants are open year-round. There is a small airfield north of town.

At the junction of U.S. 64 and N.M. 38, travelers can turn north to Red River (Tour 3), seventeen miles away. Or, taking a detour from U.S. 64, visitors can see the ruins of one of New Mexico's most famous ghost towns, Elizabethtown, five miles up N.M. 38 on the hills above Moreno Creek.

SIDE TOUR

Although little remains now to suggest ELIZABETHTOWN's past, the community once boasted seven thousand people and was the first seat of Colfax County. Many tall tales and legends speak of the town's role in the wild gold-mining era in New Mexico. Gold was first discovered in the Moreno Valley in the 1860s, near the spot where a number of creeks converge; Elizabethtown began life there also.

Called Virginia City when it was founded in 1865, the settlement soon changed its name to Elizabethtown in honor of Elizabeth Moore, daughter of a leading citizen. By 1870 "E-Town" included five stores, two hotels, seven sa-loons, and three dance halls. Desperadoes like Coal Oil Jimmy, Long Taylor, and Pony O'Neil roamed its dirt streets. Tunnels with aqueducts leading from the other side of the mountains to the town were dredged as the twentieth century dawned. A dredge called Eleanor dug a ditch from Red River to the site. Fortunes were made and lost quickly. By the beginning of this century, however, most of the accessible gold had run out. Fire destroyed much of "E-Town's" business district in 1903. Only a few overgrown foundations and the remnants of the cemetery guide the visitor to Elizabethtown now.

Aspens, *Daniel Gibson.*

Although there are no other prominent gold-era ghost towns in the Moreno Valley, abandoned mine sites are scattered throughout the foothills. "There was gold in every gulch," says one report describing the scramble to extract the precious metal from the many creeks which feed the valley.

Traveling south after the U.S. 64/N.M. 38 junction, a visitor will follow the shoreline of Eagle Nest Lake. Developments and ranches are on the right. A memorial to Vietnam veterans, the first built in the United States, stands watch over the Moreno Valley near the end of the lake. The small chapel, a soaring white presence on the mountainside, was built by hand by the Westphall family in tribute to their son who was killed in the war. It is the Vietnam Veterans National Memorial of the Disabled American Veterans and is open to visitors twenty-four hours a day.

About seven miles south of the village of Eagle Nest, N.M. 38 leaves U.S. 64 and proceeds due south to ANGEL FIRE (alt. 8,370), a year-round resort. Begun as a ski development, Angel Fire is new to the valley and includes hotels, restaurants, condominiums, and nearby camping facilities. Angel Fire is most famous, perhaps, for its miles of downhill ski trails that end at the edge of the village. Visitors can also play golf or tennis, or go cross-country skiing or snowmobiling. A lake provides fishing and boating opportunities. South of Angel Fire, N.M. 38 continues on to Guadalupita (Tour 3), thirteen miles away. However, the road is not well-maintained for much of that distance and is not recommended for passenger car travel.

SIDE TOUR

Less than a mile after the turnoff to Angel Fire, U.S. 64, climbing and winding upward, enters Carson National Forest. The road's summit, Palo Flechado Pass, 170 mi., is over nine thousand feet above sea level. It is cool when the valley floors are warm but icy and treacherous in the winter. The trail used by Taos Indians in centuries past to reach the buffalo plains to the east passes close to the road here. The summit's name means "tree pierced with arrows"; Indian legends mention a tree with arrow marks on it that once stood at the summit. Some sources say that at the end of a buffalo hunt the victorious hunters shot arrows into the tree; others contend that war parties celebrated their victories in the same way. Views from the pass down into the valley are spectacular, the colors changing with the seasons.

Wide meadows flank the Rio Fernando de Taos (Taos River) as it meanders down its valley. The small village of Valle Escondido ("hidden valley") hugs the highway. Other settlements, mainly scatterings of cabins and summerhouses, will appear along the road from here to Taos. Public campgrounds are dotted along the river, often connected to each other by walking trails. While camping areas, many with rest rooms and water, are plentiful along U.S. 64, there are also more primitive facilities off the highway, which are marked. From late spring into early fall, campers and fishermen fill this stretch of road. El Nogal Nature Trail appears just before the national forest boundary. A short bypass, which skirts the town of Taos and leads to N.M. 68 and Tour 11, soon intersects U.S. 64.

U.S. 64 becomes Kit Carson Road as it winds quietly through the Taos River valley. A wonderful grove of cottonwood trees like an immense golden umbrella in the autumn canopies the road as it enters town. Small motels, houses, and art galleries signal that Taos Plaza is nearing. The road climbs gradually and enters Taos, meeting N.M. 68 and N.M. 3 at a stoplight intersection, 188 mi., just east of the plaza. (Taos, including a walking tour and a trip to Taos Pueblo, is covered in Tour 3.)

U.S. 64 veers north at the busy Taos intersection, becoming North Pueblo Road as it passes through the business district. About a mile beyond the plaza area, the road north to Taos Pueblo appears. A few craft shops and the Children's Art Center are located along this road, which leads directly to the pueblo.

U.S. 64 curves to the left past a variety of small business establishments. Soon the settlement of EL PRADO ("meadow" or "pasture"), its boundary ill-defined, straddles the road. Surrounded by the reservation lands of Taos Pueblo, El Prado retains a number of meadows and fields, those to the east leading gently into the foothills of the Sangre de Cristos. El Prado is now almost a Taos suburb, home to artists, farmers, and summer residents.

Less than two miles north of El Prado, as the congestion of houses and traffic lessens and the wide Taos Plateau becomes more evident, three roads, U.S. 64, N.M. 3, and N.M. 150, intersect (192 mi.). N.M. 150 breaks off to the east, leading past small Hispanic villages and ultimately through Rio Hondo Canyon to Taos Ski Valley. N.M. 3 continues straight north to the Colorado border (Tour 3), about forty miles away. A left turn on U.S. 64 takes the visitor to the Rio Grande Gorge Bridge and across to western New Mexico, a continuation of Tour 2.

Valdez, *Harvey Caplin.*

Those who want to camp along the Rio Hondo, visit Taos Ski Valley, or enter the Wheeler Peak Wilderness Area will take N.M. 150 at the intersection. A paved, year-round road, N.M. 150 is nevertheless narrow and full of curves as it ascends the fifteen miles to the ski valley; winter travelers should be prepared for snowy and icy conditions.

Bordering the highway as it crosses the high plain and goes toward Rio Hondo Canyon are many examples of Taos area architectural styles. The Taos Tennis Ranch is an award-winning, adobe-like condominium complex, a recent addition to this windswept plateau. Old adobe houses, lived in and added onto for generations, share mountain vistas with newer, owner-built homes, some of them almost sculptures. Summerhouses and subsistence farms alike seem to blend into the landscape.

A small road, N.M. 230, joins N.M. 150 about two miles after leaving the earlier intersection. N.M. 230 travels directly into the valley of the Rio Hondo ("deep river") and to the small community of VALDEZ, whose name probably can be traced to José Luis Valdez, a Spaniard who joined de Vargas in the 1692 reconquest. Although Valdez lived in the Santa Cruz area north of Santa Fe, his descendants, it is said, settled this narrow valley hundreds of years ago. Once the town of Valdez was called San Antonio in honor of its patron saint. Small orchards and farms march to the river here. N.M. 230 continues east, eventually linking up with N.M. 150 beyond Arroyo Seco.

N.M. 150 remains the more direct route into Rio Hondo Canyon, skirting the sides of the dry ditch that gives ARROYO SECO, an old agricultural village turned turned crafts center, its name. Here a few simple restaurants and guest houses offer amenities to travelers and skiers. Two farmers, Cristóbal Martínez and José Martínez, founded Arroyo Seco in 1804 by planting crops along the riverbed. They commuted to their fields from Rio Arriba County, building homesteads here in 1807.

Just beyond Arroyo Seco, the highway traverses a ridge above Valdez and then winds down into the valley. Signs announce the beginning of Carson National Forest and give directions for entering the Wheeler Peak Wilderness area. Permits are required for overnight stays in the wilderness; they may be obtained either at the Taos Ranger Station or at the ranger station in Questa.

N.M. 150 follows the Hondo River, a mountain stream that is shallow and rocky. Steep gray cliffs rise on either side of the road. A number of campsites, picnic areas, and private cabins have been built along the road. Trails and forest roads wander off into the surrounding national forest.

As it parallels the river, N.M. 150 is also following the old toll road built by the William Frazer Company, developer of Twining, the mining town that long ago sat where Taos Ski Valley now bustles at the base of Taos Mountain. Gold was discovered here in 1880, and soon Amizette,

as it was then called, became a busy gold, silver, and copper town. In 1895 its name was changed to honor one of the mine's backers, Albert C. Twining, a New Jersey businessman who financed a three-hundred-thousand-dollar smelter for the operation. Unfortunately, when the smelter was fired, the molten ore stuck to the sides of the furnace. The mine, the business enterprise, and finally the town of Twining died shortly thereafter.

Taos Ski Valley marks the end of N.M. 150 and the entrance to the Wheeler Peak Wilderness Area. Climbers can reach the summit of Wheeler Peak from Taos Ski Valley in less than a day, although the climb is not an easy one.

Mountain chalets, modern condominiums, and Swiss-style lodges crowd the base of Taos Mountain. Some of the hotels are open to the public all year for snacks, meals, and refreshments. In the summer, a music school and a language institute fill a number of the lodges.

Considered one of the most challenging ski areas in North America, Taos also offers slopes and classes for beginners. The ski season usually begins at the nine-thousand-foot-high valley around Thanksgiving and extends into Easter week. When the lower slopes have lost their snow in late spring, private parties can arrange trips into the higher snow fields of the wilderness area. Racing schools are held in late summer on the upper reaches of the mountain. Ernie Blake, a European who searched the United States for the perfect site for his ski slope, founded the Taos Ski Valley and has remained at the helm of the successful operation since its inception in the 1950s. He was also a leader in bringing the ski industry to New Mexico. His weekly ski reports, delivered by radio statewide in heavily accented English, were long a source of enjoyment to skiers and nonskiers alike.

SIDE TOUR

Rio Grande Gorge Bridge, *Betty Lilienthal.*

Turning westward at the U.S. 64/N.M. 3/ N.M. 150 intersection, the traveler reaches Rio Grande Gorge Bridge after a seven-mile drive across the windy, sage-dotted plateau. The deep gorge carved over centuries by the river is not visible until just before the bridge appears. Visitors can park on either side of the span and walk across it, taking time to gaze into the depths of the gorge. Children and pets should be watched carefully.

Rising six hundred feet above the river, the Rio Grande Gorge Bridge links the eastern and western parts of northern New Mexico. Before its completion in 1965, travelers wishing to cross the Rio Grande had to wind down steep banks to cross primitive bridges at sites several miles away.

The Rio Grande Bridge is a steel and concrete structure placed at this location since the lava below provided a natural foundation for the concrete piers that soar to a height equivalent to that of an eight-story building. Because of the bridge's height—it was the second-tallest bridge in the United States when it was constructed—and because of the width of the canyon it crosses, tremendous winds often buffet the three-span structure. Travelers can take comfort in knowing that it was built to withstand gales in excess of ninety miles an hour.

On the west side of the Rio Grande, picnic tables protected from the sun and wind perch above the gorge. The panorama of the Rio Grande Gorge, its bridge, the Taos Plateau,

Rio Grande Gorge, *Harvey Caplin.*

drive of slightly more than forty miles, one of New Mexico's premier trips. The highway climbs and winds into the Brazos Range through Ponderosa forests, meadows of wild irises in the spring, and fields of purple and yellow wildflowers in the early fall. Because the road reaches altitudes of more than ten thousand feet in some places, the highway department usually closes this section of U.S. 64 in the snowy winter months.

A few miles beyond Tres Piedras, N.M. 111 (226 mi.) intersects. That road, impassable in bad weather, goes to Cañon Plaza, Vallecitos, and other small mountain villages.

Hopewell Lake, a tiny blue jewel at 9,900 feet, is located near the site of a mining town which flourished in the late 1800s. The mine and its town died long ago, but today's campers and fishermen consider Hopewell Lake a special spot. There are other scattered campsites on U.S. 64; most are primitive. Hiking trails also join the road at intervals, winding to hidden canyons and springs within Carson National Forest.

About eleven miles west of Hopewell Lake, a turnout appears at the road's summit, 10,500 feet. Here the visitor can see the smooth gray granite of Brazos Peak and can look down into the valleys and forests below. Many varieties of game—elk, mule deer, beavers, hawks, and golden eagles—still live in this mountain range. Pines, aspens, and oaks mix in the forests beneath the sides of the steep Brazos Cliffs. There will be more viewing areas along the road, some with picnic tables and descriptive signs. Soon the highway begins its descent out of the clouds into the green valleys to Tierra Amarilla. (See Tour 7 for the town of Tierra Amarilla and the journey from Tierra Amarilla to Chama, a distance of about thirteen miles.)

Heading out of Chama (281 mi.), the highway crosses a plateau of grazing land dotted with scrubby bushes. Just before the Continental Divide (7,766 feet), a dirt track juts off the road and goes to a wildlife area. Traces of the abandoned roadbed of the old Denver, Rio Grande, and Western Railroad can sometimes

and the Sangre de Cristo Mountains adds a spectacular dimension to a rest stop or picnic.

Tres Piedras is about twenty miles west on U.S. 64. A series of mountains, the Brazos Range, forms the western horizon. At Tres Piedras, 219 mi., U.S. 285 intersects. (See Tour 5.)

Many consider the route taken by U.S. 64 between Tres Piedras and Tierra Amarilla, a

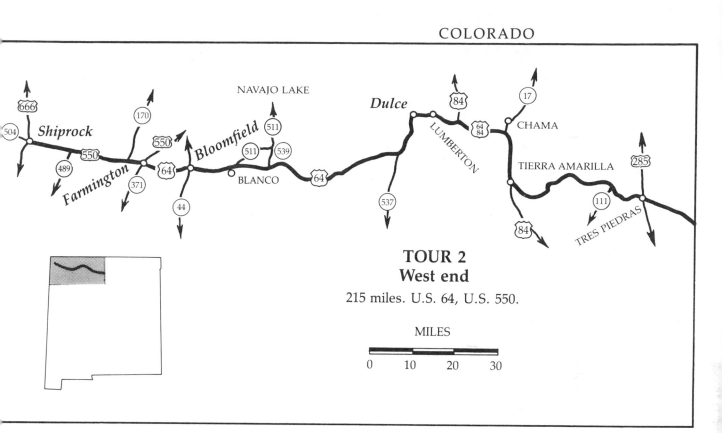

NAVAJO LAKE

Dulce

Shiprock

Bloomfield

Farmington

BLANCO

CHAMA

LUMBERTON

TIERRA AMARILLA

TRES PIEDRAS

TOUR 2
West end
215 miles. U.S. 64, U.S. 550.

MILES

0   10   20   30

be seen. The modern highway follows the path of the railroad tracks laid down in the 1880s to reach the coal fields and lumber towns in the San Juan Range. Relics of two of those late-nineteenth-century towns, Monero and Lumberton, age and crumble in their valleys. Old mine shafts, irrigation canals, and coal heaps reflect the activities once so prevalent here. It has also been established that there were Pueblo Indians in this area prior to and during the early years of Spanish conquest.

MONERO, 287 mi., whose name probably comes from the town's Italian roots (it was founded in 1884 by Italian miners), is now only a collection of log buildings, a small cemetery, and abandoned houses that cling to the old coal town's hillsides.

LUMBERTON, 303 mi., is located just beyond Monero. As sawmills and lumber camps began to spring up in the area, Lumberton was created from a large ranch by a Mr. Biggs, who

set out streets and sold building lots in 1884. A small mission church and a school still stand.

The JICARILLA APACHE RESERVATION, a vast area of close to seven hundred fifty thousand acres, begins about three miles west of Lumberton. The Jicarillas, given that name by the Spanish for their basketmaking abilities and particularly for their woven drinking cups (a *jícara* is a small cup), are members of the Southern Athapascan group, relatives of other Apaches and the Navajos. They have been living in the isolation of northwestern New Mexico for a century, placed here by the federal government.

The Jicarillas were among the last Athapascans to arrive in the Southwest. They had been nomads, wandering the northern and eastern plains until the seventeenth century, when the Spanish first mentioned them. When they settled in the northeastern part of New Mexico, the Jicarillas became farmers,

coaxing beans, squash, and corn from the arid land. By the 1850s they had moved closer to the Rio Grande. Their raids on the American wagon trains that plied the road from Taos to Santa Fe soon brought them into conflict with United States soldiers. After a number of confrontations with American troops, the Jicarillas sued for peace in 1855. For the next thirty years they were forced from place to place under the control of various Indian agencies. Promised but often not given rations to substitute for food they had traditionally gathered or hunted, they sometimes lacked adequate nourishment. Finally in 1887 they were given the land they now occupy. At the time it was not considered a desirable location, but the rising importance of fossil fuels has changed the value of the Jicarilla Reservation. Much tribal income is now derived from gas and oil leases. Tribe members also work in local timber operations or tribal enterprises, as ranchers, or off the reservation.

Horses have long been important to the Jicarilla way of life, and today many Jicarillas continue to travel and hunt on horseback. Herds of wandering horses sometimes graze close to the highway; travelers should watch for them.

DULCE ("sweet"), 307 mi. (alt. 6,767, pop. 1,651), is the capital, trading center, and population nucleus of the Jicarilla Reservation. Most of the tribe's two thousand members live in or near this mountain community in the modern houses that have replaced traditional brush wickiups. Tribal offices, a school complex, missionary buildings, and a motel and restaurant are located near U.S. 64.

Although once famous for their baskets, especially small drinking cups and larger, two-handled vessels coiled and stitched with sumac twigs, the Jicarillas sell few baskets in the

tribe's craft shop. Instead, matronly Jicarilla women preside over glass cases filled with intricate beadwork and colorful oil paintings. Visitors can shop at the craft center when they attend one of the Jicarilla celebrations open to the public, especially the Little Beaver Roundup in July and the Stone Lake Fiesta in September. The festivities at these nonreligious events include Indian dances, food, and crafts fairs.

The Jicarillas run a resort, Stone Lake Lodge, that caters to hunters and fishermen as well as to conference groups. Fishing and hunting permits are required and can be obtained at the tribe's tourism office in Dulce. Many of the smaller lakes on the reservation have simple campgrounds. There are also a number of unexcavated archaeological ruins, including remnants of pit-house cultures dating from A.D. 500, scattered throughout the vicinity. While some of the roads to the lakes, hunting areas, and campgrounds are paved and marked, it is advisable to check in Dulce on road conditions and exact locations.

High pines and meadows, green hills and valleys mark the route that U.S. 64 takes as it leaves Dulce and traverses the reservation. There are some public campsites in this area. N.M. 537 intersects from the south about ten miles southwest of Dulce. This fifty-mile paved road runs the length of the Jicarilla Reservation, passing cows grazing and pine woods, and hitching up to N.M. 44 approximately fifteen miles west of Cuba.

As U.S. 64 continues its westward path, entering Carson National Forest about twenty-five miles beyond Dulce, *arroyos*, mesas, and sagebrush create a colorful, unpopulated landscape. Soon drilling rigs and dirt roads leading to pumping stations indicate that the traveler has entered the energy-rich San Juan Basin. Ten miles beyond the N.M. 537 junction (319 mi.), the site of Project Gas Buggy is marked. In the 1960s, El Paso Natural Gas performed an experiment here designed to open underground formations to make gas more accessible. The first underground explosions were preparations for later subsurface atomic

Navajo Lake, *Harvey Caplin*.

explosions. Many experts questioned the advisability of using such a method to extract gas; the company covered over the site, and no more such experiments were performed.

Travelers will enter Carson National Forest again after passing the Project Gas Buggy area. Rock outcroppings peek through the brush beneath tall fir trees. Dry river beds and *arroyos* are crossed again and again. The Jicarilla District Ranger Station sits on the sage-strewn plain; it is not always open.

GOBERNADOR ("governor"), 347 mi., is the name of an *arroyo*, an oil camp, a canyon, and the small settlement that U.S. 64 bisects. The

area of Gobernador Canyon includes the ruins of a Navajo-Pueblo refugee site of the early eighteenth century. The land becomes drier and sandier as U.S. 64 nears the turnoff to Navajo Lake. N.M. 539, which joins U.S. 64 at Navajo City, 357 mi., and leads to the southern tip of Navajo Lake, five miles away. U.S. 64 continues on to Bloomfield.

While it is possible to reach Navajo Lake via N.M. 539, rain and snow can alter the condition of the heavily traveled road. Inquiries should be made in bad weather. Two alternate routes to the lake, through Blanco or from Aztec (Tour 9), are possible.

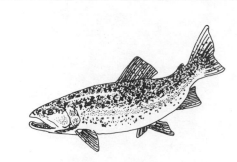

Choosing N.M. 539, the driver will cross Navajo Dam itself, an earth- and rock-filled embankment four hundred feet high and three-quarters of a mile long. By 1904 engineers were investigating the possibility of placing a dam across the San Juan River above Farmington. Construction finally began in 1958 as part of the Colorado River Storage Project. The dam was completed in 1962. Twenty-six million cubic yards of earth and rock were moved to the dam site. Highways, a railroad, and a number of small cemeteries were relocated to make way for the thirty-six-mile-long lake that was formed by the dam.

Navajo Dam and its lake serve a number of functions. Water can be stockpiled in the lake to be used for irrigation and municipal or industrial purposes downstream. Farmlands will be created on the Navajo Reservation as five hundred thousand acre feet of water per year are released specifically for the Navajos. Flooding downstream can be more easily controlled, and a source of recreation for northwestern New Mexico and southern Colorado has been created.

At the base of the lake, visible from N.M. 539 as it crosses the dam, a marina serves the many houseboaters and sailors who cruise the waterway. Pine River Campground's picnic tables overlook the lake and the marina. The visitors' center, a store, and an airstrip are near this campground. Across the lake, Sims Mesa Campground offers a more primitive but also quieter setting. A third campground, Arboles, hugs the northern shore of Navajo Lake in Colorado. The Southern Ute Tribe runs a recreation area at the northern end of the lake; it is reached via N.M. 511.

Boaters find that all parts of Navajo Lake are accessible to them. Hidden canyons become quiet weekend retreats for resting, fishing, and swimming. Houseboats can usually be rented; inquire at the lake's marina or at the boatyard and store along the river west of the dam. Fishing in Navajo Lake is considered excellent: thousands of trout and salmon have been planted there since 1962. Many fishermen and campers prefer the area below the dam where the water runs clear and cold, although special angling regulations are often in effect there.

While days are warm and pleasant on Navajo Lake in the summer, boaters especially should know that high winds and sudden electrical storms often mar summer afternoons. Many consider early fall the best time to vacation at Navajo Lake.

Leaving Navajo Dam, N.M. 511 snakes down along the earthen structure past the parking area for fishermen, along the Los Piños river, lined with cottonwoods. Campers take advantage of the easy access to the river and set up private sites along its banks. Along the route, marine supply stores and boat storage facilities cater to fishing and boating enthusiasts. The road to Aztec, N.M. 173, runs at the foot of a mesa whose layers indicate eons of geological history. Bonnie Rock looms a little under ten miles from the junction on the south side of the road. In the distance Angel and Huerfano peaks stand out from the badlands. Aztec is reached at twenty-five miles. U.S. 550 west of Aztec ends in Farmington.

Those who did not take N.M. 539 to Navajo Lake but elected to stay on the main road continue on 64 to Blanco ("white"), a small settlement named for the light-colored rhyolite outcropping in the surrounding hills. The San Juan valley begins here, a fertile area of truck farms, pastures, and fruit orchards. Just before the little town, a rough road heads south through Largo Canyon to join N.M. 44 in Cuba. For those with four-wheel-drive vehicles and a sense of adventure, a trip through Largo Canyon on a dry day provides a desert drive along a route followed by ancient Indians, conquistadors, Navajos on their way to surrender at Bosque Redondo, and, most recently, oil men. Check road conditions in Blanco.

After continuing west on 64 through Bloomfield, 393 mi. (Tour 9), look for the sign to the Salmon Museum and Ruin two miles west of the town. The museum, 395 mi., sits on a bluff overlooking the farmlands of the river valley below. It is a compact facility, built by the county with local funds and supported entirely by local residents, proud of its independence. It will eventually display many of the artifacts found at the ruins. Until then, the museum will show off a few examples of those finds as well as presenting live demonstrations of Spanish and Indian crafts and exhibits of related cultures.

A path from the museum leads down a slope to the ruin, named after homesteader George Salmon, whose property contained the ruins and who had the foresight to prevent their plunder by treasure hunters. When, as time passed, the family could no longer hold onto the land, members of the San Juan County Museum raised the down payment to buy the property and build the museum. Salmon's home, small by modern standards, was also rebuilt by the museum after the original burned. A research lab right at the site allows anthropologists and other scientists to study finds immediately and to pass them on to the museum.

The Salmon Pueblo is related to the Chaco Canyon development to the south, probably

as an agricultural colony founded by Chacoans in the eleventh century. Using one of their well-built highways, the colonists trekked north to set up a village near the San Juan River, which would give them a steady supply of water for their crops and other needs. Like the ruins at Aztec and Chaco, the Salmon Pueblo was carefully planned. The builders used sandstone, some of it quarried from thirty miles away, and *vigas* cut from the hills to construct thick, well-supported walls. The master builder directed the arrangement of two hundred fifty rooms in the shape of a squared C, two stories high, around a large plaza. Each room was spacious, twenty feet long and twelve feet high, carefully finished with adobe. Two kivas provided space for spiritual ceremonies, one a tower kiva in the middle of the C, a unique structure buttressed to support its height and weight, and the other the Great Kiva in the plaza, one of the largest kivas excavated in the Southwest. The Chacoans made a finely decorated pottery and devoted equal care to the flaking of the arrow points used for hunting rabbits, deer, and bobcats.

For all its careful design and cultured inhabitants, the pueblo was only lived in for sixty years before the Chacoans abandoned it, probably because environmental changes made it difficult to grow crops or hunt for game. Over the next hundred years a few people came and went, using the fine rooms as shelters. In the early thirteenth century several family groups moved in and the pueblo was filled

again. Called "Mesa Verde types" because their pottery resembled that of the civilization to the north, these people were simpler than the Chacoans. They divided up some of the larger rooms with clumsily built partitions and raised circular walls within others to make small kivas. Instead of burying their garbage, they simply threw it into unused rooms, even doing likewise with bodies of their dead.

Around A.D. 1250 a kiva roof collapsed and killed about fifty pueblo children who, archaeologists surmise, had climbed onto it to escape a fire. The suddenness of the tragedy fixed in time a piece of early American life, as the inhabitants left behind food and ceremonial items in their rush to get out. In spite of this loss, much of the community remained at Salmon for fifty years longer. By the end of the century, these people too had moved on, victims of the long drought. The remains of the pueblo became covered with sand and stone, and only the shape of the mounds hinted at what lay underneath until the village was uncovered by the Salmons and other settlers.

Continue west on U.S. 64 along the north side of the San Juan River and stop at former governor Tom Bolack's ranch, 405 mi. The B-Square Ranch, at the east edge of Farmington on U.S. 64, covers ten thousand acres put to a variety of uses. The five hundred acres on the south side of the river are a public showplace, devoted to growing New Mexico's most spectacular vegetables of all types, to exhibiting wildlife (living coyotes, raccoons, deer, and waterfowl), and to displaying trophies from owner and former New Mexico governor Tom Bolack's African safaris. Tours are available of the trophy room, of the greenhouses where bedding plants are grown and sold, and of a collection of well-maintained old farm machinery. At the Territorial Fair in 1892, San Juan County was awarded the prize for the best general exhibit of produce. Now the San Juan B-Square Ranch is allotted a special display case at the State Fair for its extraordinary vegetables.

Cross the Rio de las Animas Perdidas ("river of the lost souls"), a gloomy name since shortened to Animas River by the city's boosters.

FARMINGTON (alt. 5,503, pop. 31,000), once a shopping and stopping place for the farmers of the valley, is now a center of New Mexico's oil, gas, and uranium industries. The huge Kutz Canyon–Fulcher Basin, southeast of the city, was opened for gas production in 1927 but was not really worked until 1948. Since that time production of gas as well as of oil has expanded, and with it the population of Farmington. Coal mining, electric power generation at the huge Four Corners plant, and irrigated agriculture from the vast Navajo Indian Irrigation Project also bolster Farmington's economy.

Like many boom towns, Farmington looks hastily put together in places, with crowded new housing and neon-lit shops, but there are also attractive residential areas and the older Farmington, left over from when the town was indeed a "farming town" with established farmhouses and flowering orchards of peach, plum, and apple. Farmington is proud of a newly independent junior college and its Civic Center at 200 North Allen Avenue, where a growing Opera Association puts on classics and concerts are held. A small-scale hot-air balloon fiesta and the Connie Mack World Series in baseball at Fairgrounds Park are annual events. Residents boast of Farmington's location close to Colorado ski areas, ancient ruins, and the Navajo reservation, and of its access to the outdoors in general.

Farmington was known as Tohta ("among the rivers") by the Navajo; other Indians called it "three rivers" because the La Plata empties into the San Juan on the western side of the city, some three miles from the Animas. The San Juan River and the flat plains around it encouraged the first settlers to raise cattle. In 1880 rustlers rode into the area, shot men and animals, and created terror among the ranchers. The Stockton boys, desperadoes from Texas, and their henchmen, the Eskridge brothers, continued their raids through the winter of 1881. By February the ranchers had banded together to put an end to the Stock-

ton-Eskridge "wars," but the conflict stretched on until August, when fighting among the rustlers weakened their advantage and the plains could relax for a while. However continued confrontations among ranchers, settlers, and Indians and Saturday-night troubles with cowboys maintained Farmington's frontier atmosphere for several years.

Development of the fruit industry began in 1879 when William Locke moved down from Florence, Colorado, bringing peach, walnut, and other seeds. Locke later brought in small fruit trees—plum, apple, pear, and nectarine—as well as blackberry and raspberry bushes. Orchards flourished, and, along with light industries, they helped diversify Farmington's economy.

From Piñon Street, which bypasses the city at the confluence of the San Juan and Animas rivers, take N.M. 371 and head south past the Navajo Irrigation Project and into the Bisti Badlands. The irrigation project is slated to be the largest endeavor of its kind. Run by the Navajo Tribal Council, it waters the desert and provides moisture for farmers and new industries.

Further south, where the road is no longer paved, the Bisti (pronounced "bistie"; a Navajo word for badlands) Badlands lie thirty-two miles south of Farmington. The fantastic land formations of the Badlands make up a wild country, now threatened because billions of tons of coal lie so close to the surface that they can be strip-mined. A shallow sea bordered by swamps and forests once cov-

ered the area. Horned dinosaurs, or ceratopsians, roamed the area; their fossils are found in the Badlands. In this and other parts of the San Juan basin, paleontologists have a rare opportunity to trace both the end of the age of dinosaurs and the beginning of that of mammals, the first occurring 130 to 65 million years ago, the second 63 to 54 million years ago. A Farmington man, David Baldwin, spent much of his time in the 1880s looking for fossil bones. He discovered the beds in the San Juan Basin that traced the rise of mammals after the extinction of the dinosaurs. Rain poured down in the swamps, and then the sun dried the mud into the weird shapes that crowd together on the desert.

Visitors are allowed to explore on foot if

SIDE TOUR

care is taken of the fragile environment. Wilderness status has been recommended for the Bisti and for a similar area to the west, but other interests press for energy exploitation. South of C.R. 15 lies a "fossil forest," a thousand acres of fossil beds and petrified forest, also endangered by plans for industrial development.

U.S. 550 leaves Farmington and the clutter of signs at the edge of the city. At the Twin Mounds (408 mi.), N.M. 170 heads north to the Colorado border, passing Jackson Lake fishing area five miles north of the junction.

North from U.S. 550 at 414 mi. is a dirt road that parallels the El Paso Natural Gas pipeline and leads to the small rectangle of the Ute Mountain Indian Reservation. The major part of the reservation is in Colorado, but a desolate, largely roadless section lies above oil and gas fields in New Mexico. The Utes were unpopular among other Native Americans in the nineteenth century because of their frequent raids on Pueblo villages and their collusion with the Spanish in the slave trade. They were also hated by fellow raiders, the Navajo, when Utes joined Kit Carson in destructive campaigns against them. No Utes live on the New Mexico portion of the reservation, though some work there, raising livestock, farming, and leasing rights to oil and gas. The Ute culture is related to that of the Plains tribes. Now neighbors, the Navajos and Utes share an interest in the Native American Church and some joint projects.

At 417 miles, N.M. 489 goes south to Fruitland and Kirtland and the Four Corners Power Plant. Fruitland is an Anglo farming community with neat homes and graceful willow trees. It was settled in 1877 by a group of Mormons. The Four Corners Power Plant is an enormous electricity-generating unit on the south side of Morgan Lake. The adjacent Navajo Mine is the largest open-pit coal mine in the western United States. Tours are given on a regular schedule. In keeping with the grand scale of these operations, it is said that the smoke from the Four Corners Plant was the only manmade phenomenon visible with the naked eye to the astronauts on the moon.

U.S. 550 parallels buff sandstone cliffs along the cultivated river valley. Oil wells protrude to the north of the valley, and fruit trees line both sides of the road. At 427 mi. is the turnoff to the San Juan Generating Plant. Heavy truck traffic accompanies the visitor to the three-dimensional maze of pipes and towers and massive buildings. Visitors can tour the facility, owned by the Public Service Company of New Mexico.

The Shiprock dominates this area visually, but it is the San Juan River that is the truly dominant feature. The great San Juan loops into New Mexico from Colorado and then joins with the Colorado River in Utah. This is the river that spawned extensive Navajo irrigation projects and flood control programs (floods destroyed much of Shiprock in 1911). One hundred thousand acres of the most arid section of New Mexico will be irrigated by the Navajo Irrigation Project. The river water also helps serve the gigantic power plants. These plants and refineries of the local high-grade oil provide some employment for the Navajo.

SHIPROCK, 434 mi. (Navajo name Tse Bida'hi, "rock with wings"; alt. 4,965, pop, 7,228), is named for an imposing volcanic neck (described in Tour 17). As the Navajo people traditionally have lived in extended family groups, isolated from neighbors by rugged geography and the economic necessity of maintaining distance between livestock herds, a Navajo town such as Shiprock is a somewhat

316   *Tour 2:* SHIPROCK

Shiprock, *Harvey Caplin.*

artificial creation. It was established in 1903 as a northern Navajo Indian agency and remains a center for Navajo tribal business, trading, health care, and industry such as the large helium plant and a uranium-processing facility.

Nearly every fall since 1903, the Navajo nation has held its Northern Navajo Fair in Shiprock. Exceptional arts and crafts are exhibited, and rodeos and rides provide the thrills. Some older men and many women wear traditional dress to the events of the fair. Men may wear a black felt, flat-brimmed, domed hat and silver hatband with jeans, shirt, concho belt, and boots. Navajo women wear calico or satin broomstick-pleated skirts, velvet blouses, and heavy layers of silver and turquoise jewelry. It was during the detainment of Navajos at Fort Sumner that the women relinquished their black and red hand-woven blanket dresses and emulated the wives of Fort Sumner officers by wearing long, full skirts and blouses.

The Navajo blanket is now almost never used for clothing; it rarely appears as a blanket, is sometimes a rug, and most frequently serves as a decorative hanging. Weavers use complex designs and patterns true to traditional local styles, but with an individual flair.

Navajo legend credits Spider Woman with teaching the people to weave. Their Pueblo neighbors were accomplished weavers when the Navajos moved into the area, and the Navajo women eventually learned the Pueblo men's skill. Sheep were brought by the Spanish to the New World; German and English yarn and American chemical dyes were used in blankets from the mid-nineteenth century on, but the end product has always been uniquely Navajo.

Tour 2 ends in Shiprock, where it meets U.S. 666 (Tour 17), which leads north to Cortez, Colorado, and south to Gallup. From Shiprock, N.M. 504 leads northwest to the Four Corners Monument, where New Mexico adjoins Colorado, Arizona, and Utah.

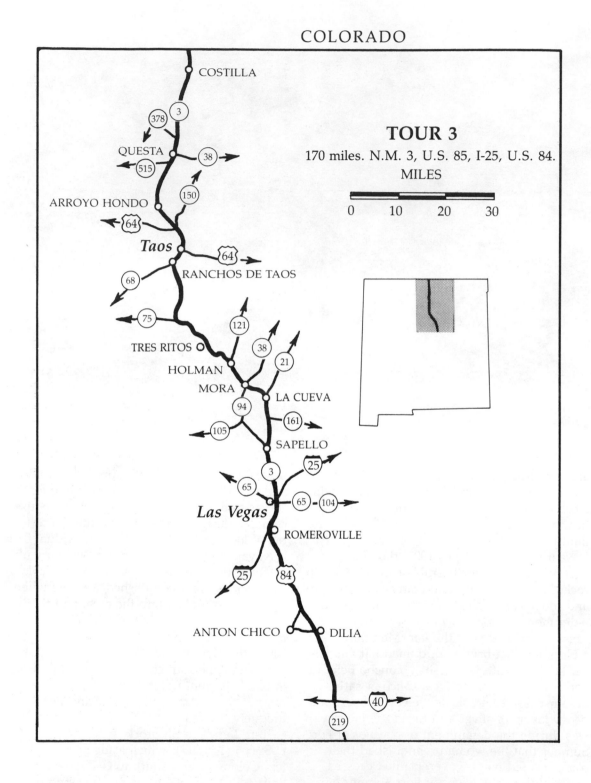

TOUR 3
170 miles. N.M. 3, U.S. 85, I-25, U.S. 84.
MILES

0   10   20   30

tour three

Tour 3 follows a scenic and historic path down from the Colorado border to Taos and through the Sangre de Cristo Mountains to the edge of New Mexico's eastern plains. N.M. 3, a wandering mountain highway, meets I-25 near Las Vegas. On the last leg of the journey, U.S. 84 connects I-25 with its east-west counterpart, I-40, nineteen miles west of Santa Rosa.

The trip begins on a broad, high plateau between two ranges within the Rocky Mountain system, enters the Sangre de Cristo ("blood of Christ") Mountains south of Taos, and drops into the Mora Valley after winding through canyons and along rivers. This is the land of mountain men and traders, of nomadic and Pueblo Indians, and of strongly traditional Hispanic settlers. The landscape throughout the 170-mile trip is predominantly rural and unspoiled. Only Taos and Las Vegas offer urban facilities, although some of the communities along the way cater to travelers.

New Mexico begins at the southern edge of Colorado's fertile San Luis Valley, with N.M. 3 leading the way across the border just north of Costilla.

COSTILLA ("rib"), 1.4 mi., is named after the

small river that passes through town. The highway once served Costilla as a main street; now, however, the settlement sits off to the west of this north-south thoroughfare, its rows of houses curving with the path of the old road, N.M. 196. Costilla was founded in 1852, when Juan de Jesús Bernal led an expedition of settlers from Taos and Arroyo Hondo to this area. They purchased their land from Charles Beaubien, one of the owners of the Maxwell Land Grant. Costilla's four plazas, laid out at the time of settlement, once stretched the length of the village into Colorado. At one time a *torreón* (watchtower) marked the location of one of the plazas. In the nineteenth century, guards kept vigil for bands of Ute and Apache through the tower's windows.

Costilla proper is reached by turning west on N.M. 196. Tourist services are available there. Travelers will find camping facilities by turning east on N.M. 196. The small village of Amalia, five miles away, is located on that road. Jeeps and other four-wheel-drive vehicles can continue from Amalia to Latir Lakes, a group of seven lakes at the head of Latir Creek.

The valley to the west and below N.M. 3 is

Latir Lake, *Harvey Caplin.*

landmark and a reminder of the Ute Indians who once roamed these plains.

As N.M. 3 traverses the broad plateau, roads break off to the east to the Sangre de Cristos and to the west toward the Rio Grande. These roads, often dirt or gravel, lead to small, tin-roofed villages or sometimes to camping areas. Once miners surged into the valley, drawn by rumors of gold and silver strikes. A few abandoned mine sites are hidden in the foothills.

Visible only as a dark scar beyond the green alfalfa fields and grazing lands to the west, the Rio Grande has carved a path through this land since prehistoric times. The deep canyon of the Rio Grande was formed in the late Cretaceous Period, 130 million years ago, and in the early Tertiary Period, about seventy million years ago. The Rio Grande Gorge, two hundred feet deep at the Colorado border and eight hundred feet deep about forty miles later, is composed of alternating layers of gravel. It is this gravel rubble which forms the Taos Plateau, part of the Rio Grande Trough of the southern Rockies.

The Rio Grande Gorge area is rich in archaeological lore. Paleo-Indians are thought to have first lived here between 16,000 and 12,000 B.C. Thousands of years later, as the climate changed and large animal herds became scarce, the area's inhabitants were farmers and then builders of pit houses who continued to hunt deer, rabbits, and antelope. Garbage heaps left by these early people have been discovered on the plain above the gorge and along many of the Rio Grande's tributaries. They provide abundant clues about the people, animals, and plants that flourished here long ago.

Forty-eight miles of the Rio Grande, from Colorado to south of Taos, have been designated a wild river, protected by the federal government from development for future generations to enjoy. Travelers can reach the Rio Grande Wild River area, a campground and park run by the Bureau of Land Management, by taking N.M. 378, 18.4 mi. This area also provides access to the Rio Grande itself.

the Sunshine Valley, formerly called Virsylvia. This is an active farming and ranching area. Ute Peak (10,151 feet), an extinct volcano, is a

N.M. 378 curves through CERRO ("peak, hill"), a small town first settled in 1854 by a group of families from Taos and Questa. It is a farm community, offering a limited number of services to tourists. The flat, wide plain through which the road travels gives little hint of the riches ahead. A series of simple campgrounds and overlooks and a visitor center in the wild river area provide spectacular views and a wealth of information about the Rio Grande, its history and geology.

The hike down to the Rio Grande, possible from a number of marked locations, takes less than an hour; hikers should assume that the ascent will require double that time. At the bottom of the gorge, paths line the river. A variety of wildlife, including muskrats, raccoons, and snakes, lives here among lichens and willow plants. Fishermen will find rainbow trout and pike in profusion. White-water canoeists and rafters enjoy the wild river's challenge. Boaters should check at the visitors' center for information about water conditions, access points, and the difficulties of the rapids.

Above the river, along its rim, different varieties of flora and fauna can be found. Big game animals, among them elk, mule deer, black bear, and antelope, roam the high plains. Ponderosa pine and Douglas fir grow at both the top and the bottom of the gorge. The campgrounds that perch above the river are sheltered by fragrant piñon and juniper trees. Carpets of wild asters, chamisa, and yellow daisies line the park's blacktopped roads in the late summer and early fall.

Back on N.M. 3, Questa lies ahead along a gravel ridge, the rocky, pine-covered cliffs of Red River Canyon forming a rich backdrop for the small mining community. To the immediate west are the Guadalupe Mountains, often confused with New Mexico's other Guadalupe range in the southern part of the state.

QUESTA ("slope, grade"), 21 mi. (alt. 7,655, pop. 734), was originally called San Antonio del Río Colorado ("St. Anthony of the Red River"). Its name was changed in 1884 when the town acquired a post office. Don Francisco Laforet came to Questa in 1829 and tried to live at his farm along the river; soon Apache and Ute raids forced him to move up to the ridge, where other settlers joined him. By 1849 there were one hundred families living above the Rio Colorado. Indian attacks continued throughout this period, prompting residents to build a six-foot wall around the town in 1854. Questa's church, erected in 1873, is its oldest building.

For years Questa was a trading and farming center. The focus of its livelihood changed with the arrival of molybdenum mining in the early part of the twentieth century. The original mine was an open-pit operation. Union Oil, present owner of Molycorp, is now constructing underground mines to extract the molybdenum, an important ingredient in lightbulbs, television tubes, and missile systems. Tailing ponds from the mine sit above Questa, fed by pipes that originate at the mill east of town. After the heavier metals settle

out of the ponds, the water is pumped back into the Red River. Molycorp is by far the largest single employer in Taos County. Its mine, located a few miles up N.M. 38 from Questa, may be visited.

N.M. 3 travels through the heart of Questa, where motels, restaurants, and gas stations can be found. Questa is also famous for its honey; beekeepers north of town sell the local product at their homes.

SIDE TOUR

At Questa, N.M. 38 enters from Red River Canyon. A detour along 38 to the town of Red River, twelve miles away, is not only a pretty sidetrip, but can be lengthened into a seventy-five-mile circle that passes through the Sangre de Cristos to the Moreno Valley, Eagle Nest, and back through the mountains to Taos. Much of that trip is described in Tour 2.

Immediately after turning east off N.M. 3 onto N.M. 38, the traveler can take N.M. 134, which heads into the mountains to Cabresto ("rope" or "halter") Lake, a small, evergreen-lined body of water high in the Sangre de Cristos. About eight miles of switchbacks and curves bring the traveler to the lake, which has campsites and picnic tables.

The Questa District Ranger Station, just beyond the N.M. 134 turnoff, provides the visitor with information on Carson National Forest as well as weather tips, campsite locations, and permits for entering Wheeler Peak Wilderness Area. A number of campgrounds line N.M. 38 as it winds through Red River Canyon before reaching Molycorp, a few miles east of Questa. Campsites are interspersed with mining activities here. Terraced molybdenum mines can be seen on the mountain sides. Campsites become more plentiful as N.M. 38 nears Red River. Soon, on the west edge of town, the first ski slope appears.

RED RIVER, 12 mi. (alt. 8,800, pop. 318), caters year-round to fun-seekers and sports enthusiasts. In the summer, its streets are filled with tourists who have come to fish, hike, ride horseback, and relax in the mountain air. An Aspen Festival in the fall draws visitors to enjoy the golden aspen leaves, a crafts festival, and other events. Winter finds the village bustling with snowmobilers and skiers, who can ski right to their hotel doors. There are plentiful accommodations, restaurants, and other tourist amenities in Red River.

Miners from Elizabethtown in the Moreno Valley (Tour 2) first settled in Red River in about 1870; they named their town after the river, which has run red since recorded time. The Mallette brothers laid out the town in 1894. It was the site of many mining attempts at the turn of the century. Red River's rebirth began with the growth of the tourist industry in New Mexico.

Beyond Red River, N.M. 38 enters Carson National Forest and ascends steeply to Bobcat Pass. At Red River Pass (9,852 feet), the road crosses the division between the Red River and Moreno valleys. Soon the highway begins its descent into the Moreno Valley, passing Elizabethtown. (Tour 2 picks up the circle here.)

Leaving Questa, N.M. 3 climbs abruptly out of the narrow valley after crossing the Red River. About three miles outside town, N.M. 515 leads to the Red River Fish Hatchery, run by the New Mexico Department of Game and Fish. At the bottom of a steep canyon, tanks and ponds of fish await planting in the state's waterways. Children enjoy feeding the fish, which range from minnows to full-sized trout. Anglers fish along the banks, and campers can hike from the hatchery to the Rio Grande. Camping is permitted along the hatchery road.

N.M. 3 continues its ascent after the fish hatchery turnoff. Garrapata Ridge brings the traveler to the beginning of Carson National Forest and to a view beyond the Rio Grande Gorge to Tres Piedras and the Brazos Range.

San Cristobal ("St. Christopher"), 31 mi., an agricultural valley settled in 1860 and still farmed today, is passed quickly. After a brief climb, signposts on the left point the way to the D. H. LAWRENCE RANCH, a property of the University of New Mexico open to day visitors. A narrow dirt road travels five miles upward to the base of Lobo Mountain, where a number of modern structures contrast with the old-fashioned log building that is the ranch headquarters.

Formerly known as Kiowa Ranch, the pine-covered property was given to Frieda Lawrence by Mabel Dodge Luhan in exchange for the manuscript of her husband's *Sons and Lovers*. The Lawrences spent about two years in Taos in the 1920s, much of it at the ranch. Lawrence, Frieda, and Lady Dorothy Brett, an aristocratic British painter who later became a beloved Taos character, often traveled to Lobo Mountain and the ranch from Taos where their benefactor, Mrs. Luhan, held court. At the ranch, the threesome kept a simple household, Lady Brett off in her own little cabin, Lawrence himself tending to many of the ranch and household chores. Three of his books were influenced by his stay in Taos: *The Plumed Serpent*, *David*, and *Mornings in Mexico*. He considered the ranch one of the world's most beautiful places.

Aspen, *Harvey Caplin*.

Lawrence died in France in 1930. His ashes were transported back to New Mexico many years later. The story, probably apocryphal, goes that Frieda (who had remarried after Lawrence's death) and some of her friends traveled from Taos to Lamy, the closest railway depot, to meet the train carrying the writer's ashes. The train was late, so the party adjourned to the nearby saloon to wait. Everyone was having such a merry time that they continued their gaiety even after they had picked up the ashes; they placed the urn be-

neath the table in the saloon and resumed their party. It was not until they had reached Taos that they remembered the urn beneath the barroom table. A messenger was dispatched to Lamy to fetch Lawrence's ashes. They now rest in an unusual handbuilt mausoleum above the ranch house.

Frieda bequeathed the ranch to the University of New Mexico, which uses it as a conference and vacation facility. The small green cottages below the ranch headquarters were some of the original housing units in Los Alamos in the 1940s when the first atomic bomb was being assembled there.

ARROYO HONDO ("deep ditch"), 34 mi., about three miles south of the Lawrence Ranch road, is the last distinct village north of Taos on N.M. 3. It lies in a fertile valley that sweeps from the mountains down to the Rio Grande. The highway bisects the village, which was built along the banks of the Rio Hondo in the early part of the nineteenth century. Arroyo Hondo was one of a string of Hispanic outposts that skirted the western flanks of the Sangre de Cristos. It was part of the Arroyo Hondo Grant established in 1815 when Nerio Sisneros and forty-two others petitioned for and then settled the area between San Cristobal and the present village.

Arroyo Hondo has always been a modest but significant center of Hispanic tradition. A number of *moradas* (Penitente chapels) attest to the strength that the Penitentes (see Religion) maintained in this little village in the mid-1800s, before the arrival of French and Ameri-

can priests forced the Catholic sect underground. The 1850s also saw a remarkable flowering of religious folk art in Arroyo Hondo. Fine examples of paintings and sculptures, many in the form of *santos* (saints) and members of the Holy Family, graced the Church of Nuestra Señora de los Dolores (Our Lady of Sorrows), built in 1833 in the upper arroyo. More such home-made art filled the walls and altars of the Penitente *moradas* and the private chapels of the Martínez and Medina families. Much of the work of the *santeros* (carvers of the saints' statues) and other artisans was judged unworthy by the priests who entered New Mexico in the second half of the nineteenth centry. Little of this indigenous work remains in the area; some of it was stolen, while many other pieces have been placed on display in the Taylor Museum in Colorado Springs. The simple adobe church of Nuestra Señora de los Dolores still stands in the upper arroyo; however, for many years, its parish activities took place in the larger village of Arroyo Seco.

While Hispanic religious and artistic traditions were flourishing in Arroyo Hondo in the mid-nineteenth century, Yankee enterprise also began to intrude. An American, Simeon Turley, came to the Taos area in 1830. Soon he had a prosperous ranch in Arroyo Hondo, with herds of sheep and cattle, as well as acres of corn and wheat. He placed a dam on the Rio Hondo and built a grist mill. He hired Taos Pueblo Indians and local Hispanics to work in his mill and on his looms. Turley was also a distiller of "Taos lightning," the famous drink that disrupted many fiestas and launched numerous brawls in New Mexico.

When the uprising of 1847 occurred (see Taos, below), Turley was convinced that his prosperity and good nature would save him from the fate facing other Americans in the area. He was wrong. A two-day battle raged at his ranch. Turley escaped as his mill burned, only to be killed at a neighboring ranch where he had sought refuge.

Gold was once discovered in the Arroyo Hondo area, bringing prospectors to the valley; however, no large strikes were made.

When hippies and other dropouts discovered northern New Mexico in the 1960s, many of them went to Taos. A few wandered into Arroyo Hondo. Tepees dotted the hillsides at the site of New Buffalo, a nearby commune. By the late 1970s few such counterculture people remained in this valley, although some tepees can still be seen to the west of N.M. 3.

Once out of the Arroyo Hondo valley, the traveler sees the Taos Plateau spread across the horizon. So level is this plain that a small cloud passing over the sun seems to cast an immense shadow over miles of sage, sand, and brush. Few houses, and perhaps a cattle pen or a ranch road, appear between Arroyo Hondo and the intersection of N.M. 3, U.S. 64, and N.M. 150, at 41 mi. Taos Pueblo and the town of Taos are a few miles straight ahead. Taos Ski Valley (Tour 2) is located east down N.M. 150. The Rio Grande Gorge Bridge is to the west seven miles away on U.S. 64 (Tour 2).

Those who continue on to Taos and to the path eastward through the Sangre de Cristos will pass through El Prado (Tour 2), where the outskirts of Taos begin. The turnoff to Taos Pueblo intersects from the left as the traveler enters Taos.

San Gerónimo de Taos is the Spanish missionary name for TAOS PUEBLO. The Pueblo selected San Gerónimo (St. Jerome), the editor of the Roman Catholic Bible, as its patron saint over Juan de Oñate's choice, San Miguel (St. Michael). The pueblo is commonly called Taos, an adaptation of Tiwa words for "in the village," and "at the red willow place."

Taos Pueblo is located at the foot of the Sangre de Cristo Mountains, less than three miles north of the village of Taos. It is Tiwa-speaking, related by language to the pueblos of Picuris, Sandia, and Isleta, and is the northernmost of the Rio Grande pueblos.

Ancestors of the present pueblo residents were in the area for centuries; archaeological sites dating from A.D. 1000 are plentiful in the Taos region. Some anthropologists speculate that as drought and other factors forced the

San Gerónimo de Taos Church, *Jean Blackmon.*

dwellers in the Anasazi villages west of the Rio Grande to flee, they moved eastward, eventually settling down along the Rio Grande, perhaps around Taos. Other experts insist that the Taos are derived from ancient groups living to the north, across the Colorado border. The Taos people have been at their present site since about A.D. 1350.

The origins of the Taos people as described in their religious traditions have not been fully revealed to outsiders. However, legends tell of the beginnings of the tribe. One story sees the Taos springing forth from sacred lakes near the Colorado border; another account tells of an eagle dropping a feather near the river that bisects the village. Taos Pueblo is reticent about its religion, traditions, and origin. "The story of my people and the story of this place are one single story. No man can think of us without thinking of this place," said a Taos Pueblo man, as quoted in the *Handbook of North American Indians.*

As the most northern and therefore among

the most isolated of the Rio Grande pueblos, Taos was not a major target of early Spanish colonial and missionary efforts. Although the Pueblo Rebellion of 1680 was plotted from Taos, there were actually few Spanish in the area in the seventeenth century. However, Taos Pueblo took part in many efforts to expel Europeans from the land, participating in both the 1680 revolt and later in the 1847 attempt to drive away the United States presence. Ruins of the old San Gerónimo Mission, constructed in 1707, stand as witness to the later battle, which Taos lost.

To the public, the multistoried Taos dwellings epitomize the pueblo world. The two large buildings on either side of Pueblo Creek (or Rio Pueblo de Taos) have stood unchanged for centuries, only recently receiving windows and doors on their lower floors. Ladders still provide a means of entrance to the upper stories. Thousands of visitors have admired the venerable adobe structures, although only pueblo residents may enter them. Scattered throughout the main dwelling area of the pueblo are kivas and other sacred places. The original mission church at Taos was constructed in 1617 and destroyed in the revolt of 1680. The present Mission of San Gerónimo was built upon the ruins of that first church. It sits at the west end of the plaza.

Taos is more conservative than many pueblos in its religious practices and traditions. It was among the last to install electricity, and it did so only after a long fight; even then, the wires were not permitted within the pueblo's ancient walls. The paving of the road to the pueblo was also steeped in internal controversy. Many tribal elders insisted that an ancient racetrack would be desecrated during the construction process.

Unlike many pueblos, Taos enjoyed a good relationship with the nomadic Plains Indians, particularly the Comanches, and embraced some Plains characteristics. Horses, important but not integral to other pueblos, are a strong symbol throughout both Plains and Taos legend and life. The more southern pueblos long relied on farming for food; however, Taos, perhaps because of its northern location and its proximity to the rich hunting grounds of the plains, has hunted and gathered as well as farmed for its food. As a result, its coffers have almost always been full, and it has shared its supplies with its more southern neighbors in times of drought, flood, or other emergency. The two groups, Plains and Pueblo, came together during the busy Taos trade fairs, held during the Feast of San Gerónimo at the end of September. Today the Feast of San Gerónimo is not only a religious celebration at the pueblo but also a continuation of those gigantic fairs.

Religious ceremonies occur throughout the year at Taos. Many feast days include events that are open to the public. During the autumn feast of San Gerónimo, visitors throng the plaza, eating food from booths set up along the perimeter and joining the Taos dancers when open drum dancing invites the crowd to participate. Residents and visitors alike look forward to the special dance in which the Koshares (clownlike figures) pick

Taos Pueblo, *Jean Blackmon*.

unsuspecting spectators and dance and jest with them, often tossing a good-natured by-stander into Pueblo Creek. Then attention centers on a tall pole erected in the middle of the plaza. A dead sheep hangs from its top. One after another, the clown society members attempt to climb the pole and seize the prize at the top. Clearly, thinks the crowd gathered around, they will never make it. Antics increase as the race to reach the top continues. Finally, a young man appears, ready to challenge his elders. The clowns pretend that he will not succeed, but the crowd knows better. In a minute, the young man leaps forward,

climbs the pole, and retrieves the sheep. That event ends, but the dances and feasting go on until sunset.

The deer dance, usually held at Christmas or near the New Year, is another favorite, a Plains vestige in which Taos men and women act out a stark winter drama on the cold, bare plaza. The men wear deer antlers and carry pointed sticks that act as forelegs. The women are dignified in buckskin dresses and elaborate feathered ornaments. The dancers come into the plaza in lines from their kivas, dancing in front of the church, hunting each other, and feigning struggles in the snow. The dance

Taos Pueblo, *Harvey Caplin*.

ends quickly, but it is repeated twice before the deer dancers leave the plaza.

Perhaps the highlight of the Taos year is the ceremony held each August at Blue Lake, high above the pueblo. No outsider has ever witnessed the rituals that take place there and at other sacred mountain sites over a period of days. Blue Lake, an important symbol for the Pueblo, was returned to the tribe by the federal government in 1970 after almost sixty years of negotiation.

About a thousand people live at Taos Pueblo today, although many members of the tribe live elsewhere. The population has risen significantly over the last hundred years. In the past, most of the men worked as farmers at Taos, with time also spent hunting and gathering food. Now, however, as the tribe has

grown and the arable land at the pueblo has decreased, many residents find that they must work in the village of Taos or even beyond the county, returning only for feast days and vacations. There are artisans at the pueblo who earn their livings creating the micaceous Taos pottery known for its glittery surface. Other craftsmen carve wooden Taos drums, topping them with cowhide and selling them to Pueblo dancers and Anglo collectors. A few women have revived the art of weaving rabbitskin blankets. At the pueblo day school, young Taos artists win prizes for their paintings and other artwork.

Taos Pueblo welcomes visitors, asking them to observe parking, photography, and touring regulations. Sometimes vendors sell Indian crafts and food in the plaza or in little stores.

taos

Transportation

The airport is located on N.M. 64 north of town. Charter and private service only. Bus service is available on Continental Trailways; there is no rail service. Taxis are usually available; check with the Chamber of Commerce.

Accommodations

Many large and small resorts, hotels, motels, cabins, and camping areas. Write the Chamber of Commerce for more information. Reservations suggested for the summer and ski seasons. Swimming: Public indoor pool at Coronado Swimming Pool north of plaza. Private pools at resorts, motels.

Sports

Horseback Riding: Inquire at larger resorts or the Chamber of Commerce. Public tennis courts at Kit Carson Park, Baca Park, and Taos Middle School. Private resorts have courts also. Public golf course at Angel Fire, 23 miles east of Taos. Skiing at Taos Ski Valley, 19 miles northeast of Taos on N.M. 150; Sipapu Ski Basin, 23 miles east of Taos on N.M. 3; Angel Fire Ski Basin, 23 miles east of Taos on N.M. 38; Red River Ski Valley, 40 miles north of Taos on N.M. 38. Hiking, camping, and fishing are available throughout the mountains around Taos, part of Kit Carson National Forest. Write the Chamber of Commerce for more information.

Information Services

Taos County Chamber of Commerce on Teresina Lane off the Plaza. Write to: Drawer L, Taos, New Mexico 87571.

Annual Events

Winter: Dances at Taos Pueblo during Christmas season. Ski events at ski areas.

Summer: Language schools at Taos Ski Valley. Taos School of Music, June and July. New Mexico Music Festival at Taos, July and August. Taos Fiesta, weekend closest to July 25 and 26.

Fall: Feast of San Gerónimo at Taos Pueblo, September 29 and 30. Taos Art Festival, early October.

The name Taos (almost rhymes with house) is probably derived from a Spanish version of the Tiwa word for "red willow place." The town's legal name, Don Fernando de Taos, honors one of its leading seventeenth-century citizens, Don Fernando de Chávez. The name was shortened to Taos in 1884 because so many variations were in use that a one-word name seemed in order.

The setting of Taos is striking. While Tour 3 enters Taos from the north, many travelers come upon it from the south, through the narrow Rio Grande Canyon, up and out of its confines and onto the wide Taos Plateau. The Sangre de Cristo Mountains rise dramatically on the northeast to shelter it and form a spectacular backdrop for the communities that huddle below.

Taos is really three villages. San Gerónimo de Taos, or Taos Pueblo, is the oldest and northernmost of them. The town, Don Fernando de Taos, is the commercial center for the three and sits between the two older settlements. Ranchos de Taos, primarily residential and agricultural, lies a few miles to the south. A highway, N.M. 3/N.M. 68, now connects the three distinct towns with a string of motels and shopping plazas. Their histories and traditions, not space, define each village today.

For many years, for many diverse people, Taos has been a mecca. It is said that an eagle first led the ancestors of the Taos Indians to the area some eight hundred years ago. Hernando de Alvarado, one of Coronado's men, came four hundred years later, in the middle of the sixteenth century. The Spanish did not

rush to colonize the Taos area, trickling into the wide valley only as the seventeenth century dawned. Anglos first wandered into Taos as trappers and traders in the first half of the nineteenth century. They married into the Hispanic community, added color to the famous Taos trade fairs, and became loyal citizens when the United States conquered the Southwest. Another colorful element of Taos life, its artists, appeared as the twentieth century began, creating an art colony and then a marketplace for the tourists who now converge, winter and summer, on the settlement beneath the mountains.

Although the Taos area was visited in the sixteenth century by Coronado's men, there is no actual record of Spanish settlement before 1617. At that time Fray Pedro de Miranda, a Spanish missionary, built an outpost close to the present Taos Pueblo. Those Spanish who first colonized Taos probably came up from the village of Yunque Yunque, south of the town near San Juan Pueblo. They built their village closer to Taos Pueblo than it is today for protection from bands of nomadic Indians who periodically raided Spanish and Pueblo settlements alike.

Relations between Taos Pueblo and the Spanish were, for the most part, peaceful in the early days of colonization. However, there were hints of tension. In 1631 a Spanish priest and two soldiers were killed near the pueblo. Later, Pueblo officials asked the Spanish to move their village away from pueblo boundaries to the site of the present plaza. Around 1650, a plot against the Spanish was uncovered in the Taos area. That rebellion never occurred, but thirty years later Popé, a San Juan Indian, led the successful Pueblo Revolt from Taos. There were no Spanish near Taos for decades after the rebellion, and de Vargas found Taos one of the most difficult areas to reconquer.

After the reconquest and the resettlement of the Taos valley, many of the Spanish abuses that had fed the 1680 rebellion lessened. The two groups once more lived peacefully side by side, farming, practicing their religions, and coming together to protect themselves from the Utes, Comanches, and Navajos who still swooped down out of the mountains to take food, and, in some cases, captives. The last such raid on a large scale, in 1760, saw Taos attacked and fifty women and children captured. Soldiers chased and massacred four hundred Indians.

In the eighteenth century, Taos was one of the busiest villages in New Spain. It was the setting for the annual trade fair, when arms were laid down and Plains Indians, Pueblos, and local villagers came together to do business peacefully with one another. Comanches traded horses, buffalo meat and skins, cattle, and even human slaves; they had swapped with the Pawnees of the Mississippi valley for many of these goods. The Pueblos traded produce from their gardens, especially corn and tobacco. They also traded horses. From the nearby Hispanic villages and from Mexico came tools, guns, axes, and cloth.

Until 1803, when the Louisiana Purchase brought the United States closer to New Mexico's borders, Taos knew little about the predominantly Anglo world to the east. Life in the valley was usually quiet and agricultural. Soon, however, the newly opened Santa Fe Trail, though it bypassed Taos itself, brought newcomers into the Taos area from the mountains to the north and east. These were the mountain men, trappers of many nationalities—French, British, Canadian, American—who, in answer to the European and United States fashions of the day, combed the streams of the Rocky Mountains for beaver and other fur-bearing animals.

Taos rivaled Saint Louis and Vancouver, according to some reports, as one of the most important markets for beaver on the continent. From a fifteen-thousand-dollar market in 1822, Taos became the trading center for over $1.7 million in fur brought in by 414 wagons in 1846. The little village was a common meeting spot for traders and trappers. Thousands of pelts and thousands of dollars changed hands during the wild rendezvous, a time for drinking, visiting, and taking care of business.

Kit Carson, who first came to Taos as a teenager in 1826, was the most famous of the mountain men. He was born and raised on the Missouri frontier. However, the sight of the wagon trains passing through Franklin, Missouri, on their way west was too much for Carson, then a saddlemaker, to resist. At sixteen he left his apprenticeship, said goodbye to no one, and easily found a job with a passing wagon train. His employer published a notice of Carson's disappearance, offering a one-cent reward for his return.

When he arrived in Taos Carson accepted any job that was offered to him. He was a teamster on wagon trains and acted as an interpreter for area merchants. Carson went on his first trapping expedition in 1829, spending the next two years hunting beaver and fighting Indians from New Mexico to California and back. For two decades he was a trapper and Indian fighter, leading bands of mountain men all over the Rockies. He seldom returned to Taos, noting in 1842 that he had been in the mountains for sixteen years. "Once a year, perhaps," he told his biographer, "I would enjoy the luxury of a meal consisting of bread, meat, sugar, and coffee."

In 1842 Carson met the explorer John C. Frémont, and he spent his next decades guiding Frémont and his troops in their campaigns throughout the west. Carson's final career was as an Indian agent based in Taos, where he became a prime force in the final subjugation of the Plains Indians. He also led the roundup of Navajos for internment at Bosque Redondo in the 1860s.

Kit Carson seldom stayed in one place for

long, although he considered the Taos area his home. He was married twice. His first wife was an Indian woman who died in childbirth. In 1843 Carson married Josepha Jaramillo, daughter of Don Francisco Jaramillo, a leading Taos citizen. Carson made attempts to settle down a number of times. First he went into partnership in the Cimarron area, but he sold the property and went off with General Frémont. In 1849 Carson and Lucien Maxwell went into business together at Rayado, east of Taos. Again, however, Carson was off in the mountains leading expeditions more than he was home raising sheep. His Taos home is now the Kit Carson Museum. Carson died in 1868.

Another famous nineteenth-century New Mexican also arrived in Taos in the 1820s. Antonio José Martínez was born in Abiquiu, New Mexico, in 1793, but he lived in Taos until his death in 1867. He was a native New Mexican, a Catholic priest, a champion of his parishioners, and a scholar who brought the first printing press to Taos and on it printed material for both his seminary and his school, the first coeducational facility in the West. Padre Martínez played a significant role in many of the events that swept through New Mexico and Taos as the nineteenth century progressed. He is said to have heard the last confession of José González, who was briefly governor during the 1837 rebellion against Mexico. After the conquest of New Mexico by the United States in 1846, an event Martínez was thought to have considered inevitable, he became the first president of the territorial legislature.

However, it is Martínez's stormy relationship with Bishop Jean Baptiste Lamy that feeds the legend of Padre Martínez as a controversial figure. Along with other Hispanic priests, Martínez resented the new rules which the French-born archbishop imposed on the diocese. A number of incidents led up to the final confrontation between Martínez and his superior. Martínez had considered tithing a voluntary gesture; when Bishop Lamy insisted that all Catholics be taxed in order to build the cathedral in Santa Fe, Martínez rebelled. He was excommunicated by Lamy and led his own schismatic church until his death.

The mid-nineteenth century was an active time politically for Taos. The Treaty of Córdova, signed in 1821, meant that Mexico (including New Mexico) was independent of Spain. Although most laws remained the same, the opening of borders to foreigners, forbidden under Spanish rule, facilitated the entrance of trappers and traders into the Taos area. However, the Mexican law was strict about taxes and trapping regulations, fostering complicated cheating schemes by the mountain men and resentment from ordinary taxpaying citizens.

Resentment grew against heavy Mexican taxes and unpopular Mexican governors. Governor Albino Pérez was especially disliked. When a rebellion centered in the Santa Cruz area began in 1837, most of Taos joined in. The revolt succeeded and a Ranchos de Taos *genízaro* (a Christianized Indian), José González, was installed as governor. His reign did not last long. Mexican forces soon came up from the south and defeated the rebels, and González and other leaders were shot.

Less than ten years after that 1837 revolt against Mexico, General Stephen Kearny's

troops peacefully claimed New Mexico as United States territory. Kearny named Charles Bent of Taos as the first territorial governor. The new laws, known as the Kearny Code, were printed on Padre Martínez's press. Most New Mexicans accepted U.S. rule, but a hard core in Taos did not. Six months after Bent became governor, rumors of a plot began to circulate. Nothing came of that whispered rebellion, but a month later, in January 1847, as Governor Bent was visiting his family in Taos, many Hispanic and Indian residents of the Taos area rose up, killing Bent and his family as well as others who were considered part of the U.S. presence. Word of the uprising sped down to Santa Fe, and soon Sterling Price was marching through mountain snows with his troops to subdue the Taos Rebellion. When he reached the town Price found most Hispanic residents hidden in their homes, so he marched on to the pueblo, where Indian rebels held the Mission Church of San Gerónimo. One hundred fifty Indians and seven U.S. soldiers died in the winter battle. The church was destroyed.

Hasty trials were called. Juries found the leaders of the rebellion guilty of treason. One U.S. observer, a young writer named Lewis Garrard, took exception to the decision: he thought treason too harsh a verdict for people defending themselves against American invaders. However, Garrard was not averse to watching the hangings of the rebels in a field north of town, and he later joined the executioners and soldiers in celebrating the event.

Taos spent the next years adjusting to its new government. The Civil War was noticed in the predominantly Hispanic village only when Kit Carson, Ceran St. Vrain, and others tacked the American flag to a pole in the plaza and took turns standing guard over it. It was clear then that Taos would remain loyal to the North.

The plaza was a bare, treeless place in those days. It was described by one visitor as having little charm, "with a few dirty, irregular lanes and a quantity of mud houses and rude hovels." Many of the mountain men settled down in Taos during the territorial period, some, like St. Vrain, establishing businesses around the plaza. The discovery of gold in the nearby mountains was expected to have an economic impact on Taos, but lack of sufficient outside capital left most of the gold mining to individual prospectors, who wandered into town only occasionally. Taos grew beyond its fortresslike beginnings around the plaza once the nomadic Indians who had plagued the region for centuries were forced onto reservations by the U.S. government.

Most of the Hispanic farmers in the Taos area during the nineteenth century raised sheep and, later on, cattle. Community lands made grazing possible. However, within a hundred years, the government had claimed that communal land as federal and state property. The holdings of most of the small farmers in the area thus dwindled progressively, until today livestock raising is limited either to large cattle operations or, as can be seen on the outskirts of Taos, modest family subsistence farms that shrink with each generation.

Taos had always been both a trading and an agricultural community. The arrival in 1848 of the Kerr brothers, who were painters, signaled that a new facet would soon be added to Taos's colorful population. Joseph Sharp, another American artist, sketched in the area in 1880. His reports to two fellow artists back east, Bert Phillips and Ernest Blumenschein, soon brought them to Taos. The "legend of the broken wheel" tells how the young men, on their way from Denver to Mexico, found themselves stranded about thirty miles outside Taos when a wheel of their wagon broke. Blumenschein, losing the coin toss, rode by horseback to Taos, carrying the broken wheel. Phillips remained behind to guard the wagon and supplies. By the time Blumenschein returned with the repaired wheel, he had fallen in love with Sharp's Taos. The two artists settled in the town and originated what is known as the Taos School, a group of established artists who made Taos their home and inspiration. The artists gave shows throughout the world, displaying paintings with Taos and

related subjects as their theme in galleries and museums and on Santa Fe Railroad calendars.

The fame of Taos as an art center was assured by the arrival in 1917 of a wealthy Eastern woman, Mabel Dodge. Drawn by her presence, invitations, and sometimes insistence, a myriad of artists came to Taos at one time or another. They included Andrew Dasburg, often considered the dean of Taos painters, Georgia O'Keeffe, Ansel Adams, Marsden Hartley, and John Marin. Mabel Dodge's greatest visitor, D. H. Lawrence, stayed in Taos for two years and wrote several pieces about the town and his hostess. A Lawrence cult thrived in New Mexico, fed in part by his widow Frieda, who returned to Taos after his death. Both Lawrence and Frieda are buried at their Lobo Mountain ranch, now called the D. H. Lawrence Ranch (see page 323).

Mabel Dodge was one of Taos's most colorful figures, still written and speculated about twenty years after her death. She and her third husband, the painter and sculptor Maurice Sterne, first went to Santa Fe in 1917. Not finding that city to her liking, Mabel motored with Sterne through Rio Grande Canyon in the dead of winter, arriving in Taos at night. Before the evening was over, she had "discovered" Taos and had rented a house from Doc Martin, another local character. Sterne soon departed. Mabel stayed on, creating an adobe estate at the north end of town, marrying Tony Luhan from Taos Pueblo, entertaining the famous, and building a wall around her ever-growing hacienda to keep out the curious. She wrote eleven books, some of which deal with her stormy relationship with D. H. Lawrence. She is buried in Kit Carson Cemetery.

Taos today is filled with painters, weavers, jewelers, writers, and potters. The artists are Indian, Hispanic, and Anglo. Some have their work displayed in famous galleries or published by large firms; others are not as successful. But they all receive inspiration from Taos.

In the 1960s, Taos saw another influx. Hippies drawn by romantic books and movies about Taos arrived in droves, living in converted buses and in tepees, and sometimes standing in welfare lines. Most left within a few years, but not before undercurrents of resentment and misunderstanding on all sides had flared into some unpleasant incidents.

Although the predominant culture of Taos today is Hispanic, as it has been for almost three hundred years, current population figures show that things are changing. In 1970, 80 percent of Taos County residents were Hispanic; in 1980, that figure had fallen to 66 percent. Many think the Hispanic population will become even smaller in the future. The county's Indian population, never large, has also shrunk. In 1980, only 6.5 percent of Taos County was Indian, compared to 8 percent ten years before.

Taos is a place where people have lived, worked, and fought for centuries. Generations of shopkeepers, teachers, and farmers have labored beneath Pueblo and Wheeler peaks. The political eruptions and social revolutions of New Mexico have, for centuries, been played out first in Taos. The three settlements—Taos Pueblo, Taos, and Ranchos de Taos—have adjusted to changing times in their own ways. Most residents of the picturesque valley would agree that the essence of Taos has remained: it is a quiet, beautiful place where individuals go about the tasks of daily life in their own ways, respecting each other and the history and environment that have brought them or kept them in this place.

taos

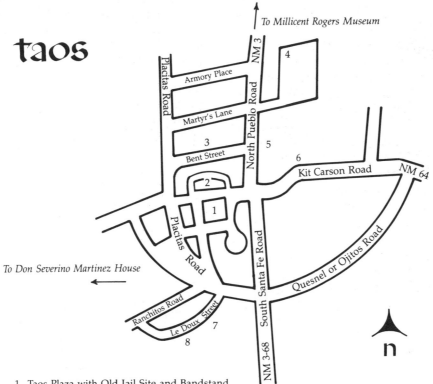

To Millicent Rogers Museum

NM 3

Placitas Road

Armory Place

Martyr's Lane

Bent Street

North Pueblo Road

Kit Carson Road

NM 64

Placitas Road

To Don Severino Martinez House

South Santa Fe Road

Quesnel or Ojitos Road

Ranchitos Road

Le Doux Street

NM 3-68

n

1. Taos Plaza with Old Jail Site and Bandstand
2. Old Taos County Courthouse
3. Bent Museum
4. Kit Carson Park and Cemetery
5. Manby House
6. Kit Carson Museum
7. Blumenshein House
8. Harwood Foundation

Walking Tour of Taos

Don Fernando de Taos, or Taos proper, is best seen on foot. Its streets were once lanes leading to the major trading routes of the Southwest. Since winding wagon trails are not suited to twentieth-century, bumper-to-bumper traffic, visitors are encouraged to park their cars either in the municipal lot north of the plaza or on side streets. The streets of Taos remain narrow and curved, often merging, sometimes bearing names that change as new neighborhoods are entered. Pedestrians will enjoy this aspect of Taos if they remember that it is small, friendly, and used to tourists.

Taos Plaza is the obvious starting point for a walking tour. It has always been the trading, gossiping, and gathering place for the Taos area. Once treeless, then shaded by immense old trees, the plaza is now, after a recent modernizing effort, changed again.

The plaza contains two focal points: its copper-covered bandstand, the gift of Mabel Dodge Luhan; and the flagpole from which, twenty-four hours a day, the American flag flies. During the Civil War, rebels attempted to take down the U.S. flag and destroy it. A number of Taos's leading citizens, including Kit Carson, rushed to the flag's defense, tacked it to its pole, and kept vigil over it. An

Act of Congress now permits Taos to keep the flag flying at all times in tribute to the loyalty of its early citizens.

A large building on the north side of the plaza is now home to small shops and galleries. It was once the Taos County Courthouse, which is currently housed in a modern structure at the south end of town. The Taos County Jail moved south with the courthouse. Until the move, the jail was under the plaza itself. Pedestrians strolling there often found it disconcerting to be hailed from below by a prisoner. Most of the buildings around the plaza are old, many with high, pressed-tin ceilings. Fires have always plagued Taos, so none of the plaza's buildings predate the nineteenth century. On the south side of the plaza, where La Fonda hotel is located, the Bent-St. Vrain Company store was built in 1832. La Fonda contains an exhibit of D. H. Lawrence paintings once banned in London. At one time women were not allowed into the gallery; now all who pay the entrance fee are admitted.

From the plaza visitors can take either of two small side streets, almost alleyways, that wind behind the buildings on the north side of the plaza. After walking through the municipal parking lot, a visitor sees the house of Long John Dunn, a colorful Taos gambler and stagecoach driver. A rambling white structure, the Dunn home is now divided into a series of shops with a boardwalk extending its length to Bent Street.

Governor Charles Bent, a Taos businessman and trader who married a member of an old Hispanic family, was the first territorial governor of New Mexico. However, his reign was short. In 1847, on a visit home from his office in Santa Fe, Bent was killed in the Taos Uprising. Other members of his family also died during the brief rebellion. Bent's home on Bent Street is now a museum and gallery containing nineteenth-century memorabilia and relics of the uprising. The famous hole in the wall, said to have been carved by hand by Bent family members in their frenzy to escape the attackers, can be seen in the museum.

From Bent Street pedestrians can cross North Pueblo Road to Kit Carson Park, which contains a playground, tennis courts, picnic tables, and shade trees. A number of Taos's most famous citizens, including Carson and Mabel Dodge Luhan, are buried in Kit Carson Cemetery. Near the park is the Taos Community Auditorium, site of many live theatrical and music performances.

Walking south on North Pueblo Road, a traveler will pass the Stables Gallery, the former home of Arthur Manby. Manby lived in Taos for thirty years, securing himself behind barred doors and snarling guard dogs that added fuel to the rumors of his own fearsome nature. He was said to have been the son of a wealthy family, to have controlled Mexican revolutionaries, to have taken part in mysterious murders. Manby's own death was a violent one. He was found decapitated one summer day in 1929, and no one ever solved his murder.

Further south on North Pueblo Road sits the venerable Taos Inn, a rambling structure with rooms wandering up the stairs and out the back around a patio. At the corner of El Pueblo and Kit Carson roads, at the stoplight, visitors who want to see the Kit Carson Home and Museum should take a left turn onto Kit Carson Road. The museum is in the middle of the block on the north side of the street. Built in 1825 and bought by Carson upon his marriage to Josefa Jaramillo in 1843, the house is a national historic landmark. The museum, open seven days a week, is not only a treasure trove for Kit Carson buffs, but also houses a fine collection of nineteenth-century Western Americana, from household and ranching utensils to archaeological relics. Artifacts from the three cultures of Taos, Indian, Hispanic, and Anglo, are displayed. A knowledgeable staff runs the museum and its gift shop.

A stroll down Kit Carson Road takes a visitor past stores, restaurants, and galleries, some housed in old buildings once home to famous Taos figures. The large gallery near the bottom of Kit Carson Road, on the south side, is the former residence of Joseph Sharp, a founder of the Taos art colony. At the base of the hill, an abrupt turn to the right leads to Ojito (also called Quesnel) Road, which climbs past hidden adobe houses, back up to N.M. 68/N.M. 3 or South Santa Fe Road. The pedestrian who crosses this highway and continues to head west will be on Placitas Road. Following it as it bends, he will come to LeDoux Street, perhaps the favorite walking thoroughfare in Taos.

Those who walk along LeDoux Street, a narrow, paved path, will find galleries, a museum and library complex, and the home of Ernest Blumenschein, another early Taos artist.

Blumenschein's house, a National Historic Landmark on the south side of the street, was built in 1797. Blumenschein bought it in 1919 and restored it, also constructing a studio and adding plumbing and electricity. The furnishings and mementos in the thick-walled house are much the same today as they were during the more than forty years that Blumenschein lived and worked here. The Kit Carson Memorial Foundation runs the homelike museum, providing guides seven days a week.

The Harwood Foundation, a library, gallery, and auditorium owned by the University of New Mexico, is located beyond the Blumenschein house. Captain Smith H. Simpson, a contemporary of Kit Carson, built the core of the structure as his home in 1860. The Harwood, a landmark, is a repository for the work of many of the artists who have lived in Taos. Its paintings and sculptures range from the works of unnamed *retablo* (painted panel) makers in the Mabel Dodge Luhan New Mexico Santo Collection to the woodcarvings of Patrocinio Barela, a prolific sculptor in wood who died in Taos in 1964. Taos painters from Oscar Berninghaus to Lady Dorothy Brett to R. C. Gorman have their works hung throughout the building. The Taos Public Library, which includes a special D. H. Lawrence collection, is also housed in the Harwood. Children tired of walking and sightseeing will find the bright children's library in the east wing a pleasant stop.

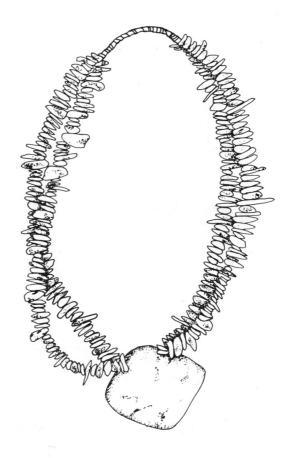

From the Harwood Foundation, visitors can stroll back to the plaza by returning up LeDoux Street to Placitas Road, following a northward path to the plaza. As an alternative, a pedestrian can meander along the paved and unpaved streets west of the plaza and north of LeDoux Street, keeping a slow pace, peeking above adobe walls into gardens and galleries. Most streets eventually veer back toward the plaza, where travelers can sit along the perimeters and watch Taos drive and walk by. Taos plaza has been providing such entertainment for generations.

Visitors may also want to see two small museums, the Martínez Hacienda and the Millicent Rogers Museum, both of which are located outside the plaza area.

La Hacienda de Don Antonio Severino Martínez is located about two miles west of Taos Plaza on N.M. 240. Don Severino, an important figure in early-nineteenth-century New Mexico, purchased his hacienda in 1804. His

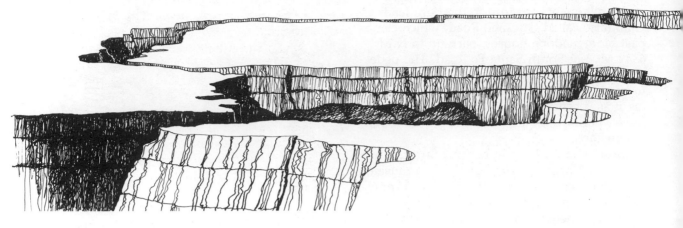

additions to the solid structure reflected his growing family and position in the community. At one time there were more than twenty rooms in the building. One of the few refurbished examples of colonial New Mexico architecture and life, the hacienda is on the National Historic Registery, and has only recently been restored.

The Millicent Rogers Museum, emphasizing Hispanic and Indian art and life, sits to the north and above the town of Taos, just south of the N.M. 64/N.M. 3/N.M. 150 intersection. Signs point the way south down Museum Road to a handsome adobe building.

Millicent Rogers, a Standard Oil heiress, came to Taos in 1947 for a visit. She stayed, making the town her home until her death in 1953. During her time in Taos, Mrs. Rogers collected a wide variety of Indian (Pueblo, Navajo, and Plains) artifacts, as well as numerous pieces of Spanish colonial art. However, the focus of her interests was on the arts of northern New Mexico. Her private collection forms the nucleus of the museum exhibits.

On display in revolving exhibits are the jewelry, weavings, clothing, pottery, and paintings of both the Hispanics and the Indians of the area. Religious figures—*bultos* (figures in the round), *retablos*, and crucifixes—are shown in a small chapel. Household articles, including tools, baskets, trunks, and utensils, adorn the rooms and fill display cases. The setting

for all the exhibits is intimate and comfortable. Guides explain how each artifact fitted into the life of the people of the area.

Taos painters Becky James, Dorothy Brett, Barbara Latham, and Tom Benrimo added a touch of whimsy to one wall of the museum. The artists spent weeks immortalizing two hundred of their favorite Taos characters in a large mural. It became a point of honor to be included in the colorful painting.

The Millicent Rogers Museum was founded shortly after its patron's death because her son Paul Peralta Ramos thought that his mother's extensive collection should remain in Taos. The museum opened in 1956, moving to its present location in the C. J. K. Anderson home in 1968. There is an admission charge. Winter and summer hours differ, and the museum is closed on major holidays.

Tour 3 continues to Ranchos de Taos (Tour 11) on N.M. 68/N.M. 3. The highway leaves the plaza area and soon plunges south into a strip of motels, restaurants, and Spanish-villa-style shopping plazas. At Ranchos de Taos, 48.5 mi., Tour 3 leaves N.M. 68 and turns east on N.M. 3 toward the mountains. (See Tour 11 for the area from Ranchos de Taos to the N.M. 3/N.M. 75 junction, a distance of about fifteen miles.)

N.M. 3 descends abruptly and meets N.M. 75 near Vadito. A sharp right turn at the bottom of the hill takes the traveler along N.M.

75 to Peñasco, Picuris Pueblo, and other villages nestled in the Sangre de Cristo Range. (See Tour 11.) N.M. 75 leads west beyond Peñasco to the Rio Grande and N.M. 68.

At the bottom of the steep hill, Tour 3 passes the junction and bears east on N.M. 3, traversing a small agricultural valley and then sweeping into a piney canyon where summer homes and camps are located. The road cuts a narrow path through here; there is barely room at some points for the picnic and camping spots along the river. Dirt trails go into the Carson National Forest to more campgrounds and trailheads. A ski area, SIPAPU, 70 mi., named after the creation myth of the Pueblos, rises above the road. This alpine-flavored resort has concentrated its gas, food, and lodging facilities within the small area at the base of its ski slope. Some of the businesses at Sipapu are open all year. The scenery in this section of the mountains is worthy of a postcard. Tall pine trees, gurgling streams, and sheer gray cliffs are juxtaposed with the open meadows that appear now and again.

TRES RITOS ("three rivers"), 74 mi., is a small resort community at the confluence of three streams, Rio La Junta ("where the rivers meet"), Agua Piedra ("rocky waters") Creek, and the Rio Pueblo ("the river of the Pueblo," or "the community"). Established as a mining camp at the turn of the century, Tres Ritos sits on a small pocket between U.S. Hill (Tour 11) and Holman Hill. In this rustic community are many private summerhouses and tourist facilities, including gas stations, restaurants, and lodges.

Beyond Tres Ritos, N.M. 3 passes more camping and resort areas that are lively and populated during the warmer months, quiet and almost deserted when cold weather arrives. A number of lodges along the road cater to fishermen, hunters, and horseback riders. The highway ascends gradually out of the many little valleys and meadows it has bisected and swoops up Holman Hill. Turnouts permit the traveler to stop and gaze down upon the scattered tin roofs of the village of Holman and across the wide Mora Valley to

the eastern plains. The settlements in the distance curve along rivers and streams, up canyons, and beside narrow roads. The Mora Valley, about fifteen miles long and two miles wide, is lush and inviting when it is green; in the winter, as it lies beneath the snows, it appears stark and almost forbidding from above.

The name MORA ("blackberry" or "mulberry") permeates this valley. It is the name of the county, the county seat, and the river that winds through the valley, and at one time Mora was the surname of some of the valley's residents. The entire district was designated Lo de Mora and De lo Mora ("pertaining to" or "belonging to Mora") in early documents describing the Mora Land Grant. At this point there is only speculation about the first use of the word *mora* in this part of New Mexico. A legend says that Ceran St. Vrain, the Taos and Mora trapper and businessman of French descent, discovered a dead man along the banks of a local river and so named the river "L'eau du Mort," or "The River of the Dead." Perhaps, and quite likely, the original settlers here supplemented their diets with the berries so abundant in the valley. However, the region's name probably commemorates early settlers who bore the Mora surname—Mora Piñeda and García de la Mora were both pioneer New Mexicans, for instance.

The immense Mora Land Grant, dated September 28, 1835, gave seventy-six settlers each a strip of land in this valley, the grant extending from San Antonio de lo Mora (now Cleveland) to Santa Gertrudis de lo Mora (now the town of Mora). Some documents take the Mora grant as far east and north as Wagon Mound. Much of the Mora grant was long ago taken from private and community hands to become part of Carson National Forest.

The Mora Valley is rich in history. Its first inhabitants were probably early Pueblo Indians, followed by Plains Indians—Utes, Comanches, and Jicarilla Apaches—who migrated south and west from the northern plains between the fourteenth and sixteenth centuries. It is likely that they hunted buffalo among the valley's tall grasses. De Vargas visited the region in the winter of 1696 in pursuit of Pueblo Indians from the Rio Grande area; he remarked on the high snowdrifts he encountered. Lonely settlements and farms dotted the valley in the first part of the nineteenth century. Early documents note that the priest at Picuris Pueblo ministered to families who lived here in 1818. As French-Canadian and American trappers and traders ventured into New Mexico at the dawn of the nineteenth century, some followed the valley's rivers and then turned west into the mountains to Santa Fe and Taos. Others stayed a while to trap beaver and other furbearing animals. No large, permanent settlements occupied the valley until almost the middle of the last century, by which time the Cimarron Cutoff of the Santa Fe Trail was beginning to carve its historic path through the valley.

Hispanics settled the Mora Valley just as the American presence was making itself felt at the borders of the Mexican colony. However, the Hispanic tradition in the valley has remained pervasive. The Penitente Brotherhood (see Religion) was long a vital religious factor here. Politics, based for years on the *patrón* system, remains an integral part of the valley's life and is a source of employment and favors. As the Anglo population in New Mexico grew throughout the nineteenth century, the valley was riddled with revolts, attacks, and counterattacks. A contingent of Texans led by Colonel Charles Warfield invaded New Mexico in 1843, when it was still Mexican territory, and fought a battle in Mora. Uprisings against the new American government also took place in the valley after 1846, when Kearny and his troops marched through and claimed the region for the United States. From the beginning of the first colonization effort until Fort Union was built to the north, the nomadic Indians whose hunting grounds the valley had been for centuries staged periodic, often devastating attacks.

Today, the Mora Valley is filled with many small farms, a number of large ranches, and vestiges of Hispanic villages whose inhabitants have left to live in larger towns where employ-ment and educational opportunities are greater. Mora County's population, 4,205 in 1980, has been declining for decades. Its per capita income has long been among the lowest in New Mexico, ranking close to the bottom nationally as well. Years of social and economic programs have barely dented the poverty and the outflow of people and dollars. However, the valley is, by anyone's standards, one of the loveliest in the state. Hunters, fishermen, and campers long ago discovered its secrets. There are campgrounds throughout the mountains that surround the valley. Fields of wildflowers and picturesque adobe houses and villages attract painters and photographers. Those born here return often, if only for summer visits and family occasions.

At the bottom of Holman Hill, N.M. 121 enters N.M. 3 from the left. The paved road leads seven miles north up a finger of the Mora Valley to the small village of CHACON, named for members of the Chacón family, who were among the valley's original settlers in the middle 1880s. Diego Chacón was the village's first postmaster, in 1894. Historically, Chacon was considered part of the larger town of Mora; its chapel, San Isidro, was a *visita* (mission) of the large Church of San Gertrudis in Mora.

HOLMAN, 88 mi., which straddles N.M. 3 at the base of Holman Hill, was founded in the late 1800s and is named after its first postmaster, Charles W. Holman. The old village actually sits off the road, its adobe chapel and school building back and to the right of N.M. 3. Holman experienced a miracle in the 1970s: residents began to see a holy image on the cracked adobe walls of the church. Crowds of believers and skeptics gathered in the small community to watch for the vision; television crews and newspaper reporters recorded the event; hot dog and chile stands filled the streets. Then the sightings abruptly ceased.

Remains of Holman's agricultural past are obvious to the visitor. Carefully laid-out fields have given way to seas of black-eyed Susans; farm implements stand rusting next to abandoned farmhouses. But the pyramidlike stacks

of firewood and gaily colored hollyhocks present all over the village are evidence that there are still a few families living in Holman.

CLEVELAND, 91 mi., originally called San Antonio but later given its present name in honor of President Glover Cleveland, seems to begin barely a mile south of Holman; the two settlements are almost contiguous. Cleveland began life as a population center for the upper reaches of the Mora Valley. Its Chapel of San Antonio was a mission for the larger church in Mora. Although its abandoned two-story general store and other massive commercial structures no longer serve its dwindling population, they are reminders of its mercantile past. A group of Irishmen led by Dan Cassidy came to Cleveland from County Donegal in the late 1800s. Cassidy operated a general store, and his countrymen settled into the community as farmers or merchants. Cleveland's population at the turn of the century was over six hundred; one guesses that fewer than half that number live there now.

At Cleveland, travelers can take the dirt roads that go into the Sangre de Cristo Mountains to Rio La Casa ("the river of the beaver dams"), Walker Flats, and other fishing and camping spots. Inquire about road and weather conditions before starting a trip on these roads.

MORA, 94 mi. (alt. 6,528, pop. 471), the seat of Mora County, is the largest and liveliest in the string of villages that lies along N.M. 3. First formally settled by the original Mora grantees in 1835, the town grew steadily throughout the nineteenth century. In the first half of that century, the Mexican government viewed Mora as a buffer between its colony and the encroaching Americans to the east. But the Americans came anyway: trappers, traders, merchants, ranchers, peddlers, and hotel and mill owners. In 1846, when U.S. troops took over the New Mexico Territory, Mora did not submit to the new regime without a fight. Although Kearny's 1846 proclamation was greeted in Mora with little activity, the Taos Uprising early the following year spread into the Mora Valley quickly. Insurgents led by a General Cortez raided villages up and down the valley, killing a number of Americans who were unfortunate enough to be present. Troops from Santa Fe arrived and quashed the rebellion, leaving the town. During the siege, many historic documents were lost in the fires that destroyed local archives and private dwellings. Official information about Mora predating the period of U.S. occupation is therefore sketchy.

The Church of Santa Gertrudis (since destroyed) was the focal point for much of the activity in Mora in the mid-nineteenth century. In the 1860s, the town became the base for a large Catholic parish that stretched almost two hundred miles north, reaching into Colorado. The priests and brothers who served this far-flung parish introduced the first version of public education into the region. From 1865 until the Dixon court decision in the 1950s (see "Education"), Mora's youngsters went to schools, both public and private, run by the Christian Brothers and, later on, the Sisters of Loretto.

While life in Mora was sometimes harsh—winters were long and snowy, and the economy was fragile—social events were not forgotten. One description of a dance in the 1850s notes that the white Mora dance hall was lit not only by a few dim oil lamps, but also by the cigarettes being smoked by the ladies in attendance. Both the men and the women were, said the onlooker, lingering along the sides of the room.

Mora was also a thriving business center a hundred years ago, with flour mills, hotels, sawmills, saloons, and a number of mercantile stores. Some of the names most prominent in New Mexico business and frontier life, including those of St. Vrain, Carson, Hanosh, Watrous, and Ilfeld, figure in Mora's history. Politics and business flourished during Mora's prime, and the town was considered an important center of political and mercantile activity in New Mexico.

Visitors can sense the colorful history of Mora as they drive slowly down its main street, N.M. 3. The highway is wide and curbed here, as befits a county seat and mercantile capital. Large stores, dance halls, and public buildings, some of them boarded up and deserted, await rejuvenation. Behind the present post office building, remains of the plaza and old, handsome adobe structures testify that Mora's heart was here before the highway passed it by.

SIDE TOUR

Travelers can delve more deeply into the Mora Valley by taking N.M. 38, which intersects N.M. 3 from the north in Mora's downtown. This paved road cuts across the broad valley and leads to the village of Guadalupita, about fourteen miles away. Coyote Creek State Park is beyond that. If nothing else, it is worth turning onto N.M. 38 to look at the massive stone St. Vrain Mill just behind Mora's storefronts on the other side of the river. This two- and three-story building, its gingerbread millwork faded and falling, once supplied Fort Union with flour. It is now abandoned.

Those who decide to venture north along N.M. 38 will look across a wide, flat valley where fields of sunflowers and miles of pastureland begin to narrow at Guadalupita. A few summer housing developments and Christmas tree farms barely interrupt the quiet landscape. Cemeteries with elaborate wrought-iron work enclosing their graves appear in the middle of alfalfa fields much more frequently than the present population would seem to warrant.

GUADALUPITA sits beneath the Rincon Range of the Sangre de Cristos. It is a farming and lumber community most of whose population has long since moved elsewhere, as is evidenced by the deserted school playground. Uneven rows of fire-blackened fir trees stand along the ridge above the valley, signs of a fire that threatened but did not consume the little village.

N.M. 38 remains paved and well-maintained as it winds past summer cabins into Coyote Creek State Park, open from May to November, and offering, from its high elevation (6,800 feet), superb vistas and fine fishing. Signs along the road indicate that N.M. 38 can be followed through the canyon to Angel Fire twelve miles away. However, the dirt road is not recommended for casual travel. Coyote Creek Canyon was formed during the Pleistocene Period, when erosion slowly cut away lava layers to reveal softer strata hundreds of feet thick. These layers fell away more easily, and thus this canyon was created.

At Mora, N.M. 94 intersects N.M. 3 and goes into the mountains through a series of small, isolated Hispanic villages whose names—Ledoux, Tierra Monte, Gascon, Rociada—are reflective of both the Spanish and the French influences in this region. Morphy Lake State Park, seven miles west of Ledoux on a narrow and rough dirt road, is a favorite, though remote, camping and fishing spot. N.M. 94 makes a circle through the mountain villages, dipping and weaving and finally exiting about fifteen miles later at Sapello. Tour 3, however, remains on N.M. 3.

ROCIADA ("dewy"), eleven miles from Mora, is perhaps the most interesting of the settlements reached via N.M. 94. It was founded in the late 1800s by Jean Pendaries, a Frenchman who also established Gascon, naming the latter village after his native province, Gascony. Pendaries started a large ranch in Rociada.

Oliver La Farge, who married Pendaries's great-granddaughter, wrote about the establishment, then called the Baca Ranch, in his book *Behind the Mountains*. Rociada was originally two villages, the lower one called Santo Niño ("holy child"). The residents of Upper Rociada dedicated their church to San José. Thousands of acres have now been incorporated into Pendaries Village, a recreation development with a golf course, a motel, and other amenities.

N.M. 21 intersects N.M. 3 at LA CUEVA ("the cave"), 100 mi. La Cueva is a National Historic District belonging to the Salmon family, owners of the large nearby ranch. What the visitor sees here is a large mill complex whose stone walls extend far beyond the immediate millworks. Built in the 1870s by Vicente Romero, founder of La Cueva Ranch, the mill ground wheat from surrounding ranches and supplied Fort Union with flour. It also generated electricity until 1949. It is said that Romero slept in caves while he built his

ranch, which was also noted for its remarkable irrigation system. N.M. 21 goes north here, past a state game refuge to Rainsville, Ojo Feliz, and Ocate.

N.M. 3 continues its southward path to Las Vegas, crossing the Mora River and bypassing the settlements that straggle along the old road to the east. N.M. 161, leading twenty-three miles across the valley and the plains to join I-25, intersects N.M. 3. The landscape changes swiftly, the pine trees that predominate at first giving way to the grays and

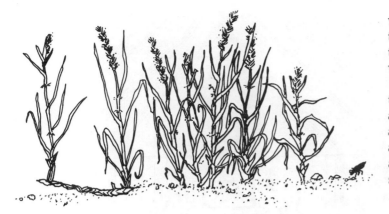

browns of the plains. The road bisects hog-back ridges of sandstone. The greens of the trees and the grasses soften 200-million-year-old red Triassic shale. Flat, smooth buttes appear in the distance.

SAPELLO, 111 mi., bears one of New Mexico's oddest names. It may have its origins in any number of languages, including French, Spanish, and Kiowa. Words ranging in meaning from "toad" to "hairbrush" to "burial" are possible antecedents. Whatever the name's meaning, the farming village is at the confluence of Sapello and Manuelito creeks and marks the turnoff for either N.M. 94 and its circle drive to Mora or N.M. 266, which goes to San Ignacio and a number of large ranches.

To the right can be seen the large granite outcropping called Hermit's Peak, a Santa Fe Trail landmark and the home for a few years of a recluse and holy man named Giovanni Marie Augustini (or one of any number of versions thereof). The hermit was reputed to be a rich Italian nobleman who had given up everything to live alone on this mesa top in New Mexico. He had come from Kansas via the Santa Fe Trail, arriving in the Las Vegas area in 1863. He first lived in a cave in Romeroville, but then moved up to one near the top of Cerro del Tecolote ("owl peak"). The hermit visited with and treated the sick at both places. He lived in a small cave, eating only *atole* (a blue cornmeal mush) and drinking from a stream whose waters, it is said, he caused to appear. A number of miracles are attributed to this stranger who left his cave

when crowds of pilgrims threatened his solitude. He walked south through the desert to the Organ Mountains near Las Cruces and was killed there in 1869.

From the crest of a hill, N.M. 3 drops onto the plains. Storrie Lake appears below, a 350-acre reservoir completed in 1924 that serves as an irrigation source for about twelve thousand acres of land. The state park along its shores is a convenient camping, boating, fishing, and swimming site for area residents.

(See Tour 1 for Las Vegas and its environs.)

From Las Vegas, travelers may take I-25 west to Santa Fe (Tour 1) or head to Conchas Lake and Tucumcari via N.M. 104 (Tour 6). Tour 3 juts south at Romeroville on U.S. 84 to end at the junction with I-40 west of Santa Rosa.

Many drivers use U.S. 84 to avoid the long connecting interstate loop through Santa Fe and Albuquerque. The road is two-lane and paved, and it meets I-40 about forty miles from Romeroville.

Although one would not guess it now, ROMEROVILLE, 119 mi., once hosted President and Mrs. Rutherford B. Hayes and General William T. Sherman. The sleepy village was the home of Don Trinidad Romero, one of a number of brothers whose father founded a freight company in Las Vegas in 1851. The enterprise grew to become Romero Mercantile Company, one of the Southwest's leading wholesalers. Two Romero sons were mayors of Las Vegas, and a third, Don Trinidad, not only became a member of Congress but was also a clever businessman who crowned his commercial achievements by building a hundred-thousand-dollar two-story mansion in this village in 1880. Romero entertained a number of prominent citizens and visitors within the rich interior of his hacienda. After his death, the large home became a sanatorium and then a dude ranch. It burned to the ground in 1932.

About midway along U.S. 84 between Romeroville and I-40, a small paved road makes a circle tour through a few outpost villages, La Loma, Anton Chico, and Dilia.

ANTON CHICO, despite its size and isolation (it is about four miles off U.S. 84), has played important roles in two incidents in New Mexico history. In 1841 Texans entered New Mexico under Colonel Hugh McLeod in an attempt to take possession of both the capital at Santa Fe and the wagon trains along the Santa Fe Trail. Governor Manuel Armijo, riding out from the capital, captured those Texans who had gotten as far as Anton Chico, executing a number of them on the spot. Six years later, when New Mexico had just become part of the United States, American troops defeated insurgents in a battle near Anton Chico.

First settled in 1822 by Don Salvador Tapia and sixteen others as part of the Anton Chico Land Grant, the town is divided into two parts, upper and lower. Both communities were built like fortresses, their rock walls high, their carved doors heavy. Anton Chico's population has shrunk over the years, but the Abercrombie Store and Dance Hall, long a shopping and social mecca for the region, continues to hold a prominent place in the community.

In making the detour off U.S. 84 to visit Anton Chico and its neighbors, travelers should be aware that there are few roadside amenities in the area. Dilia, which straddles U.S. 84, has a gas station. While the landscape is lonely, the highway produces a comforting volume of traffic. Fifteen miles south of Dilia, U.S. 84 connects with the east-west interstate, I-40, described in Tour 6.

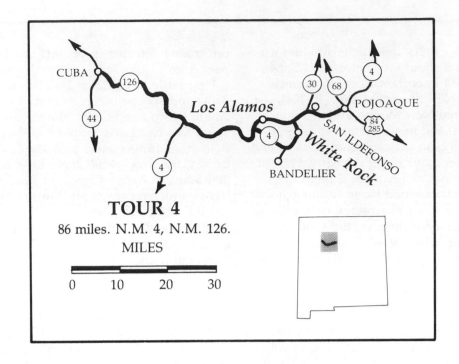

TOUR 4

86 miles. N.M. 4, N.M. 126.

MILES

0   10   20   30

tour four

Pojoaque • **Los Alamos** • *Cuba*

This trip, from Pojoaque to Cuba, starts on a modern four-lane highway and culminates in a long drive on a winding dirt road through the mountains. Prehistoric cliff dwellings, ancient pueblos, a modern city born to create the nuclear age, a vast volcanic caldera, the brightly lit strips of suburbia, and the quiet of a pine-needle-floored campground form the contrasting highlights of the journey. Side trips to ghost towns and wilderness areas can add other dimensions as well. Tourist facilities and overnight accommodations exist at both ends of the tour, and Los Alamos also offers such facilities. Forest Service rest areas are placed at intervals along the way. Tours 5, 7, and 11 are crossed by Tour 4 at Pojoaque.

At the village of Pojoaque, which lies about fifteen miles north of Santa Fe, N.M. 4, known also as the Los Alamos Road, veers off to the left from U.S. 84/285. N.M. 4 is well-marked as it heads west towards Los Alamos. The trailer–gas station–roadside bar panorama continues beyond Pojoaque, almost hiding the quiet agricultural valley that N.M. 4 bisects. Two rivers, the Tesuque and the Nambe (called the Pojoaque west of this area), mean-

der as best they can down from the mountains to the Rio Grande. Modern irrigation and engineering systems have altered their natural courses and flows, but the valley through which they have wandered for centuries continues to thrive on their moisture.

JACONA and JACONITA (related to a Tewa word for a place where tobacco is grown), 1.5 mi., two informal settlements that merge into each other, appear shortly after the intersection. Here, trailers abut old apple orchards, separated from classic adobe homes by narrow fields of alfalfa. Jacona is the site of an ancient Tewa-speaking pueblo abandoned in 1696 when most of its inhabitants allegedly fled westward to join the Hopis and escape the reconquering Spanish. Those who returned to the Pojoaque valley were integrated into Santa Clara and other Tewa pueblos. The Jacona Grant was given by Governor Cubero in 1709 to Ignacio Roybal and his wife, Francisca Gómez. Much of the land surrounding N.M. 4 is part of the Pojoaque Reservation.

About six miles west of the Pojoaque intersection, the turnoff to San Ildefonso appears to the north. Black Mesa looms ahead. The road to the pueblo is well-marked and seems

María Martínez, *Harvey Caplin*.

to lead straight to the base of the dark volcanic stem. However, it first brings the visitor to the public areas of San Ildefonso. Signs at the Y in the road point to the governor's office and to various craft establishments.

SAN ILDEFONSO was originally called Bove by Oñate, who passed through here in 1598. He later changed its name to honor the seventh-century archbishop of Toledo, Spain. The Tewa name for the pueblo is Pox Oge, meaning "place where the water cuts down through." San Ildefonso's population is estimated at about five hundred. It is best known in the rest of the world for its handmade black pottery, especially that created by María Martínez, whose descendants continue to practice the careful building and incising for which she was famous. Other craftspeople at San Ildefonso also work with black pottery as well as red-glazed pieces. A number of young artisans are also jewelers or painters. The painters usually specialize in watercolors with intricate traditional designs. Pottery and other crafts are for sale at the shops near the plaza. There is also a small museum, part of the tribal office complex near the plaza. It presents rotating displays of ancient and modern pottery and narratives of tribal customs and dances.

Public dances are held at San Ildefonso at various times during the year. January 23 is the date for a Pueblo feast that features the Buffalo and Comanche dances in alternate years. Corn Dances, held June 13 and September 16, commemorate a basic element in Pueblo life, the importance of fertility in all creatures—man, plants, and animals. The Corn Dances are usually held on the vast, dusty plaza to the northeast of the church. On the day of the dances, men go to the kivas in midmorning to dress and paint their bodies. Women dress at home, joining the men at the kivas to put on *tablitas*, the stiff headboards worn by female dancers in most of the pueblos. Meanwhile, singers are forming a circle at the south entrance to the plaza. Led by a ceremonial clown, the dancers, men and women in alternating rows, stand on either side of the singers. They enter the plaza and begin the

dancing that will continue, with a respite at noon for feasting with friends and family, throughout the day. Costumes worn in the corn dances have varied little through the years. In fact, though modified from pueblo to pueblo and dance to dance, the basic dress is much the same for all. Bells, shells, turquoise jewelry, feathers, and skunk, fox, and coyote skins are part of the males' costumes. Women generally wear the *tablita*, painted with symbols, on their heads, a one-shouldered black *manta* (dress) caught at the waist with a hand-woven sash, and turquoise and silver jewelry. Everyone carries a sprig or two of evergreen, the symbol of life. Visitors see only the public dances at San Ildefonso, yet the Pueblo ceremonial year is filled with specific days and entire weeks of rituals, including rites surrounding birth, death, and the changes of the season. The pueblo is closed to visitors at those times.

Legend says that the ancestors of the San Ildefonsos lived on the west bank of the Rio Grande along the Pajarito Plateau, possibly at the villages of Otowi and Tsankawi, now ruins. They moved closer to the river as dry periods grew longer. Certainly by the time the Spanish arrived, in the late 1500s, the present village was occupied. Its first Catholic church was built in 1617, and by the middle of the century the pueblo had about eight hundred inhabitants. In 1676 rumors of bewitching by Tewa leaders led to the arrest of more than forty Pueblo Indians. Forty-seven people were whipped and sold into slavery, and four more were executed by the Spanish. Five years later both missionaries at San Ildefonso were murdered as the pueblo took a leading role in the 1680 revolt.

When de Vargas led the Spanish reconquest of 1692, San Ildefonso did not submit readily to his troops, and it was not reconquered until 1694. Two years later, the people again protested Spanish rule, closing off the newly built chapel and convent and setting them afire. Two more missionaries were killed during that uprising, and the village itself moved up to strongholds on Black Mesa, to the north of the

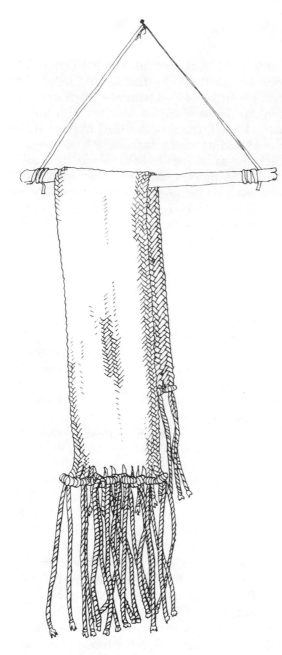

pueblo, for protection against Spanish retribution. Repeated attempts by the Spanish to bring San Ildefonso residents down from the mesa were met with strong resistance. However, once the Spanish cut off their food supply, the people had little choice but to surrender.

By the early part of the eighteenth century, a kind of peace had been acknowledged between the Spanish and the Pueblo. Missionaries moved back into the village, erecting a

chapel (the first two had been destroyed by the Pueblo in its revolts against the Spanish) that stood until about 1905, when a new church was built. Several paintings, some on buffalo and elk hide, formerly decorated the interior of the recently restored structure. The church originally was white, its walls whitewashed periodically. Now it is the color of adobe, matching most of the other buildings in the village.

At the beginning of the twentieth century San Ildefonso experienced a split, in a north-south pattern, among its members that is still reflected in ceremonial functions today. Perhaps related to a move in the 1920s by a number of families who wanted to live south of the confines of the village, the schism has lessened in impact in recent years. There were some decades at the height of the controversy when many ceremonial and governmental positions were not filled and these activities were not pursued. Many think that the split is less evident today, although the pueblo is still often described as having both a north and a south plaza, a remnant of the earlier division.

Near San Ildefonso are four sacred springs and some hilltop shrines not open to the public. The most obvious natural landmark and source of legend and tradition is Black Mesa, a volcanic neck or butte, visible from all points in the pueblo and from miles around. Stories about Black Mesa (also known as Round Mountain, Sacred Fire Mountain, San Ildefonso Mesa, Orphan Mesa, and Tunyo) are endless. Its place in history is secured by the role that the gigantic spotted butte played as the pueblo fought the Spanish. Each time San Ildefonso felt itself threatened by the enemy forces, its residents, along with members of other pueblos, fled to Black Mesa's summit, returning to the valley only when starvation set in.

San Ildefonso stories tell of the giant Tsah-ve-voh, who lived on Black Mesa. In the fall he came down from his home high above the valley to whip and punish those who had misbehaved during the year. Long ago, it is said, Tsah-ve-voh ate youngsters who had been bad the previous year. Even today, Pueblo mothers can use the giant bogeyman of the mesa to keep their children in line. In many of the Tewa-speaking villages, a man dressed as Tsah-ve-voh comes to the pueblos each autumn to punish those who have transgressed.

The top of Black Mesa is covered with ruins of pit houses and villages. Vestiges of adobe guardhouses and forts dot the ancient paths that wind up the steep lava sides of the mesa.

Back at N.M. 4, the view to the west is one of bare, yellow cliffs topped with scrubby pines. This is the Pajarito Plateau, an immense area (about four hundred square miles) of deposits of incandescent volcanic ash. In some places the ash is a thousand feet thick. This harsh volcanic blanket was laid down about five million years ago during the early Pleistocene Period. Wind and water have eroded parts of the tableland into the steep canyons and mesas that humans have inhabited for many hundreds of years. The greatest early period of population on the plateau occurred during the twelfth and thirteenth centuries. Throughout the plateau are abandoned ancient villages and dwellings, hidden from all but the discerning eye of the experienced archaeologist or the intrepid hiker. The soft volcanic rocks offered building materials and easily made hideouts for the cliffdwellers; the volcanic soil was fertile ground for crops that the ancestors of the modern Pueblo Indians grew. A number of excavated ruins of some of the homes of the ancient inhabitants of the Pajarito Plateau are included in Bandelier National Monument.

However, before reaching the start of the climb up the steep-sided plateau, a traveler must first traverse the Rio Grande at Otowi Crossing, 7 mi. Near the modern highway bridge are the remains of Otowi Bridge, a famous water gauging station. Until the 1940s the bridge at Otowi was also the freight stop for a narrow-gauge railroad, the Denver and Rio Grande Western, which ran the "Chile Express" between Santa Fe, New Mexico, and Antonito, Colorado.

For about twenty years, Otowi Crossing was also the site of Edith Warner's tearoom. Edith Warner, whose life has been celebrated in fiction and nonfiction books, was an Eastern gentlewoman who came to New Mexico for her health. She lived for a time at the Los Alamos Ranch school on the Pajarito Plateau. In 1928 she became stationmaster at Otowi, loading and unloading the trains and living next to the river in a small house she rented from the potter María Martínez and her family. Miss Warner provided tea to travelers. In time, the simple tea breaks expanded into home-cooked meals, often plain but always tasty. At one point, guests could stay overnight at the house at Otowi Bridge, and the rest stop along the banks became famous in travelers' circles.

Edith Warner was an unusual woman. She was a friend of the oldest of the area's residents, the Indians at San Ildefonso. In 1942, when scientists mysteriously appeared in Los Alamos, Edith Warner became their friend too. Her tearoom became a favorite spot for their relaxation. The warmth of the little house, the conversation, and Edith's famous chocolate cake all propelled the simple riverside place into the memories of some of the world's great scientists. They found respite in helping Edith build a new corner fireplace or tend her vegetable garden. The era of Edith Warner's tearoom ended with her death in 1951.

West of Otowi Crossing, N.M. 30 branches north from N.M. 4. This smooth, paved road is a recent addition, a means for workers at Los Alamos to get home quickly to Santa Clara Pueblo, Española, and other towns farther north. Five miles up N.M. 30 is the turnoff to Puye Cliffs, an ancient cliffdwelling and the prehistoric home of the Santa Clara Indians who supervise the site. (See Tour 5.)

Near the very base of Pajarito Plateau, at a Y formed by the dividing of two roads, N.M. 4 (the truck route) veers to the south to White Rock and Bandelier National Monument. Loop (or business route) 4 climbs on up the plateau to Los Alamos. The two roads meet again beyond Bandelier and Los Alamos and head into the Jemez Mountains.

Bandelier, *Jean Blackmon.*

WHITE ROCK, about four miles south on Truck Route 4, was originally built in 1948 as a construction site for the work going on at Los Alamos. Over the years, a suburban town has grown up out of the cluster of prefabricated buildings. White Rock is now the home of many Los Alamos employees, a middle-class settlement spread out among the pines, cliffs, and mesas of the Pajarito Plateau. There are gas stations, restaurants, and grocery stores here.

The entrance to BANDELIER NATIONAL MONUMENT, 24 mi., is beyond White Rock. The park is part of a fifty-square-mile wilderness area traversed by ancient trails and dotted with cliffdwellings and abandoned pre-Spanish villages. It is named after the Swiss-American historian and ethnologist Adolph Bandelier, who was fascinated by Indian life and lore. Bandelier lived in Arizona and New Mexico from 1880 to 1886 while he studied the culture and history of the native Americans who had dwelt in the Southwest for centuries. He visited the area of the monument a number of times during those studies. When the park, now run by the

National Park Service, was established in 1916, officials named it in his honor.

At the entrance to Bandelier visitors can obtain information about hikes, camping facilities, and fees. Juniper Campground, which sits atop the plateau near the entrance, offers simple camping spots; group camping sites can be reserved at Ponderosa Campground located a few miles down N.M. 4 from the park entrance. The road from the entrance station to the visitors center at the bottom of Frijoles ("beans") Canyon is paved, but it is narrow and winding. It descends steeply from the rim of the mesa into the cool canyon.

Visitor facilities at Bandelier are attractive and convenient. Sturdy stone structures, one of which was once a guest lodge, cluster at the base of the canyon and provide restrooms, a snack bar, and information areas. Inside the visitors' center, an exhibit hall, a theater where slide shows are given, and a rack of guidebooks and maps for the area are presided over by a staff of trained guides. Picnickers can lunch in the canyon beside Frijoles Creek. The visitors' center is open throughout the year. A mild winter day can be pleasant for hiking and picnicking at Bandelier, and crowds are absent then.

Visitors to the monument can spend a day or a week exploring its miles of trails and ruins. Most will want to take the walk through Frijoles Canyon to the kivas (subterranean ceremonial chambers) and cliff dwellings that can be seen from the visitors' center. Self-guiding tour books are free and explain points of interest along the 1.5-mile route. Children and others who are agile will want to climb the spindly ladders and trails hugging the sides of the volcanic tuff cliffs. The cave-like rooms are pleasant, protected from both summer sun and winter cold. Other trails, also comparatively easy and short, lead from the visitors' center to popular spots, among them Ceremonial Cave, about a mile up from the base of the canyon. The cave sits 150 feet above the canyon floor and is entered by climbing a series of thin ladders. Despite the "ceremonial" in its name, the cave's uses were probably more mundane; some think that turkeys were tethered inside its cool vastness long ago.

Both day hikers and traditional Pueblo Indians return often to another site in Bandelier that can be reached from the visitors' center. This is the Shrine of the Stone Lions of Yapashi, located a steep five miles from Frijoles Creek and the

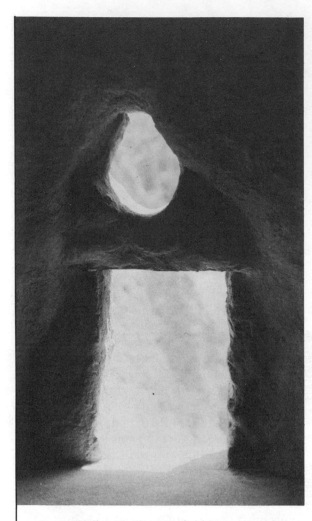

Puye Cliffs, *Phyllis Mayfield Knox.*

Bandelier parking lot. Yapashi is a Keresan word for "place of the sacred enclosure." Here two catlike stone animals are surrounded by a circle of rocks. Worshippers from Cochiti and San Felipe still come to this spot to sprinkle cornmeal on the stone lions, paint the animals' noses red, and place deer antlers between them. This is probably part of an ancient hunting ritual.

Tsankawi, an interesting ruin in a detached section of Bandelier, is also worth

a visit. It is located about eleven miles north of Bandelier's main entrance on N.M. 4. Signs mark the site. Much of Tsankawi, an extensive ruin, is still unexcavated. However, there is a self-guiding tour leading in a circular route through the prehistoric village. The path visitors follow is in many places the original trail; centuries of treading feet have worn smooth ruts in the path. There are petroglyphs along the way, and caves used by the Tewa-speaking dwellers can be seen. The two-mile round trip along the mesa top is rough in spots; in some places ladders are necessary. Most visitors find that spectacular views in all directions make the trek worthwhile.

Hikers will enjoy many trails within the confines of Bandelier. Most radiate out from the visitors' center, where those who plan to camp in areas other than Juniper and Ponderosa campgrounds can obtain permits. Hikers should heed warnings about carrying water and wearing proper clothing. It is also suggested that campers check with Park Service guides as to the state of remote trails. Books and maps, available inside the visitors' center, include information not only about trails but also about the abundant wildlife and flora in the monument.

Those who visit Bandelier will see scars from a major forest fire that occurred in June 1977. Thousands of acres of woods were destroyed during the inferno. As a result of the loss of plant life, some erosion along steep cliffs and mesa sides has taken place. The Forest Service has closed certain areas where reseeding efforts have been started. One of the most noticeable areas of fire destruction can be seen along the road between the Bandelier entrance and the junction with Business Loop 4. Miles of charred Ponderosa pine line the road. In some places the fire leaped over the highway and crept close to the fence surrounding Los Alamos Labs. No structures were damaged, however.

Bandelier Caves, *Harvey Caplin*.

SIDE TOUR

Back at the Y formed by the separation of N.M. 4, Business Loop 4 climbs up the Pajarito Plateau, winding above the narrow canyons. A turnout appears shortly after the Y. This is a scenic view area, with vistas across to the Sangre de Cristo range. Looking down, a visitor can see a patch of green, the site of Otowi Ruins, a large, abandoned pueblo that was once many-storied, similar to the apartment-like dwellings at Taos Pueblo. With the exception of one detached house, Otowi consisted of a cluster of five houses containing four hundred fifty rooms on the ground floor and an estimated two hundred fifty rooms on the second story. It was deserted prior to A.D. 1300. Archaeologists have also discovered subterranean kivas and cliffdwellings at Otowi.

When Los Alamos was a secret city, all its perimeters were guarded, either by men on horseback or by watchtowers. A uniformed patrol manned the community's eastern entrance twenty-four hours a day. Anyone wishing to enter the town was required to present a badge. The watchtower and gate have not been used for decades now, but their remnants still stand below the city, reminders of the days when the settlement was a federal encampment. Los Alamos Airport appears on the right beyond the old gate. Its runway seems to end at the edge of the plateau, sending small planes off the precipice. The airport signals the beginning of Los Alamos proper.

Los Alamos ("poplar" or "cottonwood trees"), 18 mi. (alt. 7,173, pop. 11,038), is both a city and a county, carved from surrounding

Sandoval and Santa Fe counties in 1949. Its inhabitants are involved almost exclusively in work for Los Alamos Scientific Laboratories and related support enterprises. Churches are plentiful, schools are among the best in New Mexico, and slowly the ambience of Los Alamos is changing from its army-barracks beginnings to that of a well-educated, middle-class, small city set down on a spectacular mesa with mountains and pine trees out the back door and the Sangre de Cristos visible through the front window.

Los Alamos began its days as a ranch school, the fulfilled dream of Ashley Pond, a wealthy Detroit man who believed that hardy outdoor activity was the best education for adolescent boys. Pond attempted his first ranch school in the eastern part of New Mexico, near Watrous, in 1904, but a flood wiped out the school and his dream. In 1918, after establishing a dude ranch on the Pajarito Plateau, Pond created the Los Alamos Ranch School. Young men from all over the country came there to live in log cabins, to spend their waking hours studying the classics and doing ranch chores, and to ride horseback through the Jemez Mountains on weekends. The first mounted Boy Scout troop, Troop 22, was formed at the ranch school. School uniforms—short pants, neckerchiefs, knee socks—were based on the Boy Scout outfit. Troop 22 is still an active scout troop in Los Alamos today.

Like most private schools, Los Alamos Ranch School had its ups and downs, but it continued to grow, serving young men who seemed to thrive on Pond's dictum of hard work and an outdoor life. Many of its graduates later went on to successful leadership positions in the fields of government, business, and literature. In 1941, when Pearl Harbor signaled a change for most young American men, the enrollment of the school was at its peak, but 1942 was the final year for the Los Alamos Ranch School. A decision had been made in Washington, D.C., that would have a lasting effect on the little school tucked into the mesa. With war casualties in Europe and the Pacific mounting, scientists and intelligence experts were convinced that they needed to produce a bomb to end the war. Once the Manhattan Project had been conceived and declared a high priority by President Franklin Roosevelt, it became clear that the creation of an atomic bomb in record time would necessitate the founding of a laboratory at which the brightest minds in nuclear research could work together in utmost secrecy.

General Leslie Groves became chief of the Manhattan Project. He tapped Robert Oppenheimer to head the research team. The laboratory's location was crucial: it had to be in a remote place, hundreds of miles from either of the coasts and from any international border. Many western locations were studied, and soon the search centered on New Mexico. Areas near Gallup, Las Vegas, and Cuba were quickly discarded, and Groves and Oppenheimer narrowed the choice to the Jemez valley and the Los Alamos area.

In the fall of 1942, the two men drove through the Jemez valley to the town of Jemez Springs. In many ways the little village was a good site: it was remote, yet close enough to Albuquerque for easy transportation, and there were already buildings that could be used for labs. However, its narrowness and susceptibility to flooding quickly ruled it out. The car bearing the general and the scientist team then headed up through the Jemez Mountains, past that immense volcanic masterpiece, the Valle Grande (see page 50), and down onto the Pajarito Plateau, home of the Los Alamos Ranch School and an area Oppenheimer had visited many times from his nearby vacation home.

Oppenheimer and Groves were impressed by the mesa. They could envision the addition of a few laboratory buildings to the log structures already there. Water seemed sufficient, and the site was isolated and easily protected from outsiders. A road, albeit a steep and dangerous one, wound down the mesa to Santa Fe. Later that fall, the Ranch School was given notice that its property was needed for military purposes. By February 1943 the school had closed, its final graduation ceremony held the previous month. The Los Alamos Scientific Laboratories opened formally on April 15, 1943.

Neither Oppenheimer nor Groves anticipated the growth that the Manhattan Project would soon cause on "The Hill." WACS and other military personnel joined hundreds of scientists, technicians, and their families. Workers constructed temporary barracks and laboratories, but the need for larger quarters, both for housing and for scientific research, continued. Throughout the more than two years of intense work that went into developing the bomb, the logistics of hiring, housing, and handling the thousands who eventually arrived—always in secret—was almost overwhelming.

Few who came even knew where they were going—only that they were bound for New Mexico, with instructions to check in at an office at 109 Palace Avenue, Santa Fe. Some came by car through Albuquerque; others got off the train at Lamy, a semi–ghost town south of Santa Fe. The trip through the high desert was shocking enough for the scientists and their families who were used to the green of their university campuses, but the greatest shock was still to come. The drive up the tortuous road from the Rio Grande valley to Los Alamos was worse. And then, at the top of the mesa, spread out in army-camp style along streets that were dusty or muddy, depending on the season, were the wooden barracks, log cabins, and prefabricated apartment houses that were to be their homes. However, most families adjusted well to the rigorous work schedules and shortages on the hill. Schools were organized and a hospital appeared (although the story goes that General Groves was appalled at the possibility that babies might be born and that preparations should be made for their arrival). Families enjoyed hiking and camping in the surrounding mountains, and they formed close friendships with each other as they were forced to share meager water and grocery supplies. Young, unattached scientists took on babysitting chores at night. While most of the scientists were men, their wives were soon called upon to contribute their own skills in the laboratories and classrooms. Visits outside Los Alamos were rare, but trips to the nearby pueblos for ceremonies and shopping excursions to Santa Fe gave the newcomers a chance to taste some of the area's flavor.

Work on the project, never revealed even to spouses or families, was carried on by established scientists and bright graduate students. Their research raced ahead while the pressure of the war tightened the heavy security and work schedules. By the summer of 1945, it had become clear to Oppenheimer and his team that "Fat Man," as the scientists had nicknamed the two-billion-dollar bomb, would

Modern Petroglyph, Los Alamos, *Betty Lilienthal.*

soon be ready for its final test. In July, under close security, the bomb was transported down the hill and south to the testing grounds sixty miles from Alamogordo. Trinity Site saw the first explosion of the atomic bomb on July 16, 1945. A month later, Hiroshima, Japan, across the world from Los Alamos, was flattened by "Fat Man's" brother. The Manhattan Project was a success.

The years after Hiroshima were a period of transition for Los Alamos. The big names—Robert Oppenheimer, Hans Bethe, Enrico Fermi, Niels Bohr—left. The laboratories remained in the weapons business, mainly as a research facility, continuing to operate under a contract with the University of California. Today the mesas are filled with permanent concrete laboratories that have replaced the wartime structures. Large office and administrative complexes have sprung up to serve the needs of a scientific community numbering in the thousands.

Los Alamos has changed considerably from the days when the army ran the town, when letters were opened and censored, when security badges of different colors permitted entry to specific areas. The town's water and power until recently came from the U.S. Department of Energy, but most other services are provided by the city or county. The labs and related facilities are the area's largest employer, but the population is more diverse than it was during the war years. As Los Alamos was placed in private hands, even the local archi-

tecture took on a more varied look, although the gray of government issue still seems to predominate.

Within the confines of Los Alamos are a number of interesting places to visit. Business Loop 4 runs past the district where food stores, motels, and other small-town services are located. Ashley Pond, named after the founder of the Ranch School, still retains its prominent place in the community. Fuller Lodge, an imposing three-story log building, sits behind the pond; designed by New Mexico architect John Gaw Meem, it is the home now of the local chamber of commerce, an art museum, and a community hall. The great hall soars to immense hand-carved beams nineteen feet above the floor.

Behind Fuller Lodge, in a smaller log building, is the home of the Los Alamos Historical Society. Its museum, an informal little repository of the human history of the mesa, includes exhibits on the Ranch School and the early days of the labs. The society also runs a small bookstore specializing in the history of the region. Narrow roads behind Fuller Lodge lead to other old log buildings, all of which formed the nucleus of the Ranch School. Those behind the lodge are now private residences. Other residential areas have grown out along the fingers of the mesas, connected to each other by roads and a series of bridges.

Those interested in the more scientific aspects of Los Alamos history may visit the Bradbury Science Hall and Museum, named

Valle Grande, *Harvey Caplin*.

after Norris Bradbury, one of the original scientists at Los Alamos and successor to Oppenheimer as director of the science labs. Signs along N.M. 4 indicate the location of the museum, which contains exhibits focusing on the atom and discoveries and research related to it.

About four miles beyond the last obvious Los Alamos Lab buildings, as the pines become thicker and the road less traveled by gray government cars, Business Loop 4 and Truck Route 4 merge. The Jemez Mountains are ahead. N.M. 4 becomes steep, twisting and straining through hairpin curves up and off the Pajarito Plateau and into Ponderosa forests, alpine meadows, and hidden campsites. After about six miles of climbing, forest roads begin to appear. These dirt tracks lead into the woods, and in many places cross the spine of the plateau and descend to the Rio Grande or to ghost towns and campgrounds. Check weather and road conditions before venturing onto these narrow paths.

After the boundaries of Bandelier National Monument and heavily forested areas have been passed, a green, open valley appears. This is the Valle Grande, sometimes called the

Baca Location, once considered the world's largest volcano but now believed to be part of a large caldera, a basin formed during volcanic activity in the Pleistocene Period. It was activity from the volcano that formed the Pajarito Plateau. Scientists theorize that the large mountain that finally collapsed to form the valley was probably over fourteen thousand feet high. Its basin, now a grazing area, has long been the center of a large cattle ranch. Hundreds of cross-country skiers also have enjoyed its vastness and its undisturbed trails. Access to the Valle Grande, which the federal government is presently negotiating to purchase, will be marked with signs. The Valle Grande is not always open to the general public. In fact, although much of this area appears to be open public land, many parcels of private property are located here. Travelers should heed the "No Trespassing" signs.

Camping, fishing, hiking, and cross-country skiing are favorite activities in the Jemez. A number of large campgrounds, some with trailer hookups, are located along the road. Hiking trails intersect the highway and are well-marked. Shortly after passing one of the largest camping areas, Redondo, N.M. 4 dips down off the mountain and into the steep canyon of the Jemez River. N.M. 4 meets N.M. 126 here and then leads south through Jemez Canyon to the town of Jemez Springs and to Jemez Pueblo. (See Tour 9.)

Those who wish to continue on N.M. 126 to Fenton Lake and Cuba will climb out of the area known as La Cueva, passing the San Antonio Campground (with access for the handicapped). About two miles beyond San Antonio are two dirt roads, each leading into the forest. The one on the south goes to Gilman and Cañon, while the road to the north climbs up the mountain, terminating five miles later at the Valle del San Antonio. Cross-country skiers enjoy the trek to the valley and the old YCC camp at the road's end.

N.M. 126 rises to the top of Fenton Hill, site of a hot-rock geothermal project sponsored by the federal government and operated by Los Alamos Labs. Other spots in the Jemez have also been tapped as possible sources of geothermal energy.

A few miles down the road the pavement ends. Fenton Lake, a popular fishing hole for New Mexicans, is about three miles farther. Fenton Lake has seen wilder days: during Prohibition, a local lodge defied the liquor laws and drew revelers from miles around. Today campers and fishermen quietly line the shores of the little lake.

N.M. 126 now climbs up and over the Jemez Mountains into the Nacimiento ("nativity") Range. Numerous campgrounds and hiking trails wander off the road. Trails and campsites are well-marked. Gregorio Lake and San Pedro Parks Wilderness Area can be reached by following signs that direct the traveler off N.M. 126 to smaller forest roads. Camping, hunting, and fishing in this section of the mountains are excellent and compara-

Winter Backpacking, *S. Humphries, Jr.*

tively uncrowded. However, the Nacimientos tend to receive more rain than the mountains to the east, so travelers should check road conditions and weather reports before heading into the rough terrain. The town of Cuba sits at the base of the Nacimientos, at the end of about forty miles of rough, often impassable dirt road beyond Fenton Lake. (See Tour 9 for the Cuba area.)

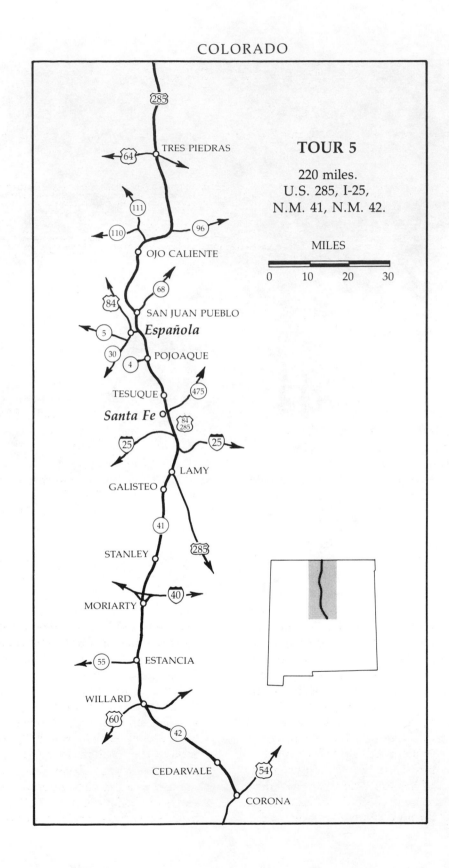

TOUR 5

220 miles.
U.S. 285, I-25,
N.M. 41, N.M. 42.

MILES

tour five

Colorado Border • **Tres Piedras** • **Ojo Caliente** • *Española* • *Santa Fe* • **Moriarty** • *Corona*

Tour 5, from the Colorado border south of Antonito to Corona, 220 miles away, can be a remarkable journey. Its first leg roughly parallels the path of a defunct branch of the Denver and Rio Grande Western Railroad (D&RGWR), which had grandiose plans in 1870 to connect Denver, Colorado, with El Paso, Texas, and with Mexico. The narrow-gauge railroad reached Santa Fe in 1881, but never went farther south. The first portion of the trip also follows the approximate route taken in 1778–79 by Governor Juan Bautista de Anza in his campaign against the Apache chief Cuerno Verde (Green Horn). South of Santa Fe, N.M. 41/N.M. 42 traces the path of the abandoned roadbed of the New Mexico Central Railroad, built in the early part of this century.

The modern trip on U.S. 285 begins on the high, lonely plains west of the Rio Grande and continues southward to Española, where a side trip to Santa Clara Pueblo and Puye Cliff Dwellings is included. After Española, the tour goes on to Santa Fe. It then leaves the congestion of the Rio Grande valley and the capital city to bear south on N.M. 41 near Lamy, passing through remote grazing land,

hardly touching a populated settlement on its southward trek. Tour 5 crosses I-40 at Moriarty, sweeps past Willard, and ends in Corona.

When the first edition of *New Mexico: A Guide to the Colorful State,* was published in 1940, it included a tour on the D&RGWR from Antonito, Colorado, to Santa Fe. Today's travelers might enjoy a recollection of that train ride as they journey down the highway. It gives a glimpse of what progress has taken from us.

> The trip on the old narrow-gauge railroad . . . is such an interesting trip and has such an old world flavor, besides affording magnificent views not possible from any of the highways in the State, that it is a tour worth taking. It is a funny sort of a road and New Mexicans poke fun at it, although they feel an affection for it, because it is part of the New Mexican scene and gives such fine, surprising views of the landscape. . . . The trip from Santa Fe, especially on up-

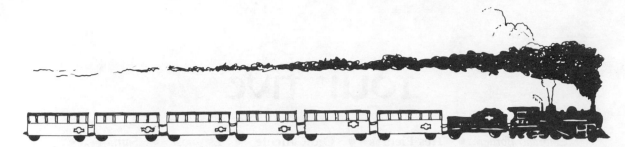

grades, is leisurely enough to give the illusion of walking through fields of grasses and wild flowers, and this is heightened by growth right up to the tracks. . . . The trip is made in daylight, but in winter it is often dark by the time of arrival at either terminus. Small coal stoves at each end of the coach furnish adequate heat. There is but one coach in regular service, the rest of the train being made up of freight and baggage or express cars. . . . It takes about seven hours for the trip from Santa Fe to Antonito. There is water on the train, but lunch should be taken. Members of the train crew speak English, but Spanish is used by a majority of the passengers. Mothers nurse their babies. . . . When migratory workers from New Mexico go to Colorado sugar-beet fields or the pea-picking plants . . . the coach is crowded. (pages 412–13)

Today the trip begins just south of Antonito, Colorado, now the eastern terminus of the Cumbres and Toltec Railroad (Tour 7). The area between the Colorado line and the New Mexico village of Tres Piedras twenty-five miles away is largely unpopulated. To the east, the view across the high Rio Grande plateau to the Sangre de Cristos is spectacular. To the west, in the Carson National Forest, the Brazos Range, a finger of the southern Rocky Mountains, extends southward. San Antonio Peak, also called Keping ("bear mountain" in the Tewa language), a significant point on the Pueblo compass, rises to 10,908 feet. It is a volcanic dome whose summit can be reached via a jutted jeep road.

The name of TRES PIEDRAS ("three rocks"), 28 mi., reflects the community's setting at the base of three granite hills. Its hunting past is remembered in its Tewa name, literally "mountain sheep rock place." The Taos Indians have crossed the Rio Grande to hunt antelope and rabbits at Tres Piedras for generations. Although the antelope herds are depleted now, the region is still a favored hunting ground for many New Mexicans. Primarily a ranching and lumber settlement, Tres Piedras was founded in 1879. It is little more than a small village offering basic services to the travelers and hunters who pass through it.

At the junction with U.S. 64 in Tres Piedras, travelers can turn east to the Rio Grande Gorge Bridge (Tour 2) and Taos (Tour 3) or west through the heart of the Brazos Range to Tierra Amarilla (Tours 2 and 7). U.S. 64 west of Tres Piedras is often closed during the winter.

Crossing the tree-studded high plains between Tres Piedras and Ojo Caliente, the traveler will see barely a remnant of the old D&RGWR railroad stations at Servilleta ("napkin") and Taos Junction. At that junction, about twenty miles south of Tres Piedras, rail travelers to Taos once debarked and crossed the plateau on N.M. 96 by motorcar, plunging down into the Rio Grande canyon and crossing the river at the present site of Rio Grande Gorge State Park (Tour 11). Taos Junction was, in the early days of the century, the closest train station to Taos. It is still possible to cross over to Taos via N.M. 96, a gravel road that passes through high, unpopulated desert, dropping down to the river with hairpin turns and rocky curves. N.M. 96 meets N.M. 68 at Pilar (Tour 11).

OJO CALIENTE ("hot springs"), 59 mi., sits along the Vallecitos River and has been a health resort for untold centuries. It is also a significant place in Tewa Pueblo myth and tradition, the site certainly of at least three pre-

Confluence of Rio Chama and Rio Grande, *Betty Lilienthal*.

historic pueblos whose ruins crumble on the mesas above town.

According to Tewa stories, Poseyemu, a mythical hero, sprang to life at Posi-owinge (Ojo Caliente) from piñon nuts (a traditional Pueblo symbol for fertility) gathered by a young virgin. He was given his name by the sun, became a fearless hunter and chief, and brought good fortune to his people. When he left, the pueblo was abandoned. It is said that Poseyemu returns to earth either every five to seven years (the cycle of the piñon crops) or every year to visit his grandmother, who lives in the green, curative waters at the spring.

The Pueblos found Ojo Caliente's mineral springs healing; so did the Comanches, Utes,

and Apaches, who thwarted early Hispanic colonizing efforts here for years. However, it is possible that the Spanish settled the area before the 1680 Pueblo Revolt. By 1735, settlers were arguing over land titles, but in 1748 residents of Ojo Caliente, along with their neighbors in Abiquiu, successfully petitioned the governor to let them abandon their village. They cited repeated Indian raids as their reason for leaving the valley. A few years later, a new governor ordered the residents to return to their farms, fining those who disobeyed. Some went back, building a defensive wall around the community. Raiders could still attack from above, however.

In 1790, José Manuel Velarde and eighteen

families asked Governor De La Concha for permission to move north from Bernalillo to the little valley. The governor agreed, insisting that adequate fortifications be made.

Zebulon Pike, arrested by the Spanish in 1807 for trespassing near Taos, was brought through Ojo Caliente. He was impressed by the warm climate, the modest brown houses hugging each other with their fortifications, the mixed Hispanic and Indian population, and, of course, the warm springs.

There are five springs in Ojo Caliente. They are located across the bridge from town. A resort has grown up around the pools where water containing arsenic, lithia, iron, and sodium bubbles forth at 48 to 113 degrees. The resort is open all year, and New Mexicans from throughout the state often make annual pilgrimages to the healing waters. Overnight accommodations at the springs or within the village are simple but adequate. Bathers can also visit by the day.

There are a number of interesting structures in Ojo Caliente: a small, restored chapel, an immense circular barn just outside town, and a row of grand adobe farmhouses sitting beneath U.S. 285 along its path south to Española.

U.S. 285 between here and Española is heavily traveled and winding. Because roads in this part of the Española Valley are numerous and confusing, travelers should watch carefully for directional signs. Fortunately, the valley is not big enough for the traveler to become truly lost.

Just north of Española, 77 mi. (see Tour 11), U.S. 285 crosses the Rio Grande near San Juan Pueblo and links up with N.M. 68. Those planning to continue Tour 5 without pausing in Española or taking the side trip to Santa Clara Pueblo and Puye Cliff Dwellings may wish to cross the river here. It is also possible to stay on the main road, which passes through the heart of Española, crossing the Rio Grande near the town's center to meet the highway to Santa Fe (U.S. 285/U.S. 84). To reach Santa Clara Pueblo and the cliff dwellings, travelers should stay on the west side of the river, watching for N.M. 30/N.M. 5 heading south.

SIDE TOUR

SANTA CLARA PUEBLO, 90 mi., is a Tewa-speaking pueblo long situated in this favored valley between the Rio Grande and Pajarito Plateau. Its population of over twelve hundred has grown considerably since the early part of this century. The pueblo traces its beginning north to Colorado where, it is said, the Tewa emerged from a lake, pausing to live at Ojo Caliente and Pecos before settling down in this spot. The pueblo was located at its present site when Coronado's expedition passed through in 1540–41. Missionaries established a church at Santa Clara between 1622 and 1629, and, after the 1680 revolt, re-established their missionary seat here.

Like the other Tewa pueblos, Santa Clara is divided into Winter and Summer groups, or moieties. Each group takes a turn at directing ceremonial activities, and, historically, religious and secular events. However, beginning in the late nineteenth century, factions within the two groups appeared, the "progressives" of each moiety objecting to the undemocratic manner in which ceremonial and work activities were decided upon. In 1894 a thirty-year schism began. Since the Summer moiety was then in possession of the ceremonial canes and thus was the ruling group at the time, the Winter moiety objected. The situation remained unchanged well into the twentieth century.

In the mid-1930s, the two factions met with the Indian service to resolve the dispute. Both accompanied by government advisers and lawyers, Winter and Summer drew up a constitution that separated reli-

gious and secular activities, providing for voluntary participation in ceremonies. Village officials, who perform both judicial and legislative functions, are now elected. Those pueblo members who guide the spiritual life of the community are called the Made People; they are like priests, and they involve themselves very little in the day-to-day workings of the pueblo.

With over forty thousand acres of farm, forest, and range land, Santa Clara has traditionally been a self-sustaining pueblo. Members have long farmed their irrigated fields along the Rio Grande, complementing indigenous crops of corn, squash, tobacco, and cotton with plants introduced by the Spanish. Farming, a communal activity, was in the past augmented by fishing with sharp sticks and yucca nets, hunting for birds, bears, and mountain sheep, and the gathering of native plants. Today, Santa Clarans work in Los Alamos, Española, and Santa Fe. They lease some of their timberlands, communal properties, and pumice deposits to outside firms. They also manage Puye Cliff Dwellings, and they have constructed a lovely campground in Santa Clara Canyon. Although few craftsmen earn a full-time living making the Pueblo's famous black incised pottery, a number of residents derive good incomes from the age-old craft, now increasingly popular in markets both local and distant. Santa Clara's painters are also famous. Pablita Velarde and her daughter Helen Hardin depict the Santa Clara life of two generations with careful, colorful, and detailed paintings.

The Pueblo celebrates its feast day on August 12 with dancing and ceremonies. Visitors are welcome to enjoy the festivities. Other religious events are marked throughout the year; some are closed to the public.

Both Puye Cliff Dwellings and Santa Clara Canyon are within the boundaries of the Santa Clara Reservation. They are located off N.M. 30 on N.M. 5 about four miles south of Española. A well-maintained road, N.M. 5 runs between piñon-dotted hills and eroded cliffs, climbing steeply to the top of Pajarito Plateau, where the vegetation thins to brush and desert grass. Ahead are the Jemez Mountains. The road continues amid tall pines to the turnoff to the Puye ruins at seven miles. Here one pays an entrance fee, either parking at the lot at the bottom of the cliffs or following a dirt road around the mesa to its top.

Puye is one of the most extensive of the cliff villages. Its site on the plateau gives it a commanding position and makes a visit there doubly impressive. Puye was the first of the Rio Grande ruins to be systematically excavated, but it was never made a national monument, having always remained under the control of Santa Clara Pueblo.

The ancient pueblo was built between 1450 and 1475, although the cliff rooms above it date from the 1200s. By 1540 its population was at its height, and Puye was the center for a number of villages built in the northern section of the Pajarito Plateau. Puye typifies Pajaritan culture in the placement of its houses and its symbolic decorations, kivas, pictographs, utensils, and red pottery, glazed in a way that shows a high development of the art. Many of the designs focus on a plumed serpent figure who guarded the springs which provided lifegiving water. Across the water jars and food bowls, a great band represented the sky path of the serpent.

There are two types of houses at Puye: cliffdwellings and the houses on the

Ruins, *Ferdinand Joesten.*

SIDE TOUR

mesa. The cliffdwellings extend along the cliff edge for more than a mile; not all of them are open for exploration. Some of the dwellings are simple caves, while others have porches or open rooms attached. A third kind of structure is the stone house, one to three stories high, built against the cliff, which is broken by a ledge wide enough for building and walking. Sturdy ladders and steps cut out of the rock provide the means of getting from one level to another and up to the top of the mesa. Visitors are encouraged to clamber in and out of the dwellings and to use the ladders and footholds to explore the living arrangements of these highly developed people.

The pueblo, a quadrangle on the mesa top, was an arrangement of four huge, terraced community houses built around a court. It is presumed that the village was designed to take advantage of the plateau's strategic location. The outside rooms in each group are noticeably small and could have been used for storing grain. All the rooms were connected by small doorways whose sills were inches above the ground. Little holes cut into the sills provided ventilation and were plugged when air was not needed. For worship Puye dwellers constructed kivas on the cliff's edge, along its base, and on the ledge halfway to the top.

Each August in the great courtyard Santa Clara Pueblo holds Puye ceremonial dances. The ruins are closed in winter.

Those wishing to continue Tour 5 to Santa Fe and points south will retrace their path back to Española on N.M. 30/N.M. 5. Cross the Rio Grande at Española and turn south on U.S. 84/U.S. 285, which takes the traveler to the edge of Santa Fe. Once on the northern outskirts of the city, inquire for directions to Old Pecos Trail going south. (For information about the twenty-five miles between Española and Santa Fe, see Tour 11.)

It should also be noted that visitors to Santa Clara Pueblo and the Puye Cliff Dwellings can continue south on N.M. 30 to N.M. 4, a distance of about five miles. Tour 4 to Bandelier Monument and Los Alamos can be picked up there.

Leaving Santa Fe and Tour 11, the traveler proceeds south on Old Pecos Trail to the entry to I-25 east. Six miles east on I-25, U.S. 285 heads southeast across the plains to Roswell. Eight miles south of the freeway, just past the turnoff to Lamy, N.M. 41 parts company with U.S. 285. The first stop on N.M. 41, GALISTEO, 128 mi., is a tiny farming village in a stock-raising area. Like a number of other towns in northern New Mexico, it has become fashionable as a peaceful hideaway for well-heeled Anglo-Americans. The town boasts vistas of the Sangre de Cristo Mountains to the north and of the piñon- and juniper-covered hills surrounding it. An old bar–general store in the center of the village serves as a repository of artifacts from Indian and Spanish colonial times.

The Galisteo Valley contains many pueblo ruins. Five of these pueblos were occupied when the Spanish came, the best-known being Galisteo Pueblo, one and one-half miles above the present village. First called San Lucas by Castaño de Sosa in 1591, it was renamed Santa Ana by Oñate seven years later. Indians from Galisteo Pueblo killed local missionary priests during the early days of the Pueblo Revolt in 1680 and established themselves in Santa Fe with their co-conspirators. After de Vargas's reconquest, the former residents of Galisteo were dispersed among the other pueblos. Re-established by Governor Cuervo y Valdez in 1706 as Santa Maria, the pueblo was deserted for the last time in 1794, its inhabitants the victims of smallpox and Comanche raids.

Leaving Galisteo, the road meanders up and down low hills covered with piñons. Fences and an occasional group of cattle are almost the sole proprietors of the magnificent views of the Ortiz and South mountains to the west and the high plains to the east.

Continuing, the road enters the broad Estancia Valley, for hundreds of years a source of salt for New Mexico's Indians and for Spanish colonists many miles away in Mexico. The salt lakes, shallow or dry, depending on rainfall, are all that remain of an eighty-three-mile-long body of water, called Lake Estancia by archaeologists, that existed in prehistoric times. Many campsites used by ancient people have been found on the shores of this lake, surrounded by the graveyards of bison, mammoths, and mastodons killed by their spears.

In the late nineteenth and early twentieth centuries the valley became important as a site of dry land farming, especially of pinto beans. Towns like Stanley, Moriarty, McIntosh, Estancia, and Willard grew as trading centers, only to shrivel again as the changes of the 1930s and 1940s led much of the population to look elsewhere for a livelihood. Only large ranchers who could afford deep wells and irrigation remained, and many fields are fallow, grazed by the few cattle that the dry range can support.

STANLEY (145 mi.), which at its peak had two hotels, numerous business establishments, a depot on the New Mexico Central Railroad, and its own newspaper, is now a town of abandoned, decaying buildings and a single general store. The large ranch of the important King family (Bruce King was twice New Mexico's governor) lies nearby.

MORIARTY (156 mi.), just south of the crossing of I-40 (Tour 6), also almost became a ghost town, but was revived largely by its position as a provider of tourist services on first the cross-country highway U.S. 66 and now the interstate highway. Its historical museum

is described in Tour 6. Moriarty also is the home town of a New Mexico governor, Toney Anaya.

ESTANCIA (172 mi.) is the seat of Torrance County and the site of consolidated schools to which most of the children from surrounding communities in the Estancia Valley and in the foothills of the Manzanos to the west are bussed. Several of the older brick and adobe buildings along the main street have been restored, and the short main street is busy on Saturday afternoons, but the town has a sleepy air. It was not always so; in the 1920s and 1930s it was a growing, thriving place, based on the warehousing and shipping of pinto beans.

Shortly before the Mexican War in 1846, the Mexican governor, Armijo, granted Antonio Sandoval four hundred fifteen thousand acres centered on what was to become Estancia. A prominent family from Los Lunas, the Oteros, claimed to have been granted a large portion of the same tract and ran sheep on their claim. Heirs of Sandoval, meanwhile, sold their rights to the Estancia grant to a Boston millionaire. In 1883, James Whitney, who represented the Bostonian, and Manuel Otero of Los Lunas held a celebrated meeting. Accounts of the encounter vary, but according to chronicler Frank M. King,

> Whitney and his men came up and took charge of the Otero property while Don Manuel was away. When he returned, he asked Whitney by what authority he was there. Whitney was seated beside a table in the room and near him was his pistol. He took it up, saying, "By this authority," and fired. The narrator of the story said he didn't remember who fired first, but that 'there was plenty of shooting.' Otero was killed and Whitney had his right jaw shot away. In addition he had two slugs in his body. Another man was killed and two were slightly wounded. According to one version, Whitney was placed in a light wagon and a team of mules were secured, then driven as rapidly as possible to Santa Fe, where he was kept in hiding in a house now owned by Judge Holloman. There he was apprehended and sent to Las Lunas by special train. At the trial that resulted he was acquitted.

After the smoke cleared, a court of private claims determined that neither claim was valid, opening the huge tract of land to homesteading and to the tracks of the New Mexico Central Railroad.

N.M. 41 then follows a section line due south to its intersection with U.S. 60 at 183 mi., which it accompanies 1.5 mi. east to Willard.

When work on the Belen Cutoff of the Santa Fe Railroad progressed up through Abo Pass and headed across the plains toward Amarillo in 1903, WILLARD, 184 mi. was already a station on the New Mexico Central. It took its name from Willard Hopewell, son of a railroad builder. The new town soon became the commercial and farming center of the southern

Willard Bank, *Jeanne House.*

end of the Estancia Valley. Two mercantile companies vied for the trade of the region. The winner of that contest, the Charles Ilfeld Company, went on to expand up and down the tracks and eventually gained quite a large share of the state's wholesale business. What remains of the scene of that activity lies a block south of the present U.S. 60. The spire of the Deo Vero Church, dating from 1912, is Willard's landmark, and is located two blocks north of the highway. Crossing the Santa Fe tracks on the southwest edge of town, N.M. 41 (unpaved and mostly unmarked) continues south across the Juames Mesa. The adventuresome traveler should inquire locally about this alternate route to Gran Quivira. Tour 8 describes U.S. 60, Willard's main street, from the Texas to the Arizona border.

On the east side of Willard, N.M. 42 heads southeast towards Corona. To the northeast the remains of an inland sea, the geologic ancestor to the landlocked Estancia Valley, are visible from the road. These are the "white sands" that become salt lakes when rainfall has been plentiful. Salt from these beds was a trade staple of the Saline Pueblos. During the

Engine, *Ferdinand Joesten.*

seventeenth century, burros carried the salt seven hundred miles to southern Chihuahua silver mines for use in smelting the ore. Paralleling the road to the southwest are the steep sides of the Juames Mesa, its name a variant of Jumanos, or Humanos, the people of Gran Quivira (see Tour 15). This mesa marks the division between the Estancia Valley and the beginnings of the Tularosa Valley to the south. Pueblo Blanco, one of the more remote of the eleven Saline pueblos enumerated by sixteenth-century explorers, once commanded the view from the northwest corner of the mesa.

In 1903, PROGRESSO (195 mi.) became the first county seat of the newly created Torrance County, a passenger car of the New Mexico Central serving as the courthouse. Only a few ranch houses remain of this once-prosperous dry-farming community. The size of the school in CEDARVALE (208 mi.) gives an idea of the number of people that nearby farms and ranches supported at one time. Nine miles northeast of Cedarvale, PINOS WELLS, named for the nearby artesian wells, now consists of a cluster of families who still maintain the Church of San José. With the exception of Santa Fe; it is older than any town on this tour. Because water was available, Pinos Wells served as a stop between Anton Chico and White Oaks on the Las Vegas stage route.

For the first forty years of this century, Pinos Wells, Cedarvale, Corona, Progresso, and towns west across the mesa to Gran Quivira and north as far as Stanley prospered with dry farming of corn and pinto beans, dairying, and livestock raising. As a former resident describes it, when the Depression hit, these products could be sold for very little money, if at all, but farm families still ate well. However, the ranges became overstocked, and when the four-year drought began in 1934, sheep and cattle began dying like flies. In the late 1930s, with no other options evident to them, many residents began migrating to California for war-related jobs. By 1942, with the draft and with war work plentiful at new military installations in New Mexico, migration from areas such as these became an exodus.

Just as soon as the war was over, however, land prices went up, making a return to the old way of life nearly impossible for many who might have wished it. The era of large ranches, begun then, continues today.

At 211 mi., the abandoned New Mexico Central roadbed heads east to Torrance, while the highway begins to climb across a ridge of the Gallinas Mountains into Corona (Tour 6).

A normally well-graded, but unpaved, road goes to Gran Quivira, one of the Saline Pueblos, at 214 mi.

At 220 mi., the tour ends at the intersection with U.S. 54 at Corona. (See Tour 13.)

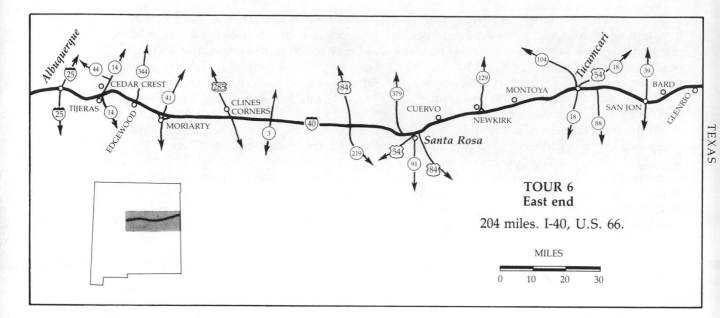

**TOUR 6
East end**

204 miles. I-40, U.S. 66.

MILES

0   10   20   30

See page 384 for western half of tour six.

tour six

Texas Border • **Glenrio** • **Tucumcari** • **Santa Rosa** • *Albuquerque* • **Grants** • **Gallup** • *Arizona Border*

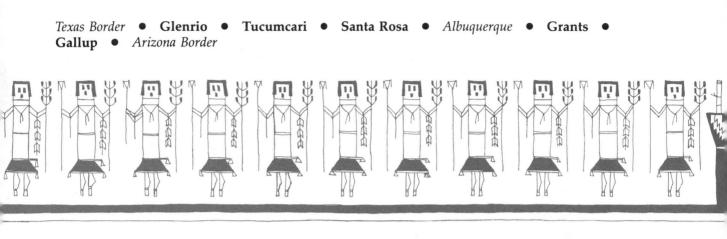

U.S. 66, famous as a route to California during the Dust Bowl and Depression days, subject of a television series, and somehow capturing the essence of what the Southwest is supposed to be like, actually came relatively late as a transcontinental highway. When the road was mapped out from Chicago to Los Angeles (via Saint Louis, Joplin, Tulsa, Oklahoma City, Amarillo, Albuquerque, Flagstaff, and Barstow) in the 1930s, U.S. 60 had preceded it across the nation and across New Mexico by a generation. The routing of I-40 west of Oklahoma City confirmed that U.S. 66 had become by the 1960s the major highway of the mountain Southwest.

U.S. 66 followed the Chicago, Rock Island, and Pacific Railroad to Santa Rosa. For the 160 miles between Santa Rosa and Laguna, the highway paralleled no railroad right of way. West of Laguna and on to Los Angeles it followed the Santa Fe Railroad tracks. I-40 enters New Mexico on the Llano Estacado or Staked Plains, usually called the high plains or the *llano*, skirts the plains' ragged edges, and crosses the Pecos River before climbing to high ground near the southern end of the Sangre de Cristo range. At Albuquerque it crosses the Rio Grande and then climbs again to the mountains and plateaus in the area of the Continental Divide.

Numerous exploring and colonizing parties traveled the western section of the route that once connected the Tiguex province (the cluster of pueblos around Albuquerque) with Acoma, Zuni, and the Hopi towns. Among the expeditions of soldiers, missionaries, and pioneers who got an early look at the lava fields and sandstone bluffs in the shadow of Mount Taylor were Coronado (1540), Rodríguez-Chamuscado (1581), Oñate (1589), and de Anza (1779).

GLENRIO, BARD, and SAN JON are three railroad towns established in the early 1900s when the Rock Island Railroad was under construction. San Jon, 19 mi., the name of the creek that flows eastward along the highway, apparently derives from the Spanish *zanjon*, meaning "a deep ditch" or "gully." The town of San Jon (alt. 3,900, pop. 339) lies just to the north of the thickly populated agricultural and livestock-raising region centering around Clovis. Some fifteen miles south of here on N.M. 39, under the overhanging limestone

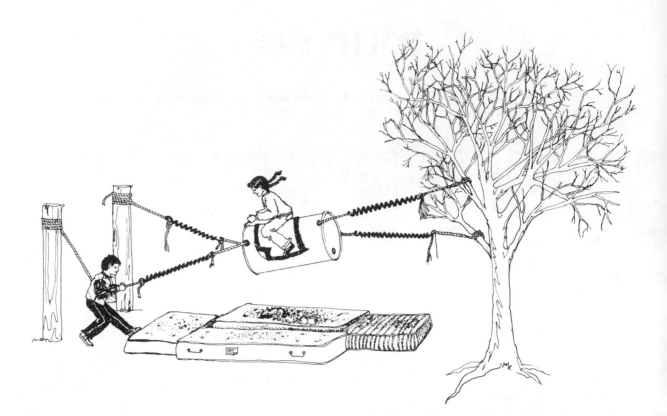

caprock, the Outdoor Drama Department of Eastern New Mexico University plans an amphitheater that will establish an outdoor theater tradition on the eastern plains. ENMU at Portales will provide information on this project.

Looking south from the stretch of highway east of Tucumcari (41 mi.), travelers can see the bluffs of the Llano Estacado, the eroded edges of the huge caprock that overlies much of the Texas Panhandle and eastern New Mexico. Tucumcari Mountain, a thousand feet above the surrounding plain, lies ahead. Of the legendary explanations for the peak's name, the most plausible is that it derives from a similar-sounding Comanche word meaning "signal peak," referring to smoke signals. When the Rock Island Railroad's main line came through in 1902 and the railroad de-

cided to build a branch from here to Amarillo, a construction camp sprang up near the base of this mountain. Eighty percent of the railroad crews in the West at this time were Mexican citizens, and Spanish was probably spoken more than English in the camp. The settlement got an English name, Six-Shooter Siding, because of a notorious element of gunfighters who frequently visited the place.

By 1908, the railroad needed a more respectable name for its division point and designated the new town—with roundhouse, depot, and growing population—TUCUMCARI (alt. 4,183, pop. 6,774). Those who prefer a good story repeat the legend about the death of Tocom, an Apache brave killed fighting for the hand of Kari, a chief's daughter. Grieving for her lover, Kari killed herself. This caused her father also to stab himself, breathing "Tocom! Kari!" as his last words. Aside from the railroad and the highway, Tucumcari owes its continued prosperity to the Conchas Dam, constructed in the 1930s on the Canadian River, and its resultant irrigation district.

Tucumcarians take pride in their new city hall and library, both built in new New Mexican style, using design motifs and features of Pueblo and colonial builders. The Tucumcari Historical Museum displays artifacts left by the Paleo-Indian big-game hunters who resided in the area as far back as twelve thousand years ago, as well as articles from the early ranching and railroad days. Also on display are gems and minerals. Over thousands of years Tucumcari Lake, on the northeast edge of town, has been a watering place for most of the people who left the things exhibited in the museum. In the last century, cattle drivers on the Goodnight and Loving trails sometimes stopped over here, as did the Comancheros (Comanche traders) who collaborated with bands of Plains Indians in driving stolen cattle over trails across these parts of the *llano*.

Quay County holds its fair in the first week in September, usually coinciding with the Tucumcari Piñata Festival. The latter features a Queen's Pageant, races, music, good food, and a parade.

A railway once hauled tons of coal from the Dawson mines to Tucumcari for use in the locomotives. Eight miles north along this abandoned rail line, old Fort Bascom, on an earlier wagon trail between Texas and Santa Fe, served as a staging area in 1868 for raids east

against the Cheyenne, Arapaho, Kiowa, and Comanche Indians. The fort's adobe ruins remain. During the 1860s it was illegal to sell whiskey within five miles of a military post, so soldiers stationed at Fort Bascom repaired to the village that they named Liberty for a taste of spirits and a sense of freedom. When the railroad created Tucumcari, people from Liberty moved over to help found the new city, leaving little behind to mark their old home, scene of Black Jack Ketchum's first train robbery. South from Tucumcari, N.M. 18 passes Mesa Redonda ("round mesa"), Ketchum's hideout during his brief but far-flung train-robbing career, which ended in his capture and eventual execution at Clayton in 1906. The road then climbs the "breaks"—canyons and boulders at the edge of the caprock—near Ragland. U.S. 54 (and Tour 13) overlaps the route of I-40 between Tucumcari and Santa Rosa.

The most direct route to Las Vegas (110 mi.) and Santa Fe (159 mi.) from Tucumcari is via N.M. 104. This course also provides a roundabout and geographically very different way to Albuquerque.

From Tucumcari it is an easy drive northwest up N.M. 104 across the plain to CONCHAS LAKE STATE PARK, 32 mi. Like most of the large lakes in New Mexico, Conchas was created in 1937 as a project of the U.S. Corps of Engineers, which dammed the Canadian River. It supplies water to a large area southeast of the project.

Because the lake is manmade in a naturally dry area, the vegetation around it is

Winter water hole, *Harvey Caplin.*

sparse, and the water stands out startlingly blue. Planned to control floods as far away as Texas and Oklahoma, the lake is also a major recreation area, easily reached from Las Vegas and Tucumcari. Fishing, boating, waterskiing, and camping also attract water enthusiasts from all over the state and from Texas. The little settlement of Conchas is home to government workers and concession owners, and supplies the recreation seekers' needs.

A worthwhile side trip from Conchas Dam is the ten-mile drive north from Conchas village to the Bell Ranch headquarters. In 1970 the ranch was designated as both a National and a State Historic Site, a well-deserved appellation since the ranch had its beginnings with the Pablo Montoya Land Grant of 1824.

Montoya was an army man, an *alcalde* (mayor) of Santa Fe who wanted space for his family. He applied to the Mexican government for a grant of land and soon received one. The grant included 655,468 acres, covered by a mixture of grasses and watered by the Canadian River running northwest to southeast across the grant.

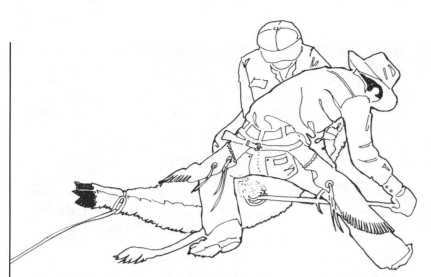

Most of the land lay below forty-five hundred feet, which ensured mild winters.

By 1844 only two of Pablo's sons still retained rights in the land, and by 1865 all of the heirs had conveyed their interests to John Watts, a Santa Fe attorney who had persuaded Congress to confirm the land grant title as the Montoyas'. Watts then transferred the title to this and an adjoining piece of property to Wilson Waddington, a wheeling and dealing cattleman who operated the ranch under several names until in 1889 it became the Bell Ranch, called after the distinctive, bell-shaped butte on the property.

Waddington may have overstepped himself in his operation of the ranch, and after a series of economic blows he was forced to sell his holding to a New York group in 1884. Nonetheless he made the range of broad mesas, canyons, and buttes into one of the "best in the west." He successfully maintained a large herd of cattle there, aided in part by his acumen and in part by the plentiful land and water.

The Red River Valley Company took over the ranch in 1899 and continued to run it until 1947, when it was broken into six pieces. The property surrounding the ranch headquarters retained the name Bell Ranch. The Bell has always worked to im-prove its cattle, as well as adopting modern range and water conservation practices. The present owners have bought back some of the original grant land so that the ranch today covers approximately one-half of Pablo Montoya's grant.

The headquarters of the ranch used to consist of an orchard and garden, a poultry yard, horse barns, corrals, a dairy, a blacksmith shop, a commissary, bunkhouses, a mess hall, the ranch office, the post office, the foreman's house, and the "White House," home to the manager and his family. Now the orchards and garden, chickens and dairy have gone, but the headquarters remains impressive. The White House sits among huge cottonwoods fronted by a lawn. Beyond it are the other units painted in warm yellows and reds, blending into the red clay of the surrounding flat land.

Back on the main road, the rest of the trip to Las Vegas is a slow ascent except at Corazon Hill, where there is a fairly rapid climb of a thousand feet. The Sangre de Cristos form a backdrop to the expansive view. In past years much of the plain was grass-covered, and there industrious bean farmers made a living. Drought has changed this; the plain is dry, covered now by desert plants.

Whatever is left of Montoya, Newkirk, and Cuervo ("crow") probably dates from the early railroad days. At NEWKIRK, 75 mi., N.M. 129 provides access to Conchas Dam from the south and west. Newkirk has the distinction of being located midway between two rivers (the Pecos and the Canadian, both gifts to the continent from the Sangre de Cristo Mountains) which appear to be about to converge here but then go on to travel their very different routes to the Gulf of Mexico. To the north, white caliche limestone caps Mesa Rica, a detached part of the original layer, as much as forty feet thick, that forms the caprock covering most of eastern New Mexico. Past Cuervo, 83 mi., the highway climbs over another piece of the *llano* before descending into the Pecos Valley. Cuervo Peak (6,220 feet) is visible to the north.

The Pecos, New Mexico's second river, was explored and settled by the Spanish as early as its first one, the Rio Grande. Coronado followed the Pecos, then bridged it in his search for the wealth of Quivira in 1541. The Rodríguez-Chamuscado Expedition, after visiting Pecos Pueblo, continued down the Pecos on its return to central Mexico. San Miguel del Vado ("St. Michael of the Ford"), a Pecos River settlement of Christianized Indians between Santa Rosa and the Pecos Pueblo, dates from the early 1600s (see Tour 1). By the beginning of the nineteenth century a string of towns, San Miguel, Villanueva (see Tour 1), and Anton Chico (see Tour 3), lined the upper reaches of the river. In the middle 1800s came Santa Rosa and Fort Sumner, and by the end of the century the bulk of the Rio Pecos population had shifted to irrigation districts in the Roswell, Artesia, and Carlsbad areas.

After breaking out of the Sangre de Cristo Mountains south of Las Vegas, the Pecos makes its way across the plains of eastern New Mexico and West Texas to join the Rio Grande near Langtry. Tales of Pecos Bill recall the days of open range and huge ranches whose boundaries were measured only by the availability and control of water sources. The Pecos also plays an indirect role in the story of Alvar Núñez Cabeza de Vaca, long supposed to have been the first person from the Old World to set foot in New Mexico. Cabeza de Vaca was shipwrecked off the Florida coast in 1528 and then spent eight years in a remarkable journey that took him across what is now the southern United States into South Texas, up the Rio Grande towards New Mexico, and then southward back to Mexico City. Older histories assumed that Cabeza de Vaca entered present New Mexico before leaving the Rio Grande, but a more recent interpretation of his journal concludes that he never crossed the Pecos nor passed its confluence with the Rio Grande (events he would not have failed to note) and thus must have turned southward before coming near present-day Las Cruces. The honor of being the first non-Indian into New Mexico now goes to Esteban, a black slave of Cabeza de Vaca, who led a later expedition to find the Seven Cities of Cibola and did cross the present state line west of Zuni.

The Pecos also had a dubious role to play in the history of relations between Texas and New Mexico. Up through the era of Mexican rule the province of New Mexico was considered to extend east at least as far as the Pecos and to include present West Texas, west of the Pecos. In the turmoil of the Texas revolt against Mexico and the U.S.–Mexican War, Texas wound up with the territory north of the Rio Grande all the way to El Paso and for a time claimed much of New Mexico east of the Rio Grande. In 1841, in fact, President Lamar of the Republic of Texas sent an armed force to take possession of the eastern drainage of the Rio Grande all the way up to its source. This force, the Texas–Santa Fe Expedition, passed near Anton Chico and present-day Santa Rosa before being disarmed and escorted home via El Paso. Since a second armed force of Texans invaded New Mexico twenty-one years later during the Civil War, one can understand the sometimes strained relations between people of the two states.

At 98 mi. (Exit 276), the tour intersects U.S. 84 south. This highway follows the Pecos

River downstream to Fort Sumner. SANTA ROSA, 100 mi. (alt. 4,615, pop. 2,477), the city of springs and natural lakes, sits in a broad section of the Pecos Valley, formed by what geologists call "condensing collapse depressions," surrounded by plains four hundred to a thousand feet above the valley floor. El Rito Creek flows through the city and waters Park Lake, "the world's largest free swimming pool." One block east, Blue Hole, an artesian spring eighty-seven feet deep and sixty feet in diameter, has long been a playground both for scuba divers and for brilliant goldfish. Underground springs also feed Hidden Lake east of town, a favorite spot for admirers of Indian pictographs. James Wallace Park and Power Dam, south of town, offers excellent free fishing (license required). The recently completed Los Esteros ("river bottoms") Dam, nine miles north of Santa Rosa on the Pecos River, backs up water to cover eighteen thousand acres with Santa Rosa Lake, providing boating, fishing, and swimming.

Settlers came to Santa Rosa during the 1860s, part of the migration of Hispanic people out of the core area of the northern New Mexico mountains. The place was called Agua Negra Chiquita ("little black water") until 1897, when Don Celso Baca built a chapel here dedicated to Santa Rosa de Lima, the first canonized saint of the New World. The chapel survives, partly in ruins. The Santa Rosa Church, built later, and the hacienda headquarters of the Baca family continue to be used. When the territorial legislature created Guadalupe County in 1891, it honored Our Lady of Guadalupe, a vision of Jesus' mother Mary that appeared with messages to Juan

Diego at the Indian town of Tepeyac, near Mexico City, in 1531. Puerto de Luna, south of Santa Rosa, became the first county seat. In 1901 four thousand railroad workers came to Santa Rosa, the point where the Rock Island Railroad connected with what was to be the Southern Pacific. The railroads brought a smallpox epidemic, a roundhouse, prosperity, the county seat, and later the highway to the new town. After the establishment, in 1903, of Roosevelt County (to honor the former "Rough Rider," President Theodore Roosevelt), the legislature renamed Santa Rosa's county Leonard Wood, for another Spanish-American War hero. The people opposed the name change, and within a few years Guadalupe County had its original name again, possibly the only county in the nation to lose and then regain its name.

The railroad shops soon moved on from Santa Rosa. Ranching and farming kept the town going until tourist trade from new U.S. 66 added a fresh element to the economy in the 1930s. When I-40 bypassed the city early in the 1970s, a panic ensued, and most of the Anglo merchants and restaurant and hotel owners sold out. However, the new Hispanic owners have managed to stay in business, and Santa Rosa has survived both the superhighway and the slump in tourism caused by gasoline price increases.

A ten-mile drive south on N.M. 91 down the valley, with views of the *llano* and canyons of the Pecos, ends at PUERTO DE LUNA. The name translates as "gate of the moon," but because the Luna family was among the village's first settlers the name is usually rendered, more prosaically, as "Luna's Gap." Coronado

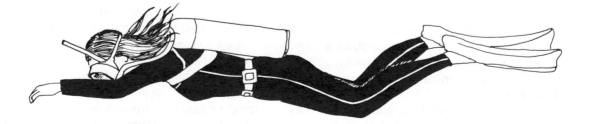

camped here in 1541, before bridging the river on the travels that would take him into central Kansas and back. The Lunas and other families migrated to the inviting spot in the 1860s, using river water to irrigate corn, bean, and chile fields. Nuestra Señora del Refugio ("Our Lady of Refuge") Church observed its centennial on July 3 and 4, 1982, with a fiesta that featured exhibits and games, a traditional community barbeque, and a Mass celebrated by the archbishop. The town enjoyed a brief decade as seat of Guadalupe County during the 1880s, when its population exceeded fifteen hundred. Puerto de Luna is now undergoing a small revival, thanks to Santa Rosa's growth and prosperity.

Rudolfo Anaya's autobiographical novel, *Bless Me, Ultima*, tells about life in Santa Rosa and Puerto de Luna in the late 1940s. It abounds with humorous and moving descriptions of the river, the spring-fed lakes and the legendary Golden Carp, the effects of the Second World War, and the faith that people live by. One of its particular themes, especially appropriate to this narrow valley in the midst of miles of plains, is the clash among the hero's relatives between the people of the wide *llano*, "where the grass was as high and as green as the waves of the ocean," and the hardworking, prudent farmers of the valley. U.S. 54 (and Tour 13) divides from Business I-40 just west of the Pecos River bridge in Santa Rosa.

Seven miles west, at 107 mi., the traveler can turn off to the nearly deserted old village of COLONIAS, twelve miles north of the highway, which predates both Santa Rosa and Puerto de Luna. The early inhabitants of Colonias ("colony") lived on buffalo hunting, subsistence farming, and ranching. Because of its exposed position, and because most of its men were *ciboleros* (bison hunters) who left for long periods of time, the village was built, with no windows facing out, around a large courtyard that enclosed the livestock and a cistern. As Colonias neared its centennial year in 1935, the Pecos River changed its course, depriving farmers of their irrigation water. Discouraged families moved out, the building

walls crumbled, and the San José Church lost its *santos*. Some of those who have an income derived from Santa Rosa commerce have now moved back to reclaim their old town.

Immediately beyond the Rio Pecos bridge at Santa Rosa, the highway begins an ascent that ends near Clines Corners, fifty-five miles west and almost two thousand feet above the Pecos Valley. On many of the Great Plains highways, drivers can climb from the few hundred feet at the Mississippi River to the four- to five-thousand-foot elevations of the high plains and hardly be aware of the ascent. Between Santa Rosa and Clines Corners, however, the climb becomes quite noticeable, especially against a strong westerly headwind. Before dipping into the Estancia Valley east of Moriarty, travelers, still on the plains, have attained an elevation of nearly sixty-five hundred feet at the point where I-40 passes between Glorieta Mesa and Pedernal Mountain.

Unlike most transcontinental roads, old U.S. 66 paralleled no pre-existing trails over the eighty miles between the Pecos and the Estancia valleys and passed no settlements in this stretch. In miles it is a short distance from Milagro, 130 mi., north to the seventeenth-century Pecos River villages of Anton Chico, Villanueva, and San Miguel. But to most people traveling the direct freeway route, they might as well be hundreds of miles away. The two existing stops, Milagro and Clines Corners, are creations of the automobile age. Even Moriarty, founded in 1901 as a stop on the New Mexico Central Railroad (the "bean line" that connected Santa Fe and Corona), changed its name and location to accommodate the new highway in the 1930s.

Northbound U.S. 84 travelers exit at 118 mi. and can refer to Tour 3 to read about Anton Chico and the mountain way to Taos and to Tour 1 to read about Las Vegas. At 144 mi. N.M. 3 leads twenty miles north to Villanueva and south to Encino and Duran. Billboards heralding the approach of Clines Corners might cause the unwary to expect more than they find—a restaurant and a gas station.

Here our tour intersects Tour 7, which travels the mostly sparsely populated 390 miles from Colorado to Texas via U.S. 285.

I-40 skirts the northern edge of MORIARTY (alt. 6,300, pop. 1,278) at 173 mi. Moriarty is a small town supplying cross-country travelers with gas, food, and accommodations, and ranchers with range necessities and opportunities for socializing. Near the junction of U.S. 66 and N.M. 41 is a historical museum that displays memorabilia from the Estancia Valley's early farming and ranching days. U.S. 66 is the business route paralleling the interstate highway through the town; N.M. 41 is the lonely, beautiful connection between Santa Fe and Galisteo to the north and Estancia, Willard, and Corona to the south (see Tour 5). Moriarty, named for one of the first Anglo settlers to come to this part of the valley, is located in a long, flat depression east of the Manzano Mountains that contained a large lake in prehistoric times, the shores of which were campsites for tribes of nomadic hunters. Although there is no relationship between early rancher Michael Timothy Moriarty and Sherlock Holmes's archenemy Moriarty, each year a group of aficionados of the great detective's exploits uses the similarity of the names as reason to meet in a local bar to revel and to read highly humorous "scientific" papers extolling their hero.

Between Moriarty and Edgewood, I-40 climbs steadily upwards to its apex, reached at about 185 mi. From the straight highway, magnificent views of the Sangre de Cristo Mountains above Santa Fe and of the South, Manzano, and Sandia mountains looming ahead to the west accompany the traveler. Turning to look back, one can see Pedernal Mountain, one of several pyramidal brown hills on the eastern horizon.

The relatively smoothly sloping, forested eastern incline of the Sandias and Manzanos contains many settlements. N.M. 14 (see Tour 15) leads north to the Albuquerque bedroom communities of Cedar Crest and Sandia Park and beyond them, to Santa Fe. South on N.M. 14 are a number of predominantly Hispanic villages and the ruins of many long-deserted Indian pueblos.

Passing Tijeras's large cement plant, the highway plunges into Tijeras Canyon along little Tijeras Creek. Just north of the town is the trailhead for the Sandia Crest Trail, which climbs to the ridge and connects with a network of mountainside paths before descending again to its northern terminus in Placitas. Information and campfire permits can be obtained at the U.S. Forest Service ranger station on N.M. 14 just south of the town of Tijeras.

At about 200 mi., the highway passes a collection of huge boulders, a reminder of the fact that the Sandias and Manzanos, when they rose from the fault plane at their western edge, were three times as high as at present; they have been worn down by the effects of millennia of wind and water erosion. The view of the mountains from the west is quite different from that seen from the east: steep and craggy, the western aspect was the vertical portion of the huge uplifted segment. Also in the canyon are remnants of an Indian pueblo, Portezuelo ("little door"), whose inhabitants may have been among the ancestors of present-day Isletans, and a small settlement, CARNUE or Carnuel (201 mi.).

Carnue has been occupied continuously since 1819, when Spanish governor Facundo Melgares formally granted a tract of land to thirty-five petitioners from Albuquerque who had been found by the *alcalde mayor* (provincial official) of the region to have no land of their own. The *alcalde* escorted a group of anxious settlers to the canyon and assigned them strips of land perpendicular to the stream, each ranging from one wall of the canyon to the other, as was the custom.

This was the second grant in Cañon de Carnue, as Tijeras Canyon was then known; the first had lasted only from 1763 to 1771. Like modern visitors arriving on the interstate highway, Apache raiders had used the canyon continuously in the eighteenth century, frequently preying upon the settlement at Carnue and the town of Albuquerque that lay beyond. Twenty-five years of Spanish tactics and warfare against the Apaches had largely controlled the menace by the turn of the nineteenth century. San Miguel de Carnue and San Antonio de Carnue were established in 1819; the grants were confirmed by the U.S. Court of Private Land Claims in 1894.

As the traveler rounds the southeast corner of the Sandias, New Mexico's largest city, Al-buquerque, comes into view (see Tour 1 which follows I-25 and the older route, U.S. 85). On the western horizon, beyond the city, are five large and thirteen smaller volcanic cones, arrayed along a fault line stretching from the immense Jemez caldera sixty miles to the north to the Wind Mesa volcanic field nineteen miles south of Albuquerque. Towering above these, as seen from the east edge of the city, is the eleven thousand-foot volcano Mount Taylor, or Cebolleta, fifty-five miles to the west. The highway meets I-25 in a spaghetti-bowl tangle of roads, called by Albuquerqueans "the Big I," at 211 mi.

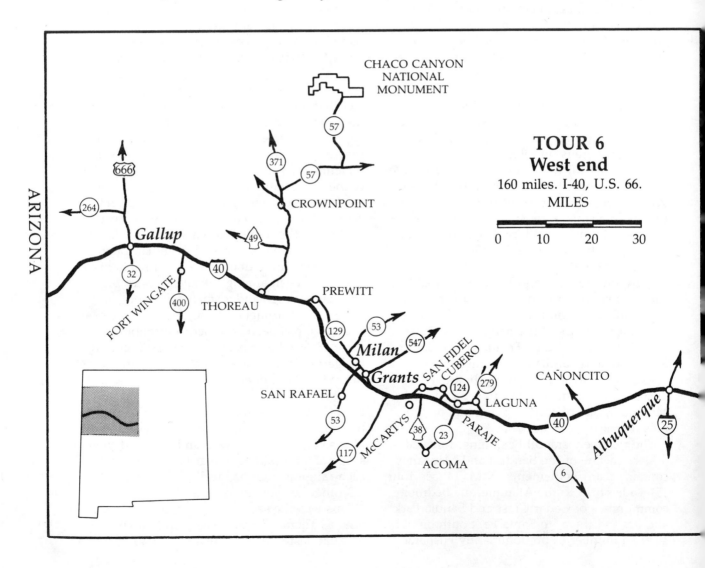

Leaving Albuquerque's sprawling environs, I-40 crosses the Rio Grande at 214 mi., affording the traveler an excellent view of the tree-lined river's sandy course, often surprising the unwary with the small size of the "great river." The highway then climbs up the Ceja Mesa past the volcanoes, meeting old U.S. 66 (Central Avenue) at the top of a long grade. Dropping off the mesa again, the road crosses the Rio Puerco at 230 mi. New Mexico sports three Rios Puercos ("dirty rivers"); the others are in Rio Arriba, Sandoval, and McKinley counties. The small, often empty riverbed crossed here drains a large, arid region to the north as well as the somewhat wetter San Pedro Mountains near Cuba and a part of the Jicarilla Apache Reservation. It flows into the Rio Grande between Belen and Socorro.

Indian reservation land begins at the Rio Puerco. For the next fifty-three miles, the highway passes through parts of the Laguna, Acoma, and Cañoncito reservations. At 239 mi. is an exit for Cañoncito, which lies north of the highway. Comprised of about twelve hundred Navajos, the Cañoncito band represents a segment separated from the main body of the largest tribe of Indians in the United States. The Cañoncito people are called by Navajos of the large reservation Diné Ana'i, or "the people who are enemies." The name derives from the betrayal of Joaquín, leader of a group of Navajos, in 1818. Joaquín reported to the Spanish *alcalde* at Laguna that a large band of Navajos planned to attack the Spanish settlers and the pueblo. He claimed to have tried to prevent the warfare but failed, and now, it appeared, he wished to join the side he expected to be victorious. He and a band of followers numbering some two hundred placed themselves under Spanish protection, as they were in considerable danger from the rebellious Navajos. They settled at Cebolleta, near their present location.

Aside from the brief period during which they were incarcerated with other Navajos at Bosque Redondo, the Cañoncito Navajos have remained in this area, an impoverished group living in scattered hogans and carrying water

long distances. They had never been fully trusted by the Spanish and were hated as traitors by their erstwhile tribesmen. Nevertheless, the group is now represented in the Navajo Tribal Council in Window Rock, Arizona. Like the Diné on the large reservation, the Cañoncito Diné Ana'i have difficulty finding work (88 percent of the work force was said to be unemployed in 1971).

MESITA, 252 mi., a small settlement of the Laguna people, lies just off the highway. Modern houses and trailers rest on a lava bed at the foot of a red-and-buff-colored mesa. Mesita was established in the late 1870s by conservative Lagunas who were threatened by the religious and social progressiveness of the dominant faction of the pueblo. The "ceremonialists" took their ritual equipment and the old image of their patron saint to their new homes in Mesita. The Laguna governor later retrieved the image and returned it to the mission church, and also ordered that some of the altars taken to Mesita be destroyed.

Around 1878 several of the displaced Lagunas moved to Isleta, but most returned to Mesita because of conflict. However, enough Lagunas remained in Isleta to form a group there called the Laguna Fathers.

The interstate then dips into the San Jose River bottom through a broken, colorful country. Here the brown and gray cliffs are formed of sandstone, while the valley itself is carved from deep red rock. Near Laguna white gypsum of the Todilto Formation contrasts with pink canyons, and the varicolored rock at the side of the highway betrays the uranium found underneath.

The exit here allows the traveler to drive through Laguna Pueblo, 256 mi., and take a detour to Paguate and Seboyeta, and to Laguna's "summer" villages before rejoining the interstate at San Fidel.

LAGUNA PUEBLO, 256 mi., lies across the San Jose River from the interstate. Just before reaching the old village, the road joins with N.M. 279, a well-paved route that leads north to Paguate, Seboyeta, and the uranium mines.

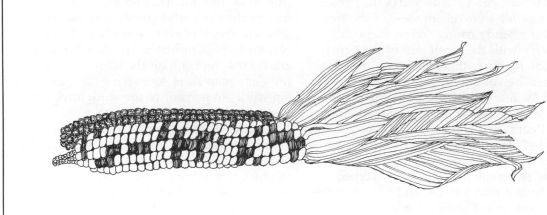

Built to accommodate the heavy mining traffic, the road twists easily through the high desert to the top of a hill. There the traveler can see the gray wastes of the Anaconda Jackpile Mine spread out below. Until it closed down in 1981, Jackpile was the largest open-pit uranium mine in the world. For twenty-seven years it provided jobs for the people of Laguna, Paguate, and the other towns nearby. Its scarred expanse is awesome.

PAGUATE, 8 mi., is built on a rise to the left of the main road, with panoramic views past the mine to the distant mesas. Ruins of stone houses, old adobes, and crumbling walls mix with the newer homes that reflect the prosperity brought by the mines. Further down the main road, a cluster of the new houses prevalent in the Laguna area injects another note of modernity. Some of them are adapted from the traditional, flat adobe style, while the soaring lines of others stand out sharply against the desert floor.

BIBO, 12 mi., is barely noticed at the side of the road, but its old church allows the visitor a glimpse into its Spanish past. The little settlement is named for a family of traders, well-known in the area in the nineteenth and early twentieth centuries. To the right signs point the way to the

United Nuclear and St. Anthony's mines.

SEBOYETA, 14 mi. (a corruption of *cebolleta*, "tender onion"), is one of the oldest settlements in the region. Remains of walls once ten feet high tell of a turbulent past. Seboyeta was first settled temporarily in 1746. Three years later the Franciscans established a mission here for the Navajos who promised to live in the town. After a year of sedentary life, the Navajos left the mission to return to their nomadic lifestyle, but although the mission failed, the town was settled further by colonists. According to one source, the settlers came from Mexico, but it is more likely that they were thirty families from the Rio Grande. They built their homes facing a plaza, with the backs forming a protective wall; the remains of this first village still stand. The colonists' presence, viewed as an encroachment on traditional territory, was deeply resented by the Navajos, who periodically attacked them. There is a long record of strife in the old archives, with the Indians raiding colonists' crops and herds, and colonists taking part in slave raids upon the Navajos. In 1804 Navajo warriors laid siege to Seboyeta, and a fierce battle followed. The governor asked for aid from Mexico, and with replacements the New Mexicans were able to subdue the Indians. Lagunas helped the colonists in many of these struggles against the Navajos, their ancient enemy.

Seboyeta is built against a hill overlooking the eastern expanse of roughcut mesas and a vast blue sky. The little town is dominated by its church, Our Lady of Sorrows, built in 1823. A skylight now illuminates the whitewashed interior of the church, where new plaster saints stand next to older wooden *santos.* To the right of the entrance a glass coffin rests on a stand. It symbolizes El Santo Entierro (the Holy Sepulchre), and inside, clearly visible, is the Cristo, crown of thorns tightly pressed to the head and bloody wounds painted on head and chest. Wooden handles make it easy for the coffin to be carried in processions. Two old paintings, depicting Our Lady of Guadalupe and St. John Nepomucene, hang on the walls. A more recent picture of a patriarchal figure includes the words "Elias Francis and Sons" on its lower left corner. Elias Francis was a Syrian peddler who visited Seboyeta about 1880, settled there, and for fifty years was its most influential citizen. His family remains well-known in the area.

North of the town, nineteenth-century colonists built a shrine to Our Lady of Lourdes in a natural grotto. The road to the shrine is unpaved. It forks just after it passes by the old walls leaving the town; the left fork goes to the shrine. About a mile up the road a sign announces "Los Portales, sacred to both our people living and our ancestors nearby." There are picnic tables near the road. A walk through a narrow canyon leads to the shrine, a natural recess in overhanging rock. A spring seeps out of the base of the stone. The shrine is supposed to have been built by colonists who, discouraged after repeated Navajo raids, had walked back to Chihuahua, Mexico. The viceroy would not allow them to return to Spain but made them go back to Seboyeta and fulfill the contract they had made to colonize the area for the mother country. On the way back, the colonists decided to build a shrine to Our Lady of Mercy and to honor her with annual feasts as long as Seboyeta stood.

From Seboyeta the dirt-packed road continues east and north to Marquez, a small farming and ranching community named for the Márquez family. Return to Laguna Pueblo on N.M. 279.

SIDE TOUR

LAGUNA PUEBLO (alt. 5,975, pop. 5,200) was named by the Spanish for a nearby lake (*lago*) that has since dried up to become a meadow. Hernando de Alvarado, an officer in Coronado's expedition of 1540, mentioned the lake in his accounts of the area. At that time there was no village at the site; the modern pueblo was not established until 1697, although earlier villages had existed in the area from the 1300s. While the Spanish governor, Pedro Rodríguez Cubero, was on an expedition to Zuni, he ordered that the small settlement be organized as a pueblo.

The original pueblo, now called Old Laguna Village to distinguish it from the new community nearby, is the most populous pueblo east of the Continental Divide, despite the fact that the extensive village as it now exists was not built until the end of the eighteenth century. Always farmers, the Keresan-speaking Laguna people planted the land around the pueblo with corn and chile, beans and squash. As the settlement grew and prospered, the farmers needed new land, and the Lagunas built six more villages. Laguna Pueblo now serves as the mother pueblo to these summer or farming villages scattered within a radius of a few miles where irrigation is available.

Laguna's patron is St. Joseph, and the pueblo celebrates his feast day twice. On

Laguna Pueblo, *Harvey Caplin.*

March 19, the traditional date, harvest and social dances are performed in Old Laguna Village. San José Feast Day, September 19, is the
occasion of a popular carnival, and Eagle,
Corn, and Buffalo dances are performed. The
outlying villages also honor their special saints
with dances.

In the 1870s tensions resulting from the
powerful influences of nearby Anglo settlers
and several Protestants who moved into the
pueblo led to the "Laguna break." The Marmon family and their cousins, the Gunns, established a flour mill in the pueblo and
intermarried with Lagunas. (A descendant of

the Marmons, Leslie Marmon Silko, has written feelingly of the Pueblo culture in her
books and poems.) Dr. John Menaul taught
and preached the Presbyterian religion. These
new arrivals determined to modernize the
Pueblo. The Marmon men wrote a constitution modeled after that of the United States
for the pueblo, and were governors for a term.
Other changes led to accusations of witchcraft
among the various factions. The leader of a
progressive faction not only introduced an
outside cult but became a Protestant. Two kivas were torn down and the Catholic church
was threatened. All of these pressures came to

a head in the 1870s, when the conservatives packed up and moved to Mesita (see above).

After railroad tracks were laid through the pueblo in the 1880s, many Lagunas worked for the railway, exposing the Pueblo to modern ways. For many years Laguna's proximity to uranium mines has also made it the recipient of royalties and jobs. Results of the uranium boom can be seen in the impressive government complex that dominates the pueblo. The road through the town is paved, and the sizes and kinds of houses that climb up and past the mission are varied. The effects of the cyclical depressions in the uranium industry are also keenly felt at Laguna.

Unlike many of the New Mexico mission churches, San José de Laguna, overlooking the town, is built of stone. Its plain, massive walls have only four openings of any size: the doorway, a window in the middle of the facade, and two small belfry openings in the false gable front. The rooms adjoining the church, formerly used as a convent, add to its massive appearance, as does the churchyard enclosed by an adobe wall.

The church, the last of the early New Mexican missions to be established, is well-preserved, although during and after the Pueblo Revolt it was used as a stable. Under Mexican rule the old convent fell into ruins but was restored in 1935–36.

The decorations of the interior are the work of Indian craftsmen. Designs in red, yellow, and green, bordered in heavy black lines, cover the walls. An animal hide on the ceiling is painted with Indian symbols of the rainbow, sun, moon, and stars, and with Christian symbols, a reflection of the efforts of the early missionaries to graft new religious ideas onto the old. As in most of the missions, craftsmen handcarved the altar from pine; it is flanked by paintings of St. Barbara and St. John Nepomucene. A painting of St. Joseph and the Christ Child on elk hide is one of the largest of its kind. Two statues are only displayed on special occasions: a statue of St. Joseph, brought here in 1699 from Mexico, is used in fiesta processions honoring the pueblo and for

Interior of Laguna Pueblo church, *Harvey Caplin.*

St. Joseph's Feast on March 19. The other statue is one of the Virgin that was removed from the mission during the revolt, hidden, and returned to the church only in 1935. The ceiling of the nave boasts carved and ornamented *vigas;* the floor is adobe.

From the Old Laguna Village the farming villages stretch west on old U.S. 66, now N.M. 129. The traveler can take this road, parallelling the interstate, until it rejoins the freeway at San Fidel. New Laguna Pueblo lies off the road to the south. Paraje is a small settlement sloping up the hillside to a new pink church, St. Margaret Mary. At Paraje the highway intersects with N.M. 23, the route to Acoma.

Just before Laguna High School, an unmarked but well-paved road branches off to the right to ENCINAL, six miles due north, whose site seems to have been chosen for its views. At one time a Franciscan mission to the Navajo existed here; today a new church stands next to the old plaza and modern homes contrast with the older adobe and stone houses. A road west of the village provides an alternate route to Cubero. Partially paved, it winds through a lonely mesa at the foot of Mount Taylor. The road forks at about four miles, the right fork, unpaved, leading to San Mateo, the left to Cubero.

The more traveled route, N.M. 129, continues straight past Casa Blanca ("white house"), named for the white clay that coated it in the past, to the Cubero turnoff. CUBERO, 10 mi., may have been named for the Spanish governor who succeeded Don Diego de Vargas. However, the town may also have been named after a family from the area. The Cubero Grant was a colony grant made in 1833 to Juan

Chaves and sixty-one colonists by the Republic of Mexico.

Cubero resembles the Hispanic enclaves of northern New Mexico more than it does its pueblo neighbors, although it was formerly occupied by Indians from San Fidel and other pueblos. The town straggles along the road before spreading out on the high ground. Old cottonwoods line the *acequia* ("irrigation ditch") and, across an aging wooden bridge that discourages traffic, a little church sits next to a Penitente *morada*. The trading post near the highway sells everything from baby furniture to farm tools.

Almost immediately, Budville's few buildings appear on the right. Bud Rice founded this hamlet as a service stop in 1928 as traffic increased on Route 66.

The road then passes stretches of desert with multicolored rock formations. Faded motels remind one of the highway's busy past. The Villa de Cubero was one of the more important stops along this section of the route. A trading post has existed here since shortly after the Civil War; like all trading posts, it takes care of a variety of needs.

SAN FIDEL, 14 mi., is the last of the little towns passed before this route crosses I-40. The town was once a small trading center for the ranchers of the district. Today a large church complex dominates the location. Just east of San Fidel, Meja Hill Lake, belonging to Acoma Pueblo, provides a recreation area.

Those travelers who do not take the side trip through Laguna's summer villages stay on I-40. At the top of a rise, just past the Laguna turnoff, a convenient lookout provides a view of Laguna Pueblo, nestling against the brown hills and uncomfortably close, it seems, to the busy interstate.

Buttes near Acoma, *Harvey Caplin.*

The turnoff to ACOMA PUEBLO, 262 mi. (alt. 7,000, pop. 3,676) comes at the junction with N.M. 23, which branches south from I-40 and winds through a settlement of modern houses on both sides of the road. The characteristic caprock formations of the Acoma area appear along the mesa tops at 4 mi., where the plain narrows into a valley. This route to the Sky City crosses fields and a sandy plain, sparsely covered with rabbitbrush and dotted with juniper trees. N.M. 23 crosses the northern boundary of the Acoma Reservation at 9 mi.

The Enchanted Mesa, called *katzimo* ("enchanted") by the Acoma, juts up to the east. Built by successive layers of different rock, ranging from pink and white sandstone at the base to a golden-brown cap of Dakota sandstone, it commands the landscape. Precipitous walls 430 feet high and sharply turreted pinnacles explain a traditional story of the Acoma Indians: Once their ancestors lived at the top of the butte. When the path was closed by a storm, the people tending their fields on the plains below were not able to regain their homes, and those who were caught on the summit died of starvation. More recently, two climbers were trapped on the top for three nights and had to be lifted off by helicopter. Such

stories illustrate why only experienced climbers should attempt the ascent, and then only with tribal permission.

A small picnic area at 10 mi. provides tables under cooling trees for a stop before or after the Acoma tour.

To the immediate south the cliffs of Acoma rise out of the valley, seemingly unassailable and uninhabited. The adobe houses crowded into seventy acres atop the mesa are barely visible, but close scrutiny reveals shapes too regular to be rocks. These are the homes of Acoma, which have perched there for centuries, making this pueblo one of the two oldest continuously occupied settlements in the United States. (The other is the Hopi village of Oraibi in Arizona.)

The turnoff to the pueblo is at a crossroads 11 mi. past the new visitors' center, where tour tickets must be purchased (there are separate charges for picture-taking). To the right the road leads to the villages of Santa Maria de Acoma, or McCartys, and Acomita, where most of the Acoma make their year-round homes. To the left the road winds up the steep rock to the pueblo. Visitors once made their way up a staircase carved out of the rock. Since the road was paved for a movie company in 1957, it has become the way for visitors to enter Acoma.

Acoma Pueblo is built on the Rock or Peñol of Acuco, a fairly level sandstone formation rising 357 feet from the plain. Once several thousand people lived here;

now only a few families remain all year to watch over their unique heritage.

Just when the pueblo was built on its natural stronghold is unknown. Shards found here suggest that it was a thousand years ago; other evidence points to the early 1300s. Indian tradition gives the time as that following the destruction of the pueblo atop Enchanted Mesa, ages ago. Acoma was here when Fray Marcos de Niza sought the Seven Cities of Cibola in 1533, but Captain Hernando de Alvarado and his soldiers of Coronado's army were the first Europeans to see the village, in 1540. Struggling up the cliffs, at times the soldiers had only toe- and hand-holds to support them, leading them to believe the mesa was impregnable. Alvarado called the village Acuco, but when Antonio de Espejo's expedition visited the pueblo in 1583 he used the spelling Acoma, from the Keresan words *ako*, meaning "white rock," and *mi*, "people."

The first Spanish foothold in Acoma came in 1598, when the Pueblo voluntarily submitted to the authority of the Spanish Crown, represented by Don Juan de Oñate. Submission soon turned to aggression, however, when the Acoma tricked Don Juan de Zaldívar into entering the pueblo to obtain cornmeal. The Acomas attacked the party, killing Zaldívar and twelve soldiers. Don Juan de Oñate marshalled the weakened Spanish force under Vicente de Zaldívar, who wanted to avenge his brother's death. A force of seventy men, protected by armor and equipped with guns, assaulted the pueblo in retaliation. Don Juan meant to punish Acoma as a lesson to the other pueblos. A fierce battle, lasting three days and resulting in as many as eight hundred deaths, ended when the Spanish overcame the pueblo.

Punishment was harsh. Seventy Indian warriors were murdered and their bodies thrown over the cliff. Sixty young girls were sent to Mexico as slaves; the other females remained in servitude in New Mexico, along with all males between the ages of twelve and twenty-five. Each older man had one foot cut off and was forced to work for the Spanish for twenty years.

The mission of Acoma had been assigned to Fray Andrés Corchado in 1598 and later to Fray Gerónimo de Zarate-Salmerón, but because of the hostilities, a church was not established here until 1629. Fray Juan Ramírez, the first permanent missionary, was escorted to Acoma by Governor Francisco Manuel da Silva Nieto on his expedition to Zuni during July and August 1629. Legend says that Father Ramírez walked alone from Santa Fe to Acoma with only his cross and breviary for defense. As soon as the Acomas saw him attempting to climb the trail, they pelted him with rocks and arrows, but not one pierced his habit. Another story describes the Acomas, by this time resigned and accepting, awaiting the priest's arrival quietly. As Fray Ramírez approached, a little girl was inadvertently pushed off the top and fell upon a pointed rock sixty feet below. The Franciscan reached her, knelt and prayed beside her, and then carried her, unharmed, up to astounded relatives and neighbors. A variation of the story describes Fray Ramírez catching the girl as she fell, earning gratitude instead of hostility.

The goodwill earned by Father Ramírez was destroyed during the Pueblo Revolt of 1680, when Fray Lucas Maldonado was murdered. Acoma remained hostile for over sixteen years. In 1692 de Vargas and his small army reached a watering place called El Pozo ("the well"), from which they could see Acoma. De Vargas wrote in his journal, "We descried the smoke made by those traitors, enemies, treacherous rebels and apostates of the Zueres (Keresan) tribe." He did not attempt to take Acoma then. The pueblo held out until 1699 when, seeing the other pueblos submit, it yielded once more to Spanish rule, the last of the New Mexico pueblos to do so.

After several decades of peace and prosperity, the pueblo experienced a spate of troubles. Battles with the Navajos, quarrels with the Lagunas over grazing and water rights, drought, and a smallpox epidemic contributed to a dramatic decline in the population of the pueblo. After the American occupation of New Mexico in 1846, the Acomas numbered three hundred fifty, down from nine hundred fifty a hundred years earlier and from two thousand in 1630. The United States confirmed the Spanish grant of 1659 on December 22, 1858, but the Acoma Indians did not formally apply for their land until 1863, when seven Pueblo governors went to Washington to confer with President Lincoln and to settle boundaries. After the conference, Lincoln presented each governor with a silver-headed cane engraved with the following inscription:

A. Lincoln
Prst. U.S.A.
1863

These canes continue to be passed to succeeding governors when they are elected in January, and constitute the badge of office.

In 1877 the Acomas possessed more than ninety-five thousand acres of land; 17,400 acres have subsequently been

Acoma Pueblo, *Billie Surmick.*

houses once were three stories high. The first story, between twelve and fifteen feet tall, originally had no openings except a trap door on top, since it was used exclusively for storage of supplies. Ladders led from the ground to the second story, which was the living area. The third level, combining the kitchen and roof, was reached by narrow outside steps against the division wall. Today single-story dwellings are more prevalent and the multilevels are not used. The rooms of the houses have low ceilings. Windows used to be made of selenite, an opaque material mined in the vicinity, but only one or two of these mica windows are left. When the visitors' center was built, Pueblo elders wanted to install traditional windows. However, no one could find the now-overgrown mining site, and modern glass windows had to be substituted.

The tour stops first at the mission church of San Esteban Rey (St. Stephen the King). This massive structure dates back at least to 1699, although some historians identify it as the original church built by Father Ramírez in 1629. San Esteban, like the other mission churches in New Mexico, was built in a pueblo that had existed for years. There was already a town center, the plaza, around which the buildings were clustered. The church therefore had to be built at the edge of the town. To make up for this distance, the friars had impressive structures built, of which San Esteban is the largest.

San Esteban is also one of the finest of all the old Pueblo missions. The building fell into disrepair as Acoma's population dwindled during the last century, and the Museum of New Mexico repaired it in 1923. The church is 150 feet long and 40 feet wide, with walls 60 feet high and 10 feet thick. All of the building material was carried up the steep passages on a burro trail chipped out of the rock under Father Ramírez's direction. Heavy roof beams, each forty feet long by fourteen inches

added by executive order. Some of this acreage below the rock is dry farmed, primarily in corn, squash, and beans. The farming villages of McCartys and Acomita, which according to oral tradition were established before 1600, irrigate their crops.

Before touring the pueblo, visitors must meet in the office opposite the parking spaces at the top of the hill. A guide knowledgeable in Acoma's history leads the group through the pueblo on foot.

Acoma's homes are built of adobe and the white stone common to the area. The

square, were cut in the Cebolleta Mountains, thirty miles away, and carried on men's backs to the top. The plain front walls of the church are sloped to form great buttresses, topped with square towers and open belfries. Inside, a richly carved *reredos* (altar) at the far end contrasts with the bare white walls of the nave. The walls are painted each year before St. Stephen's feast day. Men use only traditional yucca and sheepskin brushes to apply the paint, which is ground from pink and white stones. Twisted columns or "candles" divide the *reredos* into panels, which are surmounted by a painting of a saint placed above scroll and shell motifs. Elaborately carved scroll brackets support the huge *vigas*. No nails have been used anywhere. The wooden Stations of the Cross date from the seventeenth century. The elk-hide painting and the picture of St. Joseph, a gift from Phillip II of Spain, should be noted.

The picture of St. Joseph was the focus of a most unusual lawsuit fought through United States courts from 1852 to 1857, with the Pueblo of Acoma as plaintiff and the Pueblo of Laguna as defendant. The Acomas believed that St. Joseph had endowed the painting with miraculous powers. When the Lagunas asked to borrow the painting in order to stop the droughts, epidemics, and other calamities they were suffering, the Acomas consented. Fortunes did change, but the La-

gunas did not return the picture. After several months the Acomas sent a messenger to ask the reason for the delay, but they received no satisfaction. The Acomas held a council and all agreed that lots should be drawn to decide the ownership of the picture. Twelve slips were prepared, eleven of them blank; on the twelfth was a rude sketch of the picture of St. Joseph. The slips were shaken up in a jar, and two little girls, one from Acoma and one from Laguna, drew the slips. On the fifth drawing the Acoma child drew the sketch of St. Joseph. "So," said the priest, "God has decided in favor of Acoma," and the sacred painting was brought triumphantly to its former home.

Matters did not end there, however. One morning soon after its return the picture disappeared again. The Acomas were ready for war, but their priest counseled that the matter be taken to the United States District Court at Santa Fe. The decision was in Acoma's favor, but Laguna appealed the case to the Supreme Court. The final decision, in 1857, was in Acoma's favor. Rejoicing in their victory, the Acomas appointed a committee to bring back the painting, absent for over fifty years. The committee members had only gone halfway to Laguna when they found the painting of St. Joseph under a tree. The story concludes that St. Joseph had already learned of the decision and had started his return, but, being tired, was

Acoma Church, *Harvey Caplin*.

resting under the tree when he was met.

From the patio of the church there is a wide-angle view of the countryside, highlighted by the Enchanted Mesa ahead. The *camposanto* or burial ground off the patio was planned to give the Acoma converts a consecrated place close by in which to bury their dead. The new Christians built a stone retaining wall almost ten feet high around the outer edge of the rock, enclosing an area two hundred feet square. Then they carried up enough earth from the plain below, a sackful at a time, to make the sacred graveyard. There

are now deer heads carved into the corners of the wall, where hunters pray; formless bumps on the wall were once carved soldiers' faces, placed there as guardians of the dead. On All Souls' Day and Memorial Day, families place gifts of food on the graves.

From the church the tour continues through the almost-deserted pueblo past the old adobes, some crumbling, others showing repairs. The guide relates anecdotes passed down from elders or made up for the tourists. There is time to stop and gaze off from the cliff, to look at the

Acoma Pueblo, *Harvey Caplin*.

grinding holes, at old cisterns, at an old ladder with supposed powers of forecasting the weather, and to wonder at the wooden outhouses perched incongruously on the edges of the cliffs. For years the only water in the pueblo was that collected in the natural cisterns weathered out of rock. The largest cistern is on the south half of the mesa. Smaller cisterns still hold rainwater too.

The tour passes women selling the distinctive Acoma pottery in front of their homes. The pottery is thin and slightly less durable than other Pueblo ware, but of fine quality. Designs from nature— flowers, birds, and trees—mix with intricate geometric patterns. Some potters now use a shiny glaze, and not all pots are hand-thrown.

The guide points out the trails that used to be the only means of access to the village. The one used by Father Ramírez on his arrival at the pueblo became known as "Camino del Padre." After he was settled at Acoma, Father Ramírez also had built the less hazardous and more comfortable burro trail. The only trail accepted as existing before 1629 is the ladder trail on the northwestern side, formed by a combination of ladder and toe- and fingerholds cut into the solid rocks and narrow cracks of the cliffs. Visitors used to be able to experience these climbs for themselves; now Pueblo elders discourage the use of the trails.

While Acoma remains quiet most of the year, its people come back to the mesa, where most families own individual or

Acoma, *Harvey Caplin*.

clan homes, to celebrate the important feast days: Governor's Day, St. John's Day (June 24), Easter, and Christmas. Most important is St. Stephen's Day, September 2. Originally, St. Stephen the Martyr was named the patron saint of Acoma; but his feast is December 26, too close to Christmas. So instead St. Stephen, king of Hungary, became Acoma's patron. On his feast day there is an important procession, foot races, dancing in the plaza, and a rooster pull. Visitors are welcome at the celebration. Other ceremonial days are private, barred to tourists.

Leaving Acoma, the traveler can return to I-40 by N.M. 23 or by an alternate route, Indian Road 38, which links up with N.M. 124. At the junction, new buildings housing a community center, tribal offices, a school, tennis and basketball courts, and modern houses contrast sharply with the ancient world just left behind. A left turn here will take one to MCCARTYS, which gets its distinctly Anglo name from the contractor who built this section of the Atchison, Topeka, and Santa Fe Railroad. In McCartys, John Gaw Meem's white stone church looks down on the railroad and the busy highway. The church, though modern, is built and decorated inside in the mission style, a half-size replica of the church at Acoma. The wood carvings inside are works of art. A short jog back, N.M. 124 links up with the interstate.

Past McCartys, at 274 mi., lava beds appear on both sides of the freeway as heaps of rough black rock. This is the *malpais* ("bad country" or "badlands"), named for obvious reasons by the Spanish explorers who came across great stretches of the lava when they were picking their way across New Mexico. The lava flows extend south from here through a wide valley formed by the sandstone scarp of Acoma Reservation on the east and the Oso and Zuni mountains on the west. N.M. 117 South skirts the lava flow, providing views of extinct craters and sandstone cliffs.

Volcanic activity in the region produced the lava flows on at least three occcasions, the most recent between one and two thousand years ago. As the lava cooled, it turned black, its surface pocked and jagged. Among the tumbled rocks, caves and fissures can trap the unwary. Despite the harshness of the *malpais*, hardy bushes grow among the rocks, and in some places a green furze softens the bleak landscape.

The New Mexico Institute of Mining and Technology informs us that once away from the vent of the volcano, lava moves more slowly as its surface and base harden. The center of the lava, still soft, pushes against the hardened front, which then breaks away with the sound of "thousands of glass wind chimes," according to an observer of a recent volcano. Even though the core of the flow may be red hot, the surface of an active flow can actually be walked on.

About five miles beyond McCartys, N.M. 117 snakes southeast along the *malpais* to Quemado (Tour 17).

GRANTS, 289 mi. (alt. 6,664, pop. 32,000), for years was a railroad town and trading center for a large agricultural and ranching territory. The discovery of uranium in the area in 1950 led to a period of intense activity in uranium mining and milling and the transformation of Grants into a boom town. A subsequent slump in the industry slowed growth, but the area was revitalized in the 1970s when the Grants-Milan area produced half the uranium oxide in the United States. The boom-bust syndrome continued, with several important mines closing in 1982 as a result of declining demand.

Grants's history began in 1872 when Don Jesús Blea settled here and called his home under the cottonwoods "Los Alamitos" ("little cottonwoods"). The following year Don Ramón Baca joined him with his family. In 1881 three brothers from Ontario, Canada, constructing a right of way from Isleta Pueblo to Needles, California, established their headquarters at this point. The camp was known as Grants Camp, later shortened to Grant when a coaling station was built and a little town grew up. In 1935 the name was changed once more to Grants.

Oil from the Hospah field near Ambrosia Lake, now the scene of a huge uranium mill, was piped to a refinery just west of Grants in the early 1940s. An even more valuable commodity brought changes to the area when, in 1950, Paddy Martínez, a Navajo sheep rancher, found a strange-looking yellow rock, which he recognized as containing uranium and turned in to the authorities. The Anaconda Company, followed over the years by others, opened its huge Jackpile Mine. With the advent of uranium mining and the influx of people the town grew tremendously, suffering the growing pains of boom towns but taking an immense pride in its title of "uranium capital of the world." A museum features exhibits on the ancient Indian presence in the area, scenes of early Western life, and aspects of uranium discovery. The town actively promotes tours of places of interest nearby. Cattle ranches continue to function, with roundups at the end of summer grazing.

SIDE TOUR

North of Grants, N.M. 547 or Lobo Canyon Road climbs some eighteen miles up to Mount Taylor, where campgrounds, the Lobo Canyon and Coal Mine picnic areas, and trails have opened up the mountain for recreation. Mount Taylor (11,300 feet) is an ancient volcano, the highest peak in this area. During winter its snow-covered top is visible for miles around. The Navajos call the mountain Dził Dotłizi," "turquoise mountain," or Tso Dził, big tall mountain. Spanish settlers called it Cebolleta, "tender onion." Following the Mexican War in 1846, Anglo-Americans renamed the mountain after General Zachary Taylor. As one of the four sacred mountains of the Navajos, it marks the southern border of the traditional Navajo world. Acoma and Laguna Indians also have spiritual ties to the mountain.

Four-wheel-drive vehicles can make a five-mile trip up an unpaved road to the look-out at La Mosca Peak (11,026 feet) just below the summit; the hardy can hike it. The Forest Service maintains one of its highest fire surveillance stations on this peak. From here a forest road provides a back route to tiny San Mateo. It is advisable to check conditions before attempting to take this or other back roads in the Mount Taylor area.

Between Grants and Milan, N.M. 53 veers off to the south and west to El Morro and Zuni (Tour 18).

MILAN, 289 mi., named after the family that owned the land, is now a "suburb" of Grants, home to miners and other industrial workers.

SIDE TOUR

The exit at Milan becomes N.M. 53, the road north to SAN MATEO, 22 mi., founded either by Colonel Manuel Chaves or his half-brother, Ramón A. Baca, in 1860. One report indicates that Colonel Chaves rested at the site on his way to Seboyeta after fighting the Indians and decided to build his home and a chapel named for St. Matthew there. Another version holds that Captain Baca led one hundred Spanish settlers to a beautiful site at the foot of Mount Taylor, a place called "the meadows" in Navajo. For a century San Mateo remained a small trading center for sheep ranchers, a settlement of adobe houses surrounding a small chapel. Uranium has left its mark here too, however, with drilling taking place in the hills around the village and workers setting up their trailers and building new homes. Eight miles south of San Mateo a side road, N.M. 509, runs up to Ambrosia Lake, the huge underground uranium mining area.

Several miles on, at 305 mi., the exit signs indicate that BLUEWATER LAKE STATE PARK (not to be confused with Bluewater, a tiny residential community one exit earlier) lies some seven miles to the south. The road here is paved and climbs up and around a steep hill overlooking the valley before ending up at the lake, some seventy-four hundred feet above sea level. Before a dam was built here in 1926–27, three natural depressions in the mesa were separated by walls of solid rock. Now a lake one mile wide and seven miles long covers the area.

At its western end, Bluewater is one of the more developed of New Mexico's lakes, with several private concessions open for business.

Motorboats are permitted. Dirt roads permit access to more private areas of the lake.

THOREAU, 312 mi., pronounced "through," spreads out on the plain below the bluffs. The little ranching and lumbering community probably took its literary name from the writer Henry David Thoreau when the railroad established a station there.

A paved road, N.M. 57/N.M. 197, runs across an empty but fascinating countryside to link up with N.M. 44 at Cuba. This road provides access to CROWNPOINT, 22 mi., renowned in New Mexico and among knowledgeable buyers for its rug auctions, and Chaco Canyon, 58 mi., site of pueblo ruins.

Crownpoint lies just west of the Navajo Indian Reservation's eastern border, at the edge of a plain. Its name refers to a crown-shaped butte. The rug auctions that have brought Crownpoint fame are held several times a year, usually on Fridays, by the Crownpoint Rug Weavers Association. Both experts and amateurs attend the auctions, which take place in the public school gym. The sale itself begins at 7:00 p.m., but buyers are able to inspect the rugs, piled in the gym, all afternoon. A dinner of "Navajo tacos" served in the gym and the familiarity of many buyers with the auctions make the evening a mixture of commercial event and social engagement.

Navajo weavers submit their rugs on the afternoon of the auction. The association screens the rugs carefully to make sure they are authentic and to note whether commercial yarns and dyes are used. Buyers have a choice among small and large rugs featuring the variety of patterns used by Navajo weavers, and prices vary acccording to size, thread count, and yarns and dyes used. Depending on the size of the crowd and the number of rugs available, the auction can end by 9:00 P.M. or continue until the early

morning. Motel reservations in Grants or Gallup are recommended.

From Crownpoint, CHACO CANYON is about forty miles away, the distance seemingly increased by the unpaved, rutted condition of N.M. 57. Chaco can also be reached from the north; N.M. 57 intersects N.M. 44 at Blanco Trading Post, about fifty miles south of Farmington (see Tour 9).

As the traveler bounces and jolts the forty-odd miles from Crownpoint to Chaco Canyon, she will wonder where this narrow, isolated path is leading. Thin trails of smoke from distant Navajo homes, an infrequent pickup truck, and lonely signposts are all the traveler will see as she drives across flat, open plains and dips in and out of *arroyos*. Nothing on the road hints of the treasure ahead.

Finally, signs announce Chaco Culture National Historic Park (formerly called Chaco Canyon National Monument), an immense and rich storehouse of early Anasazi culture and probably one of the forerunners of the vigorous Pueblo culture of the Southwest.

The Chaco region has been lived in for thousands of years; archaic hunting tools have been found west of Casa Chiquita.

SIDE TOUR

Hunters and gatherers, followed by basketmakers, lived in nearby caves during later prehistoric times, 950 to 910 B.C. Pit houses were constructed about A.D. 500, followed by simple, one-story dwellings in the eighth century. By A.D. 900, the first inhabitants of Pueblo Bonito, Chaco's most famous structure, had built a low row of rooms against the canyon wall. In the next century, about A.D. 1000, construction activity matched the cultural progress being made at Chaco. Immense buildings were erected. The Anasazi created fine cylindrical pottery painted with sophisticated designs. They fashioned delicate jet jewelry and are thought to have studied solar and lunar positions from Fajada Butte. The zenith of this Anasazi civilization was reached between 1000 and about A.D. 1125 when, it is estimated, close to five thousand people lived in the canyon in the multistoried dwellings whose ruins line the valley. At the height of Chaco civilization, roads led from one pueblo to another, irrigation ditches fed the cultivated fields, and the canyon area was brimming with activity. By the end of the 1300s, however, the canyon was deserted and the massive buildings silent.

Visitors to Chaco Canyon will want to take at least one full day to explore the eleven major monument ruins (at last count there were at least two thousand ruins in and around the valley), eight of which are accessible by car. Three pueblos, Peñasco Blanco, Pueblo Alto, and Tsin Kletsin, are off the main park road but within hiking distance. An additional series of ruins lies within the park's protection. There are self-guiding tours with interpretive booklets available at the canyon's four most central and most studied ruins, Pueblo Bonito, Pueblo del Arroyo,

Casa Rinconada, and Chetro Ketl. The informative guidebooks lead the visitor through labyrinths of rooms, up stone steps to second and third stories, onto open plazas, and to the edges of subterranean kivas.

Throughout the tour of Chaco Canyon, visitors will be awed by the sophisticated level of architecture, craftsmanship, and scientific knowledge evidenced by the Anasazi people. The stonework, some of it a fine veneer placed atop an initial masonry layer, is extraordinary. Pueblo Bonito once reached five stories into the sky and contained perhaps eight hundred rooms. Other great houses were often composed of three or four terraced stories. Common areas, the most exciting of which may be the gigantic open plaza at Pueblo Bonito, were often enclosed courtyards or open, paved areas surrounded by tiers of rooms. Each pueblo contained many kivas, the underground ceremonial chambers that are an integral part of modern Pueblo life. There were great kivas as well as ordinary, small kivas at each settlement. Some, whose hidden niches yielded beads, necklaces, and other sacred gifts when they were excavated, were probably religious centers. Huge masonry columns supported heavily beamed roofs. Benches curved along the walls, and ventilating systems kept the smoke from the fire pits circulating to the outside. At the far end of the canyon, atop Fajada Butte, a petroglyph seems to indicate that the Anasazi tracked the sun, had a seasonal calendar, and marked the moon's path. Fajada Butte is no longer open to the public.

What brought the Chaco people here? What led them to create their intricate housing system? How did this dry valley

Chaco Canyon, *Harvey Caplin*.

support its thousands of inhabitants? Were there actually thousands of inhabitants? Why did the Anasazi leave so suddenly? Theories about Chaco culture are many, contradictory, and controversial. Since Chaco Canyon was first described in 1849 by Captain James Simpson, the site has been visited, studied, dug, and speculated about. The Hyde Expedition, which concentrated on Pueblo Bonito, studied the canyon from a scientific point of view in 1896 and 1899. Later expeditions, mounted by the University of New Mexico, the School of American Research, the National Geographic Society, the Smithsonian Institution, and the National Park Service, have provided a wealth of information. But there have always been nagging questions about the Chaco phenomenon that, until recently, were not answered.

In the late 1970s, a remarkable combination of groups including the Public Service Company of New Mexico, the state Historic Preservation Bureau, the Chaco Center of the National Park Service, and graduate students and personnel from the University of New Mexico studied Chaco

Chaco Canyon, *Daniel Gibson.*

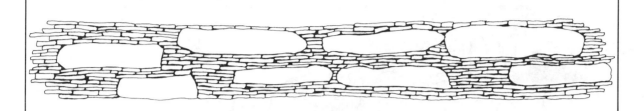

systematically. A team of scientists utilized remote sensing devices, aerial photography, pollen studies, and on-the-ground research to examine both the region and the culture. Their investigations resulted in the latest views of Chacoan society: that Chaco Canyon was the center of a vast, complicated political, social, and religious system. "Outliers," a term describing the many Anasazi ruins, most still unexplored, that lie within the San Juan Basin but outside the park, were once connected to Chaco Canyon by a series of roads. Perhaps, some speculate, Chaco was primarily a ceremonial center and Pueblo Bonito a gigantic hotel to which residents of the outliers came for religious celebrations. Maybe Chaco's buildings were food storehouses and temporary dwellings for the outliers. And perhaps Chaco never supported five thousand people at its height; rather two thousand caretakers stayed in the canyon during the year, watching over the structure and preparing for periodic influxes of visitors. Evidence is slowly accumulating that will support or refute this latest theory.

The Navajos, or Diné, who have been living among the Anasazi ruins for centuries, have incorporated the prehistoric mounds, crumbling buildings, and fading roads that dot their reservation into their own myths. They have accompanied and guided the Chaco scientists and surveyors as translators and experts on the area.

Meanwhile, potentially disruptive intruders have stepped up activity in the fifty-thousand-square-mile San Juan Basin where Chaco Canyon and the outliers are located. Energy companies have explored and leased land within a mile of the park and, in some cases, surrounded the outlier settlements. Nearby coal, oil, gas, and uranium deposits await development. The National Park Service, anthropologists, and representatives of industry are working together to see that Chaco Canyon and its outliers remain a spectacular repository of Anasazi culture and American history.

National Park Service rangers conduct guided tours of Chaco Canyon daily. They also hold evening talks at the campground to the south of the visitors' center. Campers will find park accommodations simple but adequate. Fresh tap water, essential in the hot summer months, is available at the visitors' center. Both the campground and the visitors' center are open year-round, although people will be most comfortable touring the canyon and its adjacent sites in the spring or fall. Winters at Chaco can be bitterly cold and summer days very hot. Because of the nature of the roads into the canyon, it is wise to call ahead and check weather conditions. Food and lodging are available only at Cuba, Farmington, Gallup, or Grants.

I-40 crosses the Continental Divide accompanied by a tawdry collection of buildings fronting the highway, but north of this grouping the red rock cliffs parallel the highway in spectacular fashion.

FORT WINGATE, 331 mi., is now a small munitions dump with a long history. In 1860, Fort Fauntleroy was established at this spot, called by the Navajo Shashbitó ("bear springs"). The fort was named after General Thomas Turner Fauntleroy, but when Fauntleroy resigned his commission to join the Confederate Army, it was renamed Fort Lyon. In 1866 the fort assumed the name by which it is now known, that of Captain Benjamin Wingate, who had been killed in New Mexico's only major battle of the Civil War, the Battle of Valverde. Previous Fort Wingates had existed near Grants. Beginning in 1882, the new Fort Wingate was used more for outfitting archaeological and ethnological expeditions than for military purposes. In 1914 it was used to house four thousand Mexican troops forced out of northern Mexico by Pancho Villa. When the Mexicans left, a large boarding school for Navajos became the major source of activity in the town of Fort Wingate. The fort itself now employs very few, although its function as a weapons storage site continues. Numerous houses and hogans in the area surrounding Fort Wingate are built from ammunition cases left behind from the busier days of the fort.

SIDE TOUR

A road, N.M. 400, leads south from Fort Wingate up a steep hill to a fine lookout over the red rock sandstone cliffs on the other side of the interstate. The road continues south, climbing to an elevation of eighty-three hundred feet at McGaffey, a former logging camp, now occupied by summer homes and U.S. Forest Service campgrounds. Ten miles from Fort Wingate's piñon- and juniper-clad hills, McGaffey lies among stands of spruce and Ponderosa pine. A small lake is used for fishing in summer and for skating during cold spells in the winter.

A two-lane road north of I-40 parallels the freeway from Fort Wingate to CHURCH ROCK, a distance of four miles, and on to Gallup. Church Rock is a small Navajo settlement, sheltered on the north by two magnificent landmarks of the same red sandstone that has accompanied the highway from the east side of the Continental Divide. Pyramid rock and the Church Rock, or Navajo Church, are readily visible for miles. The road north of Church Rock leads to several large caves in the rock, one called Kit Carson Cave in the belief that Carson and his men sought shelter here during their Navajo campaigns. Further north are several uranium mines, which have provided employment and problems for the people of the area. In 1979 a levee restraining the waters of a mine holding-pond broke, allowing millions of gallons of radiation-contaminated water to flow into the tributaries of the Rio Puerco, through Church Rock, and on past Gallup. The effects of this spill on the inhabitants of the area and their livestock have been and will continue to be hotly debated.

Just west of Church Rock, on land formerly owned by the century-old Outlaw Trading Post, Red Rock State Park was built in a spectacular canyon and opened in 1978. The park includes a campground, but is best-known for its big outdoor arena, built primarily for the annual Intertribal Ceremonial, and for large rodeos. A small museum of local lore is also found near the arena.

The Intertribal Ceremonial antedates Red Rock State Park by many years. It was held until 1978 in Gallup; the fifty-seventh annual ceremonial moved from the old grounds, razed for the interstate highway. The central event of the ceremonial, held in mid-August, is a performance of Indian dances by Navajos, Pueblo tribes, Plains Indians, and usually a tribe from Mexico. This performance draws spectators from throughout the country. Equally important to the local populace, including the Navajos from the large reservation that surrounds Gallup, are the opportunities to trade and to meet with one another. The ceremonial sponsors a show and sale of Indian arts and crafts, drawing entries from throughout New Mexico and beyond. Pickup trucks fill Gallup and the ceremonial parking lots. Motels and restaurants are full. The many enterprises retailing Indian goods hoard a large inventory to tempt visitors during the ceremonial. The ceremonial begins with a parade through the streets of Gallup. Costumed Indians who will participate in the colorful dance spectacular march through the town, with frequent stops to perform to the beat of accompanying drummers.

Continuing west on the frontage road past Church Rock, the traveler reaches GALLUP, 343 mi. (alt. 6,506, pop. 18,206). Gallup, named after a railroad paymaster, was built on two industries, railroading and coal, at the end of the nineteenth century. The railway reached this spot, twenty-one miles from what is now the Arizona state line, in 1881. At that time a stagecoach stop and a saloon, the Blue Goose, constituted the entire town. Within two years, it is said, the town had twenty-two saloons and other accoutrements of a boom town, including an opera house, the fading sign for which is still visible above a storefront on U.S. 66.

Coal had been discovered north of Gallup several years before the railroad arrived, and with the coming of the "iron horse" a ready market sustained growth in the mines. Immigrants from mining areas in eastern Europe, England, Wales, Germany, and Italy all found their way to Gallup. The mines in the Gallup area declined in output after World War II, as the United States moved toward the use of oil. They were eventually closed in 1950. At the beginning of the 1980s, talk of reopening them accompanied steep rises in the price of oil.

The building of highways and the availability of cheap fuel contributed, in New Mexico as elsewhere, to the decline of the railroads. In the 1940s twenty-two passenger trains per day coursed through Gallup; in 1983 the number was two, and those were in danger of being eliminated.

The railroad and coal have been replaced as major reasons for Gallup's existence by tourism and the "Indian trade," always important here. The two are related in that Gallup is a central location for visitors to several pueblos and to the Navajo Reservation. Tourists are also buyers of many of the Indian crafts, primarily Pueblo and Navajo jewelry and Navajo rugs, brought for sale to Gallup. The town serves as a trading center for Zuni Pueblo and for a large area of the Navajo Reservation. Saturday afternoon on crowded Coal Street in downtown Gallup is an experience shared by wide-eyed tourists, Gallup residents, and Indians alike. Its position as a trading center brings Gallup problems as well as prosperity: the combination of alcohol and long-distance travel makes the surrounding highways dangerous on Friday and Saturday nights. Gallup shopowners and saloon-keepers are not Indians, a fact resented by the Navajos and other

Indians trading there that has led to conflict in the town on occasion.

Gallup's position as a leading site for the wholesaling of Indian goods is unrivaled and dates to the early decades of this century, when traders like C. C. Manning and C. N. Cotton supplied goods to reservation traders and also wholesaled Navajo blankets to Eastern dealers. Navajos brought wool and piñon nuts from the surrounding hillsides to be sold. These activities continue into the present.

Gallup includes a number of important public buildings. Largest is the U.S. Public Health Service Hospital, a referral hospital for Indians and for the smaller Indian Health Service clinics of the entire eastern part of the Navajo Reservation and for Zuni Pueblo. Close to the hospital on a hill on the south edge of town is the Gallup campus of the University of New Mexico. This growing campus offers a fine view of Gallup and the surrounding mesas and rocky ridges, or hogbacks. It covers the first two years of college and makes available many night classes and courses in regional subjects, such as the Navajo language. Students may finish their education at the university's main campus in Albuquerque. Downtown, the Gallup library (115 West Hill St.) has a surprisingly complete collection, including an excellent sampling of books about the Southwest. The McKinley County Courthouse, across the street from the library, is a large and stately adobe structure, displaying on its interior walls fine murals of McKinley's early days.

A freeway interchange at the west edge of Gallup allows travelers to go north via U.S. 666 to the Navajo Reservation, Shiprock, and the mountains of southwestern Colorado. Heading south from the same intersection,

N.M. 32 leads to Zuni Pueblo and the mountain areas explored by Aldo Leopold that became part of one of the nation's first wilderness areas, the Gila Wilderness. Both roads are described in Tour 17.

Beyond Gallup, I-40 passes several small Navajo settlements outside the reservation's borders. The highway winds between picturesque sandstone cliffs into the small canyon of the western Rio Puerco, which runs into the Little Colorado River inside Arizona. The dwellings of Navajos and numerous stores offering Indian jewelry and souvenirs are set among junipers and piñons against many shallow caves in the wind- and water-eroded sandstone. At 364 mi., the highway simultaneously enters Arizona and the Navajo Reservation.

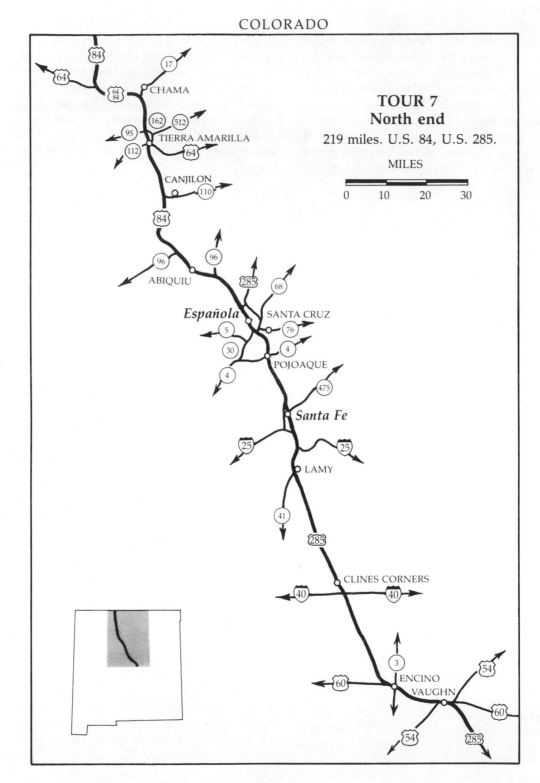

TOUR 7
North end
219 miles. U.S. 84, U.S. 285.

MILES

See page 421 for southern end of tour seven.

tour seven

Colorado Border • **Chama** • *Española* • *Santa Fe* • *Vaughn* • **Roswell** • **Artesia** • *Carlsbad* • *Texas Border*

This route winds among mountainous country and high plateaus, through quiet farming villages and places important in New Mexico history. The first part of the trip, from the Colorado border to Santa Fe, is the route followed by Fathers Silvestre de Escalante and Francisco Domínguez when they attempted to open a route between Santa Fe and California. Part of the road travels through two national forests and near hunting, fishing, and recreational areas; part passes below the fabled red cliffs near Abiquiu. South of Santa Fe, the route lies across grazing lands and farm areas dotted with oil rigs and other signs of the petroleum and gas industries that have enriched the cities of the southeast.

Just over Cumbres Pass (10,003 feet), N.M. 17 starts at the Colorado line, at a point seventy miles southwest of Alamosa, Colorado.

The highway from the Colorado state line to Chama lies in beautiful high country, sometimes passing in sight of mountain rivers and the Cumbres and Toltec steam railroad. In spring and summer, wildflowers brighten the green; in fall, the golden aspens are stunning.

CHAMA, 8 mi. (alt 7,551, pop, 1,098), is a little town settled among trees at the meeting place of Archuleta and Willow creeks. The Spanish named it after the Tewa pueblo Tzama ("here they have wrestled"), whose ancient founders must have chosen the spot for its great natural beauty and abundant sources of food. As wagon traffic from Santa Fe to Colorado increased in the 1800s, the town grew. A railroad was built over the *cumbre* or summit in 1880, and the town became a supply center for the area's ranchers. Nearby forests gave the town its early importance as a lumber center. The lumberyards, a sawmill, and general stores provide jobs for many townspeople, but recently Chama has become better known as a recreation center. Hunters and fishermen have long recognized Chama's advantages; Utes, Apaches, and Navajos hunted here. Lying as it does at the extreme north of the state, enjoying a longer and harder winter than other areas, Chama has gained a new reputation for its winter attractions. Its rolling, open spaces make it particularly attractive to the cross-country skiers and snowmobilers who have joined the hunters and fishermen in seeking winter spots. Sometimes these features also attract land developers, with resulting conflicts between those who would keep Chama for

the old-time residents and those who want to accommodate progress.

A welcome center at the junction of U.S. 64/ U.S. 84 and N.M. 17 provides information on Chama's attractions and tourist accommodations.

The best-known feature in Chama is the Cumbres and Toltec Scenic Railroad, the narrow-gauge steam railroad that chugs between Chama and Antonito, Colorado, from June through October. The coal-driven train, its steam engine built at the turn of the century, leaves the small station at the edge of Chama each morning for the six-hour trip to Osier, Colorado, where it meets its sister train from Antonito, pauses for a lunch break, and then turns around for the return trip.

Tourists have been riding the converted freight cars of the C&TS Railroad since 1971. The Denver and Rio Grande Railway Company, which had operated the freight and passenger line from Antonito, Colorado, through the mountains to Farmington, New Mexico, for almost one hundred years, found that by the 1960s its revenue from this line was falling. The D&RG requested permission to abandon the line, which had originally hauled

freight, iron ore, miners, and lumber throughout the San Juan Mountains. Citizens of Colorado and New Mexico, led by railroad buffs, petitioned their states to purchase the railroad. The legislatures of the neighboring states jointly purchased the sixty-four miles of track and equipment in 1970 for $547,120. Since then, thousands of passengers have enjoyed the day-long journey through mountains and meadows, across trestles and narrow bridges, past ghost towns, crumbling snowsheds, cowboys, and lonely fishermen. The train stops beneath wooden tanks to take on water, pauses at Cumbres Pass for picture-taking sessions, and arranges its journey around the meeting place of the two ends of the line. There, at Osier, Colorado, where Osier Creek meanders through a gentle valley, passengers from Chama and Antonito eat a hot meal in the 1885 "eating-house" or picnic on the hills along the track.

Accommodations on the Cumbres and Toltec are simple but comfortable. Photographers often congregate in the open-air car at the rear of the train to get a 360-degree view of the spectacular countryside. A trainman gives a narrative of the journey, citing snow and altitude statistics, pointing out the locations of famous train wrecks, and answering questions from train buffs and children. While the train ride is always beautiful, it is especially scenic in September and early October when the leaves are turning. It is advisable to book seats ahead. Inquire through the Chama Chamber of Commerce or the Cumbres and Toltec Scenic Railroad.

South of Chama, the route crosses the Rio Brazos and runs through high, open country.

SIDE TOUR

At Parkview, 21 mi., N.M. 95 provides a paved route to Heron Lake Dam and State Park, one of the newer of New Mexico's parks. A visitors' center offers information on Heron Lake and other recreation areas. Fine trout and salmon fishing, winter ice fishing, sailing, and camping are popular activities here. Motorized boats are permitted at trolling speeds only. A new hiking trail links Heron Lake with El Vado to the south.

Aspen grove, *Dave Wilson.*

On the eastern side of the highway at Parkview is the junction with N.M. 162, which loops through the picturesque and miniscule settlements of Brazos and Ensenada to Tierra Amarilla.

At Ensenada N.M. 512 travels up to the mouth of the Brazos Box Canyon. The canyon is an impressive natural formation, with its high, rocky walls rising straight up from the valley floor. A waterfall within walking distance of the mouth of the canyon usually flows only one month in the year, but the cliffs and creeks provide other points of interest for the hiker. The casual visitor is permitted to drive through privately owned resort areas.

SIDE TOUR

From its junction with U.S. 84, 23 mi., N.M. 112 branches west to El Vado State Park, 14.9 mi., another manmade lake that has been added to the state park system and is used for recreation as well as flood control and irrigation. The timbered mesas surrounding the lake give El Vado a distinctive alpine look. Besides the fishing and camping facilities that were provided when El Vado Dam and Reservoir were built by the Middle Rio Grande Conservancy Project, there are areas for power-boating and sailing, along with modern campgrounds and other park amenities. From here a rough road links El Vado to Regina, 28 mi., a little-traveled drive through piñon, cedar, and sage country.

Raft trips on the Chama River start below the dam. One- or two-day trips down this river, tranquil for much of its length but rough enough for white water excitement, allow travelers to experience a part of New Mexico's wilderness formerly accessible to only a few hardy hikers.

TIERRA AMARILLA, 24 mi. (alt. 6,800), named for the yellow earth of the vicinity, has been since 1880 the seat of Rio Arriba County, one of the districts settled by Spaniards and later Mexicans. When the townsite was filed in 1832, Tierra Amarilla was called Las Nutrias, probably after the beavers that populated nearby streams. The Tierra Amarilla Land Grant to Juan Martínez and his eight children was made by Mexico to encourage development of the area. However, only after 1846, when U.S. troops under General Kearny moved in, did the colony become permanent. Tierra Amarilla served as the rations headquarters, the supply source, for the Utes and Jicarilla Apaches in 1871–72, before the Utes were moved to a reservation in San Juan County and the Apaches to the western part of the territory.

The little town lies in what has in recent years become a depressed area. Once able to support settlers, the land is now farmed mainly for home vegetable gardens or used to raise a few cattle. Lack of employment opportunities has led residents to move out, as evidenced by the many boarded-up and dilapidated buildings in the town. Nevertheless, Tierra Amarilla's history and the beauty of its setting make it an interesting stopping point.

In 1967 the imposing county courthouse was the scene of a shootout that focused national attention on the aims of Reies Lopez Tijerina and his land grant movement, the Alianza Federal de los Mercedes (Federal Aliance for Land Grants). Tijerina argued that the land around Tierra Amarilla belonged to the descendants of the original grantees, not to the federal government or those who obtained the land, as Tijerina felt, by trickery and fraud. Tijerina and his followers invaded the courthouse to dramatize their objectives, and in the melee a sheriff's deputy was injured, touching off a well-publicized manhunt that employed tanks and helicopters. The resulting trial ended in a jail term for Tijerina. He was later found innocent of charges stemming from the incident. Tijerina ran for governor in 1968 as a candidate of the People's Constitutional Party,

but his name was removed from the ballot because of his earlier convictions for legal violations. Tijerina continues to work for his cause.

At Tierra Amarilla one can take U.S. 64 across to Tres Piedras and Taos, a breathtaking drive often closed in the winter, cool even in the summer months. Few signs of civilization disturb this drive (Tour 2).

CANJILON, 36 mi. (alt. 7,800), lies three miles to the east on N.M. 115. It is reputedly the town where the descendants of the conquistador de Vargas settled in 1774 and still live. Canjilon (in New Mexico, "deer antler") is now the center of a farming community set in a wide valley, with a clear view of the mountains and mesas to the south. A ranger station is a good source of information on local road conditions. Residents of the community have played a part in the land grant movement, resentful of U.S. Forest Service restrictions on what they see as their land.

From Canjilon, an unpaved and rough road runs north to Canjilon Lakes, 10 mi., where the Forest Service maintains three campgrounds. The road to the lakes parallels the Canjilon River and passes through alpine meadows where cows and horses graze among brilliant wildflowers in the spring. Traces of snow remain until June and testify to the reality of harsh winters. At 7 mi. an unpaved road leads off to the left to Trout Lakes, 23 miles away, where there is also a campground. Lower, middle, and upper Canjilon Lakes, along with the smaller ponds scattered among them, are located on the southern slopes of Canjilon Mountain (10,913 feet). The lakes were originally created by beaver dams and have been strengthened or enlarged by the Forest Service. They are still home to some beavers, but now contain many more trout. There are no hiking trails, but it is easy to walk through the woods, and a hike to the top of the mountain culminates in spectacular views.

SIDE TOUR

U.S. 84 follows the Rio Chama, winding gradually down the high plains with views of faraway mountain ranges, rolling green meadows, and tiny farms, giving way to rugged scenery where the reds and browns of ancient rock formations predominate.

A turnoff around 58 mi. leads into the Echo Canyon Amphitheater, where the Forest Service maintains a campground and shaded picnic area. A ten-minute walk, the Trail of the Echo, takes one from the parking lot to the naturally formed amphitheater. The "theater" has been weathered out of the rock over millions of years, its age attested to by successive rock layers of different colors. The aptly named canyon sends back sharp echoes of shouts and even remnants of conversations. A shorter trail, Little Echo, winds into a smaller canyon where the forces of nature are beginning the process that will eventually form a new amphitheater.

Just before Ghost Ranch Visitors Center a dirt road leads off to the west to Christ in the Desert Monastery. The hard-packed but bumpy road winds up and down to and then along the Chama River for thirteen miles before it reaches the parking lot of the monastery. Benedictine monks built their center here in 1964 in the adobe forms and colors of the surrounding land, but with a soaring, glass-walled church that is very modern. The monks work gardens, raise bees, and run a guest house for visitors in the tradition of the Benedictines. They also weave and do woodwork and pottery, occupations which bring in most of the monastery's income. Visitors are invited to Mass in the church; those who stay at the guest house can also share the prayers and physical work of the monks. A small gift shop offers unusual arts and crafts.

A short drive south down the road from Echo Canyon brings the traveler to the Ghost Ranch Visitors' Center, 51 mi., which is maintained as an attraction of the Carson National Forest. Two short walks feature a soil and water conservation project and an exhibit on the recreational, economic, and conservation uses of national forests. Examples of forest wildlife and trees and a geological exhibit about the rocky cliffs of the Ghost Ranch highlight this latter mini-tour, especially attractive to children. The well-known artist Georgia O'Keeffe owns a little house within sight of the visitors' center. The land for this center was exchanged by the Ghost Ranch for title to land claimed by 111 families who had occupied it for generations. It took six years to complete the exchange, but in 1975 the ranch gave the titles to the families in what was a unique solution to the often bitter struggles for land title in the area.

Another short ride, 2 mi., and one can take the detour east to Ghost Ranch. A well-maintained dirt road runs to the ranch, 1 mi., an adult study center maintained by the United Presbyterian Church. A fire gutted the main building in 1983. However, it is worth the detour to visit the Sundwelling Demonstration Center (a solar project), to picnic under the trees, and to learn something of the work of the Ghost Ranch. Once a working ranch, with origins dating back to 1766, it now offers seminars on a variety of topics open to all interested persons. It also offers a year-round program of conservation and land use education for local farmers and community organization and cultural education. A major goal of the ranch is to restore the overgrazed and drought-ridden land to a productive state.

The Ghost Ranch, which gets its mysterious-sounding name from the *brujas* or witches said to inhabit the canyons, is principally located on the northern third of the "Las Casas de Riano" or "Piedra Lumbre" grant (*Piedra lumbre* means "flame rock," an appropriate name for the brilliant rocks of the area.) Tomás Vélez Capuchín, royal governor of the Province of New Mexico, made the grant to Lieutenant Pedro Martín Serrano. It was a purely private grant to Lieutenant Serrano, and not part of a community grant, as were many of the other land grants. In 1893 the United States government confirmed the grant, which was gradually divided over the years. These divisions followed the Spanish inheritance system, under which estates were shared equally among children of the immediate family. Some children then conveyed their titles to others, and numerous small tracts were often traded back and forth. In 1929 all conflicting claims were bought in by the A. B. Renehan Estate.

From there title can be traced to the present owners.

In 1947 paleontologists discovered fossils of an early dinosaur named coelophysis on Ghost Ranch. A lightly built creature, no more than six feet in length, coelophysis could run fast to catch its prey. A single layer in one hillside on the ranch was packed with complete skeletons of this dinosaur, an exciting find for the paleontologists, who previously had only fragments of coelophysis to study.

The highway winds down through wonderful red and ocher rock formations. N.M. 96, 57 mi., will take the traveler to Abiquiu Dam and Reservoir, to the towns of Coyote and Gallina, and into Cuba.

A dirt road immediately cuts off the turnoff to the reservoir's boat launching area and campsites. Continue on 96 for a detour to GALLINA, 33 mi., or further to join N.M. 44, 58 mi., making a loop through Cuba to Bernalillo. The shorter trip takes you along high plains and grazing land, surprisingly green after rains. There are more corrals than houses on this drive. In front the traveler sees the massive form of the Cerro Pedernal. At Youngsville, 14 mi., trailers contrast with the old village church. The road dips into Coyote, 15 mi., where a modern adobe church can be reached by taking a trip through town on red dirt roads, sticky when wet. The town is named after Coyote Canyon, which was actually the home of many coyotes before farmers and ranchers moved in.

Past Coyote the road dips again, along eroded canyons, the Arroyo de Agua, and red, terraced cliffs. The scenery changes once more, to orchards in a lush valley whose sides are deep red cliffs balancing huge boulders. Further on, the stark cliffs take on paler hues. Around 25 mi., look ahead for the Mesa Alta ("high mesa"), whose cliffs are covered with pines. The valley widens here, and soon the road enters the Santa Fe National Forest. Wide meadows on both sides of the road feed more cattle. At Gallina houses are scattered over the meadow. The name means "hen," but it more likely refers to the many wild fowl, including turkey, that can be found in the region. The San Pedro Peaks (10,624 feet) are to the south in the San Pedro Wilderness area. Check with local rangers before attempting to enter the wilderness area from here.

At the junction with N.M. 112, 40 mi., a rough road turns north up to El Vado, the tiny community on the edge of El Vado Lake. South, the paved portion of the road continues to its intersection with N.M. 44, running through the forested country where lumbering is an important industry. One mile down this road, N.M. 95 cuts off to Lindrith, 12 mi., a tiny farming and ranching community that also has a small oil refinery. The drive here is strangely different, through rough-cut rocks, weathered and wrinkled, and delicately colored mesas.

SIDE TOUR

ABIQUIU, 65 mi., is a tiny town on a bend in the river. It is the center of a farming and stock-raising area and lies on the site of Tewa pueblo ruins that were abandoned in the sixteenth century. To reach Abiquiu, one must leave the highway and drive to the right up to the town, a cluster of adobe buildings grouped around a plaza. The old mission church of Santo Tomás dominates the open space.

Although records show settlement of Santa Rosa de Lima de Abiquiu in the 1740s, many years passed before a permanent town grew up. Indian attacks and sickness discouraged settlers. The first village lay three miles west of the present one. Barely visible ruins of the original chapel of St. Rose of Lima remain to be restored. This village was deserted after a devastating Indian raid in 1748. The same year a group of *genízaros*, captive Indians who adopted Spanish ways, was moved there, but they were no more successful at taming the area than earlier pioneers. Two more attempts at colonization were made, the last one ordered by Governor Capuchín, who also insisted that houses be built around a plaza and near soldiers. This protection seemed to work, and when the Domínguez-Escalante Expedition passed through the village in 1776 on its way to California, Domínguez recorded a sizable population.

By 1778 Abiquiu was one of the stages for those traveling to the new village of Los Angeles in California. The town also became an outfitting point for trappers and traders, both Indian and non-Indian. General Kearny established a military post here in 1848.

Padre Martínez, well-known in New Mexico history, was born in Abiquiu in 1793 and baptized in the main church of Santo Tomás. He moved to Taos when he was nine, and it was there that he began his pastorship. Padre Martínez later made his mark on New Mexico history, especially in his conflict with the powerful Bishop Lamy of Santa Fe (see Tour 3). The artist Georgia O'Keeffe is a present-day resident of Abiquiu. She has brought fame to the area by using its scenery as the subject of many paintings.

Inquire in Abiquiu for the mosque built near here for the Dar-al-Islam Foundation, which planned a Moslem community in Rio Arriba county. A prominent Egyptian architect, Hassam Fathi, designed the circular adobe building, a small replica of mosques used for worship in the Near East.

U.S. 84 continues to parallel the river on its path south through a strip of land whose bright green in the summer contrasts with the parched red land around it. Here one passes near the El Rito Campus of Northern New Mexico Community College and the little town of Medanales on the eastern side of the river. Notice the high-peaked tin roofs of the adobe houses in this area. The pitched roofs are more practical in this snowy climate than the flat ones found in the pueblos and on the adobes in Santa Fe and further south. Orchards, pastures, and chile fields spread out from the river; the oddly shaped surrounding hills are dotted with piñon.

At 79 miles, N.M. 285 crosses the river to San Juan Pueblo (Tour 11). The little town near here, Hernandez, became famous as the subject of an Ansel Adams photograph that shows a full moon rising over the houses and *campo santo* (cemetery) of the town.

This part of the tour ends in Española. Follow the signs to U.S. 285 through Española to Santa Fe, a stretch described in Tours 5 and 11.

Travelers on U.S. 285 leave Santa Fe via Old Pecos Trail. At the intersection with I-25, they have the choice of taking the freeway a few miles east to the "U.S. 285, Lamy" exit, or of staying on Old Pecos Trail to the point (126 mi.) where U.S. 285 branches off south.

Coming down the slope at 131 mi., the tour crosses the tracks of the eighteen-mile shuttle connecting Santa Fe with its train station at Lamy. The station itself lies a mile east of the highway, at 132 mi. The Santa Fe Railroad, following the Santa Fe Trail from Kansas City, had to use all the influence at its disposal to gain a right of way across Raton pass. Once in New Mexico, the railroad headed southwest, presumably via Santa Fe, making great haste to be first to the Pacific. It is possible that railroad officials and surveyors never intended to go into Santa Fe. Railroad builders, conscious of land values and political considerations and wary of what to them were the strange and old-fashioned influences of the older Hispanic communities, generally preferred to create new cities and to bypass existing ones. However that may be, when the rails reached the village founded at the time of the Lamy Land Grant, engineers declared that the south rim of the Santa Fe basin was too steep for the main line. They built the shuttle into Santa Fe but continued the main line southwest into the Rio Grande valley and Albuquerque. The railroad further honored Jean Baptiste Lamy, educator, missionary, and first archbishop of the American territorial period, by naming Santa Fe's distant station for him. Adolph Bandelier, the pioneer archaeologist who frequently took the train in his travels throughout central New Mexico in the 1880s, examined Pueblo ruins just west of the depot here.

The Amtrak system still runs one train a day

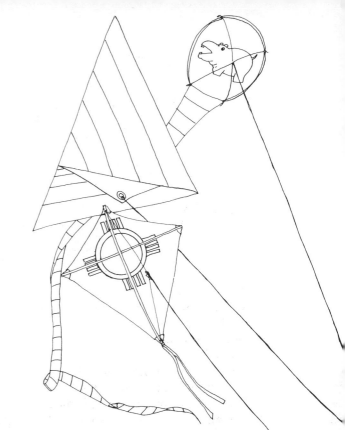

in each direction. Both trains stop at Lamy. The Tinnie Mercantile Company operates an elegant restaurant here, the Legal Tender. With long brick waiting platforms and spacious lawns, the station remains much the same as it was when a dozen passenger trains a day ran along the Santa Fe's main line. Lamy hosts a kite-flying contest annually in mid-April, with prizes for biggest, highest, and fighting kites and a separate category for children's kites.

U.S. 285 crosses the Santa Fe's main line just south of the Lamy turnoff. At 133 mi., N.M. 41 branches off to Galisteo, Moriarty, and Estancia (Tour 5). Now in the Galisteo basin, the highway parallels Glorieta Mesa, a southern extension of the Sangre de Cristo range. Along the high open stretch between Lamy and Clines Corners, mountain ranges are visible in almost every direction: immediately west, the Ortiz and San Pedros; further away to the southwest, the Sandias and Manzanos; directly south, the Gallinas; and northeast, the Sangre de Cristos. Near the road, curiously shaped, rock-capped hills challenge backseat geologists and the imaginations of travelers of all ages.

Archaeological studies still underway are revealing much about ancient ruins here in the Galisteo basin. San Cristobal Pueblo consisted of some two thousand rooms during the latter half of the fourteenth century. Historians suppose that Governor Otermín's warning of the 1680 Pueblo uprising came from San Cristobal. The pueblo, by then quite small, was abandoned during the 1680s when Pueblo people controlled New Mexico and was never reoccupied. A remnant from San Cristobal moved north to the Santa Cruz Valley. Galisteo Pueblo, another Tano-speaking town a few miles west, shared in the tremendous population growth of the thirteenth and fourteenth centuries and was also abandoned during the Pueblo Revolt. However, Galisteo was resettled early in the 1700s, and the Spanish authorities maintained a detachment of troops here against the Comanches. Tepee rings dating from this time probably belong to the Mescalero Apaches, who wintered in this area and even left women and children at Galisteo and Pecos pueblos while the men hunted bison. This Apache-Pueblo arrangement may have resulted from hostility of the Comanches towards the two groups. Comanches did regard both as enemies, and carried out fierce attacks during the middle 1700s that eventually led to the abandonment of all the pueblos east of Santa Fe.

Hispanic settlers recolonized the village of Galisteo during the period of Mexican rule and pastured sheep among Pueblo ruins all over the Galisteo basin. The San Cristobal Ranch, which now occupies a large portion of this region (and contains San Cristobal Pueblo), resulted from a battle between Ceran St. Vrain and Lucien Maxwell over the San Cristobal Land Grant. Maxwell won. Range cattle have had this corner of the world nearly to themselves ever since.

CLINES CORNERS, 167 mi., is a crossroads that has provided services for automobile and truck travel almost since U.S. 66 was first routed across the plains. Tour 6 describes I-40, Clines Corners' newer highway, throughout New Mexico.

U.S. 285 now skirts east of the Pedernal ("flint") Mountains, a small range dividing the Estancia Valley (west) from the Pecos drainage. Pedernal Peak, west at 179 mi., is named for the flint deposits and mines found at its base. A spring beneath this peak, much contested in historic times, drains into Pintada Creek, which once watered the abandoned town of North Lucy nearby, and the Pintada Ranch, forty miles downstream. During the late 1200s, Pintada Creek was the easternmost extension of Pueblo culture in New Mexico.

Between ENCINO, 194 mi., and VAUGHN, 210 mi., Tour 7 (U.S. 285) joins with Tour 8 (U.S. 60), noted along this stretch for low mountains, grazing sheep, and the Santa Fe tracks. The railway crossroads town of Vaughn is described in Tour 13 because it had its beginning on the railroad that U.S. 54 now parallels.

For the two hundred fifty miles between Vaughn and the Texas border, the traveler on U.S. 285 is almost constantly reminded of three great geographical features of southeastern New Mexico. On the west, the Front Range continues southeasterly from the Sangre de Cristos. Peaks of the Capitan, Sacramento, and Guadalupe mountains are visible from the road, weather permitting. On the east lies the Llano Estacado, or Staked Plains. When the ancient Pecos River cut through the caprock of a large plateau covering much of eastern New Mexico and the Texas Panhandle, it left an irregular line of bluffs and "breaks" (a thousand feet high in places) paralleling the river. Alongside the highway, in the wide valleys of the Pecos, are the western plains.

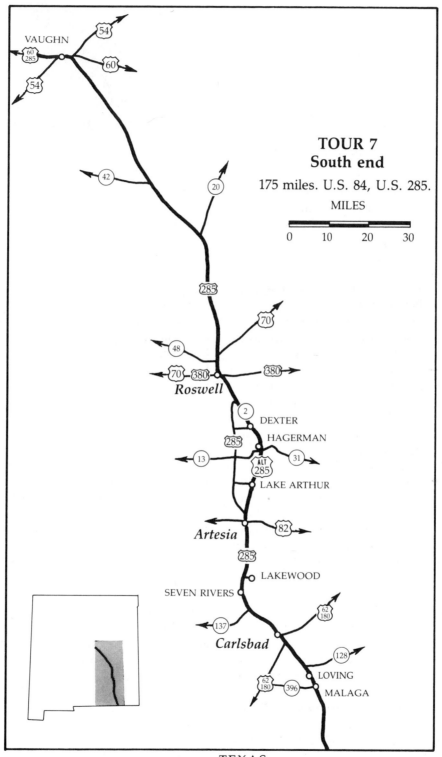

**TOUR 7
South end**

175 miles. U.S. 84, U.S. 285.

MILES

0   10   20   30

VAUGHN

54

60
285

60

54

42

20

285

70

48

70 380

380

Roswell

2

DEXTER

285

HAGERMAN

13

ALT
285

31

LAKE ARTHUR

82

Artesia

285

LAKEWOOD

SEVEN RIVERS

62
180

137

Carlsbad

128

62
180

396

LOVING

MALAGA

TEXAS

This land is changeable. Scorched in the summer heat, driven by frigid winds, usually without benefit of a snow cover in the winter, battered by spring's gusts, and overgrazed for generations, it arouses our compassion. Seen under a cloudless summer sky, in a year with late (or no) rain, it can appear miserable, unable to support life. A short month later, if August rains do come, it can be the glory of creation. Wildflowers of every color stretch to the mountains, and lush grass grows everywhere in the rich chocolate-brown earth. With care, these plains can be amazingly regenerative. Travelers, like ranchers, learn to be patient with them. Under a cloudy sky, for example, many things become visible that are hidden in the glare of the full sun.

South of Vaughn, U.S. 285 proceeds across a high, rolling prairie through Guadalupe, Lincoln, DeBaca, and into Chaves County; there are few settlements. Underlying the area beyond the town of Mesa is the Artesian Basin, where hundreds of artesian wells bring cold, pure water up from the limestone depths. Water from heavy rains and melting mountain snows, together with the drainage from basins of streams tributary to the Pecos, is caught in the honeycombed channels of porous limestone that lie under the topsoil. This porous deposit rises up on the eastern side of the Sacramento Mountains and extends underground to the bluffs east of the Pecos River, serving as a natural channel for the water flowing down to the valley floor. Water from the artesian wells, which average two hundred fifty feet in depth, has transformed some of the arid land into good farmland.

Irrigation farming has been practiced in this basin since 1880. The water was first obtained from springs near Roswell or diverted from tributaries of the Pecos, and later came from the artesian wells.

ROSWELL, 284 mi. (alt 3,557, pop, 39,698), has grown from a barren plains trading post to a modern, attractive city with parks and residential streets shaded by old cottonwoods and willows. It is situated at a major highway intersection; U.S. 285 is crossed in Roswell by U.S. 70 (Tour 10) and U.S. 380 (Tour 12), which join west of Roswell into a single route.

The grama grass that covered the Pecos River Valley made this a good route for cattle from Texas heading to New Mexico and Colorado forts in the mid-nineteenth century. The land at the mouth of the Hondo ("deep") River was a frequent campsite for Texas cattlemen Goodnight, Loving, and Chisum and their crews. A cattle pen, a house, and an adobe structure that served as the cattlemen's primitive hotel were the first buildings on this site, in the 1860s. Van C. Smith of Omaha, a professional gambler, arrived from San Francisco with his partner, Aaron Wilburn, and bought the adobe hotel and trading post. In 1870 they constructed two buildings at what are now Fourth and Main streets in Roswell, and these became a general store, post office, and guest house. Smith gave the collection of buildings his father's name, Roswell, and filed a land claim. Main Street was made very wide in order to accommodate cattle herds passing through. Smith converted this street into a seasonal race track between his store and the Hondo River, and cattlemen along the Pecos

Orchards, *Harvey Caplin*.

were attracted to Roswell as a gambling center.

Two prominent cattlemen, John Chisum and Captain Joseph C. Lea, moved into the area. Chisum headquartered his ranch six miles south of Roswell, at South Spring. It became an important social and political center of southeastern New Mexico. The Chisum Ranch, now owned by Cornell University and maintained as it was in the 1870s, may be visited by appointment.

Captain Lea built a cattle empire northwest of Roswell. In 1877 he bought Smith's holdings. Lea's father-in-law bought out Wilburn and two other settlers, giving the Lea family entire ownership of Roswell. The family registered Roswell as a townsite and turned the settlement into an important trading center.

Even now Roswell is the commercial seat of the area from Vaughn and Clovis to Carlsbad and Hobbs. The Lea family convinced the commandant of the Fort Worth Military University to locate a military school in Roswell, and it opened in the fall of 1891, receiving the name of New Mexico Military Institute in 1893. The state-supported institute is now a coeducational preparatory school housed in handsome, buff brick buildings on a spacious campus. The campus no longer has alumnus Peter Hurd's murals (they were destroyed by fire), but it now proudly displays an exceptional stained-glass window in the modern chapel.

After the accidental discovery in 1891 of an artesian water source on the Nathan Jaffe Ranch near Roswell, ditches were cut through

the plains, and irrigation began that now results in crops of staple cotton, alfalfa, apples, corn, and grain. The existence of abundant water and the construction of railroad connections to Carlsbad and Amarillo accounted for a 600 percent increase in population between 1890 and 1900. Growth based on agriculture continued steadily until 1941. The federal government then began a series of operations in Roswell. The War Department established an army flying school south of the city; Walker Air Force Base was built here in the 1950s as a permanent installation of the Strategic Air Command. Construction of Atlas intercontinental missiles began in 1960. With the closing of the air force base in 1967, the relocation of the Penn Oil Company, and the loss of the need for supportive services, Roswell sustained a great shock. Fifteen thousand people, who had made up 46 percent of the work force, left the town. One-half of the financial capital of the town departed with them. Citizens and banks rallied, however, and turned the air force base into an industrial park that houses a branch of Eastern New Mexico University, a government office complex, a hospital, an airport, residences, and, appropriately, a rehabilitation center.

Economic recovery was achieved so rapidly and with such community effort that Roswell was chosen as an All-American City in 1979 and is a frequently used example to other cities that have lost a portion of their economic base. Roswell exemplifies the conversion of defense facilities to peaceful purposes.

Roswell is the location of an extraordinary museum and art center. The museum emphasizes Southwestern art and space sciences. The permanent collection contains works by Georgia O'Keeffe, Marsden Hartley, Stuart Davis, John Marin, Ernest Blumenschein, and Andrew Dasburg. The museum also features many pieces by Roswell native Peter Hurd, best known as a regional landscape painter and portraitist who works in the medium of egg tempera. The museum's artist-in-residence program provides grants that bring innovative young artists to the area for residencies of up to one year. The Goddard Wing of the museum houses an exact replica of the Dr. Robert Goddard liquid fuel rocket workshop in Roswell in 1931. New Mexico's moon-walking former senator, Harrison Schmitt, donated his astronaut outfit to the museum. These exhibits are complemented by a planetarium.

A historical museum with a pleasant garden and carriage entrance is located in the former J. B. White home. The city has a good library and several parks, among them Peppermint Park and Zoo. A local artisan has restored the fine wooden animals on the popular carousel, and a small lake provides fishing for children. Zoo prairie dogs pay little heed to the boundary of their chain link enclosure and complete their underground tunnels wherever they please. Some pop up in the bison pen, some in front of the ostrich, and others along the zoo walkways.

The annual Eastern New Mexico State Fair in September, a tradition since 1892, brings crowds to the Roswell Fairground to show off or to admire the agricultural products of the region and the magnificent local quarter horses. The first exhibition was held in an alfalfa palace built entirely of baled hay. Visitors also swarm to the midway, food booths, or the exciting rodeos.

South of Roswell, U.S. 285 parallels the Pecos River, famed as the boundary line of Western justice. "The law west of the Pecos" is a Western idiom signifying justice summarily dealt. The range of the huge cattle ranches that flourished in the Pecos Valley in the nineteenth century has moved to the north and east; irrigation has turned the valley into a luxuriant garden spot, and the big ranches have been divided.

The Chisum Ranch is operated as an experimental station on range control and diversification of crops. John Chisum came from Tennessee to Paris, Texas, where he served as county clerk. Soon after the Civil War he drove three small herds of cattle to Little Rock and sold them to a packing house owned partly by himself. The enterprise failed and he filed papers for bankruptcy. As his only assets were wild Texas cattle, inaccessible for attachment and inconvertible into cash, Chisum started life again while judgments against him became waste paper.

Charles Goodnight and Oliver Loving had already blazed the trail up the Pecos River, and Chisum started his new drive over the same route with a motley gang, establishing headquarters in the Bosque Grande ("big woods") thirty miles south of Fort Sumner in the Pecos Valley, on a ranch site previously established by Goodnight. Chisum sold his first herd of six hundred cattle at Fort Sumner and obtained a contract to deliver ten thousand more. Realizing the riches of the Pecos Valley, he determined to make it his home, and on his second drive he made his permanent headquarters at this ranch, though he maintained two other cow camps. Between 1870 and 1881 Chisum was credited with having the largest holdings of cattle in the world. His ranch then extended from Fort Sumner on the

Pecos two hundred miles southward to the Texas line. Though his petition to President Grant for a patent to the whole area was denied, for some time no one dared dispute his rule. He enforced his edict, "Settlers are unwelcome," and the cattle with the "long rail" brand and "jingle bob" earmark (vertical split in both ears) multiplied. His ranch had more than a hundred thousand head of cattle at its zenith in about 1878, before Indian raids, rustlers, and competition from other owners diminished his power and his wealth.

After his death in 1884, litigation made further inroads into his empire. In 1893 a Colorado businessman, J. J. Hagerman, and a group bought the Chisum Ranch. Hagerman was an empire builder of another sort, and with Charles B. Eddy and other citizens of Roswell he developed the transportation facilities of the valley. The Chisum Ranch in 1894 was the scene of an elaborate party celebrating the arrival of the first railroad train in Roswell. In 1904 Hagerman remodeled the ranch house, but the main structure was left intact and made the central part of his new abode. Later, the Hagerman estate sold it to Cornell University.

Long before Chisum dominated the Pecos Valley, Indian groups lived as hunters in the area. Settled Pueblos inhabited the valley from A.D. 1000 to the thirteenth century. Spanish explorers followed the route of the Pecos River. In 1582 Father Bernardino Beltrán, a Franciscan determined to find some of his Franciscan predecessors, received permission for a rescue expedition. It was unsuccessful in finding priests or gold but brought back enticing tales of gold anyway. Gaspar Castaño de Sosa journeyed along the river from 1589 to 1591 with a party of 170 men, women, and children in an unsuccessful attempt to found a colony. It is said that during the journey, in December of 1590, Castaño de Sosa became lost east of the Pecos. His party set out *luminarias* (small bonfires), which he spotted and which guided him safely back to the camp. No Spanish remained along the river and no missions were built in the valley.

To the east along the river, the traveler can see the wispy red branches of the salt cedars or tamarisks. These shrubs, which flourish along the Pecos, were shelters for illicit stills during Prohibition. Though the salt cedars were a blessing to bootleggers, they were a nuisance to farmers. The tamarisks were first seen growing along the Pecos in 1915. The low, bushy tree was introduced to this country from Eurasia, and it is frequently considered a pest because it consumes a great deal of water and crowds out other, more desirable plants. The pretty shrub is the target of control programs of the U.S. Water and Power Resources Service.

Just east of DEXTER, 300 mi. (alt. 3,450, pop, 882), the Dexter National Fish Hatchery is located on the banks of Pecos River. Visitors are welcome at the hatchery, which has become a center for the study and rearing of endangered species of the Southwest. About 75 percent of the endangered fish species of the United States originate in this region, and many of those species are being bred at Dexter.

HAGERMAN, 311 mi. (alt. 3,419, pop. 931), named for J. J. Hagerman, is a farming community in the midst of cotton fields. LAKE ARTHUR, 315 mi. (alt. 3,366, pop. 328), is the home of the Rubio family, who received wide attention in the 1970s because of their shrine. On October 5, 1977, an image of Jesus Christ appeared on a flour tortilla made by Mrs. Rubio as she prepared burritos for her husband's lunch. The family has generously shared a glimpse of the miracle with thousands of visitors, and their home contains a shrine honoring the image.

A Union soldier, J. F. Truitt, homesteaded by a spring near the site of ARTESIA, 325 mi. (alt. 3,377, pop, 10,430). Blake's Spring, as this brook was named, is still running, and underground water was the source of the city of Artesia's present name. The Truitt homestead was part of the Chisum holding, known as South Chisum Camp. Billy the Kid worked at the ranch in the winter of 1880.

Oil was discovered in the great Abo oilfield under Artesia in the spring of 1923, and this accounts for most of the growth of the city since then. Refineries are the largest employers in Artesia, though stock raising and farming are still important industries.

A large mural on the walls of the Heritage Walkway downtown chronicles the city's history. More information about the area is available in the Artesia Public Library and the Artesia Museum and Art Center through displays of Indian artifacts, minerals, and pioneer medical equipment.

Artesia is proud of its impressive high school auditorium and the Abo Underground School. The elementary school and civil defense shelter is called an "atomic age school," and, acording to Chamber of Commerce literature, is "probably the first underground school structure built in the free world." Higher education can be gained at the campus of Artesia Christian College. Visitors are welcome to enjoy playing or exercising in any of Artesia's numerous sports facilities or tree-shaded parks.

U.S. 82 (Tour 14) crosses U.S. 285 in Artesia. Active artesian wells are not found south of this point, so irrigation is achieved by a system of dams, canals, ditches, flumes, and siphons, known as the Carlsbad Reclamation

Wagons of cotton, *Jean Blackmon.*

Project. This project spreads the waters of the Pecos that have been impounded in Lake MacMillan and Lake Avalon over the valley. The existing MacMillan Dam loses much water to underground seepage, and its capacity for flood control has decreased due to silting. The new Brantley Dam will be completed in 1988 on a natural groundwater barrier south of Lake MacMillan. The irrigated land is used primarily for cotton growing, but alfalfa, sorghums, sugar beets, grapes, and fruit trees have had some success here as well.

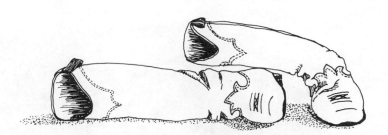

At 339 mi. is the junction with the road to Lakewood, two miles to the east. Lakewood had a tomato cannery and a population of 270 in 1915, but now is even smaller. On the east, the village overtakes old Seven Rivers, settled in 1870 by Pa and Ma Jones, who came from Virginia by ox wagon. Seven Rivers was located where seven arroyos led into the Pecos River. The spot became a stopping point on the cattle trail from Texas and a trading post for ranchers in the valley. It was a stereotype of the Wild West town of the late nineteenth century. One saloon boasted "a door with easy hinges" that could be quickly removed to serve as a stretcher for customers who had been too slow on the draw. The first settler was murdered, setting the tone for the rest of the town's history. Cattle rustlers, outlaws, and lawmen-turned-outlaws lived among the honest farmers and ranchers of Seven Rivers. Residents hoped the town would become the county seat of Eddy County, but Eddy (now Carlsbad) was chosen instead. In 1884 a Seven Rivers man, James Barrett, was the first person hanged on Eddy Courthouse Square, as one thousand people watched. Some remnants of the old adobe walls and the cemetery where, it is said, most of the men were buried with their boots on are all that is left of the old Seven Rivers community. The highway soon passes the new Seven Rivers' luxurious pecan groves.

At 348 mi., N.M. 137 heads west into Lincoln National Forest. About thirty-nine miles from U.S. 285, the traveler arrives at Sitting Bull Falls Picnic Area. The waterfall roars over a canyon wall, beautiful in all seasons but spectacular in cold winters, when the water forms frozen stalactites along the edges of rock precipices. Trails make other canyons, caves, and ridges of this uplifted reef accessible to hikers. Another branch of the road climbs over the rim, becomes a dirt road, and ends at El Paso Gap, just north of the Texas border. The rim is a narrow ridge of limestone, six to seven thousand feet high, with a gentle slope toward the Pecos Valley on the east and a sudden drop of two thousand feet on the west.

A large variety of plant and animal life exists in the national forest because of the great elevation differences. Vegetation typical of the Chihuahuan desert is found at lower altitudes. This includes mescal, agave, yucca, sotol, and creosote bush. Piñon, alligator juniper, mountain mahogany, prickly pear, and blue grama grow at elevations of five thousand to sixty-five hundred feet. Above that grow Ponderosa pines and Douglas fir. The canyons harbor ferns, bigtooth maple, walnut, and Texas madrone. A very large herd of deer browses among these plants, along with occasional elk. The wild turkeys had all been killed by 1907, but the area was restocked some decades later. The streams of the Guadalupe Mountains contain the second most southerly native trout in the hemisphere; their ancestors, the first trout in North America, were displaced to this area during an early glacial period. They were later replaced in the northern part of the continent by invading cutthroat and rainbow trout.

Shortly before entering Carlsbad, U.S. 285 passes the entrance to the Living Desert Museum (see Tour 16) and a branch of New Mexico State University. In CARLSBAD, 316 mi. (see Tour 16), U.S. 285 crosses U.S. 62/U.S. 180.

South of Carlsbad, a branch of the railroad leads east into the potash-mining area. It may be noted that the salt flats east of here and the limestone depths of nearby caves, neither of which supports vegetation, have brought forth fertilizers to supply vast areas of arable land. Potash and bat guano have been important products for the economy of the Carlsbad area in this century.

LOVING, 372 mi. (alt. 3,100, pop, 1,349), can be a rest area for travelers. The summertime green of nearby crops provides welcome relief for the parched eye. The town was named for John Loving, who was one of the first men to drive cattle up the Pecos from Texas. He was fatally wounded by raiding Comanches, whom he held off for three days and nights, only to die at Fort Sumner shortly after his escape there. A large metal cottonseed oil mill and two gins dominate the town's horizon. Abundant oil has made some of the residents of Loving wealthy. A community park is tucked inside the town, off the highway.

MALAGA, 377 mi., a trading point for farmers, is named for the sweet wine grapes grown here. The underside of a bridge in town is said to be the home of thousands of male Mexican freetail bats, who live away from the Bat Cave in Carlsbad Caverns during the season when the females are nursing their young.

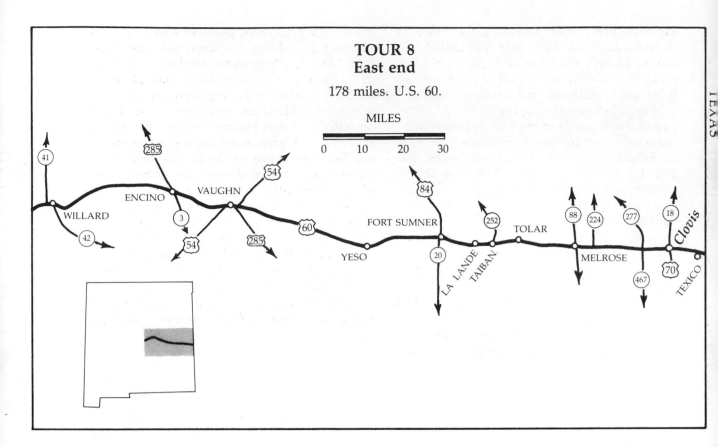

TOUR 8
East end

178 miles. U.S. 60.

MILES

0 10 20 30

41
285
54
ENCINO
VAUGHN
54
WILLARD
3
42
54
285
60
84
FORT SUMNER
252
TOLAR
88
224
277
18
YESO
20
LA LANDE
TAIBAN
MELROSE
Clovis
467
70
TEXICO

TEXAS

See page 436 for western end of tour eight.

tour eight

Texas Border • **Clovis** • **Fort Sumner** • *Mountainair* • *Socorro* • **Magdalena** •
Quemado • *Arizona Border*

U.S. 60, opened in 1917, was the first numbered automobile route to cross the nation.
Called the Ocean-to-Ocean Highway, the
marked dirt road connected Norfolk, Virginia,
with Los Angeles and the intermediate cities
of Richmond, Charleston, Louisville, Spring-
field, Amarillo, and Phoenix. Although it
missed most of the population centers in New
Mexico, it did nearly bisect the state and provide a reasonably direct route for east-west
traffic.

U.S. 60 in New Mexico divides into two almost equal portions. Heading westward as far
as Willard, it is a plains highway, running
through rich, irrigated farming and sheep-
and cattle-grazing land. Past Willard, except
for the twenty-five-mile stretch it shares as a
river road with U.S. 85 and I-25, it is a mountain highway, crossing first between the Manzanos and the Pinos and later passing among
various small mountain ranges that ring the
San Agustin Plains and straddle the Continental Divide.

Like most early U.S. numbered highways,
U.S. 60 followed the railroads: the Belen Cutoff of the Santa Fe almost to the Rio Grande
and the short spur west from Socorro. West of

Magdalena, however, it parallels no railroad
tracks, but follows instead the route used to
drive cattle to the railhead at Magdalena.

Tour 8 follows U.S. 60 across New Mexico.
Most of the route was paved during the 1930s;
pavement is now complete.

Although the Santa Fe Railroad used all the
power at its disposal to secure its right of way
across Raton Pass in order to be first in New
Mexico and the first to connect the southwest
with California and the Middle West, railroad
officials almost immediately after its completion began looking for an alternate, less mountainous route. They settled on a right of way
via Abo Pass, leaving the main line at Belen,
passing through Amarillo, and eventually rejoining the main line in eastern Kansas. Work
began on this "Belen Cutoff" eastward from
Belen in 1903 and westward from Amarillo in
1904. By 1907, the line was complete, and a
string of "cutoff towns" could be traced along
its path.

In 1900 Judge James Hamlin set up an office
in Farwell (at the Texas–New Mexico state
line) to sell off to farmers tracts of the XIT
Ranch, split by the Pecos Valley and North-

eastern Railway. One of the first settlers in this area, then known as Escavado, was Ira Taylor, section foreman of the PV&NE. He took out a 160-acre homestead in present Texico. This town boomed as a railroad construction camp but was soon eclipsed by Clovis.

CLOVIS, 10 mi. (alt. 4,260, pop, 31,344), had been named Riley's Switch when the Belen Cutoff first came through, intersecting the Pecos Valley line. Within a short time, the Santa Fe Railroad chose it as a division point and gave a railroad official's daughter the honor of naming the new town. Since she had been reading the ancient history of France, she named it after Clovis, king of the Franks, who converted to Christianity in A.D. 496. When the railroad's repair shops were moved here from Melrose, the completely railroad-created city became a four-way division point. From its central location here between Vaughn, Roswell, Amarillo, and Lubbock, the roundhouse in Clovis serviced Santa Fe locomotives coming from four directions.

When Clovis began, the surrounding high plains supported considerable ranching, and homesteaders, especially those driven west by the financial crisis in 1907, were starting to try dry farming and to experiment with irrigation methods. The dry farming remained risky and difficult, but with the advent of deep-well pumping in the 1940s, these plains quickly turned into one of the richest grain and cotton growing areas of the country, and Clovis became a leader in grain processing and livestock shipping. It has the largest grain storage capacity in the state, and manufactures more livestock feed than any town west of Kansas City. Weekly livestock auctions have been held

here since 1935. The U.S. Department of Agriculture now administers the Clovis market, among the top twenty in the nation. Horse sales are held every Monday (Clovis ranks first in horse and mule markets in the United States); cattle sales are held Wednesdays, Thursdays, and Fridays. Curry County, among the smallest in the state, leads New Mexico in volume of wheat, grain, sorghum, and sugar beets produced.

Clovis and Curry County also boast the largest county fair in the state, held early in September at the new fairgrounds southeast of town. The Clovis Cattle Festival in October features special livestock shows and sales. During the second week in June, the Clovis Pioneer Days Rodeo again fills the fairgrounds arena with young and old from throughout the high plains. Among year-round attractions for visitors is Hillcrest Park, south of town, with a zoo, sunken gardens, a swimming pool, and a trout-stocked fishing pond. The High Plains Historical Foundation maintains "the Oldest House in Clovis" as a museum, located since 1974 on the fairgrounds. Nine miles south of the city, the Blackwater Draw Museum, described in Tour 10, houses artifacts, fossils, and geologic evidence on "Clovis," "Folsom," and "Portales" people dating to twelve thousand years ago. Quail, doves, pheasants, and antelope are hunted, in season, in the immediate Clovis area. Deer can be found within thirty miles.

In downtown Clovis, the tour intersects N.M. 18, the "east side" highway that extends the length of the state north and south. North on this road, the New Mexico Outdoor Drama Association of Eastern New Mexico University,

with the help of local and distant subscribers, plans to bring outdoor theater to the high plains. The amphitheater for this project is being constructed in a remarkable setting under the rim of the caprock, between the towns of Grady and San Jon. Tour 10, following U.S. 70 and the old Pecos Valley Railroad to Portales, Roswell, and Las Cruces, branches off south from the same intersection in Clovis.

Cannon Air Force Base (turnoff at 16 mi.) dates from 1942. First known as Clovis Air Force Base, it was dedicated to General John Cannon in June 1957. The base, a component of the Twelfth Air Force, Tactical Air Command, is home of the 832nd Air Division, and provides jobs for many Clovis residents.

In the days of steam locomotives, the railroads required sources of water every twenty miles and needed repair shops to overhaul the engines and to repack wheel bearings every 90 to 110 miles. As road building progressed, they also created "towns on the front," construction camps composed largely of Mexicans, with workers of dozens of other nationalities. Many remain on the maps. The mostly vanished cutoff towns along this stretch of U.S. 60 are a reminder of those early railroad needs, and, unfortunately, of the transitory and vulnerable nature of settlement in this part of the world. These nearly deserted towns, with their empty houses and old lawns and gardens full of elm trees, are seldom places to appreciate the beauty and fertility of this land.

Santa Fe Railroad officials named MELROSE, 34 mi. (alt. 4,422, pop. 701), after Melrose, Ohio, when the Belen Cutoff reached here in 1906, and they operated repair shops here for a time. The settlement had been known since 1882 as Brownhorn because it was located midway between the Walter "Wildhorse" Brown and the Horn ranches. The Old Timer Days, held on the second weekend in August, attract fifteen hundred to three thousand visitors annually and feature an All-Girl Rodeo.

South of Melrose, aircraft from Cannon Air Force Base use the Melrose Bombing Range for practice bombing and strafing. A proposal in 1981 to treble the range's area brought out much local opposition to the Air Force's taking over fifty-two thousand additional acres of good grazing and crop land.

The Llano Estacado, the Staked Plains, the caprock, the *llano*, and the high plains are all names for a huge section of the earth's crust that was pushed up in the geologic past. This area, comprising much of the Texas Panhandle and eastern New Mexico, now is a geographic entity straddling the state line. Nomadic Indians, bison hunters, cattle ranchers, homesteaders, and deep-well farmers have successively made a life on these plains. The entire area overlies the southern end of the Ogallala Aquifer, an underground, fresh-water sea that stretches to Nebraska. The present agricultural wealth of the high plains derives from this reservoir, understood to be a depletable resource. These earthly facts help explain the sense of unity of all who earn their living on the *llano*.

On the New Mexico side, the caprock has been cut and worn by the Pecos River and its tributaries. (The same thing has happened on the east side, most visibly in Palo Duro Canyon, southeast of Amarillo.) Spectacular bluffs, loose boulders, twisting canyons, and islands of the *llano* mark the eroded edges of the caprock in many places. Local people call them the breaks and have always valued them as shelter for wildlife and for trees providing fuel and post wood. More than anything else here, the breaks, bounding the seas of grass, mean home to high plains people, as the nearness of mountains or large rivers does to people in other parts of the state.

On secondary roads such as N.M. 88 prosperous farms are evident, with dry land wheat, sprinkler farming, and livestock grazing to the sides of the road. Melrose sits on the *llano*, not far from the sharp descent into the Pecos Valley. U.S. 60 and the railroad had to make this descent, but naturally chose a gentler grade down Taiban Creek. Travelers bound for Tucumcari and those who want to get an idea of what the dropoff can be like will have a good view of the breaks at Ragland.

TOLAR, 52 mi., a cutoff town named for Tolar, Texas, provided sand and gravel for railroad construction. A terrific explosion here of a train carrying munitions flattened this town in November 1944, raining shrapnel and train parts over a large area but killing only one man.

TAIBAN (or Tivan), 56 mi., was a Comanche or Navajo word for "horsetail" and probably referred to the fact that all the tributaries of Taiban Arroyo come from the same direction, the north. The tour descends from the *llano* gradually, following this *arroyo* west to the Rio Pecos. In the geologic past, this spot was the headwaters of an eastward-running river. The uplift that created the caprock cut off the ancient river, leaving a series of lakes, gravel-filled sinks, and springs of the Portales Valley. Beginning in the 1860s, John Chisum drove cattle to Fort Sumner through the former valley, and the route became known as the Fort Sumner Trail. Springs just south of the highway here, once called Brazel's Springs, furnished water for the cattle drives. Sheriff Pat Garrett captured Billy the Kid a short way up the *arroyo* from Taiban in December 1880.

In 1917, with the creation of De Baca County, LA LANDE, 63 mi., competed against Fort Sumner and Yeso to be county seat. The town was named either for Baptiste La Lande, a Santa Fe Trail trader, or a railroad worker killed in 1905, or possibly both.

General James G. Carlton supervised the construction of OLD FORT SUMNER (4 mi. south of U.S. 60 at 67 mi.) on the banks of the Pecos in 1862. The site of the fort, called the Bosque Redondo ("round grove of cottonwoods") had been a stopping place for centuries. Comanches camped in the extensive bottomland here, Coronado stopped here in 1541, Espejo in 1583, and the U.S. Army Dragoons in the 1850s. Little of the old fort remains; floods in 1932 and 1941 carried most of it away. Since 1968 it has been partly restored as a state monument.

The museum at the monument tells a grim tale. Colonel Kit Carson sent four hundred Mescalero Apache captives to the Bosque Redondo Reservation in 1863. During the winter of 1863–64, the U.S. Army waged an all-out war against the Navajos, burning crops and homes in order to starve them into submission. Survivors were gathered at Fort Wingate (near Gallup) and marched the three hundred miles to the Bosque Redondo: "The Long Walk," still recalled with horror by Navajos. Once here, they lived five miles north of the fort on the edge of the caprock and constructed the adobe buildings of the fort itself. An agricultural experiment to make the Indians self-sufficient failed, owing to lack of water and poor soil. The Indians subsisted on rations and sickened on the river water. Finally, in 1868, Washington abandoned the "concentration camp" policy and a new treaty granted the Navajos their present reservation. The army sold the fort buildings to Lucien Maxwell, proprietor of the Maxwell Land Grant, who enlarged the officers' quarters into a lavish twenty-room house. It was at this house that Pat Garrett killed Billy the Kid in July 1881.

The State Monument Museum recounts the history of the fort, displaying floor plans and old artifacts. The bosque itself remains a stopover for migratory birds, including sandhill and whooping cranes and blue herons, travel-

ing along the Pecos. The private Old Fort Sumner Museum occupies an old building near the state monument.

FORT SUMNER, 70 mi. (alt. 4,010, pop. 1,485), became county seat when De Baca County was formed in 1917, named for Exequiel Cabeza de Baca, second governor after New Mexican statehood. As occurred near most military forts in the state, a civilian settlement grew up here. During the 1860s people raised foodstuffs, furnished meat and staples, and provided amusement of various kinds for the soldiers. After the army withdrew, Fort Sumner continued as a cattle town, situated on the Goodnight Trail. Cattle from the San Angelo, Texas, area were driven over the trail via Raton, New Mexico, and Pueblo, Colorado, to Cheyenne, Wyoming, where, fattened on New Mexico and Colorado grass, they took the train to Chicago. Fort Sumner became first notorious and later famous as a hangout for Billy the Kid and his gang. The present town dates from the coming of the railroad and received an impetus most other cutoff towns lacked with the construction of the Alamogordo Dam upriver on the Pecos. Fort Sumner now is the center of an irrigation district that produces livestock pasture and alfalfa as well as apples, grapes, melons, and sweet potatoes.

Fort Sumner celebrates the four-day "Old Fort Days" festival in mid-June. Beginning with a staged bank robbery on the Thursday and highlighted by the melodrama in the high school gym on the Saturday night, the celebration includes a black powder shoot, a "cowbelle" beef cook-off, an old-time camp meeting, a dog show, a water polo contest, an old fiddlers' contest, a western dance, a Billy the Kid marathon, and an enchilada dinner.

U.S. 84 splits off from U.S. 60 at Fort Sumner and parallels the Pecos upriver to Santa Rosa along forty-four miles of nearly uninhabited roadway. This is a principal route to Las

Vegas, New Mexico, and north. It is recommended for its views of the Pecos, the Alamogordo Reservoir, Alamogordo Creek, and the bluffs of the Llano Estacado.

YESO, 92 mi., is an impressive ruin of numerous well-constructed stone houses. *Yeso* means gypsum, and the town was named for the bad-tasting water of Yeso Creek, eight miles south, that drains east to the Pecos. In the early years of this century, Yeso thrived as a beneficiary of railroad-sponsored colonization on the Belen Cutoff. Railroad plats included land for schools, streets, churches, and a denominational college. For a time Yeso fulfilled its creators' dreams of an ideal town on the central plains. Yeso supported a high school, Tok Aker's mercantile store, and a town baseball team. Neither the drought of 1909–1912 nor the 1919 flu epidemic (which closed school for twelve weeks) defeated Yeso; but the combination of the Depression and the Second World War did. Ancient Spanish inscriptions on wind breaks, hearths, and boulders near the town remain unexplained.

Between Yeso and Vaughn, herds of sheep have the rolling plains nearly to themselves. VAUGHN, 127 mi., a transportation center rivaling Clovis but without its agricultural base, is described in Tour 13 (U.S. 54). It is also a midway point on Tour 7 (U.S. 285).

U.S. 60 intersects U.S. 285 South at 126 mi and intersects U.S. 54 South at 130 mi.

Farming homesteaders settled ENCINO, 144 mi. (alt 6,000, pop. 161), but cattle and sheep raising has been its economic mainstay for some time. As is the case with many other New Mexico towns the survival of Encino ("live oak") is closely tied to the survival of its school. The declines that have followed the closing of schools in nearby towns confirm Encino residents' fears of what will happen to their town if the state department of education decides to dispense with its school, which served fifty students in 1981. N.M. 3 here heads south past two old cemeteries to Duran and north to the eighteenth-century Pecos River settlement of Villanueva.

Just west of Encino, U.S. 285 and tour 7 branch north to Santa Fe and the back way to Denver. U.S. 60 continues west, gradually dropping into the Estancia Valley. This valley (actually a basin, since it has virtually no drainage) once lay beneath the waters of an inland sea. It has been known as a rich farming area since it was first settled in the nineteenth century.

Beginning at 174 mi., seasonal salt lakes, tangible reminders of the ancient sea, are visible from the road. In a year of good rains the lakes fill up in the late summer and can hold water during the fall months; in drier times they look like white beaches. Early Pueblo people used this salt as an item of trade that made its way to Chihuahua City and beyond, and the Spanish named the cluster of Indian towns east of the Manzanos the Salinas ("saline") Pueblos. North from the highway, Laguna del Perro ("dog lake") extends seasonally almost to Estancia. The lakes also extend south and can be seen from N.M. 42 southeast of Willard. The Tewa word for them translates "accursed." Whitish bluffs partly encircle the lakes, whose effect can be startling when they are full. At times they are the largest natural lakes in the state.

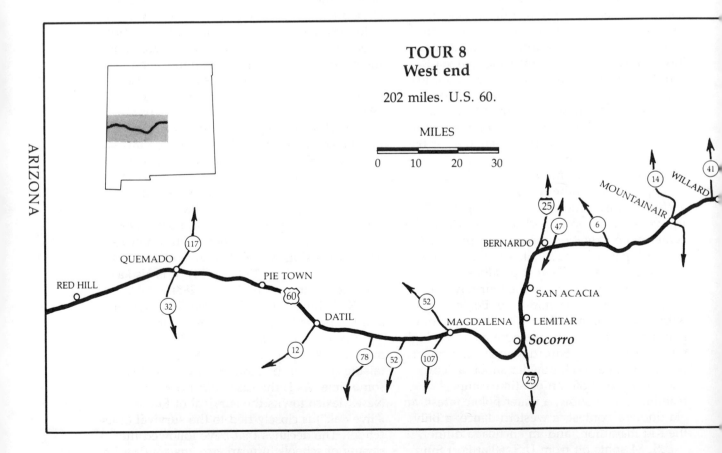

TOUR 8
West end

202 miles. U.S. 60.

MILES

0   10   20   30

ARIZONA

RED HILL

QUEMADO
117
32

PIE TOWN
60
12

DATIL
78
52

52
107

MAGDALENA
LEMITAR
Socorro

SAN ACACIA

BERNARDO
47
25
6

MOUNTAINAIR
14
WILLARD
41

25

At WILLARD, 180 mi. (alt. 6,091, pop. 164), the tour crosses Tour 5. "West of Willard are raised most of the pinto beans grown in the United States," observes *New Mexico: A Guide to the Colorful State,* published in 1940. Between 1900 and 1940 both Willard and Mountainair harvested and shelled tremendous quantities of beans, grown entirely on rainfall. Some years with little precipitation and the disruption caused by World War II put an end to the dry farming, however. The beans are gone, but the valley still produces alfalfa, potatoes, feed grains, and lawn sod raised on sprinkler irrigation.

The Salinas National Monument headquarters, which directs preservation and educational work at the three ancient pueblos of Gran Quivira, Abo, and Quarai, is located in MOUNTAINAIR (193 mi., on Tour 15) in the foothills of the Manzano Mountains. The ranger station in Mountainair provides information on trails in the Manzanos and issues permits for firewood, post, and Christmas-tree cutting.

U.S. 60 travelers reach Abo ruins a mile north of the highway at 203 mi., nearly opposite Abo Pass.

> Houses rise and fall, crumble, are
>   extended,
> Are removed, destroyed, restored, or
>   in their place
> Is an open field . . . .
> Old stone to new building, old timber
>   to new fires,
> Old fires to ashes, and ashes to the
>   earth . . . .
>   (T. S. Eliot, "East Coker")

There have been many Abos. "Old Abo," still unexcavated, was founded in the 1300s. The first for which historical records exist is the Abo of two thousand souls, largest of the Saline Pueblos, known by Coronado and visited by Oñate. Fray Francisco de Acevedo began construction of a mission church and an aqueduct here in 1629. Within a few years, Abo became seat of the Mission of San Gregorio, with a large church and organ, a monastery,

orchards, gardens, fields, and much communication with other pueblos under its care. Because of raids by Apaches, the mission and pueblo were abandoned in the 1670s. Most of the inhabitants retreated to the distantly related Rio Grande Piro towns of Senecu, Alamillo, and Pilabo. The National Park Service now cares for ruins of this Abo, stabilized and partly preserved, and welcomes inquiries about the archaeological work still underway here.

The stone buildings of a later Abo surround the older ruins and are visible along the highway. Spanish-speaking farmers and ranchers migrated here from more populated parts of New Mexico in the 1850s and 1860s. One of those pioneer families, the Cisneros, farmed and herded on land immediately adjacent to the pueblo ruin. After the State of New Mexico acquired most of the old city in 1937, Federico and Lupe Cisneros offered the state the remainder of the site for one dollar. Out of love for the place, Federico offered to work without pay to care for the treasure and to share it with visitors. The Museum of New Mexico, recognizing the tremendous asset that Federico and his family were to Abo, put him on the payroll. When the federal government took over management of the site in 1981, Federico Cisneros became the oldest ranger in the National Park Service.

In the early 1900s, the Belen Cutoff created still another Abo, a few miles east of the mission. The schoolhouse and other buildings still in use date from that time. During the 1970s settlers began reclaiming many of the old stone houses, helping to revive Abo again. Several of these buildings' foundations have probably anchored homes since the sixteenth century.

Evidence of another town built of red rock exists at SCHOLLE, 206 mi., named for Fred Scholle, a Belen merchant. During its time as a busy railroad town, Scholle had a depot, a twenty-four-hour dispatcher, two stores, a post office, and a section gang. The WPA built the green-painted rock schoolhouse. The adventuresome can turn off the highway one-

Cattle and cowboys, *Harvey Caplin*.

half mile west of the school to admire excellent pictographs by much earlier inhabitants of Scholle. Travelers willing to splash in red mud looking for original New Mexico art turn south at mile 206, follow the old road to the railroad tracks, and go back east along the tracks a little way to an underpass. After driving under the tracks and bearing left, go nearly a mile and a half and look to the right at a place where the rock stands six to eight feet high at the edge of the road. On this hill strewn with red rocks are dozens of pictures,

some very near the road, others further up the slope. The pictographs overlook a marsh of thick grass (called a *cienega* in New Mexico). The setting makes it easy to imagine camping and resting hunters as pleased with the spot as travelers are today.

At 208 mi., the Santa Fe tracks depart for Belen down the canyon, called Barranca or Abo Canyon, that U.S. 60 has followed almost since Mountainair. Railroad construction up to Abo Pass proved more difficult and costly than builders had hoped, and it took nearly two

438   *Tour 8:* SCHOLLE

years to complete the forty-mile ascent from Belen to Mountainair. The highway made its own route from here to the Rio Grande. Remaining sections of the narrow and curvy old road all through the Abo Pass region offer a lesson in comparative highway construction methods. Travelers fortunate enough to break out of the Manzanos, 211 mi., near sundown will get a spectacular view of the Rio Grande valley and its flanking mountains aglow in the sunset.

N.M. 6 branches off northwesterly at 215 mi. for Belen, Los Lunas, and Laguna, on I-40. It is also a direct route to Albuquerque and forms a leg of a possible circle tour around the Manzanos from Albuquerque via I-40, N.M. 14, U.S. 60, N.M. 6, and N.M. 47. While still making the descent into the valley one can look north along the west-facing slope of the Manzanos and clearly see alluvial fans, formed in a manner similar to river deltas. Streams carry silt and gravel down the steep mountain sides but leave it when they reach the gentler slopes. Deposits raise the level of the stream beds, causing the water to spread out. The process repeats itself, gradually building up deposits in a fan shape.

At 227 mi., the tour intersects N.M. 47, an east-bank road that approximates what was for generations the principal trail north from Chihuahua and Mexico City. Pavement extends south only six miles to La Joya, at the site of the Piro Pueblo of Sevilleta (Tour 1). Across the Rio Grande at Bernardo, 232 mi., U.S. 60 joins I-25 for the twenty-five miles south to Socorro. Tour 1 describes this section and the towns north on old U.S. 85, now N.M. 116.

Westbound U.S. 60 travelers exit in Socorro, 241 mi., and find their road at the southern end of town. The highway now approximates the route of a twenty-mile railroad line, nicknamed the elevator because it climbed two thousand feet in about sixteen miles. Built in 1884, this spur carried lead, zinc, and silver ores from the Kelly and Magdalena mines and also thousands of cattle that were driven to the shipping pens at Magdalena. The railroad

must have been spectacular. The highway certainly is, winding among boulders and gorges to emerge on the plains east of Magdalena.

In 1863 Civil War soldiers on leave from Fort Craig staked claims to silver strikes in the Magdalena Mountains. By 1870 the town of Kelly had been laid out and named for a sawmill owner and miner, Andy Kelly. The miners sent out lead and zinc first, but during the 1880s, when the town's population grew to some three thousand, silver became the principal moneymaker. After the silver boom collapsed, Kelly survived mainly as a lead and zinc mining center until the 1930s. Some oldtimers still go back to Kelly to celebrate their patron's festival, St. John's Day, on June 24.

Two miles northwest, meanwhile, miners set up another town named for the likeness of Mary Magdalene on a nearby slope. After the railroad arrived in 1884, MAGDALENA, 268 mi. (alt. 6,548, pop, 1,017), became a rowdy frontier mining town and one of the largest cattle shipping centers in the Southwest. Because the rails stopped here, ranchers to the west drove their animals to Magdalena along a huge cattle driveway, one hundred miles long and ten miles wide, across the San Agustin Plains.

The U.S. Forest Service maintains a Cibola National Forest ranger station in Magdalena. Hunters, firewood cutters, hikers, explorers of ghost towns, and rock hounds can set out in almost any direction from here: north to the Bear Mountains and Riley, on the Rio Salado; northwest to the Gallinas and Datil mountains; southwest to Mount Withington and Rosedale in the San Mateos; and southeast to Kelly, Mount Baldy, and Water Canyon in the Magdalena Mountains. Magdalena has facilities for tourists and several good rock shops. Whether or not it's the same figure seen one hundred years ago, the image of a woman, scarved as Mary Magdalene usually is depicted, does appear on a hillside facing town to the southwest.

Many of the buildings of Magdalena's early days are gone. Just north of the highway in the center of town, however, the railroad de-

Old railroad depot, Magdalena, *Paul Murphy.*

pot survives as the city hall and library. Opposite the station, the Ilfeld Company's former mercantile store continues to house a trading establishment.

Magdalena has neighbors to the northwest on the Alamo Indian Reservation. Classified officially as Navajos when the reservation system was set up in the 1870s, most of the members of the Alamo Band actually descend from the Chiricahua Apaches now living in Arizona. During the chaotic years of the late nineteenth century, this group evidently preferred to be considered Navajo in order to keep its land and to gain rights as an organized tribe. A new clinic, a school, and pavement on N.M. 52 have very recently brought the once-scattered and isolated two thousand sheep herders of Alamo closer to the outside world.

From just west of Magdalena, N.M. 52 turns northwest to Alamo ("cottonwood"); N.M. 107 (unpaved) branches off south from the center of town toward the Rio Grande, skirting the Magdalena and San Mateo mountains. At 279 mi., N.M. 52 South (unpaved) leads across the San Mateo range, then around its western and southern edges to the old mining towns of Winston and Chloride, and the junction for Monticello. N.M. 78 (also unpaved), at 287 mi., runs the length of the San Agustin Plains before entering the heart of the Gila country. Travelers should inquire beforehand about the condition of all three of these unpaved roads.

The San Agustin Plains, at one time a Pleis-

Magdalena, *Paul Murphy.*

tocene lake bed forty-five miles long and fifteen miles wide, now are a huge bowl of grass surrounded by the mountains of western Socorro and Catron counties. Besides the cattle drives, these plains were the scene of battles fought with the Apaches in the 1770s, when the Spanish were trying to resettle portions of central New Mexico. Travelers today can feel they have the plains to themselves, despite the fact that there was considerable activity here during the mining and cattle booms of a few generations ago.

The focus of the San Agustin Plains recently has shifted to astronomy. Near the old town of San Augustin, 290 mi., the National Radio Astronomy Observatory operates the Very Large Array (VLA) Radio Telescope Facility.

The VLA consists of twenty-seven two-and-one-half-ton antennas moved among numerous placement pods equipped to receive radio signals. Special cars carry the huge antennas along a Y-shaped double track railroad configuration and deposit them on the pods. The antennas are movable so that they can be focused. Clustered antennas "read" a larger area of space, while spread-out ones concentrate on a smaller sector with increased sensitivity and resolution. Physicists at VLA, working with the highly sensitive radio waves and unhindered by clouds or sunshine, can conduct research unimaginable in optical astronomy. Computers process the information received from space, allowing radio astronomers to learn quickly about phenomena such as quas-

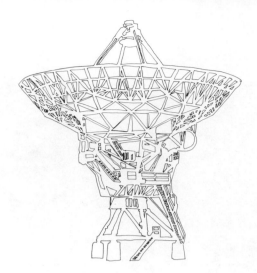
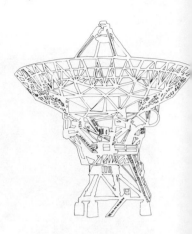

ars, pulsars, black holes, and supernovas and to pose broader questions about the geometry of space and the origin, structure, and limits of the universe. Guided tours of the facility are available to the public.

Catron County is 6,898 square miles of grazing land, national forest, bare lunar landscapes, and rich hunting grounds. It is the largest county in New Mexico, with one of the state's smallest (and dwindling) populations. Its few towns—Reserve (the county seat), Datil, Quemado, and Mogollon—are, as one resident cheerfully remarked, "twenty years behind the times." A number of ghost towns, once mining and ranching centers, have all but disappeared over the last decades. County residents live on scattered farms and ranches, in cabins up forested canyons, or along the county's main thoroughfares in its quiet, cafe-studded communities.

Catron, created in 1921 from the western part of Socorro County, then the largest county in the United States, was named after Thomas B. Catron, a powerful New Mexico Republican and U.S. senator. The Continental Divide carves a wobbly path through the middle of the county, much of which was formed by lava flows. The oddly shaped buttes and mesas that spring up in the middle of open rangeland are, for the most part, volcanic necks or other forms of igneous rock. Catron is one of the few counties in New Mexico without any land grants. More than half of its acreage is National Forest or Bureau of Land Management tracts. Most recreation areas in the county fall within the boundaries of its national forests, Cibola, Apache, and Gila.

Catron County is the site of New Mexico's earliest pit-house villages, where members of the Mogollon culture lived, farming, making pottery, and building increasingly complex dwellings. Before the arrival of settlers in the nineteenth century, and even after homesteads had been established, the Chiricahua Apaches roamed and hunted this land, retreating to a reservation in Arizona only after years of bitter battles, many of which were fought in the county.

Trappers combed Catron County's rivers and streams, hunting for beaver and other fur-bearing animals, packing out the skins and taking them to Taos or Santa Fe or even to California to trade. But Catron County is best known as cowboy country, even today. Roundups fill autumn days, cattle graze unmolested on miles of open land, and ranchers and their families lead a way of life that has remained unchanged for decades in this isolated corner of the state.

DATIL, 302 mi. (alt. 7,855), a tiny village at the intersection of U.S. 60 and N.M. 12, was named by the Spaniards, possibly for a fruit resembling dates found in the mountains of the area. In 1888 the U.S. Army built a fort here to protect settlers from Apache raids. Later the town became a trading center for ranchers and a supply point for hunters. Nowadays Datil is a quiet stop along the east-west road through Catron County and a jumping-off spot for the route south.

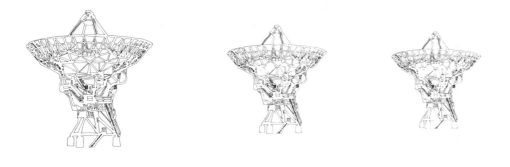

From Datil the traveler can head south on N.M. 12 to Reserve and Silver City (Tour 17). This route winds through empty countryside of rolling hills that look out over the Plains of San Agustin to the blue mountains of the south. Small working ranches and an occasional community of homes are the only signs of population. Old Horse Springs, 28 mi. (alt. 6,980), recalls a horse lost by some soldiers traveling to Fort Tularosa. They found it, miraculously they thought, at the spring that bubbles out of the ground about one-half mile west of the settlement.

Soon the highway enters the Apache National Forest and crosses the Continental Divide at 7,500 feet. Here western yellow pine, white and Douglas fir, and spruce attest to the higher elevations. Large herds of cattle, horses, and sheep graze in the forest named for the powerful tribe that left its mark through much of the region.

West of the divide the road runs through Tularosa Canyon, a winding gorge cut by the Tularosa River during thousands of rainy seasons. Most of the year the river is dry. ARAGON (alt. 7,135) is a trading center in the narrow Tularosa Valley. Small, irrigated farms make up this picturesque village, with houses and a tiny church set among lovely old trees. An old Spanish family that arrived in New Mexico in 1693 to settle the area gave Aragon its name. Americans built Fort Tularosa at the town in 1870, and it served as an Apache Indian agency when the tribe was moved here from the Ojo Caliente reservation in Socorro County. In 1874, after the Indians were moved back to the reservation, the fort was abandoned. An old burial ground for soldiers serving in the neighboring territory of Arizona is the only reminder of its existence. One mile east of Aragon, on the north side of Tularosa Canyon, Tularosa Cave was occupied for fifteen hundred years, from 400 B.C. to A.D. 1100. Pits and later masonry rooms sheltered the occupants.

Nearby APACHE CREEK's (55 mi.) name is further evidence of the influence of the tribe whose leaders, warriors called Mangas Coloradas, Victorio, Geronimo, Chato, and Cochise, for years carried on guerilla warfare in the region. At first the Apaches were hospitable to the trappers, colonists, and explorers who penetrated the area, attracted by game and the lure of gold. As later pioneers settled the countryside and took over precious land and water, the Apaches realized the threat to themselves and attacked. The burning warfare was not curbed until the final surrender of Geronimo in 1886. The area is rich with stories of encounters between Indians and settlers.

SIDE TOUR

Just west of Datil, off N.M. 60, the Bureau of Land Management has built a pleasant campground, Datil Well, which provides basic camping amenities on a tree-studded hill. It takes its name from an old well, a drinking stop on the "hoof highway" along which thousands of cattle and sheep shuffled on their way from Springerville, Arizona, to the yards of Magdalena.

The traveler will soon enter a ten-mile stretch of Cibola National Forest. The road passes through wide canyons filled with pine trees, streams, and rocky bluffs. There are a few campgrounds off the main road.

Agnes Morley Cleaveland, who came to the Datil Mountains as a child in 1886, wrote about her young life in the region in *No Life For A Lady*. She and her family arrived at their new home, a simple log cabin at the base of a mountain, in a wagon. She recalls driving across the barren plains of San Agustin from Datil to Magdalena in that wagon, in Montague Stevens's two-wheeled cart, by horseback (side-saddle), and eventually by car. She taught school when she was sixteen:

> So I answered the call of duty and a school was set up in a log cabin on the old Zaccarison place, a conveniently central point. It entailed a daily fourteen mile horseback ride for teacher, seven miles each way, but three miles was the greatest distance any of the pupils had to walk.
>
> The student body of twelve ranged from little Early Wheeler and Owen

Dean, both under six, to Gus Wheeler, who topped me in age by a few months and in stature by almost a foot. . . . The younger ones did want to do what Gus did, notably spend recess in target practice with Gus's forty-five, which he wore to school and was with difficulty persuaded to lay aside. (p. 122)

Young Agnes Morley also punched cattle, rode to town alone to get the mail, nursed the sick, and comforted those whose sick had died. She went away to school, bringing home to Datil her Stanford sorority sisters. Although she married and left the county in 1899, her book is a rollicking, valuable peek at Catron County (then Socorro County) ranch life in the late nineteenth century.

U.S. 60 crosses the Continental Divide at 7,796 feet and soon passes PIE TOWN, 323 mi. Pie Town got its name from a gas station owner who baked pies on the side. Those who stopped for gas often bought a pie and passed the word to fellow travelers about the Catron County treat. The gas station owner also posted signs along the road advertising his specialty. Soon, it is said, the hamlet became known as Pie Town. (See essay on art for a discussion of Russell Lee's photo essay on Pie Town in the 1930s.)

Nearby, the Dia Art Foundation oversees a vast outdoor sculpture by Walter de Maria called The Lightning Field. Open to the public, but on a limited, reservations-only basis, the field must be viewed over a twenty-four-hour period, and is best seen in the summer when lightning is more prevalent. The Dia Foundation brings visitors to the site from Quemado, feeding them and providing sleeping accommodations. Information on the project can be obtained by writing to: Dia Art Foundation, Box 207, Quemado, N.M. 87829. There is a fee for viewing the unusual sculpture. While the New Mexico headquarters for the Dia Art Foundation is in Quemado, many residents of the Pie Town area have worked on the art project.

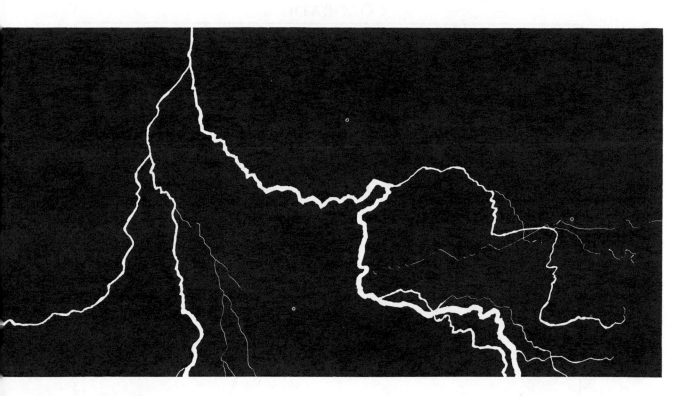

There is one town in the twenty-two-mile stretch between Pie Town and Quemado. OMEGA was established in 1870 as El Rito ("the river") by Felipe Padilla. It later became known as Sweazeville after a filling station owner, Mr. Sweaze. Its one present establishment bears a sign saying "Closed."

QUEMADO ("burnt"), 345 mi. (alt. 6,890), was part of Apache territory for a long time, its name traced in legend to an Apache chief whose hand was burned in a campfire. Another version relates that when José Antonio Padilla and his family came here to homestead in 1880, they found both sides of the local creek burned of all vegetation. Padilla, who came to the Quemado area from Belen, was responsible for bringing much sheep and cattle stock to the county.

Quemado's main street is U.S. 60. Small businesses—gas stations, modest motels and cafes, a few stores—are strung out along its two lanes. Large old adobe buildings, some with peaked tin roofs that reach almost to the ground, are reminders of Quemado's more

lively trading days. Today the village is a crossroads and a hunting and fishing mecca. The town is busiest in the fall, when ranchers are rounding up cattle and sportsmen are stalking deer, bear, elk, antelope, and wild turkeys. Cafes post notices about hunting and trapping regulations, and local gossip centers on who shot bucks and which hunters left a gate open for cattle to wander through. Like much of the far western and eastern part of New Mexico, the land around Quemado is open range, and windmills easily seem to outnumber houses.

Those going south from Quemado will take N.M. 32. (Tour 17)

Travelers heading west to the Arizona border, about thirty miles beyond Quemado, will pass through lonely, desolate grazing land. Low hills and strangely hunkering buttes add dimension to the almost flat landscape. Red Hill, 369 mi., has a population of two people (probably subject to change) and one eating and drinking establishment. The Arizona line is eleven miles ahead at 380 mi.

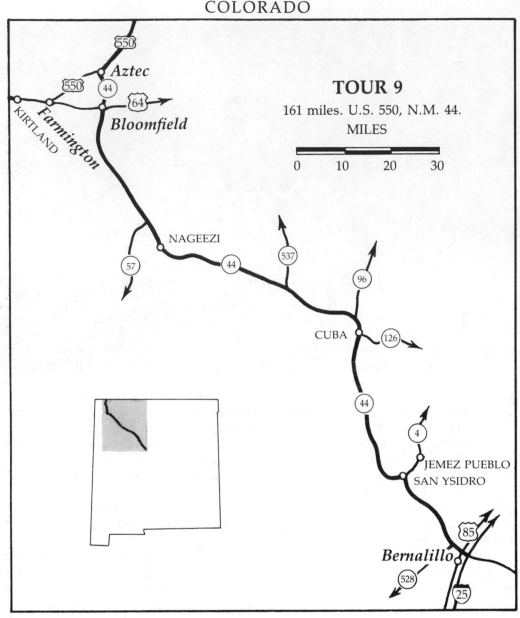

TOUR 9
161 miles. U.S. 550, N.M. 44.
MILES

tour nine

Colorado Border • **Aztec** • **Bloomfield** • **Cuba** • *Bernalillo*

The main route from Durango, Colorado, into New Mexico is via U.S. 550. This tour picks up U.S. 550 at the Colorado border and leaves it at Aztec, where U.S. 550 branches west. The traveler continues south on N.M. 44 through Bloomfield, across the wide San Juan Basin. Here one catches glimpses of the cultures of Navajo, Apache, and Pueblo peoples, and signs of energy development stand out incongruously from the bed of an ancient sea. The area takes on a fragile quality as the modern need for energy resources assaults ancient yet complex cultures and the treasures of the geological past. Pueblo ruins at Aztec and at Chaco Canyon remind the visitor of the resourcefulness and vigor of New Mexico's early inhabitants. In Cuba, Hispanic, Anglo, and Navajo cultures coexist. At the end of the tour is Bernalillo, a reminder of Spain's early colonizing efforts in the Rio Grande valley.

AZTEC, 19 mi. (alt 5,686, pop. 7,200), an attractive town whose Midwestern appearance belies its name, grew up on the east side of the Animas River. The town took its name from the nearby ruins, which were popularly believed to have been built by Indians related to the Aztecs of Mexico. The Navajos, who knew better, called the ruins Kivi K'eel, or "oblong house," because the abandoned houses were rectangular in shape rather than round like Navajo hogans. When the time came to give a formal name to the postal station, the settlers chose Aztec. The town became the county seat of new San Juan County in 1897, after Rio Arriba County was partitioned, a decision resented by Farmington and other towns but upheld by the Supreme Court.

Main Street in Aztec has resisted modernizing the facades of its shops and businesses, which remain individualistically Victorian, with pastel-colored brick fronts facing the wide, tree-lined street. At 125 North Main Street a museum preserves mementos of the pioneers of the region as well as prehistoric artifacts, exhibits of both the archaeology and the industry of the region, and an extensive collection of mineral rocks and fossils. The old city jail is another tourist attraction on Main Street. It is worth a drive through the residential areas to view the Victorian residences. The old Lovers Lane is now paved, but several dirt roads remain. Riverside Park just west of Az-

Aztec Ruins, *Harvey Caplin*.

tec's center serves both city residents and visitors with picnic tables, electricity, and water. The park skirts the river and is close to the ruins, which are located on the opposite bank near the intersection of N.M. 44 and U.S. 550.

The AZTEC RUINS NATIONAL MONUMENT includes a small visitors' center, shady picnic grounds, the main ruin and the adjacent tri-walled site, and several other ruins, as yet unexcavated. The center shows films and exhibits explaining the ruins, their inhabitants' way of life, and the vegetation of the area. A self-guided tour then takes the visitor through the ruins, back through several hundred years of history to the Basketmakers and their descendants, the Anasazi, who developed the civilizations at Chaco Canyon and Mesa Verde.

During the tenth century A.D. Indians of the area, who had previously made their homes in pits in the ground, began building above-ground pueblos scattered along the Animas River. In the early 1100s, influenced by the Chaco Canyon dwellers to the south, they concentrated their building in one U-shaped, five-hundred-room development. This multistoried structure shows in its careful design the influence of early urban planning. Using mortar and stones carried from several miles away, the masons constructed walls that would last for hundreds of years. They placed the rooms in an E shape around a great ceremonial plaza dominated by a large circular kiva. The kiva has been restored to recapture the solemnity and grandeur that those early people gave to their ceremonies.

Despite the careful planning and building, the Chacoans abandoned their pueblo less than one hundred years later, perhaps because of a drought or a shift in the river bed.

The city remained empty until about 1225, when people of the Mesa Verde–type culture moved in. The newcomers remodeled the pueblo to suit themselves and built new "apartments" to the east of the Chacoan buildings. They needed more kivas and built two large ones, tri-walled structures used for special ceremonies. One of these has been restored outside the main ruin; the other is still covered by earth. The pottery left by these people is closely related to Mesa Verde art, both in design and in the vegetable dye used. The pueblo was again deserted by 1300, perhaps because of another great drought in the last quarter of the century or the spot's vulnerability to attack by other groups. The doors were sealed in expectation of a return that never occurred.

When Domínguez and Escalante passed by the area in 1776 on their way to the West Coast, their cartographer mentioned ruins near the Animas and San Juan rivers. The area was undisturbed until settlers moving into the valley at the end of the nineteenth century poked around the remains and carted off many valuable artifacts. Shortly afterward archaeologists recognized the find; concentrated work on restoring the ruin began in 1910 under the direction of the American Museum of Natural History. The museum donated the restored pueblo and surrounding land to the United States Government in 1923.

Seven miles south, BLOOMFIELD, 26 mi. (alt.

5,500, pop. 4,835), straddles the crossroads of N.M. 44 and U.S. 64 (Tour 2). Bloomfield was first known as Porter, after a general who established trading posts in the area. The lowlands covered with meadow grass and the springtime blossoms of olives and cedars could have inspired the change of name, but more likely Bloomfield was named after one of its settlers. The young village was a violence-ridden place, with cattle rustling and terrorism leading to many deaths. The notorious Port Stockton, an outlaw of the Lincoln County War, arrived in Bloomfield in 1880 and was made a peace officer, but the town fathers demoted him when it became evident he could not be trusted with a gun. Stockton returned to his outlaw life, stealing cattle and holding up stagecoaches. The lack of peace officers in Bloomfield made the area easy pickings for Stockton's gang, and at one time forty ranchers had to patrol the area. Stockton was killed in 1881 while hiding a man sought by the sheriff. After Stockton died a man named Blaucett opened a saloon that soon became headquarters for gunmen. Although the saloonkeeper was lame, he was an effective shooter himself and caused several violent deaths.

Despite this turbulent beginning, Bloomfield settled down as the shopping center for the neighboring farmers, who grew grains, beans, and other produce. In 1906 landowners formed their own irrigation company, the Citizens Ditch and Irrigation Company, to reclaim six thousand acres of land. It was taken over in 1911 by Bloomfield Irrigation District and has functioned ever since, still irrigating some four thousand acres from a canal fed by the San Juan River. Today Bloomfield takes advantage of its location in the center of oil and gas country, these industries providing jobs and revenue.

From here N.M. 44 heads south out into the San Juan Basin, a great expanse that was covered for millions of years by a sea and, as a result, is rich in coal, oil, and gas. Fossils of clams and snails remain in the rocks, reminders of the basin's watery origins. When the waters subsided, the wind and frost continued the work of erosion, leaving jagged buttes and mesas that fascinate the traveler and geologist alike.

Thirteen miles south of Bloomfield, Angel Peak can be seen to the east rising gracefully from the surrounding badlands. Hard sandstone forms the peak's spreading "wings," remnants of a larger formation worn down by weathering processes. The mountain stands 6,988 feet tall, a landmark that can be seen for miles around. The eighty-square-mile area around it is known as Garden of the Angels or Angel Peak Recreation Area. Spanish explorers called it Nacimiento ("birthplace") despite its forbidding aspect because it had been walked over by the angel. The area is accessible by a rough but clearly marked road, exiting N.M. 44 at 37 mi., which takes one along the rim of Kutz Canyon. The blue and gray layered rocks mix with reds, yellow, browns, and purples to provide a rainbow of colors, and the wind-carved shapes give the area another nickname, the Little Grand Canyon. The Bureau of Land Management has built picnic sites with fireplaces on the canyon's southeast rim. Some of

the earliest gas strikes in New Mexico were in Kutz Canyon; rigs for oil and gas production also dot the area.

El Huerfano Trading Post, 46 mi., is situated just west of Huerfano Butte, sacred to the Navajos. The Spanish explorers named the butte "orphan" because of its solitary position, its sides jutting up five hundred feet.

Blanco Trading Post, 51 mi., takes advantage of its site at the entrance of N.M. 57, the main route off N.M. 44 to Chaco Canyon (Tour 6). Most of Blanco's fossil beds contain remains of ancient creatures; this is only one of many such burial places found in New Mexico.

The NAGEEZI Trading Post has given this spot at 59 mi. a name on the map. For a long time, the post was one of the few manmade installations in the basin. Before pickups made the trip to Farmington and Cuba easier, the local Navajos did all their shopping at posts like this one.

The Gas Company of New Mexico has built a refinery at LYBROOK, 70 mi. Trailers, a school, and stores service the residents. Around the town sandstone formations rear out of the desert, taking on alternating shades of color from the banded clays.

Soon the road intersects the southwest corner of the Jicarilla Apache Reservation. At around 89 mi., N.M. 537 cuts north, forty-six paved miles to N.M. 64 and a short-cut to Dulce, a pretty drive from the high desert up through forested country and by the fishing spots of the Jicarilla Apaches. About nine miles further on, the road crosses the Continental Divide, which here runs in an east-west direction.

As the highway nears Cuba, the landscape becomes less harsh than it has been; outlines of foothills covered with pines and scrubby sagebrush break the horizon. N.M. 96 heads north to the tiny communities in and near the Santa Fe National Forest and Abiquiu (Tour 7).

CUBA, 96 mi. (alt. 6,700, pop. 605), was originally called Nacimiento ("nativity") after the San Joaquin del Nacimiento Land Grant, which included much of the land in the area. The grant was established in 1769 for thirty-six

Badlands near Cuba, *Harvey Caplin*.

families who attempted to ranch and farm in the closing years of the eighteenth century. The mountains to the east of Cuba are called the Sierra del Nacimiento and are within the Santa Fe National Forest.

Cuba is now a ranching, farming, and tourist center. Its agricultural ties go back to the founding of the grant. Lumbering was an integral part of the area's economy until just recently, although some sawmills continue to operate and small-scale lumbering still goes on. However, tourism has become increasingly important for Cuba. Motorists on N.M. 44

pause to eat or stay, and more and more campers use Cuba as a point of departure for a vacation in the mountains.

Because it is the commercial, educational, and medical center for the northern half of Sandoval County, Cuba offers a number of services unusual for a town of its size. There are motels, restaurants, groceries, and general stores, most located along N.M. 44. A medical clinic, serving Cuba itself as well as the surrounding checkerboard area, has emergency and in-patient facilities. The Cuba School District serves children who live in the hundreds

of square miles surrounding the town. School
buses travel for miles to pick up ranch children, youngsters from the Navajo reservation,
and students at remote trading posts and
small communities.

The National Forest Service has a ranger station at the southern end of town. Persons
wishing to enter the Santa Fe National Forest
are asked to stop at the station for information
and permits. Fine hiking trails, camping facilities, and fishing lakes and streams are located
within the forest. Two campgrounds, Clear
Creek and Rio Las Vacas ("cattle creek"), are
accessible by car from N.M. 126 (Tour 4) about
fifteen miles east of Cuba. Further into the national forest, many lakes, meadows, and
streams await the hiker. In the summer there
is often the likelihood of rain. Snowshoers and
cross-country skiers are also discovering this
section of the Santa Fe National Forest.

The availability of water was instrumental in
the founding and growth of Cuba. The town
sits near the headwaters of the northern Rio
Puerco ("dirty river"), and many feeder
streams and springs also give life to the rough
terrain. Water was probably more abundant
around Cuba at the time of its settlement than
it is today. Stories are told of lush grasslands
falling away from the mountains and of six-
foot-tall buffalo grass that grew in the meadows until overgrazing and changing agricultural patterns altered the vegetation.

When the thirty-six original settlers were
given their land grant two hundred years ago,
they assumed that hard work, an abundance
of water, and strong faith would result in successful ranches and a self-sufficient life. They
tilled their land, built irrigation systems, and
constructed homes. Soon, however, Indian
raids began which continued almost unabated
for the next one hundred years. The families
fled, some going northeast across the mountains to Abiquiu, others heading downriver to
the Cañon de Jemez. Periodically a family
member would return to the grant, plant
crops, and attempt to live there again, but
continued Ute, Apache, and Comanche raids
prevented any permanent settlement. It was
almost a century before any long-term colonization was possible.

In the 1850s, the Americans came to the Cuba area. Their arrival was a mixed blessing. On the one hand, their presence brought an end to Indian attacks; on the other, the legal and bureaucratic ways of the United States government meant, in some cases, loss of water and land rights for many of the Hispanic people who had returned to work their grant.

Sheep and cattle raising was the main agricultural activity in the Cuba region until well into the twentieth century. Many people alive today remember the cattle drives at the end of summer, heading down the Rio Puerco and east along the Jemez River to the town of Bernalillo, almost sixty miles away. The weeklong trip was either excessively dusty or rainy and muddy. After their animals were sold in Bernalillo, ranchers bought supplies for the year: hundreds of pounds of flour, bolts of cloth, sacks of sugar, trinkets for the children. There are also vivid memories of floods and droughts. In the early 1900s, many ranchers were forced to leave their homes and go into the mountains at Llaves or Gallina to work in the sawmills or lumber camps because no rain had fallen on their fields and pastures.

Here, as in all Spanish colonial settlements, a Catholic church was built simultaneously with the village. Priests were rare, but the Catholic religion flourished. In fact, the Catholic Church organized and ran the first public school system in Cuba until the courts decided in the middle of this century that such a system was illegal. Until that time, Sandoval County paid the Sisters of the Immaculate Conception to teach in the county's schools.

World War II brought the twentieth century to the region around Cuba. Boys were sent away to train and fight, and farms and ranches were therefore neglected. Families joined their sons, fathers, and husbands in California, and many of them have not returned. Others left Cuba for Albuquerque or other large New Mexico towns. As agricultural activities ceased, land and water rights were bought up either by large landowners or by the federal government. A number of water

rights cases reached state courts and were settled only after long, entangled legal battles. However, there are still many ranches, large and small, active around Cuba. Water (irrigation) associations first formed at settlement still meet, many of the members bearing the surnames of the original Nacimiento grantees.

South of Cuba on N.M. 44, the land begins its descent, opening up to larger vistas, smaller trees, and withering streambeds. Spectacular rock formations mark this stretch, their colors changing as the sun sweeps across the horizon. About fifteen miles outside Cuba is the site of the old coal mining town of LA VENTANA ("the window"), 112 mi. It is barely noticeable. There were many coal mines around La Ventana when coal was in its heyday. Some mines, including those here, are now being reopened, if only on a limited basis.

Less than a mile south of La Ventana, N.M. 44 crosses one of the largest land grants in New Mexico, the Ojo del Espiritu Santo ("Holy Ghost spring"). Tradition says that the name of the grant may have come from the experience of a man who stood on guard one night after dinner. Suddenly he rushed to the camp crying, "El Espiritu Santo! El Espiritu Santo!" The others, leaving camp, saw two wraithlike spirals rising from the ground in the nearby canyon. For them, it was a manifestation of the Holy Ghost. They followed the spirals and discovered the spring, naming it after the apparition.

The Ojo del Espiritu Santo Land Grant was given to the Cabeza de Baca family, descendants of the Spanish explorer. Including more than one hundred thirteen thousand acres, it was awarded to Luis María Cabeza de Baca on May 24, 1815, by Governor Alberto Maynez. The grant extended west to the Rio Puerco and Cabezon ("big head") Peak, and east as far as the Nacimiento Mountains. Much valuable pastureland and many mineral deposits are located on the grant. The estate of the de Baca family was sold in 1934 to the United States government, which turned the acreage over to the Jemez Indians as part of a land set-

Cabezon Peak, *Ed Tilgner.*

tlement. The Jemez Tribe runs a recreation area at the site of Holy Ghost Springs. Entrance to the area is well-marked.

Thirteen miles from the site of La Ventana, Cabezon Peak looms in the near distance. The peak is a gigantic volcanic plug, rising two thousand feet above the plains on which it sits. It is visible from miles around, even from the foothills of the Sandias, almost fifty miles away. Cabezon was called Tse Najiin ("black rock") by the Navajos, who consider it the head of a giant killed by the Twin War Gods. There was once a town five miles north of Ca-

bezon Peak. It was first settled in 1826 by Juan Maestas, who called it La Posta ("the stage stop"). La Posta was an important way station on the stagecoach route from Santa Fe to Fort Wingate. Fresh horses were saddled there and riders were given a rest before continuing on their journey.

At the time of its settlement, La Posta was green and lush, and it soon became a thriving cattle town. Wheat was planted, and at one time the La Posta area was known as the breadbasket of New Mexico. In its prime, at the turn of the century, the town contained

houses, saloons, dance halls, and general stores on both sides of the Rio Puerco. Because the river flooded often, inundating the town each time, buildings were later moved up and away from the riverbanks. The name was changed to Cabezon in 1891. Cabezon was abandoned by the 1940s, and little hint of its existence is visible today. It is now in private hands and visitors are not allowed. "No Trespassing" signs announce the policy.

N.M. 44 parallels the Rio Salado ("salty river") as far as SAN YSIDRO, 137 mi. There the small stream joins the Jemez River and N.M. 4 comes in from the north. San Ysidro is now little more than a crossroads, although it is an incorporated village with remnants of its farming past visible along N.M. 4. It was settled in 1699 by Juan Trujillo, but an actual Spanish grant for the area was not received until 1786, when Antonio Armenta and Salvador Sandoval were given a strip of land twelve miles long near the site of the present village. Much of this grant was bought by the federal government in 1936 and was then deeded to Zia Pueblo.

The town is named after St. Isidore, patron of New Mexico's farmers. Statues and paintings of the saint were common in Spanish colonial times and are seeing a revival as colonial crafts are worked again. San Isidro the farmer is usually depicted wearing a blue coat and pants, a red vest, and a hat with a flat crown. That was the costume of colonial farmers in early New Mexico. The saint is often accompanied by a small angel, and together they drive a team of oxen pulling a wooden plow. May, the traditional time for planting in the central and northern parts of the state, is also the time for honoring San Ysidro. Families carry his statue through the streets of farming villages and then into the fields.

JEMEZ PUEBLO is located about five miles north of San Ysidro on N.M. 4. The road follows the winding, narrow path of the Jemez River and cuts through canyons whose colors change radically from muddy brown to brilliant red. The houses at Jemez Pueblo were once three-storied; now they are low, hugging the brown earth from which they came, outbuildings and beehive ovens matching the warm tones of the homes, the land, and all that surrounds them.

Jemez Pueblo is large, with a population of about two thousand, and is Towa-speaking. The pueblo is nestled beside the Jemez River, its fields running down below the village to the shallow stream. Its present residents are descendants of the vast tribe of Jemez that may have lived in this area and also to the north around Stone Lake, now part of the Jicarilla Reservation. At the time of the Spanish entrance into New Mexico, the ancestors of the Jemez also lived east of the Rio Grande, at Pecos and near Glorieta. Those who resided along the Jemez River before and during the Spanish conquest lived on the mountain and mesa tops. They actively resisted Spanish domination, staging battles with their conquerors even before the 1680 revolt. In one such battle a Spaniard was killed, and twenty-nine Jemez leaders were hanged in retribution. In the Pueblo Revolt, the priest at Jemez was killed. Not until the early 1700s were the Jemez Indians finally subdued and settled in their present site. They had previously lived twelve miles further upstream, with smaller villages along the mesa tops and in the canyons. Anthropologists count at least twenty-two Jemez sites in the upper part of the valley. His-

SIDE TOUR

Jemez Pueblo, *Harvey Caplin.*

torically there was friendship between the people of Jemez and the Navajos to the west. During the time of confrontations with the Spanish and their allies among other Pueblo tribes (including the neighboring Zia and Santa Ana groups), the Jemez Indians were often assisted in defending themselves by the more western Pueblos and the Navajos. For a time after de Vargas had staged his reconquest in 1692, some of the Jemez people left their land and lived with the Navajos.

Traditions are strong at Jemez Pueblo. Although most residents work outside the village at jobs in Albuquerque, a number of Jemez Indians are famous artists, writers, and craftspeople. There are also many pottery-makers at the pueblo. Their ceramic animals, bowls, and people, most shaped and painted in traditional forms, are sold throughout the state and often at the pueblo itself. During the summer and fall, N.M. 4 is lined with shaded *ramadas* (brush-roofed lean-tos) under which Jemez women sell their Indian bread, cookies, and pies. They often make fry bread on the spot, the warm smell of cooking dough mingling with the scent of a piñon

fire. While some residents farm the tribe's ninety thousand acres, hunting has always been a stronger tradition among the mountain-dwelling Jemez people; vestiges of the hunting spirit appear during dances. And Jemez is famous for its runners. Running is a tribal rite, to which cleansing and spiritual properties are attributed. Jemez runners compete in local contests (the cross-country team at the local high school often wins the state championship) and in national races.

The Jemez Indians govern themselves in a way that blends their traditional customs with those of their Spanish conquerors. A *cacique* and his assistants serve for life, enforcing and interpreting the Jemez ways that date from prehistory. Every year the *cacique* selects a tribal council—a governor, lieutenant governors, a sheriff, and aides—who will act for the tribe in its relations with outside agencies and governments.

Feast days are celebrated publicly on August 2 and November 12. The dances in August honor Pecos ancestors with the famous Pecos Buffalo Dance. San Diego, Jemez's patron saint, is commemorated with long celebrations in November. At Christmas time dances are also held which celebrate tribal as well as Catholic occasions. Other ceremonies take place throughout the year at Jemez, but many of them are closed to the public.

More than ten miles beyond Jemez Pueblo, N.M. 4 bisects JEMEZ SPRINGS, pri-

marily a resort spot. Jemez Springs offers some overnight lodging, a restaurant or two, and below the town a public bathhouse where the springs for which the town was named provide bubbling, sulfur-laden water. The geothermal spring near the bathhouse also provides heat to municipal buildings. The town has a fire department, a rescue facility, a library, churches, and a surprising number of Catholic retreat houses.

Jemez Springs, once known as Hot Springs, has seen exciting times. Sheep wars, vigilante groups, and wild gambling enterprises raged through the little town in the early part of this century. The FBI once secretly headquartered itself in the Abousleman home, the largest residence in town. Texas gunslingers were tossed bodily from local bars, their attempts at machismo rebuffed by local ranchers and bartenders.

JEMEZ STATE MONUMENT sits above the river valley beyond the village of Jemez Springs. The large stone ruin is the remains of the Church of San José, founded by the Franciscan missionary Fray Alonso de Lugo, who was followed by Fray Gerónimo Zarate Salmerón in 1621. The immediate area was the prehistoric site of the pueblo of Giusewa (a Tewa word meaning "place at the boiling waters"). Salmerón worked not only at the San José mission, but also south at the present Jemez Pueblo site, where he founded the San Diego mission. Excavations in 1921–22

Beaver dams in Guaje Canyon, Jemez Mts., *Betty Lilienthal.*

and 1935–37 unearthed a mission complex through which visitors may wander. Its walls are six to eight feet thick, culminating in a combination watchtower and belltower above the nave. The sense of the mission's need for security and permanence in this outpost is strong: window openings are small, the massive walls forbidding. One of the few fresco paintings in mission churches was found here at San José de Giusewa; both the east and west walls of the nave were once covered by an intricate, colorful design. Only stone remains.

Jemez State Monument is open to the public most days of the week. A small museum, staffed by Jemez Pueblo members, provides displays giving the visitor insight into the background of Jemez tradition and history. Strong statements about the Jemez people's place in New Mexico confirm the independence of the tribe, a characteristic they have shown since the earliest encroachment of the Spanish. There are also exhibits explaining traditional crafts and foods.

SODA DAM, a natural spring and dam, can often be smelled before it is seen. The sulfurous odor of the spring indicates its strong mineral content, down through the years thought by many—from the Jemez Indians to newly arrived residents—to have healing properties. Calcium deposits have formed the odd, mushroom-shaped dam that interrupts the flow of the Jemez River and provides a place for climbing and inspection. Visitors can park off the road. Children will want to crawl around the strange-looking, odd-smelling formation, and care should be taken. The spring bubbles even in the winter when the rocks are covered with snow, and vapors rise from the water, adding to its supernatural aura.

The surrounding mountains are part of the Santa Fe National Forest. There is also a great deal of private land in the area. The Jemez ranger station is located just north of the town of Jemez Springs; visitors can ask for weather and trail guidance there.

North of Soda Dam, the road is narrow, winding through the gorge of the Jemez River. Fishing is a popular sport along the banks, and pullouts for fishing and picnicking are marked. Camping spots are more frequent further into the mountains, where trails and sites are indicated. Those who wish to pack in to more remote country are advised to check first with the ranger for information about trails, weather and fire conditions, and precautions.

Natural wonders to look for along N.M. 4 include Battleship Rock, a sheer cliff be-

Battleship Rock near Jemez Springs, *Harvey Caplin*.

neath which the river runs; there are campsites nearby. Redondo Peak, at 11,254 feet one of the highest mountains in New Mexico, can sometimes be seen from the road. The meadows and valleys are also the sites of ancient Pueblo ruins, although none is marked as such.

At La Cueva, a picnic spot along the river about nine miles north of Jemez Springs, N.M. 4 meets N.M. 126. Those who wish to visit the Valle Grande, Bandelier National Monument, and Los Alamos will take N.M. 4 going east. N.M. 126 heads west toward Fenton Lake, and ultimately to Cuba. (See Tour 4 for the continuation of N.M. 4 and the route of N.M. 126.)

As N.M. 44 leaves San Ysidro and crosses the Rio Puerco, it traverses land that was once sea bottom and later a hunting ground for dinosaurs. In fact, within the powdery outcrops near San Ysidro, paleontologists have discovered a number of partial skeletons of prehistoric beasts, including that of a 140-million-year-old, sixty-foot-long sauropod dinosaur.

There are also prehistoric pueblo ruins in this area, some of which have been excavated and studied. Research indicates that some of their inhabitants probably were ancestors of the Keresan-speaking Zias, whose village lies about six miles down N.M. 44.

ZIA PUEBLO, 143 mi., has stood on its sandy promontory overlooking the Jemez River since at least the seventeenth century. The early Zias' ancestors may have come from Chaco Canyon and Mesa Verde and settled at a number of sites in this region. Both Zian tradition and anthropological research seem to affirm this.

When Zia was visited by Coronado's expedition in 1541, the Pueblo received Captain Juan Jaramillo politely. The relationship continued to be cordial until the Pueblo Revolt. In the years between 1680 and 1692, Zians were placed in captivity and their villages were sacked. In 1692, the Pueblo converted, en masse, to Catholicism; Zia erected a wooden cross, still standing, on the pueblo's south plaza to commemorate the event. Its Catholic church, Nuestra Señora de la Asunción de Sía, built before 1613 and still standing at the edge of the village, is used only on Catholic feast days, when a priest visits. The church is small, its front yard a cemetery, to its side a jail. Catholicism at Zia is nominal.

The pueblo has created an elaborate ceremonial and political structure to oversee what was until recently a primarily agricultural existence. There are six clans and two kiva groups within Zia, but the ceremonial responsibility for the pueblo rests with the religious societies, which guard Zia traditions, act as links with the pueblo's ancestors, supervise ceremonial hunts, perform funeral rites, and actively lead the ceremonies that control both crop and human fertility. Within the pueblo, each member has an individual responsibility to assure that his own world is stable so that, collectively, the Zia universe is balanced.

Whereas the traditional basis for Zia life was farming and, later, sheep and cattle raising, many pueblo residents now earn their livings off the reservation. The cattle association is still strong, but the amount of irrigated land has declined. There is a large market for the handsome decorated pottery made by the pueblo's women and sold throughout the country.

A symbol seen again and again on traditional Zian crafts is the Zia sun, the official symbol of the state of New Mexico. Selection of the Zia as the design for the state flag was an honor for the pueblo, but as it began to decorate plumbing trucks and tee shirts, its uniqueness as a symbol was probably lost.

There are about six hundred registered Zia tribe members, a number of whom live off the reservation. In 1540 Spanish officials counted at least five thousand Zians. Beginning in the sixteenth century, the Zia population declined steadily. By 1890 there were fewer than one hundred Zians, and many predicted that the Pueblo would not survive. By the middle of this century, however, the birth rate was climbing steadily. Today the presence of new housing and tribal offices, an active day school, and the vitality of Zia ceremonies indicate that the Pueblo is holding its own.

SANTA ANA PUEBLO's five-hundred-year-old village of Ta'ma'ya' sits on the north bank of

the Jemez River with the rugged cliffs of Black Mesa in the background (151 mi.). Ta'ma'ya' is a ceremonial village, lived in only during periods of religious observances.

Santa Ana's five hundred residents live now in the village of Ranchitos ("little farms" or "ranches"), also called Santa Ana Pueblo Number Two, ten miles southeast of Ta'ma'ya' across the Rio Grande just north of Bernalillo. This unusual arrangement begin in the early eighteenth century, when the primarily agricultural Pueblo purchased land along the Rio Grande for gardens and fields. Slowly life began to shift toward Ranchitos. At first pueblo residents commuted, sometimes by canoe, to their farms. The next century saw them spending much of the growing season at Ranchitos. By 1890 the ancient Pueblo was inhabited only during autumn and winter. An account of the time describes Santa Ana:

> A complete removal is made in March . . . . The cats alone remain, prowling like gaunt specters over the roofs and through the deserted streets." (U.S. Census Office. 11th Census 1894:431–432)

In the twentieth century, Santa Anans live in modern houses at Ranchitos, sending their children to Head Start and schools in Bernalillo and working at jobs in the area. The village is a busy place, an active farming community, the center for a number of community programs that serve other pueblos, and the home of a recreational complex that includes a swimming pool and playing fields. However, when the winter solstice draws near, during late June celebrations, and at other times significant in the Santa Ana calendar, the population of Ranchitos moves to old Santa Ana. There first the medicine societies and later the entire Pueblo take part in week-long rituals. No kivas or other religious structures exist at Ranchitos. The heart of the Pueblo is Ta'ma'ya'.

Like their fellow Keresan speakers, Santa Anans are probably descended from the Anasazi of the Chaco region. Pueblo myth and archaeological evidence link them to the vast city-states to the northwest that were deserted by the late twelfth century. The present Ta'ma'ya' was probably visited by Spanish troops in the sixteenth century. In 1598 Santa Ana formally submitted to Spanish rule.

Santa Ana joined in the 1680 revolt, fleeing most likely to the Jemez Mountains with members of other pueblos. In 1687 the village atop Black Mesa was destroyed by Governor Pedro Reñeros de Posada. By 1693 Santa Ana had settled back on its present location, aligning itself with the Spanish from then on.

Political and religious life at Santa Ana is structured and conservative. Residents are born into clans that dictate kiva affiliation. The two kivas, the squash and the turquoise, serve ceremonial functions. Overseeing Santa Ana is a *cacique*, a priestlike figure who serves for life, appointing the war priest and others who will administer the activities of the pueblo. The tribal council, chosen annually, exists chiefly to deal with the outside world.

Although a small pueblo, Santa Ana is a vigorous one. Its population continues to grow. Crafts such as weaving and pottery-making, which had almost died out, have been revived. Land at Ranchitos that lay fallow for decades is now being planted and irrigated. Each of the two Santa Ana villages is in its own way a viable place.

Sandias from Coronado Monument, *S. Humphries, Jr.*

Driving eastward after passing Santa Ana Pueblo, the traveler will be treated to an exciting panorama. Ahead are the Sandia Mountains, their color changing with the position of the sun. Below lies the Rio Grande valley and the town of Bernalillo. To the south, sometimes hidden by haze, is New Mexico's largest city, Albuquerque. The Sangre de Cristo mountain range can be seen to the north; Santa Fe sits at its feet. A small group of mountains, the Ortiz, is located to the east between the Sangre de Cristos and the Sandias. N.M. 44 follows the escarpment of Black Mesa (or Santa Ana Mesa), beneath which the Jemez River runs to the Rio Grande.

Seven miles beyond Santa Ana Pueblo, N.M. 528 enters from the south, leading eventually to Corrales and Rio Rancho (Tour 1). Less than a mile after the N.M. 528 intersection, signs point to CORONADO STATE PARK AND MONUMENT.

A large park with camping and picnic facilities, Coronado Monument perches above the Rio Grande, providing spectacular vistas in all directions at all times of the year. The monument was the site of Kuaua, one of a number of southern Tiwa pueblos that Coronado came upon during his 1540–41 expedition. He and his troops spent the winter here, making contact with a number of Pueblo groups, demanding lodging, food, and other necessities, perhaps setting the tone for the sensitive Spanish-Indian relationships of the seventeenth century.

A small museum and interpretive trails to excavated Pueblo ruins are pleasant to visit and explore. Built about A.D. 1300, Kuaua (known to the Spanish as Alcanfor) was a fortress that protected its inhabitants from the Apaches. Those who lived here were farmers, their fields planted down along the river. Kuaua was abandoned around 1700.

N.M. 44 crosses the river just below the monument and soon intersects U.S. 85. Travelers can turn south at the intersection to pass through Bernalillo and follow the old highway fifteen miles into Albuquerque. A north turn takes the driver to Algodones. Straight ahead, I-25 provides a direct route to Santa Fe or Albuquerque. Placitas is on N.M. 44 in the foothills of the Sandias. (See Tour 1 for all the above-mentioned places except Santa Fe, on Tour 11.)

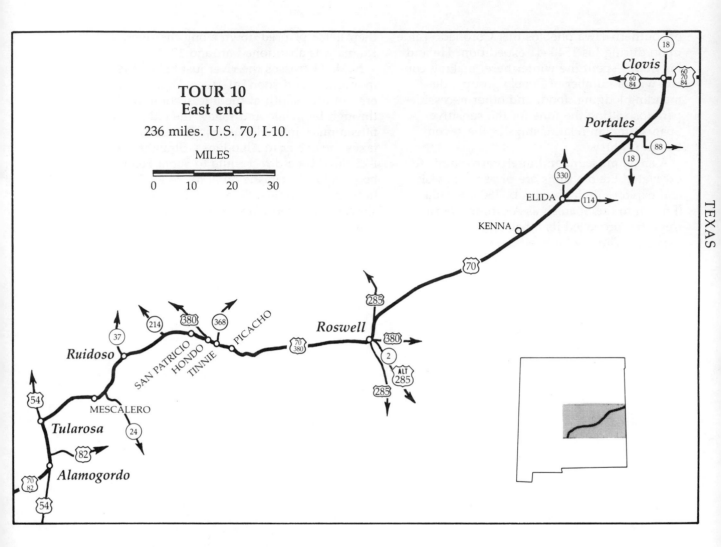

TOUR 10
East end

236 miles. U.S. 70, I-10.

MILES

0   10   20   30

TEXAS

Clovis

Portales

ELIDA

KENNA

Roswell

Ruidoso

SAN PATRICIO
HONDO
TINNIE
PICACHO

MESCALERO

Tularosa

Alamogordo

See page 476 for western end of tour ten.

tour ten

The U.S. highway system established in the 1920s gave numbers ending in zero to routes that crossed, or nearly crossed, the country east to west. One of the most indirect of these nine roads was U.S. 70, spanning the distance between Atlantic, North Carolina, and Blythe, California. This highway makes its somewhat roundabout way across New Mexico, entering the state on a common roadway with U.S. 60 and proceeding southwesterly more or less on its own between Clovis and Las Cruces. Before the construction of I-10, it shared a roadbed with U.S. 80 between Las Cruces and Lordsburg. From Lordsburg northwest it remains a back way to Phoenix, Arizona.

Tour 10 follows U.S. 70 as far as Lordsburg. The tour begins on the rich eastern New Mexico plains, descends from the caprock and crosses the wide valley of the Pecos. Between Roswell and Tularosa it climbs amid the ten-thousand-foot peaks of the Sacramento and White mountains, then traverses the plains of the Tularosa basin. Just before crossing the Rio Grande at Las Cruces it climbs to another pass between the San Andres and Organ mountains. West of the Rio Grande valley, the tour ascends among low, scattered mountains to the Continental Divide, passes through a region of seasonal lakes (playas), and leaves the state within sight of mountains in nearly every direction.

Almost all of the routes of the U.S. highway system followed railroads. The tracks that preceded U.S. 70 belonged to Charles B. Eddy's Pecos Valley Railroad, built northward from Pecos, Texas, to Carlsbad (then called Eddy) in 1891. The railroad reached Roswell in 1894 and Portales in 1898, promoting agricultural settlements and irrigation schemes all along its path. Within a few years, trading centers, cities, and county seats appeared along the tracks, and U.S. 70 soon became their main streets.

The tour begins leaving Clovis, described in Tour 8. Special Pullmans used to transport tourists roundtrip from Clovis to the Carlsbad Caverns over what was by then the Santa Fe Railroad. The motorist passes Hillcrest Park, on the southern edge of town, with a zoo, sunken gardens, a swimming pool, and a trout-stocked pond.

At a huge gravel pit in Blackwater Draw a highway crew found extinct mammoth re-

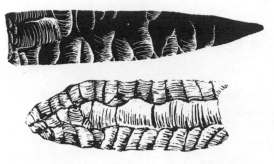

mains in 1932. This discovery shed light on the Clovis people, one of the oldest Paleo-Indian cultures known in the New world. Some twelve thousand years ago these people hunted large Pleistocene mammals using characteristic spear heads, the "Clovis Points." The BLACKWATER DRAW MUSEUM, 12 mi., is located near the archaeological site. The gravel pit once was a pond where Clovis people surprised and killed thousands of animals. Despite the fact that, according to a director of the Paleo-Indian Institute, "It has produced more evidence about early North American mammoth hunters than all other sites combined," Blackwater Draw's story is one of neglect and loss of valuable evidence, together with heroic attempts to preserve and study what has been found here. For thirty years visitors carried off bones, selling some to museums and collectors. In 1962 El Llano Amateur Archaeological Society undertook the first excavation. This work was turned over to the newly organized Paleo-Indian Institute of Eastern New Mexico University in 1965. Although many remains of the six-ton Ice Age mammoths and the weapons used to bring them down are lost, many others have been gathered here to give the public some inkling of the mystery of the earliest known life on the continent and to demonstrate the importance of these finds for further study of our hunting predecessors.

Before the uplift in the earth's crust that created the elevated caprock in eastern New Mexico and West Texas, Blackwater Draw was a river, running east to join what is now known as the Brazos River. With the geologic changes, this area of the caprock began to drain west into the Pecos River, and the old riverbed here became a series of lakes, springs, and sand-filled sinks. The old valley, now called the Portales Valley, can be traced from Taiban to the Texas line by La Tule, Tierra Blanca, and Great Salt lakes. The Civilian Conservation Corps built Eastern New Mexico State Park here. Now called Oasis State Park, it includes several archaeological sites and the museum.

The earliest settlement in this valley during historic times was at Portales Springs, six miles southeast of the present town. Cave openings looking like porch arches (*portales*) surround the springs. Bison hunters, especially the Causey brothers, who killed thousands of the beasts, frequented the springs. John Chisum stopped at them in 1866, driving steers to feed the Navajos then quartered at Fort Sumner. By 1877, eighty thousand head of cattle had passed along the Fort Sumner Trail. Doak Good settled at the springs in 1880; Billy the Kid's gang used them as a rendezvous; and by the time the railroad came through (and missed Portales Springs), a small town existed here.

PORTALES, 18 mi. (alt. 4,022, pop. 9,927), was born as a construction camp for workers on the Pecos Valley and Northern Railroad. "Uncle" Josh Morrison pulled the first store on skids from the springs, and by 1901 the new town had grown up around it. Its first newspaper, *The Progress*, was published in August of that year. Upon formation of Roosevelt County, named for President Theodore Roosevelt, in 1903, Portales became the county seat. In 1927 the state legislature authorized a normal school for the eastern plains, and in 1934 Eastern New Mexico Junior College opened for classes. This became a four-year college in 1940 and Eastern New Mexico University in 1955.

Progress in the surrounding countryside had its ups and downs, however. Railroad promoters promised irrigation water and encouraged settlement under the Homestead Act. Although this area receives more rainfall than any other part of the state suitable for agriculture, its eighteen-inch annual average was

and is too marginal for the type of grain cultivation then being imported from wetter parts of the plains. Families could not prosper for long on 160 acres without water, and irrigation projects did not become reliable or practical almost until the Second World War. The result was that many homesteaders, disillusioned and feeling themselves failures, left without "proving up," that is, staying five years, or three years with some payment. Of those who did prove up, many soon sold out to larger landholders or speculators, thus defeating the intent of the original homestead law, which was basically inapplicable to this climate. Sizable acreages reverted to grazing land. Some homesteaders were able to stay in farming by diversifying, adopting the "cow, sow, and hen" philosophy and creating a rural economy with dairying, livestock raising, and a mixture of irrigated and dry farming. The end for this way of life began with tougher sanitation requirements for dairies and the elimination of the twenty-gallon milk can, and was hastened by the dislocation caused by World War II, a disaster for small and medium-sized farms and ranches and rural towns all over New Mexico. It was at this time, also, that deep pumping (six hundred to one thousand feet) from the Ogallala Aquifer became feasible. With that water, larger farms specializing in grains, soybeans, cotton, and such crops displaced the older, diversified farms and made this area one of the richest agricultural regions in the nation. However, since water is being removed from the aquifer faster than it is being replenished, it is uncertain how long this land use will continue.

Since the 1930s, a center of Portales has been its college. The administration building, in English Tudor style, set the pattern for most later structures. In 1937 Lloyd Moylan painted there for five months to complete his mural on the Twelfth Chapter of Ecclesiastes. Three museums are located on the ENMU campus. The Paleo-Indian Institute Museum traces the beginnings of hunters in North America, displaying artifacts from the Folsom Site in New Mexico and the Hell Gap Site in Wyoming, as well as the nearby Blackwater Draw Site. The Roosevelt County Museum, affiliated with the Museum of New Mexico, exhibits household articles, tools, and antiques from the late nineteenth and early twentieth centuries. Miles Museum grew out of the collection of two weekend rockhounds, Mr. and Mrs. Fred Miles. It displays rare stones and minerals in addition to Indian artifacts, pottery specimens, and mummies. The Greyhound Arena is the principal source of basketball fever in this part of the world.

The first known grave in the county was dug on the H-Bar Ranch that predated the railroad construction camp and is now a part of the Portales Country Club. A few of Portales's original buildings remain. John Morrison's store can be found at 501 East Third Street. The original Bank of Portales is at 106 North Main Street. The home of territorial governor Washington F. Lindsey, at 1201 North Boston Street, still is used as a private residence.

Portales hosts the annual Peanut Festival, on the first weekend of October. At that time, participants cook, display, eat, and race while balancing the little vegetable, for which Portales has become famous.

At 43 mi., ELIDA (alt. 4,325, pop. 203) preceded Portales as an organized town and was for a time a better-known trading center than the county seat. By 1903 a post office, three

general stores, and many shops and restaurants had located around Elida's main square. Homesteaders came, all during the early years. They hung on "as long as the rabbits lasted," as one old settler put it, most living in dugout homes until they could build houses. In 1913 grasshoppers infested the area so thickly that trains couldn't run because the tracks were too slick. At one time Roosevelt County had 118 rural school districts; Elida now has one of the three remaining districts.

Near Elida one can see the "breaks" at the edge of the caprock. The canyons, boulders, and sometimes vertical walls surrounding the Llano Estacado or Staked Plains shelter wildlife and the trees that provide fire and post wood for a large area.

The Urton brothers from Missouri settled KENNA, 54 mi, in 1884. It was then part of the giant Bar V Ranch that extended west to the Pecos River. Littlefield, north of Kenna, was the site of the first ranch in Roosevelt County. Jim Newman established his Yellow House Ranch there in 1882, and immediately began feuding with Doak Good, another early rancher at Portales Springs, forty miles away.

San Juan Mesa, to the northwest of Kenna, is the highest point in the tableland that slopes back towards Portales. The tour continues across ranching country to the Pecos River, in whose geological youth the bluffs and mesas that characterize the fringes of the caprock were created.

The plants that dominate the area along the highway are mesquite, fourwing saltbush, and alkali sacaton, a bunch grass that survives the high concentration of salts in this soil. The grass has been a valuable ground cover, if not a good food source for livestock. Some pronghorn antelope still roam this country, eating cactus, greasewood, sagebrush, and the grasses. Those that have survived the attacks of their worst enemies, hunters, travel in herds kept together by the bucks or by family instinct. In early fall, the pronghorn bucks fight, the winners forming harems of up to fifteen does. The kids are born eight months later. Both the does and bucks are tan and have forked horns, white bands across the throat, and white rumps. The animals are very swift but fatally curious.

Where U.S. 70 crosses the Pecos River, the road also goes through the tip of one section of Bitter Lake National Wildlife Refuge. Salt Creek runs through the middle of this section, the Salt Creek Wilderness Area, the scene of an acrimonious confrontation in 1982 between oil company drillers and conservationists. The controversy regarding the extraction of minerals and leased mineral rights under designated wilderness areas is to be settled in federal courts. A large part of the wilderness is open only during hunting season. Visitors should inquire at refuge headquarters about hiking and horseback riding in the wilderness.

The old Roswell-Clovis highway, at mile 93, leads indirectly to a poorly marked entrance to the other section of the refuge and its headquarters. Between thirty thousand and seventy-five thousand snow geese reside on one of the lakes in late November and early December. Six of the seven small lakes are manmade and are fed by springs and treated effluent from Roswell's sewage disposal plant.

The lakes provide a habitat for ducks, geese, sandhill cranes, and other marsh birds. Parts of the refuge are farmed to help feed the wintering waterfowl, small mammals, and big game. During the spring and fall, the lakes are visited by hundreds of white pelicans in their migratory flight. The marshy part of the refuge is preferred by rails, bitterns, egrets, ducks, herons, and wading birds. Vegetation is predominately musk grass, a favorite food of ducks and a protective cover for fish. Fishing is permitted on some of the lakes when most of the birds have gone north again. Bitter Lake, a natural and highly alkaline lake, has long been a roosting area for the magnificent sandhill cranes. The large birds fly back to the lake, in tight formation, after a day's foraging. At dusk, the cranes wade into the water to seek safety from predators. Bobcats, foxes, badgers, and weasels are nocturnal residents, and coyotes stalk the cranes in the daytime.

Just north of Bitter Lake, the Saint Francis Natural Area contains thirty-two gypsum sinks up to fifty feet deep and filled with groundwater. An alga commonly found only in lagoons on the Gulf of Mexico grows here, along with some rare fish species. This fragile area is open only to scientific and educational groups with special permission.

U.S. 70 soon meets with U.S. 285 at 104 mi. on the outskirts of Roswell (Tour 7).

The Pecos River rises in the Sangre de Cristo Mountains northeast of Santa Fe and then follows a southeasterly course along the bottom of the slopes of the Capitan, White, Sacramento, and Guadalupe ranges. It is fed both from below ground and by living streams that come down from these mountains during the spring runoff and summer rains. One of the more important of these streams is the Rio Hondo, which waters Roswell and joins the Pecos just east of the city. Heading west from Roswell (109 mi.), U.S. 70 gradually climbs out of the Pecos valley, crosses the Diamond A Plain and then follows the Rio Hondo up toward its headwaters near Sierra Blanca.

The Two Rivers Dam is a recent attempt to control and use the water of the Rio Hondo and Rock Arroyo. It is located six miles south of the highway (turnoff at mile 123). Actually two dams, the Diamond A Dam and Rock Dam, create the Two Rivers Reservoir, which provides water for irrigation, wildlife, and recreation.

Sunset and Riverside remain on some maps at the point just before the Rio Hondo usually disappears into the sand. They are some of the first indications of the settlements that have existed in this valley for nearly a century and a half. At mile 147 the road begins a sharp ascent up Picacho ("peak") Hill, named during the days of the Butterfield Stage mail route, when the grade was steep and dangerous for inexperienced drivers. After offering a view of the canyon to the south from near the summit, the highway descends to join the cottonwoods and irrigated farms of the Hondo valley proper.

The town of PICACHO, 148 mi. (alt. 4,804), is named for the peak at whose base it sits. Settlers from the Rio Grande, hoping to avoid the big river's floods, arrived here around 1865 and began the combination of fruit and vegetable growing and small livestock grazing still popular in these sheltered valleys. A Frenchman, Leopoldo Scheney, was among the founders of the new town. By 1875 Charles Goodnight, John Chisum, and others from the Texas plains had added large-scale cattle ranching to the life of the region.

An adobe building housed a store, a post office, a Butterfield Stage stop, and a hotel for travelers between Roswell and Lincoln Courthouse and Old Mesilla. The hotel, then eighty years old, burned in 1946. During the Second World War, old Picacho was deserted, but soon afterward the present town grew up along the highway.

Five miles further west is TINNIE, 153 mi. The history of this place goes back at least to 1876, when it became known as Analla, after Joseph Analla, an early settler. A store and post office remained in the Analla family until 1906, when the buildings were bought by the Raymond family. The Raymonds built a new

adobe store and post office and, at the request of the townspeople, named it for their little daughter Tinnie.

In 1959 Robert O. Anderson of Roswell bought the Tinnie Mercantile Company and added the porch, tower, and pavillion, and the Silver Dollar Bar and Steak House. Many of the old things here were gathered by John Meigs, the artist from San Patricio who planned the new additions.

N.M. 368, unpaved, heads north from Tinnie. Connecting with N.M. 48, it is a possible alternate tour of the mostly deserted towns of Blue Water, Arabela, Pinelodge, and Encinoso. The alternate tour ends at Capitan.

HONDO, 157 mi., was once called La Junta, so named because two rivers join here. The highways divide accordingly, U.S. 70 following the Rio Ruidoso ("noisy river") while U.S. 380 (Tour 12) branches off along the Rio Bonito ("pretty river") toward Lincoln and Capitan. L. W. Coe homesteaded this part of the valley at about the same time as his Coe cousins were claiming land further upriver. A toll bridge across the Bonito was operated by Jim Gonzales, also owner of a general merchandise store.

Enterprises associated with fruit and vegetable growing—packing sheds, a refrigeration service, and a trucking company—now are the mainstay of Hondo's economy. The valley of-

fers fruit orchards and roadside stands in abundance. Just west of town, a picture-book horse ranch can be seen from the road.

When Ramón Olguín and others settled in what is now SAN PATRICIO, 160 mi., it was called Ruidoso after the river. The church was built under the care of an Irish priest. In his honor both it and the town took the name of his patron, St. Patrick. Early in the twentieth century the town got a post office. One of its first postmasters was William Brady, grandson of Sheriff Pat Brady, killed in the Lincoln County War. At one time San Patricio was the largest voting precinct in Lincoln County. The population declined greatly during World War II, and by the 1950s most of the business center had moved out to the new highway.

To see the town that has been home to such well-known people as Billy the Kid, actress Helen Hayes, author Paul Horgan, and artists Peter Hurd and Henriette Wyeth, the traveler must loop off onto the old road. San Patricio, like other towns along the Ruidoso, has had to contend with flooding. Floods upriver have cut the town off on several occasions and have been responsible for reroutings of the highway and relocations of towns in its path.

At 167 mi N.M. 214, unpaved, heads northwest to Fort Stanton. This part of Lincoln County is a fine illustration of the effect that good, but fewer, roads can have on the countryside—that is, concentration of commerce along the good roads, and isolation of the rest of the area. Where now there are only three highways, older maps show the county here crisscrossed with roads and trails connecting Lincoln and Fort Stanton directly with all the settlements in the area.

One of the early pioneering families in Lincoln county was the Coes. Originally from Missouri, several of the brothers worked the Santa Fe Trail and first homesteaded just off the trail north of Las Vegas. In the winter of 1875 they moved to the Ruidoso valley, where with the help of older neighbors they constructed irrigation ditches and harvested their first crop in 1876. The Coes—Lon, Al, Frank, Jap, cousin George, and brother-in-law Ab

Saunders—came to raise fruit and to farm. Nearby Fort Stanton was an ideal market for wild grama hay, produce, and meat. During the summer of 1877 William Bonney (alias Billy the Kid) worked for the Coes as a hand. They were soon unwillingly caught up in the Lincoln County War (see Tour 12). They sided with the losing McSween faction and left the country for a while after the shoot-out in July 1878, when their side was scattered. They soon returned, however, and Coes have farmed and raised livestock here ever since. Their story is detailed in Wilbur Coe's *Ranch on the Ruidoso: The Story of a Pioneer Family in New Mexico, 1871–1968*.

Jasper N. Coe homesteaded GLENCOE, 168 mi., in 1880. His original place is now the Bonnell Ranch. From A.D. 900 to 1200, pithouse villages of the archaeological "Glencoe Phase" occupied this area. Glencoe's town center has been moved several times, due to flooding of the Ruidoso and to changes in the routing of U.S. 70.

RUIDOSO DOWNS, 178 mi., first called itself Palo Verde and later (1946–58) that name's translation, Green Tree. Hale Spring, at the base of the mountain just to the south, was the reason for Palo Verde's existence and, many years before, for a settlement of prehistoric people. Remains said to have been a huge ancient irrigation ditch, ten feet across and six to eight feet high, can be found here, along with evidence of a large burial ground.

Heck Johnson "developed" Palo Verde in the 1930s. He sold lots and water rights, and Hale Spring did the rest. Soon there were gardens, orchards, two water-driven sawmills, and a population of five hundred in the new town. When Palo Verde citizens applied for a post office in 1946, the postal service stipulated that the town be named Green Tree.

Across the road, meanwhile, the Ruidoso Downs Race Track had grown from contests between friends and visitors to a nationally known track that featured the All-American Quarter Horse Futurity, richest horse race in the country. Eugene V. Hensley, originator of the famous race, persuaded the town to

North Fork of Bonito River, Lincoln National Forest, *Dave Wilson*.

change its name to Ruidoso Downs so that the track would have a postmark.

Racing season runs from early May to the futurity on Labor Day, with races Thursdays through Sundays. Tours of the track, stables, and practice sessions are available to the public. The three-day All American Quarter Horse Yearling Sale attracts thousands of prospective buyers and curious visitors at the end of each season.

HOLLYWOOD, 180 mi., was named for Hollywood, Florida, by its first postmaster and store owner, George A. Friedenbloom. It is now part of the greater Ruidoso resort and recreation area.

At 181 mi., the tour intersects N.M. 37 north. This highway, via Ruidoso, Sierra

Nogal Canyon, Lincoln National Forest, *Dave Wilson.*

Blanca Ski Area, Nogal, and the White Mountain Wilderness, is an alternate, more mountainous route between Tularosa and Carrizozo. It also connects with N.M. 48 to Capitan, the Capitan Mountains, and Lincoln.

RUIDOSO (alt. 6,600, pop. 4,284), at the foot of Old Baldy Peak, extends along N.M. 37 like a string of beads. Tourist signs stand out from a rich growth of spruce and Ponderosa pine. The town is named Ruidoso ("noisy") after the stream running through town, *not* for the flow of tourist traffic. The river powered a mill, now south of the highway, which inspired the town's first name, Dowlin's Mill, in 1882. Present buildings consist primarily of vacation homes and a myriad of recreation facilities. The twenty-four-hour chamber of commerce information center tells of the golf courses, both in town and nearby; of opportunities to swim, skate, eat, and play tennis; of amusement rides; of art fairs and plays; and of movies at the architecturally incongruous "castle." Several parks and a library round out the recreational opportunities in town. Immediately beyond its boundaries, one can enjoy the town's spectacular setting while picnicking, hiking, skiing, riding, or fishing.

Soon after entering the Mescalero Apache Reservation (182 mi.), U.S. 70 leaves tributaries of the Ruidoso and begins to follow the Rio Tularosa in a southwesterly direction toward the town of Tularosa. The Mescalero Reservation was established in 1873 and eventually comprised 460,177 acres between the

Sacramento and the White mountains. With timbered slopes, rich pastures, and two thousand acres of cropland, the Mescalero Reservation ranks among the best-endowed in the nation. The Mescaleros manage hunting and fishing preserves and also operate a luxury resort, the Inn of the Mountain Gods.

The Mescalero Apaches were not always so well-off, however. Their history parallels that of other Athapascan groups, who began moving from the north into present-day New Mexico in the 1400s and 1500s, at about the same time that the various Pueblos were moving east and resettling mainly in the Rio Grande valley. Both of these movements were still going on when Spanish colonizers began arriving from the south. The Spaniards found four groups of nomadic Indians. Two of them, the Navajos and the Gila Apaches, lived west of the Rio Grande, while the Jicarilla Apaches and the Mescaleros inhabited the mountains and plains to its east. At one time the Mescaleros called the White, the Guadalupe, and the Davis mountains of the Big Bend country home, and wandered over the plains from the Texas Panhandle into Chihuahua. They lived in the mountains during the summer and wintered on the desert plains.

Following a hunting, gathering, and later raiding lifestyle, the Mescaleros built brush shelters or used tepees. Their name comes from the mescal, an agave or century plant, used as a staple food. During May or June a party would chop off the larger leaves and the roots of twenty to thirty agaves. Meanwhile a fire had been built in a huge, rock-bottomed pit. The mescal bulbs were then thrown into the pit, covered with grass, dirt, and rocks and "pressure cooked" until the syrupy feast was uncovered hours later. What was not eaten on the spot was spread in thin sheets, dried on flat rocks, and taken home for storage. Fibers of the mescal plant were also used for making sandals and bags. A hallucinogen derives from the plant, as does a distilled beverage, but neither of these products is particularly associated with the Mescalero Indians.

At first the three groups, Spanish, Pueblos, and Apaches, managed a coexistence based to some extent on the need for one another's trade goods. Beginning in the 1630s and lasting up to the 1880s, however, a state of warfare prevailed. This was due partly to pressure on the Apaches from the Comanche Indians, also pushing down from the north, partly to the Apaches' inability to fit into the Spanish colonial scheme (that is, become Christian converts, pay tribute, and work), and partly to the fact that the Spanish sided militarily with the Pueblos against the Apaches.

Whatever the reasons, and however avoidable it may seem to us today, by the mid-1600s a cycle of murder and revenge had begun. Raids, counterattacks, punishment, and fear became the way of life for most of the inhabitants of the new province. Pueblo people abandoned their towns east of the Rio Grande valley and south of Isleta. During the Pueblo Revolt and for two centuries afterwards, the Apaches came to control all of present New Mexico beyond the few valleys where the Spanish and Pueblos had retrenched.

The U.S. Government inherited the "Apache problem." New settlements outside of the core area, established by English- and Spanish-speaking migrants, helped bring about the crisis of the 1860s and 1870s. During this time most of the military forts against the Navajos and the Apaches were established and attempts made to quarter the Navajos at Fort Sumner (after the Long Walk) and the Mescaleros at Forts Sumner and Stanton. By the late 1860s the government abandoned as failures these policies marked by bigotry, suffering, and bad luck, and the present reservation system began. It took more warfare to accomplish this; and when the Mescaleros finally settled on their reservation in 1873, they had to try to live on a tiny fraction of their former territory and often endured cold and hunger. Government contracts for meat (sometimes bad) and cornmeal (sometimes cut with sand) were an indirect cause of the feud between Lincoln merchants that resulted in the Lincoln County War. Undeniably, the interests of the previ-

ously nomadic Indians and the new settlers sometimes clashed. A still-unanswered question is whether another solution might have been found than the raids, reprisals, and eventual involuntary resettlement that characterized the bloody second half of the nineteenth century in New Mexico.

The reservation headquarters are located at the town of MESCALERO, 198 mi. Today the tribe numbers about two thousand people, maintains its own police force and game and fish agency, and educates elementary school children, sending high school students to Tularosa.

The Mescaleros invite neighbors and tourists to their four-day ceremonial, held annually in early July. This ceremony combines the celebration of the coming of age of young women, the coming forth of the mountain spirits for the healing of the tribe, and Fourth of July festivities. Cooking areas, booths, and tepees all are decorated with pine boughs, symbolizing the spirit of the mountains. Women serve dried mescal and mescal "pudding." Visitors are advised that dances during daylight hours usually are for fun and have no ceremonial intent. The sacred part of the event begins when celebrants dressed as mountain spirits light the bonfire at dark. Groups of spirits then begin their dancing and ritual clowning. The puberty ceremony culminates when the young women, dressed in beaded buckskin, with sacred yellow pollen on their cheeks and foreheads, dance and await the rising sun in front of their special tepee, which faces east. The last day of the celebration normally falls on the Fourth and is purely for entertainment.

As is true with ceremonials all over the country, it is often difficult in one visit to appreciate all that the festival means to the Indians themselves.

Four miles below Mescalero, Nogal ("walnut," one of several places so named in the state) Canyon enters the Rio Tularosa. This tributary was first called the "south fork of the Tularosa"; the town of South Fork began here in about 1866, when twenty ex-soldiers of the California Column decided to make it their new home.

During the Civil War, Confederate troops from Texas marched into New Mexico, attempting to distract Union forces then concentrated around Washington, D.C., and along the upper Mississippi River. Especially after the victory of General Sibley's column at Valverde early in 1862, Union strategists tried to cut the Confederates off by marching from the Pacific. One plan was to go through Mexico. Unprepared for the terrain there, a detachment did set out from Mazatlán, but only a few half-starved soldiers straggled into Presidio, Texas, some months later. The better-known and more successful force was General James H. Carleton's California Column, which marched via Camp Wright (Bakersfield), Fort Yuma, and Tucson and reached Fort Thorne on the Rio Grande (above Hatch) in August 1862. By then the Texans had been defeated at Glorieta and had scattered, but Carleton's troops regained formal control over southern New Mexico and Arizona. Many veterans of this campaign liked New Mexico well enough to stay, and they played a role in the interplay among Texans, Indians, Spanish-speakers, and Yankee newcomers that went on in the years following the Civil War.

When the soldiers came to South Fork, the nearest post office was 120 miles away in Mesilla. That same year (1866), J. H. Blazer, an Iowa dentist, moved here and took over "la máquina," a sawmill built some years previously. He is remembered as a man of peace and a friend of the Mescaleros. By 1874, the town had become known as Blazer's Mill and rated a post office of its own. In April 1878

White Sands, *Dave Wilson.*

this was the scene of one of the bloodier battles of the Lincoln County War. A later owner of a mine and mill here was George B. Bent, and the town took his name early in the 1900s. Despite the abundance of names, little remains except the walls of Blazer's old mill on the south side of the highway at 202 mi.

Whenever the highway allows a view to the west, the White Sands are visible. The road passes Round Mountain to the north, the site of an encounter between the Mescaleros and citizens of newly founded Tularosa. The outcome of this skirmish, which took place in April 1868, was considered so favorable for the future of Tularosa that construction was immediately begun on a church there. A cross marks the spot.

Below the road the Tularosa Valley stretches across the White Sands to the San Andres and Organ mountains and south as far as the eye can see. This is better described as a basin, since it is one of several "valleys" in the state that have no drainage. Downfaulting of a huge block of the earth's crust created a large hole here, which the elements have been filling up ever since with material washed or blown in from the mountains on both sides.

By mile 214 (Tularosa) the Sierra Blanca and the Sacramento Mountains have been left behind and the road continues among the fertile, irrigated fields and pastures of the valley. (See Tour 13 for the stretch between Tularosa and Alamogordo where U.S. 70 coincides with U.S. 54.)

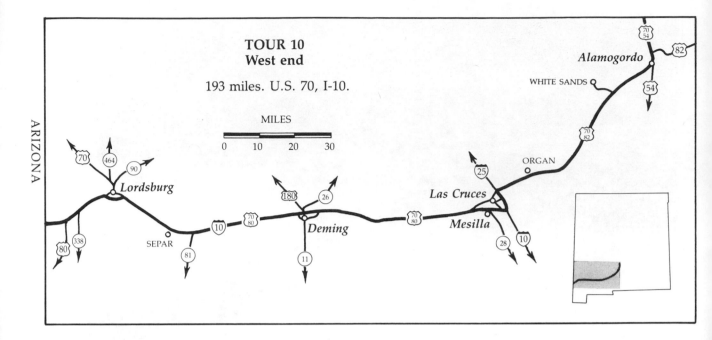

TOUR 10
West end

193 miles. U.S. 70, I-10.

MILES

0   10   20   30

ARIZONA

Leaving Alamogordo, 227 mi., the roads diverge again at mile 230. U.S. 70/U.S. 82 crosses the White Sands National Monument and Missile Range and the Organ Mountains to Las Cruces.

Ever since geologic events formed the Tularosa basin, the forces of wind and water have worn away its opposite walls, the Sacramento and the San Andres mountains, and have worked to level everything. It happens that both these ranges contain massive layers of gypsum rock. Rainwater erodes this rock, dissolving the gypsum and carrying it down to Lake Lucero, where the water evaporates. The wind and heat then loosen the gypsum, and the prevailing southwest winds move the crystals toward the northeast at a rate of up to twenty feet per year. Thus continues the creation of White Sands. Paleo-Indian hunters, then Pueblo people, and later Apaches and cattle growers have all inhabited the region.

The Holloman Air Force Base turnoff, 236 mi., reminds the traveler of one of the economic mainstays of Alamogordo. This air base, named for Colonel George V. Holloman, gained importance early in World War II with the development and testing of new aircraft. In 1942, over objections of local ranchers, adjacent range land became the White Sands Proving Grounds for experimentation with the latest form of warfare, rocketry. After emotional and tense hearings in 1948 pitted the cities of El Paso, Las Cruces, and Alamogordo against the surrounding countryside and smaller towns, the proving grounds were greatly expanded and renamed the White Sands Missile Range. With additional expansion in 1954, missile ranges now include much of the Tularosa Valley, the Jornada del Muerto, the Organ and Hueco mountains, the southern end of the Sacramentos, and the entire San Andres mountain range. U.S. 70 is closed to all traffic during short periods of missile firing.

White Sands Missile Range caught the attention of the entire nation in March 1982 when NASA officials diverted the landing of the space shuttle Columbia from Edwards Air Force Base in California to Northrop Strip here at White Sands. Thousands of space enthusiasts were able to view the landing, and later the spacecraft itself, from a safe distance.

White Sands, *Harvey Caplin.*

In 1934 Congress created the WHITE SANDS NATIONAL MONUMENT, 243 mi., comprising 224 square miles of pure surface gypsum (chemically known as hydrated sulfate of calcium). This is the largest of only three such expanses of pure gypsum in the world.

Travelers will find a picnic spot near the end of a sixteen-mile-round-trip scenic tour of the sands. (No camping is permitted in the monument without specific permission of the rangers.) Besides the strange beauty of the white, undulating earth beneath a usually blue sky, the tour makes one aware of the vegetation that grows along the fringes and on islands in the sand, and also of the fact that, since gypsum crystals differ from those of normal sand, their ripple patterns are different too. For a guided walking tour of Lake Lucero, a crucial link in the creation of the sand, inquire at the visitors' center.

U.S. 70 continues southeasterly, skirting the edge of the white sand. While still in view of the sands, one can see on the opposite side of the highway a low white rise. This is Chalk Hill, whose history evokes as much blood and passion, for those who remember it, as the Lincoln County War. Here on February 1, 1896, on a trip back from Lincoln to Las Cruces, the attorney Albert J. Fountain and his son Henry disappeared.

The story goes back to 1862, when Albert Jennings Fountain arrived in New Mexico with the California Column. Soon Fountain, then a twenty-four-year-old New Yorker, married Mariana Pérez and, with the help of his in-laws, began the Las Cruces career that would make him a power in territorial Republican politics.

In 1888 Fountain ran as a Republican for a seat in the territorial house of representatives. Here he met head-on with Albert Bacon Fall, a young Kentuckian who had moved out to New Mexico to ranch and who was seeking to become an important influence in the Democratic party. (Fall later became secretary of the interior in President Harding's cabinet and a key figure in the Teapot Dome Scandal.) The two men were to oppose each other for years. Fountain won a close election in 1888, but in 1890 Fall was elected to the first of his six terms in the territorial legislature. Supporters of the two men clashed repeatedly during this time.

City and countryside took their politics seriously in those years. By and large, the original Spanish-speaking inhabitants, plus English-speaking newcomers and ex–Union soldiers from the north and east, gave their loyalty to the Republican Party, the majority party in the nation and the territory. Southern and Texan immigrants, however, remained with the Democratic Party, discredited in the eyes of many because of the Civil War. The Santa Fe Ring, a powerful and often corrupt ruling hierarchy, dominated territorial Republican politics at that time. Democrats were seen by their opponents as a lawless, irresponsible bunch. By the 1800s the two parties came to represent the split between big and little ranchers. Republican Fountain had been hired by the (mostly big) ranchers' association to prosecute the cattle rustling that had become a serious problem. Democrat Fall and his associate, Oliver M. Lee, at odds with the larger ranchers, saw the campaign against cattle stealing as a pretext for harassment of the smaller ranchers. Lee himself was accused of being a part of a rustling operation.

People familiar with the ranching of the time note that missing cattle were a part of the business. Strays, "borrowing" a bite of a neighbor's beef, and calves following another mother were common. So, unfortunately, was outright thievery. When the issue of lost cattle got mixed in with the Democrat-versus-Republican passion, trouble lay ahead.

In January 1896 Fountain, determined to carry through with his intent to prosecute despite warnings of danger, traveled to the Lincoln Courthouse to serve indictments against Lee and others. While in Lincoln, he received a threat to his life. Fountain had taken his son Henry, age twelve, along on the trip, and the two of them set out for home alone. When they failed to reach Las Cruces, a posse was sent out. At Chalk Hill they found signs that Fountain's wagon had been forced off the road. His possessions had been rifled and his wagon wrecked. The bodies were never found. Suspicion centered on Oliver Lee, who had a ranch nearby, on his friend John Gilliland, and also on Fall himself, whose mining camp in the Jarilla Mountains just to the east saw quite a bit of activity at the time of the disappearance.

Pat Garrett, called out of retirement after his role in the pursuit, capture, and killing of Billy the Kid (see Tour 12), took on the job of settling the Fountain case as he had the one in Lincoln County. Lee traveled to Las Cruces to turn himself in, but Garrett, probably hoping to avoid bloodshed between the two factions, would not arrest him. Later Lee, Gilliland and the cowboy/novelist Gene Rhodes, pursued by Garrett, hid out in the San Andres Mountains. Matters dragged along until July 1898, when Lee's faction was surprised by Garrett at Lee's ranch at Wildy Well, south of Alamogordo. Garrett was driven off.

Finally reason, reconciliation, or higher self-interest prevailed upon territorial governor Miguel Otero to find a way out of the tense and embarrassing situation. The solution agreed to in 1898 was the creation of a new county that included the site of the Fountains' disappearance and thus removed the case from Pat Garrett's jurisdiction. The county was named Otero after the governor. By agreement, Lee and Gilliland surrendered to Judge Parker in Las Cruces and were finally acquitted of Fountain's murder at a trial in Hillsboro in May–June 1899 that was marked

Eastern slopes of Organ Mts., *John Waszak.*

by the emotion and eloquence of opposing counsels Albert B. Fall and Thomas B. Catron. At 263 mi. the highway crosses the Otero–Doña Ana county line.

Visitors may see various types of missiles at White Sands Missile Park, four miles south of the highway at 271 mi.

The San Agustin Pass, elevation 5,719 feet, divides the San Andres Mountains to the north from the Organs to the south. Both ranges feature rugged terrain that has been mined for lead, gold, copper, and silver. The traveler stands here at the western rim of the

Tularosa basin; San Agustin Peak rises just north of the highway. Five miles south, the Aguirre Spring Recreation Site offers camping and picnicking facilities and a chance to become acquainted with the flora, fauna, and geology of the Organ Mountains.

ORGAN, 279 mi., became a mining camp in the 1870s when tons of lead, copper, and silver ores were shipped here from nearby mountains. Older settlers from the slopes and from the Rio Grande valley below apparently took no part in the mining. The *Industrial Record* of 1901 sums up a widespread attitude toward people who came looking for mineral wealth:

> The old residents . . . are pastoral and agricultural, and have neither the capital nor the inclination to engage in other business, and they regard the mining industry as detrimental to their interest, and have always discouraged the development of the mineral resources, their opposition approaching persecution. (p. 40)

Controversy over a community bar that was sold and converted into a topless lounge provided residents an equally emotional issue one hundred years later in 1980.

Near mile 188, Pat Garrett was murdered on February 29, 1908. Garrett had lost his temper when his ranching neighbor in the San Andres Mountains, Wayne Brazel, allowed his goat herd to break into Garrett's pastures. The two men, both on their way into Las Cruces, met here that day and resumed their quarrel over the goats. Garrett was shot and killed. Brazel pleaded guilty to the crime but was acquitted at his trial. It was widely believed that Jim Miller, who was also present during the quarrel and who had been involved in several killings, actually murdered Garrett for hire. A Texas court later convicted Miller of another crime and condemned him to death, so the exact circumstances of and motive for Garrett's killing have remained a mystery.

Tour 1 describes Las Cruces and Mesilla, 294 mi., which sit in one of the longest-inhabited and most productive sections of the Rio Grande valley in New Mexico.

West of Las Cruces, I-10 passes through the Mesilla Valley's spreading suburbs and neat fields of cotton, corn, and alfalfa. Then the interstate begins its push across the Antelope Plains, mile after mile of high, rolling desert. In the spring the yucca plants here grow masses of creamy blossoms and the scrubland is dotted with purple and yellow wildflowers. At other seasons the desert seems barren; it is up to the traveler to discover the subtle colors, the different shapes of cacti, and the shadings of the distant mountain ranges and wide sweep of sky. Much of this area lies in the Sonoran Life Zone. Mesquite, creosote bush, grama grass, and cacti are the native flora.

Between Las Cruces and Deming, I-10 roughly parallels the old Butterfield Trail. John Butterfield was a New Yorker who laid out the route between Saint Louis and San Francisco in 1858 to provide overland mail and passenger service. From Cooke's Range the trail followed the traces of Captain Philip St. George Cooke's Mormon Battalion, one of the earliest military expeditions to pass this way. Cooke led his soldiers during the war with Mexico, and incidentally opened up this route for gold miners and emigrants. He gave his name to Cooke's Peak, a craggy landmark rising from the plain, and Cooke's Spring, a natural stop for the Butterfield stagecoaches.

The Butterfield Overland Mail would have taken the more direct route between Saint Louis and San Francisco if the postmaster general, a southerner, had not insisted that it go through El Paso. The resulting shape of the path led to its being christened the ox-bow route. The trip took a little over three weeks and was broken every nine miles by rest stops for changing horses or riders. One of the stops was Cooke's Spring. There travelers could refresh themselves, protected, they felt, by the surrounding canyon. However, the canyon also afforded a strategic lookout for the Apaches, who viewed the travelers as a threat and killed many of them during the three years that the route was open. When the Civil War broke out, Confederate soldiers from Texas began harassing drivers and stealing horses from the line. Butterfield finally moved his passenger mail route further north.

During this period Fort Cummings was built at Cooke's Spring, mainly active until 1886. Later the Carpenter-Stanley Cattle Company used the old fort as a corral. When it was built the fort was the most elaborate in New Mexico; today little remains but some walls.

DEMING, 352 mi. (alt. 4,325, pop. 10,038),

Deming, *Harvey Caplin*.

the seat of Luna County, was founded on the plain in 1881 where the Atchison, Topeka, and Santa Fe Railroad met the Southern Pacific. It was named after Mary Ann Deming, wife of a Southern Pacific magnate. Deming sits in the center of the cattle ranges and cotton and milo farms for which the flat lands of the Mimbres Valley are suitable. The expanse is broken by Cooke's Peak north of the city, the Florida Mountains forming a backdrop to the southwest, and the distinctive Tres Hermanas ("three sisters") to the south. The valleys of these mountains are dotted with old mines,

reminders that minerals were once plentiful in this area: lead and zinc in Cooke's Peak; gold, silver, copper, and onyx in the Tres Hermanas; and manganese in the Floridas, where mining still goes on.

Deming prides itself on the clear air and sunny climate that have attracted a growing number of retirees to the area. It also boasts that its water is 99.9 percent pure. The water comes from the Mimbres River, which has its source in Grant County, goes underground about twenty miles north of Deming, and continues below the surface until it drains into a

lake in Chihuahua, Mexico. The river irrigates the Mimbres Valley, allowing farmers to grow cotton and fruit.

A tidy town more typical of the eastern section of the state, Deming is laid out with wide, tree-lined streets. It is not noted for its unique architecture or archaeological treasures; instead, the Butterfield Trail Days (celebrating the pioneers of the West), the Annual Duck Races in August, and the Rockhound Roundup attract visitors. For the duck races, competitors from around the state bring their web-footed pets to compete for the purses offered. In March thousands of rockhounds descend on Deming to buy, sell, look at, and search for the semiprecious rocks for which the area is famous.

The Deming-Luna-Mimbres Museum at 301 South Silver Street is open afternoons. It is housed in the old National Guard Armory building; exhibits of classic Mimbres Period artifacts taken from sites to the north, minerals, and materials from the pioneer days represent the important facets of Deming's past. During World War II the Army Air Force took advantage of Deming's flat terrain to build an important base here to train bombardiers.

North of Deming, U.S. 180 is the route to Silver City (Tour 17).

Southeast of Deming, ROCKHOUND STATE PARK lies in the shadow of the Little Florida Mountains. Two roads lead to the park, one off U.S. 70 and the other off N.M. 11. This latter road is on the way to Columbus (Tour 17) and Mexico. Both routes cover the same distance, about twelve miles.

A private corporation donated land for this park in 1966; it is now run by the State Park Service. The park is unique in that visitors are encouraged to take home the rocks and semiprecious gem stones, souvenirs of early volcanic activity, which are scattered over the area. From a distance, the park blends into the background of the Little Florida Mountains, making it hard to distinguish the camping and picnicking units from the somewhat desolate setting. The vegetation includes desert plants like Spanish dagger, mesquite, and prickly pear. Right around the campsites, rockhounds can pick up quartz crystal, multihued chalcedony, gray and black perlite, and agate-colored spherulite.

Daytime affords a sweeping view of Deming and the plains. At night the lights of the town spread out below, giving the illusion of a much bigger city. Cold winds can sweep up from the plain and chill the camper in spring and winter.

GAGE, 371 mi., used to serve as a water stop on the Southern Pacific Railroad. Just beyond Gage, the Victorio Mountains to the south were mined in the 1880s for lead, silver, and gold.

I-10 crosses the Continental Divide (5,000 feet) at 371 mi.

N.M. 81 cuts off south to Hachita at 378 mi. From this point only rough roads traverse the empty spaces of the Sonora desert to Antelope Wells. Here bands of Apaches under Cochise and Mangas Coloradas roamed between 1862 and 1886, after war broke out between the Indians and settlers. The hunt today is for javelina and other game. At Antelope Wells there is a twenty-four-hour port of entry to Mexico.

At SEPAR, 385 mi., the old Janos trade route crossed present I-10. This trail was established in the early 1800s after copper was discovered at Santa Rita (Tour 17). The trail extended from Santa Rita to northern Chihuahua and Sonora, and was used by traders who did business in those states. When the U.S. military first operated in the extreme southwest, this route was the only one known to officers. Captain Cooke led his Mormon Battalion over it on his way to California in 1846.

LORDSBURG, 406 mi. (alt. 4,286, pop. 5,200), prosaically named after a construction engineer for the Southern Pacific, is the seat of Hidalgo County. It is a clean-looking town that spreads out on both sides of the railroad tracks. It was built on the Pyramid Valley floor, surrounded by ranching and farming country and located between the Burro Range to the north and the Pyramid Range in the south. Nine miles south of Lordsburg, Pyramid's Peak was a landmark in the early days of travel, when the Butterfield stage passed here; the peak later became the site of mining operations, which continue to be a major activity.

Lordsburg's airport was dedicated by Charles Lindbergh during his 1932 cross-country flight in the *Spirit of St. Louis.*

Three miles south of Lordsburg, the crumbling ghost town of SHAKESPEARE hangs on to life. A faded sign along the road points out the entrance to the village just before the cemetery. After a few hundred yards, the somewhat bumpy road forks; the right fork, a dirt road, goes to Shakespeare. Since the town is privately owned, by the Hill family, there are only a few tours, held every second Sunday from 10 A.M. to 2 P.M. Signs warning of dire consequences to be suffered from rattlesnakes, deep holes, and rickety buildings discourage visitors from exploring on their own.

Shakespeare began life as Mexican Springs. The Butterfield Overland Company established a route that passed through the site, and a mail company built a stop here, renaming the place Grant. After a surveyor did some prospecting in the Pyramid Mountains and found silver specimens, William Ralston financed mining operations and caused a boom. Grant was renamed Ralston in honor of its benefactor, who was also a founder of the Bank of California. Captain John Bullard prospected in Ralston until he realized that the precious ore looked very much like rocks found near his home in La Cienega and returned home to mine the area profitably, in the process establishing Silver City (Tour 18). The silver boom was short-lived here. Faced with a bust, mine owners planted diamonds in the area to promote continued mining, and for a time the ruse worked, but when the diamonds ran out, so did the miners. In the 1870s the town was again renamed, this time for the Shakespeare Mining Co., which had staked some claims in the area. Intermittent activity continued until the Depression, when Frank Hill bought the town as part of his ranch. Since that time his family has attempted to preserve what little is left of the town: a few old adobe houses, the old store, a saloon, and the Stratford Hotel are scattered around the desolate site.

SIDE TOUR

Doorway, *Jeanne House.*

Two main roads exit north from Lordsburg, N.M. 90 to Silver City (Tour 17) and U.S. 70, which terminates in Phoenix, Arizona. Three miles from Lordsburg on U.S. 70 a turnoff via N.M. 464 leads to Redrock, 21 mi., an animal preserve on the Gila River. Animals native to New Mexico mix with others brought here from out of state and abroad.

Just off the freeway at 418 mi., Alkali Flats are the remains of an ancient lake. A drive south through the Animas Valley on N.M. 338 passes through Cotton City and Animas. The flat lands of the valley made cotton king here. The road is unpaved south of Animas and joins N.M. 79 to enter the Coronado National Forest.

Just three miles east of the Arizona border, the crumbling remains of STEINS lie hardly noticed off the interstate. The Butterfield Trail passed near here in the 1850s, taking advantage of the passes that provided easy access through the Peloncillo Mountains into Arizona. The company erected a relay station in Doubtful Canyon near Steins Peak, named after a captain who was killed in the canyon. Emigrant parties on the southern route also passed by here, for the Tucson Cutoff past Steins was and is a shortcut to that city.

The station was vulnerable to attack by bands of Apaches under Mangas Coloradas. However, the Apaches did not disturb it for two and a half years, until early 1861, when a young lieutenant accused their leader, Cochise, of stealing cattle and kidnapping a child. Five of Cochise's men were seized, but the chief escaped. Angered by the insults, the Apaches responded with warfare, a conflict which was to last until 1886 when Geronimo was captured in Mexico. The Butterfield Mail Company, already harassed by Confederate soldiers in the east and fearful of the conflict, closed the Steins Peak station.

Emigrant trains, however, continued to follow the trail and were not spared by the Indians, who took advantage of Doubtful Canyon's rocks and gullies to pick off the travelers. Later in the century, mining camps sprang up after deposits of gold, silver, and copper were found in the region north of Steins Pass. One of these camps took its name from the pass and, as Steins, existed until World War II. Its maximum population was about two hundred people. At the end only a few railroaders remained. Today all that remains is a few adobe walls at the side of the highway.

The tour ends at the Arizona state line.

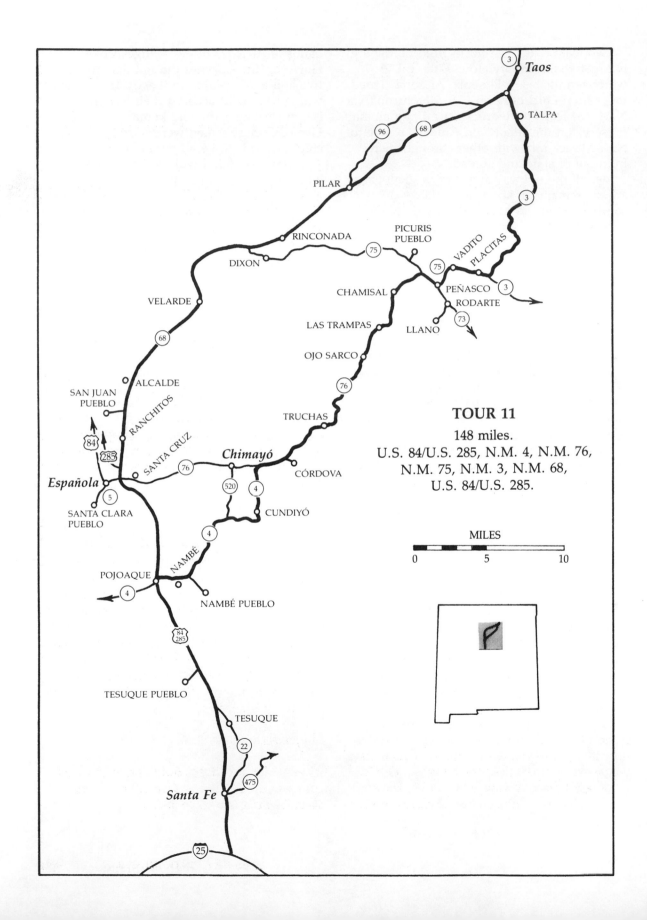

TOUR 11

148 miles.
U.S. 84/U.S. 285, N.M. 4, N.M. 76,
N.M. 75, N.M. 3, N.M. 68,
U.S. 84/U.S. 285.

MILES

0   5   10

tour eleven

Santa Fe • Chimayo • Truchas • Peñasco • Ranchos de Taos • Española • Santa Fe

One of the most popular tourist routes in the state, this elongated circle starts and ends in the small but cosmopolitan state capital, Santa Fe, passing in its course a number of little Spanish mountain villages and several Indian pueblos. It really represents two routes: the "high road to Taos," a spectacular, winding drive into the dry foothills of the Sangre de Cristo Mountains, through verdant valleys along streams emerging from the mountains; and the low road, paralleling the Rio Grande and at times occupying its east bank, through several small towns surrounded by apple orchards. Much of the early history of New Mexico took place along this route; evidence of the events of the last four hundred years is ample in the oldest capital, San Gabriel de Yunque Yunque; in the capital since 1609, Santa Fe; and in many of the smaller towns and pueblos along the way. For those more inclined to look for beauty than for historical landmarks, the route offers much: the dry, eroded hills near the river, the high peaks of the often snow-covered Sangre de Cristos, and the swift waters of the life-giving Rio Grande.

A logical place to start is Santa Fe, the state capital. However, it is so full of places to visit and walks to take that a traveler should allow at least one whole day in the city alone. Therefore, this tour includes two options: Alternative One for passing through Santa Fe and on to the mountain villages, and Alternative Two for touring Santa Fe before heading north.

Alternative One

The tour begins at the intersection of Old Pecos Trail and I-25 (exit 284 from the interstate). Old Pecos Trail heads northwest into Santa Fe, joining the Santa Fe Trail at 3.1 mi. The round state house is at 3.5 mi. on the left, the Santa Fe River at 3.7 mi. and the plaza at 3.9 mi. From the northeast corner of the plaza, Washington Street leads north and becomes Bishop's Lodge Road after passing the pink Scottish Rite Temple. See page 505 for the continuation of the tour.

Alternative Two

Leave I-25 at exit 284 onto Old Pecos Trail. Continue on Old Pecos Trail 3.9 mi. to the plaza. See map on page 488.

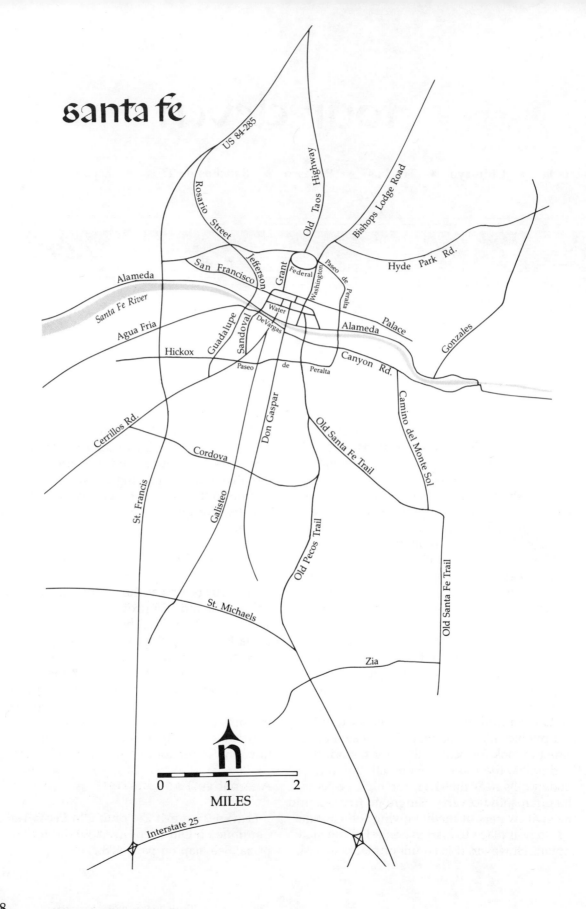

santa fe

santa fe

Transportation

Transportation within Santa Fe: taxis and rental cars. To or from the city: Air, major airlines to Albuquerque, then Shuttlejack limousine service to Santa Fe hotels. Railroad, Amtrak to Lamy, 18 miles south, then taxi to or from Santa Fe. Bus, Trailways or Greyhound from north or south, Inter-City Transit Lines to or from Albuquerque, all leaving from Union Bus Depot, 126 West Water Street.

Accommodations

Numerous hotels, motels, resorts in and near the city. Camping in private campgrounds, at Hyde State Park, and in Santa Fe National Forest.

Entertainment

Many movie theaters. Museums, frequent art exhibits in galleries and public buildings. Santa Fe Opera and Chamber Music Festival each summer. Orchestra of Santa Fe, yearly series. Several theater groups. Horseracing at Santa Fe Downs each summer. Mountain trail head at Santa Fe Ski Basin. Municipal tennis courts and swimming pools; private golf course. Libraries.

Information Service

Chamber of Commerce, 330 Old Santa Fe Trail, booth on the plaza during the summer. New Mexico State Tourist Office, Bataan Memorial Building, Galisteo Street.

Colleges

College of Santa Fe; St. John's College.

Annual Events

Corpus Christi procession and de Vargas memorial procession, June; Rodeo de Santa Fe, July; Spanish Colonial Market, July; Annual Indian Market, August; Fiesta de Santa Fe (each year since 1712), September; Festival of the Arts, September or October. Las Posadas and other Christmas activities.

The "lively market town at the base of the mountains," the "oldest capital city in the United States," the "city different," Santa Fe (alt. 6,996, pop. 52,530) started life in 1609 with the florid title La Villa Real de la Santa Fe de San Francisco. It has been, in its almost four centuries, a capital of religion, of art, of trade, and of government. Its lifetime as a center of governmental activity has seen as rulers Spaniards, leaders of rebelling Pueblo Indians, Spaniards again, newly independent Mexicans, Americans, and, for two weeks in 1862, Confederate soldiers. All have occupied the ancient Palace of the Governors, which stands along the north side of the plaza, still the center of Santa Fe.

Like other cities in the Sunbelt, Santa Fe has experienced heavy growth since World War II. Unlike many cities, however, the old capital has taken steps to preserve much of its historical past and the character of its old streets. Thus officially protected and approved, Santa Fe's brown, beige, and ocher walls melt into the colors of the surrounding foothills of the Sangre de Cristo Mountains that tower to the north and east. Santa Fe began as clusters of adobe buildings on both sides of the little Rito de Santa Fe; it has now spread across the neighboring hills. From any part of the city one may see mountains. In addition to the Sangre de Cristos, the Jemez Mountains to the west and the Sandia and Ortiz ranges to the south complete the panorama.

Never an industrial city, Santa Fe has long thrived on its attraction for travelers. The tourist trade has supplanted mercantile activities "at the end of the Santa Fe Trail" as Santa Fe's major industry. Visitors descend upon Santa Fe for its beauty and history, its art and music, its museums and displays of Indian art, its position as gateway to mountain sports. Snow lies on the thirteen-thousand-foot peaks of the Sangre de Cristos until June, when the city at the edge of the desert becomes warm. Santa Fe tempers its summer heat with cool evenings and its cool winters with the ever-present sun. Snow falls at intervals throughout the winter, interspersed with sparkling, clear days. July and August morning sun gives way in the afternoon to impressive thundershowers.

Travelers quickly succumb to the charm of the Royal City, despite the incursion of modern ways of life. Ancient, narrow streets and brown adobe houses suggest a rich past—a time when New Mexico history began and ended in Santa Fe. Seventeenth-century buildings in the city's center and well-crafted modern imitations of the once-scorned "mud huts," now very much the mode, form a largely harmonious whole. By the Santa Fe River, cottonwoods shade the historic center of the city. Throughout Santa Fe, adobe walls and carved doors hide gardens of native plants and a profusion of imported flowers. More modern adobe homes on the surrounding hillsides are almost hidden among undis-

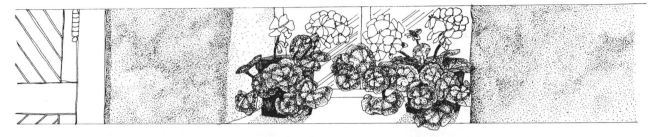

turbed piñon pine and mountain junipers, with occasional low cacti and yuccas.

This, then, is the setting for the modern visitor's rediscovery of the roots of New Mexico in its Indian, Spanish, and American cultures. There is fading evidence of ancient Pueblo settlements; of the conquest, loss, and reconquest by the Spanish and the years of Mexican rule; of the commercial invasion of the Americans and the conquest that followed. Succeeding invasions of artists, of well-heeled retirees, and of tourists have been more peaceable, but their effects have been no less profound.

The settlement was founded in the winter of 1609–10 by Don Pedro de Peralta, third governor of the province of Nuevo Méjico, at a spot long known to the Pueblo Indians. Ruins, almost obliterated when the Spanish arrived, showed that it had once been the site of a Tanoan Indian village. While digging foundations for their homes, today's dwellers frequently unearth remnants of the past in the form of pottery fragments, implements, and human bones.

When Peralta came to Santa Fe, he built the *palacio* as a fortress and seat of government, laid out the plaza, and planned a walled city. From the Palace of the Governors, built the year Santa Fe was founded and renovated many times since, sixty Spanish governors ruled New Mexico. They held dominion from Santa Fe over the vast territory from the Mississippi River to the Pacific Ocean and guarded it against an invasion from the north that did not come until New Mexico had been for twenty-five years a province of an independent Mexico.

By the time of Santa Fe's founding, the rumors of great wealth that had inspired Coron-

ado and other early adventurers had been played out. The Spanish maintained their northern outpost largely for the purpose of bringing the Catholic faith to the natives. Neither Madrid nor Mexico City supported the colony with many men or much money or equipment; estimates of the number of Spanish soldiers and colonists present in New Mexico in 1617 range from forty-eight to about a thousand. They protected a chain of eleven churches built by Franciscan friars for an estimated fourteen thousand converts. However, intolerance of the Indians' old religious customs was a common source of trouble, and conflict between Spanish secular and spiritual leaders led to unrest among the nominally converted. The historian Bancroft states that in 1645 there was a rising of the Indians near Santa Fe because forty of their number had been flogged and hanged by the Spanish for refusing to give up their ancient faith.

Disquiet grew from year to year until, in 1680, under the San Juan Indian Popé, the northern Pueblos revolted. The Spanish colonists fortunate enough to escape the well-planned uprising with their lives sought refuge in the Palace of the Governors, where they were besieged. Lacking military force adequate to break the siege, they slipped out of the palace by night and made the difficult trip down the Rio Grande to El Paso del Norte, finding signs of massacre at the scattered Spanish settlements along the way. The leaders of the revolt took the palace, defiled or destroyed the churches as the Spanish had destroyed their religious symbols, burned archives and prayer books, and turned the palace's chapel into a kiva.

For thirteen years the Indians occupied the palace. Meanwhile, the erstwhile Santa Feans

remained in rude huts by the Rio Grande at El Paso. The Spanish viceroy in Mexico City had forbidden them to abandon the settlement for more comfortable parts of Mexico, so they waited for support to come for the reconquest of the northern kingdom and the city of Santa Fe.

That support came in 1691 in the person of a new governor, Don Diego de Vargas Zapata y Luján Ponce de León y Contreras, bringing troop reinforcements, animals, and additional settlers. After one and a half years of preparation in El Paso, de Vargas led a small army up the Rio Grande. He met no resistance until he reached the palace walls in Santa Fe. His assuredness cowed his enemies, allowing the city to be regained without a battle, and with promises of absolution. Forays to retake the pueblos were also peaceful, but upon de Vargas's return the following year with the Santa Fe colonists, he met opposition from many of the Pueblos, which he overwhelmed by the quick use of force. With these victories, the

Spanish hold on New Mexico was confirmed. Tradition holds that aid in the reconquest was given de Vargas by the Virgin Mary through a small statute, La Conquistadora, that he brought from Mexico on his return.

Each June La Conquistadora is the focal point of a procession commemorating de Vargas's reconquest of Santa Fe. Following the procession, a novena of masses is said in Rosario Chapel before the statue is returned to the Cathedral of Saint Francis, her usual abode. De Vargas had been accompanied on his return by other evidence of the Catholic faith; the Franciscans went back to their posts in the pueblos. Santa Fe's position as a religious capital began again, and was finally confirmed in 1851, when Santa Fe was made the seat of the first Southwestern bishop, Jean Baptiste Lamy. Lamy replaced the bishops of Durango, Mexico, who had had difficulty controlling the affairs of the church from a distance of fifteen hundred miles.

The remaining years of Spanish rule, until 1821, were quiet, devoted to growth. Spanish policy discouraged movement to or from the French and American settlements to the north and east, but with the passage of time and the expansive nature of the young United States, increasing contact became inevitable. When independence came to Mexico in 1821, the governor in Santa Fe signed an oath of allegiance to the new nation amidst great celebration. Trappers and traders from the United States were now welcomed by the populace of Santa Fe, though they still met with official suspicion.

The Santa Fe Trail became a much-traveled highway. It ended in the muddy, open Plaza de la Constitución, as Santa Fe's plaza had been renamed in the rejoicings of 1821. Here the arriving wagon trains finished their perilous two-month journey through Indian country and American adventurers interacted with the already two-hundred-year-old society. Familiar accoutrements of a port of call appeared—saloons, dance halls, and gaming establishments—fronting on the plaza and the streets leading away from it. One of the best-known midcentury Santa Fe residents was Doña Gertrudes Barcelo, called "La Tules," the shrewd and forceful proprietress of the best-known of the many gaming houses, an observer of and frequent participant in the political intrigues of the capital city.

Santa Fe—Mexicans, Texans, Americans

Five years after the republic of Texas was established in 1836, a party traveled from the new republic to invite New Mexicans to join with them "for all the glory of establishing a new and happy and free nation." Under the territorial governor of the time, Manuel Armijo of Albuquerque, the Texans' invitation was forcefully declined. But events were brewing elsewhere. In 1846, with Texas's encouragement, the United States made war on Mexico. Stephen Watts Kearny and the Army of the West headed for Santa Fe, while Zachary Taylor drove the Mexicans from Texas and continued down the Gulf Coast. The Santa Fe militia, poorly trained and ill-equipped after decades of neglect, could have had little chance against Kearny. In any case, it was given no opportunity to resist the Americans' advance. Governor Armijo abandoned the town and fled down the Rio Grande. Some thought he had been paid by Kearny to surrender. Kearny soon departed for California, leaving a garrison under the command of Governor Charles Bent. Just four months after entering Santa Fe, Bent put down a plotted New Mexican rebellion, warned of the conspiracy by La Tules.

Santa Fe was now part of the United States Territory of New Mexico, and was to remain so except for a brief period during the Civil War, when it fell into the hands of soldiers of the Confederacy. On February 18, 1862, after the Confederate victory at the Battle of Valverde, the Confederate forces under General Henry Sibley marched to Albuquerque and then to Santa Fe. The outmanned Union forces fell back to Fort Union, regrouped, and advanced to meet the Confederates at Apache Canyon, east of Santa Fe. After a decisive victory the Union army retook Santa Fe and chased the enemy down the Rio Grande.

Santa Fe was able to resume its role as a mercantile center. In 1849, a stage line had been established over the Santa Fe Trail from Independence, Missouri. In the 1860s, with the nation's energies absorbed by the Civil War, the Santa Fe Trail was used largely for military purposes. With the coming of the railroads in the seventies, the freighters and stagecoaches began to disappear, and by the eighties the Santa Fe Trail was dead. In 1879 the Santa Fe Railroad, utilizing part of the route of the old trail, crossed Raton Pass and neared Santa Fe. However, it was found that a main line through the town would necessitate an expensive stretch of road uphill from Glorieta Pass to Santa Fe, so the Santa Fe junction was located at Lamy, eighteen miles south of the town. The only railroad connection with Santa Fe remains a freight track.

The railroad brought a new period of prosperity to Santa Fe, making trade with the rest of the United States much easier. Along with trade in foodstuffs, dry goods, books, and clothing, the railroad also brought materials that made diversity in architecture both possible and fashionable. The face of the plaza was changed in part; a formerly uniform Spanish-Pueblo style accommodated the additions that were to produce the territorial style. Millwork decorated doors and interiors, bricks dressed up and protected the tops of cornices, and double-hung windows replaced hand-hewn frames. More thoroughly different departures in architecture were made possible; the town's first bank constructed a Greek temple (now under a pueblo facade), and Archbishop Lamy, model for Bishop Latour in Willa Cather's *Death Comes for the Archbishop,* had the Cathedral of St. Francis designed in a Romanesque style reminiscent of his native Auvergne, France. In 1957, however, concern that Old Santa Fe maintain its integrity prompted its citizens and officials to draw up and pass a Historical Zoning Ordinance prohibiting the building of new structures in the downtown historical area in other styles than

Spanish-Pueblo or territorial. The pioneering regulation, which also limits the height of buildings and the types of signs permitted, has been upheld in numerous court cases, including two that reached the state supreme court. The ordinance describes "Old Santa Fe style" as follows:

> With rare exceptions, the buildings are of one story, few have three stories, and the characteristic effect is that the buildings are long and low. Roofs are flat with a slight slope and surrounded on at least three sides by a firewall of the same color and material as the walls or of brick. Roofs are never carried out beyond the line of the walls except to cover an enclosed portal, the outer edge of the roof being supported by wooden columns. Two-story construction is more common in the Territorial than in other sub-styles, and is preferably accompanied by a balcony on the level of the second story. Facades are flat, varied by inset portals, exterior portals, protecting *vigas* or roof beams, *canales* or waterspouts, flanking buttresses and wooden lintels, architraves and cornices, which, as well as doors, are frequently carved and the carving may be picked out with bright colors. . . ."

Santa Fe celebrated long-delayed and long-desired statehood in 1912 with a week-long fiesta and a new building boom, spurred by federal and state government construction. The territorial legislature became the state legislature, and the appointed territorial governor was replaced by a popularly elected governor, William C. McDonald.

Throughout these tumultuous events and continuing to the present, the Pueblo Indians maintained their presence in Santa Fe. They still display pottery, jewelry, and weaving outside the Palace of the Governors; trade and work in stores opening onto the plaza; attend schools, hospitals, and clinics in the city; and serve in state government.

Santa Fe has attracted "Anglos" for years. Tuberculosis brought many Easterners to Santa Fe beginning in the 1880s and continuing into the twentieth century. Many recovered and became prominent citizens. Painters, musicians, novelists, and photographers have come throughout the twentieth century to absorb and depict the beauty of the town and its surroundings. Los Cinco Pintores, a group of five young painters (see Art) came together in Santa Fe in 1920; they were followed by many others, including Peter Hurd, Frank Applegate, and Georgia O'Keeffe. Lew Wallace wrote *Ben Hur* in the Palace of the Governors while he was territorial governor in 1880; writers who came to Santa Fe to write of more local matters included Willa Cather, Oliver La Farge, and Mary Austin. The "eternal light" of Santa Fe has attracted photographers such as Ernest Knee, Eliot Porter, and Laura Gilpin.

Archaeologists and ethnologists, beginning with Adolph Bandelier, the Swiss discoverer of the ruins in Frijoles Canyon (now Bandelier National Monument), have made their headquarters in Santa Fe, independently or in association with the School of American Research or the Laboratory of Anthropology. These institutions remain as important coordinators and originators of Southwest archaeology. In the 1940s scientists working in the highly secret laboratories of Los Alamos began to spill over into the city. Workers at all levels of government and refugees from less colorful American cities have added to all of these streams.

Despite the contributions of Indians and Anglos, Santa Fe retains a distinctly Hispanic air. Most street names are Spanish; the surnames of most city officials and many prominent businesspeople are Spanish; architecture and cuisine remain largely unchanged from Spanish days.

As much as the old buildings and historical intrigue, the diversity of peoples encountered in the streets of Santa Fe draws visitors to the Royal City.

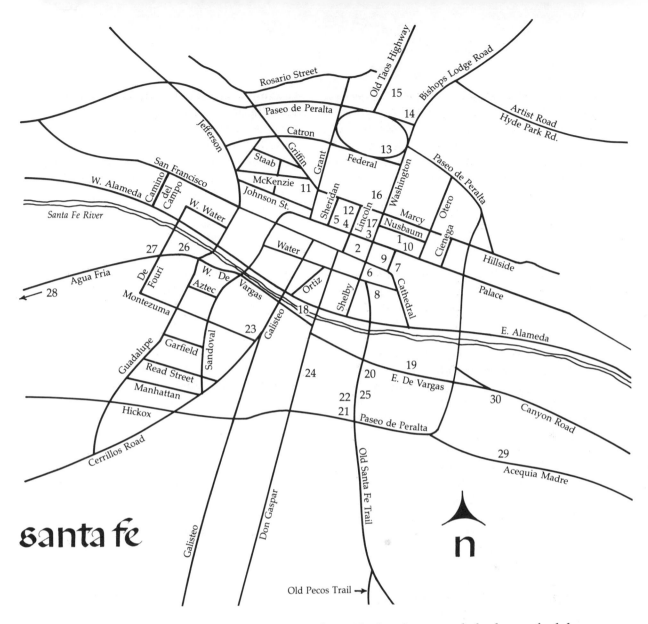

santa fe

POINTS OF INTEREST

Santa Fe is a walker's city, largely because of three qualities that set it apart: its mountain valley setting, the characteristic patterns and spaces that suggest an inviting labyrinth, and the intimate scale of the streets and buildings. On a walk through Santa Fe's neighborhoods, the observant pedestrian may encounter many visual delights. Markers and monuments abound inside and outside buildings, offering the reader bits of historic information. Mural painting is a well-developed indigenous art form, enlivening walls with bold colors and strong design. A walk can acquaint the trav-

eler with the shapes and shadows of adobe architecture throughout the city. Sitting on a bench in the plaza or in the lobby of La Fonda hotel, a visitor senses that Santa Fe continues to be a place of great characters and a wonderful diversity of people.

Neighborhoods are both varied and intriguing, having developed along ancient trails or along *acequias*. These routes have become Santa Fe's major streets, and the growing city has filled in the agricultural land between the lines of old homes. A brief description of major neighborhoods and their main points of interest follows, keyed to the numbers on the map above.

1. TRAZO/EAST PALACE AVENUE.   Spaces that were laid out in 1609 are still the center of Santa Fe today. *Trazo* is a Spanish-colonial town pattern of small buildings with interior courtyards and common walls that form a continuous facade along the streets. This area is now characterized by narrow streets and sidewalks and two-story buildings with *portales* (arcades). Near the plaza end of Palace Avenue are five restored *placitas* (buildings with courtyards). The homes of nineteenth-century American merchants line either side of the street.

2. The PLAZA, bounded by Palace Avenue on the north, San Francisco Street on the south, Old Santa Fe Trail on the east, and Lincoln Avenue on the west, is in the geographical center of town and has been the center of interest and activity for almost four centuries. It is a peaceful old square, with trim flagstones, walks, and benches, and pleasant, arching trees. In Spanish times it was much larger, including the space now occupied by the buildings, including the Catron law offices, along its east side; it was an unpaved lake of dust in dry times, a sea of mud in wet. A pyramid with a Mexican eagle atop it stood in the plaza during Santa Fe's Mexican era. Later a bull-ring graced the plaza until it was removed in 1845 because it provided shelter for invading Utes. The area also served as the marketplace for Rio Grande valley produce sold by Indians and Spaniards.

When the Americans came in 1846 they enclosed it with a white picket fence, planted it in alfalfa, reduced it to its present size, and built two-story adobe buildings with *portales* on the three sides confronting the Palace of the Governors. It was at the plaza that the wagon trains ended their strenuous journeys over the Santa Fe Trail. Here ox-drivers, cowboys, and gamblers caroused in and out of the eight saloons that at one time fronted the square; here criminals were locked in stocks, hanged from the *portal* of the Palace of Governors, or flogged in public view; here Billy the Kid once sat in chains. Hitching posts and watering troughs remain at the northwest corner of Palace and Washington streets, reminders of the trail's end.

In the center of the square stands a soldiers' monument, erected by the citizenry after the Civil War. In recent times the wording of the monument's marker has created a public furor because of its reference to "rebels" and "savages." The word "savages" was chiseled out by unknown persons, and a second marker, explaining the historic context of the first, has been placed next to it as the result of an agreement by representatives of all nineteen Pueblos, the Navajos, and the Apaches.

The plaza continues to change while it remains the heart of the city. In 1967 new *portales* were constructed around the plaza. Monuments have been removed and others added, new buildings replace those destroyed by fire, a bandstand appeared and was torn down. At the northwest corner of Lincoln and Palace avenues stands the third Spitz clock. The first one was placed on the plaza in 1881, in front of the Spitz jewelry store; the second working clock was knocked down in 1915 by Santa Fe's first motor truck; the third was brought here in 1916. The plaza provides the setting for the annual Indian and Spanish art markets, religious processions, fiestas, concerts, political rallies, dancing, roller skating, international kazoo and frisbee contests, tourist snapshots, family gatherings, and, on weekend evenings, cruising by some of Santa Fe's teenagers.

3. The PALACE OF THE GOVERNORS (north side of the plaza). The Palace of the Governors is an adobe structure that has reputedly stood since the winter of 1609–10. After a number of renovations, including one that added Victorian wooden trim to the facade, it was finally restored to its present exterior state in 1909, from plans found in the British Museum. One room in the museum it now contains has been again restored to the 1909 style to honor the archaeological, photographic, and display work of restorer Jesse Nusbaum. Originally the palace was the most imposing and impor-

tant part of the royal presidio, an all-purpose fortress built by followers of Don Pedro de Peralta. It extended east and west along the north side of the plaza for a distance of four hundred feet, and north and south more than double that span. A pair of low towers stood at either end of the plaza side. The west tower was used for the storage of powder and military equipment, and the east tower housed a chapel for the use of the garrison. Adjoining and connecting with the tower at the west end were the dungeons. A *portal,* under which many prisoners of war were hanged, extended the whole length of the building along the south facade. The ends of the building were shortened and the towers removed after the Pueblo Revolt of 1680.

Spanish settlers who found their way to the palace during the great revolt were besieged there for five days by a force of Indians from the northern pueblos. The Spanish governor of the time, Don Antonio Otermín, led the survivors out of the city, leaving everything to the Indians, who burned much of the property of the European intruders who had made themselves so unwelcome. Twelve years later the reconquering governor de Vargas retook the palace, which served as the seat of government well into the American era.

The story of the palace during the eighteenth century is a narrative of military activities and a succession of Spanish governors. The Mexican regime, which lasted from 1821 to 1846, quartered its governors in the palace. After Kearny's peaceful conquest in 1846, American territorial governors occupied its rooms until 1907.

The palace now serves as a museum that includes changing exhibits and a photo gallery. Permanent exhibits comprise the Mexican governor's office, the office of American territorial governor Prince, a story of the evolution of the palace, "Four Hundred Years of New Mexico History," "The Frontier Experience," a nineteenth-century New Mexico chapel, and the stagecoach area.

4. THE MUSEUM OF FINE ARTS (West Palace and Lincoln avenues). Dominating the northwest corner of the plaza, the museum building was erected in 1917 on the site of the old Fort Marcy military headquarters building. Funds for its construction were raised by public subscription and individual donations, matched by the state legislature. Because of this public effort, it was the policy of the museum to offer any artist the use of its exhibition space. Now the museum contains an extensive permanent collection of works of well-known artists, primarily those who have worked in New Mexico. Changing exhibits are selected to represent fine work of contemporary artists as well as excellent retrospective shows of arts, crafts, and photography.

Built around a grassy patio with cloistered walls, the museum is an architectural composite of six of the Spanish missions built by Franciscan friars. Its towers and balcony were inspired by the church at Acoma, and details were adapted from the missions at San Felipe, Cochiti, Laguna, Santa Ana, and Pecos. A prototype of the structure, designed by the Santa Fe architectural firm of Rapp and Rapp, was built at the 1915 Panama-California Exposition as the New Mexico Building; the current museum is a replica of this design.

5.   THE ST. FRANCIS AUDITORIUM (West Palace Avenue).   The St. Francis Auditorium resembles an old chapel and occupies the west end of the Museum of Fine Arts. Its mural paintings depict scenes from the life of Saint Francis of Assisi, planned and sketched by the artist Donald Beauregard and finished after his death by Kenneth Chapman and Carlos Vierra. The auditorium is used for a diversity of concerts and lectures and is the home of the Santa Fe Chamber Music Festival and its resident composers and musicians.

6.   LA FONDA (San Francisco Street and Old Santa Fe Trail) stands on the site of the old *fonda*, or inn, the adobe building that was a hotel from the beginning of the American occupation in 1846 and marked the end of the Santa Fe Trail. The most notable landmark of the trail days, the old structure was the rendezvous of Spanish grandees, trappers, traders, pioneers, merchants, soldiers, and politicians. Like most buildings of the time, it was one story high and built around a central patio, with a large corral and stables to the south. The stables often served as lodgings for those travelers without cash for a room.

During the American military occupation, Santa Fe was noted for the brilliance of its society, which gathered at the inn. La Fonda was the scene of the Victory Ball, celebrating the entry into the city of Kearny's Army of the West. It is said that La Tules, whose gambling house was on the site of the present county courthouse, attended the ball, her reward for a loan she gave Kearny to pay his troops.

The patronage of the old hotel dwindled as more modern accommodations became available, and the building gradually fell into disrepair. During this period Billy the Kid is said to have washed dishes in La Fonda's kitchen.

The inn changed names and owners several times until, during a Victory Bond rally in 1919, the building was demolished to make way for the present hotel. Citizens of Santa Fe bought stock to build the new La Fonda, but the venture soon went bankrupt. The Atchison, Topeka, and Santa Fe Railroad acquired the hotel and leased it to Fred Harvey. As a Harvey House, it became the center for a busy tourist trade. The hotel continues to serve Santa Fe's visitors, surrounding them with the rich tones of Gerald Cassidy paintings, handsome murals, hand-made tile and carved wood decorations, and a variety of Indian- and Spanish-style kitsch.

7.   THE CATHEDRAL OF ST. FRANCIS (San Francisco Street and Cathedral Place) stands as an enduring monument to Archbishop Jean Baptiste Lamy, his priests, and the Catholic people of New Mexico. The cornerstone was laid in 1869, eighteen years after Archbishop Lamy arrived in Santa Fe. The site he chose was first occupied by the church and monastery erected in 1622 by Fray Alonso Benavides and destroyed during the Pueblo Revolt. A second church, known as the Parroquia, was built there in 1713. Lamy, whose statue stands at the entrance to the cathedral, built the new walls around this second edifice and used it during the construction operations, so that not a Mass was missed while the cathedral was rising. The sacristy in the rear of the cathedral is an actual part of the old Parroquia.

The native sandstone used in the walls has a richness of color that adds to the beauty of the cathedral's Romanesque lines. The height of the middle nave is fifty-five feet. Its ceiling is arched in the Roman style and made of a very light volcanic stone obtained from the summit of a hill about twelve miles from Santa Fe. The interior of the cathedral is dominated by the high altar, under which Archbishop Lamy and other clergy lie buried.

To the left of the altar, in the Sacred Heart Chapel, is the statue of La Conquistadora, almost three hundred years old. A painting done by Pascualo de Veri in 1710, depicting Christ at Gethsemane, is in the narthex. A stark concrete and glass addition and a new entrance to the south of the cathedral were completed in 1967.

With the encouragement of then-archbishop Byrne, Igor Stravinsky's music resounded through the cathedral four times in 1959–63, conducted by the composer himself.

8.   LORETTO CHAPEL (Old Santa Fe Trail near Water Street).   The small Chapel of Loretto, once part of a Catholic girls' school, is of Gothic design, inspired by the Paris Sainte Chapelle, the home chapel of Archbishop Lamy. Above the altar is a golden statue of the Virgin. A spiral staircase winds upward, apparently without support, and has given rise to mystic legends about its construction. It is said that an unknown carpenter appeared to build the stairs with only a hammer, a saw, a T-square, and tubs of water in which to soak the lumber. He disappeared after its construction.

9.   THE FEDERAL BUILDING (Cathedral Place). Formerly the post office, this structure was constructed in 1921, one of the few federal buildings in the United States designed in a local architectural style.

10.   SENA PLAZA (East Palace Avenue).   In 1831 José Sena built this large home for his bride. The building has been successfully restored in territorial style, as evidenced by the slender posts supporting the portal and the brick coping surmounting the walls. W. P. Henderson was the architect for the restoration. Offices and a variety of shops fill the many adobe rooms, facing the street and surrounding an inner courtyard.

11.   MARCY/MCKENZIE (McKenzie and West Marcy streets).   This area was the site of the Fort Marcy Military Reservation, dating from 1846, and of Spanish military establishments before that. Narrow, detached barracks surrounded an open parade ground, the entry into which is now Lincoln Avenue. Elm trees line the rectangular blocks of the neighborhood, whose small red brick homes, set back from the street, typify the McKenzie area.

12.   OLD FORT MARCY AND THE GARITA. Fort Marcy once dominated the city from a hilltop but is now only a group of mounds. Townhouses cover much of the fort site. Here, in 1846, American soldiers of the Army of the West erected an elaborate system of earthworks for the protection of the town. The fort was named for Captain Marcy of the U.S. Army, discoverer of the Canadian River in

Zozobra, *Harvey Caplin*.

northeastern New Mexico. The Garita, some-what lower on the slope, was a diamond-shaped prison with towers at its corners. Originally a Spanish stronghold for prisoners condemned to hang, it was later used by the Americans as a guardhouse.

13. THE UNITED STATES COURTHOUSE (South Federal Place at Lincoln Avenue).   The court-house at the north end of Lincoln Avenue, two blocks from the plaza, was begun in 1850. Funds allotted by Congress for its construc-tion, however, were sufficient to raise the building only one story and a half. The Civil War interrupted both the work and the flow of funds to carry it on, and it was not until the late 1880s that Congress appropriated enough money to finish the structure. Between 1926 and 1930 a carefully matched stone addition was built on the north side. Its halls were painted with six large murals by William Pen-hallow Henderson in 1935–37. Structural de-tails of wood, brass, and marble abound, including handsome brass doors and a marble staircase that winds down to the soda ma-chine. In front of the south entrance to the building stands an obelisk, a monument to Kit Carson. The oval street surrounding the build-ing was originally a race track for mules.

14. THE SCOTTISH RITE TEMPLE (Paseo de Peralta and Washington Avenue).   Built in 1911, this conspicuous pink stucco building of Moorish design is the Masonic meeting place, containing classrooms and an auditorium. A mural above the proscenium arch portrays Boabdil delivering the keys of the Alhambra to Ferdinand and Isabella.

15. THE CROSS OF THE MARTYRS.   This cross, crowning a low northern summit of the city, commemorates the slaying of twenty-one Franciscan missionaries in the Pueblo Revolt.

16. CITY HALL (Lincoln Avenue near West Marcy Street).   A remodeled public school is now the city hall. It occupies the site of the old parade grounds and military complex of the Spanish and, later, of the American Fort Marcy. The bell of the U.S.S. *Santa Fe*, a rep-lica of the Spanish royal banner, and a sea-sonal New Mexican *santos* calendar decorate the halls.

17. THE PUBLIC LIBRARY (Washington Street).

The library opened in 1907, founded by the Santa Fe Women's Board of Trade. The building was remodeled in territorial style in 1932. Stairwell decorations in true fresco were executed by Santa Fe artist Olive Rush. The library maintains an active calendar of events, has extensive information services, and operates with the motto *Con buenos libros no estás solo* ("With good books you are not alone").

18.   WATER STREET; THE ALAMEDA; and the SANTA FE RIVER.   Although the riverbed is often dry, the park bordering the Santa Fe River is green throughout the summer, and winter snows decorate branches of its many trees. Historically, the area has been used for goods-hauling activities. The bus station, car repair shops, and parking lots have replaced the wagon and carriage repair shops, stables, and warehouses along Water Street. The area also offers shops and galleries, many in small shopping malls.

19.   BARRIO DE ANALCO; GOVERNMENT SITE; GUADALUPE (De Vargas Street).   The appellation Barrio de Analco stems from a Nahuatl word meaning "the other side of the water," which area (south of the river) was home for Mexican Indian slaves early in the history of La Villa Real de Santa Fe. This section of humble, centuries-old, randomly sited homes is strung out along De Vargas Street between the Chapel of San Miguel and the Santuario de Guadalupe. The narrow streets of the area open up onto lawns and entryways of dignified government buildings. The houses edging lower San Francisco Street and Agua Fria ("cold water") Street have a handmade appearance. Several walls are enlivened by brilliant murals.

20.   SAN MIGUEL CHURCH (Old Santa Fe Trail and De Vargas Street).   A church built at this site in 1636 for the use of the Indian slaves of Spanish officials was all but destroyed in the Pueblo Revolt. De Vargas partially restored it when he recaptured the province in 1693. Later, in 1710, it was completely rebuilt by the Marqués de la Peñuela, the Spanish governor of the time. The exterior of the building has changed its appearance many times since. The old walls remain, however, and the back of the church retains its original massive lines.

21.   The STATE CAPITOL (Paseo de Peralta between Old Santa Fe Trail and Don Gaspar Avenue), one of the newest state capitol buildings in the United States, was designed in 1966. The circular kiva of the Pueblos and the Zia circular sun symbol inspired what is popularly known as "the Merry Roundhouse." Its four entrances represent the four winds, the four seasons, the four directions, and the four stages of life. The legislative and executive branches of the government function in this building. Visitors can take guided tours, view historic and cultural displays, see the governor's gallery, and attend the annual legislative sessions in the winter. It is not yet known how its circular design affects the destiny of New Mexico.

22.   THE GOVERNOR'S GALLERY.   The reception room of the governor's office in the State Capitol Building houses a gallery of rotating exhibits, primarily the works of New Mexican artists and craftsmen.

23.   BATAAN MEMORIAL BUILDING (Galisteo Street at Montezuma Avenue).   The old state capitol, with its silver dome, has been surrounded by the Bataan Memorial Building, which contains state government offices.

24.   STATE LIBRARY BUILDING (Don Gaspar Avenue near South Capitol Street).   The collections of the State Library and History Library (Washington Street at Palace Avenue) are open to the public.

25.   LAMY BUILDING (Old Santa Fe Trail near De Vargas Street). During the construction of the cathedral, skilled European workers came to Santa Fe and remained. The European style is evident in the adobe structure of St. Michael's Dormitory, now the Lamy Office Build-

ing. The Christian Brothers founded St. Michael's College, a Catholic school for boys, in 1859 and built the dormitory thirty years later. Long, narrow windows, gray shutters, a balcony, pegged railings, and French-style trim adorn the building. St. Michael's College is now the College of Santa Fe and is on St. Michael's Drive.

26. SANTUARIO DE GUADALUPE (Guadalupe and Agua Fria Street).   Situated on a low bluff between the Santa Fe River and what was once the Camino Real or Chihuahua Trail, among new herb gardens, the present *santuario* (sanctuary) is the result of many reconstructions. Built in the late eighteenth century, the church was extensively remodeled in 1882, again after a fire in 1918, and again in 1976 for the United States Bicentennial. It had been closed for many years prior to its last remodeling, and is now the setting for a display of Spanish colonial art and religious artifacts and a series of choral and chamber music concerts. Fine old carved *vigas* and corbels adorn the high ceiling; adobe walls almost three feet thick and small barred windows are features of the interior. In the sanctuary hangs a painting of Our Lady of Guadalupe, patron saint of Mexico, dated 1783 and signed by the Spanish colonial artist José de Alzíbar. The building also contains fine stained-glass windows, a history exhibit, a graceful Victorian staircase, and a library, which was the original sacristy. The sacristy has been dedicated to Jean Baptiste Lamy, first archbishop of Santa Fe, who often celebrated Mass in the church. Many of the room's furnishings were Lamy's.

27. AGUA FRIA.   An area of once-prosperous farms is now a line of adobe homes, alternating with modern trailers and makeshift animal barns along Agua Fria Street. Prehistoric Pueblo peoples preceded the Spanish farmers here in their dependence on the now nearly dry Santa Fe River. A sense of community continues in the area that was the village of Agua Fria, today engulfed by Santa Fe.

28. AGUA FRIA CHURCH (Agua Fria Road). San Isidro Church, built in 1835, is still used by the people of the district, who celebrate the feast of their patron saint, the guardian of farmers, each May. At Christmas the walls of the church and the boundaries of the little cemetery are covered with *luminarias.*

29. ACEQUIA MADRE (between Canyon Road and Old Santa Fe Trail).   The Acequia Madre, a usually dry irrigation ditch, borders a residential area of adobe houses in soft earth colors, with native vegetation enhancing their rural character. While no longer important to Santa Fe residents, this and similar ditches throughout New Mexico once served vital agricultural, sanitary, and social functions. The villager in charge of ditch maintenance and water allocation, the *mayordomo,* was often the most powerful settler in the area.

30. CANYON ROAD.   El Camino de Cañon, or Canyon Road, is an ancient thoroughfare extending from the Alameda, off the Paseo de Peralta, and along the Santa Fe River for ten or twelve miles into the mountains. A walk along Canyon Road is a re-enactment of walks probably experienced by Pueblo Indians before the founding of Santa Fe. In pre-Spanish days, the road is said to have been part of the Indian trail from the lower Rio Grande valley to Taos. More recently it was the burro trail to the hills for those seeking pinon firewood. However, Pueblo and Hispanic travelers saw the mountains rather than the shops, galleries, and restaurants that now line the street. For many years, Canyon Road has supported a concentration of artists and craftsmen. If the

traveler turns north at the point where Camino del Monte Sol joins Canyon Road, or returns west in the direction of the plaza, he passes many fine adobe houses, which often enclose garden patios.

31. CAMINO DEL MONTE SOL. This street takes its name from a nearby conical hill, Monte Sol, so named because it catches the first and last rays of the sun. This street was once known as the center of the artists' colony. Their houses were scattered along the street and were, for the most part, built by the noted artist, architect, and writer Frank Applegate.

32. CRISTO REY CHURCH (Canyon Road and Camino Delora). One of America's largest adobe buildings, the Cristo Rey (Christ the King) Church was built in 1940, designed by John Gaw Meem. The reredos, or altar screen, is a masterpiece of stone carving. The 32-foot-high, hand-carved screen was a gift to the Catholic church by Don Antonio de Valle in 1760. Originally placed in the military chapel near the plaza, the reredos was moved in 1850 to cramped quarters in the cathedral, and then to Cristo Rey Church in 1940.

33. OLD SANTA FE TRAIL AREA. The piñon-studded foothills of the Sangre de Cristos are the setting for several of Santa Fe's excellent museums, St. John's College, and the National Park Service's Southwest regional headquarters.

34. MUSEUM OF INTERNATIONAL FOLK ART (Camino Lejo) is a gem in the cluster of mu-

seums in the hills. Opened in 1953 through a gift of Florence Dibell Bartlett, it was the first folk art museum in the world designed to be fully international in scope. In 1983 a wing was opened to include the extraordinary and often whimsical folk art collection of Santa Fe architect Alexander Girard. A reference library of books about costumes, textiles, folk art, and ceramics, and much of the stored collections, are open to the public. The spectacular changing exhibits, however, provide most of the viewing. Folk costumes, majolica (tin-glazed pottery), Spanish colonial arts, textiles, and Alpine art are among the richest parts of the museum's holdings. The facility's goal of stimulating and preserving folk art is accomplished through such exhibits as the Southwest Craft Biennial and such workshops as the Rio Grande Weaving and Dyeing Workshop and the Villanueva embroidery project.

35. THE LABORATORY OF ANTHROPOLOGY (Camino Lejo) was organized in 1923 by a small group of enthusiastic citizens of Santa Fe. Fearful that in another decade the opportunity might be gone forever, they started to assemble, by gift and purchase, a collection of Southwestern Indian pottery that would demonstrate, scientifically and chronologically, the development of the art from earliest times to the present. Built in 1931, the Spanish-Pueblo style buildings include a museum, lecture hall, laboratory unit, and storage facility, all designed by John Gaw Meem.

Important museum features of the laboratory are the great collections of Pueblo pottery, Navajo and Pueblo textiles, silver, basketry, and the arts and crafts of other tribes. Museum attendants encourage their study by pupils of Indian schools and adult Indian crafts workers, as well as by artists, writers, students, and all who can, in any way, promote an interest in the revival and improvement of native arts.

Construction on a new Indian Arts Museum, to be adjacent to, and associated with, the Laboratory of Anthropology, is to begin in 1984.

36. The WHEELWRIGHT MUSEUM (Camino Lejo). The intent of the Wheelwright Museum has been in preserving and indeed nurturing the spirit of Navajo ceremonialism. Founded in 1937 by Mary Cabot Wheelwright to contain a collection of six hundred sandpainting replicas and ceremonial items for students of Navajo religion, art, and culture, the museum now houses the works of the famed Navajo medicine man Hosteen Klah. It has a large collection of Apache items, Pueblo, Plains, California, and Athapascan Indian materials, and fine weaving, silver, and basketry collections. The vitality of the museum is enhanced by the changing exhibits in the main hall, the working trading post at the lower level, and student access to the library's books, films, tapes, and Edison cylinder recordings of Navajo ceremonial and social songs. The museum structure was designed by William Penhallow Henderson to resemble a Navajo hogan, with its entrance to the east and a cribbed roof of pine logs, to achieve a Navajo sense of harmony with nature.

37. ST. JOHN'S COLLEGE (Camino Cruz Blanca). A small, four-year liberal arts college whose main campus was founded in Annapolis, Maryland in 1696, St. John's occupies beautiful foothill grounds at the southeastern edge of Santa Fe. Students pursue a curriculum centered in the Great Books. The college is also an arts center for Santa Fe.

38. The NATIONAL PARK SERVICE REGIONAL HEADQUARTERS (Old Santa Fe Trail). More than two hundred thousand adobe bricks were used in the construction of this imposing structure, housing National Park Service headquarters for the parks of the Southwest. An information center and display area are open to visitors.

39. CERRILLOS ROAD. Not a street for walking, Cerrillos Road is the site of the Institute of American Indian Arts and the State School for the Deaf, both near downtown Santa Fe. It boasts a string of franchise outlets, motels, and neon signs extending toward Albuquerque—or to the state penitentiary.

40. The NEW MEXICO SCHOOL FOR THE DEAF (Cerrillos Road). The graceful green campus of the state school for the deaf stretches along Cerrillos Road. The institution was founded in 1887, and many of its Pueblo-style buildings were built during Work Projects Administration days.

41. The INSTITUTE OF AMERICAN INDIAN ART, SANTA FE INDIAN SCHOOL (Cerrillos Road). The institute is in a period of transition. It has been a federally supported school for artistically talented students of all tribes, aimed at the development of individual skills and styles through a basic knowledge of traditional arts and crafts. More Indian control and a wider curriculum are current trends. The classes are now held at the College of Santa Fe. The Santa Fe Indian School campus includes a large outdoor amphitheater designed by the innovative architect Paolo Soleri.

42. The COLLEGE OF SANTA FE (St. Michael's Drive). The Christian Brothers operate the College of Santa Fe as a four-year coeducational liberal arts college. Outstanding features are the Fogelson Library and the Greer Garson Theater, at which the actress Greer Garson, who lives not far from Santa Fe, has often appeared.

43. The INTERNATIONAL INSTITUTE OF IBERIAN ARTS. The College of Santa Fe is home for a collection of paintings dating back to the sixteenth century from mission churches along the Pecos River.

Leaving Santa Fe to begin the tour of the Sangre de Cristo mountain villages, follow Bishop's Lodge Road (N.M. 22) northeasterly, out of Santa Fe.

N.M. 475, 4 mi. east, leads to Hyde Memorial State Park and the Santa Fe Ski Basin. The state park, eight miles in, has camping facilities and hiking trails, and contains many fossil rocks and other noteworthy geological features. The ski basin, on the edge of the Pecos Wilderness, is a seventeen-mile trip.

Jean Baptiste Lamy, first archbishop of the diocese of New Mexico, lived for a time at Bishop's Lodge, 7 mi., built in 1854. The lodge is now a well-known resort, its grounds straddling the clear, cold water of the Little Tesuque River.

The route continues north, following the course of the Rio Tesuque. The Shidoni Foundry and workshop, at 9 mi., has recently become the site of an annual summer outdoor show of metal, stone, wood, and other sculpture. The foundry is open to visitors.

The village of TESUQUE, 10 mi. (alt. 6,800, pop. 1,000) dates from 1740 and now thrives as an art and woodcarving center. *Tesuque* is a Tewa word referring to the river's alternating appearance from and disappearance into the sand. The village is situated several miles upstream from the present pueblo.

After joining the main road from Santa Fe, U.S. 285/U.S. 84, at 12 mi., the tour proceeds to the TESUQUE PUEBLO turnoff, 14 mi. (pop. 300). Located a mile west of the highway, Tesuque is the southernmost of the Tewa-speaking pueblos. When first visited by the Spanish in the late sixteenth century, the town was located three miles east of its present site. The murders of Cristóbal de Herrera and Padre Juan Baptista Pío, which began the Pueblo Revolt, occurred here on August 9 and 10, 1680.

Noteworthy features of Tesuque Pueblo are its resistance to government-sponsored "suburban" housing and its attempt to keep the central village intact. Some of the buildings around the plaza still rise to two stories.

The church at Tesuque pueblo is named for San Isidro Labrador, a twelfth-century saint whose feast day is celebrated in early May. His legend, that of a poor farmer helped by

Camel Rock, *Harvey Caplin.*

angels, mingles with one of Tesuque itself in which a poor farmer who insisted on plowing during Mass was visited by an angel predicting grasshoppers, floods, and drought unless the poor man left his hungry family in God's hands and went to church. The man was not moved. Finally the angel threatened him with the gossip of a bad neighbor. Terror struck; the farmer ran to join his family at church. When Mass was over, the field had been mysteriously plowed. Tesuque also claims as patron San Diego, the fifteenth-century Spanish Franciscan, and celebrates his feast day on November 13.

The traveler can easily recognize Camel Rock, at 15 mi., an eroded sandstone formation. Fossil bones are numerous in the ancient stream deposits of this area. Camping and picnicking facilities are available here, just north of the formation.

POJOAQUE, 20 mi. (pop. 130), is an ancient Tewa pueblo, abandoned after the Pueblo Revolt and partially resettled in 1706. Without a discernible village center, the present town surrounds the old pueblo and church. Like the residents of Tesuque and Nambe, many Pojoaquians work with the Northern Pueblo Enterprises or other industries brought to the area in the 1970s. The annual feast is celebrated in honor of Our Lady of Guadalupe on December 12.

The tour turns at 21 mi. onto N.M. 4 East and proceeds up Nambe Creek to NAMBE, 23 mi., another settlement near an ancient Tewa site. Scattered among cottonwoods and adobe walls, this spacious pueblo lies two miles southwest of the highway. *Nambe* means "people of the roundish earth," a reference to the topography of a more ancient location of the pueblo several miles to the northwest.

NAMBE FALLS is a series of three waterfalls five miles up Nambe Creek from the pueblo. The falls and reservoir now have fishing, hiking trails, camping, and picnicking facilities available. Commemorating the falls is a legend about a maiden courted by a warrior and a hunter. The jealous warrior killed the hunter, and both were swallowed by the earth in answer to the maiden's prayers for her lover's revenge. These falls and smaller pools are said to have been formed by the girl's tears as she wandered, weeping. Ceremonial dances honoring St. Francis of Assisi, Nambe's patron, are held here annually in October.

N.M. 4 has been running through what geologists call Santa Fe marl, pinkish deposits of clay, gravel, and loam. At lower elevations, the thinly clad hills are dotted with juniper trees (Rocky Mountain red cedar). Approaching 28 mi., where N.M. 520 forks north to Chimayo, the road climbs and turns east to face the Sangre de Cristo range, which extends two hundred fifty miles from central Colorado nearly to I-40, south of Santa Fe. To the west, across the Rio Grande, stretch the Jemez, older mountains of volcanic origin. Peaks visible from vantage points along this part of the road are, north to south, Trampas, Truchas, Pecos Baldy, and Santa Fe Baldy. In the foreground the stands of juniper thicken and become mixed with piñon, *Pinus edulis,* the state tree of New Mexico. Adjacent to the pavement, true sagebrush grows.

The rainfall in the towns and valleys hereabout ranges from ten to fifteen inches per year, occurring primarily in July and August. Although this provides more moisture than is received by most other populated areas of the state, it is still not generally sufficient for growing crops without irrigation. The nearby mountains, however, receive twenty or more inches per year and support such large trees as Ponderosa pine, aspen, Douglas fir, and blue and Englemann spruce.

CUNDIYO, 28 mi., is one of the several villages on this tour that appear to have survived almost intact from another century. Just below another old Tewa site (possibly ancient Nambe), Cundiyo perches above the Rio Frijoles and overlooks almost vertically the fields in the valley below.

After crossing the Rio Medio, 32 mi., the road climbs again to the turnoff (west) to SANTA CRUZ LAKE, 34 mi. This reservoir, fed by several streams, sits in a beautiful basin 1.5 mi. west of the highway. Here are campsites, picnic tables, hiking trails, and a boat-launching ramp. Almost directly opposite the Santa Cruz Lake turnoff is Forest Road 306 (east) into the Pecos Wilderness, Borrego Mesa and

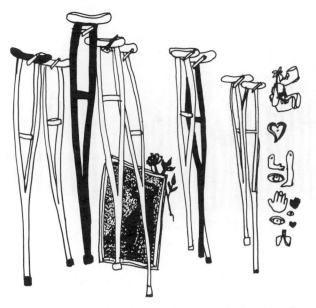

the upper Rio Medio. Within a mile begins the sharp descent to the Rio Quemado, 35 mi., and the valley settlement of Rio Chiquito.

Left from the junction of N.M. 4 and N.M. 76, at a distance of 2 mi., lies CHIMAYO, famous both for its weavers and for the Santuario de Nuestro Señor de Esquipulas. Hundreds of pilgrims and visitors each month find the santuario, a mile south of N.M. 76. The turnoff (south) at Chimayo is well-marked. This church was built in 1813–16 by Don Bernardo Abeyta in a style that had not changed substantially since the first churches of two hundred years earlier. It has been cited as an example of the "cultural crystallization" that resulted from the extreme isolation and precarious economic situation of the New Mexico province. The chapel exhibits the classic features of Spanish-Pueblo church architecture: twin towers, a choir loft, *vigas* (roof beams), a window over the altar, *retablos* (paintings), and a *campo santo* (cemetery) in front.

One legend claims that when Don Bernardo was deathly ill a vision beckoned him to a spot on the ground beneath the cottonwoods, where he was immediately cured. He built a chapel over the spot in thanksgiving. Whatever the circumstances of its construction, the sanctuary is now cherished throughout the region for the healing power of the earth in the floor of a room to the left of the altar. Numerous crutches, braces, and messages of thanks-

giving line the anteroom, attesting to the restorative value of the holy mud. The setting itself, amid cottonwoods, irrigation channels, and a view of the little Quemado valley, certainly has a curative effect. Many New Mexicans take part in an annual Easter pilgrimage to the shrine, some walking for miles on foot.

Next to the *santuario*, and competing with it as a source of supernatural power, is the chapel of the Santo Niño (Holy Child). To the robes of this child Jesus are pinned notes and photographs of those for whom special blessings are asked. The chapel is privately owned but open to the public.

Between the *santuario* and Chimayo nestles one of the state's historic eating places. El Rancho de Chimayo, in the Jaramillo family since early this century, is worthy of a visit for its food, for its decor, for its feeling of an old country inn.

Chimayo itself was established around an old Tewa pueblo after the reconquest in 1692. The word means "good flaking stone," i.e., obsidian. For over two hundred years Chimayo has been known for its weaving, an art that continues here today. Most early Spanish residents of New Mexico wove, if only to make their own clothing. In 1805 the inhabitants of Santa Fe imported two fine weavers from Spain to help them develop their craft. Juan and Ignacio Balzán soon moved from Santa Fe to Chimayo, which became the capital of the weaving industry in the province. At least seven generations of weavers have continued the tradition. The original weavers used local wool, but more recent artisans have made use of yarn, often brightly colored, obtained from the eastern United States. Their products are characterized by stripes, at least near the ends of the rugs, with the warp tied off in fringe beyond the ends of the rug proper. Complex patterns such as the eight-pointed star called a Trampas design are often woven into the creations. In 1940 there were almost one hundred families engaged in the weaving business, usually within their own homes. Now the number is smaller, but their products reach Santa Fe, Albuquerque, and beyond. They can also be purchased in the weaving shops in Chimayo, where children and adults alike are entertained by the skill of the weavers.

Chimayo was the eastern boundary of the province of New Mexico from 1598 to 1695 and the frontier place of banishment for offenders, which in those days was a greater punishment than prison. After the reconquest it was known as San Buenaventura de Chimayo.

Returning on N.M. 76, the traveler follows the high road to the crest of a hogback dividing two small valleys, with Truchas Peak (13,306 feet) and the Taos Mountains ahead. At 38 mi. a paved road branches down to the right into a small valley, where the village of CORDOVA, 1 mi., hugs the slope above the Rio Quemado.

Cordova boasts a tradition of distinguished woodcarving families who have been carving for several generations. Signs along the road mark their workshops, and visitors are welcome. The López family sign is prominent; back in the 1920s and 1930s José María López fashioned birds, squirrels, and beavers from juniper and piñon, as well as the religious figures for which the area is famous.

Settled soon after the reconquest and known as "El Pueblo Quemado" until 1900, the village originally was built in a defensive *placita* pattern: houses end-to-end, opening upon a central area but protected from outside by a common exterior wall. Cordova today appears to follow no definite plan, with its narrow dirt-packed road twisting among tiny homes.

Near the center of town, the Church of San Antonio de Padua is well worth the effort of a visit. As is the case with some of the other churches in the area, visitors must obtain the key from the postmaster or the *mayordomo* (caretaker) of the church. San Antonio is in excellent condition and is still used for occasional services, including those during the feast day of San Antonio on June 13. Inside, there are fine *reredos* painted around 1834 by

Chimayo, *E. A. Scholer.*

José Rafael Aragón, a well-known *santero*. The church also houses primitive *santos*.

The road continues out of Cordova to rejoin N.M. 76, which then climbs until it reaches TRUCHAS ("trout"), 43 mi. (alt. 7,622, pop. 672). A Spanish archive of 1752 refers to it as Nuestra Señora de Rosario de las Truchas, a name longer than the village's main street. A 1762 archive tells of the transfer of its people, together with those of Las Trampas, to the parish of Picuris. The history of Truchas is fairly well documented, as another archive, dated 1772, records the requests of the villagers for twelve muskets, powder, and protection from the Comanches. "Denied" is written in answer to both requests. Because of

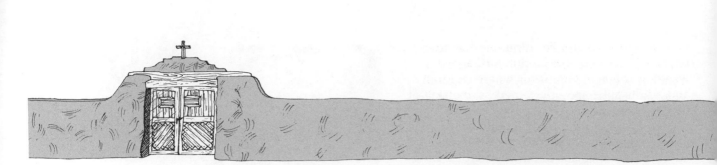

fears of Comanche raids, Governor Vélez Capuchín ordered that the settlement be built around two plazas instead of in scattered *ranchos*.

A dirt road runs off the highway along the high ridge through the little town. Thick-walled adobe houses, small shops, and businesses give way to vistas of the Sangre de Cristos and other ranges in the distance. The entire Tewa world and a magnificent panorama of the Rio Grande valley spread out below.

Numerous trails branch out from Truchas into the Carson National Forest. East of Truchas, a gravel road leads into and through the forest, linking up with the small Trampas Canyon Recreation Site. This camping area is open from May to October, with room for four units. Fishing and easy access to the wilderness areas are its attractions. Another primitive forest road north runs over mountain trails and across canyons to Las Trampas. It is best to inquire locally or of the Forest Service about driving conditions, as the roads are not paved.

The more conventional route to Trampas is N.M. 76, which turns left at Truchas. The Carson National Forest covers much of this area and forest roads lead off the main road on both right and left. These go to camping areas, trailheads for backpackers, and logging roads. Some roads permit motorized travel; others do not.

OJO SARCO ("clear blue brook"), 48 mi., is a tiny farming community that spreads off to the left of the road, following the bed of the canyon of the Rio Sarco.

N.M. 76 corkscrews up and down the mountains, settling into LAS TRAMPAS ("the traps"), 50 mi., founded in the 1700s and now most renowned for its Catholic church, San José de Gracia, which sits on a rise near the road.

Built in the eighteenth century with the permission of Bishop Tamarón, who stipulated that the church be within a walled compound for defensive purposes, San José de Gracia (also known as the Church of the Twelve Apostles and as Santo Tomás de Río de Las Trampas) is considered a good illustration of early New Mexico religious architecture. Legend says that only twelve men were allowed to work on the church at one time, although the entire village set aside one-sixth of its crop yields to pay for the materials. The result of their labors and sacrifices is a large, traditional adobe structure with twin belfries, an outside choir balcony, and painted *vigas* and corbels in the interior. Inside the simple planked floor contrasts with the ornate *vigas* that form the ceiling; the plain benches counter the elaborate paintings, some probably brought from Spain. At one time a Penitente death cart, with Doña Sebastiana (a skeleton dressed in black) seated inside it, warned parishioners of death and punishment. The cart is no longer in the church. Also missing is one of the two bells, María de Gracia, which had always called people to feast days and weddings. The other bell, María del Refugio, is now safe atop the church inside one of the belfries.

The Church of San José de Gracia was almost the victim of progress. As state highway department engineers surveyed for the widening and paving of N.M. 76 in 1966, the villagers of Las Trampas were faced with a dilemma: if the road was widened and upgraded, asphalt would come dangerously close to the venerable church. On the other hand, a modern road accessible to all vehicles in all weather was certainly needed. Las Trampas citizens were ready to give highway officials the go-ahead when word of the problem reached Santa Fe. A group of preservationists, led by architects Nathaniel Owings, John Gaw Meem, and Alan McNown, rushed to form a committee to work with the villagers, the highway department, and federal officials. They placed the church on the National Register of Historic Places, thus saving it from destruction, and worked out a compromise. The road was rebuilt and widened, curving around the church and preserving its integrity. And the Santa Fe group then helped the villagers to reroof and replaster the structure. A villager showed Nathaniel Owings a family photograph of the church complete with its belfries, which had been gone for years. No one had been able to re-create them. With the photograph, weathered wood, and a carpenter supplied by Owings, the twin belfries were constructed. On the day of the fiesta that celebrated the new road and the repaired church, María del Refugio was rung again in the belfry.

Although the church is closed except for services, a visitor can inquire in the village, often at the little store across from the church, for the *mayordomo,* who will open the heavy doors and let a visitor step into the cool, hushed interior.

Much of Las Trampas is not visible from the road. The old plaza, once in front of the church, no longer exists as a focal point. Houses are scattered up and down the valley formed by the Las Trampas River. Settled first by a Santa Fe Spaniard, Juan de Arguello, who was given a grant for twelve families in 1751, Las Trampas until recently has been a predominantly Spanish-speaking village. However, although its heritage is still Spanish, many of the villagers now are summer visitors who have bought and restored old adobe homes. Others are young people who are trying, as the Spanish did, to do subsistence farming in the area. Once there was a great

deal of agricultural activity throughout the Las Trampas Land Grant; now there are few working farms and orchards. Much of the land grant became Carson National Forest in 1906, reducing the land available for private or communal farming and grazing. In fact, the entire village is surrounded now by the national forest.

Heading north out of Las Trampas, back into the mountains, the road passes an old log flume. An important part of the *acequia* system, the carved-out log brings water down from the mountains into the valley to water fields, gardens, and orchards. Not many such log flumes can be found any longer, but the ditch system of irrigation is still an important part of agriculture throughout New Mexico.

CHAMISAL, 56 mi., is the next little settlement that appears as the mountains open up and give room to a valley for a while. Although it does not appear on most highway maps, Chamisal actually may have more people and farms than many of the other, better-known villages. It is part of the Picuris Land Grant and was established as a settlement in

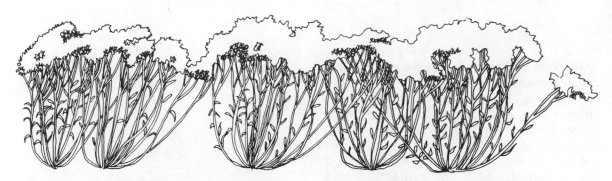

1851. Its name comes from the chamisa, or rabbitbrush, the large round plant with narrow leaves that lines the road. The thin branches of the chamisa support tiny yellow flowers in the late summer, and the plant appears golden then; autumn finds it covered with a white fluff. Chamisa dyes—yellow from the flower and green from the inner bark—have been used throughout the West for centuries. Although it is not a good forage plant, chamisa can be used for fuel.

Like other villages in the Sangre de Cristos, Chamisal spreads itself up and down the valley, and the road that bisects the community passes only a fraction of the town. Many of Chamisal's homes and farms are off the paved highway, but some houses, with tin roofs steeply pitched to ward off snows, flank the road and are sometimes connected with a few business enterprises—a gas station, the post office, a little grocery—that Chamisal supports.

Shortly after leaving Chamisal, winding in and out of scrub pines and tall spruce trees, a traveler can see the peaks of the Sangre de Cristo range, although the summits are often obscured by the same clouds that make the pitched roofs on the houses in the area so important. Snow and rainfall, accompanied by gray days, are more plentiful in this area than on the wide valley floor to the west or on the open plains to the east.

N.M. 76 intersects with N.M. 75 at 59 mi. One-half mile after turning west at the intersection, the traveler finds a paved road, Tribal Route 120, that leads to PICURIS PUEBLO.

A Tiwa-speaking village, Picuris Pueblo has existed since prehistoric time, isolated from other pueblos by the surrounding mountains. *Picuris* is a Tiwa word for "at the gap in the mountain." The village sits in a valley, its fields fed by the Rio Pueblo since before the first visiting Spaniard, Gaspar Castaño de Sosa, received a noticeably cold reception there in 1590.

The present pueblo population of somewhat more than one hundred fifty is drastically less than Fray Martín de Arvide claimed he ministered to in 1621; his figure of more than two thousand baptized souls gives credence to other Spanish observations that there were multistoried apartment dwellings and thousands of people active in the valley during the time of Spanish exploration and colonization.

The white-facaded church, which can be seen as soon as Tribal Route 120 crests the hill above the village, is the third or fourth Catholic church erected in Picuris. It was built, say historians, between 1770 and 1776. The first church, built by de Arvide in 1621, was desecrated and burned during the 1680 rebellion. A new, smaller chapel is presumed to have been built nearby after 1706, when the Picuris people returned from the plains where they had gone to escape their colonizers. Another church may have been constructed shortly thereafter, but was leveled by 1744, leading to the need for the present church. San Lorenzo de Picuris, built more than two hundred years ago, has been in constant use, its good condition belying its age but testifying to the fine care that it has received.

Before the Spanish appeared in Picuris, the pueblo was a strong, active village, a link between the Pueblo and the Plains Indians. Spanish intrusion on Pueblo life was not taken quietly by the Picuris, who rebelled in 1680, 1694, and 1696. The entire pueblo was deserted from 1696 to 1706, when residents fled eastward to the plains, living among the

Apaches to escape the Spanish. After their return to Picuris, the tribe became friendlier with their conquerors. The good relationship that Picuris had enjoyed for centuries with neighboring Indians ended in the eighteenth century, when Picuris joined the Spanish to fight the Comanches, Utes, and Apaches. The late eighteenth and early nineteenth centuries found the Spanish appropriating many Picuris lands and passing along epidemic diseases; soon the Picuris, like other Pueblos, were outnumbered by their European neighbors. By the end of the nineteenth century, the pueblo was poor and underpopulated, a sharp contrast to the strong village Castaño de Sosa first visited. Today, however, Picuris is an active, growing pueblo, its new homes and young families attesting to its health.

A tribal museum operated by the Picuris tells the story of the Pueblo and offers guided tours through the ruins of the old village. The museum is located to the right and beyond the church. Signs guide the visitor to various areas open to the public, including a campground that has picnic and tent sites, water, rest rooms and even fishing possibilities. The Feast of San Lorenzo, August 10, is the time of greatest public celebration at Picuris.

After visiting Picuris, it is easy to retrace the drive back to N.M. 75, turning east at the intersection of 75 and Tribal Route 120. Just before the junction, N.M. 75/N.M. 76 there is a cemetery with a sign above its entrance that says *Dios Da Y Dios Quita* ("The Lord Giveth and the Lord Taketh Away").

N.M. 75 leads to PEÑASCO ("rocky outcroppings"), 60 mi., actually one village composed of a number of smaller settlements. Peñasco was founded in 1796 by three families who petitioned the governor, Fernando Chacón, for permission to build two towns in the valley. Seventy-seven people received his permission and founded three villages, Llano ("plain"), Llano Largo ("large plain"), and Santa Barbara. Much of the town stretches to the east, and the sense of many small villages, dating back to its founding almost two hundred years ago, remains.

Even at its founding, Peñasco was not a typical walled, plaza-centered Spanish town. Because it was settled at a time when many of the more serious Indian raids had ceased, the villagers could afford to spread themselves out; they built their homes in family compounds, often placing them on ridges above the Rio Chiquito, leaving the arable bottomlands for crops and orchards.

The old village church has been replaced now by a modern building. There are, however, many other traditional adobe structures along the road—homes, dance halls, gas stations, and restaurants. Many Peñasco residences were once showcases for the entire Embudo Valley. Large abandoned movie theaters, inactive car dealerships, sleepy mercantile companies all attest to the fact that Peñasco was once bigger and more prosperous than it is now. It was formerly the commercial center for all the little villages strung back through the mountain valleys. Peñasco still retains its role, however, as the educational center for the area; bright yellow school buses ply the narrow roads, bringing in kindergarteners through high schoolers to the modern complex of school buildings at the east end of town.

In a sense, Peñasco typifies what has happened in this century to many small mountain communities. In the past its residents had lived by subsistence farming, raising fruits, vegetables, and sheep and cattle, primarily for their own use. Some also were sheep ranchers, taking their animals up to the mountains for the summer and selling their wool each year. However, as the economy of New Mexico diversified and public schools and other institutions made their way into village life, employment and value changes occurred.

Many of the people who live in the mountain villages now are old. They are still subsistence farmers, but most of their children and grandchildren work in Santa Fe, Los Alamos, Española, or Taos. Other families have moved to Albuquerque or even out of the state to find jobs. While a few ex-villagers do return, their jobs in the larger towns are usually such that

Northern New Mexico, *Harvey Caplin.*

farming can only be done on a part-time basis, if at all. This disuse of agricultural land often leads to controversies over water rights. In some cases rights have been lost by landholders, making a return to farming in the future almost impossible. Land owned by absentee farmers is often sold for back taxes, usually to summer residents who will not farm. It is said that entire villages have been bought for back taxes by people from outside the area. Llano Largo, a part of Peñasco, is largely owned by summer residents, and other parts of the valley are now summer home sites.

However, there is vitality in the mountains, typified by the resurgence of interest in many traditional village crafts and customs. Art shows in Taos and Santa Fe often feature woodcarvings, *santos*, weavings, embroideries, and paintings by local artists. Other cultural awakenings, in dance, drama, and song, are played out in the villages. At Christmas time, *Las Posadas*, the singing pageant that dramatizes the search of Mary and Joseph for a room, has been revived after decades of neglect. The Penitentes Brotherhood, a conservative Catholic society most active in the late

1800s and early 1900s, is meeting again (see Religion). Many Penitentes are now professional men who left the vicinity for schooling and work but did not forget their traditions.

At Peñasco N.M. 75 bears north. Straight ahead N.M. 73 leads into the mountains and to a number of hiking trails and campgrounds. The small village of RODARTE, a traditional woodcarving center, lies just ahead. Hodges Campground is four miles beyond Rodarte on Forest Road 116, a dirt road. Open from May through October, Hodges is small, with picnic tables, rest rooms, and tent sites. Santa Barbara Campground, three miles past Hodges, is larger, with more tent sites, picnic tables, restrooms, and drinking water. Its season is the same, May through October. It is possible to take simple day hikes or extended backpacking trips from both of these areas.

More detailed camping and area information can be found at the Peñasco ranger station, located on N.M. 75 just beyond Peñasco. Forest rangers will supply visitors with free highway maps and forest tips, sell guide maps to Carson National Forest for a small fee, and give drivers, hikers, and skiers information about weather and road conditions and campground availability. Wilderness permits for travel into the Pecos Wilderness can be obtained here.

Barely two miles northeast of Peñasco, another valley, the home of VADITO ("small ford"), 62 mi., opens up. Surrounded by mountains, Vadito was primarily a farming community; its present population still farms to an extent. It was once also a stronghold of the Penitente Brotherhood, and there are probably still some Penitente *moradas* and crosses in the valley. There is a small adobe chapel on the left.

Two miles beyond Vadito, a scattering of houses indicates that the valley is widening and that once there were many active farms here. The fields are still neat and well-tended, and many of the houses have been restored, their tin roofs shining, their gables newly painted. The wide spot in the road that was a village soon narrows again, and N.M. 75 climbs into forests of tall pines and spruce.

The road winds down out of the mountains to the intersection of N.M. 75 and N.M. 3, 76 mi. A wall built of rocks gathered in the valley forms the junction. N.M. 75/N.M. 3 goes east to campgrounds (Comales campsite is closest, just down the road, and has tent sites, restrooms, and picnic tables, but no water; it is open May through October), a ski area (Sipapu), and the Mora Valley (Tour 3).

The road to Taos, N.M. 3, climbs steeply into the mountains. Meadows appear, and picnickers, hikers, and cross-country skiers can be seen in season taking advantage of the trails that lead from the highway into the forest. The road continues to ascend until it reaches eighty-five hundred feet at U.S. Hill. A turnout, rest room, and vista point make this a good spot at which to stop and look at the mountains, valleys, and rivers that extend in all directions. To the west lies an ancient road used for more than a thousand years, first by Indians as a trading link, then by Spanish explorers and settlers. Later the Mexicans traveled the *camino* (road) between New Mexican outposts like Taos to the north and the capital of Mexico to the south. French trappers and traders also trekked the historic road as early as 1739, using it extensively during the heyday of the Taos fur trade in the 1820s and 1830s. Its last important role came in 1847, when Colonel Sterling Price and his troops hauled heavy weapons over the trail through the snow to Taos to squelch a rebellion against the American occupation. Colonel Price's experience hastened the building of a new, easier road, the Camino Militar (the military road or highway), which lies to the west along the Rio Grande. It was completed in 1875.

Meadows and streams now signal the approach of the wide Taos Plateau. Pot Creek, the north fork of the Little Rio Grande, meanders through the high valley. Pot Creek Pueblo, probable ancestral home of the Taos Indians, was located near here in the 1200s. Now Fort Burgwin Research Center straddles the road. Burgwin, built in the 1850s to protect Taos from the Jicarilla Apaches and the Utes, was never officially designated a fort and was abandoned in 1860. It has been restored and is now a research facility of Southern Methodist University. A museum, open to the public, operates here in the summer.

Just past FORT BURGWIN, 76 mi., Carson National Forest ends, the road rises, and houses appear. The village of TALPA ("knob"), 80 mi., sits along a ridge overlooking a valley. It was the site of prehistoric pit houses and small pueblos from A.D. 1100 to A.D. 1300. Settled in the late eighteenth century by the Spanish, Talpa grew up with houses strung along the ridge in family compounds. Below, the Rio Chiquito brings water to the orchards and to fields of alfalfa, corn, and chile. An elaborate eighteenth-century hacienda, belonging to the Durán family, is a former local showplace; it boasted a private chapel. There was once a resort built around the hot spring here; bathers could enjoy the waters, have lunch in the tearoom, or spend time swimming in the indoor and outdoor pools. The hot spring still exists, but the surrounding luxuries do not. There are a number of artists' studios and large, restored homes in Talpa. Private and public cemeteries, or *descansos*, can be seen from the road.

Talpa also includes the settlement of Llano Quemado ("burnt plain"), site of excavations carried out by the Smithsonian Institution; it

is thought that this was one of the early homes of the Taos Indians.

Soon N.M. 3 forms a junction with N.M. 68, 82 mi. A few miles to the north on N.M. 3 is Taos (Tour 3); gas stations and fast-food restaurants lining the road attest to its proximity. To the south, a turn south on N.M. 68 brings the visitor to Ranchos de Taos, perhaps once the farming center for local Indians. It was settled by the Spanish in 1716. Like much of northern New Mexico, Ranchos de Taos and Taos Pueblo were intensively raided by nomadic Indians in the 1700s. At one point the residents of Ranchos de Taos abandoned their village and lived for a time, in mutual fear, with the Indians at the pueblo north of Taos. However, by the end of the eighteenth century both the Spanish and the Taos Indians felt secure enough to resettle Ranchos de Taos, although the plaza was well-fortified.

The Church of St. Francis of Assisi at Ranchos de Taos is one of the Southwest's most famous churches, and certainly one of the most frequently photographed buildings in the United States. The Ranchos church, as it is often called, sits to the east of N.M. 68; its enormous rear abutments can be seen from the road. Built in 1772, well after the initial mission-building phase in New Mexico, the church is fortresslike. Its adobe walls are four feet thick, with large buttresses at its transepts and apse. Inside the traditional cruciform structure are enormous *vigas* and fine corbels. Large *reredos* contain very old paintings, and there are numerous European and New Mexican art pieces throughout the church. One of the paintings is said to glow miraculously at night. The Ranchos parish is an active one; in 1979 parishioners themselves replastered the exterior walls of the church with mud adobe, the traditional way of protecting adobe walls. Cement stucco, a harder, harsher finish, had been applied over the original adobe in 1967. The feast of St. Francis is celebrated at the church and in the village on October 4. The church is always open to visitors, and guides are sometimes available to conduct tours.

Much of the village of Ranchos de Taos ex-

tends to the east and west on either side of N.M. 68. The view in all directions is splendid. To the north Taos can be seen crouching beneath its protective mountains. To the west is the Rio Grande; beyond its gorge, the plains and mesas climb to distant mountains. South and east lie the Sangre de Cristos and the canyon through which the Rio Grande wanders or surges, depending on the season and the bedrock. Within Ranchos de Taos are many fine old adobe buildings. Some have been restored, while others have become ruins, stables, or shells, their *vigas*, door frames, and window finishings taken to dress up another old home or lend authenticity to a new one. The dirt roads that intersect N.M. 68 can be wandered along for glimpses of adobe walls, old homes, and interesting gates and fences.

Heading south, the road climbs and winds around the foothills and tablelands that form the Taos Plateau. The Rio Grande flows below; its canyon walls begin to close in above. The highway moves closer to the river. Shortly after Ranchos de Taos, the N.M. 96 turnoff west to Rio Grande Gorge State Park appears, at 83 mi. The park, which sits along the banks of the river, is open all year and offers campsites, drinking water, rest rooms, and excellent fishing.

The Rio Grande soon rushes alongside N.M. 68. The canyon walls are steep here. An occasional wide spot in the river's path leaves room for a small farm, an orchard, or, in some cases, an old mining camp. There are turnouts and picnic areas along the river; fishermen, canoeists, and white-water rafting parties sometimes appear, the river their playground.

Where the river is wide, a small, deltalike piece of land juts into it. This is Pilar, 96 mi. Once a Jicarilla Apache farming community, it

was sacked and burned by Oñate and his troops in 1694. In 1795 Governor Fernando Chacón gave a grant to twenty Spanish settlers, and here they founded a village, perhaps naming it after Nuestra Señora de Pilar, a famous shrine in Spain. As part of the grant stipulations, the settlers were to share this land with the Jicarillas, who were still there. They never did, and suffered the consequences of that choice by being raided frequently. After much bloodshed on both sides, the Jicarillas conceded defeat, signed a treaty, and left the area in the mid-1800s. Both sides of the river have been farmed at Pilar; the earliest in a series of bridges spanning the river at this spot is said to have been built in 1598.

Three miles south of Pilar is a suspension bridge that leads to Glen-Woody Bridge, 99 mi., on the west bank. In 1902 a sophisticated mining venture was attempted here. High hopes brought the spot a hotel, homes, a street layout, and even a turbine engine to run the mining equipment. The mining venture never succeeded, and the town fell into ruins. It is now privately owned property, almost a ghost town.

Near Rinconada ("place at the corner"), 103 mi., the river valley widens between towering cliffs on both sides of the river. The highway here is built very close to the Rio Grande, and there are places where a car can drive onto the banks for a close-up view of the river or for a picnic.

N.M. 75 intersects N.M. 68 at 105 mi. and heads east to Dixon, 2 mi., and on to Picuris and Peñasco, following the route of the Embudo River between hills and canyons. Dixon is a pretty little town that has made use of local stone in its buildings.

At Embudo ("funnel"), 107 mi. (alt. 6,500), a

former Indian pueblo, the river rushes through a funnel formed by the high walls of the gorge. Embudo is now no more than a few ranches and, across the river, an abandoned station of the Denver and Rio Grande Western Railroad, part of the old Chili Line, which carried wool, hides, piñon, chiles, and other agricultural products out of the valley. The complex of structures around the old railroad station, erected in 1880, is known as the Embudo Historic District. Privately owned now, the buildings can be viewed with permission of the owners by those brave enough to cross the wooden trestle bridge that links the highway with the historic site. (The bridge also has a history: it originally spanned the river at Española but was carried away by the flood of 1920 and replaced upstream.) The water tower once replenished locomotives on the Denver and Rio Grande line here, and the old turntable was used to help trains over the steep grades.

Part of the Historic District and a landmark in its own right is the Embudo Gauging Station. John Wesley Powell, famous Western explorer and pioneer, built the original station to measure the river's depth. It was the first of its kind to be built anywhere. The present station is sixty years old and still measures the stream depths.

At 109 mi. the highway leaves the canyon and enters the wide Rio Grande valley, a taming influence on the river. Don Diego de Vargas defeated the Taos Indians here in September 1696, the final victory after the Pueblo Revolt.

VELARDE, 110 mi. (alt. 5,600), center of a farming community with fine peach and apple orchards, was formerly called La Jolla but was later renamed for Matías Velarde, who had founded the community in 1875. During the growing season fruit stands abound on both sides of the road; in the winter these stands display red chiles and gourds. Velarde proper lies off the main road closer to the river, not readily observable from the highway but accessible by several dirt roads.

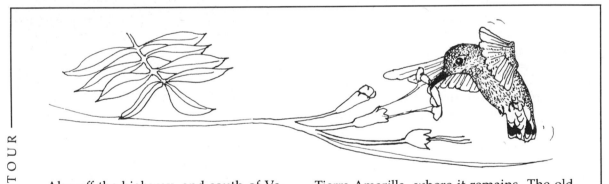

SIDE TOUR

Also off the highway, and south of Velarde, LOS LUCEROS, 115 mi., named for a prominent family of the area, was once the capital of the *departamento* (a political division established by the Mexican government in 1836) of Rio Arriba, and from 1855 to 1860 was the seat of Rio Arriba County. In 1860 the county seat was transferred to Alcalde (see below), then called Plaza del Alcalde, and in 1880 to Tierra Amarilla, where it remains. The old Los Luceros county courthouse is now a private residence in excellent condition and one of the original two-story territorial-style homes. The building may have been begun as early as 1601. It was later used as a fort, and then converted into a great hacienda. It is open to the public by appointment only.

ALCALDE ("magistrate, judge"), 118 mi., once a healthy trading point, now consists of a few houses scattered along both sides of the highway.

A turnoff here links up with the Old Velarde Road, a paved road paralleling the river and passing by San Juan Pueblo. It is a picturesque route to the pueblo (but slower than taking N.M. 68 to the San Juan turnoff), passing small gardens and high-walled old adobes, winding under the poplars and cottonwoods common along the Rio Grande. Of interest here is the old Swan Lake Ranch, once a gracious hacienda, well-known for the elegant and literary parties given by its owner, a dancer, and the writer Hamlin Garland.

SAN JUAN PUEBLO, 120 mi. (pop. 1,181), is a large, built-up Tewa pueblo hidden among huge cottonwoods and rabbitbrush near the banks of the river. Traditional adobe houses now mingle with more modern homes, and modern architectural styles have influenced the new government buildings on the plaza, including the headquarters of the Eight Northern Pueblos and their crafts outlet. Another contemporary structure is the crafts cooperative of the San Juan residents, Ohke Oweege (the Tewa name for San Juan, which means "the capital of the Tewa people"), one of the first Pueblo cooperatives. The old mission church no longer exists here; instead a pseudo-Gothic brick structure dating from the early twentieth century dominates the plaza, facing a smaller stone chapel. As in all the pueblos, residents appreciate respect for their privacy, and visits are limited to the plaza unless permission is obtained from tribal officials.

Another pueblo existed earlier across the river at Yungueingge ("mockingbird-place pueblo"), but after the Spanish arrived in 1598 and Oñate made it his military headquarters, the Tewa inhabitants moved to the present site, taking with them the name of San Juan de los Caballeros ("St. John of the gentlemen" or "knights") for their new pueblo. The title of *caballeros* was supposedly earned by the Tewas for their gracious behavior in giving up their homes to the Spanish, but the name could

San Juan Pueblo, *Alejandro Lopez.*

have honored the Spanish gentlemen who rode with Oñate, or, more likely, the Knights of Malta, whose patron is St. John the Baptist. His feast day is celebrated in San Juan on June 24 with a special Mass and dancing. Visitors are welcome at the dances; cameras are not. The feeling here, as at all pueblos, is that the dances are personal celebrations and not exhibitions.

The Spanish who remained at Yungueingge renamed it San Gabriel de Yunque Yunque.

Oñate established the first capital of New Mexico here in late 1598 or early 1599, and settlers lived here several years, building it into a fairly large town. Oñate left his capital several times on exploratory trips. The poverty of the land and other difficulties led the majority of the colonists to return to Mexico during Oñate's absences. When a new governor was named, the handful of remaining settlers moved the capital to Santa Fe, a more convenient site, in 1609. The ruins that remain are significant as those of the first European settlement in what is now the United States. However, they are barely visible and remain under the custody of San Juan Pueblo.

Spanish rulers remained at San Juan, according the population a repressive government that overworked the Indians through forced labor and tried to stamp out their religion by burning the kivas. In 1676 a San Juan religious leader, Popé, was taken with forty six others to Santa Fe, where he was jailed and flogged. Four years later Popé led the Pueblo Revolt.

After the Spaniards returned to the area, San Juan became a Roman Catholic parish center as well as a trading center because of its central location at the convergence of several trade routes. These routes remain today as major highways, coming together a few miles south in Española.

Modern San Juan residents no longer rely on the old subsistence agricultural and trade economy. Many work in government pro-

grams in Santa Fe or Los Alamos, or for the Pueblo Council.

Leaving San Juan Pueblo, the tour can continue on the Old Velarde Road to the river, where a bridge leads to U.S. 84 (Tour 7) and south to ESPAÑOLA, 125 mi. (alt. 5,585, pop. 10,800). An alternate route is via N.M. 68, east of the pueblo and linked to it by a paved road south of the plaza.

Española (a shortened version of San Gabriel de los Españoles, another name given to Oñate's first colony) lies on the banks of the Rio Grande. A late-nineteenth-century town, it suffers architecturally from its newness, lacking the charm and history of other towns on this tour. Española's city hall, Bond House, is of interest, however. Franklin Bond, a Canadian-born merchant who found considerable success in diverse ventures in the Española Valley and beyond, began construction of an adobe house with Victorian trim and decorations here in 1887. Gradually many rooms were added to the original two-room structure. The rambling result was donated to the city after Bond's death, becoming the city hall in 1957.

Española is now the modern, urban center of Rio Arriba County, serving as a nucleus for the nearby ranching and farming communities and replete with fast-food outlets, motels, and other conveniences for its citizens and visitors. The town's major arteries, especially on weekend evenings, become showplaces for the "low and slow, mean and clean" cars known as "lowriders." Lowrider clubs, rallying points for Hispanic teenagers and young adults, abound in the Española Valley. Associations made up of the youth of the town and nearby villages take great pride in their customized vehicles, which often feature welded-chain steering wheels, crushed velvet upholstery, wire wheels, and candied and metallic paint with painted murals, geometric designs, and irridescent decals. The car clubs often are focuses of community pride and good works.

The lowrider concept seems to have emerged in the early 1950s in Texas and in the Los Angeles area to improve the image of the

"pachuco gangs" of the 1930s and 1940s and to contrast with the Anglo hot rodders of the same period. Unlike the hot rodders, lowriders prefer cars that are indeed low (almost scraping the ground) and slow, rarely approaching speed limits. In recent years the cult has spread to all of the Mexican-American Southwest; in New Mexico it includes recently arrived Mexican nationals as well as the New Mexican descendants of the conquistadors. On weekend evenings the shining vehicles, lovingly polished and chromed, parade slowly around Española, just as they do around the plaza in Santa Fe and on Central Avenue in Albuquerque.

Periodic contests are held in each of these towns. Cars are judged on appearance and on two more athletic properties: hopping and scraping. To hop, a lowrider must be powered by hydraulic pumps requiring as many as eight storage batteries. At the touch of a button, usually on a show ground or when pulled up at a traffic light, the front or back end of the car will leap up as high as twenty-nine inches off the ground and then fall back to the pavement, scraping the ground with a shower of sparks.

Española is the home of Northern New Mexico Community College. The town is also a highway crossroads. U.S. 84 (Tour 7), U.S. 285 (Tour 5 and 7), and N.M. 68 all converge from the north at this point.

Travelers not crossing the Rio Grande at San Juan Pueblo will continue south on N.M. 68. At the junction with N.M. 76, 125 mi., a short detour to the left takes the visitor to the historic "city" of SANTA CRUZ, which lies just

north of N.M. 76, one-half mile east of N.M. 68. It is now a village of adobe houses around a plaza with a large, modern concrete cross in the center.

For over three hundred years Santa Cruz was on the main road between Santa Fe and Taos, but it has now been bypassed to the west by the newer highway. The village was first settled by colonists who came with Oñate in 1598 and established haciendas on the fertile lands along the Santa Cruz River. Abandoned by the Spanish at the time of the Pueblo Revolt, it was occupied by Indians from the Tano pueblos of San Cristobal and San Lazaro. They established new pueblos here and remained in possession of the area until the reconquest in April 1692, when de Vargas ordered them to leave. The first settlement had been on the south side of the Santa Cruz River, but the new village was built on the north bank, becoming, in 1695, the second official "royal villa" (Santa Fe was first, in 1610; Albuquerque third, in 1706). The 1695 resettlement, assisted by de Vargas, consisted of sixty families from Zacatecas, Mexico, who were accompanied by Antonio Moreno, a Franciscan friar. The "colonies" of Chimayo and Cordova originated from Santa Cruz.

The formal-sounding "Villa Nueva de Santa Cruz de los Españoles Mexicanos del Rey Nuestro Señor Carlos Segundo" ("new city of the Holy Cross of the Mexican Spaniards of our lord, King Charles II) actually witnessed several outrageous events and colorful characters. One such episode was the successful Chimayo Rebellion against an 1837 law of the Mexican government which, opposition leaders claimed, would tax consummation of the marriage vow. On this occasion two hundred troops led by Governor Pérez were routed by the incensed insurgents.

Following the American occupation of New Mexico, Santa Cruz was the scene of another battle, this one during the Taos Revolt of 1847. At this time an American force en route from Santa Fe to avenge the killing of Governor Bent in Taos was met by a large force of Indians and Mexican troops. The Americans, under Colonel Sterling Price, prevailed. They then proceeded to Taos to suppress the revolt.

During territorial days Santa Cruz's reputation for disorder increased. Thomas A. Janvier, writing in Santa Fe's *Partner,* said:

> Santa Cruz de la Cañada . . . was said to have took the cake for toughness before railroad times. It was a holy terror Santa Cruz was! The only decent folks in it was the French Padre—who outclassed most saints—and hadn't a fly on him—and a German named Becker.

Dominating the plaza in Santa Cruz is the Spanish Mission, a massive, cruciform church erected in 1733, one of the largest in New Mexico. The interior is a treasury of Spanish-Mexican art. The walls of the nave are adorned with Mexican pictures of Our Lady of Sorrows, St. Joseph, St. Stephen, and Our Lady of Guadalupe. On the north wall is a long niche containing figures which represent Christ in the tomb. Near it is a remarkable seventeenth-century Spanish woodcarving, a figure of St. Francis. The side of the altar is richly painted. Paneled doors lead into the chapel of St. Francis. On the north side, the chapel of Our Lady of Carmel contains a modern image of the Virgin and two paintings on metal, one of St. Anthony of Padua, the other of St. Joseph.

The church originally had a flat dirt roof, but after several disastrous rains the present hip roof was constructed. Preserved here are historical and ecclesiastical records beginning in 1695, described as the most perfect and complete in the Southwest. In 1979–80, the church was renovated with the help of parishioners and advice from an expert in Spanish colonial art.

On Santa Cruz Day, May 3, the feast of the finding of the Holy Cross, the cross in the plaza is always draped in white, and every second year *Los Moros y Christianos* is presented. This play represents the conquest of the Moors by the Christians and is enacted on horseback.

Legend explains two missing fingers on a *santo* in the Church of the Holy Cross. At one time, when the Santa Cruz River overflowed its banks and threatened the town, a finger was broken off the statue and thrown into the flood. Soon the sun shone and the water subsided. A second finger was burned during a particularly terrifying smallpox epidemic and its ashes rubbed on the foreheads of the faithful on Ash Wednesday. A statue of Our Lady of Carmel, "La Madrecita" ("little mother"), also resides here and performs acts of mercy.

From the junction with N.M. 72 at 125 mi., the tour continues south for one half mile on N.M. 68 to the busy intersection directly across the Rio Grande from Española. Here the traveler has several choices: to go west to Española and proceed northwesterly on U.S. 84 (Tour 7) towards Chama; or to follow Tour 5 north from Española on U.S. 285 via Tres Piedras and Antonito, Colorado; or to continue the present tour south towards Santa Fe via U.S. 84/U.S. 285.

The intersection with N.M. 4 West at 132 mi. marks the beginning of Tour 4 to Los Alamos, Bandelier Monument, and the Jemez Mountains.

The Santa Fe Opera, 144.6 mi., is a unique experiment and success story for John Crosby, its founder and director. Its first season (1957) included Stravinsky's *Rake's Progress*, directed by the composer himself. In the original theater, artists performed to the elements as well as to enthusiastic opera lovers; after a disastrous fire in 1967, the building was enlarged and **redesigned** as a soaring open-air amphi-

theater, with more protection for artists and patrons. Now seating 1,765, the Santa Fe Opera performs five to six operas annually from late June to mid-August, mixing familiar works with lesser-known compositions and premieres.

Among the opera's educational services are the Apprentice Artist Program (for training singers), the Student Technician Program (lighting, costuming, scenery, and so forth), and the New Mexico Opera Guild, which provides educational programs for schools and groups throughout the state.

At the top of Tesuque Divide, 146 mi., the Old Taos Highway joins U.S. 285/U.S. 84 as the tour re-enters Santa Fe.

The National Cemetery is the burial place of New Mexico soldiers who fought in every American war.

The Church of Santo Rosario is said to be a part of the chapel which de Vargas raised in his camp after the reconquest of Santa Fe in 1692. La Conquistadora, the image of the Virgin that de Vargas brought with him when he returned with Santa Fe's colonists and to which he credited his victory, is carried each year in the De Vargas Procession to this chapel before being returned to the Cathedral of St. Francis.

Old Taos Highway leads, via Federal Place and Washington Avenue, to the Plaza, 148 mi., at the end of the tour.

The traveler who wishes to avoid Santa Fe's busy downtown streets may continue along the truck bypass route, St. Francis Drive, which circles southwest of the city and meets I-25 three miles beyond it. Southwest along this route, a portion of the Pan-American Highway, are Albuquerque, Las Cruces, and El Paso (Tour 1), and Mexico City. To the northeast lie Las Vegas and Raton (Tour 1) and Denver. Other routes south from Santa Fe branch off the interstate highway: N.M. 14 to Cerrillos, Madrid, and Mountainair (Tour 15); U.S. 285 to Clines Corners and Roswell (Tour 7) and Carlsbad (Tour 16) and N.M. 41 to Moriarty and Estancia (Tour 5) and Corona (Tour 13).

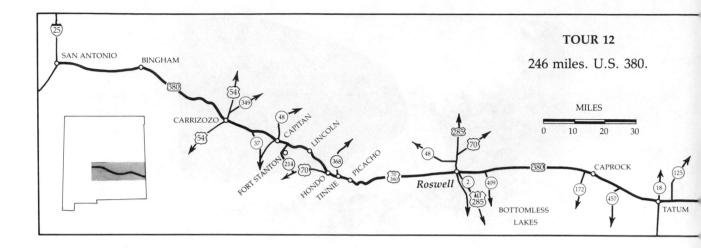

TOUR 12

246 miles. U.S. 380.

MILES

0   10   20   30

SAN ANTONIO
BINGHAM
380
54
349
CARRIZOZO
54
48
CAPITAN
37
LINCOLN
214
FORT STANTON
70
368
HONDO
TINNIE
PICACHO
70
380
Roswell
285
70
48
2
409
ALT
285
BOTTOMLESS
LAKES
380
CAPROCK
172
457
18
125
TATUM

tour twelve

Texas Border • **Tatum** • *Roswell* • **Hondo** • **Lincoln** • *Carrizozo* • *San Antonio*

U.S. 380 traverses the flat country of the Llano Estacado or Staked Plains, where cattle and sheep grazing, agriculture, and oil production are the main industries. Going down the Mescalero Ridge and across the Mescalero sands and the Pecos River valley into Roswell, the tour then continues through mountainous country and the scene of the Lincoln County War. The highway crosses the once-treacherous Malpais, travels north of the Trinity Site, and ends at San Antonio and the *bosque* (woods) of the Rio Grande.

The Staked Plains are said to have been marked by stakes driven into the ground by the local Comanches to guide the Great Chief who was to come from the East to deliver the Indians from their enemies. Others say that the name came from the stakes of yucca rising up from the flat terrain. Along the north and west rim of the plains is the caprock, with corrugate cliffs formed like an *estacada* (stockade), the most likely source of the name Llano Estacado. The desolate, dry land is also said to have been marked with stakes to guide early travelers to water sources. Sources are now marked by the giant stakes of windmills and the plains are spiked with oil derricks.

A treeless expanse of the *llano* is finally broken by the appearance of the trees and towers of TATUM, 15 mi. (alt. 3,986, pop. 897). This sleepy crossroads town has grown very slowly and rather steadily since James Tatum filed for a homestead on 320 acres here in the summer of 1909. He opened a general store and a post office within the year and hoped that cattle drivers heading north and south and travelers between Roswell and Brownfield, Texas, would be his customers while he worked at dry farming. Gradually other homesteaders joined Tatum, a school was built with funds from box suppers and socials, and a small community formed.

The oil boom of Lea County came to Tatum last, with the drilling of a sizable production well in the 1940s, but oil company offices and service operations remained in other Lea County cities. The community of Tatum continues to depend financially upon agriculture and the occasional traveler. Rodeos are a frequent entertainment, and the town enjoys two parks and a community building with a library. Silvered storage tanks of spherical, oblong, and cylindrical shapes and varied sizes emerge like mushrooms throughout the town.

Sheep, *Harvey Caplin*.

The work of a blacksmith whose silhouetted scenes adorn businesses and mailboxes adds another touch of whimsy to Tatum's appearance. In Tatum is the junction with N.M. 18, which heads north through four small communities to Portales. Southward, N.M. 18 goes past McDonald, an old farming community, and Hillburn City to Lovington.

U.S. 380 continues across the *llano*. The vast, arid flatness of the plains offered more challenge to settlers than the state's rugged mountain areas. A settlement map of the southeast corner of New Mexico would have been empty one hundred years ago. Drilling, first for water and then for oil and gas, has enabled the area's settlements to grow. A century ago, the vast herds of game animals were gone; the unpredictable rainfall made dry farming a gamble; and a large range area was needed to support each cow or sheep, necessitating an immense area for a ranch to prosper.

In the 1880s the whole of northern Lea County was the Four Lakes Ranch. The ranch had one huge cottonwood from which, in ter-ritorial days, there swung a noose for horse thieves. The ranch was split into several huge parcels at the turn of the century. At one of these, the Jones Ranch, the Debouillet sheep was developed. Several handsome ranches now spread across the area.

Sheep and cattle dot the horizon. A lone Baptist church at 38 mi. indicates the religious affiliation of most Lea County residents. Before churches were built in the county, many homesteaders used cattle watering tanks as baptismal fonts. In Caprock, 40 mi., cottonwood trees surround the isolated post office.

At about 43 mi. is a shady rest area. Paleo-Indian hunters were the first to seek bison across the *llano*. Many centuries later Kiowas, Apaches, and Comanches hunted here, leaving campsites, flint mounds, and animal traps but no signs of permanent habitation. The bison was target of their bows and arrows. Before the Spanish brought the horse to the Southwest, the Plains Indian hunter met the challenge of killing a beast that could be up to six feet tall and weigh up to twenty-five

hundred pounds. He may have disguised himself in a wolf skin in order to get within arrow-shot distance of his prey; or he may have performed antics wearing a bison skin to attract the attention of the beast, then darted behind a cliffside mound built for the purpose while his fellow hunters frightened the herd from behind. This would cause them to stampede over the Mescalero Ridge. The introduction of the horse facilitated this method of killing.

The woman's role among these Indians was to prepare meat and hides. In cold weather the meat could be frozen and stored; in warm weather it was sliced thin, smoked, and dried in the sun to make jerky, still popular in New Mexico today. Dried meat was often pounded with fat and seasoned with herbs and berries to make pemmican. The tanning of hides was a laborious process of soaking, scraping, oiling, and rubbing the skins, but the finished product was an exceptionally fine, light, soft

leather that rain would not harden. It is said that the bison supplied the bowstring with which to kill himself, the tools with which to carve himself, and the fuel, bison chips, with which to roast himself. When Anglo hunters destroyed the bison by 1880, the Indians also left the area.

A definite break in the caprock of the Staked Plains occurs at about 45 mi. Mescalero Ridge, named for the Apache hunters, is a north-to-south uplift marking the western boundary of the higher plains with the Pecos river valley below.

The sides of the highway are covered with interwoven buffalo gourd vines. Their gray-green, triangular leaves grow along stems up to twenty feet long; the giant yellow or orange blossoms of the summer give way in the fall to foul-tasting, slightly toxic fruit, resembling tennis balls. Water for the gourds is drawn up through enormous root systems, weighing as much as several hundred pounds.

At 77 mi. U.S. 380 meets N.M. 409, which goes south to BOTTOMLESS LAKES, New Mexico's first state park. Seven small lakes, bordered by high red bluffs, were formed when water dissolved gypsum and salt deposits in underlying rock formations. A network of underground cavities resulted. The roofs of some of these caverns collapsed, and the resulting sink holes filled with water. Early cowboys who tried to determine the depths of the lakes with weighted lassos found that even two ropes tied together would not come to rest; hence the name. The lakes actually range in depth from seventeen to

ninety feet. Mysterious aspects of the lakes are enlarged upon in many local stories. New Mexico's version of the Loch Ness monster is said to live here and is occasionally sighted. Underground caverns supposedly connect the lakes with Carlsbad Caverns ninety miles away. Indeed, a baby who fell into one of the lakes happily reappeared in those caverns, according to local folklore.

The true wonders of the lakes are the rare species of animals that live here. The two-inch-long Pecos pupfish and the eastern barking frog are among the endangered species. The park is home to rare

SIDE TOUR

rainwater killifish, who eat mosquito larvae, and the remarkable, tiny cricket frog, which can jump up to eighty-four times its length. Deer, skunks, snakes, and jackrabbits are plentiful, but they try to avoid meeting visitors.

The deepest of these bodies of water is

Lea Lake, where there are good facilities for fishing, picnicking, camping, scuba diving, and boating. An attractive visitors' center houses descriptions of the natural history of the area and is the center of a network of nature trails.

Just east of Roswell is the Roswell Test Facility Office of the Water Research and Technology Saline Plant. The long name denotes a processing system for experimental recycling of brackish water. Visitors are welcome at the facility and tours are available. The plant has lured many interested visitors from the Middle East to the area.

In Roswell, 87 mi. (see Tour 7), are junctions with U.S. 285 and U.S. 70. U.S. 70 runs westward together with U.S. 380 between this point and Hondo, where 380 branches to the north. The section between Roswell and Hondo is described in Tour 10.

HONDO, 134 mi., sits at the junction of two rivers, the Rio Ruidoso ("noisy") and the Rio Bonito ("pretty") which, after uniting here, flow east to the Pecos as the Rio Hondo ("deep"). This tour follows the northern tributary, the Rio Bonito, northwest up towards its headwaters high in the Sierra Blanca range. For the first twenty-five miles, U.S. 380 sticks faithfully to the narrow, fertile valleys of rivers that in other parts of the country would probably be called mountain streams.

Like other valleys in the south-central mountains, the Bonito valley has supported a settled way of life, with orchards, pastures, and corn and bean fields, since the middle of the nineteenth century. Large fruitpacking sheds and beautiful horse ranches are still the basis for the town of Hondo's prosperity. (See also Tour 10.)

LINCOLN, 144 mi. (alt. 5,600, pop. 0,000),

was first settled in 1849 by Hispanic villagers from the east side of the Manzano Mountains. Until the creation of Lincoln County in 1869 and its designation as county seat, the new village was called Las Placitas ("little settlements") del Rio Bonito. The establishment of nearby Fort Stanton in 1855 encouraged more settlers to come during the 1850s and 1860s. A chapel dedicated to San Juan became the center of an area of small farms up and down the river, with sheep raised in the adjacent mountains.

The arrival of ranchers and their cattle from the Texas plains challenged this kind of life in the early 1870s. The newcomers, mainly English-speaking and Protestant, certainly differed from their predominantly Spanish-speaking, Catholic neighbors. More important than ethnic distinctions, however, was a conflict that has taken many forms throughout New Mexico: that between tractable farmers on the one hand and ranchers, whose sense of duty rarely extended beyond the cattle under their care, on the other. To the Hispanic settlers, the code by which these newcomers lived must have seemed lawless and dangerous. They laughed at hardship, scorned civil order, and considered killing a man (under "proper" circumstances) far less serious than other moral offenses. It can be argued that such a code, ideally, could work as well as many others. What often resulted, however, was bloodshed.

In December 1873 a group of cowboys attended a traditional dance in Lincoln. A commotion arose and the Harrell brothers, whose record of felonies could be traced across central and West Texas, killed four Hispanic men. This incident was a forewarning of events to come. The Lincoln County War held sway over this town during the years 1878–81 and has dominated popular accounts of its history ever since.

Unfortunately, the Lincoln County War was not the bloodiest squabble of this kind in New Mexico's history. In this area of the state alone, two "wars"—a cattle war centering around La Luz between the Good and Lee factions in the 1880s, and a political war in Las Cruces during the late 1890s—each probably cost more lives than the war in Lincoln. The Lincoln County War is remembered and its episodes celebrated in song and story chiefly because of the involvement of Billy the Kid.

This was not a cattle war. Of the principals, only John Chisum was a Texas cattleman, and he was not an active participant. It could be better characterized as businessmen's war, but the general willingness to resort to any available firearms made it seem like a typical cowboy-movie brawl. The Lincoln County War began over rivalry between the mercantile stores of John Tunstall and L. G. Murphy. These two vied for contracts with the army and also with the Mescaleros and for one another's customers. In 1877 Murphy hired Alexander McSween to collect the $10,000 insurance money he claimed Tunstall owed him. McSween and Murphy fell out, and McSween became Tunstall's partner, and was accused by his former employer of stealing the $10,000. Murphy, who was friendly with county political leaders, had a warrant issued for Tunstall's arrest. While riding from his ranch into Lincoln to submit peaceably to the authorities, Tunstall was taken by surprise, shot, and killed on February 18, 1878.

Some of Tunstall's cowboys witnessed their boss's death, among them William Bonney, alias Billy the Kid. Bonney swore revenge for Tunstall's death and declared his intention of

killing all the men associated with the murder. Ambushes and counterattacks soon became part of the life of the area. All the citizenry began to take sides in the conflict, willingly or reluctantly. Juan Patrón, the owner of a third smaller store, tried to remain neutral and make peace, but in the end he felt compelled to side with Murphy. This is the way things stood in Lincoln by July of 1878: Murphy and his partner James Dolan, both former Union soldiers, had become the principals of one faction; McSween and John Chisum led the other. The Murphy-Dolan group had the backing of the sheriff's department and the corrupt "Santa Fe Ring," which included many state officials. Sheriff Pat Brady and Deputy Hindman had been killed in front of the Wortley Hotel by Billy the Kid's gang on April 1. Later that month, a bloody battle had been fought at Blazer's Mill, now in Otero County. The entire town was tense and divided.

Many of the buildings in Lincoln that were involved in a five day shoot-out that occurred July 15–19, 1878, are still standing. On the last day the McSween house and headquarters were burned, and McSween himself was added to the list of casualties, shot while apparently trying to surrender. Most of his faction escaped and dispersed. General Lew Wallace became governor of the territory in August and proclaimed amnesty "to all who had taken part in the war, except those under indictment for crime, on the understanding that they would lay down their arms." A unit of black troops patrolled Lincoln town. The Lincoln County War was over, but Bonney and seven others refused to quit. They set up a reign of terror in the surrounding countryside.

Numerous unsuccessful attempts were made to trap Billy's gang and force their surrender. In October 1880 Pat Garrett became sheriff of Lincoln County. Garrett captured Billy at Tivan Arroyo, near Fort Sumner, on December 21 of that year. Bonney was jailed in Santa Fe, then moved to La Mesilla to be tried. In March 1881 he was convicted of Pat Brady's murder and sentenced to be hanged

Torreon at Lincoln, *Harvey Caplin.*

in Lincoln on May 13, but in late April he escaped from the Lincoln County jail. At Pete Maxwell's house near Fort Sumner, a bullet from Pat Garrett's gun ended Billy the Kid's short career on July 15, 1881. Legends claim that Bonney killed a man for every year of his life, but since both his birthdate and the number of men he actually killed are unclear, this is impossible to corroborate.

Lincoln celebrates Billy the Kid's jail break during an annual pageant held on the first weekend of August. The parade, fiddlers' contest, arts and crafts fair, and forty-two-mile

pony express race from White Oaks to Lincoln attract thousands of visitors each year. Many of the buildings from the 1880s have been restored and are open to the public. The Murphy store, converted in 1880 to the courthouse and jail from which Billy escaped, is now a museum. The Tunstall store, at the east end of town, also survives, and contains many original stock items from the nineteenth century. The Wortley Hotel, across from the old courthouse, burned in the 1930s but was faithfully restored in 1960. It is now open as an inn, furnished in the style of the late 1880s.

Ironically, Lincoln today owes much of its charm and prosperity to the young desperado from New York City, William Bonney. Daring, humorous, likeable, moody, cruel, he symbolized for some the spirit of the Southwest frontier. By the time of his death in 1881, however, most of the inhabitants of Lincoln and surrounding counties, whatever their sympathies in the war, had had enough of Billy the Kid's killing. Curiously, he then became a hero to people outside New Mexico and was the subject of legends, ballads, books, and a ballet. This process of glamorization finally returned to New Mexico in the mid-twentieth century, and several places, notably Lincoln, Mesilla, and Fort Sumner, began to play up their roles in the life of Billy the Kid.

At 152 mi., N.M. 214 leads to FORT STANTON, located 2.5 miles south of U.S. 380 on the banks of the Rio Bonito. It was established in 1855 to encourage settlement in this part of New Mexico. The Mescaleros, who signed a treaty with the U.S. government in 1852, were quartered here for a short time, but they soon set out on their own and eventually were resettled, in 1873, on their present reservation thirty miles to the southwest. The fort was deserted and burned by Union forces in 1861 upon the advance of General Sibley's Texas troops; volunteers under Kit Carson reoccupied the post in 1863. Fort Stanton was rebuilt in 1868 and for thirty years served as both a military post and a social and economic center of the region.

Originally planned to lie halfway between Fort Union (Las Vegas) and Fort Bliss (El Paso), Fort Stanton was built in a high valley of the Bonito surrounded by the Capitan Mountains and the Sierra Blanca and watered by numerous mountain streams. Plentiful wild game, good water, and pasture made it a natural stoppng place. In 1857 the fort became the first, and for many years and many miles around the only, post office in south central New Mexico. At various times this post office served the communities of Lincoln (Las Placitas), Ruidoso, White Oaks, Roswell (Seven Rivers), Capitan, Nogal, and Peñasco. Wagon roads and later stage coach routes connected Fort Stanton to the towns of Roswell, San Antonio (situated on the Rio Grande to the west), Santa Fe (to the north), and Mesilla (near present-day Las Cruces).

By 1898 the Army no longer needed the military post, and Fort Stanton became a U.S. Marine Hospital for tubercular patients. It later served as a public health hospital, a state hospital for the tubercular and, after 1966, a school for the mentally retarded.

CAPITAN ("captain"), 157 mi. (alt. 6,600, pop. 769), takes its name from El Capitan Peak (10,083 feet) near Arabela and the mountain range that U.S. 380 has paralleled since leaving Lincoln. The Capitan Mountains are among the few ranges in the country that extend east and west rather than north and south; they are also one of the few without a major stream.

In 1884 Seaborn T. Gray homesteaded here on Salado Flat. The town and post office that grew out of this settlement was called Gray until 1900. During the same period the El Paso and Northeastern Railroad, pushing northward from Carrizozo, built a coal line up to the nearby Phelps-Dodge coal mines in 1899. "Coalora" was the name of the mining town there, one mile northwest of Capitan. By 1905 these mines had played out, many buildings were moved to Dawson, and Coalora was abandoned. Capitan got its name in 1900, and has survived to the present as a small mountain crossroads. N.M. 48, unpaved, curves north and east around the Capitan Mountains. It once connected the towns of Encinoso, Richardson, Spindle, and Arabela with the outside world; it now serves ranches and recreation areas. N.M. 48 also heads southwest from Capitan as a paved road towards the fishing, hunting, and resort areas of Angus, Alto, Nogal, and Ruidoso.

A day in May 1950 had important effects on Capitan's recent past. It was then, after a five-day fire that burned seventeen thousand acres in the Capitan Mountains, that firefighters found a small bear cub and nicknamed him Hot Foot Teddy. The bear, renamed Smokey,

was flown to Santa Fe for medical care and later to Washington, D.C. He soon became the most famous bear in the country, as a survivor of a devastating fire that had been started by a careless person and as a symbol of the nation's concern over the protection of our forests. The town of Capitan built the Smokey Bear Motel and Cafe, and, without any federal or state assistance, constructed a log museum to tell the story of the cub's beginnings. At about the time that a state park was created in 1976, including the museum, a picnic spot, and a playground, the original Smokey died at the National Zoo in Washington. He was buried at the new Smokey the Bear Historical State Park. A second bear, Smokey Junior, then assumed the role of representing fire prevention to the country.

After crossing Indian Divide at 164 mi., U.S. 380 begins to descend into the Tularosa basin. From points along the road, one can look across the lava flow, the Oscura ("dark") Mountains, and the Jornada del Muerto to the mountains that line the eastern bank of the Rio Grande. Closer at hand, the old railway cuts are occasionally visible. At 169 mi., N.M. 37 doubles back (southeast) to Nogal and Nogal Lake. Here the road descends between Nogal Peak, to the south, and Vera Cruz Mountain, immediately on the north. Beyond this mountain lies White Oaks, at one time an important small city and gold mining center. U.S. 380 intersects U.S. 54 on the northern edge of Carrizozo, at 177 mi. (See Tour 13 for Carrizozo and White Oaks.)

A few miles west of Carrizozo black volcanic rock becomes visible and the road crosses what is believed to be the youngest lava flow in the continental United States. Some fifteen hundred to two thousand years ago, at a time when our ancestors were well-established here, lava pouring from Little Black Peak, to the north, created a "valley" forty-four miles long, up to five miles wide, and seventy feet deep. At 184 mi. a turnoff leads a short distance to the Valley of Fires State Park. A *malpaís* ("badlands") is unsuitable for plant, animal, or human habitation. The state park is located on the fringe of the black rock, and the Malpais Nature Trail indicates numerous varieties of plant life that grow here on soil blown onto the lava. The trail also explains the pecularities of the rock itself, including "collapse pits," bubbles in the hot magma whose tops caved in upon cooling.

The sharp descent of U.S. 380 begins at 200 mi. and crawls down the wall of Chupadera Mesa. The road then bounds across the foothills of the Oscura Mountains; a sign points out North Oscura Peak on the left at 204 mi. These mountains were profitably mined for copper at the turn of the century; coal had been discovered on their western slopes before the Civil War. In 1881 the Santa Fe Railroad built a line out to the Carthage coal fields from San Antonio, but these rails were torn up. Later the New Mexico Midlands Railroad built another line on the same roadbed. The town of BINGHAM, 213 mi., now consisting of a few old buildings and a rock shop, grew up to provide services for the Carthage mines.

For twenty-five miles between Bingham and the Rio Grande, U.S. 380 crosses the northern edge of the infamous Jornada del Muerto ("journey of the dead man"), a mostly flat, dry, treeless intermountain plain. It was used by early travelers between Mexico City and Santa Fe to cut several days off their trip, bypassing the uninhabited bend of the Rio Grande from the Las Cruces region to Fra Cristobal (now under the water of Elephant Butte Lake). Stories of thirsty marches, Apache attacks, and dead men's bones are

San Antonio, *Toby Smith*.

part of New Mexico folklore. Despite the fact that several towns and large ranches have prospered on the Jornada, its reputation for sinister barrenness was enhanced when the first atomic bomb was exploded south of the White Sands Missile Range in 1945. The entire plain became part of the White Sands Missile Range in 1948. A section of this military reservation, the Stallion Range Center, lies south of the marked highway turnoff at 230 mi.

Tokay Mine, another extensive coal deposit, once straddled the New Mexico Midlands Railroad, two miles south of U.S. 380, at 235 mi. The coal from the Carthage and Tokay mines fueled the growth of San Antonio during the late 1800s. One San Antonio resident who did well during this period was Gus Hilton, father of the more famous Conrad. Gus established a stagecoach line to White Oaks (approximately the route of the present highway) and, in dealings with miners and trappers in this area, became the "merchant king of San Antonio."

A Piro village existed on or near the spot later occupied by the town of San Pedro, 240 mi., on the east bank of the Rio Grande. The Piros were a Tanoan-speaking Pueblo group who built small and medium-sized towns in the valleys of the Rio Grande and its tributaries between present-day Belen and Truth or Consequences. They abandoned the entire area due to Apache raids in the mid-1600s and the upheaval in 1680.

SAN PEDRO became a farming community during the resettlement period in this area during the 1830s. It was known for wine grapes and contributed a large share of the 250 barrels of native wine shipped yearly out of San Antonio at the turn of the century. Eutemio Montoya of San Antonio operated a coal mine here, from which he and San Pedro prospered for a while in the 1880s.

Tour 12 ends at the intersection with I-25, two miles west of San Antonio, 242 mi. (See Tour 1.)

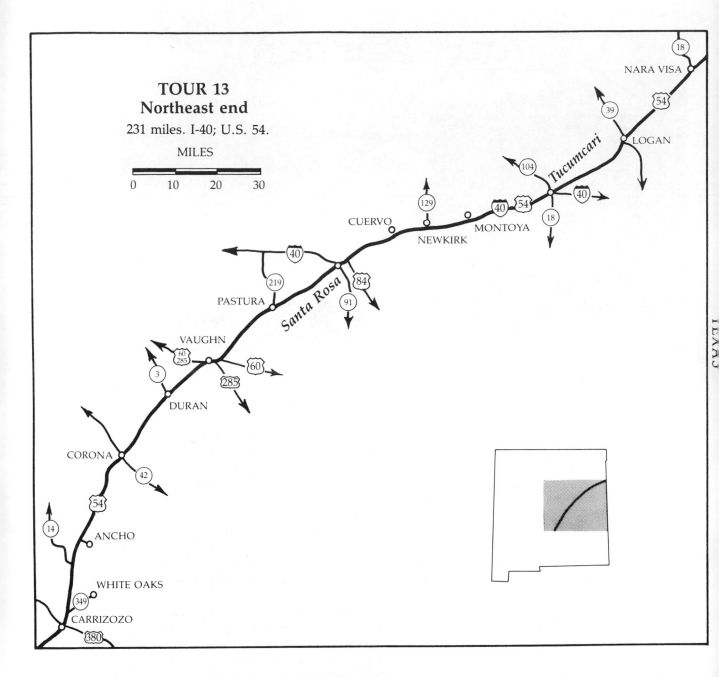

TOUR 13
Northeast end
231 miles. I-40; U.S. 54.

MILES

0   10   20   30

NARA VISA

LOGAN

Tucumcari

MONTOYA

CUERVO

NEWKIRK

PASTURA

Santa Rosa

VAUGHN

DURAN

CORONA

ANCHO

WHITE OAKS

CARRIZOZO

TEXAS

See page 542 for southwestern end of tour thirteen.

tour thirteen

Texas Border • **Nara Visa** • *Tucumcari* • *Santa Rosa* • **Vaughn** • **Carrizozo** •
Tularosa • **Alamogordo** • *El Paso, Texas*

The Santa Fe Railroad gained its right of way over Raton Pass in 1878, and by 1881 had completed a somewhat roundabout and mountainous route (via Las Vegas, Albuquerque, and Deming) across New Mexico on its way to Los Angeles. Within a few years the Chicago, Rock Island, and Pacific Railroad (the "Rock Island"), working across southern Kansas and heading for the same destination, had its eye on a more direct path across New Mexico: The Rock Island route would connect with the Southern Pacific tracks at El Paso, Texas. In 1899 entrepreneurs began building northward from El Paso, while the Rock Island pushed southwest from Liberal, Kansas. The two lines met in Santa Rosa in 1902. The railroad bypassed the existing towns of Puerto de Luna and Tularosa which lay in its path, preferring instead to create its own cities. Tucumcari, Santa Rosa, Alamogordo, and numerous towns in between are direct beneficiaries of railroad building and maintenance.

U.S. 54 links Chicago with El Paso, crossing Illinois, Missouri, Kansas, the panhandles of Oklahoma and Texas, and New Mexico, following the just-mentioned rail connection over the western two-thirds of its length. Tour 13 covers this route through the state, from Nara Visa to Newman. It enters New Mexico on the high plains, crosses the Canadian and Pecos rivers, then climbs to travel the entire 150-mile length of a large intermountain basin, the Tularosa Valley.

Narvaez, a sheepherder, lived near the Texas line here in the late 1880s and left his name, changed to Nara Visa, on a nearby creek. The town of NARA VISA, 4 mi., grew with the Rock Island's arrival in 1902. New Mexico's extreme eastern highway, N.M. 18, turns north from this point to Clayton and the Colorado state line. To travelers coming from the Oklahoma and Texas panhandles the land hereabout might appear unproductive and underused. The fact is that in the long run New Mexico probably manages its land better, due to its stringent water laws, which tend to limit irrigation and plowing on land such as this that is better suited for grazing.

The Sangre de Cristo Mountains spawn two great rivers, the Cimarron and the Canadian, which head eastward across the plains and together water most of the state of Oklahoma. Just southwest of LOGAN, 29 mi., the highway

Catholic church, Nara Visa, *Toby Smith*.

bridges a shallow gorge of the Canadian. Even when practically dry, rivers such as this remind one, with their rocks, mud, trees, undergrowth, and trickles of water, that they are the source of life for the plains. A few miles upriver from here on N.M. 552, 31 mi., Ute Dam and Ute Lake State Park provide fishing, sailing, and water skiing. N.M. 39 follows Ute Creek up toward the Harding County towns of Mosquero and Roy and the western section of the Kiowa National Grasslands.

SIDE TOUR

Harding County, the least populous county in the state and one of only two not served by the U.S. highway system, began officially on March 4, 1921, the day President Harding was inaugurated. Both Roy and Mosquero, the only settlements that have survived to the present, owe their early growth to the 146-mile Dawson Railway, built in 1906 from Tucumcari to the Dawson coal fields west of Raton by the Southern Pacific Railroad. New settlers dry farmed here successfully until the 1940s. Roy and Mosquero ("swarm of flies"), as well as the older town of Bueyeros ("oxdrivers"), also prospered from the production of dry ice in the 1920s and 1930s since the area overlies the Bravo Dome carbon dioxide gas field. The field is now being mined again around Clayton for use in the tertiary recovery of petro-

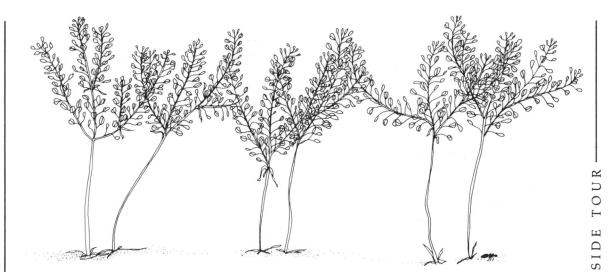

leum; see Tour 2. The county now depends entirely on livestock raising.

A converted schoolhouse serves as the Harding County courthouse in Mosquero (pop. 196). Roy (pop. 383) was established by Frank and William Roy in 1901 and later moved over to the new Dawson tracks. A fire destroyed many of its buildings in 1916. Travelers on N.M. 39 will also pass near Chicosa Lake State Park (camping and picnicking) north of Roy and Mills Canyon on the Canadian River, headquarters of Melvin Mills's political, cattle, and fruit- and vegetable-growing empire at the turn of the century.

Returning to the main tour, Tucumcari Mountain, standing nine hundred feet above the plain, is visible from afar, lending credence to the name's probable derivation from the Comanche word meaning "signal peak." U.S. 54 joins with U.S. 66 and I-40 (and Tour 6) between Tucumcari, 53 mi., and Santa Rosa, 110 mi. Travelers on U.S. 54 get off the interstate in Santa Rosa and, after crossing the Pecos River on the west side of town, turn south toward Vaughn.

The tour climbs again to the plains, pastureland for cattle and sheep as it has been since the bison disappeared. PASTURA ("hay"), 132 mi., once supported the Pastura Trading Company, an outlet of the Charles Ilfeld Company, which dealt in sheep, cattle, and wholesale and retail goods in mercantile stores throughout the state. In addition Pastura served as the railroad station for the large Ilfeld holdings at Pintada Ranch, northwest on Pintada Arroyo. Because of a lack of water fit for use in its locomotives' boilers, the Southern Pacific Railroad piped water to Pastura and intermediate watering stations at twenty-mile intervals all the way from Bonito Lake, 125 miles to the southwest.

At 151 mi., VAUGHN (alt. 5,965, pop. 1,060) is the intersection of the central plains. Seven hundred ten miles to the east and 5,200 feet lower down, along routes that parallel the old Santa Fe Trail, lies Kansas City. Following the Pecos River and then the Rio Grande downstream a distance of nine hundred miles and dropping almost six thousand feet, one reaches the Gulf of Mexico. A Merchant's Wagon Trail once connected Las Vegas and El Paso, passing through what is now Vaughn. Other ancient routes, of course, connected El Paso with Mexico City. Vaughn remains on a direct rail and highway link with Mexico City, a distance of 1,455 miles. Tour 8 describes U.S. 60, Vaughn's main east-west artery, and Tour 7 provides information on places to the northwest and the southeast along U.S. 285.

In the early 1900s, as now, this area was the center of good grazing land and extensive sheep and cattle ranching. Within the space of five years, the building of two transcontinental railroads created the town of Vaughn. The El Paso and Rock Island Line came first in 1902 from the south, joining El Paso with Kansas City. Epris (derived from EP–RIS) was the name given to the construction center and saloon town that was at that time a few miles west of the present town. Then in 1907 the Belen Cutoff of the Santa Fe Railroad (Belen to Amarillo) crossed the El Paso and Rock Island, and the town of Vaughn was founded, named for Major G. W. Vaughn, a civil engineer for the Santa Fe.

Although most of the Santa Fe repair shops are gone, the tracks still dominate Vaughn, which stretches along them for a mile. Sheltered residential streets lie south of the highway. Tourist accommodations, the school, and livestock shipping on the railroad provide livelihoods now for Vaughn residents. Travelers with children may appreciate the good-sized park with playground equipment at the western edge of town.

U.S. 54 runs mostly east and west between Chicago and El Paso. After Vaughn, however, it heads nearly straight south to the international border and becomes an extension of Federal 45 in Mexico. Together the two roads connect central Mexico with the central United States. In this century, people from the Midwest and South, heading originally for California, often stayed in New Mexico. Meanwhile railroad workers and others were coming into the United States from Mexico and settling here, too. The two groups mingled with each other and with the older inhabitants of the area, learning something of one another's ways.

When it was first laid out in the 1920s, U.S. 54 followed what were by then the Southern Pacific tracks almost curve for curve. Pavement along most of this stretch was not completed until the mid-1950s.

Around mile 160 there are signs that the tour is leaving the high plains and entering the transition to mountain vegetation. Hardy varieties of three common trees, pine, juniper, and oak, characterize this zone, which hereabout extends roughly from elevations of six thousand to seventy-five hundred feet. The piñon represents the pine family and is valued for its edible nuts and firewood. Junipers (better known as cedars) which begin as small, scattered bushes, are excellent firewood and unsurpassed as fence posts. The brighter green of scrub oaks, and in the fall their golden brown, distinguishes the lesser relatives of the mighty oak.

DURAN, 166 mi. (alt. 6,000, pop. 100), dates from 1901, when scores of workers were employed at the railroad repair shops located here. The roundhouse is gone, but several large buildings remain. These houses, built like the Biblical house "upon stone foundations," have not fallen but now are mostly vacant. Duran was a ranching center, but larger and fewer ranches and less employment on the ones that remain account for the decline in its population. The San Juan Bautista Church, dated 1916, remains open. N.M. 3 leads northwesterly to Encino on U.S. 60. The small mountain to the west is called Duran Mesa.

At 177 mi., Camaleon ("horned toad") Mountain rises like an island in the ocean of the plain. Early Pueblo people chose it as a townsite, but it was abandoned soon after the Spanish arrived.

The town of Torrance once thrived one-half mile west of the highway, 180 mi. Torrance was the terminus of Francis J. Torrance's New Mexico Central Railroad, which Tour 5 follows south from Santa Fe. Beans and cattle provided livelihoods for some time for fifteen hundred residents. The old hotel remains, now a private residence. The first U.S. mail contract for rural delivery by automobile in the nation was a daily route from Torrance to Roswell.

The elevation of 6,724 feet at CORONA ("summit"), 186 mi. (pop. 238), is given by the Southern Pacific Railroad as the highest point on its line and on the rail link between Chi-

cago and Los Angeles. Corona is a survivor. It lies near the southeast corner of an area that extends west to Claunch and Gran Quivira and northwest along the New Mexico Central and the Juames Mesa to U.S. 60, where the Estancia Valley proper begins. From the coming of the railroad until the Second World War, this area was settled as thickly as the Midwestern plains. Dozens of communities, most with their own schools and post offices, prospered here on the dry farming of pinto beans and corn, cattle and sheep raising, and dairying. Corona itself annually shipped out hundreds of carloads of cattle and sheep, scores of carloads of beans, up to ten carloads of wool, and as much as five thousand gallons of cream. Bean shellers, treating one hundred pounds a minute, ran sixteen hours a day during the August/September harvest in Corona, Torrance, Claunch, Cedarvale, and Mountainair.

Contrary to what one might expect, the complete abandonment of agriculture in this region cannot be explained by a lack of rainfall. Average annual precipitation now is substantially the same as it was during the decades of successful farming (1900–1940). What caused families to get out of farming were the two- and three-year droughts, when there was nothing to fall back on, and the dislocation caused by the military draft and the search for war-related jobs during the Second

World War. After the war, people who knew the ups and downs of farming a marginal area such as this would not or could not reinvest in land and equipment to start over again.

The end of farming is also associated in the minds of early Corona settlers with a climatic change in this region. Ponderosa pines once grew on nearby slopes, and snow sometimes lay all winter. The fact is that logging, dry farming, and overgrazing, three pursuits that contributed to early prosperity, also resulted in exposing the land and increasing wind erosion, soil temperature, and evaporation. This means that the rain that falls now probably doesn't do as much good as before, which may account for the difficulty that some of the original plant growth (large trees and native prairie grass) has in re-establishing itself. The soil is still good, but it is best suited for grazing. In order for the land to regain its former productivity, however, ranchers need to adopt methods that take better account of the interaction of high quality grasses and the herd animals that graze them.

Corona was originally built on the east side of the railroad tracks. When U.S. 54 was laid out in the early 1920s, the main street was moved across the tracks and the commercial structures built where they now stand. However, a fire destroyed much of this downtown in 1928, and most of the stone and brick buildings visible now have been constructed since

then. The town now depends for its survival on a trade area and school district as large as a small state but consisting of scattered ranches measured in dozens of sections.

Approaching Corona, the N.M. 42 junction marks the end of Tour 5 from Tres Piedras, Santa Fe and Estancia. Near the southern edge of town, N.M. 42 leads east to U.S. 285, sixty miles north of Roswell. Near the intersection here, a good-sized natural lake provided early Corona residents with fishing, boating, and swimming.

The site of Greathouse Tavern is three and one-half miles up Red Cloud Canyon from the Red Cloud Campground turnoff, 192 mi. During the 1870s, the Greathouse Ranch served as a stagecoach stop between Pinos Wells and White Oaks. Here, in 1880, Billy the Kid hid out, pursued by Jim Carlyle, deputy of Sheriff Pat Garrett. Following an attempt at negotiation, Carlyle was killed. Another posse soon returned from White Oaks and burned Jim Greathouse's place to the ground, but Billy the Kid (and Greathouse) escaped. Shortly thereafter the village of Red Cloud was established nearby. Both early pit house dwellers and later Pueblo people have left abundant evidence of their presence in the Gallinas Mountains area. Local residents have long known about two especially extensive sites, Pueblo Bonito and Pueblo Colorado, now protected by the state but not yet excavated or open to the public.

After crossing the foothills of the Gallinas Mountains at Corona, U.S. 54 has become an intermountain road. For the two hundred miles south to El Paso, the front range—the Jicarilla, Capitan, White, and Sacramento mountains—forms the eastern side of the corridor. To the west stand the Oscura, San Andres, Organ, and Franklin ranges. This "valley," narrow and indistinct here, widens at Ancho, becomes a "plain" at Carrizozo, and from near Tularosa south emerges as a great continental basin.

At 196 mi., the road drops and winds through Tecolote ("owl") Canyon, opposite Tecolote Peak just east.

ANCHO ("broad" or "wide") turnoff at 210 mi., was left two miles off the highway when U.S. 54 was paved and rerouted in 1955. The railroad created this town in 1899, but considerable mining in the nearby Jicarilla Mountains had already been going on for some time. A huge brick factory here made the cream-colored bricks that built many houses and stores throughout central New Mexico. In fact, after the San Francisco earthquake and fire in April 1906, trainloads of Ancho bricks traveled the 1,460 miles to reconstruct that city. "My House of Old Things" is an excellent private museum that completely fills the old railroad station with tools, photographs, furnished rooms, clothing, and other artifacts of the past century.

N.M. 14, 212 mi., unpaved, parallels the Chupadera Mesa northwest to Claunch and Gran Quivira on Tour 15.

The Malpais lava flow is visible from points along the road for more than forty miles, beginning about mile 220. Little Black Peak, which erupted some fifteen hundred to two thousand years ago, forming the youngest lava flow in the continental U.S., lies directly to the west.

White Oaks, *Harvey Caplin.*

At 229 mi., N.M. 349 leads to the newly rediscovered ghost town of WHITE OAKS. Gold finds near the springs between the Patos ("ducks") and Carrizo ("reed") mountains in 1879 caused the rapid growth of the city of over twenty-five hundred inhabitants. White Oaks was a stop on the stage line from San Antonio (on the Rio Grande) to Roswell, as well as on the Las Vegas stage road to old Mesilla and El Paso. Partly because coal was also found here, railroad builders planned to continue the main line from Carrizozo north via White Oaks in 1898. Land prices in White Oaks, it is claimed, forced them to reconsider and instead run the line via Corona, where more mountain construction would be required. It is an open question whether White Oaks would have survived had it been on the railroad. In any case, before the town disappeared in the 1950s it served as trading center, school, and post office for such mountain and farming communities as Raventon, Texas Park, Vera Cruz, Encinoso, and Jicarilla.

Numerous buildings dating from 1890s still are standing or are being renovated. Former residents include governors, congressmen, cattle queens and barons, and Lincoln County War refugees. Annually in early August a "pony express" horse race runs the forty-one miles from White Oaks to Lincoln, the old county seat. Emerson Hough, a reporter for a Lincoln paper, set his novel *Heart's Desire* (1903) in the high time of White Oaks.

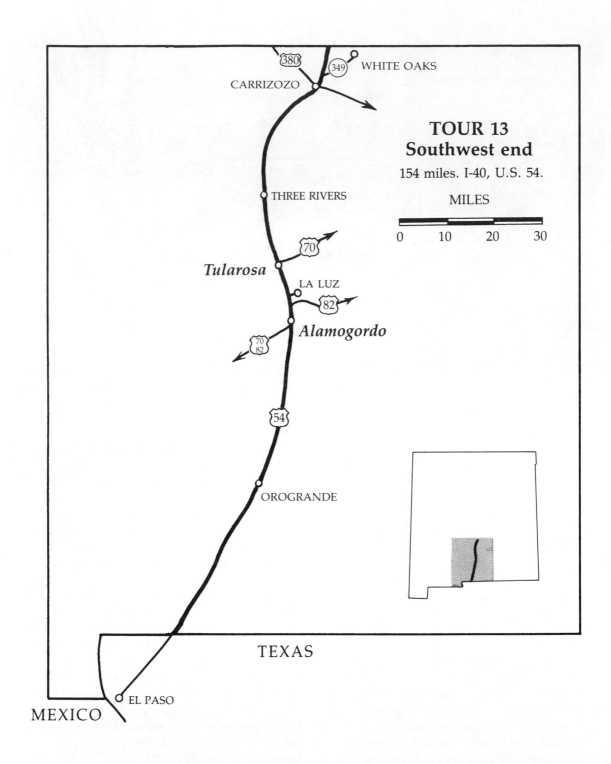

TOUR 13
Southwest end
154 miles. I-40, U.S. 54.

MILES

0   10   20   30

WHITE OAKS

CARRIZOZO

THREE RIVERS

Tularosa

LA LUZ

Alamogordo

OROGRANDE

TEXAS

EL PASO

MEXICO

The intersection of U.S. 54 and U.S. 380 is on the north edge of Carrizozo, 232 mi. U.S. 380 goes east to Capitan and Lincoln and connects with paved roads to Nogal, Bonito Lake, and Ruidoso. Five miles west on the route is the Valley of Fire State Park, on the bank of the Malpais. (See Tour 12.)

CARRIZOZO (alt. 5,429, pop. 1,217) is named for the carrizo grass or reed, excellent livestock feed that is native to the plain and foothills here. The town owes its existence to the fact that the railroad bypassed White Oaks and instead created a division point at Carrizozo. The roundhouse and repair shops soon led to the development of a sizable city, the supply center and shipping point to a large area and seat of Lincoln County. Carrizozo had its peak population of over two thousand in the decade 1910–20.

A railroad strike in 1923 had serious effects on the economy of the area. Advances in railroad technology, especially the advent of diesel locomotives in the 1940s, also reduced employment since less maintenance of track and rolling stock was required. Today, Carrizozo contains county offices, a clinic, a library, several parks, and an inviting soda fountain and ice cream store, restored to its original 1920s appearance.

OSCURO ("dark"), 248 mi., first established as a pumping station on the Southern Pacific, was settled soon thereafter by a group of Chicagoans. Forty-five miles west of here, across the Oscura range, the first atomic bomb was exploded on July 16, 1945. This event, which changed the course of history, also signaled that this remote valley would never be the same again. The White Sands Missile Range was created that same year, and, together with Fort Bliss Military Reservation and the McGregor Range, now occupies most of the land between U.S. 380 and El Paso and between the Sacramento Mountains and the Rio Grande. A tour of the Trinity Site, the spot at which the blast occurred, is conducted annually by the Army. (See Alamogordo, below.)

THREE RIVERS, 259 mi., was the rail station for the Three Rivers Ranch, established in the

1870s by Patrick Coghlan, "king of Tularosa." Among other profitable ventures here, Coghlan fenced cattle stolen by William Bonney, alias Billy the Kid. After the killing of William McSween during the Lincoln County War, his widow, Susan McSween Barber, acquired part of the valley above Coghlan and became known as "the cattle queen of New Mexico." By 1915 Senator Albert B. Fall had bought out both Pat Coghlan and Susan Barber. Its name now translated as Tres Ritos, the ranch became a desert paradise under Emma Fall's horticultural care. The Falls enlarged Coghlan's mansion, and this was the scene, in 1921, of the discussions that created the Teapot Dome Scandal. Whether Fall was guilty of accepting a bribe from his business associates Doheny and Sinclair in return for granting them oil drilling contracts in the Elk Hills Reserve in Wyoming, or whether he was a scapegoat who paid for the low public morality of the times, is a still-debated issue. Fall, broken and ailing, spent six months in prison in 1931.

Thomas Fortune Ryan was the next to be captivated by Three Rivers. He acquired the ranch in 1941, tore down all of the Falls's mansion except the library, and built a Span-

Petroglyphs, Three Rivers, *Patrick Lauth.*

ish-style house surrounded by poplar and cottonwood trees. Despites its magnificent setting—the broad Tularosa Valley below, clear creek water underfoot, and Old Baldy towering over all—an aura of sinister mystery hangs over this "magic valley." Murders, suicides, unexplained corpses, hair-raising tales, and ruined millionaires have been a part of the ranch from the 1870s to the present.

The traveler proceeding east up the Forest Road from Three Rivers will see Ryan's house at three mi., Susan McSween Barber's "rock house" at 8 mi. Near the eastern limits of the ranch are Ryan's hunting lodge, built for survivors of the Bataan March, and the Shanta Indian Community of the Mescaleros. At 15 mi. the White Mountain Wilderness begins.

The Department of the Interior recently has opened the Three Rivers Petroglyph Site, five miles up the valley from U.S. 54. Here, on a ridge between the mountains and the Tularosa Basin, a mile-long marked trail winds among the over five hundred beautiful and intricate rock pictures, some one thousand years old. Partially reconstructed pueblo and pithouse-style dwellings dating from A.D. 1000 to 1350 also are visible along the trail. The petroglyph site has picnicking and camping facilities.

The Tularosa Basin proper opens south of Three Rivers. It is one hundred miles long, lying between two huge mountain ranges, the San Andres on the west and the Sacramentos on the east. By now the vegetation is characteristic of the Chihuahuan desert: creosote

bush, large yuccas, and flowering sotol mix with prickly pear, smaller cacti, frail tentacles of ocotillo, and precious native grass. This is the home country of Eugene Manlove Rhodes, author of several novels and numerous short stories set in central and southern New Mexico.

Four facts help clarify the early history of TULAROSA, 277 mi. (alt. 4,500, pop. 2,521): (1) The U.S. Government, after a period of armed conflict with the Mescalero Apaches, established a military post at Fort Stanton, in the mountains to the east, in 1855. (2) In late March 1862, Texas volunteers under General Sibley, recently victorious at Valverde, were defeated near Glorieta Pass by a combination of U.S. Army regulars and mostly Spanish-speaking New Mexico militia units. (3) During the summer of 1862, the lower Rio Grande flooded, destroying many homes and villages on its banks. (4) Toward the end of the Civil War, Lincoln's blockade of the South was becoming effective enough to prevent Texas cattle from reaching market, resulting in overstocked ranges.

On November 1, 1862, one hundred men from several washed-out Rio Grande villages had gathered at Mesilla and set out on the dangerous journey across the Tularosa Valley. About a week later they reached the place

(which the Apaches evidently considered theirs) where the Rio Tularosa comes down from the Sacramento Mountains. Here, in the relative security that Fort Stanton provided, they set out orchards and built houses. The following spring, women, children, and additional families arrived, and the forty-nine blocks of the new village (which in 1979 became a registered historic district) were plotted and irrigation rights allocated. Despite occasional hostilities with Indians from the mountains, these first years were the idyllic period of Tularosa's history. Crystal-clear river water irrigated the fields and orchards, which thrived in the moderate climate. Cottonwoods shaded the low adobe houses and the plaza of the Church of San Francisco de Paula.

As early as 1874, however, Texas cattlemen heard of the grass of this valley and began arriving with their families and herds after a trip which usually took them, in slow stages, across West Texas and the Pecos Valley near Roswell. On their heels came merchants, former Union soldiers, professionals, and promoters. From then on in Tularosa as elsewhere in central and southern New Mexico, the three main groups—the Spanish-speaking farmers, the cattle people, and the Anglo townspeople—had to get along together as best they

could, usually, as at Glorieta, with the "Mexicans" and "Yankees" in uneasy alliance against the "Texans." Meanwhile, the valley grass disappeared and, especially after the 1889–92 drought, the river ran silty when it ran at all. Cattle wars, notably one in 1888 between the Good and Lee families and their respective allies, terrorized the population. Political factions and feuds corrupted public life.

Somehow Tularosa has managed to survive as a beautiful little city. Fruit trees are still watered by ditches that branch through the town. Block-long adobe houses (Eugene Rhodes's "recumbent skyscrapers") remain, especially west of the highway. Corn, cotton, and alfalfa grow in the surrounding valley, irrigated, as before, by mountain streams. As was common in New Mexico, the railroad missed Tularosa. A small center sprang up around the station a mile and a half to the west, but because of the moderate expansion of the community the two towns never grew together. Besides Rhodes, Tularosa has another worthy chronicler in C. L. Sonnichsen, author of *Tularosa: Last of the Frontier West* (1963).

Three festivals celebrate Tularosa's history and unite residents and visitors. Although the city and river were named for the reedy places hereabouts (*tule* means reed; a *tular* is a reedy place), Tularosa is known as the "City of Roses," and a Rose Festival is held annually the first weekend in May. The Rose Queen, an old-timers' picnic, and arts and crafts exhibits help celebrate the blossoming of the flowers, which *do* grow well here. The following weekend is usually the St. Francis de Paula Fiesta, commemorating the building of the first church, an event that followed a showdown with the Apaches at Round Mountain in April 1868. On Christmas Eve *luminarias* glow on the church and the plaza, and on the highway for almost two miles through the village. At a fourth annual celebration, Tularosans are invited to share the Fourth of July with their old rivals, the Apaches, at the Mescalero Festival (seventeen miles east up U.S. 70 on Tour 10).

LA LUZ, turnoff at 284 mi. (alt. 4,819, pop. 1,183), the oldest living settlement in the Tularosa Basin, dates at least from 1719, when two Franciscans built a chapel here in honor of Our Lady of Light. Its more recent history parallels that of Tularosa, since colonists from another Rio Grande town, Jarales ("thickets") near Socorro, settled here in 1863. Among the new settlers from the East who came in the following decades was Roland Hazard, a Rhode Island emigrant, who built a large pottery plant that produced great quantities of urns and roof tiles. Ruins of this plant and Hazard's inn, Mi Casa, lie up La Luz Canyon, now badly eroded. Mi Casa served in the late 1800s as a stagecoach stop, and in the early 1900s as a popular eating place. In La Luz itself, the small church of Our Lady of Light is a well-preserved marvel. Nearby El Presidio Park, like the town bearing the date 1863, is surrounded by the adobe walls and buildings of the village. Its present calm belies the fact that La Luz was the home of John Good, one of the principals in a ferocious range war that bloodied this town in 1888.

Tour 14 from Lovington, Artesia, and Cloudcroft ends at the junction with U.S. 82, at 286 mi.

In 1898 Charles B. Eddy purchased Alamo

Space Hall of Fame, *Jeanne House.*

Ranch from Oliver M. Lee (John Good's range war antagonist) for a division point on his El Paso and Northeastern Railroad. He also envisioned an ideal city, his own "ALAMOGORDO," 240 mi. (alt. 4,303, pop. 23,035). He was not disappointed. Within months 960 acres had been subdivided, and new residents began to pour in. By 1902 the town had a population of four thousand, complete shopping facilities, and the Alamogordo Baptist College. The railroad employed three hundred people, and lumbering, including a railroad tie plant that supplied the entire state, provided jobs for as many more. Its growth tapered off when the

railroad shops were moved to Carrizozo in 1907. However, the young city received another boost from the wartime activity at Holloman Air Force Base; during the 1950s, with the reactivation of the base and White Sands Missile Range, Alamogordo's population quadrupled to twenty-four thousand people.

The novelist Gene Rhodes humorously describes the early growth of Arcadia, his fictitious name for Alamogordo, in his novel *Bransford of Rainbow Range.*

Arcadia's assets were the railroad, two large modern sawmills, the climate and printers' ink. The railroad found it a patch of bare ground, six miles from water; put in successively a whistling-post, a signboard, a depot, townsite papers were confirmed, established machine shops and made the new town the division headquarters and base for northward building. . . .

The railroad, under the pseudonym of the Arcadia Development Company, also laid out streets and laid in a network of pipe-lines, and staked out lots until the sawmill protested for lack of tie lumber. It put down miles of cement walks, fringed them with cottonwood saplings, telephone poles and electric lights. . . . It decreed a park, with nooks, lanes, mazes, lake, swans, ballground, grandstand, bandstand and the band apertaining thereunto—all of which apparently came into being over night. Then it employed a competent staff of word-artists and capitalized the climate.

The result was astonishing. The cottonwood grew apace and a swift town grew with them—swift in every sense of the word. It took good money to buy good lots in Arcadia.

People with money must be fed, served and amused by people wanting money. In three years the trees cast a pleasant shade and the company cast a balance, with gratifying results. They discounted the unearned increment for a generation to come.

It was a beneficent scheme, selling ozone and novelty, sunshine and delight. . . . Arcadia became the metropolis of the county and, by special election, the county-seat. Courthouse, college and jail followed in quick succession.

Besides White Sands, one of the tourist attractions Alamogordans are proudest of is the International Space Hall of Fame. Set against the hills east of Alamogordo, the hall of fame displays equipment used in space exploration, provides historical information, and features a marble tablet honoring each of the more than thirty-five members from eight countries. Since its dedication in 1976, the hall of fame has expanded beyond its original cubical building, and it includes a planetarium, auditorium, and meeting rooms.

Annually in October, military police conduct a tour through White Sands Missile Range to

the Trinity Site, the location of humankind's first atomic explosion. The 150-mile trip from Alamogordo takes about six hours. Tours also leave from the Tularosa Gate and the Stallion Range Gate (on U.S. 380, east of San Antonio) the same day. Travelers who would like to leave the Missile Range through a different gate from the one they entered should let the military escort know their intentions. The Alamogordo Chamber of Commerce will provide specific details.

Two miles southwest of Alamogordo the highways separate, 293 mi. U.S. 70 continues to the southwest past Holloman Air Force Base and White Sands National Monument to Las Cruces. (See Tour 10.) U.S. 54 heads almost due south toward El Paso. At the old railroad station of Valmont is the turnoff (east) to Dog Canyon and the newly developed Oliver M. Lee Memorial State Park. Dog Canyon, in places an almost-vertical cleavage in the west face of the Sacramentos, was named in the 1860s by settlers who pursued Apaches up this canyon and found only a dog left behind.

In the mid 1880s a Frenchman, François-Jean Rochas, settled in Dog Canyon, and without much help or communication from anyone raised cattle and cultivated grapes, olives, figs, apples, cherries, peaches, and plums. He was killed late in 1894 by cattlemen because of a disagreement over water. Meanwhile, Oliver M. Lee established his ranch headquarters one quarter mile south of "Frenchy's" cabin. Lee, rancher, promoter, state legislator, and friend of Albert B. Fall, was also involved in the controversy surrounding the disappearance of Albert J. Fountain. (See Tour 10.) The state park here includes ruins of old settlements and irrigation systems and a nature trail that points out some rare and endangered plant species.

Two mountain ranges are visible to the west, fifteen miles north of Orogrande. The further, many-pointed mountains are the Organs, just east of Las Cruces. The nearer, low ones are the Jarillas ("bushes") which were from the 1880s to the 1920s one of the most productive mining districts in the state. Abundant gold from these mountains created the town of Orogrande, 328 mi., once called Jarilla. In the early years of the twentieth century, this town's two thousand people, with the aid of nearby miners and ranchers, supported a thirty-two-bed hospital, a sixty-three-room hotel, and a weekly newspaper, *The Jarilla Enterprise*. Remains of a smelter still exist northeast of town. Orogrande also witnessed the construction of the "big ditch," an ambitious project to channel and pipe water down from the Sacramentos, in 1904–5. In addition to gold and copper, turquoise had been mined here since preconquest times.

Now the town is entirely surrounded by missile ranges. When the McGregor Range was extended to over one thousand square miles in 1954, some two hundred people east of here were displaced, and the highway connecting Orogrande with the south end of the Sacramentos was closed. One old rancher, John Prather, refused to leave. He had worked to improve his ranch since settling here in 1903, and took pride in his grass that grew in places to car-top height. During a tense encounter at the ranch in July 1956, the government backed down and left Prather the fifteen acres around his house and a check for over two hundred thousand dollars for the rest of his land. Up until his death in 1965, John Prather continued his ranching, and he never acknowledged the existence of the government check.

U.S. 54 continues south through the Fort Bliss Military Reservation to the state-line town of Newman. Low mountains on the left are the Hueco and Cornudas ranges. The

Franklin Mountains at El Paso lie ahead on the right. Newman, 358 mi., once was a pueblo and later, during and after railroad building, a town.

Since Juan de Oñate first crossed the Rio Grande in May 1598, just above the narrows downriver from the present town, El Paso del Norte played an important role in the province, territory, and state of New Mexico. Franciscan brothers founded a mission for the Mansos Indians here in 1659, administered from their home convent in Socorro. Within a decade this mission was dedicated to Our Lady of Guadalupe. The mission, and all El Paso until the nineteenth century, was situated on the right bank of the Rio Grande, where Ciudad Juárez, Mexico, now is located. The stone facade of the present Cathedral of Nuestra Señora de Guadalupe dates from the early mission days.

In the fall of 1680 El Paso became the capital of New Mexico when the two thousand refugees from the Pueblo Revolt were resettled in three new communities downriver from the mission. This state of affairs lasted until Santa Fe was reconquered in 1692; but three of the pueblos who had retreated here with the Spanish established new towns which still exist today, Ysleta del Sur, Socorro del Sur, and Senecu del Sur.

Paso del Norte, a garden spot in the wide valley of the Rio Grande, gained importance as a stopover on the long road between Mexico City and Santa Fe. Into the nineteenth century it was the only settled community between Chihuahua City and Albuquerque and was located about halfway between them. By the 1830s a settlement (first called Franklin) had begun on the left bank of the river, and Anglo-American influence became increasingly felt.

Invading Americans moving down the Rio Grande from Santa Fe gained control of El Paso after a relatively bloodless battle north of the city (at La Salineta, in New Mexico) on Christmas day, 1846. From that time on, the small town on the north side of the river was separated from its mother city by an international boundary, and soon thereafter from the New Mexico Territory by the Texas state line. Many families sympathetic to the Confederate cause waited out the Civil War on the Mexican side while Union troops occupied El Paso, Texas.

For some nine months in 1865–66, Paso del Norte served as the capital of the Republic of Mexico. This happened when the French conquered central Mexico for the Emperor Maximilian and pursued Benito Juárez, the constitutional president of Mexico, and his cabinet and staff, north to the border city. Juárez was offered asylum and hospitality by friendly North Americans, notably by General Carleton in Santa Fe; but he remained steadfastly on Mexican soil. Juárez and his loyalists went on to reclaim the actual government of Mexico, aided in some measure by arms left at border crossings such as El Paso by the recently victorious Union forces in the United States. The Mexican city, Paso del Norte, was renamed Juárez in 1888 to honor the beloved president. "El Paso" thereafter referred only to the Texas city, which by then was prospering with the New Mexico mining, railroading, and cattle booms of the 1870s and 1880s. It quickly became the metropolis serving southern New Mexico, rivaled by Albuquerque only after the Second World War.

Two one-way bridges connect downtown El Paso and Juárez, while a newer bridge, two and one-half miles east, leads to shopping plazas and museums built in part to attract and accommodate North American tourists.

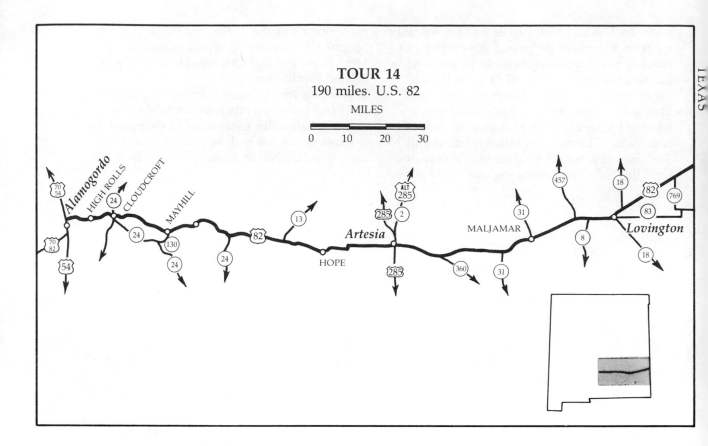

TOUR 14
190 miles. U.S. 82

MILES

0   10   20   30

Alamogordo
HIGH ROLLS
CLOUDCROFT
MAYHILL
Artesia
HOPE
MALJAMAR
Lovington

TEXAS

552

tour fourteen

Texas Border • **Lovington** • *Artesia* • **Cloudcroft** • *Alamogordo*

This route connects the oil-producing Staked Plains around Lovington with the mountain recreation areas of Otero County. There is heavy traffic from Texas to the mountains for escape from summer heat and for winter skiing and sledding. From Cloudcroft to Alamogordo, the road descends at an awesomely steep grade.

U.S. 82 crosses the Texas line and heads into the level plains covered with growth of shinnery oak and sedge. Pumpjacks and cattle echo each other's slow, dipping movements. Coyotes, jackrabbits, skunks, and badgers populate the flat land. The homesteaders who followed the Texas cowmen to the area built their homes partially underground. An example of the dugout home can be seen at the museum in LOVINGTON, 20 mi. (alt. 3,908, pop. 9,766). Robert Florence Love built his family's dugout home on the site of Lovington in 1903. When he moved to Knowles, his brother Jim and family moved in. Florence Love came back in 1907 and deeded part of his homestead land for a town site. The community has followed the pattern of other Lea County settlements: it grew as the land was

taken by homesteaders and used for dry farming. By 1910 the town had twelve hundred residents and boasted churches, a bank, a reading club, a hotel, and secret societies. Five years of drought drove a great many homesteaders away, but oil brought people back in the late 1920s. The population again decreased when the price of oil dropped dramatically during the Depression; post-Depression growth has been steady.

Lovington residents built themselves a grade school in 1908 and a high school in 1911, the first on the *llano* ("plains"). In the same spirit, fifty years later, the people of Lovington and other Lea County cities took action to stop the export of their "most valuable resource," their children, who left the area for higher education. New Mexico Junior College was the first two-year college in the state and enrolls a high proportion of the county's youth.

The divided highway, N.M. 18, between Hobbs and Lovington is one of the most heavily traveled in the state. Only in 1912, however, was the first grading of roads done on the *llano*. In 1936 the section between the two cities became the first paved road in the

county. Sandy, nearly impassable roads greatly hampered communication and transportation between Lovington and any other community. The first automobiles arrived in town around 1912, and had to have gasoline brought for them from Lamesa, Texas, by means of wagons pulled by teams of eighteen to twenty burros. Those first cars, Buicks, Hanes, Coles, and Fords, traveled around Courthouse Square. Today the square is still the quiet, attractive center of the city. Off one corner of the plaza is the old brick hotel-turned-museum, which houses an enormous stuffed grizzly bear as well as furnishings reassembled in separate rooms to show the character of homes, businesses, and the school in the early days of Lovington. A block west of the square is the city's fine library.

Throughout the oil boom, Lovington has also continued to emphasize agriculture in the area. The annual Lea County Fair in Lovington proudly displays agricultural products and provides entertainment at a rodeo and a midway.

Between Lovington and Artesia, U.S. 82 crosses the lower end of the Staked Plains and the Mescalero Ridge, a region of ranches and vast grazing lands where mirages are often seen in the summer. A water mirage is essentially a reflection of the sky. Light rays from

just above the horizon are sent upward by the surface of extremely hot air just above the road or sand. The optical illusion for the traveler is of a shimmering reflection that resembles a body of water. The great heat of summer here is tempered by pleasant nights and cooling thundershowers. Cold spells in the winter do not last long. There are also sandstorms. When asked why there are no cyclones, an old-timer replied, "Humph! There couldn't be. Our straight winds would blow the hell out of a cyclone."

Just beyond the Mescalero Ridge is MALJA-MAR, 45 mi., the site of New Mexico's first successful oil well, which started gushing oil on December 9, 1926. Maljamar is also the name given to a phase of Indian occupation. Archaeological remains in the area, including pit-house villages, date roughly from A.D. 950 to 1150. West of Maljamar, the route traverses the plains to the Pecos valley, crossing the Pecos River at 78 mi.

In Artesia (see Tour 7), 83 mi., U.S. 285 intersects U.S. 82. West of Artesia U.S. 82 goes through open range country, covered with short, coarse grass and occasional cane cactus, clumps of soapweed, and Spanish dagger. As the road rises gently at 100 mi., Lombardy poplars, orchards, and cottonwoods appear.

HOPE, 103 mi. (alt. 3,450, pop. 111) was called Badgerville when it was settled in 1885 because the homes were earthen dwellings dug out of the ground with only the roofs made of timber. The name was changed to Hope when the post office was established in 1888. In order to decide on a new name for the town, two settlers, Elder Miller and Joe Richards, threw a dime in the air and shot at it. Richards said, "I hope you lose." Miller did, and Richards chose Hope. A railroad bed was laid to Hope from Artesia about 1906. In April 1912, while the station was being built, Lord Pierson, head of the group of English capitalists that provided the financing for the railroad, was aboard the ocean liner *Titanic*. Pierson and hopes for the completed railroad went down with the ship. Hope holds regular, lively reunions for those who have left the

Aspen in Sacramento Mts., *Laurel Drew.*

farming and ranching community. A primitive road from Hope heads south into the Guadalupe Mountains and eventually along the mountain ridge, passing places with names like Buzzard Canyon, Strychnine Draw, Freezeout Canyon, and Last Chance Canyon.

From Hope west, U.S. 82 follows the Rio Peñasco ("full of boulders") up toward its headwaters in the Sacramento Mountains. At 130 mi., N.M. 24 loops south past Dunken to Piñon and rejoins the tour at Cloudcroft. Before the federal government closed off large sections of southern New Mexico for military firing ranges, this road continued over the southern foothills of the Sacramentos to Orogrande, on U.S. 54.

LOWER PEÑASCO ("rocky"), 135 mi., is a farming community that overlooks a deep gorge of the river. It once shared this narrow valley with the villages of Peñasco and Culbertson's Sawmill, formerly located a few miles upriver. Throughout the arid Southwest, except during periods of heavy runoff, moun-

tain streams such as the Peñasco normally disappear underground when they reach the gravel and sand of the lower foothills. Settlers here succeeded in extending the Peñasco an additional twenty-five miles by ditching it away from the sink holes and driving cattle over the new river bed to compact it.

ELK (142 mi.) is named for the many elk in the canyon that joins the Peñasco here from the northwest. A group of Texas families created the town in 1885 and first called it Yorktown after the York ranch, which was nearby. Archaeological evidence found since, including well-made black-on-red bowls dating from the 1200s, has indicated something of the lives of much earlier settlers.

During the middle 1800s, when people from the Midwest and South were homesteading this valley, the Mescalero Apache Indians still used all the surrounding mountains as their summer home. Frequent clashes occurred between the two groups. Captain Stanton, for whom Fort Stanton was named, met his death

in 1854 on a punitive raid against the Apaches hereabouts.

MAYHILL, 155 mi., is situated on a mesa above the junction of the James and Peñasco canyons. Former soldiers from Fort Stanton settled here in 1876 and called it Upper Peñasco. John F. Mahill immigrated from Missouri in 1881, married into the Coe family of the Ruidoso valley, and lent his name, with a "y" added, to this sheep-, fruit-, and vegetable-raising community.

N.M. 130 continues southwest along the Peñasco toward the villages of Weed and Sacramento. U.S. 82 follows James Canyon nearly all the way to CLOUDCROFT, 173 mi. (pop. 533), one of the highest towns in the state at an elevation of 8,640 feet. The name means "cloud in a field." Cloudcroft began when the El Paso and Northeastern Railroad reached Alamogordo and acquired three thousand acres in these mountains for cutting cross-tie timber. The EP&NE built a lodge here as a summer resort for El Pasoans, and a vacation village grew up around it. The lodge burned in 1909, was later rebuilt, and is still open, providing rooms and meals.

The Sacramento Mountains Historical Museum, located in a cabin on the main highway, provides information about Cloudcroft's past and present. Two festivals begin and end the summer season. The Mayfest, over Memorial Day weekend, features an art show, hayrides, chuck wagon dinners, and horseback riding. Four months later, on the first weekend of October, the Aspencade attracts thousands of visitors to an arts and crafts fair, a community barbecue, motorcycle races, and Western-style dancing, in addition to nature walks led by Lincoln National Forest personnel in cooperation with the chamber of commerce. Two art schools open for summer courses each June. Cloudcroft also boasts the southernmost ski area in the country, operating four lifts from November to April. The ski slopes receive an average of eighty-nine inches of snowfall annually.

SIDE TOUR

A recommended side tour begins two miles south of Cloudcroft on N.M. 24. There one takes Forest Service Road 64 (paved) to the Nelson Canyon Vista Trail for a marked walking trail and splendid views of the White Sands. The side tour continues south past Russia Canyon, the end of an old logging railway, and concludes at Sunspot, home of the Sacramento Peak Observatory. With the world's largest coronagraph (sixteen inches), astronomers can study the sun's gaseous outer envelope and sunspots, as is possible at few other observatories in the world. Tourists can take self-guided tours daily and look across the Tularosa and Hueco basins below. The observatory conducts guided tours Saturday afternoons, May through October.

The sixteen miles between Cloudcroft and the junction with U.S. 54, at 190 mi., near Alamogordo, are some of the steepest and most remarkable in the state. The highway approximates the path of the cog railway built to the logging camps in Russia Canyon. The spur climbed six thousand feet in twenty-seven miles, twisting from trestle to tunnel and back, one of the most vertical railroads imaginable. The tracks are gone, but U.S. 82 still descends almost forty-five hundred feet after leaving Cloudcroft and, in so doing, passes through all the vegetative zones that characterize North America from the Hudson Bay region of Canada to the Sonoran desert.

Halfway down are the apple-, peach-, pear-, and cherry-raising twin towns of MOUNTAIN PARK and HIGH ROLLS, 181 mi. Settled in the 1880s, Mountain Park was first named Fresnal ("ash grove") after Fresnal Creek. A short way upstream, the Fresnal Rock Shelter has yielded important archaeological evidence of the early "archaic" period (A.D. 700–900), the time when prehistoric people here began to quarry rock, build hearths, and fashion stone tools (*manos* and *metates*) for grinding grain. High Rolls's name refers to the rapids on Fresnal Creek. The two towns sponsor an apple festival the second weekend in October, with crafts booths, fiddle music, and apples in every conceivable form. Bill Mauldin, whose cartoons amused and enlightened millions during the Second World War and on through the 1960s and 1970s, grew up in High Rolls.

A short distance west of Mountain Park, the tour enters the only highway tunnel in the state. From the rest stop nearby one can get a panorama of the White Sands, a large portion of the Tularosa Valley, and the mountains beyond.

The turnoff for La Luz (described in Tour 13) is at 188 mi. Tour 14 ends at the junction with U.S. 54, 190 mi.

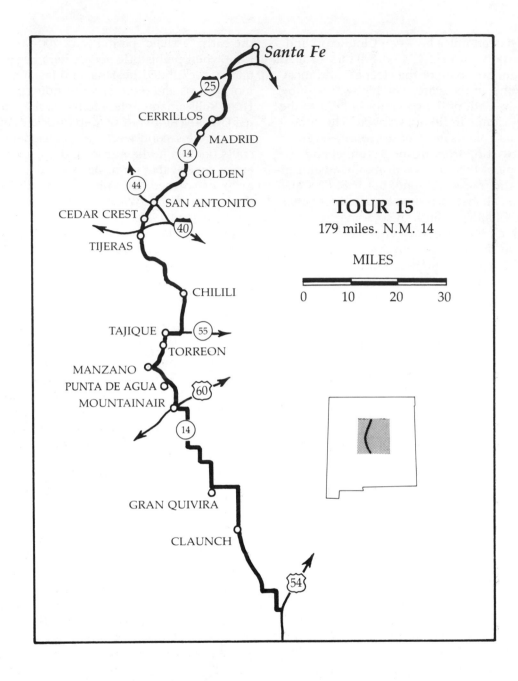

Santa Fe

25

CERRILLOS

MADRID

14

44 GOLDEN

SAN ANTONITO

CEDAR CREST

40

TIJERAS

CHILILI

TAJIQUE 55

TORREON

MANZANO

PUNTA DE AGUA

MOUNTAINAIR 60

14

GRAN QUIVIRA

CLAUNCH

54

TOUR 15
179 miles. N.M. 14

MILES

| 0 | 10 | 20 | 30 |

tour fifteen

Santa Fe • **Cerrillos** • **Madrid** • **Chilili** • **Mountainair** • **Gran Quivira** • *Carrizozo*

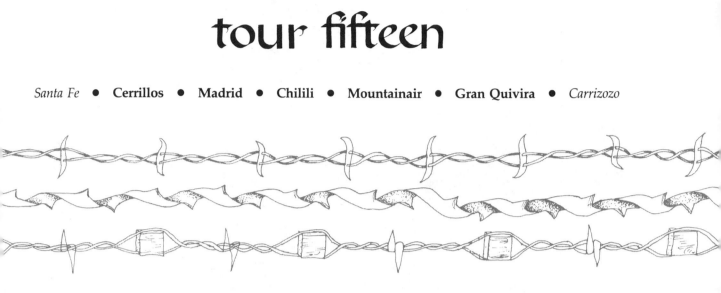

This route, up and down the Ortiz Mountains and the foothills of the Sandias and Manzanos, is often used as an alternative to the faster interstate between Santa Fe and Albuquerque, as well as a means by which to reach the ruins of the "Saline Pueblos," Abo, Quarai, and Gran Quivira. In the north it travels through small, almost deserted mining towns; in the south it traverses the hilly Spanish farming communities at the foot of the Manzanos.

Cerrillos Road, a busy franchise row, passes under I-25 (see Tour 1) nine miles south of the Santa Fe plaza. It continues south through low hills dotted with piñons, houses, and the State Penitentiary, crossing the Santa Fe Railroad's main line just north of Cerrillos at 23 mi.

CERRILLOS was once an important stop on the railroad; the depot was the point from which much of the lead, silver, coal, and turquoise mined in the surrounding hills was shipped. The mines were played out, and a small town was left with its boardwalks and boarded-up false-front stores. Some of these stores have been reopened as antique shops, and artists and other seekers of quiet have re-stored some of the town's old homes. The Cerrillos area contains the ruins of San Marcos, a large pueblo, known at the time of the Spanish conquest for its fine pottery. The pueblo was abandoned during or shortly after the Pueblo Revolt of 1680.

MADRID, three miles beyond Cerrillos, was also a mining town, as the huge slag piles all around it attest. The miners' wooden houses, deserted when the mines shut down for the last time in 1954, are still largely closed; in fact, the town was for sale as a unit in the 1970s. A buyer was not found, but a number of young people have renovated several of the houses along the highway and have opened general stores or outlets for their arts and crafts. Madrid was a bustling community not long ago, and was known to many not only as a supplier of coal, but also as a town united around the display of spectacular Christmas decorations each year from the 1920s to 1941. Air traffic on the fledgling Transcontinental Airlines (now TWA) was rerouted over Madrid during the Christmas season so passengers could see the lights. A new Christmas-time tradition has recently been started: an arts and crafts weekend is scheduled during December,

Madrid, *Ernesto Burciaga*.

during which artists' studios throughout the little town are opened to visitors. The old stone baseball field at the north end of Madrid is still in fine condition; its stands are used each summer for weekend jazz concerts, spotlighting musicians from throughout the state.

Southward, the road climbs through the Ortiz Mountains, a region of long-abandoned mines, toward views of the Sandia and Jemez mountains. GOLDEN, 38 mi., was active during the short-lived development of a placer mining district in the San Pedro Mountains. It has a history of gold mining dating to the sixteenth century, when Spanish colonists worked small deposits, using enslaved Indians as miners. In 1933 contractors used power shovels idled by the Depression in an attempt to locate larger yields, without success; but it is said that local residents have found free gold in gulches after cloudbursts. Nearby are several ruined pueblos, inhabited for many years before being abandoned during the early Spanish period; a tiny adobe church; and, on the west side of the road, a house surrounded

by its owner's collection of colored glass. Across the road is the general store, which displays a fine collection of Pueblo pottery.

N.M. 14 passes through the small settlement of San Antonito. Just beyond it is the junction with N.M. 44 at 49 mi.

SIDE TOUR

N.M. 44 passes through forests of Ponderosa and spruce to wind fourteen miles to Sandia Crest. The road goes past several picnic grounds, favorite points of escape for Albuquerqueans fleeing the city's summer heat, and reaches the ski area at 7 mi. (The top of the ski area is also the upper station of the Sandia Peak Tram, which ascends the steeper west side of the mountains.) The pavement ends at a parking lot just below an overlook, 13 mi., which allows an unparalleled view of Albuquerque and the plains and mountains in a full circle around it. Looking to the west, one sees a very steep drop, with spires attesting to the much larger mountain that formed from the uplifted strata. These same strata are exposed at many places along the road to the top, and in several spots the knowledgeable can find fossils dating back millions of years, to the time when the area was under water.

Eight miles from the base of the Crest road, a dirt road numbered N.M. 44 branches off to the north, following Las Huertas Creek down to the town of Placitas, in the foothills at the north end of the Sandias. This road is not plowed and is often snow-covered in winter, making it passable at times only for intrepid sled and inner-tube riders. Placitas is a small community, favored in the 1960s by counterculture communes and by the 1980s increasingly inhabited by Albuquerqueans escaping the noise and pollution of the city for the quiet and sweeping views of the villages.

Along the winding dirt road to Placitas is Sandia Man Cave. An anthropology graduate student, Kenneth Davis, exploring the area in 1936, found several shallow caves in a sandstone cliff a short distance from the road. Looking through these openings, he discovered a longer, narrow cave extending in tunnel-like fashion two hundred yards back into the rock face. From the inside of this tunnel he took back to the University of New Mexico's museum a cigarbox full of remnants from prehistoric Pueblo days: basket scraps, woven yucca footwear, and a deer antler scored with a knife.

Although these finds were not remarkable in themselves, a team from the university set out to determine if there was other evidence of human habitation in the caves. The first find was the jawbone of a

Sandias, *Daniel Gibson.*

giant sloth, extinct in New Mexico and elsewhere for thousands of years. Digging down through the fine dust blown into the cave over many years, they reached a travertine layer, formed during an earlier period when the area had been much wetter than it is now. They broke this layer with sledgehammers, suddenly coming upon arrowpoints and animal bones characteristic of Folsom Man (see Tour 2) ten thousand years before.

They continued digging through a layer of yellow ocher, into the trashpile of even more ancient people. Here were arrow points of a very different type not known before, cruder than the finely fashioned Folsom points, along with skin scrapers, other implements, and the bones of long-extinct animals. Neither here nor elsewhere in New Mexico were any remains of the Paleo-Indians themselves found, however.

Initial estimates placed the age of the Sandia Man trashpile at twenty-six thousand years, far older than any other evidence of human activity in the New World. These dates, however, at first confirmed by the radiocarbon process, have since been called into question. It now appears that Sandia Man and the first inhabitants of the Clovis region were probably contemporaries, living only one to two thousand years before Folsom Man roamed New Mexico's eastern plains.

Nothing remains at the site of these momentous findings but the caves and a commemorative plaque. The long, shaft-like cave from which the relics were gathered has been sealed off to prevent injury to inexperienced adventurers. But standing by quiet Las Huertas Creek in the shadow of the cliff is as pleasant to modern man as it must have been to the primitive Indians ten to twelve thousand years ago.

Continuing south on N.M. 14 a wider highway passes through Cedar Crest, the first of a short string of "mountain suburbs" of Albuquerque. Just beyond the junction with I-40 (see Tour 6), the town of Tijeras ("scissors"), 55 mi., lies at the crosspoint of two canyons that gives it its name.

From Tijeras, the road climbs steeply up wooded slopes, giving occasional views of the Manzano Mountains to the west and of tiny farming communities. Descending the long hill into Chilili, one glimpses, on the plains to the east, the large, usually dry lakes from which salt was transported for many miles around. Two pueblos near the present site of Chilili were among ten called by the Spanish the Saline Pueblos. Like the others, Chiu and Alle, the two at Chilili, were abandoned under intense Apache pressure in the seventeenth century.

CHILILI, 75 mi., is a small mountain village, newsworthy in the 1970s for a conflict over the management of its land grant. The grant, made in 1841 by the Mexican governor and confirmed by President Theodore Roosevelt in 1909, specified eleven named and twenty unnamed families as owners of forty-two thousand acres of land in the pretty valley where the village stands. In the 1930s grant holders lost title to the land when they were required to cede it to the state in lieu of taxes, but a portion was repurchased by some of the original grantees' descendants in 1941. Since then persistent fighting—verbal, legal, and occasionally physical—has characterized the town, dividing it into the three factions of Anglo newcomers, grantees wishing to sell the land and realize a profit, and grantees desiring to retain title to the land to use for the traditional

activities of grazing and woodcutting. In 1977 the last-named group blockaded a road leading to the subdivision where the newcomers lived; after a year or more of legal battles, the barricades were removed in 1978. The debates simmer on.

At 86 mi., N.M. 14 takes a right-angle turn to the west. N.M. 55 to the east takes the traveler to Estancia (see Tour 5). TAJIQUE, 88 mi. on N.M. 14, is the oldest of the Spanish villages at the east edge of the Manzanos. It was built on the site of a Tiwa pueblo, Tashike, which for a short period served as refuge for Pueblo tribes escaping Apache raids. In 1675, however, Tashike also came under Apache domination and was deserted. The town was resettled under a Mexican community grant in 1835. From Tajique, a gravel road runs west to the campground in Fourth of July Canyon. The canyon is spectacular in the fall when its stand of maple, unique in New Mexico, turns red. From the campground the hiker has access to the network of trails going north and south along the Manzanos.

TORREON ("round high fort"), at 90 mi., is another mountain village of small ranches and farms. Here are also ruins of a Saline pueblo, so-called because of proximity to the salt lakes to the east.

The road progresses up and down the piñon-covered hills, offering magnificent views of the mountains until it reaches MANZANO, 97 mi., where it begins its descent to the plains. Manzano sits at the base of 10,608-foot-high Manzano Peak. The town, the peak, and the range are named for the apple trees (manzanos) found in the area when the town was established in 1829. Archaeologist Adolph Bandelier, who surveyed the area in the 1880s,

thought that the trees were planted by Franciscan friars in the seventeenth century, but more recent tree-ring analyses date them to about 1800. Manzano has had a reputation as a querulous town of political passion, despite the leavening presence of the well-known archbishop's nephew, Father Lamy, as pastor in the nineteenth century.

A short-lived newspaper, *The Gringo and the Greaser*, was published in Manzano for several years after the Civil War. Its acerbic publisher and principal writer, Charles G. Kusz, campaigned bitterly against many local customs, including the Penitente ceremonies and cattle rustling, until his assassination in his print shop in 1884. Passions have now cooled, leaving Manzano quiet in its beautiful valley. A road at the south end of the small town leads up steeply to Manzano Lake State Park and to a cool, wooded forest campground.

PUNTA DE AGUA ("water point," named for a spring in this hamlet), 102 mi., is a tiny settlement at the junction of the road to Quarai, one mile west. Quarai was the first of the Saline Pueblos to be abandoned; it was deserted in 1674 under pressure from the Apaches. It had been a large village; Juan de Oñate, who brought the first Spanish settlers to New Mexico in 1598, found six hundred Tiwa Indians living there. Franciscan friars established a mission at Quarai in the early seventeenth century, and in about 1629 the magnificent Mission Church of the Immaculate Conception was built.

One of the best-loved of Spanish priests in New Mexico was Father Gerónimo de la Llana, who died at Quarai in 1659. When the pueblo's inhabitants fled to Tashike in 1674, the priest's remains accompanied them. After

Tashike too was abandoned, the casket was left undisturbed until found intact, with ancient inscriptions, in Santa Fe in 1880. Details of its final journey are lacking.

The mission church has been stabilized by experts from the University of New Mexico; it and several partially excavated portions of the pueblo form a unit of the Salinas National Monument (see also Tour 8 regarding Abo, and below regarding Gran Quivira, other portions of this same monument). The twenty-foot-high stone walls and large wooden beams of the ancient structure are still visible. A cool grove of cottonwoods and grassy fields surround the ancient ruins and a small picnic ground.

Indians who fled the pueblos in this area are said to have settled, in the seventeenth century, near El Paso del Norte, where they formed the village of Ysleta del Sur and where their descendants live today. Other accounts state that the inhabitants of the small Texas pueblo are remnants of a group of Isleta Indians who fled the Pueblo Revolt with the Spanish in 1680.

The road now continues across fields and pastures to MOUNTAINAIR, 109 mi. (alt. 6,492, pop. 1,152). This town, at the junction of N.M. 14 and U.S. 60 (Tour 8), was founded as the Santa Fe Railroad's "Belen Cutoff" approached Abo Pass in 1903. Mountainair was once an important railroad junction between the Santa Fe and the now-defunct New Mexico Central railroads. Both offered special fares to Mountainair to encourage New Mexicans to vacation at the annual Chatauqua lectures held here between 1908 and 1917. At that time the town supported several hotels. The last survivor was the now-boarded-up Hotel

Gran Quivira, *Harvey Caplin.*

Shaffer, unique in its Southwest–Art Deco splendor, adapting Indian designs in garish colors. Headquarters for the Salinas National Monument are in Mountainair.

South of Mountainair, N.M. 14 zigzags along section lines to Gran Quivira, 135 mi. Several settlements were once found along the road. Many are now deserted, victims of the drying trend of the 1920s and 1930s. The pueblo at Gran Quivira, built in a commanding position on a mesa, was named Cueloze by its inhabitants. Its first Spanish visitors, who came in 1598 under Oñate, called it the Pueblo de los Jumanos ("the pueblo of the striped ones") because the natives decorated themselves with a stripe painted across the nose. To later Spaniards it was Gran Quivira, the object of Coronado's and Oñate's futile search for gold, a name obviously assigned in error. Multiple names for a single pueblo were common in the days of early Spanish exploration of New Mexico. Several expeditions encountered various groups of Indians between Coronado's conquest in 1540 (he described

Three centuries later, their community was incorporated into a larger village by more advanced Pueblo Indians from the north. They built adobe houses above ground, and a distinctive pottery style, Chupadero black and white, evolved. As the settlement grew, masonry communal buildings replaced the earlier individual homes. The village, by 1600 the largest in the area, probably was comprised of fifteen hundred Indians at its peak. The large population subsisted on corn and bean farming and hunted the bison, whose range ended nearby.

After the Spanish discovery of the pueblo, Franciscan missionaries were assigned to convert its Indians. They found Gran Quivira to be a group of three- and four-story stone houses separated by narrow streets. In 1627 Father Alonso de Benavides toured the Saline Pueblos, reporting that he had preached a sermon in the plaza of the Pueblo de los Jumanos that "converted all the Indians." The first church was built in 1629 but deteriorated rapidly, and in 1659 Father Diego Santander supervised the construction of the massive church of San Buenaventura, with a large adjoining *convento*. However, this church and the entire pueblo, like Quarai and Tashike, were abandoned in the 1670s under heavy Apache attacks.

Gran Quivira has been extensively excavated by teams from the University of New Mexico, allowing the visitor to observe the construction styles of several ages. In several parts of the tour, one can see down through more recent buildings to older and more primitive habitations. In some of the rooms are the *metates* used to grind corn. The splendid Church of San Buenaventura is open for inspection. Its walls tower thirty feet above the ground; mighty timbers used as lintels must have been transported from miles away. The small museum offers exhibits, explanations, and audiovisual programs that enhance a visit to this enchanted, peaceful spot.

South of Gran Quivira the road is unpaved, traveling through ranching country with very infrequent dwellings. CLAUNCH, 154 mi., is es-

about seventy pueblos) and Oñate's tour of 134 pueblos in 1598. The various expeditions may have transcribed the Indians' names for their towns differently; they sometimes also gave them new names on the basis of characteristics of the people or their situations, such as Jumanos and Isleta ("island"). In addition, patron saints were later assigned by the Spanish missionaries, adding to the confusion. For these reasons it is not possible to be certain to which groups the descriptions of these early explorers apply. For example, it is known that a group of Indians, perhaps the Jumanos, ambushed a party of Spaniards at a small pueblo near Gran Quivira, and that the Spanish retaliated by killing nine hundred people and taking four hundred more as prisoners, probably to be sold as slaves, but it is not known from which village these warriors originated.

The area where the pueblo now stands was probably first settled in the ninth century by pit-house dwelling Indians related to the Mogollon tribes from southwestern New Mexico.

sentially a ghost town now, with several interesting old buildings. In its heyday, in the 1910s and 1920s, high-priced Case tractors and Cadillacs "littered" the landscape here, which consisted largely of pinto bean fields that supported the town's wealth. The surrounding area also contains evidence of several long-deserted pueblos.

The road meets U.S. 54 (Tour 13) at 179 mi., seventeen miles north of Carrizozo.

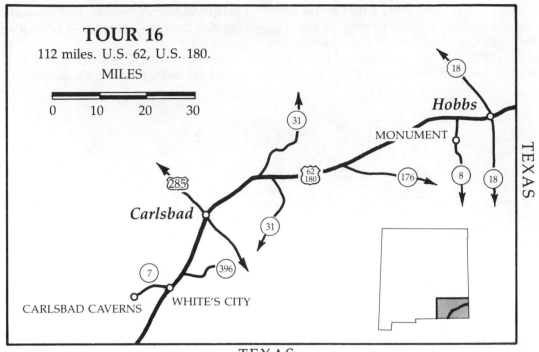

TOUR 16
112 miles. U.S. 62, U.S. 180.

MILES

0   10   20   30

285

Carlsbad

7   396

CARLSBAD CAVERNS   WHITE'S CITY

31

31

62
180

176

MONUMENT

Hobbs

18

8   18

TEXAS

TEXAS

tour sixteen

Texas Border • **Hobbs** • **Carlsbad** • *Texas Border*

From the Texas border to the Texas border, Tour 16 goes through the area known as Little Texas. A majority of the residents were born out-of-state, mostly in the neighboring state. The area is topographically, culturally, and linguistically linked with West Texas.

U.S. 62/U.S. 180 traverses the high plains and the Pecos River valley and approaches the Guadalupe Mountains. There is little change in elevation along the route. Such vegetation as exists without irrigation consists of sparse grasses and drought-resistant plants. The eroded land surfaces of the entire route have yielded many Paleo-Indian sites and artifacts between seventy-five hundred and ten thousand years of age. More recently, Comanches and Apaches hunted bison extensively in the area but had no known permanent settlements here. They left completely upon the disappearance of the bison by the 1880s. The true wonders of the region lie beneath the surface: in the east, natural gas and oil; in the valley, saline potash; near Carlsbad, the extensive and magnificent caverns.

Beginning at the Texas border, motels and restaurants usher the traveler into HOBBS, 3 mi. (alt. 3,659, pop. 28,708). A Texan named James Hobbs built his dugout home on the site in 1907, and the school he began became the center of social activities for homesteaders in the area. A store and post office followed, then small establishments for molasses- and broom-making, but the town remained tiny until the Midwest Oil Company discovered the Hobbs oil pool in 1928. Not only individuals but also whole towns moved to Hobbs in the "black gold rush." Knowles, which had been the largest settlement in the county, was dismantled and moved south to Hobbs. The Texas and New Mexico Railroad line, one of the last to be completed in the United States, reached Hobbs by 1930. Tent houses with wooden floors, corrugated iron sides, and fabric roofs, along with all manner of other shacks, appeared overnight. Some more substantial brick structures, a hotel, and some elegant shops were constructed. Over twelve thousand people had moved into the area before 1930 was out. New residences filled in the gaps among four small communities to make one sprawling town. Many hangers-on followed those associated with the oil industry, bringing all-day and all-night activity to the oil-slicked streets. (Oil was spread on the streets to keep the dust down.)

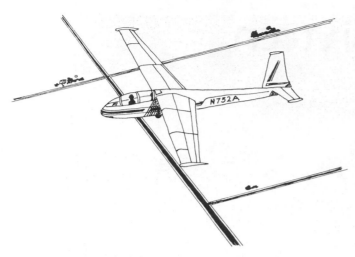

In spite of Prohibition and a restrictive town ordinance, numerous taverns—rollerskating rinks by day and dance halls at night—were opened. Many oil drillers went directly to these establishments from work, necessitating extensive wardrobes of gowns for the dance-hall girls. Brothels, domino parlors, nineteen pool halls, and other gambling spots flourished. Competition among taverns inspired publicity stunts, including the "auction of a live baby," who at the time of the sale was revealed to be a live baby alligator. The raucous nightlife was facilitated by gaudy neon lights and burning gas flares; at the time, natural gas was regarded as a noisome byproduct of the oil wells. An all-metal tank, chained to posts and set in the sun, served to house prisoners. Other "undesirables," those with infectious diseases, were kept in the local pesthouse.

Within a year the price of oil dropped from $1.05 to ten cents a barrel, and the migrant fortuneseekers turned away. Their temporary homes were lifted onto truck beds and hauled off. More than three-quarters of the population left Hobbs; its remaining residents struggled through the Depression and built a more stable community. They were ready then for the return of intense oil drilling, with improved technology, in the mid-1930s. The first oil well, Midwest No. 1, continues to produce within the city, and Hobbs is still a boom town. The importance of the oil industry to the present city is reflected in the thick section of the yellow pages devoted to drilling operations. The community's prosperity is shown in its extensive shopping centers, which help make Hobbs a trading center for surrounding farming and ranching towns. Business in Hobbs has diversified to include chemical production, feedlots for livestock, and the raising of thoroughbred horses. Further diversification is important to Hobbs as oil and gas reserves decrease.

Hobbs's extended second boom has lured to the area many people for whom there are no jobs or only very low-paying jobs. The contrast between the numerous attractive, large houses and the ramshackle dwellings of the poor is great. Services are slowly catching up to the needs of the fairly new, predominantly Hispanic and black low-income population.

Hobbs has many educational opportunities, including good public schools with outstanding sports facilities, the New Mexico Junior College, with a rich continuing education program, and the private College of the Southwest. The large, modern campus of New Mexico Junior College houses the Cowboy Hall of Fame.

The "perpetual flying weather" that brought an air base to Hobbs in 1942 has continued to serve the area well after the base's closing in 1946. Commercial aircraft and a multitude of private planes use the Hobbs airstrip, and the industrial air park is home to several glider clubs. Hobbs hosts national and international sail-planing events.

One large hangar at the air park shelters the Confederate Air Force Museum. Although a few hot-air balloons were used in the East during the Civil War, this museum has nothing to do with that venture. The Hobbs Confederate Air Force members rebel against the government's plane disposal policy by purchasing and restoring government rejects for the air museum. The mythical commander, Colonel Jethro Culpeper, oversees air shows that display much of the museum's collection of military aircraft built between 1939 and 1945. The airfield also has other recreational facilities for adults, including drag strips, a ri-

Hobbs, *Harvey Caplin.*

fle range, a pistol range, and a skeet range. The Hobbs Chamber of Commerce has information about the dates of air shows and competitions.

N.M. 18 goes through the center of Hobbs. The northward route to Lovington (see Tour 14) is almost continuously crowded, and the highway is one of the most heavily traveled in the state. The cities of Hobbs and Lovington are linked by their importance to the oil industry, their importance in Lea County government, their railroad, and their shared interest in education. Both New Mexico Junior College and the College of the Southwest are on N.M. 18 between the two cities. Earlier in this century, however, the towns contrasted greatly. Hobbs became known as a hot spot, while Lovington had one of the strictest blue laws in the country, which outlawed meeting, working, engaging in sports, horseracing, cockfighting, and disturbing anyone on Sundays, and outlawed dancing anytime.

Recreation facilities for both communities also lie along N.M. 18. Lea County State Park provides picnicking, camping, and fishing sites around two small lakes.

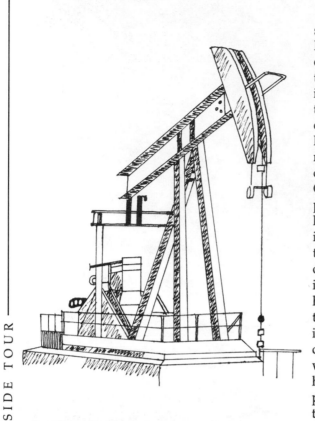

South on N.M 18 is the route leading to Eunice (18 mi.) and Jal (34 mi.). Leaving the divided highway, Alternate N.M. 18 dips into EUNICE (alt. 3,569, pop. 2,962). Pumpjacks scattered through the town provide a slow background rhythm. The town is so small that the orderly, white-enameled street signs display neither the whole alphabet going in one direction nor the numbers up to twenty-five in the other. The park (with a bandstand) and the library are the sites of potluck suppers, fiddling contests, square dances, and rodeo celebrations.

In 1908 John Carson claimed 320 acres to homestead by making a furrow around the perimeter. He applied for a post office; the standard conditions for approval then were that mail be carried for three months without charge and that a name be chosen for the office. Mail was delivered and Car-

son's daughter Eunice provided the name. He promptly added his home and a general store to the site, but it was the addition of a school in 1910 that turned Eunice into a real community. At that time the town was known for weekly musical productions which might last all day. The Eunice Literary Society held monthly dramatic presentations and readings. The tradition of musical gatherings started by the Carson family, with Eunice then at the piano, continues today. An annual highlight is the fiddling contest, usually held in August, featuring old-time, fancy, and trick fiddling. Contestants and audience come hundreds of miles to hear fine playing, perhaps a man playing fiddle with his work gloves on or a boy playing "Listen to the Mockingbird" while doing various acrobatic stunts. The serious competition includes the rendition of a waltz, a breakdown (square dance or hornpipe), and another chosen dance piece. Most players have learned to play their lively tunes by ear and are accompanied by guitar, piano, banjo, mandolin, or bass. Food and dancing always follow the friendly competition.

The population of Eunice dwindled during years of severe drought, during which the farmers and ranchers used acorns and hard, bitter pie melons as food for their livestock and themselves. After many failed attempts, a well drilled near Eunice began producing oil in 1929, and the town began life anew. The Depression squelched growth until 1935, when oil again brought people and business to Eunice. Several companies here began producing carbon black, a byproduct of burning natural gas and an ingredient of ink, paints, fertilizer, carbon paper, cement, and dark chocolate. Today, oil drilling service companies are still the town's main employers.

Alternate N.M. 18 rejoins N.M. 18 near

Pickhandle Flat, which was named for the weapons used in a feud between two homesteading groups.

Old-timers say that in the 1930s one could drive from Eunice to Jal at night without headlights because of the light provided by flares, the lighted natural gas then considered a mere byproduct of oil production. The present road parallels the Texas and New Mexico Railroad. In the 1920s and 1930s some people drove their cars on the rails rather than using the bumpy, unpaved road. They let the air out of the tires and "doodlebugged."

Just south of the junction with N.M. 128 lies JAL (alt. 3,115, pop. 2,671). The brand of the old Jal Ranch, A headquartered six miles east of present Jal, appears all over town, most dramatically as the shape of the local lake. Geese, ducks, fish, and summer swimmers are at home in the lake, which was built along with a surrounding park and playground in 1973. A small bridge to the island inside the letter A is the only bridge in Lea County, which has no running streams within its 4,738 square miles. (The iron brand of the old Jal Ranch lacked the crossbar on the A because the concentrated heat would have been too intense and could have caused sores on the cattle.)

The chamber of commerce profile of Jal shows the town's sense of humor when it states, "Population—approximately 4000 people within a five mile radius and three soreheads."

The earliest human inhabitants of the area were Indian hunters. Nearly twelve thousand years ago, Clovis Man hunted mammoths, straight-horned bison, camels, dire-wolves, antelopes, and ground-sloths here. Folsom Man hunted the land around Jal for three thousand years, until about 7000 B.C., when a period of terrible drought may have occurred. Other Indian peoples periodically grew some of their food, hunted bison, and gathered wild

plants in the area from the eighth to the fifteenth century A.D. The Kiowas and Comanches hunted in the region during the nineteenth century, but neither they nor their ancestors appear to have made any permanent settlements here. However, they did leave numerous artifacts, which give clues to their culture and hunting methods. The shores of what were once playas ("rain-filled lakes") still yield arrowheads.

Indian and Anglo bison hunters roamed the plains simultaneously only briefly during the second half of the nineteenth century. Overzealous hunting eliminated the animals, and Indians headed for settlements to the north. Many of the Anglo bison hunters became open-range ranchers here in the 1880s. Fences were illegal, and the range was governed by water rights. When a rancher dug a successful well, the grassland within the radius of a one-day cow walk (usually about ten miles) then belonged to him. Horsepower turned the waterwheels at first, but soon windmills replaced them. A new wave of people, homesteaders, came in 1912. These "nesters" were permitted by law to claim and fence 160 acres (one section) apiece if they also lived on the property. Many people built houses directly on section lines so two family members could live on the land, thus claiming 320 acres rather than 160. The homesteaders were dry farmers who supplemented their produce with quail, jackrabbits, and antelope. The breaking up of the land was not always peaceful, and range wars of theft and reprisal sometimes ensued.

Schools were often built at the corners of sections in order to be close to several families. Where schools were built, small communities grew. One of these, Ochoa, west of present Jal, was notorious for its moonshine whiskey. During Prohibition, distilling became so profitable that a small syndicate functioned in Jal to take advantage of the profits. Ochoa also had one gas pump. A rancher one day tied his horse to the pump; the horse bolted at the sound of a backfiring car and pulled the pump away. Now the entire town is gone. The traces of habitation that remain date from four hundred seventy-five to six hundred years before this most recent exodus. The "Ochoa archaeological phase" refers to the occupation of the area by a hunting society from A.D. 1300 to 1450.

Many of the area's small communities and schools disappeared during the Depression, in spite of the discovery of oil, but the Jal school remained open. An area rancher, Mederer, earned brief national attention for his practice of flying his son in a private plane fifteen miles to school in Jal and back in the afternoon.

Jal followed the pattern of Lea County's other cities by becoming a boom town, shrinking during the Depression, and becoming a boom town again. Brothels, gambling dens, and taverns came with the first boom in spite of efforts, by refugees from some of Texas's Sodoms and Gomorrahs, to outlaw them. Feuding land developers in 1927 deliberately platted the town so that streets would not meet. Giant jogs remain today in Jal's flat main streets. Much of the rowdiness left town with the Depression. Jal was revived by continued expansion of the El Paso Natural Gas Company, which is still its largest employer. Most of the gas from the area is piped to California. "The Company" is responsible for the airport and golf course. The town also boasts several parks and a striking library. Beyond Jal to the south lies the vast Chihuahuan desert.

West from Hobbs, U.S. 62/U.S. 180 forms a junction with N.M. 8 thirteen miles from Hobbs. South on this road is MONUMENT, which is named for a thirty-by-thirty-by-twenty-foot pile of stones that has marked a spring for centuries. The Jornada people, a branch of the pottery-making Mogollons, did some farming and built pit houses near here, possibly from A.D. 200 to 400. They developed a culture but disappeared from the *llano* ("plains") for unknown reasons. Both earlier Paleo-Indian and later prehistoric hunters lived in the area. Because of the availability of water, other peoples have been attracted to this site as well. The population peak came between 1909 and 1912; when all available homesteading land was claimed and drought lingered, Monument almost disappeared. Beginning in 1928, it was reborn because of oil, lost to the Depression, resurrected because of more oil, and then lost its population to the more prosperous Hobbs. The town tavern, known as "the pepperbox" because of numerous bullet holes in the walls, has also been hauled away to Hobbs. Some staunch residents remain, as do the massive Hat Ranch house, built in the 1880s, and a sculpted monument of an Indian that does not resemble but is named for Geronimo.

Much of southeast New Mexico is within

the Permian Basin, the bed of which was an inland sea covering New Mexico, Arizona, Colorado, and Utah 250 million years ago. As the water evaporated, it left layer upon layer of dead marine life, which was eventually covered by strata of rock and earth. This marine life was to become the petroleum wealth now being tapped in Lea County. Scientific methods exist that can find rock formations that may hold crude oil, but there is no sure way to know where the petroleum lies until an exploratory, or wildcat, well is dug. These wells are bored with drill bits, while the cutting tool is lubricated and rock fragments flushed away by mud pumped from the surface. The initial release of pressure on the crude oil often brings it to the surface, but most wells require pumps, the giant grasshoppers of the plains, to extract the bulk of the oil they contain. Water is added to the well in a second step to recover the oil, and then polymers are introduced to release more oil. Natural gas is a vaporized fraction of crude oil, often separated naturally in this area. Other fractions of the oil are separated at the refineries in the order of their temperatures of vaporization. The fractions are natural gas, gasoline, benzene, naphtha, kerosene, diesel fuel, light heating oils,

heavy heating oils, and tars. As the oil is heated and sent into a tower, the vapors of the fractions condense on collectors at different heights and are drawn from the collectors for further processing.

The enormous sky and flat horizon of the roads in this part of the state are interrupted by oil wells, pumps, refineries, and the wells for the other precious underground commodity, water. The water of the Ogallala Aquifer that serves the region is ominously low, and because of a shielding layer of caliche (calcium carbonate crust) most ground water from rainfall cannot reach or replenish it.

At the junction with N.M. 31, 57 mi., a region of potash mining begins. The Carlsbad area is within the lowest part of the Permian Basin, and therefore a great concentration of evaporated saline brines occurs here. Potash, K_2CO_3, is of prime importance to agriculture as a plant food and to the chemical industry for use in the manufacture of soft soaps, glass, and other potassium compounds. The name "potash" comes from the way the product was first manufactured: a solution leached from the ashes of wood or kelp burned in pots was evaporated to obtain it. The Carlsbad field was first mined in 1931. Ore is now removed from

a bed of halosilvite averaging eight feet thick and found one thousand feet below the earth's surface. The brine pockets in these salt beds have complicated the federal government's controversial plans for storage of nuclear waste in the Carlsbad area.

In CARLSBAD, 75 mi. (alt. 3,102, pop. 25,592), the junction with U.S. 285 (see Tour 7) intersects Tour 16. The city has taken advantage of its location on the Pecos River by establishing a network of parks along both sides of the water with a wealth of picnic areas, fishing spots, and playgrounds. The most elaborate of these is President's Park, a small, attractive collection of amusement rides and shops. The giant carousel is a fantasy of carved wood pigs, ostriches, and horses.

Real animals native to the Chihuahuan desert are kept in natural-looking settings at the Living Desert Zoological and Botanical State Park north of the city, off U.S. 285. The park serves to protect rare and endangered species of plants and animals. The walk-through aviary includes a saucy jay and many timid desert birds. The nocturnal house displays the elusive night creatures of the desert, including the coatimundi, kangaroo rats, and foxes. Prairie dogs' antics amuse, and reptiles intrigue visitors. The park includes hoofed animal, cat, and bear exhibits. The desert botanical gardens and the propagation house display extraordinary and beautiful plants. Mineral, archaeology, art, and animal exhibits fill the entry building.

The Carlsbad Municipal Museum, within the city's library, emphasizes the history of the area from prehistoric times to the present.

The mineral content of a spring northwest of the city was said to rival that of Karlsbad Springs in Czechoslovakia, so citizens voted in 1899 to change the name of their eleven-year-old community from Eddy to Carlsbad; the county retained the name of the ranching brothers, John and Charles Eddy, who helped organize and promote the town. Although the county courthouse is decorated with the cattle brands of area ranchers and cattle ranches are still important to the area, much of the grassland has been turned over to alfalfa and cotton. The Carlsbad Reclamation Project provides irrigation for the valley and serves to ensure flood protection on the Pecos River.

Tourism and potash mining remain the town's most important industries. In the late 1960s Carlsbad suffered an economic depression because of the world oversupply of potash. However, intensive farming has created potash deficiencies in the soil, and demand for potash increased throughout the 1970s, only to decrease again in the 1980s.

The establishment of the federal Waste Isolation Pilot Project for burial of nuclear waste would bring many new jobs and also possible dangers to the area. The WIPP officials have a permit to build storage tunnels in salt beds near Carlsbad to demonstrate the feasibility of salt as a repository medium. Environmental and political concerns, as well as geological surprises, have delayed the project.

On U.S. 62/U.S. 180 south of Carlsbad is a U.S. tourist information center. A private auto museum with a large collection stands east of the highway.

Carlsbad Caverns, *Harvey Caplin.*

WHITE'S CITY, 94 mi., is at the junction with N.M. 7, the road to Carlsbad Caverns. Tourist services and a private museum cluster at the national park boundary. Inside the park, the road winds up the Capitan Reef with several pulloffs for vistas, interpretive exhibits, and developed nature trails. Deer are frequently seen among the spiky, garden-like growth of sotol, yucca, and ocotillo. Banks of prickly pear, pitaya, and strawberry cactus grip the limestone palisades.

At the top of the limestone reef is the park headquarters and visitors' center. Information is available here about cavern tours and thirty-nine other caves within the park. These caves may be entered only with permission of the superintendent of Carlsbad Caverns National Park. Hiking permits are required for overnight trips within the park.

The caverns are open every day of the year, with tour schedules varying according to the season. A modest admission fee is charged. A nursery and kennel are available at the headquarters. Visitors may purchase food and film in the depths of the cavern. Comfortable walking shoes and a sweater are recommended, as the temperature in the caverns remains at

SIDE TOUR

fifty-six degrees summer and winter. Access to the Big Room is by a long, steep, and safe walking trail or by elevator; the trail through the Big Room will accommodate wheelchairs.

Events leading to the formation of the Caverns began during the Permian period of geologic history, around 250 million years ago, when the southeastern corner of New Mexico and West Texas were covered by a shallow sea and had a climate similar to the present one. In this sea lived countless generations of lime-secreting algae. The remains of each successive generation built up to form a lime reef more than one mile across and hundreds of feet thick. The fossils of many types of sea life are scattered throughout this reef mass. The lagoon between the Capitan Reef and the land mass filled gradually with deposits from rivers flowing from the higher land into the sea. Layers of salts and gypsum also were deposited in the basin as the lagoon water evaporated, and the whole area became deeply covered with sediment. The land rose, beginning about sixty million years ago. The Guadalupe Mountains formed as the earth's crust shifted upward.

Movement of the crust millions of years ago caused two systems of small cracks to appear in the reef, one perpendicular and one parallel to the reef's axis. Water, which had become a weak acid from collected chemicals and humus, seeped through these fissures and dissolved some of the limestone. The seepage created gradually enlarging cavities filled with water. Large parts of the reef resembled a giant, water-saturated sponge. The water table dropped, and slowly the rock "sponge" emptied, causing collapse of large sections of the network and opening great chambers.

The most common cave deposits are stalactites and stalagmites of many shapes and sizes, formed by weakly acidic groundwater containing dissolved limestone. This water appeared in the chambers as drops on the ceilings. The carbon dioxide in the solution was then released into the air, and the water, no longer an acid, was rendered incapable of carrying the lime in solution. At that point the lime in the water became the first trace of a stalactite or, if the water was flowing fast, of a stalagmite, built up by drops on the floor. On the ceiling the limestone deposit began in a circle at the edge of the drop of water. The next drop appeared in the same place and added another miniscule layer to the ring. Many layers resulted in a hollow tube of limestone called a soda-straw stalactite. Some soda straws grew longer than seven feet, as one can see in the caverns today. If the hollow tube was plugged or there was too much water at once, the stalactite took on the more common conical shape. If the opening in the center of the straw was too small for a

drop to form, capillary action caused the limestone deposit to form by chance rather than by gravity. The irregularly deposited particles formed great tangles of limestone called helictites, which grow in all directions. Cave pearls (layers of limestone formed around a small foreign object like a bat bone) and helictites are rare formations.

Repetition of these processes caused the stalactites and stalagmites to grow, some to more than fifty feet in height and twelve feet in diameter, over thousands of years. Sometimes stalagmites and stalactites met, forming columns. A small amount of iron or other mineral matter in the limestone produced delicate tinting. The brilliant and translucent growing formations result from saturation with water; the dull and dry stones are called "dead" formations.

Erosion eventually stripped away much of the rock overlying the highest level of the cave. The roof collapsed in two small places, one a narrow rift with a vertical drop of over one hundred feet and the other the opening through which one may enter on the Carlsbad Cavern walking tour.

A swarm of bats emerging from this opening led cowboy Jim White to rediscover the cave in 1901, though early Indians apparently knew of its existence. White told anyone who would listen about his fantastic explorations in the cave. Word got to government officials Robert Holley and Dr. Willis T. Lee, who investigated. Dr. Lee's expedition reports were published in the *National Geographic* magazine in 1923 and 1924. A photograph in the report was printed upside down,

but almost no one caught the error since the rock formations were so extraordinary. In 1930 President Hoover signed the bill making the area a national park.

Bats still inhabit the caves, emerging each evening except during the winter, when they migrate to Mexico. There are five species of bat, the most common of which is the Mexican freetail. Their immense number is decreasing rapidly, in part because of the use of pesticides in their feeding areas. It is estimated that one hundred thousand bats eat one and one-half tons of insects nightly on a nonstop flight of about ten hours. A seasonal evening program informs visitors about the tiny, flying mammals; meanwhile the bats release their grip on their roost at the ceiling of the cave and come up the final 150 feet to the outside in a counter-clockwise spiral at the rate of between five and ten thousand per minute.

The bats' enormous appetites and their droppings, guano, have assisted area farmers greatly. In 1933 the Carlsbad Bat Guano Company began the manufacture of fertilizers from thousands of tons of guano removed from the cave. Most of the fertilizer was sent to California for use on the citrus groves The bulk of the droppings left from seventeen thousand years of habitation by bats has now been removed, and the fertilizer plants are closed. A slight odor lingers as the visitor walks into the gaping entrance to Carlsbad Caverns. The bare, high-ceilinged entrance gives little hint of the extent of the cavern chambers or of the delicate rock tracery, grandiose obelisks, monoliths, pagodas, and festoons of stalactites to be seen below.

U.S. 62/U.S. 180 continues through a rolling terrain, with the Guadalupe Mountains to the west. Many stories of secret gold mines are told about these mountains. One of them concerns a man named Old Ben Sublett, a water witch for the railroad, who located wells along the right of way with a hazel wand. It is said that one day his wand served him even better and he returned from a trip into the Guadalupe Mountains with a sack of gold. Ben refused to tell where he had made the find. Repeated efforts to discover his secret were unsuccessful, for Sublett was a good shot and left no tracks. After his death, a shepherd told gold seekers that the mine had been found by a man named Long, and express office records revealed that an Ed Long had consigned $30,000 in gold to himself in California.

Two major sites in the Guadalupe Mountains, Hermit's Cave and Burnet Cave, have been found to contain Paleo-Indian remains that indicate Indian habitation in the area for ten or twelve millennia.

The Butterfield Trail, a main route from San Francisco to Tipton, Missouri, during Gold Rush days, rounds the southern point of the Guadalupe Mountains. This route through El Paso was used to avoid the snows of the Rocky Mountains. Limestone caves in New Mexico were favorite haunts of bandits who preyed upon wagon-train shipments of gold and merchandise. Later the same caves served as hideouts for cattle rustlers and outlaws, including Billy the Kid, whose name appears on the wall of one of the canyons.

SIDE TOUR

Travelers will find the turnoff to New Cave at 100 mi. Tours of New Cave and Slaughter Canyon are given only by reservation with the National Park Service at Carlsbad Caverns.

"New" is not an appropriate name for a formation that is several million years old. In relation to its age, the cave was discovered only moments ago, in 1937, though Indians had used it long before. Tom Tucker, a bat guano miner, found it when his goats wandered to the entrance. Tucker's main interest in the cave was its supply of bat guano, so he filed a mineral claim on it. He and a partner mined the cave intermittently for twenty years, until chemical fertilizers replaced bat guano on the market. In 1973 the Park Service opened the cave's vast interior to flashlight tours. There is a strenuous one-mile uphill hike to reach the entrance and a one-and-one-quarter-mile walk through the interior. A visitor should have good shoes, water, and a flashlight. The limestone formations within New Cave are worth the trip; the sparkling Christmas Tree Formation and the nefarious-looking Clansman are highlights.

The J. Slaughter Ranch headquarters were along the highway near the Texas border. This was the starting point of the important east-west Slaughter Cattle Trail, which began in 1879.

Beyond the Texas line, where the mountain range extends into Texas, Guadalupe Mountains National Park can be seen west of the road. Dirt roads head off U.S. 62/U.S. 180 back into New Mexico and to the Cornudas ("horned") Mountains. On their southern slope there are plastered and painted caves, now blackened with soot, and many thousands of petroglyphs. Early Indians have left traces of their culture on the east side of the Cornudas, and raiding Apaches took secret shelter in the caves centuries later.

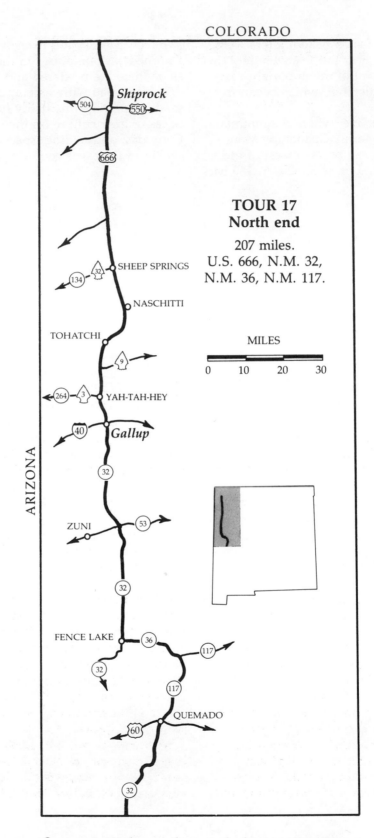

COLORADO

Shiprock

504 ●550→

666

**TOUR 17
North end**

207 miles.
U.S. 666, N.M. 32,
N.M. 36, N.M. 117.

134→ 32 SHEEP SPRINGS

○ NASCHITTI

TOHATCHI ○

9→

MILES

0   10   20   30

←264 3 ○ YAH-TAH-HEY

←40 ○ *Gallup*

32

ZUNI
○ 53→

32

FENCE LAKE ● 36 117→

32 117

QUEMADO

←60 ○

32

ARIZONA

See page 589 for southern end of tour seventeen.

582

tour seventeen

Colorado Border • *Shiprock* • *Gallup* • *Quemado* • **Reserve** • **Silver City** • *Deming* •
Columbus • *Mexico Border*

Paralleling the western border of New Mexico, this tour passes through six counties on its way from the Colorado state line to New Mexico's only full-service international border crossing at Columbus, New Mexico/Las Palomas, Chihuahua. Unlike most of the tours, which follow the course of a single highway, Tour 17's route requires eight different numbered roads. In so doing it encounters few large towns but much magnificent and widely varied scenery.

Between the Colorado border and Gallup, the traveler crosses the high plain of the Navajo Reservation on U.S. 666. To the east is an open, sparsely vegetated, rolling basinland stretching for miles to the Bisti Badlands and Chaco Canyon. To the west one passes the towering monolith of Shiprock, sacred to the Navajos, and several other remarkable rock castles before the Chuska range comes into view. Numerous trading posts and Navajo tribal chapter houses are placed near the road; the great rug-weaving districts of Two Grey Hills and Crystal are nearby. Between Gallup and Silver City, on six different highways, most of the route is mountainous, forested largely with Ponderosa pine, with piñon and juniper at lower elevations. There are only small villages on this portion of the route, with few accommodations except at Gallup and Silver City. Catron County, through which the route winds for 125 miles, is known for its mountain wilderness, ranching (including ranches where Butch Cassidy and the Sundance Kid once stayed), played-out mines, and very few people. South of Silver City, U.S. 180 and N.M. 11 traverse the desert, passing through Deming to the town of Columbus, raided by Pancho Villa's revolutionary band in 1914.

U.S. 666 leaves Colorado and the Ute Reservation to travel through arid country on its way to Shiprock. Four miles north of the state line, U.S. 160 heads west to the Four Corners Monument, marking the only spot in the United States where four states (New Mexico, Colorado, Arizona, and Utah) come together. The monument can also be reached by N.M. 504 from Shiprock.

SHIPROCK, 15 mi. (alt. 4,965, pop. 7,228), the largest town on the Navajo Reservation, has grown rapidly due to the building of small tract homes on barren land. The town is the

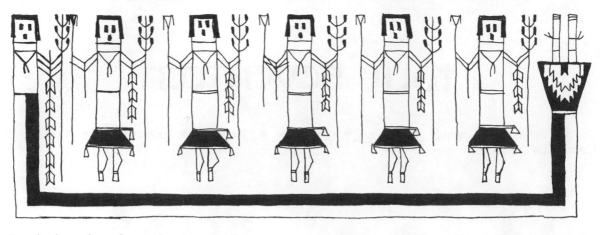

site of a large boarding school, an Indian Health Service Hospital, and a number of trading posts. These specialize in Yeibichai and Two Grey Hills rugs from nearby weavers, but textiles from other parts of the reservation are also available. Since areas within the reservation are no longer as isolated from one another as they once were, weavers may learn and execute patterns more characteristic of other areas. Therefore any discussion of regional styles presupposes that the styles described may actually originate in any part of the Navajo Reservation, even if they once came solely from one area.

Navajo weaving for a time seemed to be a dying art, as fewer and fewer weavers pursued the painstaking work on the upright loom. Spurred by nineteenth-century traders such as Don Lorenzo Hubbell in Ganado, Arizona, however, weavers gradually improved the quality of their work, for these traders paid premium prices for well-designed, well-executed works. Hubbell and others sold these rugs by mail order, priced according to weight. It was not until the second half of the twentieth century that rug prices began to escalate, ensuring the entry of talented young weavers into the field. The price structure now strongly rewards quality: knowledgeable buyers check for symmetry, consistency of materials, natural dyes, and other indicators of quality when offering to buy. Higher prices are also paid for rugs characteristic of one of the regional types, thus strengthening these styles.

Typical of the Shiprock area are the Yei and Yeibichai rugs, portraying religious figures—

tall, slender, sticklike, with stylized arms and legs, usually lacking true religious significance. The rugs generally are woven with commercially dyed yarn, and may be coarse or fine in texture.

Two other locally produced types of rugs are also available in Shiprock, easily identifiable as to origin. Teec Nos Pos, an area close to the Four Corners Monument, produces a bright and busy rug with a broad, figured border and intricate geometric designs, largely using commercially dyed wool. It is said that a missionary to the area early in the twentieth century circulated pictures of Persian rugs among weavers, influencing them to adopt a similar style. One of the most popular and most costly regional rug types is the Two Grey Hills rug, named for a trading post twenty-five miles south of Shiprock. This style emerged in the twentieth century after area weavers threw off an attempt by a trader from Crystal to introduce bright commercial colors. The Two Grey Hills rug uses black, a commercial color, and the natural colors of brown, gray, and white, woven with a dark (usually black) border and strong, geometric designs within the border. Some of the finest Two Grey Hills rugs can be classified as tapestries rather than floor coverings; the works of Daisy Tauglechee, for example, may have 120 threads of her hand-spun wool to the inch and a buttery texture.

Further south, a small community on the west side of the Chuska Mountains produces the Crystal rug. Although the art of weaving in the Crystal area was fostered and revived by the famous early trader John B. Moore, the

Gallup-Shiprock highway, *Harvey Caplin.*

designs that he favored—colorful, bordered, with features such as arrows and swastikas (a traditional Navajo design element)—are no longer seen. The current Crystal product is very different, borderless and comprised largely of contrasting bands of vegetal-dye colors. The bands themselves are made through a technique called the "wavy line," formed by the alternation of strands of different colors. Within some of the bands are such other decorations as arrows, feathers, or geometric designs. Many of the regional styles from elsewhere on the reservation (across the Arizona border) are available in trading posts in the larger towns, such as Shiprock and Gallup, as well as in Albuquerque and Santa Fe, as are the specialty rugs—pictorials, double weaves, and storm patterns.

As the traveler heads south from the town of Shiprock, the monolithic formation called Shiprock (because of its resemblance to a sailing craft with wind-filled sheets) looms to the west. Tribal route 13 heads west from U.S. 666 to Red Rock, Arizona, at 21 mi. Follow this road 7.8 miles, turning north just before reaching a spectacular hogback, or rocky

ridge, of vertically oriented strata. About three miles of this twisting dirt track will bring the traveler to the base of Shiprock. A climb around the base affords many fine views of the hogback, the monolith itself, and the barren canyons, walled by red rock, to the west. As with all such rock monuments in Navajo country, it is forbidden to climb the Shiprock because of its religious significance. The rock itself soars 1,450 feet above the dry plain. Like the other monoliths that dot the northern part of the Navajo Reservation, Shiprock is composed of dark igneous rock that once plugged the core of a volcano. The softer rock of the surrounding volcano long ago eroded away.

Several other spectacular monuments of volcanic stone front U.S. 666 as it continues south; the first is Barber Peak, at 26 mi. At 39 mi. and 41 mi., small roads head west to the trading posts at Sanostee (from the Navajo for "surrounded by rock") and Two Grey Hills. Sanostee weavers have altered the basic Two Grey Hills rug design by incorporating colors other than the characteristic black, grey, brown, and white. The added colors are all obtained from vegetal dyes derived from wild plants growing in the area.

U.S. 666 is almost entirely straight in this stretch, with numerous small dirt roads leading east and west at irregular intervals. Until the 1960s and 1970s, almost all roads on the Navajo Reservation were similar to these unmarked tracks heading to unknown places across open country. Now many of the more important roads have been paved, but travel for Navajo families living among the tangle of dirt roads becomes impossible when summer

rains or melting snows turn their long "driveways" into quagmires. Despite the almost universal replacement of horse-drawn wagons by pickup trucks, spring thaws often bring out government helicopters for the transportation of food and animal fodder to mud-stranded families. The combination of paved roads and the pickup truck has revolutionized Navajo life. The local trading post still exists throughout the reservation, but it is not the sole gathering place it once was; many Navajos meet for shopping, trade, and socialization at newly accessible towns ringing the reservation.

East of U.S. 666 is a large, barren area, very sparsely settled. In the 1980s an energy-hungry country and coal-mining concerns were pressing strongly to open the starkly beautiful area to the strip mining of coal. Navajos living in the area, largely on Bureau of Land Management land, joined groups of environmentally concerned citizens in opposing the coal companies, but it seemed inevitable that at least some of the area would be mined, perhaps including sensitive areas near the prehistoric sites of Chaco Canyon (on Tour 6).

Near U.S. 666 are a great number of ruins of prehistoric dwellings, belonging to early Pueblo, not Navajo, civilizations. Many are directly related to the remarkable Chaco culture; the sites at Crumbled House and the extremely dense cluster of sites at Skunk Springs were probably among the hundreds of "Chaco outliers," villages at the ends of the spokes of the giant wheel controlled by the hub at Chaco Canyon. The ruins at Skunk Springs contain several great kivas; these suggest that this settlement may have housed a religious or administrative center of the Chaco culture. Other sites around the rim of the wheel cover large parts of the arid northwest corner of New Mexico.

The Navajos may not have arrived in this area by the time all of the Chaco civilization had departed, although the Navajo creation legend specifies that the Navajos emerged from another world into their present homeland bounded by their four sacred mountains. Archaeologic and linguistic evidence, on the other hand, suggests that the Navajos and Apaches are descended from a large group of Indians living in northwestern Canada, who speak a similar Athapascan language. The nomadic Navajos and Apaches are thought to have come south along the Rocky Mountains more than one thousand years after Christ, filling the vacuum left by the departing Anasazi, ancestors of the Pueblo Indians of today, in the fourteenth century.

SIDE TOUR

At 59 mi., Tribal Route 32 climbs rapidly west from the Sheep Springs Trading Post and chapter house. (Navajo tribal government consists of a tribal chairman and a tribal council, with councillors selected from each of the fifty-six chapter houses, which form social and governmental units throughout the reservation.) The road, now paved, climbs from the arid plain, through piñon- and juniper-covered foothills, to Washington Pass, twelve miles west of Sheep Springs, sheltered by tall spruces and Ponderosa pines. Near the pass are several beautiful lakes, of which Blue Lake and Todacheenie Lake are the best-known. There are fine tribally maintained public campsites near the pass, excellent for escape from the summer heat along U.S. 666. Descending the west face of the Chuska (Navajo for "white spruce" or "pine") Mountains, one comes across the community of Crystal at 16 mi. The route described here has been traveled by Navajos and traders for years.

At numerous times in the late nineteenth and early twentieth centuries entrepreneurs attempted to establish trading posts along the route, but heavy winter snows limited their endurance. Trader John B. Moore, who settled in Crystal in 1896, used the long, cold winters to circulate among Navajo weavers, working with them to improve their wares. Crystal is a year-round settlement; many Navajos establish summer camps in the upper reaches of the Chuskas to escape the heat and pasture their sheep.

The road continues past Crystal, reaching Tribal Route 12 at 21 mi. from Sheep Springs. Six miles south of this junction is the town of Navajo, New Mexico, site of the large tribal lumbering enterprise. Twelve miles farther south is the tribal capital and administrative center at Window Rock, just across the state line in Arizona, named for a formation in its spectacular red rock backdrop.

Continuing south from Sheep Springs on U.S. 666, the highway passes the trading posts of Naschitti and Buffalo Springs and enters TOHATCHI (alt. 6,100, pop. 1,036)—the word means "scratch for water"—at 83 miles. Tohatchi was built on a site of ancient ruins and has been a center of schooling and missionary activity for years. The Reverend L. P. Brink, a Christian Reformed missionary who came here in 1900, was one of the first to put the complicated, tonal language of the Navajos into print. His *Ethnologic Dictionary of the Navajo Language* has been a much-used reference for decades; Franciscan fathers at St. Michael's mission near Window Rock furthered Brink's linguistic work in later years. Above Tohatchi looms Chuska Peak, at 8,795 feet the highest mountain in the Chuska range. A shadowy group of "Navajo witches" is said to inhabit the peak, thus making it off-limits for traditional Navajos.

At 91 mi., Tribal Route 9 heads east through the small communities of Brimhall and Standing Rock to Crownpoint and Chaco Canyon (see Tour 6). At 99 mi., Tribal Route 3 (also numbered N.M. 264) leads into the reservation and past a large coal strip-mine to Window Rock, seventeen miles to the west. The junction of this road with U.S. 666 is called Ya-Ta-Hey; the name is a corruption of the Navajo greeting, *Ya'ateeh,* which also means "beautiful" or "good."

At 103 mi., U.S. 666 passes the settlement of Gamerco, named for the Gallup American Coal Company, which mined actively here from 1921 to 1950, attracting immigrant workers from all over Europe. The miles of underground passages are abandoned now, awaiting further increases in the price of coal that will make their exploitation profitable once more. The road reaches Gallup (see Tour 6) and I-40 at 107 mi.

At the end of the overpass over the interstate highway, U.S. 666 becomes N.M. 32, which bypasses Gallup and climbs through wooded hills before dropping again into the valley of the often-dry Zuni River. Scattered Navajo settlements and Anglo ranches dot the hills on both sides of the road until it crosses the boundary of the Zuni Reservation at 127 mi. At 130 mi. is a junction with N.M. 53 (Tour 18). To the west is the pueblo of Zuni, the first of the pueblos to be visited by Spanish explorers seeking vainly for the Seven Cities of Cibola, said to be made of gold; to the east are the Ramah Navajo band's major settlement and El Morro National Monument.

Continuing south past the intersection, the traveler can occasionally see the hogans of the Ramah Navajos among the piñons and junipers. The circular or octagonal house, its door always looking east, is traditional for the Navajos, who for centuries have built similar structures of materials close at hand—in some areas of stone, here of logs.

FENCE LAKE is a tiny settlement at a crossroads in western Cibola County, 163 mi. Land near the lake has recently been promoted for vacation-home sites. Fence Lake once included a large reservoir fenced in by stockmen; now the only lake, usually dry, is in a parched riverbed several miles north of the small community.

As N.M. 32 becomes quite rough past Fence Lake, the traveler is well-advised to take N.M. 36 east from its intersection with 32, just past the school. In hilly country similar to that between Gallup and Fence Lake, N.M. 36 meets N.M. 117 twenty-one miles to the southeast. It is possible from this point to drive the spectacular and very lonely route northeast to a point nine miles east of Grants, traversing mountainous country and the black lava fields of the Malpais. Heading south once again on N.M. 117, one reaches U.S. 60 (Tour 8) at QUEMADO, 204 mi. In Quemado is a ranger station from which information can be obtained about the Gila National Forest south of the little town. Quemado's tiny high school made headlines in the late 1970s for its football team, which included the only female to have played the sport in one of the state's high schools.

South of Quemado, N.M. 32 resumes, traveling amid magnificent mountain scenery through the Gallo Mountains within the Gila National Forest. At 227 mi. the traveler reaches Quemado Lake, a beautiful, large reservoir suitable for boating, fishing, and camping in the adjoining Forest Service campground. Several small logging and lumber mill operations and cattle ranches account for the few dwellings along the remainder of the thirty-nine-mile stretch to Apache Creek. The road passes through alpine scenery, climbing to eighty-five hundred feet at Jewett Gap. It then plunges through oaks, aspens, and cottonwoods, past pine trees to Apache Creek. (See Tour 8.)

Five miles before reaching that small town, and just before leaving the national forest, the traveler may explore Lee Russel Canyon, a five-mile hike across Apache Creek from N.M. 32. Nearby, archaeologists have found a treasure trove of colorful agates of many types and potsherds from the cookware of prehistoric Indians and of the Chiricahua Apaches, who used the area as a hideout in the 1880s. One mile north of Apache Creek's store and a three-mile walk up Apache Creek is a fine waterfall. The walk along the creek reveals many forms of wildlife in a shaded, pretty habitat.

Beyond Apache Creek, N.M. 12 continues to wind through sparsely populated country. The hills to the left of the road are topped with flat, fort-like ridges of stone. Ahead the traveler glimpses plains edged by mountains.

RESERVE, 262 mi. (alt. 6,380, pop. 437), the seat of Catron County, lies along the banks of the San Francisco River, surrounded by pine-covered hills. The tiny town, named by a U.S. Forest Service employee for the forest "reserves" in the area, was founded by Mormon cattlemen in the 1860s and has retained the flavor and atmosphere of those days, when gold strikes and cattle drives promoted wild Saturday nights. There were originally three

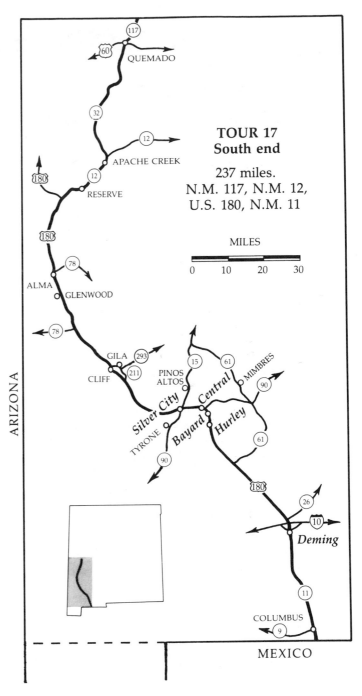

TOUR 17
South end

237 miles.
N.M. 117, N.M. 12,
U.S. 180, N.M. 11

towns, Upper, Middle, and Lower San Francisco Plaza; the Upper Plaza alone survives as Reserve, whose streets are wide enough for fabled Western encounters with gunmen and whose false-front buildings house friendly saloons and the businesses necessary for cattle raising.

Back when Reserve was still three towns, the Middle Plaza provided the setting for a famous gunfight, from which emerged a New Mexican folk hero, Elfego Baca. Baca, a deputy sheriff from Socorro, had a reputation for being a tough law-and-order man. He came to the Middle Plaza in 1884, when he was eighteen, to help a friend, also a deputy sheriff, who was having trouble controlling the Texas cowboys who accompanied the cattle drives. Baca arrested one cowboy for shooting up the town. After the local justice let the cowboy off, some of his friends threatened to "get" Baca. They cornered him in a shack and besieged him for thirty-three hours. Baca held off his attackers singlehandedly, killing three Texans and wounding several more. A truce was finally called. Baca was arrested and taken back to Socorro, where he was tried for murder and acquitted. He later continued to bring his brand of law and order to New Mexico as sheriff in Socorro, after being variously a county clerk, a mayor, a school superintendent, and a district attorney. He died at the age of eighty in his law office in Albuquerque.

Reserve's main street follows the river as it winds through the valley past the old Frisco Store in what was Middle Plaza, past the old church, and past fields of grazing cattle and horses, coming to an end beyond the old Lower Plaza, now called San Francisco Plaza. An unpaved road continues through the Gila National Forest to link up with N.M. 78.

Near Reserve a number of archaeological sites belonging to the Mogollon culture have been excavated. Named after the mountain range that cuts across the Gila National Forest,

the culture evolved around 300 B.C. and lasted until A.D. 1250. Archaeologists are not yet sure of its origins, but they believe that the Mogollon people were basically food gatherers and hunters. After A.D. 900 the Anasazi influenced the Mogollon, as can be seen in the T-shaped doors found in the Gila cliffdwellings and the designs on the Mogollon black-on-white pottery. Archaeologists believe that Anasazi immigrants in the thirteenth century caused overcrowding of the Mogollon area, which led to eventual movement up to Zuni country.

The Pine Lawn phase (named after a local cattle brand) is an early branch of the Mogollon culture, evolving around 250 B.C. The SU site about seven miles west of Reserve on top of a ridge dates from that era. Here remains of pit houses, circular dwellings partially dug out of the earth, yielded up a variety of pottery and artifacts that gave archaeologists some idea of the development of the Mogollon people. The pit houses were built of logs and chinked with mud and branches. Today all that remain are depressions in the earth. The Starkweather Ruin, three and a half miles east of Reserve in the Gila National Forest, was inhabited much later, around A.D. 927. Here the pithouses were dug deep in the ground; there was also a round "great lodge." Like SU, this site has not been restored.

A few miles southwest of Reserve, U.S. 180 joins N.M. 12 from Springerville, Arizona. The highway continues south as U.S. 180, traveling through roughhewn Starkweather Canyon and then through an open, rolling valley where tall pines and stands of juniper sometimes close in on the road.

ALMA, 293 mi., is the next stop on the route, more than twenty-five miles past Reserve. Only a few families reside in what was once a prosperous supply town for nearby ranches and mining camps. In spite of the unsettling fear of Apache attacks, the town grew and was thriving up to 1913. One member of

Butch Cassidy's Wild Bunch made Alma his home after serving time in the penitentiary. He stayed for two years before going straight in Wyoming.

Surrounding Alma, the W-S ranch spreads over many acres. W-S stands for Wilson and Stevens, the names of the original partners. Montague Stevens had come from England for a vacation when he decided to join the hunt for Geronimo. He was fascinated by the land around the Mogollon range and decided to start a cattle ranch there with his friend Harold Wilson. The W-S was unwittingly the headquarters for the Butch Cassidy gang when the famous outlaw and his cohorts worked there for a time in the late 1890s. Gang members earned reputations as good workers, and Butch was even offered a permanent job here. He declined, not wanting to ruin the good name of the ranch. Stevens later became a partner in the Stevens-Upshur ranch, which eventually included holdings in an eighty-by-thirty-mile area. He continued to take part in the army's efforts to capture Geronimo, who with his bands was hiding out in the Mogollons during the 1870s, leaving camp to attack travelers and settlers in the valley.

Stevens was also on the final expedition to Mexico that culminated when Geronimo chose capture by U.S. soldiers over death at the hands of Yaqui Indians. Stevens wrote with admiration of the chief, who had eluded some eight thousand U.S. soldiers for eight years.

Alma gives its name to the first pottery of the Mogollon area, a plain brown ware called Alma Plain and Alma Rough.

A detour to the east of the highway at Alma on N.M. 78 leads to MOGOLLON, 9 mi., a well-preserved ghost town, now once more home to a few people, including some artists and craftsmen. To get to Mogollon, the traveler must endure a drive on a narrow road that climbs up the side of a hill, along a high meadow, and down the steep side of Silver Creek Canyon. Hairpin turns as the road dips down to the valley floor make it advisable to take this trip in the daytime. There are spectacular views for those who can look. Watch for the new mines working in the canyon. Mogollon itself is picturesque, the old buildings lining a rough road that labors up the steep canyon to the Little Fanny Mine at the top of the hill. Abandoned mine shafts and sluices, an old hotel and general store, the cemetery, and the residences of the miners make wonderful pictures and provide colorful places where imaginations can wander.

Mogollon takes its name from the Mogollon range, rough mountains that hem in the west side of the Gila Wilderness and include Whitewater Baldy (10,892 feet) and Mogollon Baldy (10,778 feet). The mountains were the scene of Apache raids, gold strikes, and pioneer settlements, and today provide trails for backpackers. They were named after Don Juan Ignacio Flores Mogollón, who governed the Spanish territory from New Mexico to the West Coast in the early eighteenth century. The town itself grew up in the

SIDE TOUR

Mogollon, *Joan Larson.*

1870s, when silver was found in its canyons. Sergeant James Cooney, stationed at Fort Bayard in 1870, discovered a gold quartz rock while on patrol in the area. He said nothing about his discovery, but upon his discharge returned to the site to work his claim. Others followed, not only miners but camp followers, gamblers, and other picturesque characters. Several mining towns sprang up on Mineral Creek.

The whole district became known as the Cooney mining district, and the sergeant also gave his name to the settlement of Cooney, a few miles from present-day Mogollon, and Cooney Canyon, where he was buried after Apaches killed him in 1880. Cooney's friends blasted a hole in the rock to make a tomb for him, which can be visited in Mineral Creek.

By 1880 the major activity had shifted to Silver Creek, and Mogollon became a rowdy mining town. Floods and fires wiped the town out several times, but it was always rebuilt. Mogollon's tenacity is understood when the production figures for its mines are known: in 1913, for example, gold and silver from them accounted for 40 percent of New Mexico's

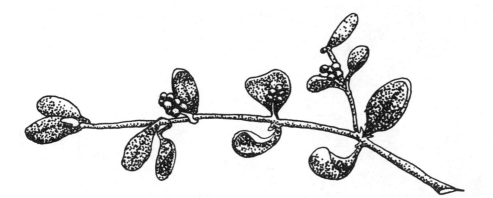

production. Nowadays the old mines are quiet.

Past Mogollon the road remains paved for about five miles and then continues unpaved to several campgrounds, popular for fishing and for their accessibility to the Gila Wilderness area: Bursum (ten miles from Mogollon), Ben Lilly, Willow Creek, and Gilita (twenty miles in from Mogollon), are only open from April or May through November. The drive from Mogollon to Willow Creek is lovely, particularly in the fall when the trees change color. A rough, graveled, but scenic road continues on to Beaverhead, some forty miles, where a paved road provides access to the ghost towns of Winston and Chloride. From this point N.M. 61 runs south past fishing spots and campgrounds, completing this 130-mile loop through the Gila when it joins N.M. 90. This is just one of a network of routes through the Gila Wilderness and Black Range that should only be taken after careful checking with forest rangers.

Once back on the main road there are only five miles to the next detour at GLENWOOD, 300 mi., a small resort town hidden among the trees and site of a fish hatchery.

Turn east here and take a winding country road up to WHITEWATER CANYON and the CATWALK. Twisted trees shade the picnic ground at the entrance to Whitewater Canyon, which was used as sanctuary by Apache leaders Geronimo and Nana during the years of the Apache wars. After Cooney's find of gold and silver and the subsequent development of mining, a town was built at the mouth of the canyon to service the mines. Named Graham, it was also the site of a mill, which had to be located here since the terrain closer to the mines was so rough. Because the creek often dried up, miners built a pipeline from about three miles up the canyon, where there was always water, down to the mine. This first line ran along the west side of the canyon; as more water was needed, the miners built a larger pipe which hung directly over the creek. This was nicknamed the catwalk by the men who had to walk along it to repair it.

The Graham mill closed in 1913. Much later, in 1961, the Forest Service built the present steel catwalk, making repairs since then as necessary, as when heavy rains wash out major parts of the walk. Such rains can cause flash floods; hikers are warned to be cautious.

A short way up from the picnic area the walk begins on a steel pathway hugging the rock face above the canyon's flow. Railings provide security for the walk which crosses the creek and continues up the western edge of the narrow, tunnel-like gorge. When appropriate the walk is cut out of the rock itself or constructed of hardy planks. The two-and-one-half-mile walk is not difficult; children es-

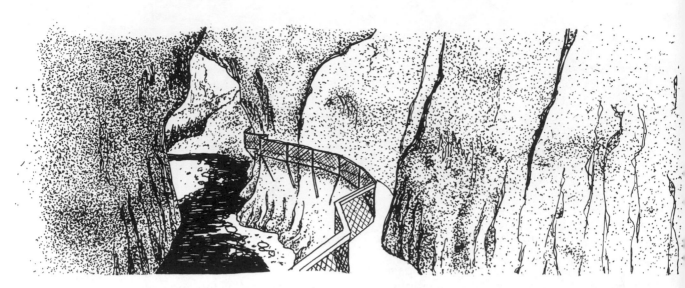

pecially will enjoy clambering up the rocks and along the narrow steel walkway as it hangs over the creek.

Return to Glenwood and continue south, passing Pleasanton, 302 mi., an aptly named settlement on the San Francisco River sur-rounded by small farms, orchards, and cattle ranches. Some thirteen miles farther on, N.M. 78 branches off to the west to Mule Creek and the Arizona border. U.S. 180 now runs along a plain where homesteaders built their houses and planted their crops.

SIDE TOUR

At CLIFF, 331 mi., the road joins N.M. 211, which loops around and through tiny Gila before rejoining the main road, a detour of some five miles. This side trip takes in the Kwilleylekia ruins, an ancient city of the Salado Indians. The Salados were a minor culture of the area, named for the salt river where they settled. Because the ruins are located on private land, they are not clearly marked; neither are they always open. (Hours are 8 A.M. to 6 P.M. in the summer.) However, the detour to get to the ruins is not long.

Follow N.M. 211 for a few miles east until it branches off as N.M. 293, where a sign advertises "Ruins." Here, down a dirt road is Kwilleylekia, where the Saladoan people lived for some one hundred fifty years from about A.D. 1325 to 1475, while farming in the fertile valley. A flash flood forced them to abandon their homes. While this event was tragic for the Indians, it has proved of tremendous worth to archaeologists. Although the flood destroyed the adobe buildings, the emergency caused the inhabitants to leave most of their belongings behind, and archaeologists have been able to study mounds of tools, utensils, and weapons, at the same time reconstructing the ancient town. After the Saladoans left, nomadic Apaches camped in the remains of their city, and the bodies of those who died there were abandoned; at one time those viewing the ruins were able to see whole skeletons simply leaning against the walls of the rooms.

The loop route on N.M. 211 through Gila, a jumping-off point for backpacking and pack trips into the Gila Wilderness area, leaves the lush farmland for more desolate scenery: bare hillsides covered with scrub and eroded *arroyos*.

Back on U.S. 180 the countryside changes again; corrals and windmills are evidence of farming activities, and new adobe homes show that people are still moving to the area.

SILVER CITY, 360 mi. (alt. 5,851, pop. 9,887), is approached from a hill, and the first view of the town shows it spread out below, the streets laid out in dutiful blocks even as they straggle up and down hills. While the modern outskirts of the town sprawl, the center remains an old Western town, preserved as a historic district. The Silver City Museum at 312 West Broadway is a good place to start a visit; its extensive display of old photographs shows the city from its beginnings. Other exhibits feature frontier furnishings and Indian artifacts. The museum itself is located in the H. B. Ailman House, former home of a prominent Silver City family. Partly owing to the efforts of museum supporters, local historic preservation is an ongoing process, and the buildings of a core area around the museum are examples of Victorian architecture. The historic area is expected to grow as more buildings are designated part of the town's cultural heritage.

Two blocks west of the museum the Grant County Courthouse sits on a hill at 100 West Cooper Street. Murals by Theodore Van Soelen decorate the walls of the lobby. They are interesting examples of mural art of the 1930s, when the WPA employed artists to paint on government buildings. East of the museum, Bullard Street's brick business buildings and Western facades are solid reminders of Silver City's past.

Silver City is also the home of Western New Mexico University, on College Avenue. Begun as a normal school or school for teachers, the university now boasts an expanded curriculum and new buildings that straddle the hilltop.

The modern town is a shipping point for the nearby mines and the business center of southwestern New Mexico. However, in the middle 1850s the site was a marsh known by its Spanish name of La Cienega de San Vicente ("St. Vincent's marsh"). Gila and Mimbres Apaches who had camped there claimed ownership of the area, and settling of the region by Easterners provoked violent fights with the Indians. In spite of these conflicts, prospectors crowded the area after the Civil War, attracted by gold in Pinos Altos and other sites north of La Cienega. Some used the cool stream and springs just to refresh themselves, while others stayed to farm.

In 1870 a group of such farmers, led by Captain John Bullard, rode south to investigate the excitement of the silver find in Shakespeare, then called Ralston (Tour 10). The story goes that Bullard and his men recognized the ore as being plentiful back where they came from, and they returned immediately to dig in familiar territory. The first mining district was Chloride Flat, just west of the city. Bullard's group, formalized as the Bullard Mining Company, staked its first claim behind the present county courthouse and called it the Legal Tender.

When word of the silver claims spread, prospectors poured into the pleasant valley, and soon a tent city had sprung up, giving way gradually to more permanent structures. Instead of retaining the name of its more peaceful past, La Cienega, the burgeoning city christened itself, aptly it thought, Silver City. In 1874 Silver City was named the county seat and in 1878 was granted a charter, the first of its kind in New Mexico. Unlike other boom towns, which died as mining fell off, victims of decay and fire, Silver City survived the busts. Although the town declined in the late part of the last century, modern irrigation and farming methods introduced into the Gila and Mimbres valleys increased the importance of agriculture, and Silver City was also established as transportation center for the region. The discovery of more gold in the Mogollon Mountains and iron at Fierro, as well as the revived cattle and copper industries, all served to help Silver City retain its place as a focus of diversified business interests in the region.

Billy the Kid's family lived in Silver City, where he was known variously as Henry McArty, Billy Antrim, and later Kid Antrim. Billy's mother, Catherine Antrim, is buried in the old Memory Lane Cemetery at the western limits of the city, just off U.S. 180. Billy left town after his mother's death, to begin his notorious life as an outlaw two years later in Arizona. When he returned to New Mexico he ignored Silver City.

Until the 1800s the Apaches raided the town that had been built on land they considered theirs. Soldiers from the army post at Fort Bayard, as well as posses of townspeople, helped protect the citizenry. During one chase, leading citizen John Bullard was shot through the heart. The townspeople named Bullard's Peak and one of the main streets through town after him. Bullard Street later became the main thoroughfare after huge floods made a river out of Main Street.

There had been floods from time to time, but by 1895 the slopes of Silver City's hills had been stripped of vegetation by man and his mules. When the rains fell that year there was nothing to hold the waters back. A twelve-foot wall of water swept through the town, taking everything with it and leaving behind a thirty-five-foot-deep ditch, the "Big Ditch." After another bad flood in 1903, Main Street was stripped to fifty-five feet below its original level. The city grew accustomed to this scar. Not until 1936 did the Civil Conservation Corps institute measures that could check future floods by lining the sides of the ditch with masonry. The Big Ditch survives one block east of and parallel to North Bullard Street (notice that buildings now facing Bullard Street still have fronts on the ditch, or old Main Street). Citizens of Silver City in 1980 dedicated the ditch as a park, a delightful river walk shaded by large trees, cooled by waterfalls, and lit at night by lamps.

SIDE TOUR

Cooper Street South in Silver City turns into N.M. 90, the direct route to Lordsburg. About four and one-half miles from the city limits, modern TYRONE boasts an all-new underground utilities system. It is a pleasant town, home to workers of the Phelps-Dodge copper mine. Five miles further south, a turnoff leads to the mine itself, once the setting of old Tyrone, known in its time as "the million-dollar mine camp" and more recently as a million-dollar ghost town. Copper had been discovered in the Burro Mountains in 1871 and was mined on and off until the Phelps-Dodge Corporation bought the property in 1912. Supposedly, wives of two executives encouraged officials to construct a model town, and old Tyrone was in fact designed by Bertram Goodhue, the architect for the 1915 San Diego Exposition, and modeled after Spanish colonial architecture. The railroad station featured a marble drinking fountain and splendid chandeliers; there was a modern hospital, and the homes, built of substantial materials, boasted indoor plumbing. A library and an early shopping center also served the population of five thousand.

After World War I the demand for copper lessened, and Tyrone became a ghost town. No one wanted to tear it down, but in the end it was too unprofitable to move it. When the mine was reactivated in 1966 as an open-pit operation, Tyrone was sacrificed. Millions of tons of overburden were removed, the beautiful Spanish homes among them, to be replaced by the large open pit and mill. A visitors' lookout point, reached from the turnoff, straddles a hill overlooking the operation.

Continuing south on N.M. 90, the traveler will pass White Signal, where one of the first uranium deposits in New Mexico was found. The road here is desolate, with few homesteads.

Along the way a sign describes the killing of Judge H. C. McComas and his family by Apaches, who under the leadership of Geronimo had rebelled against their enforced living conditions and banded together in the Sierra Madre of Mexico. In the spring of 1882 a group of warriors went north to forage for horses and guns. The hapless McComas family, on a business trip from Silver City to the Lordsburg area, got in their way. The judge's little boy, Charlie, was taken by the band to be raised as their own. Over the years he was reported sighted in Mexico, once by archaeologists who described a blue-eyed chieftain. However, a member of the Apache band before his death in 1963 described Charlie's end at the hands of a

warrior enraged by the killing of his mother by soldiers.

The scrub-covered hills of the region give way to a vast plain as Lordsburg (Tour 10) comes into view at 404 mi.

Instead of following the direct route to Lordsburg, the traveler can return to Silver City from old Tyrone and take Hudson Street, which becomes N.M. 90/U.S. 180 East. Very shortly N.M. 15 intersects it on the east. At this point the traveler can make a short side trip to Pinos Altos, an old mining town currently being restored and occupied by artists and craftspeople. A longer trip on the same road takes in a drive to Lake Roberts, up to the Gila Cliff Dwellings Monument, and down N.M. 35 to San Lorenzo and back past the giant copper mine of Santa Rita.

PINOS ALTOS, 7 mi., is tucked away among the trees some six miles in on a winding road that forks at this point, the left fork passing through the village, the right fork bypassing it. The name, meaning "tall pines," lingers from an old Mexican gold-mining camp of the 1830s. In 1860 some Americans discovered gold in nearby Bear Creek. The resulting gold rush was slowed down by Apache attacks, and in 1861 chiefs Mangas Coloradas (Red Sleeves) and Cochise led a major raid on the settlement and frightened the miners away. Major activity did not resume until 1866. Several mines then produced gold into the 1920s; silver, zinc, lead, and copper were also mined. The tall pines that gave the town its name were used to build houses and businesses, and Pinos Altos became an attractive and important town. When Grant County was formed in 1868 from Doña Ana County, Pinos Altos was the first county seat. The old Eckhart house at the north end of town housed the government.

Both lode mining and placering were carried out here. Lodes are "veins" of gold; placer gold deposits form when gold from the veins is carried away by a stream and deposited. After placer gold was found in the area, miners went on to find the "mother lodes" and to develop mines with colorful names like Wild Bill, Deep-

Down Atlantic, and Kept Woman. The activities in the mines supported an opera house in town, as well as the necessary saloons and hotels. Today the opera house has been restored, as have a saloon and an old mill. A forest, not part of the original settlement, has been grown here as a tourist attraction. Several people live in the older miners' homes, and the shops are busy selling artists' and craftspeople's products.

From Pinos Altos the narrow drive winds through the forest, past isolated houses tucked among piñons and junipers. The lower vegetation of the forest is cholla, agave, and mescal cacti typical of the high desert. Views of the wilderness beyond open up to the east.

About three miles from Pinos Altos a small parking area has been set off for the Ben Lilley monument, which is a short but steep walk from the road. Ben Lilley was a successful bear- and lion-hunter, famous in the region for his knowledge of animal trails and his ability to bring in the mountain lions that plagued the ranches. The monument is a fitting one for a mountain man: a great pile of rocks that invites climbing and provides views of distant ridges and valleys.

Two miles north, the road skirts the edge of Cherry Creek Canyon and McMillan public campgrounds. The road continues to twist north through the forest until, at about the twenty-six-mile mark, it

joins N.M. 35. The well-constructed road winds on through a wild and broken country of deep gorges and rough canyons until it descends to the Gila National Monument.

The GILA NATIONAL MONUMENT, 44 mi., lies in the Gila National Forest at the edge of the Wilderness Area. Aldo Leopold, a forester with the National Forest Service, had long urged the service to preserve the Gila River area as a wilderness. In 1924 the government took his advice and named the Gila Wilderness as the first such area in the United States to be set aside and kept in its natural state. Primitive areas have also been designated as possible additions to the wilderness. Permits for hiking the trails that crisscross the seventy-five thousand acres of the wilderness are obtained at the ranger stations north of Mimbres, Glenwood, and Reserve. The trails cover a variety of geographic zones, from desert foothills through spruce and fir forests. Some of them follow the Gila River.

Early settlers in this area came across pottery fragments and ruins, the remains of people who had lived and farmed in the narrow valley of the Gila. In 1884 Adolph Bandelier wrote of the discovery of the Gila dwellings themselves, homes built in large caves in a narrow canyon of the West Fork of the Gila River. In 1907, President Theodore Roosevelt signed the bill designating the dwellings a national monument.

The Gila cliffdwellings are a short walk from the parking area and visitors' center of the monument, along the canyon where the water that supplied the cliffdwellers still runs. Visitors can walk along the outsides of the apartments and climb ladders to explore the insides. Built of masonry in the caves high up in the stone walls of the canyons, the dwellings were the homes of a people who lived there eight hundred years ago. Walls of stone still front the larger caves. Their inhabitants also built earthen roofs beneath the ceilings of the caves; holes in the walls show where the supports were placed. Natural archways connect the small caves to larger ones.

The Indians who lived here are believed to have been part of the Mogollon culture. They settled the area between A.D. 100 and 400, the date of the earliest ruin within the monument, at this time farming corn and beans, hunting a little, and making plain brown pottery. They built pit houses, round underground homes with long, ramplike entrances. Pit houses of varying styles lasted until A.D. 1000, when, perhaps under the influence of the Anasazi from the north, people began to build square, aboveground dwellings of masonry or adobe. Late in the twelfth and thirteenth centuries, the Indians built cliffdwellings like those found in the north. Built along the cliffs for protection, these dwellings are more spectacular than other types of Indian sites and therefore attract the most interest; they are, however, among the rarest type. By this time the Indians were producing a finer pottery, white with black designs. A protracted drought in the late thirteenth century probably caused the settlers to leave their attractive home. The visitors' center exhibits explain the archaeology and the history of the area.

Besides exploration of the caves, easy hikes up the river are a delightful way to spend a hot day. The river provides cooling ponds and smooth rocks for climbing, and hikes can be extended into backpacking trips. A national park campground and sites along the river on the approach to the area provide space for overnight stays.

Back at the junction with N.M. 15, the road snakes to the east, parallelling Sapillo ("little toad") Creek, which empties into Lake Roberts, 63 mi. Here concession stands and boat rentals encroach on the wilderness. But the lake is pretty, and

rowing or motorboating on it is a pleasant adventure. There is a tiny island on the lake, good for picnicking, and places all along the shore for sunbathing and fishing.

The rest of the trip down to N.M. 90 meanders through forests of low piñon and juniper, past private ranches, homes, and pleasant meadows. Backpacking trails cut off from the road; the ranger station just north of Mimbres is a good source of information on the area.

The Mimbres River parallels the road here across N.M. 90 and down the Mimbres valley. Beginning in the third century A.D., Mogollon people in the area built pit houses along the river, cultivated the flood plain of the valley, and hunted in the surrounding hills. Known as the Mimbres branch of the Mogollon culture, this people by the tenth century had begun to make a different kind of pottery, exquisite black-on-white vessels that they buried with their dead under the house floors. The distinctive designs created by these artists are copied today on pottery, cloth, and in other arts and crafts. Later, in the twelfth century, the Mimbreños left their valley, long before the extended drought that drove away their Gila neighbors. Mimbres ruins were overrun by pot hunters years ago; none have been restored.

The Black Range, *Harvey Caplin*.

The Harris Village, a quarter of a mile east of MIMBRES, 84 mi., contained over one hundred pit houses of varying types of construction, revealing the different phases of their builders' development. Also well-known are the Mattocks and Galaz ruins near Mimbres. Because, like other Mimbres sites, they were almost totally destroyed by vandals, much information about the Mimbres culture has been irretrievably lost.

From Mimbres a rough road leads east to the ghost town of GEORGETOWN, which once yielded three million dollars' worth of silver from the Naiad, Queen Commercial, and McGregor mines. Saloons and gambling halls flourished in the get-rich-quick atmosphere, and a busy passenger service ran between Georgetown and Silver City by stage and rail. All that is left today of the second-richest camp in the territory are scattered foundations and an adobe wall. The cemetery provides the most complete information on what used to be a thriving town.

Bear Canyon Lake is a good stop at the edge of the forest. Near San Lorenzo, 89 mi., the road intersects with N.M. 90. A heap of rubble nearby attests to the existence of Fort Webster. This military outpost had a short life here; in 1853, after only two years of service, it was moved to Fort Thorne, near Hatch.

Eight miles west on N.M. 90 about three miles to the south, the Kneeling Nun prays before a giant altar. This famous landmark was noted by the Spaniards when they first arrived in the area and saw the resemblance of the slim rock to a nun. Here the dumps and headshafts of various mines attest to underground activity; the vast pit of the SANTA RITA copper mine, 97 mi., makes them insignificant. An observation point overlooks the huge hole; a sign warns of blasting between 2 and 3 P.M. On a clear day the activity of the mine is evident; when mists and rains obscure the view, the vastness and color of Santa Rita can only be imagined. A mile and a quarter across and more than a thousand feet deep, the cavity is divided into terraces or benches of varicolored earth, each fifty feet high and wide enough for trucks, shovels, and drills to work in. The open pit allows the visitor to see what goes on in the mine, which uses a mass mining method, one in which the ore and waste are removed from the ground and carried away together, in contrast to the selective method used in other mines, in which only the ore is removed.

Long before the Kennecott Copper Corporation began its operations here, local Indians probably mined the copper, which had been deposited as a result of millions of years of geologic activity. Old copper ornaments and implements have been found in the area. When Spanish parties arrived in the region to man military outposts at the turn of the nineteenth century, one of the commandants, Lieutenant Colonel José Carrasco, was told of the copper deposits by an Indian. He realized the possibilities in mining and resigned from the army to invest his energies in copper. The venture proved too ambitious for him, and in 1804 he sold his interest to Don Francisco Elguea, a rich banker from Chihuahua. Elguea had the finances for a major operation, and with a grant from the Spanish government he built a town, Santa Rita del Cobre ("Saint Rita of the copper"). A fort-prison nearby kept Apaches out while keeping the Indian slaves who worked the mines in check. The high-grade Santa Rita ore was used in the royal mint in Mexico City.

Mining methods were crude, and between work hazards and frequent raids, keeping the mines going proved difficult. There were a succession of Mexican and American lessees until, in 1873, Martin Hays cleared title to the mine from Elguea's heirs, later leasing and finally selling the mine to Kennecott Copper's Chino Mines Division.

By this time most of the high-grade ore had been removed, and using the same underground method to get at the lower-grade ore would have been too expensive. A young mining engineer, John M. Sully, tested ore samples from the area and advised open-pit mining with steam shovels. In 1910 open-pit mining began, saving the village of Santa Rita from becoming a ghost town. However, as operations continued, the town was first isolated on an island in the center of the pit and finally removed as the island was swallowed up.

A short side trip to the faded towns of Hanover and Fierro can be made by a paved road that joins N.M. 90 about two miles west of Santa Rita. Gray and rust predominate in these towns, the colors of the old mines, the old houses, the slag heaps, and the abandoned machinery. But some Victorian houses remain in HANOVER as reminders of a more glamorous past. And there is some life still in the zinc deposits that have been mined since the late nineteenth century, when the Santa Fe Railroad reached Hanover and made mining profitable.

Up the hill FIERRO ("iron") rusts, the shell of a once-industrious town of iron mines. It looks abandoned, shafts leaning against the hills, empty mines and houses and an old cemetery to the right on a slight hill. However, a small railroad still moves mining materials through the town from an active mine. At the junction with N.M. 90, a sign indicates a rough road to Georgetown.

About seven miles east of Silver City, signs point to FORT BAYARD, to the north. The army built this fort in 1866 as a center of its operations against Apache chieftains Mangas Coloradas, Victorio, and Geronimo. The site was a strategic one, sitting on the war trails of the Apaches, and it was natural for the Army to take advantage of it. Fort Bayard remained an active army post until 1900, when it was converted to an army hospital mainly treating tuberculosis patients. In 1920 the Veterans Administration took it over, and since 1955 it has been run by the state as a hospital for the care of the chronically ill. Two national recreation trails run out of Fort Bayard into the Gila Forest. Inquire about these trails at the Forest Service office in Silver City.

The old officers' quarters, heavy stucco duplexes with whitewashed verandas, still stand along tree-lined streets. The soldiers' families lived in small white wood bungalows, dwarfed by the rambling hospital building. All the buildings on the huge grounds are well-preserved.

CENTRAL, 368 mi. (alt. 6,000, pop, 2,500), a village set around dirt-packed streets, is situated across the highway from Fort Bayard. Central grew because of its proximity to the fort, providing residences for the settlers who followed the troops. Originally known as Santa Clara, it received its present, more prosaic name from its location in the center of the populated area. Now the nearby Phelps-Dodge and Kennecott mines provide jobs for residents as the economy and activity in the mines dictate.

To complete a tour of the mines, take U.S. 180 south to BAYARD, 370 mi. The waste dumps of the Santa Rita mine loom to the east; Kennecott's leaching plant is between the dumps. The plant removes copper from the waste in an attempt to get as much valuable ore as possible from the earth before dumping it. The copper precipitate recovered by the leaching process goes to Hurley to be smelted. Ore cars travel the ten miles over a small Atchison, Topeka, and Santa Fe line to Hurley. Bayard itself lies about a mile from the plant.

From Bayard the highway continues south to HURLEY, 376 mi. (alt. 5,732, pop. 2,200), founded as a company village by the Chino Mines Division, which still has its general offices here. Hurley is now an incorporated town. Its fortunes have risen and fallen with the mining operations at Santa Rita; since it is the current site of a smelting operation for the Santa Rita mine, its population is stable at present. The smelting operation separates valuable minerals from the rock taken out of the Santa Rita pit. The tower of the smelter rises out of the plain and provides a landmark visible from miles away.

Two miles west of Hurley, the Cameron Creek ruins are the remains of a Mogollon village excavated between 1923 and 1928 by the Universities of New Mexico and Minnesota. The village was located on a short ridge projecting into the Cameron Creek valley and occupied from about A.D. 700 to an undetermined date. When the village was excavated, archaeologists found unusual burial grounds—oval pits, under the ground floors of the rooms, in which bodies were placed in a flexed position. Their belongings were buried with the deceased, including personal jars with holes drilled perfectly through the bottoms to allow the spirit of the jar to escape with the soul of the dead. Today practically nothing remains of the ruins.

About fourteen miles down the highway, a historic marker and signs indicate the way to City of Rocks State Park, another worthwhile detour. Turn east on N.M. 61 and pass Faywood Hot Springs, 2 mi. In the late nineteenth century a resort hotel was built here to take advantage of the curative power of the springs (which still bubble out of the ground), but the springs had been used long before this; prehistoric objects left by the Mimbres Indians have been found in the area. Stage lines connected the resort to far-off cities, and the Hudson Hot Springs Sanitarium Company, as it was then known, flourished. The hotel burned in 1891, but the company was taken over by Messrs. Fay and Lockwood, who rebuilt the complex as an elegant and modern resort. Unfortunately the clientele never returned in great numbers. Lack of business caused it to shut down in the 1950s, and nothing remains of it today but portions of foundation. Recently the area has been developed to serve the handicapped, and new pools have been built for the public to enjoy.

Two miles beyond the springs a good road from the highway leads to the CITY OF ROCKS STATE PARK, (alt. 5,200). As its name implies, the park appears from a distance to be a city. Closer up, it is seen as a fantastic jumble of huge rocks formed from fine volcanic stone. Erosion of the overlying harder volcanic rocks exposed the tuff (rocks formed from the compaction of volcanic ash flows). Further chemical and physical processes formed the "streets" along which crowd the rows of "houses." The effects of erosion are also seen in the weird shapes suggesting mythical creatures and monsters from prehistory.

Live oak trees give cooling shade from the desert sun, and there are plenty of hiding places among the rocks. Ancient Indians also used these natural shelters; remains of their homesites have been found under the sand. Table Mountain rises to the northeast, a perfect mesa formed out of welded tuff with sheer upper cliffs and a softer base sloping outwards. Standing on top of a rock, one can see Cooke's Peak to the east, a landmark for early travelers and drivers of the Butterfield Trail (Tour 10), and other peaks, which will mark the rest of the trip south: the Black and Red mountains, the Floridas' jagged peaks, and the Tres Hermanas ("three sisters").

SIDE TOUR

City of Rocks, *Harvey Caplin*.

—— SIDE TOUR ——

Back on U.S. 180, the road from Hatch, N.M. 26, enters at 411 mi. Deming, 412 mi., sits at the intersection of U.S. 180 and I-10 (Tour 10). Thirty-two miles ahead, Columbus lies almost at the end of N.M. 11, which runs straight through fields of cotton and a plain unbroken except for the hazy blue peaks in the distance.

COLUMBUS, 444 mi. (alt. 4,024, pop. 414), is a town that evokes more recognition than its size and appearance would indicate. Early settlers named it for Columbus, Ohio. Situated just three miles north of Mexico, it is famous as the scene of the only attack in history on the United States mainland by a foreign power. On the morning of March 9, 1916, a group of some five hundred followers of the Mexican revolutionary General Pancho Villa attacked Columbus. In the battle that followed, eight American soldiers, ten civilians, and one hundred Villistas died. In reprisal the U.S. Army sent the Punitive Expedition, led by General John "Black Jack" Pershing, into Mexico to find Villa. A fight at Carrizal, Mexico, almost led to war between the two nations, and the search for Villa was called off. He was never captured, and his men continued raids along the Texas border for almost a year.

During this time Columbus was headquarters for Pershing's group. After the Punitive Expedition left town in 1917, Columbus remained field headquarters for some five thousand troops, but by 1923 almost all the soldiers had departed.

Columbus today remembers those times with two museums and a state park. The old Pancho Villa Museum displays photos and exhibits relating to the raid; a newer museum in the former railroad depot also shows photos and cards, as well as general mementos, of the era.

It may be startling to find a state park named after the invader, and Pancho Villa State Park did indeed arouse some controversy when it was opened. Today it is Columbus's main attraction. Landscaped with cacti, it features a botanical garden of some five thousand varieties of desert flowers and cactus, as well as campsites. The good weather attracts campers from all over, some of whom winter here. Besides the desert flora the park contains reminders of the beginnings of the mechanized armed forces. The first grease rack installed to service army automotive equipment holds a place of honor in the park, a

tribute to the mechanic who provided the first motorized link between headquarters and forces in the fields. A few old adobe buildings from the original headquarters are protected in the park. Across the road, the military airbase that sent off biplanes to punish Pancho Villa is now used for modern aircraft.

Columbus provides easy access to Mexico, with a twenty-four-hour crossing to Las Palomas, a small town directly across the border. Paved roads link Palomas and Nuevo Casas Grandes to major roads into the interior of Mexico. There is also a road from Nuevo Casas Grandes to Juárez. Inquire in Deming or Columbus about the current state of highways before attempting them. Columbus hopes to capitalize on its border location should Mexican plans for industrializing the area materialize. Although ambitious dirt roads have been laid out in expectation of growth, Columbus remains a very small town, still living on memories of a few exciting days.

From Columbus a paved road, N.M. 9, leads across the plains to Hermanas, and, unpaved, on to Hachita.

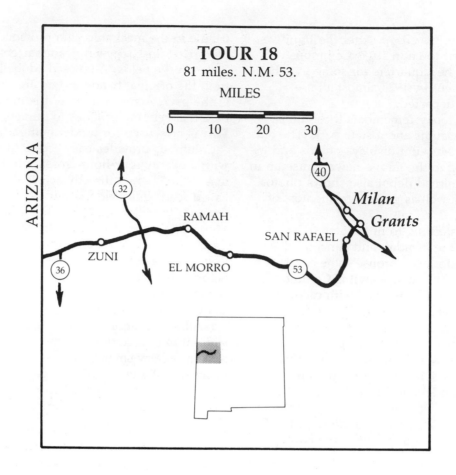

TOUR 18

81 miles. N.M. 53.

MILES

0   10   20   30

ARIZONA

32

36

ZUNI

RAMAH

EL MORRO

53

SAN RAFAEL

Milan

Grants

40

tour eighteen

Milan ● **El Morro** ● **Zuni** ● *Arizona Border*

N.M. 53, extending from San Rafael, south of Milan, to Zuni and the Arizona border, roughly traces the old Zuni-Cibola Trail, the route followed by Indian travelers between Acoma, Zuni, and the Hopi villages beyond. Later, Spanish explorers and American wagoners used the same road to take advantage of the cooling spring at El Morro. Today tourists travel the well-paved road to wonder at the Ice Cave, pore over the signatures carved on El Morro, and visit the old village of Zuni. This route can be hazardous in winter.

Four miles from the junction of I-40 and N.M. 53, old SAN RAFAEL (alt. 6,462, pop. 2,000), hides among trees. When the second Fort Wingate was built here (the first was at Seboyeta, Tour 6), the fort commander invited Spanish-Americans to settle near the fort. Kit Carson used the fort as his headquarters during his Canyon de Chelly campaign, when he rounded up the Navajos for the Long Walk to Fort Sumner. In 1869 the army abandoned the fort and moved to Gallup, but the little settlement remained populated. The old town is little changed today, while a new San Rafael is springing up across the road on the plain.

The Cibola National Forest begins at 20 mi.

Some of the hills here are surrounded by lava, a feature called "steptoes" by geologists. One particularly distinctive steptoe has been named the "Hole in the Wall"; the lush green that grows within the steptoe contrasts strangely with the bleak lava. From this point the Zuni Mountains stretch northwest. A little further on, lava flows spread out over the valley, the black crust striking against the underlying red rocks.

The ICE CAVE, 26 mi., has been a tourist attraction since Francisco Coronado was taken there by his Zuni guides. In the area are other caves like it, where low temperatures keep water frozen all year round, but this one is the most accessible from the main road and the only one safe for the public to visit. The cave and adjacent Bandera Crater are located on private land; the owner charges an entrance fee. An old trading post, camping facilities, and tourist cabins line the parking area.

A short walk south of the store through a pine forest and heaped lava leads to the Ice Cave. Years ago, after the nearby volcano erupted, molten lava draining from the crust formed tunnels. Caves were created when the tunnels collapsed.

Wooden steps lead down to the Ice Cave,

paso por aqi el adelanzado aon ju
de oñaze Dedesscubrimenzo adela ma
del sur a 16 dea 621lool 605

into which visitors look from a platform. For those who have seen the vast Carlsbad Caverns, the cave may be disappointing because it is so small. Its attraction lies in the layers of green ice that line the walls, only a few feet from the open air above. Several factors explain why the ice is preserved even in summer: the low temperature at this altitude (7,600 feet); the fact that the opening is placed in such a way that sunlight enters for only a few minutes on a few days of the year; the shape of the cave; and the direction of the winds. All of these conditions prevent air from circulating and keep the cold air in the cave. Water freezes in the winter months, and the cold air and insulating lava above keep it frozen. Indians supposedly used this kind of cave, fairly common in the *malpais* (badlands), as an icebox. Algae in the water colors the ice blue-green; the layers result from alternate freezing and thawing. The thick layer of basalt at the top of the ice probably fell off the roof of the cave and was cemented in place by the ice.

About a hundred yards back toward the store, a clearly marked trail leads to the volcano. The walk to the crater is about one and a half miles, an easy walk. From the trail the visitor has a close-up view of the results of the volcanic activity that occurred five thousand years ago from this and dozens of similar volcanoes in the area. Along the trail lava is piled up in jagged heaps, the result of crust breaking off as it hardened. As the trail nears the cone of the volcano, it snakes through a narrow canyon where a lava river once flowed. The trail ends at the crater, about halfway up the 450-foot-high cone. The walls inside are smooth, all the rough spots having fallen off

and collected at the bottom. Below this debris a hard core of lava remains; after erosion has worn down the rest of the volcano, this core will be left jutting up, a "volcanic neck" like Cabezon Peak and Shiprock. On the trail back to the store, smaller eruptions of lava have formed "spatter" cones.

Less than a mile down N.M. 53, the road crosses the Continental Divide at Oso Ridge (7,882 feet) before descending through pine groves into a valley. Red shale and sandstone formations limit the valley and stand out sharply against the sky.

About twelve miles beyond the divide EL MORRO ("headland, bluff") protrudes to the southwest. It was formed at two different times, fifty million years apart, and the newer Dakota caprock has slowed the wearing down of the older Zuni sandstone. The road to the monument and the National Park campsite exits to the south at 42 mi. From the camp, pleasantly sheltered among pines, one can look across to El Morro and the jagged peaks of Los Gigantes ("the giants").

The National Park Service administers the monument, created in 1906 to preserve Inscription Rock, and a small visitors' center provides information on El Morro and the area. Trails to Inscription Rock and to the top of the mesa start from the center. It is a short walk to the base of the cliff; a longer hike leads across the mesa. Elevation here is 7,200 feet; it is advisable to take plenty of time on the longer walk.

Inscription Rock, a massive sandstone, preserves the names of many travelers who passed here, stopping for shelter and for the water held in the natural basin at the foot of the rock. Don Juan de Oñate was the first non-Indian to carve his name in the soft sandstone. *Pasó por aqui*, his long inscription begins. "The governor Don Juan de Oñate passed by here." This was in 1605, fifteen years before the Pilgrims landed at Plymouth Rock. Long before Oñate, Indians who lived on the mesa and nearby etched petroglyphs—pictures of people, birds, and symbols of Indian life—into the stone.

After Oñate, hundreds of Spanish soldiers and priests traveling the route between Santa Fe and Zuni passed by El Morro. Many of them could not resist leaving the messages that now provide a historical register of the era. Some boasted: Don Francisco Manuel de Silva let everyone know he had overcome the impossible; de Vargas that he had conquered all of New Mexico. Others just wanted to leave their mark: thus "Felipe de Arellano, soldier," and, in 1774, the last Spanish inscription, reading simply "Andrés Romero."

The next dated writing is that of an officer of General Kearny's Army of the West and a Philadelphia artist, R. H. Fern, who copied all the inscriptions in a book. A few years later Lieutenant Edward Beale brought his experimental camel train by the famous headland for water. After that, emigrant trains, cattlemen, surveyors, and settlers passed by. Their signatures varied from rough lettering to neat block print. The fanciest is that of a Mr. Long, who carved his name in flourishes.

From the base of the cliff a longer trail leads around the headland and steeply up the side. At the top of the trail the outlines of ruins being excavated are visible. Following the trail carved across the rock, the visitor can look down into the surprising box canyon that runs deep into the rock. Children will enjoy scrambling along the walk; adults can savor the wide-angle view of the countryside.

The ruins of Atsinna (Zuni, "writing on rock") on the eastern edge of El Morro have already been uncovered. A self-guided trail leads through the ruins, which Indians occupied during the thirteenth and fourteenth centuries, probably choosing the site for its ready

water supply and excellent natural protection. They built some structures three stories high, dwellings that sloped down on the southern side to take advantage of the sun. Atsinna Indians built both a round and a rectangular kiva for their ceremonies. They abandoned the pueblo in the fourteenth century, perhaps moving over to the better farmland around Zuni.

N.M. 53 continues on to Zuni. Just past El Morro, the road to the south runs into the population center of the Ramah Navajo Reservation. Ramah is the largest of several groups of Navajos who live off the main reservation, governing themselves while keeping cultural and social ties with the main group. Navajos had lived in this area before their Fort Sumner captivity, and several returned afterward to settle.

The highway cuts through pretty farming country and through the quiet town of Ramah, 57 mi., not to be confused with the reservation. A large Mormon church testifies to Ramah's origins, which go back to 1876, when Mormon missionaries persuaded the Navajos to let them settle there and named their town after a religious figure in the Book of Mormon. Beyond Ramah the road descends into less verdant countryside, through piñon and juniper and into sagebrush and cactus. Here the Ramah Navajo Indian Reservation ends and Zuni Pueblo begins.

The road passes through the Zuni village of Pescado, 62 mi., and crosses the Rio Pescado. An unimproved road here goes off to the north, up to Nutria Lake and villages, the old summer residences of Zuni Pueblo. At the end of the road, 18 mi., the Village of the Great Kivas is the site of three ancient pueblos, the largest of which contained two kivas similar to the great kivas of Chaco Canyon. This site and the lake can be visited with permission of the Zuni tribal government. Some seven miles past Pescado, the road from Quemado, N.M. 32, enters from the south (see Tour 17) and, half a mile on, cuts off to the north to Gallup. Look for Pierced Rock on the south with its window opening and a thin sandstone known as Feather Rock in front.

Near Zuni Pueblo, at Black Rock, the narrow valley opens out to views of the Zuni Butte to the north and wide plains where sheep and cattle graze and crops spread out. The Zuni River runs through the valley. To the south Taaiyalone ("corn"), the sacred mountain, provided refuge for the Zunis when they had to flee from the Spanish. Remains of pit houses on top of this mesa could date from A.D. 700. At Black Rock a Public Health Service hospital has been built in this "suburb" of Zuni. Modern housing overlooks the Zuni reservoir, a bright blue spot against the brown and gray plain. Some volcanic rock left over from a fairly recent flow is visible here.

ZUNI PUEBLO (alt. 6,400, pop. 5,760) is the largest of the pueblos. Its people speak Zuni, which is unrelated to any of the other Pueblo languages. The tribal fairground and government offices are built just inside the pueblo. Signs prohibit picture-taking and buying jewelry without a permit. At first the pueblo looks like any New Mexican community. The business district mixes modern shops with older enterprises, while cinderblock and adobe houses dominate the residential areas. But off the main road old Zuni remains, although one-story homes have replaced the multistoried buildings of the past. Beehive-shaped *hornos* (ovens) in backyards are still used for baking. Some of the houses are built of stone and resemble those found in ancient Pueblo ruins. Trees shade the streets and some of the homes; a creek runs through the center of town.

At the first crossroads, just to the south, the restored mission church, Nuestra Señora de Guadalupe de Halona, is almost hidden among its neighbors. The church is usually closed; visitors must go to the newer St. Anthony's rectory, on the east end of town, to get a guide who will open it during certain hours.

The original mission, like other New Mexico churches, was established by Franciscan friars between 1630 and 1666. It was later destroyed during the Pueblo Revolt and rebuilt. The Franciscans returned to Zuni and stayed on through the 1700s but left in the early nineteenth century, feeling that the Navajo and Apache tribes of the area had become too "intrusive." After the Franciscans returned to Zuni in 1921, they built St. Anthony's Mission and school in the northwest section of Zuni. These attractive red-brick structures contrast with the adobe homes of their neighbors. Meanwhile, after over a century of neglect, the old mission church had deteriorated to a shell. It was rebuilt between 1966 and 1972, the restoration uncovering many older features of the church as well as remains of the faithful who had been buried in the church. Mass is celebrated here on special days, including the feast day of the patron, St. Anthony.

The walls of the old mission had been decorated with murals between 1775 and 1780, and Zuni artist Alex Seowltwa has transformed the restored walls with his vision. Beginning on the south wall, the scenes portray the mesas south of the village and follow the seasons from spring to winter, with figures representing each season: Mudhead from spring; Father of the Kivas; the rain dancers; and the Shalako from winter. The paintings are remarkable for their color and fine detail. They picture the main figures of the Zuni religion existing in harmony with the Catholic saints who take their places in the front of the church. Traditional Stations of the Cross line the walls under the murals; two large metal candelabra hang from the *vigas* (roof beams). The altar is simple, without the *reredos* (elaborate altar-

Zuni, *Harvey Caplin*.

piece) found in other mission churches.

Visitors can purchase Zuni crafts from the village cooperative. Zuni artisans have developed distinctive styles of silversmithing and pottery. Jewelry is made of turquoise, mother-of-pearl, and coral by a technique known as inlay whereby the stones are placed in depressions in a silver crown and ground to fit a given space. Needlepoint is a style resulting from tiny stones placed very close together in various patterns. Silversmithing received its impetus from the Spanish. Tourists discovered Zuni jewelry in the 1920s, but the quality of the work reached a peak only in the 1970s. Although silversmithing used to be a strictly male activity, both men and women share now in jewelry making.

Here as in all the pueblos, pottery was traditionally a practical art, and many examples of Zuni bowls, jugs, and vases can be found in New Mexico's museums. With the renewal of interest in Indian works, Zuni potters produce pieces for both the tourist trade and collectors, so that cute owls now have their place beside classic bowls. Zuni pottery is characterized by black and red stylized plant, bird, and

deer designs on a white background.

Craftspeople also fashion images of the *kachinas* that figure strongly in the Zuni and other pueblo religions. *Kachinas* are the deities that accompanied the ancestors of the Pueblo peoples from the womb of Mother Earth to the surface. Like humans, they share good and bad qualities and are not above humor. Spanish missionaries tried to replace the *kachinas* with Catholic figures but never succeeded. Today *kachinas* are prominent in ceremonial dances. Zuni artists create "dolls" representing the kachinas for parents to give their children. In most pueblos except Zuni and the Hopi villages the figures are not supposed to be seen outside the pueblo.

The Zuni religious year, punctuated by the solstices, includes many intricate and impressive ceremonials. Visitors are permitted to see those parts of dances which are open to the whole pueblo.

The most elaborate of all Pueblo rituals is the Shalako. The Shalako ceremony, held in late November or early December, closes the Zuni year and dedicates new houses. The final ceremonial dance, with many god-impersonators, is the culmination of a year of planning and forty-nine days of ceremony. The person who acts as the Rain God of the North (Sayatasha) and the leader of the Mudheads, each with a cord knotted forty-nine times, begin the countdown by untying one knot every day. The Mudheads, or Koyemshi, are the grotesquely comic clowns who participate in rituals all year, but are seen by most visitors at the Shalako. Men with mud-smeared torsos wear ragged skirts and mud-daubed masks with knobby protrusions and circular mouths. These Mudheads announce the imminent arrival of the gods and the Shalako and then retreat to the Mudhead house for days of chants and prayers.

A ten- to fourteen-year-old boy is chosen each year to act as the Fire God, the central figure in the next portion of the ceremony, the pilgrimage to shrines on the surrounding mesas. Perfection is expected of him in his performance of chants, races, and fire lighting. It is he, painted black with red, yellow, blue, and white spots, who begins the finale by visiting the ceremonial houses and leaving prayer plumes at each. The Council of the Gods then enters the village, each member with a freshly painted and fantastic mask. The Zunis receive the council members with reverence and sprinkle them with sacred cornmeal. At dusk the Shalako appear.

Shalako are imposing, ten-foot, bird-like creatures, wearing white embroidered ceremonial clothing, massive black ruffs fashioned from glossy raven feathers, and long black hair. Eagle feathers form the crown and plume framing the giant, blue birds' faces. The heavy superstructure of the masks places great responsibility upon the Shalako dancers, who must not miss a step or fall in their dance lest they be lashed with yucca rods by the whippers and bring misfortune to the entire pueblo. Despite the difficulty of the dance, the Shalako step and dip adroitly, swooping and diving while clacking their wooden beaks and rolling their wooden eyes.

Each of the six Shalako enters the new house that has been prepared for him and for the night-long dancing. The figures dance to the pervasive rhythm resounding from cottonwood drums in the houses chosen to represent all new homes of the pueblo. The flooring of a host home is not put in until after the ceremonial so that the dirt can be dug low enough to allow the huge Shalako to dance. The walls of the new home are covered with brilliant blankets and shawls. Stuffed antelope and deer heads, draped with a wealth of silver and turquoise jewelry, stare mutely from their wooden mounts on the walls. The Shalako and visiting Mudheads continue to perform in front of the Zuni in the main room and the many Anglo, Navajo, and other Pueblo onlookers pressing at the windows and doorways. The beat of the drum, the rich vision of color and movement, and the smell of cooking stew, bread, and coffee enter into all present with greater intensity as the night wears on.

At dawn the final prayers are said and the Zuni sprinkle the dancers with sacred cornmeal. The "going out" of the Council of Gods, led by the Fire God, occurs at about noon. The great Shalako race, pray, and demonstrate their role as couriers of the gods to carry Zuni prayers for rain and crop fertility.

After the departure of the gods, dancing continues for four more days, and finally the clowns or Koyemshi receive payments of food and goods for their year of service. All of the participants and their hosts have spent a fortune in time and goods to successfully orchestrate the intensely complex Shalako ritual.

Those who wish to watch the all-night finale of Shalako should be prepared for cold, possibly wet weather, hours of standing on tiptoe, welcome coffee and food offered at the host home, and strict observance of requests for quiet.

N.M. 53 continues west to Arizona. Reservation Road 2 (N.M. 36) South branches off to the ruins of Hawikuh, 14 mi., and a camp-ground at Ojo Caliente, 15 mi., following the Zuni River valley. About two miles north of Ojo Caliente a dirt road to the west leads to Hawikuh. Permission to visit this site may be obtained from tribal headquarters. Be careful of the unpaved roads after rain.

HAWIKUH was one of the "Seven Cities of Cibola," known to the Spaniards in Mexico City in the early 1500s as places of great wealth. Mexican Indians had long traded with the Indians of "Cibola," exchanging shells and tropical bird feathers for salt, turquoise, and red paint. These Indian traders knew the cities as small adobe villages, but the Spaniards were impressed by the reports of Alvar Núñez Cabeza de Vaca. This explorer had been shipwrecked off the coast of Florida and had wandered throughout the Southwest, where he heard stories of cities whose streets were paved with gold, silver, and precious stones. The Spanish associated these cities with Cibola.

In 1539 Fray Marcos de Niza, guided by the Moor Esteban, who had accompanied Cabeza de Vaca, arrived at Hawikuh, the westernmost of the villages of Cibola. Zuni Indians had lived here for some two hundred years, and had probably occupied the Zuni valley from A.D. 700, living first in pit houses below ground and then in above-ground villages. Esteban antagonized the inhabitants and was killed. De Niza was forced to retreat without really seeing the pueblo, although he described it in exaggerated terms on his return to Mexico. One story explains de Niza's impression as the result of his viewing Hawikuh at sunset, when the walls of the village shone gold.

The following year Coronado arrived at the village. The Zuni took to arms immediately, but Coronado conquered the village easily and the Zuni fled to Corn Mountain, their retreat. They soon returned to their homes, however, and the Spanish and Zunis coexisted for a time. Some Mexican Indians also remained in the pueblo, making their homes there.

Coronado returned to Mexico in 1542 with the truth about the cities of Cibola. Although

he had traveled as far as Kansas and Arizona, he had found nothing resembling the fabled cities reported by Cabeza de Vaca. Gold-seeking expeditions no longer bothered Hawikuh, but other groups stopped by the villages on their explorations throughout the Southwest. They were well-received by the Zunis (some attribute this warmth to the influence of the Mexicans who had stayed in Hawikuh). One member of the 1581 Rodríguez-Chamuscada Expedition wrote the first descriptions of the villages, establishing their number as six. The explorer called the present-day pueblo of Zuni Alongua, from the Indian Halona, and noted that it had "forty-four three- and four-story houses." By this time, one village had already been abandoned.

By the time of Oñate's second trip in 1605, the villages were in disrepair and almost empty, but enough inhabitants remained for the Spanish government and Franciscan friars to establish a mission in Hawikuh and Halona. The Zunis did not accept this presence; they burned the church in 1632 and killed a brother and two soldiers. A small force was sent to punish the rebellious Indians, who reportedly fled once more to their retreat at Corn Mountain. The missionaries returned in 1660 and rebuilt the mission in Hawikuh.

Soon Apache attacks sent both the Zuni and their priest away again, the Zunis returning just before the Pueblo Revolt of 1680. During this bloody period the Zuni rebellion was not as fierce as that in other pueblos, but they killed the priest at Halona and burned the church. The turmoil of the revolt and continued Apache attacks drove the Zunis once more to Corn Mountain, where de Vargas met with them in 1692 for their surrender. After

this the Zunis did not return to Hawikuh; instead the remaining inhabitants all moved into Halona, now Zuni Pueblo. The name Zuni is adapted from the Keresan Suni'tsi, meaning "unknown."

The burnt-out church was rebuilt as a much larger structure than before. This fresh start was disrupted in 1703 when the Indians protested against mistreatment by Spanish soldiers assigned to protect the mission. After yet another sojourn on Corn Mountain, they returned to their pueblo in 1705 and were joined by a priest. The life of the mission and village resumed.

The Franciscans left Zuni in 1820, discouraged by resistance to conversion and by Apache and Navajo raids. Other religious groups sent missions from time to time but had no lasting influence. The Franciscans returned one hundred years later.

Zuni has been continuously occupied since 1692, far from the mainstream of Spanish and later American activities but not completely cut off, since the pueblo was located on several strategic trade routes.

Traders, teachers, and government officials settled in Zuni toward the end of the nineteenth century. The traders helped the Pueblo shift from a purely subsistence to a cash economy. Each group of outsiders influenced Zuni life in some way; sometimes they were fairly disruptive. In 1902 some non-Indians were instrumental in calling in troops to control the Bow Priests. The priesthood had changed its focus from protecting the Zunis against the enemy to protecting them against witches. The harsh treatment of witches disturbed the non-Indians, and troops were called in to calm the resulting conflict.

Zuni tries to keep ties to the old ways by maintaining its ceremonial system and world-view order. Zuni religion continues to be extraordinarily rich. (Author Tony Hillerman has helped increase knowledge of Zuni beliefs, as well as those of the Navajos, in his book *Dance Hall of the Dead*. See Literature.) Zuni is also modernizing as much as possible. Thus political power now lies in the hands of tribal politicians; attempts to attract industry have been made, and the tribe is now in charge of its own educational system.

bibliography

The following New Mexico bibliography is by no means comprehensive. The authors referred to many sources in preparing essays and tours; the books listed here are the basic ones. Some books were used in more than one section; they are listed under only one topic. The authors also relied on many periodicals, too many to list, but special mention must be made of the *Albuquerque Journal*, the *Albuquerque Tribune, Artlines, Artspace, Century*, the Public Service Company of New Mexico's *Electric Lines, El Palacio, New Mexico Business Journal, New Mexico Historical Review, New Mexico Magazine*, and *The* (Santa Fe) *New Mexican*. "F. Stanley's" series of slim volumes on little known towns of New Mexico was another frequently used source, as was the original *New Mexico: A Guide to the Colorful State*.

History

Beck, Warren. *A History of Four Centuries*. Norman: University of Oklahoma Press, 1962.

Cooke, Philip St. George. *The Conquest of New Mexico and California*. 1878. Reprint. Oakland, Calif.: Biobooks, 1952.

Davis, Ellis Arthur, ed. *The Historical Encyclopedia of New Mexico*. Albuquerque: New Mexico Historical Association, 1945.

Debo, Angie. *Geronimo: The Man, His Time, His Place*. Norman: University of Oklahoma Press, 1976.

Dozier, Edward P. *The Pueblo Indians of North America*. New York: Holt, Rinehart and Winston, 1970.

Ellis, Richard N. *New Mexico, Past and Present: A Historical Reader*. Albuquerque: University of New Mexico Press, 1971.

Fincher, E. B. *Spanish-Americans as a Political Factor in New Mexico, 1912–1950*. New York: Arno Press, 1974.

Goodchild, Peter. *J. Robert Oppenheimer: Shatterer of Worlds*. Boston: Houghton Mifflin Co., 1981.

Gregg, Josiah. *Commerce of the Prairies*. 1844. Reprint. Norman: University of Oklahoma Press, 1974.

Hibben, Frank. *The Lost Americans*. New York: Thomas Y. Cromwell Co., 1968.

Jenkins, Myra Ellen, and Albert H. Schroeder. *A Brief History of New Mexico*. Albuquerque: University of New Mexico Press, 1974.

Keleher, William A. *Memoirs: 1892–1969*. 1969.

Reprint. Albuquerque: University of New Mexico Press, 1983.

———. *Turmoil in New Mexico, 1846–1868.* Albuquerque: University of New Mexico Press, 1952.

Kessell, John L. *Kiva, Cross and Crown: The Pecos Indians and New Mexico, 1540–1840.* Washington, D.C.: National Park Service, 1966.

Lange, Charles H., and Carroll L. Riley, eds. *The Southwestern Journals of Adolph F. Bandelier, 1880–1882.* Albuquerque: University of New Mexico Press, 1966.

Larson, Robert W. *New Mexico's Quest for Statehood, 1846–1912.* Albuquerque: University of New Mexico Press, 1968.

Myrick, David F. *New Mexico's Railroads: An Historical Survey.* Denver: Colorado Railroad Museum, 1970.

Oliva, Leo E. *Soldiers of the Santa Fe Trail.* Norman: University of Oklahoma Press, 1967.

Ortiz, Alfonso, ed. *Handbook of North American Indians,* vol. 9. Washington, D.C.: Smithsonian Institution, 1979.

Schaefer, Jack. *Adolphe Francis Alphonse Bandelier.* Santa Fe: Press of the Territorian, 1966.

Sonnichsen, C. L. *Tularosa: Last of the Frontier West.* 1960. Reprint. Albuquerque: University of New Mexico Press, 1980.

Stuart, David E., and Rory P. Gauthier. *Prehistoric New Mexico: Background for Survey.* Santa Fe: Dept. of Finance and Administration, State of New Mexico, 1981.

Westphall, Victor. *Thomas Benton Catron and His Era.* Tucson: University of Arizona Press, 1973.

Land

Calvin, Ross. *Sky Determines: An Interpretation of the Southwest.* Albuquerque: University of New Mexico Press, 1965.

Christiansen, Paige W., and Frank E. Kottlowski, eds. *Mosaic of New Mexico's Scenery, Rocks and History.* Socorro, N.M.: New Mexico Bureau of Mines and Mineral Resources, 1972.

Soils of New Mexico. Las Cruces, N.M.: New Mexico State University, 1978.

Tuan, Yi-Fu, Cyril E. Everard, and Jerrold G. Widdison. *The Climate of New Mexico.* Santa Fe: State Planning Office, 1969.

Westphall, Victor. *The Public Domain in New Mexico, 1854–1891.* Albuquerque: University of New Mexico Press, 1965.

Williams, Jerry L. and Paul E. McAllister. *New Mexico in Maps.* Albuquerque: University of New Mexico Press, 1981.

People

Between Sacred Mountains: Stories and Lessons from the Land. Chinle, Ariz.: Rock Point Community School, 1982.

Casaus, Luis, Max Castillo, and Miguel Arciniega. *Parenting Models and Mexican Americans.* Albuquerque: Pajarito Publications, 1982.

Chavez, Fray Angelico. *Origins of New Mexico Families in the Spanish Colonial Period.* 1954. Reprint. Santa Fe: William Gannon, 1975.

Cleaveland, Agnes Morley. *No Life for a Lady.* 1941. Reprint. Lincoln: University of Nebraska Press, 1977.

Curry, Ella Banegas, and Shan Nichols. *Our People: Selections from the Mesilla Valley.* Las Cruces, N.M.: Curry and Nichols, 1974.

Fergusson, Erna. *New Mexico: A Pageant of Three Peoples.* 1964. Reprint. Albuquerque: University of New Mexico Press, 1973.

González, Nancie L. *The Spanish-Americans of New Mexico: A Heritage of Pride.* Albuquerque: University of New Mexico Press, 1969.

Holmes, Jack E. *Politics in New Mexico.* Albuquerque: University of New Mexico Press, 1967.

Kutsche, Paul, and John R. Van Ness. *Cañones: Values, Crisis, and Survival in a Northern New Mexico Village.* Albuquerque: University of New Mexico Press, 1982.

Motto, Sytha. *Madrid and Christmas in New Mexico.* 1973. Reprint. Albuquerque: Alpha Printing, 1981.

Rittenhouse, Jack D. *The Santa Fe Trail: A Historical Bibliography.* Albuquerque: University of New Mexico Press, 1971.

Weigle, Marta. *Hispanic Villages of Northern New Mexico.* Santa Fe: The Lightning Tree, 1975.

Food

Cameron, Sheila MacNiven. *The Best from New Mexico Kitchens.* Santa Fe: New Mexico Magazine, 1978.

Chavez, Tibo J. *New Mexico Folklore of the Rio Abajo.* Portales: Bishop Printing Co., 1972.

Chile. Circular #396. Las Cruces: Cooperative Extension Service, New Mexico State University, 1966.

Douglas, Jim. *The Complete New Mexico Cookbook.* Santa Fe: Elena's Kitchen, 1977.

Gilbert, Fabiola Cabeza de Baca. *Historic Cookery.* Santa Fe: The Shed, 1965.

The Good Life: New Mexico Traditions and Food. Santa Fe: Museum of New Mexico Press, 1982.

Hughes, Phyllis. *Pueblo Indian Cookbook.* Santa Fe: Museum of New Mexico Press, 1977.

Romero, Philomena. *New Mexico Dishes.* Los Alamos. New Mexican Dishes, 1970.

Sinclair, John L. *New Mexico: The Shining Land.* Albuquerque: University of New Mexico Press, 1980.

Tipton, Alice S. *The Original New Mexican Cookery.* Santa Fe: R. L. Polese, 1965.

Religion

Brackenridge, R. Douglas, and Francisco O. García Treto. *Iglesia Presbiteriana: A History of Presbyterians and Mexican-Americans in the Southwest.* San Antonio: Trinity University Press, 1974.

Brugge, David M., and Charlotte J. Frisbie, eds. *Navajo Religion and Culture: Selected Views.* Santa Fe: Museum of New Mexico Press, 1982.

de Aragon, Ray John. *Padre Martínez and Bishop Lamy.* Las Vegas, N.M.: Pan-American Publishing Co., 1978.

de Cordova, Lorenzo. *Echoes of the Flute.* Santa Fe: Ancient City Press, 1972.

Domínguez, Fray Francisco Atanasio. *The Missions of New Mexico, 1776.* Translated and annotated by Eleanor B. Adams and Fray Angelico Chavez. Albuquerque: University of New Mexico Press, 1956.

Fergusson, Erna. *Dancing Gods: Indian Ceremonials of New Mexico and Arizona.* 1931. Reprint. Albuquerque: University of New Mexico Press, 1966.

Gilpin, Laura. *The Enduring Navajo.* Austin: University of Texas Press, 1968.

Hodge, Frederick Webb, George P. Hammond, and Agapito Rey. *Fray Alonso de Benavides' Revised Memorial of 1634.* Albuquerque: University of New Mexico Press, 1954.

Kessell, John L. *The Missions of New Mexico Since 1776.* Albuquerque: University of New Mexico Press, 1980.

Kluckhohn, Clyde. *Navaho Witchcraft.* Boston: Beacon Press, 1967.

Myers, Lewis A. *A History of New Mexico Baptists.* New Mexico: Baptist Convention of New Mexico, 1965.

Ortiz, Alfonso. *The Tewa World.* Chicago: University of Chicago Press, 1969.

Roediger, Virginia More. *Ceremonial Costumes of the Pueblo Indians.* Berkeley: University of California Press, 1941.

Salpointe, Jean Baptiste. *Soldiers of the Cross.* 1898. Reprint. Albuquerque: Calvin Horn, 1967.

Scully, Vincent. *Pueblo: Village, Mountain, Dance.* New York: Viking Press, 1975.

Tyler, Hamilton A. *Pueblo Gods and Myths.* Norman: University of Oklahoma Press, 1964.

Waters, Frank, *The Masked Gods: Navaho and Pueblo Ceremonialism.* 1950. New York: Ballantine Books, 1975.

Weigle, Marta. *Brothers of Light, Brothers of Blood: The Penitentes of the Southwest.* Albuquerque: University of New Mexico Press, 1976.

Politics and Government

Ellis, Richard N., ed. *New Mexico Historic Documents*. Albuquerque: University of New Mexico Press, 1975.

Garcia, F. Chris, and Paul L. Hain. *New Mexico Government*. Rev. ed. Albuquerque: University of New Mexico Press, 1981.

Simmons, Marc. *Spanish Government in New Mexico*. Albuquerque: University of New Mexico Press, 1968.

Education

Barber, Ruth K., and Edith J. Agnew. *Sowers Went Forth*. Albuquerque: Menaul Historical Library, 1981.

Multicultural Education and the American Indian. Los Angeles: American Indian Studies Center, 1979.

Smith, Anne M. *New Mexico Indians: Economic, Educational, and Social Problems*. Santa Fe: Museum of New Mexico Press, 1969.

Szasz, Margaret. *Education and the American Indian: The Road to Self-Determination Since 1928*. Albuquerque: University of New Mexico Press, 1979.

Wiley, Tom. *Politics and Purse Strings in New Mexico's Public Schools*. Albuquerque: University of New Mexico Press, 1968.

Arts

Amsden, Charles Avery. *Navaho Weaving: Its Technic and Its History*. 1934. Reprint. Glorieta, N.M.: Rio Grande Press, 1974.

Aspen Center for the Visual Arts. *Enduring Visions: 1,000 Years of Southwestern Indian Art*. New York: Publishing Center for Cultural Resources, 1969.

Bedinger, Margery. *Indian Silver: Navajo and Pueblo Jewelers*. Albuquerque: University of New Mexico Press, 1973.

Berlant, Anthony, and Mary Hunt Kahlenberg. *Walk in Beauty: The Navajo and Their Blankets*. Boston: New York Graphic Society, 1977.

Boyd, E. *Popular Arts of Spanish New Mexico*. Santa Fe: Museum of New Mexico Press, 1974.

Brody, J. J. *Mimbres Painted Pottery*. Albuquerque: University of New Mexico Press, 1977.

Cerny, Charlene. *Navajo Pictorial Weaving*. Santa Fe: Museum of New Mexico Foundation, 1975.

Dickey, Roland F. *New Mexico Village Arts*. Albuquerque: University of New Mexico Press, 1949.

Fox, Nancy. *Pueblo Weaving and Textile Arts*. Santa Fe: Museum of New Mexico Press, 1979.

Garman, Ed. *The Art of Raymond Jonson, Painter*. Albuquerque: University of New Mexico Press, 1976.

Jernigan, Earl Wesley. *Jewelry of the Prehistoric Southwest*. Albuquerque: University of New Mexico Press, 1978.

Light and Color: Images from New Mexico. Santa Fe: Museum of New Mexico Press, 1981.

Mather, Christine. *Baroque to Folk*. Santa Fe: Museum of New Mexico Press, 1980.

Maxwell Museum of Anthropology. *Seven Families in Pueblo Pottery*. Albuquerque: University of New Mexico Press, 1974.

O'Keeffe, Georgia. *O'Keeffe*. New York: Viking Press, 1976.

Robertson, Edna C. *Los Cinco Pintores*. Santa Fe: Museum of New Mexico Press, 1975.

The Santa Fe New Mexican. *New Mexico Artists and Writers: A Celebration, 1940*. Santa Fe: Ancient City Press, 1982.

Schaafsma, Polly. *Indian Rock Art of the Southwest*. Albuquerque: University of New Mexico Press, 1980.

School of American Research. *Representative Art and Artists of New Mexico*. Santa Fe: Museum of New Mexico Press, 1976.

Performing Arts

Frisbie, Charlotte J., ed. *Southwestern Indian Ritual Drama*. Albuquerque: University of New Mexico Press, 1980.

Larkin, Margaret. *The Singing Cowboy*. New York, 1931.

Robb, John Donald. *Hispanic Folk Music of New Mexico and the Southwest: A Self-Portrait of the People.* Norman: University of Oklahoma Press, 1980.

Literature

Dobie, J. Frank. *Guide to Life and Literature of the Southwest: Revised and Enlarged in Both Knowledge and Wisdom.* Dallas: Southern Methodist University Press, 1952.

Major, Mabel, and T. M. Pearce. *Southwest Heritage. A Literary History with Bibliographies.* Albuquerque: University of New Mexico Press, 1972.

Powell, Lawrence Clark. *Books West Southwest.* Los Angeles: Ward Ritchie Press, 1957.

———. *Southwestern Book Trails.* Albuquerque: Horn and Wallace, 1963.

Architecture

Bunting, Bainbridge. *Early Architecture in New Mexico.* Albuquerque: University of New Mexico Press, 1976.

———. *Of Earth and Timbers Made.* Albuquerque: University of New Mexico Press, 1974.

———. *Taos Adobe.* Santa Fe: Museum of New Mexico Press, 1964.

Dewitt, Susan. *Historic Albuquerque Today.* Albuquerque: Historic Landmarks of Albuquerque, 1978.

———. *Santa Fe Historic Structure and Townscape.* Santa Fe Planning Dept., City of Santa Fe, 1976.

Economy

The Economy 1979. Albuquerque: Bank of New Mexico and the Bureau of Business and Economic Research, 1980.

Flora and Fauna

Findley, James S., Arthur H. Harris, Don E. Wilson, and Clyde Jones. *Mammals of New Mexico.* Albuquerque: University of New Mexico Press, 1975.

Koster, William J. *Guide to the Fishes of New Mexico.* Albuquerque: University of New Mexico Press, 1957.

Lamb, Samuel. *Woody Plants of New Mexico and Their Value to Wildlife.* Santa Fe: New Mexico Department of Game and Fish, 1971.

Ligon, J. Stokeley. *New Mexico Birds.* Albuquerque: University of New Mexico Press, 1961.

Martin, William C., and Charles R. Hutchins. *Flora of New Mexico,* Vols. I and II. Vaduz, Lichtenstein: J. Cramer, 1980.

Tours

Alsberg, Henry G., ed. New Mexico: *A Guide to the Colorful State.* 1940. Reprint. New York: Hastings House, 1962.

Anaya, Rudolfo A. *Bless Me, Ultima.* Berkeley: Quinto Sol Publications, 1972.

Appelt, Norman T. *Guide to Prehistoric Ruins of the Southwest.* Denver: Pruett Publishing Co., 1981.

Badash, Lawrence, Jos. O. Hirschfelder, and Herbert P. Broida. *Reminiscences of Los Alamos: 1943–1945.* Boston: D. Reidel Publishing Co., 1980.

Balcomb, Kenneth C. *A Boy's Albuquerque, 1898–1912.* Albuquerque: University of New Mexico Press, 1980.

Baldwin, Brewster, and Frank E. Kottlowski. *Santa Fe.* Socorro: New Mexico Bureau of Mines and Mineral Resources, 1968.

Baldwin, Gordon. *The Apache Indians: Raiders of the Southwest.* New York: Four Winds Press, 1978.

Bancroft, Hubert H. *History of Arizona and New Mexico, 1530–1888.* 1889. Reprint. Albuquerque: Horn and Wallace, 1962.

Bandelier, Adolph F., and Edgar L. Hewett. *Indians of the Rio Grande Valley.* Albuquerque: University of New Mexico Press and School of American Research, 1937.

Batchen, Lou Sage. *Las Placitas: Historical Facts and Legends.* Placitas: Tumbleweed Press, 1972.

Beck, Warren A., and Ynez D. Haase. *Historical Atlas of New Mexico.* Norman: University of Oklahoma Press, 1969.

Benrimo, Dorothy. *Camposantos.* Ft. Worth: Amon Carter Museum of Western Art, 1966.

Bolton, Herbert E. *Coronado: Knight of Pueblos and Plains.* New York: Whittlesey House and Albuquerque: University of New Mexico Press, 1949.

Boyd, E., and Frances Breese. *New Mexico Santos: How to Name Them.* Santa Fe: Museum of New Mexico, International Folk Art Foundation, 1966.

Bullock, Alice. *Living Legends of the Santa Fe Country.* Santa Fe: Sunstone Press, 1972.

Bryan, Howard. *Tours for All Seasons.* Albuquerque: Calvin Horn, 1972.

Calvin, Ross, ed. *Lieutenant Emory Reports.* 1848. Reprint. Albuquerque: University of New Mexico Press, 1951.

Caplin, Harvey. *Enchanted Land: New Mexico.* Albuquerque: Bank Securities Inc., 1973.

Carleton, James H. *Diary of an Excursion to the Ruins of Abo, Quarai, and Gran Quivira in New Mexico in 1853.* Reprint. Santa Fe: Stagecoach Press, 1965.

Chavez, Fray Angelico. *But Time and Place.* Santa Fe: Sunstone Press, 1981.

———. *My Penitente Land: Reflections on Spanish New Mexico.* 1974. Reprint. Santa Fe: William Gannon, 1979.

Church, Fermor S. *When Los Alamos Was a Ranch School.* Los Alamos: Los Alamos Historical Society, 1974.

Church, Peggy Pond. *The House at Otowi Bridge.* Albuquerque: University of New Mexico Press, 1960.

Cleland, Robert Glass. *This Reckless Breed of Men: The Trappers and Fur Traders of the Southwest.* 1950. Reprint. Albuquerque: University of New Mexico Press, 1976.

Coe, Wilbur. *Ranch on the Ruidoso: The Story of a Pioneer Family in New Mexico, 1871–1968.* New York: Alfred A. Knopf, 1968.

Coles, Robert. *The Old Ones of New Mexico.* Albuquerque: University of New Mexico Press, 1973.

Conron, John P. *Socorro: A Historic Survey.* Albuquerque: University of New Mexico Press, 1980.

Cordell, Linda S. *Tijeras Canyon: Analysis of the Past.* Albuquerque: University of New Mexico Press, 1980.

Davis, W. W. *El Gringo: New Mexico and Her People.* 1938. Reprint. Lincoln: University of Nebraska Press, 1982.

Dodge, Nathan N. *Flowers of the Southwest Deserts.* Santa Fe: Southwestern Monuments Assoc., 1952.

Dutton, Bertha P. *Navahos and Apaches: The Athabascan Peoples.* Englewood Cliffs, N.J.: Prentice-Hall, 1975.

Eisenstadt, Pauline. *Corrales: Portrait of a Changing Village.* New Mexico: Cottonwood Printing, 1980.

Elmore, Francis H., and Jeanne R. Janish. *Shrubs and Trees of the Southwest Uplands.* Globe, Arizona: Southwest Parks and Monuments Assoc., 1976.

Espinosa, Gilberto, and Tibo J. Chávez. *El Rio Abajo.* Pampa, Tex.: Pampa Print Shop, 1966.

Evans, Max. *Long John Dunn of Taos.* Los Angeles: Westernlore Press, 1959.

Fergusson, Harvey. *Home in the West.* New York: Duell, Sloan and Pearce, 1944.

———. *Rio Grande.* 1933. Reprint. New York: William Morrow, 1967.

Furman, Agnes Millere. *Tohta.* Wichita Falls, Tex.: Nortex Press, 1977.

Garrett, Pat. *The Authentic Life of Billy the Kid,* edited by M. G. Fulton. 1927. Reprint. Norman: University of Oklahoma Press, 1967.

Gilpin, Laura. *The Rio Grande: River of Destiny.* New York: Duell, Sloan and Pearce, 1949.

Gregg, Kate L., ed. *The Road to Santa Fe.* Albuquerque: University of New Mexico Press, 1952.

Groueff, Stephane. *Manhattan Project: The Untold Story of the Making of the Atomic Bomb.* Boston: Little, Brown, 1968.

Grove, Pearce, Becky J. Barnett, and Sandra J. Hansen. *New Mexico Newspapers.* Albuquerque: University of New Mexico Press, 1975.

Hackett, Charles W., ed. *Revolt of the Pueblo Indians of New Mexico and Otermín's Attempted Reconquest, 1680–1682.* Albuquerque: University of New Mexico Press, 1942.

Hallenbeck, C. *Spanish Missions of the Old Southwest.* Garden City, N.Y.: Doubleday, Page and Co., 1926.

Hester, James J. *Early Navajo Migration and Acculturation.* Santa Fe: Museum of New Mexico Papers in Anthropology, no. 6, 1962.

Hinshaw, Gil. *Lea, New Mexico's Last Frontier.* Hobbs: Hobbs Daily News Sun, 1976.

Historic Preservation Program for New Mexico, Vols. I and II. Santa Fe: State Planning Office, 1973.

History of Lincoln County Post Offices. Lincoln County, N.M.: 1962.

Hoard, Dorothy. *A Hiker's Guide to Bandelier.* Albuquerque: Adobe Press, 1977.

Horgan, Paul. *Great River: The Rio Grande in North American History.* New York: Holt, Rinehart and Winston, 1960.

———. *The Centuries of Santa Fe.* 1956. Reprint. Santa Fe: William Gannon, 1976.

———. *Lamy of Santa Fe: His Life and Times.* New York: Farrar, Straus, & Giroux, 1975.

Horn, Calvin. *New Mexico's Troubled Years.* Albuquerque: Horn and Wallace, 1963.

Hughes, John T. *Doniphan's Expedition: Containing an Account of the Conquest of New Mexico.* 1847. Reprint. New York: Arno Press, 1973.

James, H. L. *Cumbres and Toltec Scenic Railroad.* Socorro: New Mexico Bureau of Mines and Mineral Resources, 1972.

———. *Southwest New Mexico.* Socorro: New Mexico Bureau of Mines and Mineral Resources, 1971.

Johnson, Byron A., and Robert K. Dauner. *Early Albuquerque.* Albuquerque: Albuquerque Journal, 1981.

Jordan, Louann, and St. George Coe. *El Rancho de Las Golondrinas: Spanish Colonial Life in New Mexico.* Santa Fe: Colonial New Mexico Historical Foundation, 1977.

Kidder, Alfred V. *An Introduction to the Study of Southwestern Archaeology.* New Haven: Yale University Press, 1964.

Kubler, George. *The Religious Architecture of New Mexico in the Colonial Period and Since the American Occupation.* 1940. Reprint. Albuquerque: University of New Mexico Press, 1972.

Kunetka, James W. *City of Fire: Los Alamos and the Atomic Age, 1943–1945.* Englewood Cliffs, N.J.: Prentice-Hall, 1978. Revised edition. Albuquerque: University of New Mexico Press, 1979.

La Farge, Oliver. *A Pictorial History of the American Indian.* Rev. by Alvin B. Josephy, Jr. New York: Crown Publishers, 1974.

La Farge, Oliver, and Arthur N. Morgan. *Santa Fe: The Autobiography of a Southwestern Town.* Norman: University of Oklahoma Press, 1981.

Lange, Charles H. *The Cochiti Dam Archaeological Salvage Project.* Santa Fe: Museum of New Mexico Press, 1968.

Lange, Charles H., Carroll L. Riley, and Elizabeth M. Lange, eds. *The Southwestern Journals of Adolph F. Bandelier, 1885–1888.* Albuquerque: University of New Mexico Press, 1975.

Leonard, Olen E. *The Role of the Land Grant in the Social Organization and Social Processes of a Spanish-American Village in New Mexico.* Albuquerque: Calvin Horn Publishing, 1970.

Lucero, Barbarita, Aurelia Gurule, and Antonio De Lara. *Placitas del Pasado/Conversations of the Past.* Placitas, N.M.: Tumbleweed Press, 1976.

Luhan, Mabel Dodge. *Lorenzo in Taos.* New York: Alfred A. Knopf, 1932.

———. *Winter in Taos.* 1935. Reprint. Denver: Sage Books, 1981.

Lummis, Charles F. *The Land of Poco Tiempo.* 1928. Reprint. Albuquerque: University of New Mexico Press, 1966.

MacDonald, Eleanor D., and John Arrington. *The San Juan Basin.* Denver: Green Mountain Press, 1970.

Marshall, Michael, John R. Stein, Rich W. Loose, and Judith E. Novotny. *Anasazi Communities of the San Juan Basin.* Santa Fe: Public Service Company of New Mexico/Historic Preservation Bureau, 1981.

McAllester, David P., "Indian Music in the Southwest." McAllester, D. P., ed., *Readings in Ethnomusicology,* Johnson Reprint Corp., N.Y., 1971.

McFarland, Elizabeth. *Wilderness of the Gila.* Albuquerque: Publication Office of University of New Mexico, 1974.

McNitt, Frank. *Richard Wetherill: Anasazi.* Albuquerque: University of New Mexico Press, 1966.

————. *The Indian Traders.* Norman: University of Oklahoma Press, 1962.

————. *Navajo Wars: Military Campaigns, Slave Raids, and Reprisals.* Albuquerque: University of New Mexico Press, 1972.

Moorhead, Max L. *New Mexico's Royal Road.* Norman: University of Oklahoma Press, 1958.

Morrill, Claire. *A Taos Mosaic: Portrait of a New Mexico Village.* Albuquerque: University of New Mexico Press, 1973.

Nabokov, Peter. *Tijerina and the Courthouse Raid.* Albuquerque: University of New Mexico Press, 1969.

Nahn, Milton C. *Las Vegas and Uncle Joe.* Norman: University of Oklahoma Press, 1964.

New Mexico Historic Sites Survey. Santa Fe: Museum of New Mexico Press, 1967.

New Mexico Tourist Bureau. *Mission Churches of New Mexico.* Santa Fe: New Mexico Tourist Bureau, 1939.

Nichols, John. *If Mountains Die: A New Mexico Memoir.* New York: Alfred A. Knopf, 1979.

Noble, David Grant. *Ancient Ruins of the Southwest.* Flagstaff, Ariz.: Northland Press, 1981.

Osterwald, Doris B. *Ticket to Toltec.* Lakewood, Colo.: Western Guideways, 1976.

Parish, William J. *The Charles Ilfeld Co.* Cambridge, Mass.: Harvard University Press, 1961.

Parsons, Elsie Clews. *The Pueblo of Jemez.* New Haven: Yale University Press, 1925.

Patraw, Pauline, and Jeanne R. Janish. *Flowers of the Southwest Mesas.* Santa Fe: Southwest Parks and Monuments Assoc., 1977.

Pearce. T. M. *New Mexico Place Names: A Geographical Dictionary.* Albuquerque: University of New Mexico Press, 1965.

Pettitt, Roland A. *Los Alamos Before the Dawn.* Los Alamos: Pajarito Publications, 1972.

Perrigo, Lynn I. *Historic Las Vegas, New Mexico.* Las Vegas: San Miguel Chamber of Commerce, 1975.

Quaife, Milo Milton, ed. *Kit Carson's Autobiography.* Lincoln: University of Nebraska Press, 1960.

Ratkevich, Ronald P. *Dinosaurs of the Southwest.* Albuquerque: University of New Mexico Press, 1977.

Reeve, Frank D. *New Mexico: Seventeen Short Illustrated Histories.* Denver: Sage Books, 1961.

Rhodes, Eugene Manlove. *The Rhodes Reader: Stories of Virgins, Villains, and Varmints.* Norman: University of Oklahoma Press, 1975.

Russell, Marian. *Land of Enchantment: Memoirs of Marian Russell Along the Santa Fe Trail.* 1954. Reprint. Albuquerque: University of New Mexico Press, 1981.

Schaefer, Jack. *New Mexico.* New York: Coward-McCann, 1967.

Schilling, John H. *Taos–Red River–Eagle Nest Circle Drive.* Socorro: New Mexico Bureau of Mines and Mineral Resources, 1956.

————. *Silver City–Santa Rita–Hurley, New Mexico.* Socorro: New Mexico Bureau of Mines and Mineral Resources, 1967.

Schroeder, Albert H. *A Brief History of Picuris Pueblo.* Alamosa, Colo.: Adams State College, 1974.

Shalkop, Robert L. *Arroyo Hondo: The Folk Art of a New Mexico Village.* Colorado Springs: Taylor Museum, 1969.

Sherman, James E., and Barbara H. Sherman. *Ghost Towns and Mining Camps of New Mexico.* Norman: University of Oklahoma Press, 1975.

Silko, Leslie Marmon. *Ceremony.* New York: Viking Press, 1977.

Simmons, Marc. *Albuquerque: A Narrative History*. Albuquerque: University of New Mexico Press, 1982.

———. *Fighting Settlers of Seboyeta*. Cerrillos: San Marcos Press, 1971.

———. *New Mexico*. New York: W. W. Norton & Co., 1977.

Sonnichsen, C. L. *The Mescalero Apaches*. 1958. Reprint. Norman: University of Oklahoma Press, 1980.

———. *Pass of the North*. Vols. I and II. El Paso: Texas Western Press, 1980.

Southern Sandoval County League of Women Voters. *This is Sandoval County*. Bernalillo: Bernalillo High School Printing Class, 1978.

Southwest History Class, 1974–75. *Viva El Pasado*. Bernalillo: Bernalillo High School, 1976.

Stevens, T. Rorie. *The Death of a Governor*. Jacksonville, Tex.: Jayroe Graphic Arts, 1971.

Tate, Bill. *Truchas: Village with a View*. Santa Fe: Tate Gallery, 1972.

Torrance County. Estancia: Torrance County Historical Society, 1979.

Truslow, Edith C. *Manhattan District History*. Kasha V. Thayer, ed. Los Alamos: Los Alamos Scientific Laboratory, 1946.

Twitchell, Ralph Emerson. *Leading Facts of New Mexico History, 1911–1917*. Reprint. Albuquerque: Horn and Wallace, 1963.

Ungnade, Herbert E. *Guide to the New Mexico Mountains*. Albuquerque: University of New Mexico Press, 1972.

Vivian, Gordon, and Paul Reiter. *The Great Kivas of Chaco Canyon and Their Relationships*. Albuquerque: University of New Mexico Press, 1965.

Waters, Frank. *The Woman at Otowi Crossing*. Chicago: Swallow Press, 1970.

Watson, Dorothy. *The Pinos Altos Story*. Silver City: The Enterprise, 1960.

Weber, David J. *The Taos Trappers: The Fur Trade in the Far Southwest*. Norman: The University of Oklahoma Press, 1970.

Woods, Betty. *101 Trips in the Land of Enchantment*. Santa Fe: New Mexico Magazine, 1973.

index

Major discussions of a given location are indicated by **boldface.**